SENATOR POTHOLE

Other Books by the Author

The Kingmakers
The Running of Richard Nixon
The Impeachment of Richard Nixon
Party Politics: Why We Have Poor Presidents

SENATOR POTHOLE

The Unauthorized Biography of Al D'Amato

Leonard Lurie

A Birch Lane Press Book
Published by Carol Publishing Group

TO DORIS

A Birch Lane Press Book
Published by Carol Publishing Group
Birch Lane Press is a registered trademark of Carol
Communications, Inc.
Editorial Offices:
600 Madison Avenue, New York, N.Y. 10022
Sales and Distribution Offices: 120 Enterprise
Avenue, Secaucus, N.J. 07094
In Canada: Canadian Manda Group, P.O. Box 920,
Station U, Toronto, Ontario M8Z 5P9
Queries regarding rights and permission should be
addressed to Carol Publishing Group, 600 Madison
Avenue, New York, N.Y. 10022

Carol Publishing Group books are available at
special discounts for bulk purchases, sales
promotion, fund-raising, or educational purposes.
Special editions can be created to specifications.
For details, contact: Special Sales Department, Carol
Publishing Group, 120 Enterprise Avenue,
Secaucus, N.J. 07094

Manufactured in the United States of America
10 9 8 7 6 5 4 3 2 1

Library of Congress Cataloging-in-Publication Data
Lurie, Leonard.
    Senator Pothole : the unauthorized biography of
Al D'Amato / by Leonard Lurie.
        p.   cm.
    "A Birch Lane Press book."
    ISBN 1-55972-227-4
    1. D'Amato, Alfonse. 2. Legislators—United States
—Biography. 3. United States. Congress.
Senate—Biography. I. Title.
E940.8.D36L86   1994
328.73'092—dc20
[B]   93-47232
                                              CIP

CONTENTS

Foreword   ix

Acknowledgments   xi

Source Notes   xii

1. Growing Up in Island Park   3
2. Betrayal   13
3. Is "the Tiger" an Animal?   22
4. The Not-So-Civil Service   34
5. How American Politicians Stay Out of Trouble, or District Attorney Cahn in the Can   44
6. The D'Amatos Give and Take   51
7. D'Amato Commits Perjury   60
8. How Al Wins   64
9. D'Amato's Ascension   72
10. How to Become a Judge, or Drinking Beer in Astoria   79
11. Oh, Those ABSCAM Sheiks   89
12. D'Amato Bets on a Sure Thing   97
13. It Takes More Than Luck   105
14. "D'Amato's Folly"   111
15. The Unnamed Official   123
16. The Squire of Old Brookville   138
17. Two Pols in Tuxedos   146
18. How Senator Pothole Operates   156

CONTENTS

19.	The Boss's Second Shot	168
20.	D'Amato and Margiotta Fight for Power	176
21.	Forming Battle Ranks	185
22.	Finally After Eleven Years	194
23.	How to Get a Job in Government	202
24.	The Emperor's Clothes	213
25.	The Spear Carriers	226
26.	Cullen and Jund—Their Day in Court	234
27.	For the Defense	243
28.	The Senator Redefines Perjury	251
29.	Damage Control	270
30.	The Pit in Which Scores Were to Be Settled	278
31.	Summing Up	284
32.	The Verdict	296
33.	A Higher Authority	306
34.	How D'Amato Planned to Win Reelection	316
35.	Why D'Amato Won Reelection	326
36.	The Lethal Threat	335
37.	The Prospering of the D'Amatos	341
38.	Appointing Safe Prosecutors	349
39.	Blowing Up His Mistake	358
40.	The Fast Track	362
41.	Turning a Friend Into an Enemy	370
42.	The Mafia Connection	377
43.	Al's HUD House of Cards	383
44.	The Cover-up	392
45.	The Senator From Puerto Rico	398
46.	The War at HUD	404
47.	Scandal Rockets Bursting in Air	411
48.	Al's Doomed Lemmings	419

CONTENTS

49. A Night in Island Park   430

50. His Friends Call Him Richie   435

51. Prosecutors on D'Amato's Cases   440

52. The Senate's Ethics   447

53. The Survival Frenzy   463

54. The D'Amatos' Trial   474

55. Out, Out, Damned Spot   494

56. To the Members of the Class   512

    Epilogue   532

    Index   537

Iago:
Heaven is my judge, not I for love or duty
But seeming so, for my peculiar end; . . .
But I will wear my heart upon my sleeve
For daws to peck at; I am not what I am.
                                    Othello
                              Act I, Scene I

FOREWORD

When Mafia godfather Paul Castellano was gunned down in front of Sparks Steak House in Manhattan in 1985, no one would have imagined that a U.S. senator might feel the slightest sense of loss. The front-page pictures of the man designated by the Federal Bureau of Investigation (FBI) as America's leading gangster dead on the sidewalk under the open door of his black limousine summoned up no thoughts of senatorial intrigue. Paul Castellano ordered murders and arranged extortions and the distribution of drugs. He was a one-man assault on society.

Four years later, in preparation for his first campaign to become mayor of New York, Rudolph Giuliani told reporters that in early 1985, a few months before Castellano's gangland execution, he had had a "disturbing" conversation with Sen. Alfonse D'Amato about Castellano. Giuliani was then U.S. Attorney for the Southern District of New York and was about to bring Castellano to trial for murder. Senator D'Amato had spoken to him for about "five minutes in person" about Giuliani's decision to prosecute the Mafia chief. D'Amato urged him to reconsider his decision.

D'Amato is a man capable of using formidable persuasive powers, and the topic itself was freighted with ominous, if not threatening, overtones. D'Amato warned of what he considered the likely loss of the case and the "embarrassment" that would cause.

Since D'Amato had picked Giuliani to be U.S. Attorney, Giuliani considered the senator a friend: They had vacationed in Italy together; D'Amato had been a guest at Giuliani's wedding. Nevertheless, Giuliani found the conversation so disturbing that he delivered "a lecture" to D'Amato, warning him never to make such an approach to him again.

This was D'Amato's second attempt to gain Giuliani's help for a mafioso. Giuliani told reporters that a few months before D'Amato had tried to end the Castellano prosecution, D'Amato had asked him to get the sentence of convicted Mafia captain Mario Gigante reduced. Mario was the brother of Vincent "Chin Chin" Gigante, the head of the Genovese crime family, and had received an eight-year sentence for extortion. For years "the Chin" had saved himself from prosecution by posing as mentally incompetent. He would appear on the street in Manhattan's Little Italy wearing a bathrobe, leaning on the arm of a burly escort, mumbling incoherently, his eyes blank.

The FBI, which did not admire the Chin's acting ability, had been told that the godfather turned to Roy Cohn to see if a fix could be arranged to reduce his brother's sentence. Cohn, a major mob attorney, would soon be disbarred for a number of betrayals of his clients, including illegally using escrow money that had been entrusted to him and borrowing $100,000 from a client that he never repaid. According to the FBI informer who handled the pay-off, Cohn told the Chin it would cost $175,000 to shave two years off Mario's sentence.

In the fall of 1984, soon after the jail doors closed on Mario, Cohn filed a motion for the two-year reduction. Then Senator D'Amato placed his call to Rudy Giuliani. Giuliani's response: "I told him immediately that we would oppose and oppose it in strong language."

Giuliani filed a document fighting Cohn's motion. In a harsh comment that had implications for Alfonse D'Amato, he informed the court, "A reduction in this sentence would be greeted in these same criminal circles as evidence that crime pays and that justice can ultimately be bought and sold."

Despite Giuliani's opposition, the court granted Cohn's motion. The *Village Voice*, which broke the story, described the subsequent events:

> Following the sentence reduction, Vincent ('Fish') Cafaro [the Mafia informant] later told the FBI, he delivered $175,000 in cash to Cohn's office in three installments of $75,000, $50,000, and $50,000. Cafaro said he delivered the last payment to Tom Bolan, Cohn's law partner and a D'Amato confidant.

Giuliani's 1989 revelation about D'Amato pleadings on behalf of Paul Castellano and Mario Gigante resulted in a series of critical editorial comments about the senator. D'Amato's intervention was viewed as a violation of Senate ethics. Senators are prohibited from even making inquiries into any ongoing legal action. But this wasn't a minor civil action whose innocuous content might lead a senator concerned about a constituent into committing an error in judgment. D'Amato's interventions involved criminal cases, and Giuliani's targets were not minor hoodlums.

Senator D'Amato's support of Mafia causes and unaffiliated criminals goes far beyond these two incidents. The question is, how could someone so compromised reach the summit of political power in America?

ACKNOWLEDGMENTS

Thanks to my brother-in-law Max Martey, who told me how to get to the Uniondale courthouse in 1985, where the 1 percent case was about to begin, the starting point of this book, and for the years that he has spent clipping articles and reading journals not normally available to me.

I am deeply grateful to Deborah Brudno and David Bernstein for their helpful, on-the-spot Washington research.

Hillel Black, editorial director of Carol Publishing Group, is the most skilled editor with whom I have ever worked. His suggestions about the final draft of the manuscript were invaluable.

And, finally, homage to my wife, who read and edited at least ten major drafts of this book. She has given love and texture to the two-thirds of my life we have spent together.

SOURCE NOTES

I feel that writers have an obligation to identify the source of the material they use. Conventionally this has been done by the use of footnotes or notes listed at the end of a book. My last book had thirty-five pages of notes. Those pages contained several items that I later regretted not putting directly into the text. No one ever commented on them, and I concluded that they were overlooked.

The remedy applied in *Senator Pothole* has been to include sources directly in the work. This has been done as unobtrusively as possible in an endeavor not to disturb the narrative flow.

SENATOR POTHOLE

ONE

GROWING UP
IN ISLAND PARK

lfonse Marcello D'Amato was born into a world of economic squalor on August 31, 1937. The first year of his life was spent on Greene and Lafayette avenues in the Bushwick section of Brooklyn. Bushwick consisted largely of jerry-built tenements lining dark, narrow streets. Immigrants and their offspring trudged its filthy sidewalks looking for work. In the nineteenth and early twentieth centuries Italians had built New York's sewers and subways and paved its endless roads. During the Great Depression most residents of Bushwick still earned their bread with their muscles and hands. Alfonse's father, Armand, was an exception. He was small, five feet four, and at a disadvantage in the manual-labor market.

His slight stature was no hindrance when he wooed Antoinette, his wife-to-be, who barely reached five feet in height. Antoinette described her first meeting with Armand to me in terms of traditional romance. "I was introduced to Armand by some girlfriends. They brought him to my house." Her somber face and unemotional eyes did not reflect the happiness of that moment more than fifty years in the past; too many periods of painful dissatisfaction with her spouse had intervened.

3

Alfonse's parents were born in America—Armand in 1913, Antoinette shortly before the United States entered World War I. Despite their Yankee status, they maintained an Old Country atmosphere in their household. Although they spoke English, Armand with a tough Brooklyn accent, Italian was the preferred tongue at home.

Armand's parents came from Naples and settled in Newark, New Jersey, where they brought up ten children. But most of Armand's family history was written in Sicily, and he believed you could survive if you understood that everyone not your blood relation was your enemy.

Antoinette's father, Alfonse Cioffari, grew up in Italy. Antoinette told me that hard times in Rome had caused him to seek his salvation in America. Once settled in Brooklyn, he became a fur merchant and invested his profits in 'Brio,' a Manhattan theater-district restaurant that for years attracted a wealthy clientele.

Antoinette and her younger sister, Violet, were brought up in Island Park near Long Island's Atlantic coast. The Cioffaris lived at 14 Ostend Road, directly across the street from Antoinette and Armand's present house. The family patriarch was considered wealthy by Island Park standards. Old-time neighbors say Alfonse Cioffari made a good impression. He was stately, well-dressed, with a pointy waxed mustache. In the village he was thought of as a charming man with an unassuming continental style. A neighbor whose husband handled some of Cioffari's legal business said, "He was family-oriented, appeared to be well-educated, spoke with a slight Italian accent, but spoke grammatically. His wife was pretty and petite." A family friend remembered: "Besides English and Italian, he was fluent in French and Spanish."

When life became too hard in Brooklyn for Armand, Antoinette, and one-year-old Alfonse, they moved across the Hudson to Newark. Armand Paul, their second son, was born there in 1945, when Alfonse turned eight.

Antoinette's father thought the struggling couple, with their newborn second child, would do better in Island Park. In order to make the move tempting, Alfonse Cioffari put a generous down payment on a house across the street from his. It was a large two-story wooden house with a two-car attached garage that occupied the entire half-acre triangle encompassed by Ostend Road, Sagamore Road, and Nassau Lane. Thoughts of "trading up" had no allure for them, and they lived there for the next fifty years.

Antoinette became an excellent cook who prided herself on Southern Italian pasta dishes and sauces freighted with tomato and garlic. Her friend of many years, Catherine Fazio, spoke of her with affection. "Ann is a very domestic woman. Talented in knitting, crocheting, sewing, cooking, baking. She was always helpful in the community, cooking for the San Gennaro street festival or donating food for dinners at our church." She was credited by those who knew the family with strength of character and was recognized as the real head of the D'Amato household. Armand had not yet gotten his feet on the ground.

Although Armand and Antoinette conversed in Italian, young Alfonse was never comfortable with it. His father's coarse vocabulary, however, did provide the few phrases Alfonse needed when answering to challenges from neighborhood boys.

Grandpa Cioffari's petite wife suffered from diabetes and became blind in later life, at which point the Cioffaris turned their Island Park home over to their younger daughter Violet's family and moved to an apartment in nearby Hempstead, where Alfonse died. Grandma Cioffari went into a nursing home, where she ended her days. "The two daughters were devoted to her," a neighbor recalled, "but the situation got beyond their ability to handle."

Antoinette and Armand's last child, a daughter, Joanne, was born in 1948, three years after the move to Island Park. In an attempt to meet his growing family responsibilities, Armand had enlisted in that generation's army of insurance agents. Each day he dressed in a business suit and tie and sold policies to anyone who thought a twenty-five-cent-a-week payment to a man who came knocking on their door would protect them against life's terrors. He affected his father-in-law's continental style, sported a pointy waxed mustache, and was already struggling with a drinking problem that was to become more serious.

The Island Park in which Alfonse grew up is less than one square mile in area along the South Shore bays of Long Island, bounded by water on three sides. The main part of the village is occupied by people of Italian and Irish extraction, a few of whom lived there in waterfront shanties before World War II but most of whom moved from Brooklyn after the D'Amatos came from Jersey in 1945. Westward across the Island Park Canal is Harbor Isle, with a much smaller, politically impotent Jewish population; it is joined to the village by two small bridges. To the east is Barnum Island, the most recently constructed area of the village. It is named after P. T. Barnum, who lived in a large Victorian house on the beach and quartered his circus there from 1889 to 1893.

The movers and shakers in Island Park think of themselves as part of an extended family. They are white lower-middle-class tradespeople and pride themselves on the virtues of village life: stoicism in the face of misfortune, great piety, loyalty to members of the group and their leader. They spend much of their free time socializing in the volunteer firehouse in the village center. Al D'Amato has for decades been the firehouse's titular head. The fire department offers access to government jobs and a jock environment where a quickly assembled back-room bar is an adjunct to the floating crap games. It's a den in which gossip can be exchanged and plots are hatched. Membership is restricted to the politically well connected.

The old-timers are called "clam diggers" by "outsiders and newcomers." The hostility between them is open and often violent. Political feuds are common and split the village into warring camps. The Sacred Heart Church is a weekly meeting place for the fractious groups but has only an ameliorating impact on the vendettas.

World War II, which did so much to end the Great Depression across America, did little economically for Island Park. Armand found the new environment unpromising. In an endeavor to improve his prospects, he became active in local politics, joining the nonpartisan Public party in 1950, formed to capture village offices, which were becoming a source of power in the growing hamlet. He also joined the county Republican party.

Jim Fazio, a Democrat who twice ran for the state assembly, became the leader of the Public party. Jim grew up in the Red Hook section of Brooklyn, where he lost his right arm up to the shoulder when a glass transom fell and severed it. The settlement money from that disaster put Jim through Syracuse University and Harvard

Law School. His wife, Catherine, described him as "an Italophile who loved to help people." When the Fazios moved from Manhattan's Greenwich Village at the end of the 1940s, they bought a house across the street from Armand and Antoinette. Catherine became Ann's friend, and Jim became Armand's benefactor.

Armand was an aggressive salesman whose public life was shaped by his professional needs. He sold insurance to the Fazios, and Jim helped him get accounts from Fazio's law clients and friends. Catherine felt that Armand cultivated them solely because of what they might do for him. "We socialized a bit. We went to dinner at each other's houses, dinners at the American Legion. I liked Ann. She was a pleasant person to be with."

Catherine Fazio said that Armand "was a family-oriented man. He had, after all, a very good wife." But Ann's sweet nature made no impression that outsiders could detect on her husband. "Armand was extremely egotistical," Mrs. Fazio said. Another neighbor agreed. "His speech turned you off. He talked down to you."

Speaking in a calm, thoughtful manner that characterized her at age seventy, Catherine Fazio added, "People didn't like him. He had a superior attitude. Once in a while when people would say, 'Oh, is Armand connected to you?' we'd pretend he was not part of our group, since people were really turned off by him."

The Public party was supporting urban redevelopment, the building of a high school, and the creation of a strong summer beach program for teenagers. Catherine Fazio said, "When we would have political meetings trying to set up a strategy, Armand would always have suggestions for what other people should do, but he never chaired a committee or really actively spearheaded anything. He gave the impression of wanting to be on both sides of every issue, on both sides of the fence . . . wherever it was better for him. He was an opportunist."

When the Public party elected a mayor in the early 1950s, Armand sought his reward. Jim Fazio gave him a share of the village insurance business but refused to provide him with the monopoly he wanted. "I know that Armand was very angry at my husband because he didn't immediately get all the insurance business," Catherine remarked. "Jim and the other men in the party said that Armand was interested only in the insurance and himself."

While the Public party was dominant in the 1950s, Armand sought a seat on the village school board. Catherine felt that his motivation had nothing to do with education. "He was always trying to get acquainted with people to pick up insurance customers." His campaign issue looked like a sure winner in this predominantly Catholic community. St. Ignatius Catholic High School was in Rockville Centre, where Armand had his insurance office, and he wanted Island Park kids who went there transported with public funds. He lost.

The two families were also united by the friendship of Armand Paul and the Fazios' son Frank. They were toddlers together, shy by nature. Catherine recalled with delight the first time Armand Paul came knocking on her door to play with Frank. "I said, 'What's your name?' And I thought he said, 'I'm Paul.' Of course, he was saying, 'Armand Paul.' He lisped and continued to for many years. He was a good-looking fellow—better looking than his brother. Alfonse isn't nice looking. I think his personality shows through his face. Armand Paul was very likable. He had his mother's sweet nature."

Catherine still thought of Armand Paul fondly. "He spent so much time in my house as he was growing up. He and Frank liked to play baseball, catch frogs—by the bucketful. They made rafts out of clothespins and floated them in big basins. Frogs would leap off the rafts into the water. At the end of the day they released them. Innocent pleasure."

The relationship between Alfonse and Armand Paul was not so innocent. From the first, Alfonse established a lifelong pattern of bullying that reduced Armand Paul to a subservient position. "Alfonse acted the older brother," Catherine remarked, "and had little to do with Armand Paul."

When Alfonse involved himself with Armand Paul and Frank, it was to stir up mischief. Catherine said, "If these two close friends would get into an argument about a ball or whatever, Alfonse would egg them on to fight each other. I can still hear him yelling out, 'Hit him,' He was not a well-liked youngster, and that might have made him mean."

In our second interview Catherine told me another frog story, this time involving "thirteen- or fourteen-year-old" Al. She summarized what she thought it illustrated about his character. "Meanness. It was cruel. . . . He showed it. He really did. He was a mean kid."

Alfonse went to the Radcliff Road Elementary School, where he was frequently in trouble. In speaking of him during those times, his mother has said, "He was no angel." She was often called to the school because of his behavior. In an attempt to solve that problem, Antoinette suggested to Principal James A. Lynch that he hire her in some minor capacity so that she could be present in the building to control her Alfonse.

The D'Amatos had inadvertently burdened their oldest son with a name that embarrassed him. "I absolutely hated my name," he has said. "When I was a kid in the third grade, whenever the teacher wanted me to settle down, she would say, '*Allllll-fonse*,' and the whole class would go into hysterics."

According to D'Amato, his teachers repeatedly teased him about his name. He also vividly recalled being "ribbed unmercifully" during his childhood by his classmates and taunted by neighborhood kids who would call out in falsetto voices, "After you, *Alfonse*." He was twelve years old when he claims to have finally gotten up the nerve to ask his father, "Dad, why did you call me Alfonse?"

He quoted his father as replying, "Son, your Uncle Alfonse was a very wealthy man, and that's how we got the down payment on this house."

D'Amato avoids discussing his youth. Instead, he offers a biography that paints his adolescence in glowing colors. In an endeavor to maintain control over his image, D'Amato instructed close associates in Island Park not to talk to anyone about him. Interviews with his village cronies during the years of research for this book were often aborted by D'Amato's unwillingness to reveal anything about his early years.

Mike Masone, D'Amato's closest ally in Island Park, revealed the extent of D'Amato's determination to hide his youthful self. In 1991, Masone was a convivial seventy-six-year-old retired village supervisor of public works who played poker with the senator throughout most of the year every other Sunday night in the Volunteer Fire Department. Masone had invited me to his modest Island Park house to discuss what were stipulated to be positive recollections of D'Amato's youth. Talk about the latter-day D'Amato was understood to be out-of-bounds.

The conversation with Mike and his wife, Sue, took place in their living room. The window was a few feet from the back of the Volunteer Fire Department. He occasionally rose from his chair and called out to some friend parking his car in the adjacent lot. Our conversation went along pleasantly for over an hour—until it was interrupted by a phone call from the senator's Manhattan office. That ended our discussion of the young D'Amato.

Within minutes, Masone got a call from "the village hall" telling him to end the interview. A tape of that conversation has Masone telling me what D'Amato's village cohort informed him: "You know, Mike, you're going to get your fanny in trouble if you say— you know—without Al's blessing. So that's it."

In an endeavor to escape from the oppressive Alfonse label, the youngster asked to be called by a nickname. The family pet was an irascible, fidgety dog named "Tippy," and relatives thought their similar personalities called for matching names.

D'Amato explained why he went along with the slightly pejorative diminutive. "If you were in school and had a choice between Alfonse and Tippy, you'd choose Tippy." To this day Island Park old-timers call him Tippy.

Brother Armand told a reporter about a minor example of Al's feverish behavior in those days. "We slept in the same room when we were kids, but he didn't snore so loudly then, though sometimes he woke me up in the middle of the night chewing hard candy."

Armand Paul recalled that his father used them in political campaigns. "I can remember going door-to-door delivering circulars advertising who was going to be running, and I think that it was that early indoctrination into politics from my dad that got Al and eventually myself involved in politics."

Years later, under oath at his trial for mail fraud, Armand Paul described his place in the family. "I'm not as gregarious as other people." His face became pensive. "They say the middle child is the quiet one."

During the early 1950s things began to look up for the D'Amato family. Jim Fazio's helping hand made life easier for them. There was money for piano lessons for the three siblings. Armand played the piano. He told me, "When I grew up in Newark, all of my nine brothers and sisters played some musical instrument. Didn't you know that all Italians are interested in music?"

His children followed his lead. Joanne was the only one who did so eagerly. Armand Paul told me, "I hated it. We went to Rockville Centre for private lessons. The teacher was a tyrant. I had to learn a certain way. If I made a mistake, he hit my knuckles with a ruler. I'd come home with my knuckles cut up. I kept telling my parents, I hate it. Finally, they let me quit."

Joanne continued her music studies in college, Antoinette said proudly. She eventually married a Spanish-born concert violinist who made his primary living teaching at Northwestern University. "She's the smart one," said Armand Paul, commenting wryly about the stressful lives of the Island Park D'Amatos. "She lives in Chicago."

After graduating from eighth grade, teenage Alfonse had exhausted Island Park's educational possibilities; there was no local high school. In the mid-1950s about 650 students had to travel ten miles to West Hempstead High School; few went on to college. Young men in Island Park looked forward to earning their livelihood in some trade. However, a handful of ambitious youngsters, among them Al D'Amato, applied to Charminade High School, run by the Catholic Marianists in Mineola. Charminade had a reputation for demanding hard work from its students. D'Amato described himself at that time as "pretty much an average kid, although a little hyper."

D'Amato claims those years were a lark. His hyper nature had produced a sinewy youth, thin as a rail, who sported a crew cut. "I had a tremendous sense of spirit, attending every ball game and rooting for the home team." He played tuba in the school band and was a sprinter on the track team.

Before our interview was broken off by D'Amato's office, Mike Masone reminisced about the small number of village students in those days who went to Charminade, where *tuition* was demanded. "It was an uppity thing then."

Although the young D'Amato was a mediocre student, he was extremely competitive in sports. He described that characteristic, which was already well defined at Charminade. "I'm very aggressive by nature. It goes to the essence of what I'm about."

11

The D'Amatos had planted their robust seed in the sandy terrain of the South Shore. A hundred years earlier, Walt Whitman had trod the pathways along which young Al impetuously sought his way. The poet would surely have marveled at the tenacity of the D'Amato vine, which had found soil perfectly suited to its needs.

TWO

BETRAYAL

Island Park is a tiny part of Long Island's Nassau County, an area with town names supplied by Indians and seventeenth-century Dutch and English settlers. Nassau is inhabited by the rich and by people of less modest means whom most of the world's inhabitants would consider wealthy. The county rests uneasily against New York City's eastern boundary, separated from its neighbor by a superhighway Nassauites like to think of as a high-tech moat capable of keeping out Gotham's slum dwellers, who loom as a constant threat.

More than 1,300,000 people live in this north-south slice of Long Island, although many of them work in nearby Manhattan; its population is equivalent to the eleventh largest state. From the early 1900s America's economic aristocracy—the Vanderbilts, the Whitneys, the Tiffanys, and the Guggenheims—occupied estates on the county's North Shore "Gold Coast."

With their scant possessions, Armand and Antoinette D'Amato joined other urban pioneers in a massive trek, participated in primarily by Brooklyn Catholics, to the Protestant potato lands east of New York City. For them, Long Island, with its rolling North Shore wilderness hills and the ocean to the south, was an earthly paradise, and so they accepted Grandpa Cioffari's tempting offer.

The post–World War II boom filled in the village's empty lots with middle-class homes. The senator's house reflects the new prosperity. It occupies a third of an acre, just out of sight of the

13

coarse grass that clogs the nearby bay. The front of the modest house is covered with shingles painted a bright brick red; its sides are simulated white clapboards made of aluminum. There are a handful of wealthy people living in Island Park, some of them members of organized crime, but most village residents still pay their bills out of their current salary checks.

During the summer, residents swim in the channel off Park Beach; families take part in evening barbecues at the picnic area; fishing for snappers at Hog Island Channel is a popular pastime. In early September, the four-day feast of San Gennaro dominates village life. A week in advance, hundreds of volunteers cook meatballs, bake ziti, assemble deep fryers, and hammer together plywood games of chance that annually raise about $80,000 for the Sacred Heart Church. The D'Amatos had settled into a comfortable nest.

As graduation day at Charminade approached in 1955, Alfonse was getting desperate. His grades made him uncertain about getting into college. Once again the D'Amatos turned to Jim Fazio, their one-armed neighbor. Jim was a 1938 graduate of Syracuse University and as a frequent contributor to the school's scholarship fund had a certain standing with the admissions committee.

Catherine Fazio recalled D'Amato's pilgrimages. "Alfonse used to come to our house on a Saturday evening or Sunday. He was having difficulty getting into Syracuse. Jim loved helping people. He encouraged people who needed advice to come and talk."

Although Jim was a leader of the Nassau Democratic party and the D'Amatos were aggressively Republican, young Al cultivated Fazio with the same self-serving intensity displayed by his father. Jim wrote a letter of recommendation to Syracuse. He also got the president of the Oceanside Bank, a contributor to the university, who had never met Alfonse, to write a glowing letter for him.

After his acceptance, Alfonse displayed the modesty of his academic aspirations. He chose the university's least demanding major, business administration, at that time not the ticket to Wall Street it was to become in another generation. Even in that noncompetitive academic atmosphere, D'Amato found it hard to maintain a B- average.

Despite D'Amato's lack of academic achievement, Jim Fazio encouraged the struggling student to become a lawyer. With the aid of Jim and his Syracuse undergraduate degree, Al gained admission to Syracuse Law School, where he spent an additional two years. During those six years, D'Amato lived above a pizzeria on Marshall Street and held a part-time job as a janitor.

Occasionally during the school year he would return to Island Park and invariably visit Fazio. Jim had one piece of advice for the law student who was already talking about becoming a politician. " 'I'm active in politics,' " Catherine recalled her husband saying, " 'but I don't depend on politics for my living. I think that's what you should do. Because if you depend on politics for a living, then you're not your own man.' "

While in law school, D'Amato met Penelope Collenburg, known as Penny. She was from New Rochelle, New York, a straight-A high school student. She went to Syracuse's Fine Arts College on a scholarship, maintained an A average, and went on to earn a master's degree in art education. The Fazios attended their wedding reception in Armand and Antoinette's home. It was a marriage of opposites: a sensitive, cultivated woman; a crude, self-centered man. Penny's teaching job in a Syracuse public school supported them while Al finished his studies.

After his graduation, the couple moved to Island Park, where Penny continued to teach. D'Amato passed the bar exam in 1962 and sent out the usual employment applications to Wall Street firms. Poor law school grades ensured rejection, which he spoke of bitterly years later, implying that someone from southern Italian stock never stood a chance.

Island Park harbored few clients in need of an expensive lawyer's talents; D'Amato's prospects were unpromising. At this point, his father, whose financial success resulted from ties to the clubhouse, came to his aid. Armand knew Joe Carlino, the State Assembly's Speaker and most powerful figure. Carlino also served as Nassau County Republican leader and in those two capacities seemed unable to recognize the most obvious conflict of interest. Carlino lived just a few minutes to the south, over the Long Beach Bridge; he was happy to get Armand's son a clerk's job in the county attorney's office.

The Nassau Republican organization nourished itself in this manner, filling government offices with semicompetents who were frequently unable to pass civil service exams or were too impatient to take that demanding route. D'Amato came to his entrance-level job with much better credentials than most political appointees and as a result expected to rise rapidly.

The year 1961 proved chaotic for the Nassau Republican party. Democrat Eugene Nickerson threw Carlino's cadre into disarray by capturing the county executive's office. The county executive is in most respects equivalent to the mayor of a large city. He is head of the six-member county board of supervisors, which controls much of the financial and government policies of the county's five major towns and their sixty-four village subdivisions, such as Island Park. Democrat Nickerson's victory was an event never before recorded in Nassau history; the Republicans were always masters of that office and its patronage.

Jim Fazio, a close friend of Nickerson's, ran against Joe Carlino for the assembly and almost beat him. Nassau Republicans were in shock. Soon after Nickerson took over, he cleared out some of Carlino's appointees in the county attorney's office, all of whom gave at least 1 percent of their salary to the Republican party, none of whom had civil service status; Al D'Amato was one of them.

Republican Ralph Caso, who was then supervisor of Hempstead, the largest of the county's five major towns, remembered the moment vividly: "You have to realize what happened in 1961, when Nickerson came in—we Republicans panicked. We had lost the top position in the county, with the tremendous powers that the county executive has: the appointment of judges, commission-ers—top positions, high-salaried positions. So what we did was to set up in the town [Hempstead] government services the county was giving. It created a lot of jobs."

It also made Nassau County one of the highest-taxed counties in the country, with the highest ratio of government workers to tax-payers. Hempstead taxpayers were suddenly paying for two departments, in most service areas, instead of the one that they needed. But from Al D'Amato's perspective, it was a scheme that proved the genius of Republican leaders, ensuring as it did that he would not spend a day off a government payroll.

It took no more than a phone call from Armand Sr. to Boss Carlino to get Al a job as a warrant clerk in the Republican-con-trolled district court. Soon afterward, Armand prevailed on Carlino to move his son into the family court as a law assistant, where he worked for two years. Al now knew the secret to success: A penniless boy with barely visible prospects who had connections to the party could look forward to better days. The party could provide him with a job he might otherwise not get and, if he was fired, could find him another one instantly.

D'Amato formally enlisted in the county Republican ranks in 1962 when he became a block captain in the Island Park Club. Still in his twenties and incredibly energetic, D'Amato was a political whirlwind. Since his area of churning diligence was small—the size of a city block—and its working-class residents were easily impressed by the status of a credentialed professional, by 1964, D'Amato was chosen by the club leader to become a committeeman.

Committeemen are the rock on which Nassau Republicanism rests. They are in charge of an election district consisting of no more than three residential blocks, each with a block captain, who reports directly to his committeeman. The committeeman treats the block captain like a flunkie: He supplies him with literature to distribute to residents in his area; he gives him election petitions requiring voters' signatures; he assigns him a monthly quota of raffle tickets and then makes sure the money is collected and deposited in the club's Committeemen's Council checking account.

In return, the committeeman rewards his block captains with as little as he can to still keep those hungry soldiers marching to the party tune. The rewards most avidly sought are a government job, or if one has that prize, a raise or a promotion. The committeeman's problem, and that of the club's leader in the hierarchy above him, is that there is never enough to go around. The more successful the party, the more soldiers it will attract, but there is a limit to the number of jobs even the most inventive Nassau bureaucrat can supply to the party boss who has placed him at the head of a government department.

A successful committeeman must have a persuasive tongue that will enable him to convince the block captain he is championing his cause with the clubhouse leader and that patience will produce results. If the committeeman is a glad-hander, is adroit at bending people to his will, and likes to party, then the bad medicine goes down easier; D'Amato was the perfect committeeman.

On May 2, 1975, D'Amato testified before a federal grand jury in Brooklyn that was investigating allegations that "employees of the town of Hempstead have been forced to give portions of their salary to the Republican party." Referring to those early clubhouse years when he had been Island Park's most active committeeman, Assistant U.S. Attorney James Drucker asked whether D'Amato knew "about employees [of the town] being expected to give a portion of their salaries to the Republican party." Although his answers to most questions that day were a model of evasiveness, he responded, "Yes . . . there is a general knowledge which really permeated the area that a one percent contribution did serve as a guideline. . . . It was a general thing which most people were aware of. You are on the team—you want to be a team player." As a committeeman, it was his responsibility to inform new team members that 1 percent was the guideline for their kickbacks.

So adept was he at playing the team game that in 1965, little more than a year after he had become a committeeman, he was chosen by Island Park's ten committeemen to head the club and was designated the executive leader.

Al quickly engineered the appointment of his father as village insurance broker. Armand Sr. was now the chief beneficiary of the village business, a circumstance that annually added thousands of dollars to the family income.

In 1962, the year D'Amato started his ascendancy in the county Republican party, he plunged himself even more vigorously into Island Park politics. It was a smaller pond in which to swim; there were no competing Republican big fish.

Jim Fazio's Public party and its opponent, the Unity party, enrolled Republicans and Democrats. Republican Armand D'Amato was still a member of Democrat Fazio's party. Al was free to join either village party without jeopardizing his standing with the county Republican organization.

The Fazios expected Al to join their party. Armand was still dunning Jim for insurance clients, Armand Paul was always in their house, and Antoinette and Catherine chatted daily. There were even more direct ties: The Fazios had trusted thirteen-year-old Al to escort their daughter Karen to school, for which they paid him $2 weekly. During his adolescence Al had often sought advice from Jim; by 1962, Jim had been Al's mentor for over seven years. When the young man whom they had helped so much joined the opposition Unity party, the Fazios were disappointed. "It didn't mean anything to him," Catherine remarked about D'Amato's sense of obligation. "He was anxious to gain his own stature, and he knew he could not supplant Jim in local politics."

However, Catherine admitted, she and Jim were not surprised. "His father was interested in what he could get out of the Public party, and I just put it down to the son was just going to be as opportunistic. I didn't like the father and the son."

Terry Boyle, a wholesale-milk deliveryman, was leader of the Unity party from 1959 to 1962 when Al cast his lot with Fazio's opponents. Boyle, who describes himself as "a hardheaded Irishman," lived two houses down Nassau Lane from the D'Amatos for almost forty-five years and had seen young Alfonse grow into manhood. He remembered him as a wild kid. "He would run through buildings while they were being constructed. The construction men would kick him out." He was always taking a shortcut to his friend's house over Boyle's fence. "I used to holler at him and tell him not to do it again." To no effect. "He was arrogant and pugnacious: 'I know everything.' " Despite his bad opinion, Boyle welcomed Al to the Unity party. In a guild composed mainly of beer-drinking tradesmen, a lawyer became an attractive prize.

Boyle was a taskmaster. He insisted that D'Amato had to knock on every door, keep in close contact with the village voters, hand out literature on street corners. Al worked hard, and Boyle appreciated his efforts. In late 1962 problems arose in the Unity party, and Boyle decided to form the Village party. He sought allies, and Al D'Amato became his main confidant. During a discussion with D'Amato about his plans, the young recruit agreed to join Boyle's insurrection but startled the older man by demanding to be made president of the new party.

Boyle reflected sourly, "I told him, 'Get your feet on the ground, relax. Don't push things. Don't rush them.' He was an eager beaver even then."

The eager beaver seemed to take Boyle's advice without offense. "Alfonse and I decided before the meeting that during the meeting I would say my piece, and we would walk out, and five or six others would join us." The climactic meeting took place in the village

American Legion hall. Boyle's confidence remained high, although he was surprised to see over fifty people present at a meeting normally attracting less than a third that number.

"I was chairing the meeting," Boyle recalled. "I said my piece—I was resigning as president of the party. It was a nasty meeting. Strangers harassed me."

Boyle expected that as he walked out Alfonse would join him. Instead, Boyle found himself striding down the aisle alone. "I thought, as I walked, I got double-crossed. Alfonse set me up. He told me he was going to walk out with me. He knew he wasn't going to get what he wanted from me in the Village party, so he stayed and took over the Unity party."

Later that month, Boyle ran into Al and Penny in the bar of the Island Park Hotel, formerly P. T. Barnum's Victorian home. "I told him just what I thought of him," Boyle said. "I didn't use any fancy language. I'm just sorry for Penny."

As soon as D'Amato took over the Unity party, his demeanor became arrogant. His behavior disheartened the Fazios. "When we had a public meeting," Catherine Fazio said, "D'Amato would be very loud and talk about how Jim was not doing the right thing for the village and speak against whatever views Jim was espousing. He used street language."

Under Al's whip, Catherine said, "there were brawls very often at village meetings."

Catherine Fazio described the issue generating much of the bitterness. "The Public party was trying to use federal funds to knock down some buildings and build senior housing to revitalize the village. Alfonse was definitely against this. He rallied the people against urban renewal." His chief tool: racial prejudice. D'Amato warned that although federal money would lower village costs, it would open the way for minority people to take over.

Catherine Fazio scoffed at his tactics. "I don't know where minorities would have come in. We don't have enough room for projects housing large numbers of people. But this was the scare tactic he used."

Catherine described his attacks against Jim as being "vitriolic." The past relationship meant nothing to him. Jim was an opponent, and opponents had to be obliterated.

In 1968, Jim suffered a heart attack. He could not work for months. When he went back to practicing law, he curtailed his Manhattan work and concentrated on his nearby Lynbrook office. Nevertheless, as head of the Public party he remained active in local affairs. Although much weakened, he was determined to carry on as normally as possible.

"The village meant so much to him." Catherine said. "He felt that Alfonse was selling Island Park short."

Jim's heart attack brought about no change in Alfonse's behavior toward him.

"Whenever Jim came to a public meeting, Alfonse would attack him mercilessly," Catherine recalled.

In 1969, as Alfonse D'Amato's career prospects brightened, Jim Fazio had a second heart attack and died.

THREE

IS "THE TIGER" AN ANIMAL?

When D'Amato was elected Island Park Club leader in 1965, he became one of sixty-nine members of the Republican County Executive Committee, a genuine minor dignitary of the Nassau party. A man in such a position could insist that he no longer be forced to mark time in family court. He was appointed deputy attorney in the Hempstead town attorney's politically staffed office.

It was at this point that Jim Nagourney, one of Nassau's leading Republicans, first met him. He would work closely with D'Amato for fifteen years. Nagourney was on Supervisor Ralph Caso's staff in Hempstead Town Hall writing press releases. "I was sitting at a table having lunch at 'The Greeks,' a storefront diner across the street from town hall, and he sat down at the table with me and introduced himself. He knew who I was. He said, 'I'm Al D'Amato. You work in the public relations department, don't you?'

"This was the first political conversation I had with him. And he suddenly said, 'After this November, we're all going to lose our jobs.'

"He thought Caso wouldn't win the election. The impression I was left with was: Gee, what a down thing to say. That's treasonous. That has always stayed with me, because—talk about incredible pessimism. It was totally out of character with everything I know about Al D'Amato."

Nagourney's conversation with D'Amato revealed a man deeply scarred by his firing by Democrat Eugene Nickerson. Fortunately for D'Amato, Ralph Caso won, and the deputy town attorney was allowed to remain in his job for two years, being watched by, and carefully and reverentially watching, the new Republican party boss, Hempstead town chairman Joseph Margiotta. Joe Carlino had by this time left the state assembly, had abandoned elective politics, and was officially registered as a paid Albany lobbyist.

Margiotta and D'Amato got on splendidly. Ralph Caso, Hempstead supervisor, became D'Amato's boss. He told me about the nature of the relationship: "D'Amato ingratiated himself with Margiotta. He was articulate. An opportunist. He was able to work his wiles on Margiotta. Margiotta used to call him his 'Tiger.' D'Amato was the kind of guy who could pick up a phone and talk to you about nothing and make you feel . . . important: 'Hi, bub. What'cha doin' today? You were great last night.' "

As a sign of his pleasure, Margiotta had twenty-seven-year-old D'Amato appointed public administrator, a post in which he supervised the estates of persons who died without specifying their heirs. Prior to 1962, those duties were carried out by the county treasurer, but that year, in an attempt to cut down on Nickerson's powers, the Republican-controlled county board of supervisors created the new job. Nickerson denounced the switch as "a bald patronage grab."

Shortly after D'Amato's appointment, New York's senator Robert F. Kennedy called for an investigation of the state's surrogate system. He charged it had become a patronage device for paying off politically connected lawyers, jurists, and former officeholders. D'Amato was now the youngest surrogate in the state and showed his gratitude to Margiotta by appointing as conservators anyone the boss suggested.

Margiotta had by then taken over Carlino's job as county leader. Caso described Margiotta's attitude toward D'Amato: "He [Margiotta] felt that the executive leaders were sacrosanct. And here was one of his demigods . . . a guy who was eager to go anyplace, do anything, and he had been floundering around, going from one job to another."

Margiotta's feeling for D'Amato had a deeper emotional layer. He publicly announced, "I like him like a son." Margiotta had also been born in Brooklyn's Bushwick section, where he lived until he was ten, and seemed to see in the Island Park go-getter an unpolished replica of himself.

Margiotta's profession was *distributor of government jobs*, although he was *not* a government official. He had positioned himself as a gatekeeper between applicants and the government work they sought. But county Republican leader Margiotta, who was also Hempstead Republican leader, knew he could remain head of the party only if he found slots on the public payroll for those who held a party IOU.

For example, in 1967, when Sol Wachtler, Republican supervisor of the town of North Hempstead, ran, and lost, against Eugene Nickerson for county executive, Margiotta was obligated by party etiquette to see that Wachtler landed on his feet. The occasional party-supplied job as executor for some estate wouldn't be enough for this Kings Point bon vivant with whom Joe Margiotta liked to carouse. Wachtler had done the party's work; now it was time for the party to work for him.

Margiotta proudly told me that he had asked his party member, Gov. Nelson Rockefeller, to make Wachtler a judge. Despite the Bar Association's "unqualified" rating for Wachtler because of his seamy political background, in January 1968, Rockefeller obliged: Clubhouse leader Wachtler was appointed to the state supreme court. In 1972, with Margiotta's help, he won election to the state's highest court, the court of appeals; he was appointed its chief judge in 1985.

Having been trained by Margiotta to break the law, Judge Wachtler was now in charge of determining whether accused criminals had done so. When Wachtler was arrested by the FBI on November 7, 1992, for extorting money from his former lover by threatening to kidnap her fourteen-year-old daughter, Margiotta was preparing the strategy for making him New York's governor. And if Wachtler had not entered federal prison on September 28, 1993, to serve fifteen months, Margiotta would still be scheming to advance the political career of his most prestigious and dependable servant.

Margiotta's decision in 1969, two years after Al D'Amato had started serving as public administrator, to promote the Island Park executive leader to the interim post of receiver of taxes was a similar exercise of his extralegal gatekeeper's function: Dependable party functionaries had to be found to fill vacancies. However,

Margiotta's order to Republican town board members that they should appoint D'Amato reflected a more sincere demonstration of the boss's affection. In doing so, Margiotta had announced that D'Amato had become a rising star. The receiver of taxes held an elective office and therefore had a place in the limelight. In the election six months later, "incumbent" D'Amato's name appeared on a ballot for the first time.

It was a billboard-sized sign of Margiotta's confidence in his protégé: The receiver of taxes held sway over an office employing almost a thousand people. "It became a patronage mill," Caso said. He went on to explain that this was possible because "the civil service was always being manipulated."

James Nagourney was also a Margiotta favorite. Since the early 1960s, tall, handsome Jimmy had been making his way up the administrative structure of the Republican organization. He ran several party campaigns and developed a reputation for being smooth, efficient, and brainy.

Nagourney left the county payroll in 1969 and went to work in Washington as head of an information-gathering business owned by his friend William Casey, the future head of the CIA, whose North Shore Nassau estate was located in Glen Cove. By the end of the year, Nagourney became bored. A phone call from Margiotta in 1970 summoned him back to Nassau. The boss wanted Jim to "run the campaigns for all our 'nonincumbent' candidates." The incumbent candidates didn't need Jim's help, since none of them were seriously opposed. It was Jim's task to pick up another seat for a Margiotta handpicked state senate candidate.

The newly married Nagourney moved back to Lido Beach, a short distance from Island Park, sublet an apartment, and promised his bride "a honeymoon after the campaign."

Nagourney described an encounter with D'Amato shortly after he returned from Washington:

"People in my building knew that I was in politics," he said zestfully. "They came to me with a problem. 'We're responsible for cleaning our own beach. It's very inefficient and costly for us to do it. Can you work something out where we could pay the town or the county. The county cleans to the left of us, the town cleans to the right, can we work something out?' "

Nagourney saw this as an opportunity to win support from people who were not normally Republicans. "I called Al D'Amato. I said, 'Al, here's a chance for you to make some hay. The people in my building have a problem. They want the town to take over the maintenance of the beach. I don't see any reason why it can't be done, but it's a chance for you to be a hero and do something.' It was the summer of 1970—he's the temporarily appointed receiver of taxes, but it's understood that he's in for something better."

D'Amato agreed, and a meeting was arranged in Nagourney's apartment. Nagourney said he was "surprised" at the manner in which D'Amato addressed the petitioners, most of whom were Jewish.

" 'Look,' " Nagourney quoted D'Amato as saying. " 'I'm in politics and I'm in the business of doing favors for people and expect them to remember and do me a favor sometimes.

" 'Yes. I will try to get the town to take this over, and at some point I'm going to want to have something in return. It may just be your vote. It may be that I want you to help me, but if I go for you, I expect that sometime in the future you will help me.' "

Nagourney said, "I was shocked. I expected him to deliver that message, but with some subtlety. Boy, if that isn't bold-faced, I said to myself. Here you are with a guy who says, *A deal is a deal.*

"At that time I was reading *The Godfather.* The lines seemed to have been taken directly out of it. It was appropriate because *The Godfather* took place at Lido Beach."

D'Amato tried to deliver on the deal but failed. Even so, he had made some Lido Beach converts. With their aid he won his first election, receiver of taxes, with a startling seventy-two thousand victory margin. At an election-eve rally in the Garden City Hotel, Margiotta introduced the thirty-three-year-old victor as "my tiger."

"There is no question about it," Nagourney commented, "He was Margiotta's tiger. But the rest of the party, behind his back, called him 'the Animal.' He'll eat you alive if you're in his way or if he's hungry and you're standing there. He had that nickname by that time."

In 1971, Eugene Nickerson concluded that the Democrats didn't have either the interest or the capacity to make him governor or a senator and decided not to seek reelection. His consolation prize, which he arranged for himself, was a lifetime appointment to a judgeship.

Consequently, Ralph Caso ascended to the county executive's office; Francis Purcell became presiding supervisor and in the process left a vacancy in Hempstead for a supervisor. Waiting only until Boss Margiotta indicated his preference, the town board appointed D'Amato to that position.

In a court trial years later D'Amato detailed his duties: "It is a very interesting development, because Hempstead is the only town in the entire state—and there are about, approximately, nine hundred towns in the state—that has two supervisors; the presiding supervisor and supervisor. . . . The supervisor of the town . . . really is a councilman. He has the same vote as a councilman. No more, no less. And the duties that he has are really those that may be assigned to him by way of the presiding supervisor."

In order to execute these amorphous duties, D'Amato had an appropriately unimposing staff: a secretary and two clerical assistants. There was one additional occupant of his outer office whose presence revealed something about D'Amato's plans for the future. Richard L. Miranda was hired on January 3, 1971, two days after D'Amato took office, as D'Amato's $20,500-a-year press secretary. He was the only "councilman" with a press secretary.

Presiding Supervisor Francis Purcell, a mild-mannered, hands-off administrator, was D'Amato's superior in town government. He resented the young supervisor's constant attempts to use Press Secretary Miranda's skills to grab the limelight. An anonymous "Republican source" gave the following opinion about D'Amato to *Newsday*: "He's completely political. I've seen him do things purely for their public relations value. Maybe, if he's lucky, he'll be burned a few times before he is forty. Maybe it will help him to mature." For the record, Purcell sourly commented: "He's had more publicity than any other supervisor in town history."

D'Amato's dedication to politics took its toll at home. Penny complained, "The hours are terrible." She was seeing less and less of Al. He admitted that being a politician was a twenty-four-hour-a-day obsession with him. Declaring that politicians' wives were "the unsung heroes," he explained why Penny fit that role. "Look what she puts up with: me, the kids, me in and out. Politics is a family affair. Don't let anyone tell you differently. You can't do a job unless your partner is equally committed."

Penny's commitment was less than Al demanded. She was well educated, living during an era when women were being "liberated." During the early 1970s, NOW leaders proclaimed that women could "have it all": children, a career, an identity all their own. But while Bella Abzug was in Congress telling the big boys where to get off, Penny was at home, she told *Newsday*, "making all of her own clothes [and] most of the children's clothes." And although she stated she was content being "the woman behind the man," she added, "No one can say doing housework is fun."

While he was describing under oath the inconsequential burden of his work as town supervisor, D'Amato added that he was paid somewhat more than a Hempstead councilman. "About, I recall, three to five thousand dollars." But there was more for Margiotta's tiger. "Then I believe I received fifteen thousand dollars in addition for sitting on the county board."

What were the heady responsibilities for which the county paid its servant? Caso described how decisions were made on the county board after he and D'Amato became members:

"Margiotta would not come to my office in the county executive building. He told me if he did that people would say an unelected politician was running the government. Instead, weekly we'd meet for lunch at the Golf Club on Front Street in Hempstead. It was there that the word was passed to us from Margiotta as to how to vote at the supervisor's weekly meeting."

Margiotta ruled Nassau, yet he drew no salary from the county. Instead, he settled for the pleasures and advantages associated with the real, though unauthorized, exercise of power.

How circumscribed were the powers of D'Amato, Purcell, and Caso and how unlimited were those of Margiotta can be illustrated by Caso's description of how he selected one of the key members of the county government after he took office on January 1, 1971:

"The County Treasurer holds a very sensitive office. He decides in which bank the county's funds are going to be deposited during the time that it takes for the county employees to deposit their pay checks and for the bank to clear them for payment. That usually takes the banks three days. During that time they have, and can use, the money that the county has deposited with them. It amounts to millions of dollars each pay period. Believe it or not, the bank that gets this windfall pays the county no interest on those millions. You can imagine how badly the banks want that money.

"When I took office, Margiotta recommended John Scaduto, political leader of Long Beach, for the job of county treasurer. As in the case of all Margiotta recommendations, I appointed him.

"Scaduto deposited the county funds in European-American Bank. After a while I began to get complaints from other banks around the county: 'Why is it that the county payroll always goes to European-American?'

"I called a conference with Scaduto and representatives of the complaining banks. I tried to argue with him: 'Why do you always use the same bank?' He'd tell me . . . other banks couldn't provide the service. They [the complaining banks] said they could. I discussed it with Margiotta. He backed up Scaduto and told me we had to use European-American."

Why Margiotta was so determined to give European-American Bank the exclusive use of Nassau County's money is a matter he has never discussed. Such deals between politicians and friendly banks are a common arrangement around the country. But what Caso made clear was that once Margiotta had decided European-American should get this valuable municipal favor, the county executive was the last person in the world who could dissuade him.

With Nickerson gone and no one in government left to protect Democrats, the Republican guillotine worked overtime; Caso—or more accurately, Margiotta—suddenly had hundreds of jobs to fill. Al D'Amato felt one of them might suitably be occupied by his father, whose insurance accounts allowed few luxuries. The senior D'Amato was by this time identifying himself as an alcoholic at meetings of Long Beach's Alcoholics Anonymous. D'Amato asked Boss Margiotta to put in a word for his floundering father with Caso.

"Margiotta recommended him," Caso recalled. "He had no specialty or professional expertise. I put him in the Department of General Services, which is the county's housekeeping department; it had charge of changing light bulbs and keeping the heat turned on. He had a low-level administrative job." Armand continued to run his insurance business.

Having delivered Armand Sr. to a safe berth, Al turned his attention to brother Armand Paul, twenty-six years of age, a graduate of St. John's law school and therefore eligible for a better job than his father. Soon Armand Paul was working as Albany counsel for Joe Margiotta. The boss had been in the state assembly for seven years; it was an environment congenial for deal-making pols. By this time the relationship between the brothers had stabilized. Strong-willed Al gave the orders; passive Armand Paul took them.

In 1972, the year after Al became a member of Margiotta's hierarchy, bother Armand found himself tapped by the party to run for a safe seat in the state assembly. Armand Paul was elected and faithfully served those responsible for his success, doing as much for the welfare of the state as most of his peers.

One of the reasons well-connected lawyers like Joe Carlino, Joe Margiotta, and Armand Paul D'Amato like to be in the assembly is that while collecting a substantial salary and benefits jocularly labeled by them "lulus," the state's ethics laws allow them to have private law clients doing business with, and being regulated by, the state. It is possible for an assembly speaker like Joe Carlino, once retired from that body, to spend the next twenty years of his life using his Albany legislative connections to lobby on behalf of a long list of corporate clients. Many of these clients had him on their payroll when he was Speaker.

With brother Armand Paul now safely ensconced in the state assembly, Alfonse could turn his attention to other "requests." As the executive leader of Island Park, he was constantly bedeviled by members of the local party who knew how things worked.

Catherine Fazio was skeptical about what D'Amato's patronage did for the village. "Some people got little jobs that weren't worth very much. A number of people I know got little jobs after they retired. They were pretty much no-show jobs. They worked on Long Beach Road and at the beach club or at the golf course."

One example of D'Amato's influence peddling, which later came back to haunt him, was the case of Robert Marcus, an Island Park Club member. Soon after he became supervisor in 1971, D'Amato was approached by Marcus—a garbageman working for the Hempstead Sanitation Department—with a request that D'Amato get him a raise. Marcus has been described by D'Amato as "unsophisticated."

Marcus was a problem for D'Amato, since he was one of the ten Island Park Club committeemen. Despite his title, however, Marcus was not in a position to put much pressure on his club leader. He was married, a father of young children, earning $7,500, living with his in-laws in an Island Park bungalow, unlikely ever to rise above his humble position and therefore, clearly, never to be of much use to D'Amato. He was merely a supplicant, depending on the generosity of a man who was basically disinterested. Fortunately for Marcus, two of his more influential fellow committeemen were willing to lend a helping hand. They spoke to D'Amato, and his previous indifference turned to concern.

D'Amato described—years later, again under oath—what he then decided to do under the whip of Marcus's colleagues: "I called the commissioner of sanitation [William Landman, soon to be convicted of extorting money for the party from sanitation workers]. I told him that I understood Bob was doing a good job. He was having some difficulties. Could he recommend him. He said that the had no trouble in doing that. And he was submitted for a raise through that process."

D'Amato allowed the exact nature of "that process" to remain obscure. In essence, what happened after D'Amato's call was that the commissioner of sanitation—who had the power to effect the raise merely by sending an authorization to his payroll department—contacted Joe Margiotta and asked whether Marcus should be given his raise. Margiotta's answer: "No!"

Every day of the year the boss of bosses received requests for approvals of pay raises or promotions for individuals who were doing "a good job." The problem was how to differentiate between those who, by his private standards, were really deserving and those merely judged deserving by others. The test of merit, in his eyes, was simple: Did the applicant contribute at least 1 percent of his salary to the party coffers? Did Margiotta have a receipt in party headquarters verifying Robert Marcus's payment of that essential bribe? A routine check had resulted in information that didn't put supplicant Marcus in a good light.

Club leader D'Amato informed the two committeemen of Margiotta's rejection; one of them was Daniel V. Kikkert, D'Amato's eventual successor as executive leader (soon to become a Hempstead town attorney), a man whose opinion could not easily be ignored. D'Amato discussed his problem with the boss. Although D'Amato claimed to have no recollection of the actual conversation, the import of Margiotta's response seems to have been: "Rules are rules."

The sovereign of Nassau had spoken, though only about the destiny of one unsophisticated fallen sparrow. Rather than plead Marcus's case any further, D'Amato decided on an elegant solution: he paid the required bribe with money Committeeman Marcus had collected for the Committeemen's Council checking account.

We know this from a letter D'Amato was indiscreet enough to write on June 9, 1971, which has since come to be known as "the smoking-gun letter." It is addressed to Donald Woolnough, Margiotta's lieutenant at Nassau County Republican headquarters in the Garden City Hotel, and reads in full:

Dear Don,

I have spoken to Mr. Margiotta and he has indicated to me that the raise for Mr. Robert Marcus of the Sanitation Department would be approved if he took care of the 1%.

Accordingly, please find check for $75.00 from the Island Park Republican Committeemen's Council.

> Warmest personal regards,
> Cordially,
> (signed) Al
> Alfonse D'Amato, Supervisor

D'Amato was buying his clubhouse member a government raise by paying a bribe to Margiotta. Aside from the illegality of what he was proposing, D'Amato revealed a numbed, if not absent, sense of morality. There were hundreds of other Hempstead garbagemen who wanted a raise, yet Marcus's request, endorsed by D'Amato's bribe, was sufficient to deny them fair treatment.

Although he was writing to a party official about a party matter, D'Amato used official town supervisor's stationery, an indication he viewed himself as so impervious to retaliation that it was unnecessary to be cautious.

By January 1972, Jim Nagourney considered Al D'Amato somewhat out of control. As Nagourney's reward for electing some of the Republican "nonincumbents" in 1970, Margiotta had arranged to appoint the campaign strategist city manager of Long Beach, the town bordering Island Park on the south. Nagourney recalled that he and D'Amato had both been in office only a few weeks when "one day my secretary told me Al D'Amato was on the phone. I said, 'Hi, Al,' and that was the last word I got in. I just heard three minutes of screaming, and all I said was 'But, Al . . . but, Al . . . I don't know what you're talking about.' "

Between bursts of vulgarity, Nagourney pieced together that D'Amato was upset "about what one of my deputy city attorneys was doing in his private practice and how it affected some D'Amato friend. He was yelling and screaming and ended by saying that 'you just remind that guy that the world is round.' I said, 'Al, I don't even know what you're talking about. You're telling me to stomp on this guy and you've never explained what he's doing.' "

Nagourney shook his head.

FOUR

THE NOT-SO-CIVIL SERVICE

Most new Nassau residents were Democrats, but they were
soon visited by a Republican committeeman who warned
that if they wanted their son to get a summer job at the
beach or have their garbage picked up, it would be wise to visit
the board of elections and register Republican. Al D'Amato was not
offended by such requests. His father was a loyal Republican, and
Al was pleased that his beliefs and his advantage were so neatly
joined. He knew that politics for the professional was not the politics described in civics classes.

But who gave young Al his graduate political training? What
were the standards they urged him to adopt? What kind of party
was Republican county leader Joe Margiotta running?

Nassau County officials in the early 1970s had come to the point
that county officials all over America are now reaching. Having
convinced the voters that their minimal services were indispensable
for the preservation of democracy, party leaders were busy dipping
their hands into a variety of public treasuries.

In 1971, when Al D'Amato became Hempstead town supervisor,
he had the disadvantage of a bad role model on the party ladder
above him; Joe Margiotta had simultaneously made his obedient
servant Ralph Caso county executive. In the secrecy of his soul
Ralph Caso dreamed that someday he might be the first Italian-
Catholic president of the United States.

34

When I first met Caso at the end of 1985 in his shabby office in a three-story commercial building near the Long Island Railroad tracks in Merrick, that dream was just another source of despair. He had been out of office for eight years. The unimposing, ruddy-faced Caso now spent his time regretting the past, trembling at what was to come, and reading prayer cards he had spread out on his otherwise empty desk.

Caso had made the mistake of alienating Boss Margiotta in 1974 when, despite Margiotta's objection, he accepted the state party's nomination for lieutenant governor. He then went on to defeat, the victim of a voter backlash against the crimes of Watergate and President Richard Nixon's resignation. In an endeavor to teach those indentured to him that ignoring his command was a sure way to end one's career, Margiotta hounded Caso out of public life.

But in 1971 the boss and Caso seemed content with each other. Margiotta had picked Caso as county executive because he knew Caso would take orders. Caso told me that Margiotta never let him make a single decision about job assignments. "No one got a job unless he [Margiotta] sent them as someone who must be appointed."

To the casual observer, it looked as if Caso were in charge of appointing commissioners and deputy commissioners: He was the one who submitted their names to the six-member board of super-visors. Caso explained the real process: "The board of supervisors had to approve, by resolution, all the appointments made by the county executive. But that's a technicality. Before the person gets on the calendar for approval, he had to get the political approval of Margiotta."

Caso might have added that to become a *Republican member* of the board of supervisors you needed Margiotta's approval. D'Amato already had that approval. As Hempstead's new supervi-sor, he was automatically on the board, as were the heads of the county's five major towns, a majority of whom were Margiotta's puppets. Should Caso have an impulse to occasionally submit a name Margiotta had not approved, the boss was in a position to have D'Amato, and the other members of the board he controlled, exercise his veto.

In order to tighten his grip on county government, Margiotta had Caso set up a new "personnel agency" that would screen job appli-cants who had passed civil service tests and were awaiting

35

appointment. He then had Caso designate Al Riehl, a party hack, head of the new agency. Riehl was recommended for this pivotal job by Al D'Amato, who assured Margiotta of Riehl's reliability. Riehl had been mayor of Island Park and still lived there. He was a member of D'Amato's club and talked to Al every day.

The Unity party's former leader, Terry Boyle, offered a compelling reason why Al Riehl was bound to take orders from D'Amato and Margiotta. Boyle called it "the five-year bit." After pointing out that Island Park mayors earn a modest $3,200 annually, while trustees receive just $1,200, he explained, "Most of the Island Park trustees and mayors, like Al Riehl, go on the county payroll at a high salary for the last five years of their work career. Then they have a pension and benefits based on their total service with the village and the county and retire as if they had been earning the last five years' salary for their whole work career." Riehl knew that the only way he could get those last five years of exorbitant pension credit was to perform the way Margiotta wanted him to.

Margiotta wanted the new personnel agency because it tightened his control over government appointments. Caso understood Margiotta's motives and endorsed them but years later claimed that the new agency was his attempt to gain some independence from the party's stranglehold on appointments. "I had set up the employment agency in the county so that they [job seekers] wouldn't have to go to a political boss . . . but the stupidity of that was I let him [Margiotta] pick the guy who was going to run the agency—Riehl. Who as I sat and talked to him, as I'm sitting and talking across the desk to you—I'd tell him, 'I don't want you going to headquarters. I don't want you talking to Woolnough [Margiotta's assistant at party headquarters].You're to advertise if jobs are available and let people come in off the street.' And he would say, 'Okay.' "

Caso pictured himself as being deceived by people he trusted, all of whom were secretly taking orders from Margiotta. "You see, I never believed people could be so rotten. That they would betray me." In order to be betrayed, however, one must be deceived. Caso knew exactly why Riehl was heading the personnel agency and to whom he owed his primary allegiance.

In a confessional mood that sometimes visits traumatized sinners, Caso admitted that not only were Riehl and D'Amato taking orders from Margiotta; he was on the same leash. Soon after being sworn in, Caso sent a directive to all personnel officials. He ordered them, before hiring anyone, to send Al D'Amato's clubhouse buddy Al Riehl copies of graded civil service lists requesting his preference. He told Riehl to check the voter rolls and determine the party affiliation of the successful test takers. Riehl would then print next to each name on the list—before returning it to the personnel office—an "R" for an endorsed Republican, a "D" for a rejected Democrat, or an "neD," indicating that the individual was not enrolled but had nevertheless failed the test of employability because an enrolled Democrat had been detected at the same address.

What made this tampering possible was a loophole in the state civil service law, the "one-in-three rule." It gave the department head the right to fill a vacancy with *any* of the top three persons on a civil service list. Although the number-one man might have scored substantially higher than his nearest competitor, the third man on the list could get the job. Caso dictated that if the first two candidates were not Republicans but the third one was, the third candidate was to be selected. Only if all three candidates were Democrats was it theoretically possible to assign the job to such a person.

Margiotta maneuvered to avoid letting even that stray dissident make it onto a Nassau payroll. If some troika of Democrats were on the top of a list, the list would be allowed to expire, and the vacancy would be filled by a provisional appointee with a new title but the same duties. Since new titles could be created by a majority vote of the three-member Nassau County Civil Service Commission—and those members were picked by Margiotta—he only had to tell the commissioners what new provisional title was required to see it authorized.

A March 1972 State Civil Service Commission audit of the Nassau County Civil Service Commission concluded that the county commission allowed too many patronage jobs to be created—60 percent of all jobs under its jurisdiction. It also charged that the Nassau commission gave too few examinations, let provisional employees work beyond the nine-month state limit, and frequently failed to use exam lists to fill jobs held by provisional employees.

The auditors documented a method of bypassing civil service laws. There were "more than one hundred examples . . . in the county service alone of a practice of granting additional provisional appointments, usually to a higher-level title, after the provisional has failed the examination for the lower-level title."

The party man from Island Park who had been given a provisional job by his executive leader, Al D'Amato, having been incompetent enough to fail a test for the position he had been working in, often for years, then felt justified to ask Al for another even more prestigious provisional job. In the unlikely event that the Nassau County Civil Service Commission felt moved to schedule a test for that provisional job, the incompetent worker had no reason to panic. Failure in one position merely provided the loyal party worker with a promotional opportunity.

The audit commented: "Neither the State Constitution nor the Civil Service Law contemplated the making of careers based on provisional appointments."

The auditors were particularly critical of the commission's decision to issue a blanket "exempt" classification covering 101 positions, with total annual salaries of $1,397,000, in offices of the county's board of supervisors—where Al D'Amato maintained a second staff—and in the county executive's office. "There is nothing in the Civil Service Law that contemplates or permits the wholesale allocation of jobs in these two offices to the unclassified service," the auditors said.

The key figure on the Nassau County Civil Service Commission over a period of many years had been its executive director, Adele Leonard, a diminutive blonde lady who had the knack of pleasing politicians.

In 1968, as part of Hempstead Republicans' attempt to create duplicate town jobs that could be distributed without interference from county Democrat Nickerson, the town board voted to set up its own civil service commission. Assemblyman Margiotta led the fight in Albany to get the legislature to authorize the secession of the town from the county commission. In an endeavor to find out why Hempstead politicos had been allowed to capture the civil service, I interviewed Mrs. Leonard on August 22, 1985, in the witness waiting room at the Uniondale courthouse, after she had testified at a trial on behalf of the Republican party. She was wearing a black suit with a gold pin on her left lapel. She seemed weary, perhaps ill. Her eyelids were normally hooded, but now her right eyelid drooped. I prefaced my first question by remarking, "You had a working operation in the 1960s in Nassau County. You gave tests for the whole county." Under those circumstances, I wanted to know, "Why did the town of Hempstead set up its own shop?"

She responded with obvious approval for their initiative. "Of course, Hempstead filled all their vacancies with the people we tested, but they wanted to do their own testing. The legislature allowed them to do it, so why shouldn't they?" Nassau's civil service watchdog seemed less like a Doberman pinscher than a somewhat self-absorbed poodle.

A crisis occurred in Democrat Adele Leonard's career when the Republicans reclaimed the county executive's office from Eugene Nickerson in 1971. Mrs. Leonard soon found an opportunity to ingratiate herself with Nassau's new rulers. Nassau Coliseum—the future home of the Islanders hockey team and Wrestlemania high jinx—was to be completed on a portion of what was once Mitchell Field in January 1972. Mrs. Leonard knew that the prospect of staffing that facility made visions of sugar plums dance in Margiotta's head.

On August 13, 1972, *Newsday* printed the results of an investigation by a team of reporters, led by Brian Donovan, into staffing irregularities at the new stadium.

> With the cooperation of the supposedly nonpolitical commission, the GOP has turned the Coliseum into a rich source of political patronage. Those placed on Coliseum-related payrolls have included 22 GOP committeemen, several relatives of influential Nassau Republicans, and other active party workers and contributors.

Donovan went on to name names, among whom were Ralph Caso's sister, Virginia, who had previously dipped her foot into the patronage pool when she worked for the board of elections. She became confidential assistant to John Pingle, the Coliseum's director, who screened applicants and was himself a committeeman and former president of Margiotta's Uniondale Club.

When asked to comment about this example of nepotism, Caso responded indignantly that he was embarrassed that his sister's $13,125 salary was not higher. "Why," he demanded to know, "should my sister be prejudiced against from working—to support my mother, if you want to get into hearts and flowers—just because I'm county executive?" Caso seemed to imply that without this job his sister would be permanently unemployed.

Donovan explained how "neutral" civil service procedures had been bypassed:

"The commission's actions in staffing the Coliseum were supervised by Adele Leonard, the agency's executive director [who] stood to lose the job when the GOP took over the county last year.

"But the Republicans have been pleased with her performance. On May 2 [1972], after the majority of Coliseum jobs had been created and filled, the GOP-controlled commission board voted to clear the way for her to remain in her $31,900-a-year post until August 5, 1974."

Coliseum workers interviewed by *Newsday* said they had first been screened for their jobs by their political leaders. When *Newsday* asked Mrs. Leonard about violations of the civil service law, "she said she felt that any of the commission's violations were 'victimless crimes.' " The phrase became chic at that time but was usually applied to bookmaking and prostitution.

When asked, "What about the person who wanted to take a test and get a job?" She replied: "Who's he?" In her defense, Mrs. Leonard remarked, "All I can say is, we don't do things without reasons."

Mrs. Leonard, the designated defender of the civil service, protested that she did not understand the nature of the problem. "If this is patronage, then it's a big plus for patronage."

The benefits Adele Leonard was to receive from her new Republican bosses were never certain, nor were their demands ever permanently satisfied. The Coliseum staffing concessions were merely viewed by Margiotta as the first installment on what was to be a steady source of political favors.

The next installment came due in August 1972. Mrs. Leonard announced she was going to campaign for Al D'Amato's brother, Armand Paul, who was running for a seat in the state assembly. Since Mrs. Leonard's nonpartisan position as head of the county's civil service commission called for her to distance herself from politics and since she had never before taken part in a campaign, her partisan declaration raised eyebrows.

Mrs. Leonard explained that she had come to know the young D'Amato—only recently out of law school—in his brief role as counsel to Assemblyman Margiotta, with whom she occasionally conversed about civil service matters. However, the callow law school graduate's "sterling" qualities had not caused her to abandon her politically inactive status. Rather, it had been a conversation with Al D'Amato, during which the town supervisor requested her support. She felt she could not refuse.

When Ralph Caso was asked what he thought of Democrat Leonard's decision to endorse Al D'Amato's Republican brother, he said with a broad smile, "That's always refreshing, when someone sees the light."

Hempstead's secession from the Nassau County Civil Service Commission had become final in 1970, and the state consequently had reviewed Hempstead's independent commission's actions from January 1972 to January 1975. On July 18, 1975, the state commission issued a report charging that the town—under the leadership of Margiotta's henchmen Presiding Supervisor Francis Purcell and Supervisor Al D'Amato—was permitting hundreds of provisional workers to hold jobs without taking qualifying tests. During that time, when D'Amato became the de facto leader of Hempstead's government, the state audit found that the number of provisionals grew from 393 to 558, which meant that 53 percent of the town's employees had gone untested "in direct violation of state law."

The report concluded: "Most importantly, the provisional situation in Hempstead is without exception the worst of any of the 108 local civil service agencies [in the state]."

Meanwhile, Adele Leonard, on the county level, functioned with a serenity that could only be based on the assurances she was getting during her conversations with Chairman Margiotta. On March 14, 1976, *Newsday* revealed part of the reason the chairman was satisfied with her. In her 1975 report to the New York State Civil Service Commission, Mrs. Leonard had listed 630 provisional *county* appointees. Under the heading "Original Appointment Date in

Title," Mrs. Leonard claimed that only 4 of those 630 provisionals had served more than nine months, which roughly seemed to conform to the state civil service law.

Newsday discovered that a large number of the 630 provisionals actually held their jobs for several years, and these favorites included "Republican committeemen and politicians' relatives."

Mrs. Leonard's habit of allowing competitive jobs to be permanently filled with provisional appointees was first denounced by the state auditors in 1972. At that time she was asked by *Newsday* to comment on the state's criticism. She responded defiantly:

> Mrs. Leonard told *Newsday* that people also can be kept at the same job provisionally, simply by laying them off at the end of the nine-month period, and hiring them the next day for the same job. In practice, she said, "It's a joke," since the commission simply assumes each nine months that this has been done and thus saves on red tape.

Some comedians claim that the old jokes are the best; apparently, Mrs. Leonard subscribed to that school of comedy. Three years after the state auditors pointed out the error of her ways, she was still listing under "Original Appointment Date in Title" the most recent reappointment date. Her explanation this time was: "Original doesn't mean what you think it means."

Well, then, what did it mean? It meant, she explained, that when a provisional's nine months expired and there was no replacement for him from a certified list, the provisional was merely resuscitated, like the phoenix, from the ashes of his former appointment. "The old appointment doesn't exist anymore, so this becomes their original date." So much for people who don't understand English.

Mrs. Leonard, however, did not hint at an explanation for why so many committeemen and relatives of politicians were the beneficiaries of this new definition of the word "original"; good jokes don't require explanations.

Joe Margiotta and Al D'Amato's control over the lives of county workers depended on the willingness of Mrs. Leonard and the three members of the Nassau County Civil Service Commission to define words in a manner that would meet with their approval. The state civil service law had been passed in 1883 precisely to thwart men like Margiotta and D'Amato, but they had discovered that as long as Adele Leonard and her counterpart in the town of Hempstead played the game according to their rules, the law was unlikely to present any obstacle that a phone call couldn't remove.

Periodic audits by the New York Civil Service Commission reveal that every violation of the state law in the 1970s was continued into the 1990s. Exhortations to be honest, unaccompanied by specific penalties, didn't prevent politicians from illegally, and unfairly, handing out approximately twenty thousand jobs in Nassau County.

By the mid-seventies, Al D'Amato had graduated from Margiotta's finishing school for politicians. He would soon be teaching the master some new tricks.

FIVE

HOW AMERICAN POLITICIANS STAY OUT OF TROUBLE, OR DISTRICT ATTORNEY CAHN IN THE CAN

Al D'Amato, Joe Margiotta, and Al Riehl were illegally placing unqualified party hacks on government payrolls, but Nassau county district attorney William Cahn didn't seem to care. Why was Cahn, who was charged with protecting the public against lawbreakers, in effect protecting *these* lawbreakers?

William Cahn was a flamboyant figure on the Nassau scene from the day he had been appointed county district attorney by Governor Rockefeller in 1962. He came out of the same county Republican apparatus as state chief judge Sol Wachtler and displayed the same tendencies. He specialized in arrests of "international bookmakers" and housewife-prostitutes, always making sure the press knew the time and location of these events. His favorite speech focused on the need for "old-fashioned virtues." The papers often had stories about his trips, typically to places like Argentina or Mississippi, to make law-and-order speeches or interview potential "secret witnesses."

Like his friend Judge Wachtler, who phoned one of his demands for $20,000 to his former Manhattan mistress, Republican fund-raiser Joy Silverman, from Harrah's Casino in Reno, Cahn found that attending "legal conferences" allowed him to secretly indulge passions other than the law. He was an obsessive gambler, and his rising debts made him desperate.

During the time of his unchallenged public rectitude, Cahn was accused of concentrating on sensational single-act crimes, which gave the appearance of a busy prosecutor's office but had no impact on systematic corruption within the county. His pledge to the voters, through four successful campaigns, was that he would protect the utopia Margiotta and D'Amato were building from organized crime, pornography, drugs, bookmaking, and prostitution. Despite his pledge, often proclaimed from the same political podiums from which D'Amato had just made identical promises, all of these crimes increased during his administration.

Speaking about the need to do something about crime had become the standard campaign tactic of Nassau Republicans. When Sol Wachtler sought election to the New York Court of Appeals in 1972, he ran a television commercial showing him slamming a jail door and in a rich baritone vowing to "get the thieves and muggers and murderers into these cells." Strong words about crime camouflaged an absence of action and offered politicians the rhetorical equivalent of Fourth of July orations favoring patriotism. Throughout his career, Al D'Amato's success in winning voter approval can partially be attributed to his vigorous anticrime speeches.

Cahn never tired of boasting that although two hundred members of organized crime lived in Nassau County, because of their fear of him they did their business elsewhere. Cahn's claim that these mafiosi were inactive in Nassau was as invalid as his pretension that they feared him. Soldiers of the Mafia had infiltrated Nassau County during the 1920s, when Prohibition made the unguarded beaches of Long Island ideal for smuggling booze. After repeal, organized crime made its presence felt in the construction and garbage industries and in a variety of trade unions.

Cahn ran the district attorney's office as if it were a branch of the Republican party. Of his ninety-two assistant district attorneys, ninety-one were Republicans; the different drummer was a token Liberal. When accused of being tied to the Margiotta-D'Amato apparatus, Cahn responded, "Look, I know the argument that politics are bad for a D.A. In some states a D.A. who runs has to raise the war chest himself. Suddenly, a D.A. becomes the tool of just a few." Which summarized the accusations leveled against him.

Cahn ignored all charges that Margiotta and D'Amato were illegally rezoning the county in exchange for payoffs or giving out contracts to party contributors, but liked prosecuting misdemeanors that would attract the notice of a tabloid audience. His priorities were revealed by his assignment in 1971 of his chief lieutenant, Assistant District Attorney Robert Roberto, to an undercover probe of Executive Relaxation, a Syosset massage parlor. Roberto later commented that he had viewed his assignment as "a public service" which "had to be done, so I did it."

Normally this type of drudgery would have been handled by the police who specialize in vice, but Roberto made up in enthusiasm for his lack of experience. The forty-year-old prosecutor entered the Jericho Turnpike massage parlor and was introduced to Sandy, a sixteen-year-old dressed provocatively. Sandy had Roberto strip, then escorted him to a bathroom, where she bathed and powdered him.

The assistant district attorney was then led to a cubicle whose only furniture was a bed. Stressing the informal aspect of the occasion, Sandy removed her top and, after coating the dedicated public servant with baby oil, began massaging him with her breasts and manipulating his genitals.

At her prostitution trial, Roberto testified that he had allowed Sandy to exercise her professional skills on him "from my private parts up to my neck" and had ejaculated after thirty minutes.

Since Section 230 of the New York State Penal Code stated that a person was guilty of prostitution if he or she merely "agreed to engage in sexual conduct for a fee" and sexual conduct was defined as "physical contact of the person's clothed or unclothed genitals," it seemed that Roberto's dedication to his assignment had been carried to an extreme.

Cahn's vice investigator eventually paid the twenty-five-dollar fee and tipped Sandy five dollars. Several former assistant district attorneys stated that Roberto didn't have to engage in such extensive contact with the sixteen-year-old in order to meet statutory requirements of this bordello episode.

But Cahn was so pleased with Robert Roberto's performance that he took him on two overseas junkets; their cost to the Nassau taxpayer has never been divulged.

Cahn served as an important cog in the Margiotta-D'Amato operation, a role performed for politicians by Cahn's counterparts in district attorneys' offices across the country. He effectively warded off demands for investigations of Margiotta's and D'Amato's activities that, in the absence of a sympathetic county attorney, would have sent them to jail.

In April 1972, *Newsday* reported that county employees were required to pay 1 percent of their salaries to the Republican party. A charge of this nature from such a responsible source should have led Cahn to assign some of those ninety-two assistants, if not his most trustworthy traveling companion Robert Roberto, to conduct an investigation. Instead, one year later, Norman E. Blankman, a wealthy builder and independent candidate for county executive running against Caso, charged that Cahn was still refusing to investigate the accusation.

Margiotta and D'Amato were perfectly content with Cahn. Prosecution for corruption is a peril of political life. Margiotta and D'Amato accepted the risk as a potential cost of doing business, reassured by the thought that most, if not all, prosecutable offenses they had committed would remain the dirty little secret of themselves and their unindicted coconspirators. District attorneys like Cahn provide ample reason for that sanguine attitude.

The 1974 campaign occurred at a bad time for the Republican district attorney; it was played out against the cacophonous background of the national party's Watergate scandal. During the campaign, Ralph G. Sorley, a Rockville Centre physician who had appointed himself unofficial county ombudsman, charged that Cahn was guilty of double-billing the county and the National District Attorneys Association, which Cahn had once served as president, for $45,179. Dr. Sorley turned over the documents related to his charges to Denis Dillon, Cahn's Democratic opponent.

Denis Dillon, a former New York City policeman, lacked experience but attacked Cahn as a "pleasure seeker" who was absent from Nassau County five hundred days during the previous four years and in the course of his wanderings had charged the county $200,000 for his expenses.

Since the duplicate bills for identical expenses to the same events could not be denied, Cahn's explanations became tortured exercises in hair splitting. "We're not talking ethically or morally," he responded to Denis Dillon. "We're talking legally. Who was defrauded? They both expected to pay."

The Brooklyn-based Eastern District federal grand jury, which had begun its investigation of *Newsday*'s allegations of 1 percent kickbacks demanded from government workers, also began scrutinizing Dr. Sorley's charges against Cahn.

It was too much even for the citizens of Nassau County, some of whom, in the process of denying they were the victims of swindlers, had learned to accept numerous reasons why politicians do unsavory things—excusing the thieves who were cheating them even as they were being plundered.

Meanwhile, Al D'Amato was developing his network, tightening the chains that shackled him to Margiotta, making sure his Island Park committeemen were canvassing door-to-door to ensure control of his satrapy in the upcoming election, and eying the next meal on the political menu.

After election day, William Cahn became "the former district attorney," and Denis Dillon became the hope for the future. In August 1975 the federal grand jury indicted William Cahn for mail fraud, a felony he engaged in while he was double-billing. He was also indicted for perjuring himself before the grand jury and for income tax evasion.

The double-billing trial began in Brooklyn Federal Court on February 10, 1976. Cahn told the following phantasmagoric tale: It seems that between 1970 and 1974 he had a "secret informant" whom he knew only by the code name "Sam Houston." According to Cahn, Houston was in his late forties and appeared to be of Italian descent. They would meet every month or two in various cities, since Houston made it a condition of their relationship that they could meet anywhere except New York; furthermore, he insisted on not being paid for his services by county voucher.

Cahn claimed that all his problems stemmed from Sam Houston's insistence on those two points. He alleged that in 1970 he spoke to the county controller, Angelo D. Roncallo, about the possibility of paying Houston without turning in authorizing vouchers to Roncallo's office.

Roncallo was a close friend of Joe Margiotta's and was executive leader of the Oyster Bay Club. The ever-attentive Dr. Sorley charged that when Roncallo was the county controller, "he was consistently a no-show," concluding, "He made a shambles of the controller's office." A beefy extrovert, Roncallo was elected to Congress in 1972. He was tried for extortion in federal court in May 1974 and acquitted. The voters delivered a more critical verdict: He was defeated for reelection several months later.

Two weeks before Cahn's trial was to begin, Margiotta had Ralph Caso name the unemployed Roncallo to the Nassau Board of Assessors, a part-time post for which Roncallo was paid $22,300. The four Republican members of the board of supervisors, led by Al D'Amato voted to approve the nomination. Roncallo gratefully acknowledged: "It puts bread on the table, and until I build up my practice, it will be helpful."

Roncallo was now called on to help party stalwart Cahn. Testifying so soon after assuming his untaxing responsibilities as county assessor, Roncallo, under pressure from federal attorney James Drucker, insisted he didn't know whether duplicate payments would have been wrong. Had he known about them, in order to determine whether to pay, he would have sought the advice of the county attorney, who at that time was Bill Cahn.

When Cahn finally entered the witness box, Prosecutor Drucker supplied a different motive for Cahn's submission of duplicate bills, one having nothing to do with the ghostly Sam Houston. Drucker asked Cahn whether the real reason for his double billing was to get money for "the gambling losses you incurred in Las Vegas and Reno?"

Appearing astounded at the accusation, Cahn was alternately angry and patronizing, but he did concede that during sojourns to the gambling meccas of Nevada, he most often stayed as a guest in the free suites reserved for heavy hitters.

Drucker felt that gambling was the major reason for many of Cahn's trips. At one incendiary point, Drucker charged that "much of the $155,000" paid to a California detective agency on a county contract "was used to pay your gambling debts." Nassau's district attorney was on the hook to the underworld, and in one way or another he had to pay. The two hundred county mafiosi—who had been doing business in Nassau since the 'Roaring Twenties'— understood his problem and probably could not stop smirking.

In his charge to the jury, Judge John F. Dooling advised that it was illegal to collect twice for expenses incurred once. "Each organization was entitled to be told the facts so duplicate payments could be avoided and the single expense properly allocated between the two."

Despite Judge Dooling's almost explicit instruction to find Cahn guilty, on February 27, 1976, the frustrated jury told him that they stood eleven to one for conviction but that one man was insisting he had a "reasonable doubt." That doubt led Judge Dooling to set a new trial date for May 3.

At the second trial, Cahn, stating that he could not afford an attorney, defended himself. County assessor Angelo Roncallo— who would eventually become a state supreme court judge under Chief Judge Wachtler's supervision—again came to his aid, recalling that Cahn had once spoken to him about paying an informant without vouchers, a procedure, Roncallo said, he opposed.

On May 22, 1976, after a two-and-a-half-week trial, Cahn was found guilty, sentenced to a year in prison, and fined $2,500.

The mail-fraud charge was merely a device to bring Nassau's former district attorney before a jury. The trial record abounded with references to other crimes; indictments for perjury and income tax evasion still hung over his head.

The lesson of this scandal was that Margiotta and D'Amato, who used a multitude of illegal practices to hire and promote government workers, had also debased the legal office charged with prosecuting organized crime and political corruption. District Attorney Cahn was in their pocket. His job was to keep Margiotta, D'Amato, and their friends out of jail by ensuring that his office never took notice of their transgressions, or if some whistle-blower insisted on redress, making certain that the only action was a cover-up.

SIX

THE D'AMATOS GIVE AND TAKE

In the summer of 1971, property owners living near the coastal swamps of Oceanside, New York, twenty-five miles east of Manhattan, began to complain about the local muskrats. The muskrat is a large water-dwelling rodent with thick light brown fur and webbing between the toes of its rear feet. When muskrats live near houses, they destroy lawns, ruin vegetable plots, and tip over garbage cans looking for food. Residents of this Long Island community also suspected them of carrying diseases, some as yet uncataloged.

The Oceanside complaints reached Al D'Amato, Hempstead's new supervisor. Oceanside is part of the town of Hempstead, and thirty-four-year-old Supervisor D'Amato had jurisdiction over the half-submerged muskrat burrows. Usually such a complaint would have been handled by the extermination department, but D'Amato chose to intervene.

He phoned the press and announced that he would set out on an expedition to trap muskrats in Oceanside swamp. Shortly before noon the next day, D'Amato, wearing knee-high rubber boots and a white safari outfit, led a bustling group of reporters and cameramen in search of the prey.

D'Amato carried a wood-framed, chicken-wire trap two feet long and six inches high and wore a grin on his face that did not suggest seriousness of purpose. His trap, in fact, was too small for a fully grown muskrat, which normally is ten inches tall.

D'Amato soon emerged from the swamp with an empty trap. A reporter pointed out that muskrats only came out at night and so the supervisor had staged his show at the wrong time, if he actually wanted to catch anything.

D'Amato had in fact come back with what he set out to capture: publicity. The next day, the papers carried a picture of the smiling supervisor, trap in hand, trekking through the bog, seeking the muskrats' nests. Accompanying the picture was the comment of a householder who lived on the border of the swamp—he was "glad somebody did something about" the muskrats.

This was the kind of *something* in which D'Amato specialized: a well-publicized media event aimed solely at capturing attention. His skill at organizing such extravaganzas throughout his career partly explains his extraordinary electoral success. That Al D'Amato spent much of the rest of his time feathering the family nest is made clear by his behavior, in 1973, in the case of the proposed janitorial contract for the Nassau County Medical Center.

The medical center had traditionally managed its own janitorial services, but the attempt by private companies to obtain that potentially lucrative contract attracted the attention of the D'Amatos.

Armand M. D'Amato, family patriarch, had been promoted in his short period of employment with the county to director of commerce research, for which he was paid the then respectable salary of $23,439 per annum. His duties didn't completely occupy him, and he continued to run his insurance business.

In early 1973 he had a conversation with a friend, William E. Pyne, who had been a vice president of a Delaware firm that had earlier tried to interest the medical center in its services. According to *Newsday*, the elder D'Amato urged his friend Pyne to "start your own business," advising him that "it doesn't hurt for you to know the right people."

Pyne accepted Armand's advice and on May 31, 1973, formed CCS Services. Assemblyman Armand Paul D'Amato took his father's friend in hand and drew up the incorporation papers, for which he was paid $1,400.

In order for Pyne to get the medical-center janitorial contract, it was necessary to change deeply imbedded ways of doing things. The center's director, Dr. James Collins, opposed awarding the contract to any outside firm—he was especially opposed to the $140,000 bid by CCS, considering it too costly.

Pyne's hopes rested on knowing "the right people." D'Amato, by then town supervisor for two years, was also a member of the county board of supervisors, which controlled the center. What heartened Pyne even more was that Supervisor Al D'Amato was chairman of the board's health and welfare committee; as such, he introduced all of the county's legislation involving the center, including resolutions awarding its contracts.

Pyne submitted the proposed CCS contract to the center's board of managers in August 1973. On September 12 he met with Supervisor D'Amato to see what Armand's older son might be able to do for him. Later that day, Al arranged a meeting between Pyne and John O'Shaughnessy, then a member of the center's board of managers but soon to be promoted to county attorney and, subsequently, to a judgeship in Nassau's district court.

On October 10, Assemblyman D'Amato and his father became CCS directors, and Armand Sr. wrote out a $100 check in payment for his purchase of company stock.

Despite the aggressive support of the D'Amatos, approval of the contract was delayed: Dr. Collins's opposition had not abated. Pyne complained to the D'Amato board members. In answer to his complaints, Pyne told *Newsday*, "Assemblyman D'Amato and his father explained to him [Pyne] several times that Collins's opposition to the CCS proposal was the only problem . . . and that once Collins left, it would be approved." Since Collins was retiring in a few months, the D'Amatos' request for patience seemed credible.

In April 1974, as Dr. Collins's retirement approached, Pyne formed AHA Consultants, a corporation that would seek janitorial contracts with other hospitals. During the months that followed, he issued free shares of AHA stock to the assemblyman and his father. Armand Paul once again handled the incorporation papers.

With Collins out of the way on June 1, CCS's biggest fans, the D'Amato family, were looking forward to collecting their first dividend check. Instead, someone told *Newsday* that CCS and the D'Amatos were involved in a deal that might interest the public.

On September 11, one day after a *Newsday* reporter went to the center and asked to see a copy of the CCS contract, Pyne was told that his proposal was rejected. The FBI began to look into charges concerning CCS and the D'Amatos.

On October 27, *Newsday* reported:

> In an interview, Assemblyman D'Amato acknowledged that he suggested to Pyne, after learning of the *Newsday* and federal investigations, that Pyne "rip up" those stock certificates. Later, Pyne said, the assemblyman told him to make what Pyne considered misleading entries in the company books.

To support his allegations, Pyne gave *Newsday* a recording of a phone conversation he had made with Assemblyman D'Amato on September 27—after the elder D'Amato had feverishly returned his stock certificates—during which the assemblyman had discussed how to make the corporate records less damaging to the D'Amatos.

Assemblyman D'Amato assured *Newsday* that " 'it never entered my mind' that his brother, the supervisor, might ever have to vote on a CCS contract."

Newsday reported that Alfonse defended himself against possible skeptics with the same note of bold indifference. "Supervisor D'Amato denied any wrong-doing and said nobody in their family ever had intended to benefit from the proposal." His father had apparently bought a share of CCS stock with no intention of collecting a profit.

The Nassau ethics code decreed that no county employee should "become interested directly or indirectly in any manner whatsoever . . . in any business or professional dealings with the county." It further required that any county employee "who has knowledge of any matter being considered" by the county "in which he has any direct or indirect financial or other private interest" must file a public disclosure statement revealing "the nature and extent" of that interest.

The elderly D'Amato was clearly covered by this provision but had never filed a disclosure. Since Alfonse, as a member of the county board of supervisors, received $15,000 a year from the county, it seemed that he also overlooked the obvious responsibility to report his involvement—"directly or indirectly"—with the CCS deal.

The CCS affair represented the first time Alfonse was connected to a corrupt deal of the sort that in one form or another has dogged him most of his career. But since District Attorney Bill Cahn was then still in office, D'Amato was forced only to endure some criticism, which (since none of it was voiced by Joe Margiotta) was easy to ignore.

Jim Nagourney, Margiotta's other favorite in the Republican organization, remembered the events of that period with painful clarity because of what he considers to be D'Amato's "cruel nature." The uproar caused by the D'Amato family over the medical center janitorial service contract had not yet subsided when political bosses of the county decided to introduce legalized gambling and Nagourney found himself embroiled with D'Amato.

Early in the decade, the state legislature had authorized counties so inclined to institute Off-Track Betting (OTB), but Nassau didn't get around to opening horse-betting parlors until the beginning of 1975. Since Nagourney's job as city manager of Long Beach had ended after the previous election, when Democrats regained control of the town, Margiotta had been looking for a place for his protégé. He decided that the efficient Nagourney was the perfect man to be executive director of the fledgling OTB operation. Someone of his caliber was needed. OTB was important to the party. There were plans to open twenty-five branch offices, which meant that Joe Margiotta had twenty-five branch manager jobs to hand out to party soldiers. There would also be supervisor jobs, teller jobs, bookkeeper jobs, and loads of uncategorized jobs, all at the discretion of the party. At lunch at the Hempstead Golf Club, County Executive Caso was informed of the boss's decision, and Nagourney was hired.

Nagourney decided to open a betting store in Hempstead directly under his OTB offices and another one in Island Park, where, he explained, "the demographics were right."

He immediately contacted D'Amato and discussed his plans. "We always cleared it with the [Republican] leader," Nagourney said. "That wasn't just good politics. That was good business sense. He's going to know that town better than I do. And it would be highly discourteous not to."

They had a number of lengthy conversations. "I described the whole plan. How we were going to handle the parking and everything like that."

Nagourney stressed that he had D'Amato's approval. As a result, "we negotiated [with a store owner] and signed a lease. We then

55

announced the location. There was an outcry. 'You're too close to the school. This is terrible. What are you doing.' "

Nagourney continued: "D'Amato then starts to get nervous. He called and said, 'Hey, you can't say that I approved this. You guys have to recognize that nobody has a job if the guy whose name goes on the ballot doesn't get elected. So when you're protecting me, you're protecting yourselves as well.' " The practical Nagourney responded, "I have no problem with that, Al."

D'Amato then spelled out what price Nagourney must pay to get the Island Park OTB opened. "Well, they want to have a public hearing."

"Okay, we'll have a public hearing."

"It's going to be at the Oceanside High School auditorium. I'll handle it, but you'll have to be there."

Nagourney wanted to send his deputy, since he was going to be opening the Hempstead OTB betting office with a big ceremony the next morning, January 30, 1975. But D'Amato insisted. "Absolutely not. You can't delegate. You've got to be there yourself. I don't care about your other problem."

Nagourney pressed on: "I thought Al was going to look after me. I felt it was not going to be a pleasant meeting, but my experience is that it's always worse thinking about them than it actually is—all those life experiences that you don't look forward to. But this was the only time where my worst expectations were too conservative. Every time I get in trouble since then I think, Remember Island Park. Things aren't necessarily as bad as you think they are. They're worse."

The nearby Oceanside High School auditorium had been chosen because no facility existed in Island Park large enough to accommodate the five hundred people who showed up. Nagourney felt sanguine. "We were sitting next to each other on the dais. The only thing he said to me in a whisper was: 'I'll do all the talking. You don't say anything.'

"I'm not particularly concerned. I'll sit there and they'll heap abuse on me and Al will defuse it. And then we'll go and open up the office. Let them let their steam off."

Nagourney was unconcerned because he knew that OTB wasn't *his* project; it was *the party's* project. As long as he had been scrupulously careful to clear everything with D'Amato, what difference could this meeting make? Nassau County wasn't a stronghold of participatory democracy.

"Al gets up to speak. He's the first speaker. And he's going through his presentation. 'Well, despite the fact that Mr. Nagourney did not speak to me personally . . .'

"I'm not bothered by that. I'm a big boy and I understand politics. He starts describing why, despite that, the idea may not be that bad."

As I watched Nagourney reliving those events, his voice lowered, and he became tense, dramatic. "He [D'Amato] senses by the body language of the crowd he's on the wrong side. I have never in my life seen such an artful change. You couldn't find the seam in it. 'But on the other hand . . .' He then goes into a vicious attack on me. Totally switching position, he attacks me for not having spoken to him, for picking the worst location. What a despicable human being I am and he won't let this happen. He's glad the community has brought this to his attention in time.

"This was after starting a speech where he was expressing his support. I was the only one who knew what was happening. I was the only one who knew what his real position was."

As Nagourney sat dumbfounded on the platform, speakers lined up at the floor microphone to express their hostility. "I have never been as physically frightened as I was that night," Nagourney said. "The way that crowd was abusing me. One speaker after another was saying what a son of a bitch I was. 'But what was the worst thing of all was how you could do this to such a wonderful human being like Al D'Amato.' "

As far as Nagourney was concerned, D'Amato had become the leader of a lynch mob. "The physical fright came as I was leaving the auditorium. I had so many people purposely banging into me, trying to hurt me, trying to make sure I understood how they felt. I've never been jostled like that in my life. I thought I was going to be physically attacked in the parking lot. It was totally unexpected. I had never experienced a verbal beating such as I had taken." Compounding D'Amato's betrayal was "that I had to sit there while Al was telling those incredible lies."

Nagourney's ordeal continued the next morning when he arrived at OTB Hempstead headquarters for the ceremony opening the first betting store. "A half hour before the public ceremony, officials were going to gather in my office, have some coffee and cake, and then go downstairs as a group. So Caso and Margiotta and D'Amato are there, and D'Amato is telling the story about what happened the night before: 'It's the funniest thing that ever happened.' "

Nagourney paused momentarily and then continued. "I've told you about the terrible position he put me in with the way he lied, and he thinks it's the funniest thing that ever happened. He's telling this to the whole political leadership in Nassau County. He's telling them about this marvelous, funny experience he had and what a terrible evening Jimmy Nagourney had. 'Jim Nagourney really suffered last night. It was a funny show. You should have been there to see how Nagourney had to suffer.' "

The shock that he experienced at D'Amato's hands still bothers him. "Now, it's fifteen years later, and I've never told the story publicly—how I suffered like that and covered for Al in one of his great lies."

I asked him, "D'Amato, even in this semiprivate moment, never said, 'Thank you'?"

"Not only did he not say thank you; he took pleasure out of my pain."

"What happened to the office in Island Park?" I asked.

"We didn't open it. Even though we had a signed lease. I told the landlord: 'Al D'Amato will do anything he has to do to stop this. If this goes through, in one way or another, you're going to suffer. My advice is, cancel the lease, although we have no legal grounds to do so. You have to do business in town.' He [the landlord] never said another word."

Less than a month later, on February 23, 1975, *Newsday* revealed that Presiding Supervisor Francis Purcell and Supervisor D'Amato were involved in a major rip-off of Hempstead taxpayers. They had been authorizing large payments to dozens of Republican party officials and their family members under a no-bid system that allowed party favorites to monopolize the rental of dump trucks to the town. The town owned seventy dump trucks but spent $500,000 a year to rent, without bidding, ninety more trucks, whose model, specified by Purcell and D'Amato, was owned by those party members who somehow knew which would be the favored model.

In *Newsday*, reporter Dan Hertzberg, who later won a Pulitzer Prize for investigative reporting at the *Wall Street Journal*, identified "57 GOP committeemen or members of their families who have rented trucks to the town in the past eight years." The town had paid $3 million to these people; not one was a truck driver. Numbered in their ranks was Nassau's deputy county executive— Ralph Cuso's right-hand man—Thomas DeVivo; also, the executive director of Hempstead's civil service commission, Sidney Rosenthal.

In an endeavor to discover how widespread the practice had become, Hertzberg contacted other local heads of government. "Officials in Nassau's two other towns and the county government," Hertzberg wrote, "all of which are Republican controlled, say they stopped renting trucks long ago because it was too costly."

The right to rent trucks to the town was frequently passed down in Republican families from one generation to another. When Elizabeth Hilgendorff of Elmont died in 1970, having been an active member of the Nassau County Federation of Republican Women to the end, her estate tax return listed five trucks and explained: "The unincorporated business, if it could be called that, consisted solely of a political favor afforded the decedent by the Town of Hempstead, cancelable at will. The decedent's late husband, John Hilgendorff, was an Executive Committeeman."

Husband John, who had died in 1952, had been renting the town trucks since the 1940s, and even after the death of his wife, the estate continued to rent the family inheritance to the town at a biweekly rate in excess of $900.

Al D'Amato did not invent this scam; he merely nourished it. In the process, he benefited in the fashion unique to politicians who have control over the public treasury. By covertly distributing taxpayers' dollars to a group of influential members of the party, he was, at no expense to himself, preparing for the moment when he would ask them to return the favor.

SEVEN
D'AMATO COMMITS PERJURY

At the end of 1974, U.S. Attorney David G. Trager, head of the Eastern District, located in Brooklyn, sought an indictment against Nassau County Republicans, charging they were forcing government workers to kick back 1 percent of their salary to the party. The grand jury heard testimony from Paul Clark, a former deputy commissioner in the party's favorite patronage pantry, the Department of General Services, that in addition to his 1 percent kickback, he had been ordered to buy a $500 ticket to an affair honoring Assemblyman Joe Margiotta. He had also been forbidden to dismiss his assistant, Margiotta's mother-in-law, Agnes Crean. He claimed that when he refused to do what the party asked him to do and threatened to do otherwise, he was fired.

By January 1975, Trager's deputy, Assistant U.S. Attorney James Drucker, brought an average of fifteen witnesses into the fourth-floor chambers of the Brooklyn grand jury every Friday to outline the dimensions of Nassau corruption. Each day, Margiotta and D'Amato could read accusations made against them in the New York press.

There was an outpouring of witnesses—politicians, civil service employees, businessmen, and a cross section of Nassau society. Over a period of months, several hundred of them lined up in the dimly lit corridor outside the paneled grand jury room, prepared to describe—many with great reluctance—how government functioned under the fist of the Republican party.

On May 2, 1975, it was Hempstead supervisor Al D'Amato's turn to testify. He prefaced his remarks to the grand jury with phrases such as: "To be quite honest with you," "To be quite candid," and "Again being very honest."

Prompted by Drucker's questions, Al D'Amato told the jurors it was "general knowledge" that Nassau employees were expected to give the Republican party 1 percent of their salary. However, although he knew from "1961 or '62" what every loyal employee was expected to contribute, "to be quite honest with you, I don't recall what I gave in the early years. . . . But I did, as the years proceeded, use one percent as a guide."

Since D'Amato had already said that he knew about the 1 percent kickback from "1961 or '62," Drucker asked whether anyone had told him that 1 percent was the guideline for those wanting raises and promotions. Disingenuously, he responded, "When I came to the employ of the town in the period mentioned, about 1965, no one ever mentioned that to me." No one had to, since he already knew the size of the kickback for at least four years.

Subsequently, he informed the jurors, he had heard about it from talks with "employees" whose names he no longer remembered. D'Amato was uncomfortable with his evasions, and *"Again being very honest"* and *"To be quite candid"* made their appearance.

Drucker tried to pin him down: "What we are trying to determine is whether the contributions were voluntary or forced."

At this point, D'Amato could have testified that he knew that at least one contribution of 1 percent had been forced: the one paid when Robert Marcus had wanted a raise in Hempstead's Department of Sanitation. The smoking-gun letter written on Marcus's behalf by club leader and Town Supervisor D'Amato on June 9, 1971, was already in Drucker's possession, having been swept up by FBI agents in a raid on Nassau Republican headquarters in preparation for this investigation. But the incriminating missive lay buried, and undiscovered, among crates of eye-glazing documents.

In reality, D'Amato in his role as executive leader of the Island Park Republican Club, had been forcing such payments from the easily coerced and the more reluctantly giving for at least ten years. His circle of extortion had widened during his two years as receiver of taxes, riding herd over hundreds of docile civil servants.Each year, he assigned section enforcers to collect the 1 percent from intimidated workers and ordered punishment for the tardy.

Attempting to avoid self-incrimination, D'Amato confined his convoluted answer to his present job as Hempstead supervisor. "I never collected. The three or four employees directly under my responsibility—I have no recollection of ever collecting from any of them. I think they, you know, of their own—one girl lives in my town. I have known her for many, many years. She may have given me a check to hand in. I can't even recall that."

Several sections of D'Amato's testimony were perjured in that they were not simple—perhaps accidental—misstatements of facts but were deliberate attempts to lie to the grand jury. Drucker, however, had his eyes set on more tempting targets: Boss Margiotta or the more easily convictable friend of the ectoplasmic Sam Houston, Nassau district attorney William Cahn.

An example of D'Amato's perjury occurred when Drucker asked the usually verbose supervisor, "Have you put pressure onto anyone under you?" Although years later, when the statute of limitations had run out on a possible indictment, D'Amato answered the same question differently, he now responded, "No."

Further along the following exchange took place:

DRUCKER: Do you yourself know of any policy within the town of Hempstead or with any of the departments whereby supervisors in the departments ever expected to collect from the men and the men are expected to give at the risk of possibly losing overtime or other benefits? [It almost seemed as if Drucker knew about the Marcus affair.]

D'AMATO: I am not aware of any and only recently where certain statements have come out. But to my knowledge, officially and unofficially, *no one has ever come to me and complained to me and made known that type of policy [italics mine]*, and I think if it is the case, it certainly should not be collected. I would certainly use my influence to see to it that it would not be collected.

That he had used, and continued to use, his influence to see that it *was* collected was something that D'Amato gambled the jury would never find out.

The jurors' interrogation proved to be no problem for D'Amato. The first question was: "Do you have anything to do with the preparation of the budget for the town of Hempstead?" A question so far from D'Amato's personal involvement in corruption did not call for a simple no answer. Suddenly, D'Amato, who had no responsibility for the budget, was intent on explaining the intricacies of its formulation. "I will say no, but let me give you a more detailed answer." He then delivered a lecture on how budgets are prepared.

Another juror asked a typically off-the-target question: "How much is the total budget?" After D'Amato's unilluminating answer, highlighted by his candid remark "I wasn't prepared to go into those questions," the next juror's question was: "What part of that [the budget] is salary?"

The jurors' queries left little doubt that they had scant knowledge of the matters before them and less than an all-consuming interest in correcting that deficiency.

Clearly relieved when Drucker said he was finished, D'Amato exuded, "I would like to thank you, Mr. Drucker, for giving me an opportunity to get in here early and maybe escape the media." The politician's concern for image shone through.

While the federal grand jury privately listened to Al D'Amato's dubious testimony, a small group of Nassau County government workers had gone into state supreme court to file the 1 percent case against the Republican party that was to last for the next nineteen years. The party immediately hired a battalion of lawyers, headed by its former leader, the ethically numb Joseph Carlino. The man who got young Al his first county job was now deputized by the party to see if he could preserve the income of the rest of the brethren.

EIGHT

HOW AL WINS

On March 5, 1976, the federal grand jury, which had been interviewing witnesses for over a year, returned indictments against seven Republican party officials. Alfonse D'Amato counted his blessings: Although five of those indicted were his employees, his name was not on the list of the accused.

Those five officials were charged with extorting money from government workers for the party, a practice that had consumed an enormous amount of D'Amato's energies for over a decade. Four of the accused were also charged with lying to the Brooklyn grand jury—as had D'Amato—about their involvement in the extortion.

The indictments also hit central figures in the party organization. Chief among them was Donald Woolnough, Margiotta's office manager. Assistant U.S. Attorney James Drucker said that Woolnough was his major target, but his proximity to Margiotta and D'Amato suggested that Drucker hoped to turn Woolnough on his superiors and by that classic stratagem land the real prizes.

Woolnough, Raymond Graber, the deputy commissioner of conservation and waterways, and August Cosenza, a Hempstead sanitation supervisor, were arraigned in Judge John F. Dooling's Brooklyn court on March 18, 1976. They pleaded innocent.

The fourth accused perjuror, former water commissioner William Phears was absent. His attorney, and the attorney for all the indicted men, was John J. Sutter, who was among a handful of prosperous lawyers in Nassau County most often called on by the Republican party to tidy up its legal messes. Sutter said that Phears was traveling in Africa, but when Judge Dooling stated he would issue a bench warrant for Phears's arrest, Sutter said, if the judge held off, he might be able to contact the fugitive.

The first to be tried was August Cosenza, described by Attorney Sutter as a "lower echelon" party worker. Rather than face the more serious perjury charge, Cosenza accepted Sutter's advice and pleaded guilty to a misdemeanor: violating the civil rights of town employees. Cosenza admitted to Judge Dooling that when seeking contributions for the party he told workers whom he supervised that it would be helpful to them, if they wanted promotions or overtime, to kick back 1 percent of their salaries.

Attorney Sutter, concerned that the party might be besmirched by its association with an admitted criminal, told the press that his client "thought it was his duty to get money for the party," *but*, Sutter insisted, no one *instructed* Cosenza to shake down town workers. Sutter wanted the press to believe that lower-echelon Cosenza had hatched the 1 percent kickback plot himself.

From Al D'Amato's viewpoint, Augie Cosenza's case had been handled with the least possible personal distress. Cosenza was fined $500 and given three years' probation. A mild-mannered, retiring individual who wanted an end to the public exposure, he compliantly accepted the guidance of the attorney the party had supplied. D'Amato must have regretted that the 1 percent kickback was now described in a court record as a crime; but it was, after all, Cosenza's court record, not his.

Cosenza illustrated a reason why Al D'Amato, though often accused of crimes and clearly the beneficiary of crimes committed by others, was for twenty years an elusive target for an army of prosecutors. Early on D'Amato had learned that political leaders must never directly tell those in the lower echelons what to do. Orders to extort money from workers originated with D'Amato, but those orders were given directly only to his commissioners. They knew that their jobs depended on reelecting D'Amato. Therefore, they protected him. But the commissioners never spoke to the likes of Augie Cosenza. They told their *deputies* what level of extortion D'Amato demanded. They in turn told their *foreman*, and it was only after at least four levels of deniability had been established for D'Amato that the toilers in the field heard from Cosenza what was required of them.

Even if Cosenza wanted to turn state's evidence, what evidence did he have to offer the state? And why should he attack the all-powerful party apparatus? The party had provided him with a job and a promotion. If he kept silent, his penalty would merely be a suspended sentence. In exchange for a slight stain on his reputation, which party leaders would consider a badge of honor, D'Amato would make sure he kept his job; in fact, in the future his salary would increase, and his pension would be paid out. Entrenched behind such a wall of self-interest, D'Amato had little to fear from prosecutors. Equally important, the voters would never understand his role in the unlawful acts of which others were accused. It was one of the strategies that made possible D'Amato's unbroken string of electoral victories.

Within the month, on August 31, 1976, a second Republican went on trial in Judge Dooling's court, and the party found that its luck had run out. In place of the compliant Cosenza was the erratic Raymond Graber, Deputy Commissioner of the Conservation and Waterways Department. A skeletal-like, balding man, he became hysterical whenever charged with being a bagman for Margiotta; his Dickensian name added to the unsavory image.

Graber was anxious to please anyone in the hierarchy above him and equally convinced that anyone in a grade below his should be just as anxious to please him. A man with this attitude was perfect, in Margiotta's eyes, for collecting what he once described to *Newsday* as "union dues."

According to Graber, each October, when "that time of the year" rolled around before election, his boss, Commissioner Harold Udell, would call him into his office and hand him printouts showing the salaries of his workers. Next to each name was a sum, exactly 1 percent of that worker's salary. Udell instructed Graber to see that at least that amount was collected from everyone on the list. Graber would then divide the list and give a portion to each supervisor under his control; thereafter, he assiduously checked the returns, making sure to pressure those who were delinquent. The neatly tallied list of "voluntary" contributors and their checks was sent to the county Republican Finance Committee.

Although his trial was scheduled to start on August 31, Graber didn't appear. Judge Dooling issued an arrest order, and the next day, Graber was dragged into court in handcuffs. He stood before the judge weeping and denouncing Attorney Sutter, who he claimed "represents the Republican party, not me." Judge Dooling adjourned the trial to the following day, first warning Graber that if he did not appear he would forfeit his $10,000 bond.

The twenty-four-hour delay did not improve Graber's frame of mind. The gaunt deputy commissioner renewed his attack on his lawyer, emotionally complaining, "For months I have begged to have meetings with my counsel." How else could he prepare his defense, Graber asked in a quavering voice. "There were appointments set up, and I sat and cooled my heels in the outer office."

Graber charged that Sutter did not seem concerned that potential witnesses "fear they might lose their jobs if they testify for me." It seemed incredible to him that his lawyer wanted him to appear in court without any witnesses. "They simply want assurances from Mr. Sutter that they would be protected."

Sutter calmly replied that one of his law clerks had met with Graber to prepare for the trial. "I don't want to get involved in political infighting in a case like this," he said.

Judge Dooling, in a humanitarian gesture, philosophically advised Graber, "Something like this that overhangs a life is best met and disposed of. It's not going to go away."

He arranged an adjournment so that Graber could finally talk to his attorney. Forty minutes later, they returned, and Sutter informed Judge Dooling, "We're friends again."

The trial was postponed for a week. After Judge Dooling left the courtroom, under the watchful eyes of the press Sutter embraced the tearful Graber, clinging to him for several minutes, repeatedly saying, "Hold on to a friend."

When the trial resumed, Graber was the sole witness Attorney Sutter presented in his defense. Had Commissioner Udell appeared to affirm he had ordered his dutiful subordinate to collect the 1 percent or had been questioned as an uncooperative witness on that subject, the court might have seen Graber's behavior in a more sympathetic light; however, that was not to be. Instead, Graber tried to explain his perjury to the Brooklyn grand jury by claiming that on July 11, 1975, "I was in a bad state of mind."

Why had he been so perturbed? Because Assistant U.S. Attorney Drucker had said something to him as soon as the already petrified deputy commissioner was sworn in. Drucker habitually informed each person being interrogated whether they were being called as a potential witness to crimes or as a target of the investigation, and Drucker—unlike the manner in which he had put Al D'Amato at ease—had started his examination by advising the hollow-eyed Graber that he was "a target."

It suddenly occurred to Graber, he claimed, that he might become the only target. That fear had been generated by a conversation he had with his boss, Harold Udell, several months before the grand jury subpoenaed him. Udell told his malleable underling that if he [Udell] were ever asked whether he had instructed Graber to serve as a "transmitter" of the 1 percent collections, he would deny doing so. Was there any other way that he could protect the interests of his boss, Supervisor D'Amato?

Graber remembered from the witness box in Judge Dooling's court that Udell had told him, " 'I'm not like these other fellows,' " referring to the thirty-odd commissioners working for D'Amato. " 'I'm not a politician. You understand why I can't be involved. I can't admit that I assigned you to this each year.' "

His voice rising, Graber exclaimed, "I said, 'Mother of God,' " He sobbed and added, "I realized what was happening."

Then came that awful confrontation with Drucker before the grand jury, and all Graber could remember was Udell's betrayal. He felt deserted and became "unglued" under "accusatory, loud, and rough" questioning from Drucker about whether he had forced town workers to kick back their salaries.

Graber claimed that Drucker would not allow him to complete his answers. "I was being rushed," he contended, adding that Drucker had told him, "There's a hallway full of people out there that we're trying to get out of here by lunchtime." Sutter depicted Drucker as the cause of Graber's unintentional perjury. It was a plausible explanation, which is all one can expect from an attorney who knows his client is guilty.

In his summation, the prosecutor referred to Graber as "Mr. One Percent." More appropriately he might have labeled him "Mr. Fall Guy." The prosecutor went on to describe Graber as "an articulate individual with a responsible position" and accused him of lying to the grand jury "to protect himself . . . and, in essence, to cover up the role that he played in collecting that one percent." The jury agreed; Graber was convicted in October 1976.

The members of the town board, pressed by public clamor, decided something must be done now that the jury had rendered a guilty verdict. But a board consisting of Al D'Amato and four party executive leaders, all with dirtier hands than Graber's, was hardly in a position to play the role of the offended. Some hard-noses, not in town government, wanted Graber fired. The board stalled for two months; then, on December 14, 1976, two days after Dooling sentenced Graber to three years' probation and a $1,000 fine, the board demoted the deputy commissioner to administrative assistant and cut his salary from $24,000 to $20,000. But since he was no longer on a managerial line, it was possible for him to recoup the shortfall by earning overtime.

Judge Dooling's limp punishment had validated Graber's attorney's assurance that there was no need to call witnesses in his defense. Graber's recognition that he was being taken care of by D'Amato also kept him working at his government lathe, still a loyal, dues-paying, ticket-purchasing party member. If the town supervisor was willing to shelter a convicted felon who extorted money from his hardworking, penurious coworkers, then the least Graber could do was keep his mouth shut. Such restraint paid off; by 1990, Graber's annual salary was in excess of $60,000.

While his employees and political associates were struggling to disengage themselves from justice's net, D'Amato occupied himself in numerous unpublicized ways. Jim Nagourney, at OTB headquarters in Hempstead, frequently heard from the town supervisor about whom he should hire and how he should distribute raises and promotions, although OTB was officially an "autonomous public benefit organization."

Nagourney told me of an incident involving a clerk D'Amato had pressured him into hiring at OTB headquarters. Soon afterward, the young woman had asked her immediate boss for a promotion. She was turned down and arranged to see Nagourney, assuming that on his politicized level she had more influence.

"I also turned her down," Nagourney said. "I thought I had a very rational discussion with her. 'What you're getting now is fair. For your experience and age I think you are being properly compensated. You want more, but what I think you're looking for is more than would be appropriate at this time. I like the job you're doing, and I think you're being properly paid.' "

The young lady left his office without further protest, which Nagourney took to mean that she had been placated but which actually meant that she was taking her appeal to a higher court.

"The next day, I got a yelling and screaming call from D'Amato. It was not just a leader calling me and saying, 'Why didn't you give this gal more money,' and my giving an explanation. When he wanted one of his people to get a promotion, he called yelling and screaming.

"I told him, 'I can't do this. It would be out of proportion. She's getting a fair salary now. We did you a favor by hiring the person. The person is capable of handling the job she is in now. But she's not qualified for a promotion or a raise. The money is what it should be.' "

Nagourney held his ground, but D'Amato let him know that he wouldn't forget being turned down. "He became vulgar," Nagourney said, shaking his head. "It was a very, very rough phone call."

This wasn't Nagourney's only confrontation at OTB with an aroused D'Amato. Nagourney particularly remembered a 1976 call from a raging D'Amato. The town supervisor had gotten Nagourney to hire one of his relatives. The young woman worked in Nagourney's office, and she and a married man also working in the office became somewhat involved. When the relationship was not going to the satisfaction of the young woman, she went to see the most powerful member of her family.

D'Amato was furious. He screamed at Nagourney, demanding that Nagourney "stomp" on the miscreant. "He had personal reasons he felt strongly about and wanted me to fire the guy. I didn't agree. I felt it was something that had nothing to do with Off-Track Betting. 'You want me to fire a married man with children. I won't do it. Besides, this matter took place outside business hours. The guy does his work well. You want me to punish him for something in his private life. I don't think that's right.' The man had done nothing as an employee to warrant being discharged, and I said I wouldn't consider doing it."

D'Amato's vituperative reaction startled Nagourney. "I don't remember the words he used. I think I don't remember because I was stunned at the barrage that was suddenly directed at me."

From that point on Nagourney found that "Al was totally cold to me." When I suggested that D'Amato reacted in this manner because a relative had been involved, Nagourney disagreed. "That was almost a secondary issue. The real issue was that I had committed the sin of saying no to Al D'Amato."

D'Amato was unlike any of the politicians with whom Nagourney regularly dealt. "There were a lot of political leaders who were calling me for favors who I was saying no to with the blessing of Margiotta." The boss, Nagourney said, had a different standard from D'Amato's from which he never wavered. " 'All things being equal, if you can do the favor, okay,' " Nagourney quoted his mentor's instructions when he selected him for the job. " 'If it's a favor that you think should not be done, say no.' "

But saying *no* to D'Amato was not acceptable. Nagourney added, if you stood in his way, he would crush you. You said no to your mother, your father, your wife, even to Joe Margiotta, but you never said no to him. Because if you did, Nagourney said, "he's very upfront in telling people that 'I'll fight you. I'll haunt you. You know me. You know my energy. I'll fight you twenty-five hours a day.'

"At that point," Nagourney went on, "most people give in. Because there are other things in life. Because it was not a bluff. He was giving a recitation of just what he would do."

Nagourney felt that the use of threats was another reason D'Amato was a consistent winner. Threats win out in local politics; opponents live in the same area and see each other frequently. It was commonplace in Island Park or Hempstead town board meetings for Al D'Amato to scream at his adversaries to "Shut up!" when they rose to mildly question something he was proposing. Though he is a charming, smiling man to supporters, foes characteristically speak of being fearful of opposing him.

Underlings were prosecuted and convicted for exactly what D'Amato did every day of the year—in fact, precisely what he had ordered them to do—but everything about the way he conducted himself broadcast that he was convinced that no one in the U.S. Attorney's office would ever lay a finger on him.

NINE

D'AMATO'S ASCENSION

The cases of the remaining members of D'Amato's group of town felons were disposed of in 1977. Hempstead highway commissioner Harold Haff and sanitation commissioner William Landman were convicted in May on charges that they pressured their employees into making contributions to the party. Within a few months, William Phears, Hempstead water commissioner, pleaded guilty to the same charges. Former town controller William Smith died in Florida before his case came to trial.

Politically, forty-year-old D'Amato was rarely more active than he was in 1977; he was getting ready to take a leap. Ralph Caso and Joe Margiotta had become enemies, and party boss Margiotta had determined to dump the county executive; he had not hidden his animosity. At the first sign of Margiotta's intentions, Caso announced that if denied the Republican nomination he would run as an independent. Margiotta's candidate was the flaccid Francis Purcell, Hempstead's phlegmatic presiding supervisor, who was attentive to nothing more than playing golf and the latest telephone call from headquarters.

D'Amato had been supervisor since 1971, having perfected his kowtowing to Margiotta. Margiotta's "Tiger" knew his career was on a single-line track; his progress was fixed by the speed of the two trains in front of him, Purcell and Caso. As a result, he watched blissfully, early in 1977, at the impending derailment of Caso's caboose.

Caso remembered the midyear county nominating convention with ill-concealed distress. He recalled the sight of his two brothers-in-law, Lou and Sal Milone, rising at Margiotta's bidding on the convention floor and, in response to Margiotta's question as to whom they were supporting, hearing them tell their fellow executive leaders and two thousand committeemen, "The party comes before family feelings. We support Purcell!"

Purcell had won the support of party loyalists by numerous acts of generosity, all of which had been paid for by unaware taxpayers. In quest of the nomination he was about to receive, Purcell had distributed 93 percent of the 601 town summer jobs to young people with connections to delegates in the hall. When asked by the press about the fairness of distributing these jobs as patronage sops, the presiding supervisor responded, "Is everything fair in life?" And then, on a typical banal note, Purcell mused aloud, "There are many unfair things in life."

Purcell had also tried to buy delegates by asking the state legislature to exempt three hundred town employees from the rigors of civil service testing. Many of them, or their patrons, had the power to vote at this convention. Purcell had little difficulty in snatching the county executive's nomination from incumbent Caso. If Lou and Sal's brother-in-law wanted to run for reelection, he was going to have to do so on a ticket that wasn't put together by Joe Margiotta.

Now that the track was cleared, Al D'Amato got nominated for Hempstead's top job. Pausing long enough only to thank the beaming Margiotta and his applauding marionettes, he set out to win the November election. Never a man of wider vision, D'Amato followed the party's traditional tactic of condemning crime, promising to increase the productivity of town workers, and lowering the always rising town taxes. Each of these problems had grown during the seven years he had held town office, but he spoke with a detachment that suggested that none of it was his fault.

He did have one original issue; his favorite project, which he first proposed in 1972 and which he now spoke about with squeaking intensity in each campaign speech. He wanted to build a gigantic garbage-disposal plant; it was to be located on fifteen acres of the northeast corner of vacant Mitchell Field. D'Amato wished to place it on the side of the landscaped Meadowbrook

Parkway, next to Roosevelt Raceway. George Morton Levy, president of the racetrack, already owned two-thirds of the parcel, which he planned to use as part of an eighty-acre development "for commercial use." Dreams of a bonanza to be made from converting the 170-acre track to office buildings and other commercial establishments were dancing in Levy's mind long before D'Amato announced, in 1972, that he was intent on building a $30 million garbage plant. In 1973, as D'Amato selected Black, Clawson, Inc. to construct the plant, Levy voiced his strenuous opposition. "The taking of our land changes our whole development picture. This is very serious."

Nevertheless, D'Amato spoke glowingly of the advantages such an edifice would confer on Hempstead's citizens. It would not merely be an incinerator; the town had several of those. It was to be a resources recovery plant, capable of handling up to 600,000 tons of garbage each year, from which it would extract recyclable metals and glass. In the process of incineration the plant would manufacture electricity that the *private* operators would sell to the Long Island Power Company, returning "40 percent" of the profits to the town. D'Amato's actual deal with Black, Clawson limited Hempstead's share to 15 percent of whatever Black, Clawson's accountants described as profits.

The first step in the process was to get the state legislature to pass a law waiving the five-year limit on municipal contracts with waste-disposal companies; Black, Clawson wanted twenty years. Al didn't have to search for a sponsor of the bill. Brother Armand Paul, in his first year as an assemblyman, stepped forward. The Hempstead Resources Recovery Plant was a D'Amato family affair from the beginning.

Technical problems caused delays during the mid-1970s, but by 1977, D'Amato had cleared away all obstacles. The concept, D'Amato breezily insisted, guaranteed success; private investors would provide the $73 million now needed—up from $30 million—to finance the project. Tax-exempt 10.5 percent bonds were issued and bought by three insurance companies: Equitable, Aetna, and Connecticut Mutual; they, he inaccurately stated, assumed the risk. D'Amato told Island Park residents that soon the Oceanside Mountain garbage dump would stop growing on their northern horizon and fly ash from its incinerator would stop raining down on their roofs. In exchange for these blessings, Hempstead was required only to provide the fifteen-acre site in the heart of the county's richest real estate and bind itself to a seventeen-year garbage-processing contract with Black, Clawson, *at a yet-to-be-determined per-ton fee.*

The problems arising from the use of an unproven technology on such a massive scale were obvious: What were the health hazards of burning that much garbage in the midst of a densely populated area? Less important but more practical, was the experimental plant for which the town was providing $3 million of free land and which it was committing itself to use ever going to work up to the level of D'Amato's glowing claims? And finally but most intriguing, why was D'Amato so determined to give the contract to a company that had no experience in recycling garbage?

D'Amato waved aside all criticism. He saw no potential problems, only potential profits. The town would receive "after the first year of operation," he predicted, "about $3.5 million annually." Even OPEC was cooperating with him: The 1973 boom in oil-cartel prices had increased U.S. inflation, taking away billions of American dollars. He said confidently that the plant would generate 1,200,000 kilowatts of electricity daily, and he called this "a most vital asset during the current energy crisis." Building the plant was not only a good dollars-and-cents endeavor; it was a patriotic necessity.

The attention of sanitation engineers around the world focused on the iron girders and blank walls of concrete rising on the east bank of the Meadowbrook Parkway. Honolulu's mayor, whose island metropolis had a population of 700,000 that was beginning to smother in garbage, sent two representatives in the summer of the 1977 to visit the state. The plant was till ten months short of completion. The chief of Honolulu's delegation told the members of the press that D'Amato had assembled, "This is a tremendous commitment on the part of Hempstead and Black, Clawson. We are looking at millions and millions of dollars. Everyone is going to be watching it—everyone."

Alfonse D'Amato soon wished that all those eyes had been averted. The most noticeable off-kilter aspect of the operation, which even casual watchers detected, was that D'Amato's 1977 cost estimate of $73 million quickly ballooned to $93 million. Less than two years later, at the plant's completion in October 1978, the cost had doubled to $140 million.

Where had all the money gone? No doubt a portion of it had gone with some offshore wind to the Middle East, but the cost overruns far exceeded the rise in inflation. As explanations were sought, D'Amato attempted to quiet criticism with even loftier promises of benefits: Only 2 percent of the trash, after processing, would remain as an irreducible ash; he made it sound like garbage-disposal magic.

But the clamor against the enormous cost overruns caused by political corruption continued to rise. The Margiotta machine was extracting, so these allegations went, a 10 percent kickback from anyone doing business with the plant. The Federal Organized Crime Strike Force, stationed in Brooklyn, was informed that D'Amato was the organizer of the kickback operation. You could be the most competent builder, but if you didn't pay off the party, if you didn't use party-approved lawyers, if you weren't willing to bribe union leaders favored by the party, then don't bother to bid on contracts. Moreover, party clearance was needed to get one of the four hundred construction jobs, and in order to be a supervisor, it was almost obligatory to be a committeeman. It was the good old days of the Coliseum's construction and OTB's dream parlors—a new source of jobs for the party faithful.

Who would pay for the additional cost? Since the profits would not meet D'Amato's prediction, was the town's share of the nonexisting profits also nonexistent? Did the increased debt caused by the cost overruns mean that all of the receipts, for years to come, would have to be devoted to repaying the additional tax-exempt bondholders?

These questions were not answered during the 1977 election campaigns. The widespread hope that D'Amato's prestidigitations might prove beneficial to the community was supported by the sight of the monstrous structure actually taking shape on the side of the otherwise sylvan Meadowbrook Parkway. Perhaps it would work.

Such hopes, attached to the doubts citizens have of their ability to influence government, created a spirit of indifference about the charges. The Republican party was thought to be beyond redemption or correction. Wasn't the party's continuing 1 percent extortion from government workers conclusive evidence that even the most blatant criminal behavior by its leaders would never be punished?

Reinforcing this negative view was the extraordinary reaction to an attack made on the 1 percent scheme during the campaign by one of the party's leaders. State senator John R. Dunne, of Garden City, former head of the Nassau County Bar Association, was challenging Caso and Purcell in the September 8 Republican primary for the county executive nomination. In the midst of the supercharged campaign, on June 2, the hitherto loyal Dunne broke the oath of silence. At a press conference he charged that for years he had been coerced into giving 1 percent of his salary to the Nassau GOP. The only way he could advance his political career, he said, was to pay this extortion. Dunne, a party regular who had been in the state senate for a decade, was suddenly blowing the whistle on what he referred to as "the one percent kickback scheme." He was the highest-ranking Nassau Republican ever to admit being forced to make that annual payoff. He said he would be willing to repeat his charges to a federal grand jury without a grant of immunity.

Francis Purcell had his press aide hand out a written one-sentence statement that ignored Dunne's accusations. "I no longer consider Sen. Dunne a serious opponent, and I will no longer respond to any of his charges."

Nassau district attorney Denis Dillon, the first Democrat to occupy that office in sixty years, whose lack of response to any allegations of Republican corruption had ceased to surprise Democratic leaders, informed inquiring reporters that he would look into the matter. However, he said, "the talk that has come up in political campaigns about the pervasive nature of corrupt officials in this county is exaggerated. The criminal statutes are not a panacea for solving what problems there are." That tone of prosecutorial detachment caused Margiotta to say that he was thinking of adopting Dillon as *his* candidate and boded poorly for the vigorous investigation of Dunne's charges.

Meanwhile, Senator Dunne continued his attack. He ran advertisements in county newspapers with photographs of Margiotta, Caso, and Purcell, declaring that "these men are defendants . . . in a legal action against the one per cent kickback scheme."

Margiotta was in a fury: Not only was he under continuous siege by the "kooks" in the civil service, but Dunne, a member of his own party, from whose trough he had fed for years, had launched a full-scale attack on him.

The messy three-way primary resulted in the nomination of Purcell, Margiotta's candidate for county executive; Caso's political career was destroyed. Senator Dunne endorsed the party's nominee and attempted to act as if all those stones he had been hurling at Margiotta had been thrown by someone else.

Al D'Amato won the primary without opposition. Since everyone's attention was focused on the drama being enacted on the county stage, D'Amato had no difficulty in November defeating the Democrats' candidate for Hempstead's presiding supervisor.

The Island Park Republican Club's leader had finally achieved a genuinely powerful position. He controlled approximately three thousand jobs, half of which were under the nominal protection of the politically obedient Hempstead Civil Service Commission, all of whose members were susceptible to the presiding supervisor's whimsical or malevolent—but always political—decisions about promotions, raises, transfers, evaluations, even the size and furnishing of each individual's work space. All heads now bowed lower when Al D'Amato swept by.

There was, indeed, only one man in the county who was more powerful, and he was the new presiding supervisor's best friend.

TEN

HOW TO BECOME A JUDGE, OR DRINKING BEER IN ASTORIA

In December 1976 five aggrieved Nassau workers brought the 1 percent case into the federal court of the Eastern District. The case was listed on the calendar as *Cullen v. Margiotta*. Lorraine Cullen, a county probation worker, had spearheaded the original assault on the party, and her name was therefore attached to the plaintiff's case. Margiotta was the shorthand label for several handfuls of party defendants. Judge Jacob Mishler, the senior judge in the twelve-judge Eastern District panel, took charge of the case.

Over the next nineteen years Judge Mishler was to be the most authentic threat to Al D'Amato's serenity; in fact, a threat to the careers of both D'Amato brothers.

Judge Mishler—"Jake" to his old friends in New York City's Astoria Republican clubhouse—stared at me through his left eye; his right eye was almost completely closed. I first interviewed him in autumn 1985 in his chambers in the Uniondale courthouse. The story circulated that the judge had suffered a stroke. At first glance, the rumors seemed true. The right side of his face sagged. His ragged mouth was twisted in a downward slope, shut from the right corner to the center and then open in a gaping oval.

As a youth, the judge told me, he found socializing hard. The pain of those memories still seemed to bother him. "I was timid. I was shy. That was all through high school." He did not consider himself scholarly. "I was a quiet boy that worked hard."

As I looked at his pale, thin face—there was a drop of moisture clinging to the rim of his closed eye—I wondered whether he would be able to endure the rigors of the seemingly endless 1 percent case. "I've seen several outstanding villains, a few clowns, and a great number of people with indecipherable motives," I told him. "But, Judge," I continued, "I'm still looking for a hero."

The judge smiled with half his face. "Are there any heroes in the Bible?" he asked, and then added: "Was Moses a hero?"

Judge Mishler had lived seventy-four years and had seen enough of human behavior to make him doubtful even about that emancipator of slaves. It was clear that through his off-centered, Cyclopean eye, the former president of the Astoria Republican Club viewed the world with a great deal of skepticism.

The son of immigrants, he graduated from New York University (NYU) Law School in 1933, at age twenty-two, and was admitted to the bar the following year. It was an inauspicious time to be looking for a job; the Great Depression was at its fearful worst. Franklin Roosevelt had just delivered his first inaugural address in which he offered the not entirely reliable counsel to the class of 1933: "The only thing we have to fear is fear itself."

During his first years in practice, Mishler modestly remarked, he did "ordinary stuff. Contracts to buy or sell a house, landlord and tenant claims. I did a lot of that."

Of greater significance, in terms of the 1 percent case, however, was Mishler's decision in 1938 to join the Astoria Republican Club, one he made on the most practical, nonideological grounds. "In my opinion, you had to have a hand in politics just to further your law business, your law practice, your law profession. You should have contact with everyone that was in government, and that was an easy way for me because, as I said, I was quite a timid soul."

But why not join the Democratic party, which was then enrolling most New York Jews?

"Well, I reasoned this way: If I wanted to go anyplace politically, there were a hundred Democrats ahead of me. I knew fellows that were there for years. When a party is in power for a long, long time, it's a long wait. And I wasn't interested in politicking. I was interested in being associated with politics."

He also had a friend in the Astoria Republican party, and that made the difference between the Democrats and Republicans substantial. "I knew the leader, Frank Kenna, who ultimately became the county leader. He was a powerful leader. We became very friendly. We went out socially. I had a certain admiration for him."

Kenna, a thin, unimposing man, was the ruler of a political banana republic. He never elected anyone in Queens County except occasionally one member of the borough's twelve-man assembly delegation. He was ignored by the city's feisty mayor, Fiorello La Guardia, who, although a former Republican congressman, was elected four times primarily with Democratic, Liberal, and American Labor party votes.

Kenna's power came from his association with Republicans who controlled the legislature, from Republican governors like Thomas Dewey and Nelson Rockefeller, who distributed Albany statehouse patronage, and from Republican occupants of the White House. He was the authentic representative of the state and national party in Queens, and it wasn't necessary for him to elect local officeholders in order to be the beneficiary of their generosity. Kenna controlled the votes of delegates to state and national Republican conventions, and that made him, in the eyes of his party's potential New York governors and aspiring presidential candidates, a truly powerful man. Queens delegates' votes at state and national conventions were just as valuable as the votes of delegates from areas that regularly elected officeholders.

The Astoria Republican Club was the most ineffectual precinct of Kenna's domain. On election day, its supporters were outnumbered at the polls, sometimes five to one. "In Queens County, it was just a Republican club," Mishler remembered fondly. "It was in an old one-family house that was converted into club rooms. It was very adequate, and it was a good meeting place. If you wanted to, you came in and you joined, and we had a meeting once a month. If you came in on any day in the week, you'd find some card playing and beer drinking. And the people were having a fine social time."

The club offered Mishler a change from his daytime routine of drawing up contracts and negotiating deals. In addition, he was unhappily married; the club provided a social outlet. Moreover, although not an aggressively ambitious man, there was the hope that by keeping "a hand in politics" something might turn up.

After twenty years of attending meetings and socializing with the boys, Kenna made his friend president of the club in 1958. It was a splendid time to be active in Republican politics: Dwight Eisenhower had become president; Nelson Rockefeller, governor.

Destiny now played a role in Mishler's life. "Came 1959 and a friend of mine, who was a supreme court justice, suddenly dropped dead. I was appointed for the interim term. I served from September through December. But the election intervened. I think it was the Tenth Judicial District. We never lost an election in that district, because Nassau and Suffolk were tied in with Queens; and Suffolk and Nassau always brought in the majority that overcame the Democratic majority in Queens."

The Democrats were ready to concede Mishler's victory. Before the Democratic convention, at which his opponent was to be chosen, Mishler got a call from the Democratic leader, Pat Clancy, "who I knew very well. Pat said, 'There are three openings. All we want is one of them. We want to give you bipartisan endorsement.' I said, 'I'll get back to you. . . .' I got hold of Frank. Frank said, 'Jake, we'll take all three.' I called Pat and said, 'Sorry, Pat. I can't do anything for you.' "

A wry look covered the part of Mishler's face that was still mobile. "But that year they had the so-called Islip scandals. There were a lot of land deals and frauds. Suffolk did not come through with the usual majority. So I went down to defeat."

In that defeat grew the seed of a future victory, nourished by Frank Kenna's bad conscience. "I'll never forget the day after the election," Mishler said. "I could hear the tears in Frank's voice, and he said: 'I don't know what to say to you.' I said, 'What do you mean, *what to say?* I've been a judge; I'll go back to making money,' He said, 'Gee I'm so relieved.' Because he felt terrible about it. So he said, 'The next opening, you're getting bipartisan endorsement.' "

Shortly after he lost the state supreme court election, Mishler was on the platform of the Astoria Republican Club with Kenna when a member brought in a *Journal-American* story stating that a federal district court judge was taking senior status. That left an opening on the Eastern District bench. Appointment to that vacancy didn't require a deal with Democrats. The U.S. Senate voted on federal judgeships, and a majority of the Senate would accept any nomination that had the approval of the state's Republican senators, Jacob Javits and Kenneth Keating, and President Eisenhower.

Mishler recalled the triumphant moment in the Astoria clubhouse when his career was restructured. "The *Journal-American* story was read to Frank as the three of us were walking down the aisle. He said, 'That's the position for Jake.'"

That simple sentence settled any questions Jacob Mishler had about hiss future. Because of Frank Kenna's benevolent concern, for the next third of a century Mishler led the prestigious, reclusive, imperious life of a federal judge, exactly the life he most yearned to live and which, despite advanced age and health problems, he had no intention of ever relinquishing.

Judge Mishler was left with nothing but roseate images of the unpressured camaraderie of the Astoria Republican clubhouse. Nostalgia for the good old days was mixed with a conviction that political parties had to do all those untidy things they did in order to make the process of government work. Party politics had, after all, made him the senior member of an exalted court.

Under these circumstances, was there any federal magistrate the Republican party of Nassau County would have preferred to have presiding at its trial?

As one of his first acts after taking control of the 1 percent case, on June 27, 1977, Judge Mishler granted class-action status to the twenty-two thousand Nassau County civil service workers who had never filed a complaint. He did it for a technical reason, almost absentmindedly ignoring the consequences his decision had for those defendant-politicians whose problems he so well understood. He stated that granting class status to all these unnamed workers would forestall future individual litigation that "would create the possibility of inconsistent adjudications."

Suddenly, Judge Mishler's concern for consistency had placed the party in serious financial jeopardy. In addition to individual complainants such as Lorraine Cullen, "the class"—numbering twenty-two thousand—now sued to have all the money its members were forced to contribute returned, plus triple damages; abruptly, millions were at stake.

Judge Mishler told me that he considered this decision the most important one he made in the case; he felt it broke new legal ground in cases involving political parties; clearly, he believed he had acted in a daring manner.

Once he got his teeth into the case, Mishler began to sympathize with the horde of Nassau workers who had for decades been squeezed by the Republican party. That was clearly indicated in his class-action decision when he wrote that the allegations "suggest that the defendants have trampled on the First Amendment rights of countless numbers of civil service employees."

The party attorneys saw the threat implicit in Mishler's class-action decision and moved to reverse him in the court of appeals; Mishler was upheld, and new rules of the game were established involving complaints against political parties.

There are 3,070 counties in the fifty states, and clearly Judge Mishler, then in his late sixties, felt he was confronted with a case affecting all of them.

Months after Mishler created "the class," he held an open session in his court on the burgeoning 1 percent case. In the audience was Burt Neuborne, NYU law professor. In his other more melodramatic role Neuborne was assistant legal director of the American Civil Liberties Union (ACLU). He had come at the invitation of Mishler's law clerk, a former student of Neuborne's at NYU; the clerk explained that the judge wanted to consult with him. Neuborne had followed the case in the *New York Times* and in law journal articles. He complied with Mishler's request with no understanding of why the judge wanted him present except his student's reference to "problems" Mishler had with the case.

Neuborne, born in Brooklyn, was thirty-six. He had a cherubic face, which reflected an intense desire to be of help to whomever he was addressing. His most frequently used philosophical concept was *fairness*. In adversarial situations, Neuborne often said, "I think that's fair," or would ask, "Do you think that's fair?"

His rounded cheeks quivered as he spoke or as he shook his head with staccato motions in an effort to emphasize some point. He had a tuft of dark, Iroquois-styled hair on top of his balding scalp; and his puffy lips, protruding from an ordinary, pleasant face, seemed always prepared for a lucid explanation of some arcane legal matter. He wore metal-rimmed glasses, was habitually attired in a neat blue pencil-striped suit, and listened with complete attention to anyone speaking to him.

Numerous interviews I had with him produced conflicting signals about his approach to life, although the underlying pattern was clearly that of a man concerned with society's neglected and with his role as the defender of free speech.

"I'm very cynical. My wife thinks the world can be saved," he said, and then added in his open manner, "I look at myself as the quintessential realist. I have few illusions about what I can do. The only true existentialists in the world are civil rights lawyers. They know in their hearts the system is corrupt, and they can do little to change it. I have no romantic illusions; no lawyer ever changed society. If you're here to snatch a little out of the flood, then the system leaves room for that."

While at undergraduate school at Cornell, Neuborne considered himself "apolitical." He was a fraternity member, since "it was the way to have fun at Cornell"—but took the matter of having fun seriously enough so that he ran for, and was elected, president of Tau Epsilon Phi, a group exclusive only in that it was a refuge for Jews who were excluded from most campus frats.

The Vietnam War was the shaping event in his life. "I volunteered for the reserves for six months at Fort Dix to keep out of the army," he said in an endeavor to describe his revulsion to the conflict.

Three years at Harvard Law School worked against his liberal impulses. "You knew that the whole world was waiting for you. We were the cream. There was a perceived opening. It was an intoxicating moment." However, he found that "Harvard is intellectually corrosive. Politically dead—unrelentingly unromantic. It made you question your sentiments."

Nevertheless, he graduated cum laude in 1964 and admitted, "I wanted to make money." The best place to do that was at a prestigious New York law firm: Casey, Lane & Mittendorf. After three years of struggling with his conscience, he decided, "I couldn't see spending my life working for the financial interests of a particular class. I knew I had to get out."

In 1967, as Lyndon Johnson escalated the Vietnamese conflict, he applied for a job with the ACLU. "I handled the Vietnam-demonstration cases," he recounted proudly. "I did the first voter-rights cases—the first student-rights cases. I loved it."

He filed over a hundred briefs with the U.S. Supreme Court, where he appeared in a number of landmark cases, perhaps the most dramatic of which was his 1973 argument against the legality of President Nixon's order to bomb Cambodia. Most of his cases were the newly popular class actions, ideally suited for masses of arrested student protesters or large numbers of blacks whose voting rights had been violated.

Soon after court was called to order, Mishler proclaimed a judicial edict, "Mr. Neuborne, you are the counsel for the class."

Mishler, who was a graduate of NYU Law School, later explained, "I appointed him by reputation. Neuborne is a good lawyer. And he has a rare quality as a litigater. He gives the jury the impression of being almost neutral. It's a very good attribute to have."

"I was itchy," Neuborne offered as a partial reason for accepting. He had been a civil rights attorney for a decade. "I had tried private practice and didn't like it." Mishler was essentially giving him a private case, but one that had an overriding public interest.

"I think he [Mishler] wanted everything to come out. Mishler believes in that system; he believes in patronage. I think he doesn't like Margiotta, not personally; I think he just feels that's not what a person should do, that he had overstepped. It's the annoyance that a team player feels for somebody who is making it harder for the team. When somebody abuses it to the point where it calls the legitimacy of the whole process into question, he wants that guy to get what's coming to him."

Neuborne asked for access to the thirty-one cartons of documents FBI agents had swept up from Nassau Republican offices during the 1975 grand jury investigation. Mishler was reluctant to grant Neuborne's request. He operated on the premise that the case had a life of its own and that its course should not depend on material gathered in other actions. This attitude affected decisions he made during the trial and had an enormous impact on its outcome; however, at the beginning of Neuborne's participation—an involvement Mishler had forced on him—the judge was more open to persuasion.

Nevertheless, it took Neuborne months of arguing with Mishler to win access to the thirty-one cartons. Even then, Neuborne was bound by wearying restrictions: The documents could only be viewed in the U.S. Attorney's office, and perusal of them would have to be done entirely by him.

Neuborne started that massive exploratory expedition in December 1977. He quickly discovered that a great deal of the material in those dusty cartons had never been examined: Original wrappings had been left undisturbed. For six weeks, through the Christmas vacation and into 1978, he immersed himself in this incredibly rich storehouse of evidence. What emerged was an understanding of how a political party operated; but for the first five weeks there was no conclusive proof that the huge amounts of money Margiotta's tong had routinely collected from government workers was anything but voluntary contributions. None of the thousands of receipts specified that the contributor had met his or her annual *obligation*; none of the requests for money threatened *retaliation* if the prospect failed to ante up.

One night, at the end of the fifth week, after hours of studying documents under the glare of a desk lamp in the small office made available to him, Neuborne picked up a neatly labeled file from the office of Robert Livingston. Livingston had been Hempstead's receiver of taxes since 1971, when Al D'Amato gave up the office in exchange for the title of town supervisor. As he lifted Livingston's file, Neuborne felt there was a sheet stapled to its back, and when he turned it over—lo and behold—there was D'Amato's 1971 smoking-gun letter, describing in the most direct terms how the 1 percent extortion worked.

"Livingston was responsible for the D'Amato letter," Neuborne said. "All copies of the D'Amato letter had been destroyed. Livingston had gotten a Xerox copy of it—I don't know how—and it was stapled to the back of one of his files. When I asked him why, he said he never threw papers away. He didn't believe in throwing away records. He was a *real* accountant," Neuborne remarked with a tone of gratitude. "Without that D'Amato letter, I'm not sure I would have ever been able to establish enough credibility to get the case moving."

He added, "The irony was that I didn't find it until the statute of limitations had run out on the perjury for D'Amato (his 1975 grand jury testimony), and . . . the statute of limitations that would have enabled me to sue him for civil damages had run out as well. It was a three-year statute. That's why he got off.

"I never heard of Al D'Amato when I was appointed in 1977. It was not until I found the letter that I realized that he was a central person in the case."

There is no doubt that luck plays a major role in politics. Had Trager's staff unearthed D'Amato's 1 percent solution for Robert Marcus's financial problems, there is little doubt that the U.S. Attorney would have zeroed in on this "central person in the case." There was never to be a more conclusive piece of evidence about the Republicans' shakedown operation than this personalized stationery from the office of the Hempstead supervisor. But Trager's staff did not discover it, and by the time Neuborne's eyes fell upon it, the legal system, which Al D'Amato had spent his entire career abusing, had placed a shield about him.

Even as Neuborne came to understand the nature of D'Amato's criminal involvement, Island Park's executive leader was assuming his new office as Hempstead's presiding supervisor. Since the letter remained hidden from sight while Neuborne waited for the moment when he would present it to a jury, D'Amato's public pose of rectitude went unchallenged.

As the summer of 1978 approached, Neuborne knew it might be two years before preliminary motions on the "amended complaint" were decided by Judge Mishler and—if Mishler did not object—he could begin to present his case to a jury. In America, crime is instantaneous, but its remedy has the patience and otherworldly preoccupation of a saint.

ELEVEN

OH, THOSE ABSCAM SHEIKS

In October 1978 the tree-shaded lawns of Salisbury and the cloistered homes of Garden City were smothered under an odoriferous cloud that, regardless of the wind's strength, seemed never to disappear. Citizens of East Meadow, accustomed to refreshing breezes, found themselves coughing in an attempt to clear constricted throats; toddlers in Hicksville, with red and rheumy eyes, gazed at their frantic mothers in helpless discomfort.

On calm days, the cloud hung heavy over Levittown, and Sol Goldfarb—the custodian of the truck scales at the Oceanside dump—wondered why the air coming in the windows of his modest home, once spiced on cool evenings by Atlantic gusts, now smelled like the mist rising from the latest deposit on Oceanside Mountain.

Then it was noticed that Al D'Amato's pride the Hempstead Resources Recovery Plant, situated in the center of these bedroom communities, had started on its mission. Though the furnaces were scarcely functioning at half capacity, a terrible stench jetted from the warning fingers of its two smokestacks. Parsons & Whittemore (P & O)—now the named owners of the plant—dealt with the phone calls alleging a connection between the foul odor and the opening of the plant as any bureaucracy deals with *complainers*: The discontented were offered blanket assertions of innocence, combined with an alchemist's listing of theories about what might be creating this enigma.

In terms of the short range, P & W and their public defender, Al D'Amato, were lucky: The plant opened as the cold weather descended on Long Island, and the residents of Nassau closed their windows for the winter, thus insulating them from the full impact of the plant's rancid product. Presiding Supervisor D'Amato, now in charge of Hempstead's dealings with his Frankensteinian creation, could only be grateful that the monster—rumors of whose foul-smelling conduct were quick to reach his sensitive political ears—was still shackled to the dungeon wall.

From his viewpoint, the 1978 election went off as smoothly as most, with the usual acceptable results. There seemed to be no reason to worry about the occasional suggestion that some kind of problem was being generated, along with a disappointing number of kilowatts, on the east bank of the Meadowbrook Parkway.

In early 1979 the threat of outside intervention at the recycling plant was not taken seriously by D'Amato: after all, the padding of costs to pay off politicos and the distribution of legal business to favored lawyers had been going on for at least fifty years. Despite the occasionally publicly exposed scandals, hadn't all of his predecessors prospered, and weren't they remembered by the amorphous public as honorable gentlemen?

Party leaders were sure nothing could affect their control over the generally distracted electorate; business as usual remained the order of the day. But in the secrecy of the Brooklyn Organized Crime Strike Force offices an investigation was being conducted into the construction of the Hempstead plant that didn't bode well for the party's complacent leaders. By January 1979, Thomas P. Puccio, head of the strike force and his chief prosecutor, Lothar R. Genge, were certain they had enough evidence to indict at least two key Nassau Republicans.

Simultaneously, Puccio was even more deeply involved in another major national scandal—file name, ABSCAM—whose tentacles had wound themselves around Hempstead's town hall. Puccio had reason to suspect that perpetrators of the ABSCAM crimes in Suffolk County, to the east of D'Amato country, and in New York City, New Jersey, and Pennsylvania, to the west, had not overlooked the fertile ground in between.

Puccio's sting man, con artist Mel Weinberg, operated out of a dummy business office in Holbrook, Long Island, called Abdul

Enterprises, Ltd. Weinberg had already convinced a bevy of politicians along the eastern seaboard that two playacting sheiks, Kambir Abdul Rahman and Yassir Habib, were Mohammed's direct descendants. They had, Weinberg crooned to his pigeons, billions in OPEC gold ready to invest in enterprises, no matter how shady, that could be created by bribing public officials.

Politicians by the score had lined up with hands extended for cash, which some of them stuffed into their pockets while FBI video cameras recorded the obscene moment. The dialogue in these political minidramas was always marked by grandiose expressions of loyalty to the posturing sheiks and cries of joy from the participants over their success in selling their public trust.

Eventually, the list of convictions included six members of the House of Representatives: Cong. Michael J. Myers (D-Pa.), Raymond F. Lederer (D-Pa.), Frank Thompson Jr. (D-N.J.), John M. Murphy (D-N.Y.), John W. Jenrette, Jr. (D-S.C.), and Richard Kelly (R-Fla.); one member of the Senate, Harrison A. Williams (D-N.J.), also went to jail.

Several individuals involved in the prosecution said that if top Justice Department officials had not called a stop to the sting operation, dozens of other members of Congress and members of local governments around the country were prepared to follow the example of their more agile, and less prudent, colleagues.

Also involved in the ABSCAM conspiracy was a friend of Al D'Amato's, Alfred Carpentier, a businessman from East Meadow. Carpentier, a roly-poly extrovert, had proudly posed for a picture with one of the "sheiks" in Florida at the beginning of March 1979. He was offering the services of his friend Al for the usual price.

In published transcripts of tapes made by Puccio's agents, Carpentier is quoted as saying he had done business with Hempstead's presiding supervisor for many years. Familiarity had apparently not bred respect. "I've been contributing to these bastards for years, y'know," his voice booms out clearly on the ABSCAM tapes. "No big amounts—five, ten grand—they kiss your ass. D'Amato may look to shake you down for a little more."

The tapes, made in the Holbrook offices of Abdul Enterprises on March 9, 1979, dealt with Carpentier's offer to Mel Weinberg, and two burnoose-cloaked FBI agents, to obtain Mitchell Field for the sheiks. Carpentier claimed that D'Amato had given him "the inside door" on the development contracts. The Hempstead Resources Recovery Plant had only used up a few acres in the northeast corner; there were still five hundred acres of town land left. D'Amato controlled the destiny of those choice acres, since no work could be done until he approved zoning changes. Carpentier quoted D'Amato as telling him, " 'Find me somebody to build the fuckin' thing, we'll give them fuckin' deals. I'm telling you they can rob it from us. . . . If you find somebody who wants to invest in this thing, we'll give 'em a deal they can't refuse.' "

Carpentier was so sure of his relationship with D'Amato that he offered to arrange a meeting with Weinberg and his associates. "Now, with D'Amato, I would like, if possible, for you to meet with him. By the way, the guy is definitely taking contributions. He's on the take. If you want to give him something, we'll weigh that when the time comes. You make your analysis based on what he's giving us."

Weinberg had encouraged Carpentier by confiding that he had Camden, New Jersey's mayor, Angelo J. Errichetti, in his pocket. Twice on the tapes, Carpentier compared D'Amato to Errichetti. He claimed that the relationship Weinberg had with Errichetti "we have with this guy down in Nassau." Carpentier assured the conspirators that D'Amato was like Errichetti—"a guy you can relate to."

Later that day, in an Atlantic City hotel, the same group was joined by Mayor Errichetti and Carpentier's business associate, attorney Kenneth Boklan. Boklan provided a second witness to Carpentier's connection to D'Amato. After bragging that D'Amato "runs the [obscenity] town," Boklan can be heard on the tape loudly advising, "The way to establish the relationship, the way to introduce it to him, is to give him a contribution and he'll tell Al [Carpentier] how far it should go, how much he will do for how much, basically is the way it runs."

Carpentier interjected that *the relationship* would be consummated in D'Amato's office in Hempstead's town hall but cautioned that such acts of bonding are best done in private: He recommended that Tony DeVito (the assumed name of the FBI agent then in the room with them) be the one chosen to represent the sheiks, since D'Amato preferred to be "with his own kind."

Once the relationship was established, the sky was the limit; D'Amato would do anything in his power to help his generous

Arabian friends. Carpentier was specific: If they paid off, D'Amato would enable them to build a business/industrial/hotel complex at Mitchell Field. He guaranteed that zoning and environmental problems—all of which had to be settled before a spade of Mitchell Field dirt could be dug—would be taken care of by D'Amato. "He said you can develop that whole goddamn thing. That whole thing comes to, like, a $240 million development. You can have any part of it or the best pieces, whatever you want."

Puccio listened to the tapes and knew that Nassau politicos were as susceptible to his sting man's con as politicians in neighboring Suffolk and New York City. In mid-1979, he went to Judge Jacob Mishler, who was scheduled to preside over some of the major ABSCAM cases, and told him of aspects of the case that required him to ask for more time. In order to obtain that time and protect ABSCAM from exposure, Puccio informed Mishler of the full scope of the sting operation; as a result, Mishler granted the time but disqualified himself from hearing any of the cases.

Before the trap could fully be closed on D'Amato, the energetic sheiks became diverted by other, more prestigious clients in the bazaar—a gaggle of congressmen and a senator. There were bigger camels to be caught with their $50,000 stacks of government marked bills. From D'Amato's viewpoint, it was vital that the probe into his connection to the ABSCAM conspiracy took place out of sight. It was destined to remain for years the private knowledge of the conspirators and federal prosecutors trying to work up juryproof cases against D'Amato and a multitude of politicians.

Jim Nagourney had another view of D'Amato's machinations at Mitchell Field. In 1977, when Francis Purcell was elected county executive, Nagourney decided it was time for him to leave OTB and take a bigger job in county government. He asked Margiotta to make him deputy county executive. Since the boss was grateful for the job Nagourney had done with the OTB hot potato, he informed Purcell about his new deputy. Purcell put Nagourney in charge of disposing of Mitchell Field, thereby again placing D'Amato and Nagourney in direct conflict.

Nagourney knew nothing of Carpentier's conspiracy with the ABSCAM sheiks, but he did know that each time he made a move to arrange a deal at Mitchell Field, D'Amato put a roadblock in his way.

Nagourney wanted to get a private operator to run the Coliseum, "because we were losing two million dollars a year for seven years." It appears there was a price to be paid for the bloated payrolls the party had forced on the Coliseum management.

Nagourney's second concern was to keep the Islanders hockey team from moving to the New Jersey Meadowlands. "If I didn't keep them as a tenant, nobody would take over the Coliseum." He also wanted to get Marriott to build a hotel next to the Coliseum. "It was a very, very complicated deal. If the Islanders leave, the Coliseum will be a white elephant. If the Coliseum is a white elephant, all of Mitchell Field will be a white elephant. We're talking about hundreds of millions of dollars and a very essential part in the future of Nassau County.

"It was a very tough balancing act. I spent the better part of two years working almost exclusively on those projects. All the time being belittled by Al," who was publicly and privately griping: " 'What the hell does Nagourney know about negotiating a lease?' " Nagourney tried to explain why D'Amato was sabotaging his efforts. He felt D'Amato was grandstanding at his expense. "He had to take credit."

D'Amato tried to retain control of Mitchell Field by constantly complaining: "Nagourney has been going around saying that I'm holding up the deal. That's a lie." Nagourney told me, with some regret, that he had not been able to say this for fifteen years: "*That was a lie. D'Amato* was holding up the deal."

Nagourney knew that D'Amato had set up "his own negotiating team" in opposition to his county's team. "It became very clear that Al wanted to produce the first lease." D'Amato's proposed client was the United Parcel Service. "When the offer of United Parcel came along," Nagourney recalled, "my first thought was: What a horrendous use of that land. Some of the potentially most valuable land in the world—totally irreplaceable—vacant land within an hour of fifteen million people. But, for the very first use of it for a warehouse." His voice sounded incredulous.

Nagourney settled back in his office chair and continued: "He wrote the whole deal. The lease was sent to me because it had to get county executive approval. I looked at it. I knew that I had appraisals of $200,000 an acre. You should get $20,000 an acre for rent. The only lease I did at Mitchell Field was for the Marriott Hotel, and we got $20,000 an acre.

"So I said, 'He's starting to rent for five or six thousand dollars. And look at the escalators; the escalators are so far below what the consumer price index seems to be, and what you can expect to happen for the next thirty years, that this is an incredible cheap price these people are paying.' " At that point Nagourney wrote what he described as "that infamous memo" to Purcell denouncing the giveaway as a rip-off of the taxpayers and hyperbolically describing it as "unconstitutional." Despite his protestations, the deal went through. "The whole pattern for Mitchell Field was set by D'Amato." All the subsequent rentals were based on that first "bad deal."

Despite his public relations circuses, rumors constantly surfaced about D'Amato's probity. Occasionally, an irate taxpayer would rise at a meeting of the town board and complain to the presiding supervisor about some zoning variance D'Amato proposed that smacked of payoffs. The taxpayer would invariably be treated to an ill-tempered response.

What bothered D'Amato was that stench emanating from the Hempstead garbage plant, which, as the summer of 1979 approached, could be detected by the most congested allergiacs. Something in the plant's emissions irritated tongue, inner cheeks, throat, and lungs. The presiding supervisor had ambitious political plans that made it imperative that citizens' disgust with the stench did not develop into a personal irritation with him.

In fact, antagonists were already referring to the plant as "D'Amato's Folly." On June 6, 1979, D'Amato began to disassociate himself from his offspring: The plant, he warned, might have to be shut down if its management failed to correct a serious odor problem. Too many people, he told the *Times*, were complaining. He made no reference to his previous unrestrained advocacy, the $140 million already expended, or the pivotal role he had played in getting a large section of Mitchell Field turned over to the developers. The residents' dissatisfaction posed a threat to his latest political plans, and the loss of millions of other people's money was no reason to allow that threat to continue.

When it was also reported that the acrid discharges from the plant's smokestacks contained potentially harmful amounts of dioxin—a chemical that had forced the permanent evacuation of a midwestern town—the plant's originator and decade-long chief supporter became one of its most vocal critics.

Displaying the same unbounded enthusiasm with which he had built Hempstead's garbage recycling pork barrel, D'Amato shouted that the poisonous machinery must be decommissioned, and a padlock was quickly clamped on the door.

TWELVE

D'AMATO BETS
ON A SURE THING

Sen. Jacob Javits thought of himself as an irreplaceable national resource, a venerable sage whose finer qualities were so manifest that he was respected even by his enemies, all of whom were impressed by his honesty and intellect.

Javits was born to immigrant parents on Manhattan's Lower East Side, and his career embodied the American dream. He became a Manhattan congressman in 1947. By the time he left the House in 1955 to seek election as New York's attorney general he had firmly established himself as a Republican liberal. Recognized then as a loquacious party spokesman who made compromise his preferred tool, he became a protégé of Nelson A. Rockefeller's. Rockefeller was making his first bid to become governor, an office he subsequently held for eleven years and which he used as a springboard for repeated attempts to capture his party's presidential nomination. As New York's attorney general, Javits was considered Rockefeller's strongest supporter, a service returned in kind over the next twenty-five years by the leader of "the eastern liberal establishment."

With Rockefeller's financial aid, Javits, in 1957, became the successor, in the U.S. Senate, to New York's Depression-era governor, Herbert H. Lehman. For the next twenty-four years, Javits added to his reputation as a thoughtful legislator who was primarily interested in broad national issues and international affairs. He performed the normal services for his New York constituents but seldom trumpeted his role in these mundane affairs.

He was reelected with substantial majorities three times and as he was approaching the end of his fourth term in 1979, at age seventy-five, indicated he wanted another term. It was his hope that with the upcoming presidential victory of Ronald Reagan the Republicans would finally capture control of the Senate and he would become chairman of the Foreign Relations Committee. This was a reasonable ambition for a man of Jacob Javits's accomplishments. However, Nelson Rockefeller's death during the early stages of the campaign invited all sorts of mischief to Javits's ambitions.

Suddenly, Al D'Amato began to suggest he would make a better senator than the incumbent of his own party. He said he was considering a run against Javits in the Republican primary. But the manner in which Margiotta had dispatched the disobedient Ralph Caso little more than a year earlier made it clear that the forty-one year-old "Tiger" had to win the boss's approval before he made any move against the state's most renowned public servant.

On December 10, 1979, Joe Margiotta signaled his approval. He called a meeting of the sixty-nine-member Nassau Republican Executive Committee, which, on the boss's command, unanimously approved the "exploratory" senatorial candidacy of one of its own members, Hempstead's presiding supervisor, Al D'Amato.

Javits phoned Margiotta soon after the result of the meeting was announced. He expressed his determination to run regardless of who opposed him and predicted the loss of his Senate seat to the Democrats if a divisive primary took place. The Democrats were in the process of nominating one of two well-known women, Cong. Elizabeth Holtzman or former Miss America and then New York City's consumer affairs commissioner, Bess Meyerson, either a formidable candidate. Javits's attempt at persuasion failed: Margiotta told the *Times* that few members of the County Executive Committee knew Javits, because he rarely visited Nassau. He revealed he had informed Javits that if the senator made the error of trying for reelection, the mutiny Margiotta was leading would most likely go on to the bitter end.

Vincent Albano, Manhattan's Republican leader, angrily blasted Margiotta's dump-Javits move. "Joe Margiotta has become the Don

Rickles of the Republican party," he roared. "His joke is that he is supporting an unknown to be the Republican nominee for senator from New York; his insult is that he is placing this unknown against our great United States senator, Jack Javits."

Ralph Caso explained why Margiotta and D'Amato were actually pursuing a shrewd, if rather daring, strategy: "There was no secret to the fact that Jake Javits could never win a Republican primary. The Republicans knew that all the time. Javits was a popular vote getter, but not with Republicans. He was too liberal for Republicans. And with the swing to conservatism that took place with Reagan, this made Javits all the more vulnerable."

For years Javits had actually been a helpless prize waiting to be captured by someone ruthless enough to place his own ambitions above the shallow concerns of political etiquette. Buffalo's Jack Kemp, the conservative's favorite Republican, showed the power that this antiquated etiquette had even as D'Amato was about to deliver it a deathblow: The former professional football quarterback took himself out of the game by saying that unless Javits voluntarily withdrew, he would not challenge him.

Caso recalled the realities of early 1980 as the primary battle took shape: "Rockefeller's death was the political demise of Jake Javits, because while Rockefeller was alive, no one would dare threaten Jack Javits, and Rockefeller made that very clear. I can remember many conversations in which Margiotta would say, 'We can't stomach that Javits.' And Rockefeller would say, 'Don't you touch Javits. He's a great vote getter. He's my friend. He's a wonderful man . . . an intellectual.' And he is. But Javits was never considered a Republican. He was too liberal."

Margiotta's memory of those days emphasized the practical reasons for opposing Javits and ignored the ideological. After describing himself as "a moderate," which would have placed him at Javits's side, Margiotta coolly told me, "Javits might have been a very fine statesman, but Javits never produced the way Al had." What the Senate needed, in the view of Uniondale's most prominent employment agent, was not a statesman but a ward heeler.

Caso described the sequence of events in D'Amato's strategy: "So . . . Rockefeller dies, and D'Amato starts playing footsie with the conservatives to pull off the designation of the Conservative party as the candidate against Javits. He had given jobs in his administra-

tion to Conservative party people. They would have done it any-
way, because the only reason for the Conservative party coming
into being was they were against Nelson Rockefeller—he was too
liberal—and they hated Jacob Javits."

Jim Nagourney ridiculed the idea that D'Amato was a conservative, or, for that matter, a man with any kind of immutable philosophy or ideology. "I'm sure that as soon as things go back to the
left—and everything is cyclical in politics—Al will be on the left."

Nagourney found it hard to understand why otherwise sophisticated people did not understand that D'Amato's political stance was
entirely opportunistic. "And the biggest joke of all was Al running for
the Senate as a conservative. Look at the way he spent money as a
supervisor. All you had to do in those days was show up at a board
of supervisors meeting and demand something. You want a new
community center, you got it. These people want a raise, they got it.
Any group that came in and wanted something done for them, Al
would say yes. He wanted their vote. That isn't the conservative way
of running government: The candy store never closes, and someone
else will pay."

Terry Boyle, former leader of the Unity party, provided an example of D'Amato's willingness to buy votes with tax money. "Alfonse
spoke to me when he was running for the Senate," Boyle remarked
sarcastically. D'Amato and he had not exchanged a word in eighteen years, since Boyle had cornered D'Amato in P. T. Barnum's
old homestead and cursed him out as a betrayer. But here he was,
in front of Boyle's house, across the street from Armand and
Antoinette's place, chatting as if nothing had happened.

D'Amato offered Boyle a substantial bribe. " 'If you want a job with
the county,' " Boyle quoted him as saying, " 'I can get you one.' " It
was the old "five-year bit." D'Amato was inviting Boyle to paste
together the time that he had worked as a village trustee and whatever time he would put in with the county to come up with a pension he didn't deserve. "He was offering everyone something,"
Boyle said. "I told him I always earned my own way. I didn't need
his favors."

The conservatives' endorsement, although it provided window
dressing, was not sufficient to win D'Amato a Senate seat. He
needed the Republican nomination in order to seriously challenge

the Democrat's nominee. What most observers failed to understand but what Margiotta and D'Amato took as a given was that D'Amato would have no difficulty winning the GOP nomination. Javits would certainly get reelected if he were *on* the Republican ticket; without Rockefeller and with any certified Republican who would challenge him in the primary, it would be easier for that seventy-five-year-old recreational tennis player to win the Wimbledon Cup.

D'Amato hired Roger Ailes as his media consultant. Ailes would eventually earn the championship belt in the field of effective advertising with his contributions to the Willie Horton commercial during Mike Dukakis's 1988 bid for the presidency. In 1980 he had already established his credentials as one of America's slickest creators of negative campaigns.

A number of county leaders, mostly from downstate, lined up behind D'Amato. Javits saw the handwriting on the convention wall and announced that he would not "live or die" by the results of the now unavoidable Republican primary. The primary was scheduled to take place on September 9, 1980. D'Amato took every opportunity to draw attention away from Javits's distinguished record and focus it on the aging senator's health. Javits had for years suffered from a neurological condition that progressively weakened his muscles; six years later, it led to his death. It had, however, no impact on his intellect or his ability to function in the largely sedentary life of a U.S. senator.

D'Amato's campaign against Javits was mean, his attacks slashing, always aimed at Javits's physical condition. He often finished his assaults by shouting, "And now, at the age of seventy-six and in failing health, he wants six more years."

Attempting to counter D'Amato's thrusts, Javits tirelessly swept around the state, jocularly remarking that he wasn't running for an office requiring him to lift heavy objects.

Although D'Amato had reason to be optimistic, a political land mine went off on September 5. Word emerged from a source in the labyrinthine 1 percent case that Burt Neuborne had filed papers with Judge Mishler that destroyed D'Amato's credibility. There was, according to the source, a smoking-gun letter on D'Amato's official stationery that had been in Judge Mishler's possession for two years. Reputedly, the letter so conclusively tied D'Amato to the Nassau Republican's extortion plot and so clearly showed he had lied to the 1975 federal grand jury that this time there was no way for him to explain away his corrupt activities.

The previous Sunday—several days before word of the Marcus letter began to surface—D'Amato had angrily denied he knew of the Nassau kickback scheme. That furious denial was still fresh in reporters' minds as they questioned him about the letter at a Rochester television station; it was the Friday before the upcoming Tuesday primary. D'Amato's initial reaction was to deny any memory of such a letter. "This is obviously a desperate late-minute attempt to create political embarrassment. The alleged letter is nearly ten years old, and I have no recollection of it."

Margiotta took the same tack, calling the letter a "last-minute political smear." Unlike D'Amato, however, he did not seem to doubt the authenticity of the "alleged" letter. "It is very odd," he said, "a few days before the primary election that a letter pops up after ten years. We've been hearing charges by the opposition for years and years, and we keep on winning elections."

According to Margiotta, the important thing was winning. He brushed aside the accusations of extortion and bribery, remarking that these charges had been made "for years and years."

At the same time, it had become obvious that Javits was feeling uncomfortable about the emergence of the letter: These were, after all, accusations being made against the party to which he had pledged allegiance; the party that had given him a lifetime of rewards and acclaim and from which he still expected additional laurels. Amid the gloom, D'Amato noticed Javits's overanxious denial that he was responsible for the letter's disclosure.

By the time D'Amato had traveled the few miles between Rochester and Syracuse, he was on the offensive. Of course, he did not recall writing the letter but insisted its release "speaks to the fact that the Javits people are absolutely desperate." The diversion worked; Javits issued a statement: "Until I read this story in the newspaper I was not aware of any such matter, and I am satisfied that neither was any member of my staff. I regret very much that this matter has arisen during the primary campaign."

Margiotta issued a statement intensifying the attack. "We assume that this is what the Javits people are doing after looking at the polls. This is the general tactic we have encountered over the last ten years from the Democrats when they would break something in the final days of the campaign." Though he had no proof of Javits's involvement, he added, "Who else would do this?"

By the next day it was clear to D'Amato that there was no possibility of denying the authenticity of the Marcus letter; copies had appeared in newspapers all over the state. Reporters were phoning and reading it to him or calling out at campaign stops the implications of a Byzantine conspiracy: *"Dear Don, I have spoken to Mr. Margiotta and he has indicated to me that the raise for Mr. Robert Marcus of the Sanitation Department would be approved if he took care of the 1 percent . . ."*

In a press conference in his Hempstead Town Hall office Saturday morning, three days before the primary, D'Amato confessed that he now remembered the letter; his memory had been jogged, he said, when it had been read to him. But—he seemed to be saying—let's look at this from another angle. Marcus was "a pathetic, poor soul, but a nice guy. I think he had some disabilities. This would seem like an effort on our part to help this guy out, since he was apparently unable to make a contribution. For many years *this* [workers kicking back 1 percent of their salary to the GOP] was an accepted practice." He reiterated, "It was a very common practice at the time."

So Marcus had been the beneficiary of a generous act by a kindhearted soul. His missing "contribution"—which was holding up his salary increase—was being paid by an eleemosynary D'Amato, who recognized the special circumstances of this unusual case. There were, unfortunately, twenty-two thousand other needy Nassau employees who wanted raises but were beyond the special dispensation that Hempstead's leader had granted to Marcus.

"When I look back, sure, it was an error in judgment," D'Amato told the assembled press corps. Over the years, and as recently as the previous week, he had repeatedly told the same reporters that he had never taken part in, or knew anything about, the 1 percent kickback. Then, with an aggressive sweep of his arm, he flung a handful of Santa Claus dust in their eyes: "I'm not going to hang my head in shame because nine years ago I tried to help someone."

This mixture of flimflam and posturing saw D'Amato through; as the professionals in the party knew, Javits could not win a Republican primary. The September 9 turnout, as in the case of all such organization functions, was small.

Going into the primary, Javits had carried another ace in his hand: the Liberal party. As they had in the past, the Liberals nominated Javits and declared they would support him in the November election even if he ran only on their ticket.

But once D'Amato had won the Republican nomination, the Liberal party ace became a card D'Amato held: There was no way Javits could win an election in which up to 6 million votes might be cast, only on a ticket that normally polled 300,000 votes. His prospects were especially dismal, since most of those liberal votes would be siphoned off from D'Amato's Democratic opponent, who the Democrats had finally decided was going to be the sober congresswoman Elizabeth Holtzman.

Caso explained: "It was the ego of Javits, and I say this with feeling, because I know how Javits felt, as the incumbent, because I did the same thing. Javits stayed on to run on the liberal line; he got 600,000 votes. Now, any idiot can figure out that of those 600,000 votes, at least a couple of thousand would have gone to Liz Holtzman, enough for her to beat D'Amato, because he only won by 3,000 votes. People who had voted for Javits never would have voted for D'Amato: They would have gone for Holtzman. She would have won."

To his dying day Javits was forced to contend with the fact that he was responsible for placing D'Amato in the Senate.

On the night he won the primary—and, again, on the night he won the election—D'Amato staged victory parties at an Island Park nightclub. The club was owned by Philip Basile; Basile, in fact, was D'Amato's master of ceremonies. Basile was a good friend of Al's; they often dined together. Over the years, Basile had given thousands of dollars to D'Amato's campaigns. D'Amato's brother, Armand Paul, was Basile's attorney. Basile was also a friend of Paul Vario's, leader of the Lucchese organized-crime family, with whom Basile dined as frequently as he did with his good friend Al. Godfather Vario lived in Island Park.

There was an obligation in this Mafia relationship that only the passage of time would reveal. On election night in Basile's club, as the Chianti glasses were raised in a victory toast, the farthest thought in the new senator's mind was that there might be some reason to worry about that obligation.

THIRTEEN

IT TAKES MORE THAN LUCK

ormer county executive Ralph Caso moved his hands restless-
ly over his desk, touching one prayer card and then another.
The hurt that Margiotta had inflicted years before was still
eating away at him in 1985, yet the comfort that he sought in this
gesture of supplication seemed to elude him most as he fingered
the cardboard talismans.

In an attempt to distract him, I asked what he thought had led to
D'Amato's great success. "Luck, and being in the right place at the
right time," he responded with the certainty of a man who had
pondered that question at all hours of the day and night.

Support for Caso's "luck" theory was supplied by the events of
the week following D'Amato's election. U.S. Attorney Ed Korman,
who had been dogging D'Amato and Margiotta's tracks for years,
announced, on November 11, 1980, that he was investigating
Margiotta's direction of an insurance racket in Nassau County.
According to Korman, Margiotta had picked the private broker who
wrote Nassau's lucrative insurance policies. In return, he had
demanded that the broker allow Margiotta to distribute 50 percent
of the broker's fees to party faithful selected by Margiotta. These
party members did nothing to earn their payoffs, and the 50 percent that was added to the cost of the policies was passed on to
Nassau taxpayers. Since one of these hacks was Al's father, Armand
Sr., had Korman made that announcement a week before the elec-

tion instead of a week after, the few thousand votes Elizabeth Holtzman needed to beat Margiotta's emotional "son" would very likely have materialized.

The day after Korman revealed his Margiotta probe, Senator-elect D'Amato announced at a Washington luncheon for congressional reporters that he had news for Korman: He would not be automatically retained until the end of his term as U.S. Attorney for the Eastern District. Korman's term ran to August 1982, leaving the energetic prosecutor ample time to do a great deal of damage to D'Amato and his friends.

As D'Amato introduced a note of uncertainty into Korman's career plans, Lyn Nofziger, press secretary to President-elect Ronald Reagan, said Reagan would soon ask for the resignations of all Democratic U.S. Attorneys. U.S. Attorneys were particularly vulnerable to political pressure, unfortunately for the administration of justice, since their four-year terms could be aborted at any time by a note of dismissal from the president. Within the year President Reagan had replaced ninety of the ninety-four U.S. Attorneys across the country.

To fill each of those U.S. Attorney vacancies, the state's senator from the president's party, if there was one, suggested a nominee, whom the president routinely accepted, sending on the nomination to the Senate, where it was almost invariably confirmed. Therefore, D'Amato was in a position, if he asked Reagan to fire Korman, to dictate who would be the U.S. Attorney deciding whether action would be taken against his political father and possibly his real father and himself.

After D'Amato announced his reservations about retaining Korman in office, reporters asked about Korman's inquiry into Margiotta's rigging of Nassau insurance fees. The senator-elect would not comment on the connection the reporters seemed to be drawing between the two events. He responded that he was going to appoint a "panel of distinguished citizens" who would screen names and advise him of possible appointees. The panel would include Michael F. Armstrong, D'Amato's personal attorney, and attorney Thomas A. Bolan, who was a founder of New York's Conservative party and law partner of the soon-to-be-disbarred Roy Cohn.

D'Amato was asked whether it would not be better, if only for the sake of appearances, to retain Korman until the Margiotta investigation had run its course. He responded that he couldn't answer such a question because his appointment of a "distinguished" screening panel made the question "hypothetical."

It was obvious to those reporters at the luncheon that Ed Korman would soon be in private practice.

Unfortunately for D'Amato and Margiotta, New York's senior senator Daniel Patrick Moynihan had made it difficult to peremptorily jettison Korman. Four years earlier, when Democrat Moynihan had taken office under Democratic president Carter, he had permitted New York State's four U.S. Attorneys—all Republican appointees—to complete their terms.

On WCBS-TV's *Newsmakers*, November 16, 1980, Senator-elect D'Amato said that after conversations with members of the legal community and reviewing Korman's record, he had decided to let Korman finish his term. "I want to avoid any appearance of politicizing this office," he declared.

From Margiotta's point of view, the man who owed everything to him, the man who everyone conceded had the right to replace Korman and thereby crush his tormentor, was instead allowing Korman to continue his restless prosecution. Especially galling to Margiotta was the thought that D'Amato could have protected his patron with little risk to himself. Similar political debts were being paid off across the country. U.S. Attorneys who were about to be replaced had previously taken their offices by stepping over the dispatched bodies of their predecessors. It was a tradition. Besides, D'Amato wouldn't have to run again for six years, and by that time, few voters would remember, or care about, what he had done in those ancient days. Forgetfulness, not luck, would be his savior.

For the beleaguered Margiotta, this blow came after a week of setbacks. He had sent his attorneys to Washington to persuade Justice Department officials that the case against him was weak and that whatever he had done did not technically violate the law; all to no avail. A Justice Department source told the press that should Korman be removed in two months, when Reagan was sworn in, Margiotta's case would *probably* have gone too far to be stopped.

D'Amato could claim he had little chance to head off Margiotta's indictment; under such circumstances, why get involved? That type of practicality strains political friendships, and Nassau Republicans began to mutter that D'Amato was trying to distance himself from the besieged boss. They reasoned that if D'Amato had kept the pressure on Korman, the U.S. Attorney would not have been so anxious to move ahead.

Word also went out that in the two weeks since the election D'Amato had called Margiotta only twice, both times speaking to him briefly and perfunctorily; this in contrast to his normal practice of phoning every day on any pretext that offered an excuse to whisper into his ear.

Margiotta's spokesman, Levittown's executive leader Robert McDonald, declared, "There's no rift." For those who were by nature skeptical, he added, "They have great respect for each other." Gary Lewi, D'Amato's public relations man, straining to indicate how intimate the relationship remained, said that the two men continued to have "close personal respect" for each other.

McDonald nevertheless conceded that Margiotta and D'Amato were at odds over selection of D'Amato's successor as Hempstead's presiding supervisor. Hempstead was D'Amato's home turf and was the Nassau party's strongest power base; he wanted to control it. If James Bennett, who had served as supervisor under him, was selected, that control was guaranteed. Margiotta preferred Assemblyman Thomas Gulotta of North Merrick. Margiotta was determined to show that he, and not Senator-elect D'Amato, was the most powerful Nassau Republican. Senator D'Amato could only appoint four U.S. Attorneys, a handful of federal judges and marshals, and members of his own staff. He might attend ceremonies to which Margiotta would not be invited, and he could, along with his ninety-nine colleagues, speak for hours in the usually empty Senate chamber. But Margiotta knew, and consoled himself with the thought, that he remained the final arbiter of the destiny of twenty-two thousand county employees, the careers of thousands of judges and politicians, and the distribution of contracts worth hundreds of millions of dollars.

Moving swiftly to clear up any uncertainty about who was boss in Nassau, Margiotta called a meeting of the Hempstead Republican Executive Committee, which, at the wave of his baton, chorused a unanimous vote of approval for Margiotta's Gulotta. Two months later, in January 1981, as D'Amato was preparing to be sworn in as senator, the town board showed how government affairs were decided in Hempstead; they accepted the Republican Executive Committee vote as a command and turned the town over to Assemblyman Tom Gulotta.

However, on January 8, D'Amato again had reason to feel that his luck was holding: Nassau's district attorney, Denis Dillon, awakening from a lethargy about political corruption that had now gone on for six years and a reelection campaign, announced that his office was questioning executives of a Pennsylvania firm, Kravco, Inc. of King of Prussia, about a $5,100 contribution made by executives of that company to Senator D'Amato's campaign fund. It seemed that Kravco had wanted to build a $30 million addition to its Nassau Green Acres shopping center in Valley Stream, and Dillon had received complaints that in return for the contribution Kravco had been exempted by the leaders of Hempstead from filing an environmental impact statement.

Having been accused so frequently of corruption, the still-euphoric senator brushed aside the allegation, apparently perceiving no threat from any investigation launched by Denis Dillon. He remarked that he was surprised to hear that Kravco hadn't been required to file an impact statement, declaring, "At no time did we ever solicit or contact Kravco personnel in any way for contributions. They did it on their own." Sufficient layers of deniability had clearly been put in place.

The Kravco incident was merely the tip of the D'Amato fund-raising iceberg. His senatorial victory was due in part to the $3 million he had raised to sponsor mindless, but winsome, television commercials showing Mother Antoinette reassuring those waiting for the resumption of their favorite soap opera that her son was a good boy. There were few reputable ways for a poor boy from Island Park to raise that kind of money, and simply because D'Amato had possibly found one seemed to his admirers to be slender reason to call him once again before a grand jury.

D'Amato's greatest advantage as a politician had not been his luck; rather, his ability to sell off chunks of the commonwealth to raise money for his next campaign. In keeping with that priority, D'Amato asked the new Senate Republican majority leader, Howard Baker, to place him on the Finance Committee; failing that majestic appointment in his freshman semester, he would settle for the Budget, Banking, or Commerce committee.

Should any of those appointments come through, he would be able to influence legislation affecting Wall Street firms, where his slush-fund list included a large number of addresses. He would immediately become the target of intense lobbyist activities on behalf of those firms, and he could then tap into the richest segment of American society.

Baker yielded three choice assignments: Banking, Housing, and Appropriations. With a maximum amount of added pressure, D'Amato convinced Baker to make him chairman of a Banking subcommittee, a position of such importance that a senator less obsessed about accumulating money would have relaxed, sat back, and watched the "contributions" pour in from banks across the country. Membership on the Senate Banking Committee was most often desired precisely for that reason.

D'Amato had hit the jackpot with his committee assignments; characteristically, he prepared to use his leverage aggressively. Phone calls were made, and soon after Baker's largesse was announced, a Wall Street committee to raise funds for Senator D'Amato's reelection materialized.

Ironically, the one man who was most responsible for placing D'Amato beneath that golden faucet was now bleeding from a wound inflicted by him.

FOURTEEN
"D'AMATO'S FOLLY"

A l D'Amato came close to being indicted for his role in building the Hempstead Resources Recovery Plant. Lothar Genge, the special attorney for the Department of Justice's racketeering section was one of thirteen federal prosecutors working with the revitalized Brooklyn Organized Crime Strike Force. He spoke of the lost opportunity with regret during several hours of conversation we had in his fortresslike Florida office.

In 1983, Genge had been transferred out of Brooklyn, the place where the investigation of D'Amato and the Hempstead plant was centered. The strike force functioned within the judicial area covered by New York's Eastern District, which included Nassau County. When I interviewed him on February 23, 1987, he was working with the Fort Lauderdale strike force. Political corruption was no longer on his agenda. Instead, he waged war on drugs. I reached his office through the twisting corridors of the mammoth, cement-terraced Federal Building. The plate-glass window at the entrance to Genge's office was bulletproof. The receptionist, a stocky FBI agent with a pistol strapped to his left buttock, sat behind the window. Thick armored plate backed the door to his office and protected the wall surrounding the plate-glass window.

Lothar Genge, who stood six feet three inches, came to America from Germany in 1951 at the age of ten. His parents had given him the name of a thirteenth-century Germanic king, hoping that their

111

Lothar would also be a conquering hero. He was raised in one of Nassau's richest communities, Great Neck. After graduating from Columbia Law School in 1966, he worked for Frank Hogan, the legendary Manhattan district attorney. In 1977, U.S. Attorney Ed Korman and Tom Puccio, head of the Brooklyn strike force, convinced Genge to transfer to the federal prosecutor's office by telling him they would mount an all-out campaign against organized crime. The U.S. Attorney impressed Genge, who said of Korman, "Ed is a very capable, honest individual and an outstanding scholar. He didn't care who got credit for cases. He wanted convictions. He's also a nice guy, down-to-earth."

Genge believed in harshly punishing corrupt politicians. "There are politicians out there ready to turn their local Hempstead recycling plants into a good thing for themselves. The only thing that restrains them is the thought that they might get caught. But catching them won't do much good if all they get is a slap on the wrist and some pleasant time at Allenwood or some other correctional institute–country club. A short sentence at one of those places is just an opportunity to get your tennis game in shape."

Genge described the origins of the probe into D'Amato's garbage plant. "When I started to work in '77, '78, we were investigating George Boylan. He was head of the International Boilermakers Union, Local 5. Although the Boilermakers were a small union— only about fourteen hundred members—they were extremely important in the making of power plants. Basically, Boylan supplied all of the boilermakers in the greater Metropolitan area, New Jersey, and upstate New York. We had information that Boylan was shaking down contractors. As it turned out, over a period of time Boylan had gotten in excess of a million dollars in payoffs. Essentially, what he did—unless they paid him, and he had rule-of-thumb prices for particular facets of the job—he would give them workers who were, I think his term was, 'whiskey sticks.' You would get the dregs, as opposed to making sure that there was labor peace.

"During the investigation we found out that some of his people were working at the Hempstead recycling plant. And so it was our investigation of Boylan that took us into Hempstead."

Payoffs and extortion at the Hempstead plant were divided into at least two separate operations. George Boylan and other racketeering labor leaders controlled the first of these operations. They ran their own scam, which extorted money from contractors. The amount of money they robbed—and their effectiveness in collecting it—did not depend directly on aid from the other group: the politicians and their agents. It did, however, require their acquiescence.

Earlier word about Boylan's shady practices had been confirmed by Organized Crime Strike Force investigators in the summer of 1977, when Robert Spitzer, the head of Treadwell Corporation, a Manhattan-based company that erected power plants, informed them that for over ten years he had been subject to Boylan's extortion.

Robert Spitzer cooperated with the government in all subsequent investigations. In an interview in his East Side apartment in Manhattan, he explained to me how he became involved with Boylan.

It all started in 1964–65, Spitzer recalled. His company, Treadwell Corporation, was erecting two large steam-generating boilers for the Long Island Lighting Company (LILCO) in Northport. He said, "It was a six-million-dollar contract. We employed two hundred to four hundred Local 5 boilermakers. From the start, we found them unproductive. At that time, I was vice president of Treadwell, and I had a number of meetings with Boylan about the problem. During the course of one of those meetings Boylan stated he had emphysema and suddenly asked, 'And who will support my wife and kiddies?' He then told me that productivity could be improved at Northport if he was paid off. The payoffs usually took place over lunch or dinner at various restaurants and sometimes at Treadwell's office. The payments kept getting larger. My jobs always overlapped. It was an impossible situation to extricate yourself from."

"The *feds* came to *me*," Spitzer went on. "I was afraid of Boylan. Two of my superintendents were killed in the late 1960s. One was dynamited in his car; the other was beaten with pipes by a bunch of thugs. He was in the hospital for a long time—fractured skull, seven blood clots, broken bones. He was never the same. He died two years later."

Spitzer had asked the FBI to investigate, but "they showed very little interest," he said. "The city police never came up with anything."

Lothar Genge built his case against Boylan on leads provided by the irate Spitzer and several other contractors. Once Genge had convinced Spitzer of their determination to pursue Boylan, he became an active participant in putting the case together.

Boylan was indicted on June 7, 1979, on eleven counts centering on the charge that he had "conducted the affairs of Local 5 through a pattern of racketeering activity"; in effect, that he had violated the federal Racketeer-Influenced and Corrupt Organizations Act (RICO), which had been passed to strengthen the government's hand in Mafia-related prosecutions.

Spitzer became the chief witness against him. "He was an excellent witness," Genge said. "Unshakable and utterly convincing." Officers from his company corroborated his testimony, and the heads of six other construction companies from around the country also declared they had been extorted by Boylan. Boylan was convicted on all counts and sentenced on November 19, 1979, to ten years in a conventional federal prison. "After a while, he cooperated with the government," Genge said. "He decided to see if there was a little something he could do to help himself."

Spitzer's fear of retribution by Boylan's associates had somewhat abated by the time I interviewed him, but he knew that he continued to live in jeopardy. "I've cooperated with the government on many things," he said slowly, and then added with emphasis: "And still do."

Although he was unaware of it, Spitzer's continued cooperation with Lothar Genge was a substantial threat to Al D'Amato and his pet project, the Hempstead Resources Recovery Plant. On close inspection by the Organized Crime Strike Force, that rusting erector set seemed to have been conceived by Boss Tweed, engineered by Rube Goldberg, and financed by Ivan Boesky.

George Boylan told Lothar Genge that Nassau County had become a gold mine for anyone with a scam who needed a political connection. It was an area in which politicians mixed with businessmen, labor leaders, and racketeers. They would meet at Margiotta-arranged dinners, cocktail parties, and golf outings. Deals were hatched during social gatherings at local country clubs, over feasts at neighborhood restaurants, on vacations, and while vows were exchanged at the weddings of each other's children.

Genge gave one explanation why these men on the make found Nassau such a friendly place to arrange deals. "DA's on the Island get reelected by prosecuting street crime, not white-collar crime. As a result, when we turned our attention to Nassau County, the prosecution of political corruption was virgin territory."

As Boylan strove to impress the U.S. Attorney's office, he told Genge of bribes paid to him during the building of the Hempstead plant. Genge recalled, "It soon became obvious that there was corruption at *all* levels in the building of that plant."

Striving to prove the value of his information, Boylan began to mention names—among them, Raymond Walter, president of the Clayburn Construction Company. Although Clayburn was based in New York City, it did most of its business in Nassau County. Genge discovered that Walter, whom he had heard about from other sources, was associated with most of the key figures in the building of the recycling plant. He developed a strategy to convert Walter into a witness against corrupt Nassau politicians.

Raymond Walter became habituated to paying off politicians. He considered it a "business necessity." Since the mid-1960s, he had spread his checks and cash in a wide circle. His most frequent extortioner was Francis O'Connor, the executive leader of the Locust Valley Republican Club. In the 1960s he also served as Oyster Bay's chief engineer. From the beginning of his dealings with Walter, O'Connor acted mainly as a bagman for the party; he was a conduit for the payoffs. At O'Connor's "request," Walter made "political contributions . . . almost on a monthly basis." The money went into Margiotta's coffers.

O'Connor had learned during the 1960s that Walter was reliable and that he would "play ball." However, after January 1971, when O'Connor became head of the county General Services Department and took on new duties, his relationship with Walter, never a personal one, faded. Despite this, Walter was not surprised on May 5, 1972, when he returned to his Long Island City office, to be handed a telephone message from O'Connor informing him that he should return O'Connor's "very urgent" call "at once."

The events leading to that message began in Hempstead the previous month, on April 13, 1972. On that day, two representatives of Black, Clawson, Inc., a paper-manufacturing company with substantial holdings in Europe, came to Presiding Supervisor D'Amato's office. They proposed to build a large garbage-recycling plant, which would employ techniques so innovative that the machinery for the plant would have to be imported from Europe. Hempstead's would be the first of dozens of recycling plants in the metropolitan area, where landfill sites were rapidly disappearing. Also present in D'Amato's office was William Landman, the town's soon-to-be-jailed, bribe-taking sanitation commissioner. Black, Clawson's missionaries were extremely persuasive; although D'Amato has said that there was a period of extended discussions between him and the company, he apparently made up his mind almost instantly that this could be an extraordinary opportunity.

How D'Amato, schooled mainly in fund-raising, could have so effortlessly made such a borderline technical decision remains a mystery. A man never concerned with details, he was untutored in the intricacies of garbage disposal, much less the technical aspects of the largely untried technology of generating energy while separating and recycling metal, glass, and other materials.

Nevertheless, certain aspects of this possibly useful community project seemed particularly attractive to D'Amato. For one thing, Black, Clawson was no fly-by-night outfit. Its fine reputation lent an aura of respectability to an enterprise that, if it carried only the burden of his endorsement, might flounder. More important, he had developed a close relationship with Peter Alevra, vice president of Black, Clawson. D'Amato described him as the company's "top man." Alevra would be in charge of building the plant. According to D'Amato, although Black, Clawson would decide who would be hired, before any decision was made his "advice" would be sought in this "joint venture."

That Black, Clawson decided it did not want to deal with any of the unions working on the site further weakened the company's role in hiring. Word of payoffs to union racketeers like George Boylan was widely disseminated in business circles, and the owners of Black, Clawson had determined they would not allow themselves to become the extortionists' target. The plant would be built by subcontractors, a species of businessmen who had been successfully squeezed by D'Amato for many years. In effect, this procedure gave D'Amato control over the distribution of contracts; if a subcontractor wanted a slice of the action at Mitchell Field, he first had to pass D'Amato's "contribution" test.

On April 26, 1972, D'Amato and Sanitation Commissioner Landman flew to Ohio, where they were shown Black, Clawson's small experimental plant. On May 5, nine days later, Francis O'Connor left his "very urgent" message on Raymond Walter's desk. Since

Walter was aware that any discussion with O'Connor usually led to a profit for his construction company, he hastened to arrange a meeting with the general services commissioner at his Nassau County office. O'Connor told a startled Walter about D'Amato's new project, word of which had not yet been made public. O'Connor informed Walter he was in a position to ensure that Clayburn would receive a "financially desirable" contract to do a major part of the plant's construction, which he estimated would cost between $26 and $30 million. Walter said he was interested. O'Connor promised that Black, Clawson would be in touch with him.

The extraordinary aspect of this meeting was that Francis O'Connor was not then, nor was he ever, a Hempstead official. His salaried work was being done solely on behalf of Nassau County's General Services Department. O'Connor had no legitimate way of knowing that such a project was under consideration by Hempstead's presiding supervisor, Al D'Amato, the chief force behind the project. Yet he was seeking to peddle a town contract for a portion of the construction worth $12 million.

Equally startling was O'Connor's demonstration of his "clout" with D'Amato, which he frequently bragged about. Within a week of O'Connor's promise that Black, Clawson would be in touch, Walter received a call from Black, Clawson's chief engineer, Dean Kohlepp. O'Connor did not work for Black, Clawson. His only connection to the firm was through Al D'Amato. Walter knew that the call had been approved by D'Amato and that the deal was set.

Black, Clawson's engineer Dean Kohlepp and Raymond Walter arranged to meet on May 19, 1972. Subsequently, under oath, Kohlepp revealed that he had been instructed by one of his bosses—he thought it was D'Amato's friend Peter Alevra—to contact Walter and give him technical information so that the Clayburn Construction Company would be able to prepare cost estimates.

Walter and engineer Kohlepp held a series of meetings at which Walter submitted budget estimates, which were modified as Kohlepp produced additional technical data. The advantage that this personalized treatment gave Clayburn over its potential competitors was obvious. All of D'Amato's conspiratorial maneuverings took place *before* Black, Clawson officially submitted its proposal to the town of Hempstead. Black, Clawson believed that without discussing their proposition with the board of supervisors, in

117

whose hands the decision supposedly rested, they had a commitment from D'Amato equivalent to a signed contract.

On May 23, 1972, four days after Walter's first meeting with Kohlepp, Walter was summoned to a meeting in O'Connor's county office. After first asking Walter about the progress he was making, O'Connor dropped the other shoe: He wanted a cash payoff equal to 10 percent on any contract Clayburn obtained at the recycling plant. He told Walter that he was splitting the 10 percent with D'Amato.

Walter claimed to have found the size of the extortion "shocking." He couldn't conceive of delivering a minimum of $2.6 million in cash over the next two years. A series of negotiations ensued; the haggling resulted in an agreement on a 2 percent kickback. Walter never doubted D'Amato's involvement, since it was obvious to him that a county official of O'Connor's minor status could not possibly have the power to produce the results he had witnessed without the connivance of Hempstead's leader. In order to ensure that the citizens of Hempstead, and not himself, paid the 2 percent bribe, Walter included it in his final cost estimate.

Primarily because Black, Clawson was unable to successfully float a bond issue, a contract to build the plant was not signed. For several years it looked as if D'Amato's fantasies about the greatest boondoggle in Nassau history would never become reality, but single-handedly he managed to breathe life back into the project, and in 1975 Black, Clawson—now metamorphosed into Parsons & Whittemore (P & W)—signed a contract with the town to inflate D'Amato's South Sea Island bubble.

By that time the original Clayburn Contracting Corporation had been dissolved, and Walter's new firm, Clayburn Construction, was unable to undertake such a sizable job. Although Walter and O'Connor again drifted apart, their more significant encounters were still to come.

Replacements for Walter were easy to find. D'Amato told prosecutors that he had been "deluged" with requests from local concerns that wanted a "piece of the action." Since all of the local concerns were acquainted with the rules of the game, it is understandable why the cost of the plant kept escalating as the feeding frenzy among the contractors took hold and the extortionist's expectations grew.

Actual construction of the recycling plant did not begin until 1976, four years after D'Amato started lobbying for it. There was some feeling that the site had been selected because a majority of nearby downwind Salisbury residents were Democrats. Therefore, the nostrils of the offended—if the plant stank as much as other garbage plants—would belong to those whose outraged sensibilities would not cost D'Amato many votes.

The degree of thievery surrounding what *Newsday* labeled "D'Amato's Folly" can be illustrated by describing the antics of Terrence Shine. Shine was hired by P & W as superintendent on the site in April 1976, after D'Amato had exercised his right of approval. As such, he was the official with whom subcontractors dealt when any problems arose; he also evaluated their work. Although Peter Alevra served as his superior, the subcontractors understood that Shine was "the man in charge."

In May 1976, Shine awarded the first contract to Leon deBremont; it involved demolition of existing buildings and clearing the site. Since P & W did not want to deal directly with the workers, Shine offered deBremont the payroll contract, under which deBremont was to receive 15 percent of the gross salaries paid; in return, Shine demanded one-third of deBremont's share, eventually receiving $8,500.

DeBremont chafed under Shine's ultimatums. He was particularly upset when Shine told him to put "phantom" workers on the payroll. At first, he refused, but Shine got his way by threatening to blackball him if he did not cooperate.

DeBremont reached his breaking point in late October 1977. It was "that time of the year" when the political apparatus was mobilized to raise money for the November elections. Shine suddenly demanded $30,000 from deBremont, saying it was for "Alfonse D'Amato and other politicians."

DeBremont protested; enough was enough! Didn't these politicians know when to stop squeezing?

In response to deBremont's display of outrage, Shine contemptuously told him, "You're too small. There's too much at stake here. Get off the job."

This challenge to his masculinity and his pocketbook was sufficient to send deBremont in search of help. He showed his lack of sophistication about politics in his choice of a savior; he went to Sanitation Commissioner William Landman, one of the party's warhorses. In his agitated state, deBremont blurted out that Shine had demanded cash payments for D'Amato.

Landman recognized trouble when he saw it; he would take the matter up with Peter Alevra, the manager of the plant, he told a fuming deBremont. For some reason, which the suspicious will trace to complicity, Landman did not suggest that he would present deBremont's charge of criminality to the Nassau district attorney or even to the plant's owners.

Instead, Landman arranged a meeting the next morning between deBremont, Peter Alevra, and himself. DeBremont was extremely nervous and excitedly told Alevra that Shine had demanded money for D'Amato; he was, of course, unaware of the close relationship between Alevra and D'Amato. For good measure, deBremont described Shine's personal use of construction materials and labor, the bilking of P & W on landfill contracts, and Shine's attempt to put phantom workers on his payroll. Alevra took the matter up with Shine and finally discharged him; in Alevra and Landman's world extortion and theft were handled administratively.

Lothar Genge discovered that Shine was immediately rehired by another plant subcontractor. The culprit, Shine, who Alevra conceded was a thief when he fired him and whose criminal activities should have been reported to the county prosecutor, was, instead, merely shifted to a different payroll. This is surely the type of punishment all criminals would prefer.

DeBremont's complaint had instantly made its way from Landman's office to Presiding Supervisor D'Amato. Much later, when the matter became public knowledge, Gary Lewi, D'Amato's public relations aide, said that when D'Amato "found out about the matter, he immediately notified Parsons & Whittemore, who subsequently discharged Mr. Shine." Lewi insisted that there was a vast gulf that separated the two men: "Mr. Shine is certainly not a friend or an intimate." And he wanted it known that Shine had never been authorized to raise funds for the presiding supervisor.

But why, the reporters wanted to know, hadn't D'Amato informed law enforcement authorities about the extortion attempt? Lewi averred that his boss had only heard "of the allegations at second hand." Lewi's account established that the "secondhand" allegations had been enough to convince D'Amato to tell P & W to fire Shine but not enough to make Hempstead's supervisor refer the matter to the district attorney.

Lewi also wanted everyone to believe that D'Amato had not been aware that Shine had gone to work for another plant subcontractor after initially being discharged.

D'Amato's luck held when U.S. Attorney Ed Korman authorized Lothar Genge to proceed with his prosecution of Terrance Shine on charges of extortion and income tax evasion. Korman's authorization was given at the beginning of January 1981, less than two months after D'Amato had won his narrow victory over Liz Holtzman.

On January 15, 1981, as D'Amato hired staff for his new Senate office in Washington, Genge made his opening remarks to the Shine jurors. Genge's description of the corruption surrounding the building of the Hempstead Resources Recovery Plant proved damaging to D'Amato's reputation, but in practical terms it had no impact on his fortunes. For the next six years he would be able to ride the Senate subway to the Capitol Building.

The Shine case was ready and could have been prosecuted two months earlier. Its delay was an act of prosecutorial discretion on the part of the Eastern District U.S. Attorney's office, which may partially explain why D'Amato did not go after Ed Korman's scalp more vigorously.

D'Amato was anxious to avoid a fight with the formidable U.S. Attorney: He had to fear Korman's ability to retaliate. Earlier, in September 1979, at George Boylan's trial, Lothar Genge had asked a witness if he knew about $140,000 in payments to obtain contracts at the Hempstead Resources Recovery Plant. Genge then asked the witness if he knew Alfonse D'Amato. The judge, George C. Pratt—Margiotta's former party attorney—hammered his gavel and cut off the line of questioning. When reporters asked D'Amato why he thought his name had been connected by the U.S. Attorney to a $140,000 bribe, the future senator responded that he had no idea.

D'Amato understood that FBI agents had been investigating the Hempstead recycling plant for two years, since 1977, with increasing zeal since the plant had permanently closed in April 1978. In addition, associates of D'Amato had been questioned about his role in the disaster; equally alarming, any contractor unfortunate enough to have touched the sticky surface of that suspect project had been asked about his D'Amato campaign "contributions."

Furthermore, in the spring of 1979, as D'Amato fought Javits for the nomination, reporters came to him with pointed inquiries about the plant. The questions focused on the charge that D'Amato had accepted the plant as completed before it was functioning properly and in doing so had released P & W from their contractual obligations to turn it over in perfect working order. He was accused of prematurely releasing the company, although the plant had substantial design problems and repeatedly broke down. The problems were so severe that instead of burning garbage and generating electricity, as he had promised for years, the plant actually burned oil to generate electricity owed to LILCO.

Particularly horrifying to D'Amato was an interview in which a reporter asked him whether his brother or father had any law-firm or insurance connections to the plant. Although he acted indignant and threw the reporter out of his office, it was clear that he would soon be assailed by damaging stories about him, his family, and the failed plant.

Adding to D'Amato's stress was the news that U.S. Attorney Korman had decided to pursue Margiotta. Since D'Amato had been completely involved in Margiotta's insurance racket, selecting pet brokers he wanted paid off, including his father, D'Amato knew that Korman must also be investigating him. Shine's trial was merely another sign of potential disaster. Caution demanded that he abandon Margiotta to the pursuing pack. To a class of men often found at the summit of their vocation, betrayal is always preferable to sharing the blame.

FIFTEEN

THE UNNAMED OFFICIAL

S hine's conviction in 1981 and two-year sentence were treated by D'Amato as a nonevent: He did not testify at the trial, and he issued denials about references to himself at the trial through his press agent. He was, however, not able to remain aloof when Ed Korman targeted his next Nassau politician. It was the senator's good friend and close party associate Francis F. O'Connor, the county's commissioner of general services.

The decision to prosecute O'Connor grew out of the same Organized Crime Strike Force investigations that had sent George Boylan and Terrence Shine to jail. It was essentially an outgrowth of the 1 percent grand jury investigation initiated by the FBI in 1974.

For several years U.S. Attorney Korman had received allegations that D'Amato was using the recycling plant as a cash machine for his campaigns. In order to safely collect the cash, D'Amato used Francis O'Connor as his chief bagman. People who wanted to buy influence with Al D'Amato would not hand him an envelope filled with cash. They would speak to bagman O'Connor, who would tell them how much that influence would cost. A check made out to the party then went into *his* bag. If there were any legal difficulties caused by the check, O'Connor would have to face those difficulties, not D'Amato, for whom the check had been collected.

During Shine's trial, contractors testified that Shine had claimed that whatever money he squeezed out of them was extorted on behalf of Al D'Amato. From Boylan—and other informants—and the 1974 grand jury records, Korman also knew that bribery was a way of life in the Margiotta-D'Amato precincts. "Everybody paid off in Nassau County to do business with the county," he told me. "You couldn't do business without paying."

In order to close the loop around O'Connor, Korman authorized Lothar Genge to use Robert Spitzer, who had been cooperating with the Organized Crime Strike Force and the FBI since 1977. Genge felt Spitzer was the ideal person to infiltrate the extortion consortium, since Spitzer's role in cracking the Boylan case was unknown in late 1978 to anyone outside the U.S. Attorney's office. Genge had not yet taken the Boylan case to the grand jury, and the union racketeer would not be indicted until June 7, 1979, at which time Spitzer's role as informant might become public knowledge. This gave Spitzer at least several months at the beginning of 1979 to see if he could develop an opening to the Hempstead gang.

Spitzer easily gained entry to the plant. A number of local boiler concerns that had worked on the project were no longer bidding on contracts; Treadwell was almost the only company capable of doing the work. Spitzer was approached by Raymond Walter, offering to broker a contract at the recycling plant. Walter was acting as an agent for Francis O'Connor. Spitzer had known Walter for years and told Walter he was interested, but he kept him in the dark about his true purpose. They arranged a collusive bid on the installation of a small P & W boiler. Walter's bid was slightly higher than Treadwell's, and when Spitzer got the contract, he paid Walter $10,000. "We took a little contract to gain access for the government," Spitzer explained.

Spitzer went out to Westbury to look at the plant and was shocked at what he saw. "The odors were horrible. Paper-mill equipment, unsuitable for handling ground municipal waste, had been used. If all the garbage in Hempstead had been nothing but old newspapers, it would have worked fine. They ground up everything—tried to remove metal by gravity and magnetism. Then the glass was to be separated out, and the remainder was to be burned. But it just didn't work. The glass was grinding up everything. There was glass everywhere. The workers in that plant would have eventually gotten silicosis. It was a horrible place.

Mechanisms were not correctly mounted, piping not correctly supported. Pipes were carrying abrasive substances they were not built to handle. This wasn't a maintenance problem. The place had to be rebuilt. People were running around moving materials with wheelbarrels because the conveyers had failed. Everything was falling apart."

Following Genge's plan, Spitzer was wired with recording equipment by FBI agent Michael Shay, who had been working on the 1 percent case since 1974. Shay had been the pivotal federal investigator in many Nassau political corruption cases. The wired Spitzer met with Walter and asked for help to get the plant's annual $3–4 million maintenance contract. In response, Walter boasted about his past dealings with O'Connor and of O'Connor's claims of "pull" with D'Amato. Walter said he would speak to O'Connor and Landman, asserting that he was sure O'Connor would want to be paid "in long green" for any recommendation he made.

Walter met with O'Connor on January 9, 1979, and told him that Treadwell wanted the maintenance contract. O'Connor hesitated. Despite Spitzer's small P & W boiler contract, Treadwell, he said, had no "track record" with him. Walter pressed the button he knew activated O'Connor; he promised him money.

At meetings between Spitzer and Walter on March 20 and in the following weeks, all of which were secretly taped by Spitzer, the two decided that $50,000 a year was a figure to which O'Connor "could relate." On April 5, 1979, the day after Walter transmitted Spitzer's "offer" to O'Connor, Spitzer paid Walter $10,000 for his "consulting services." Walter was now neatly skewered. Lothar Genge invited him to his office and played Spitzer's tapes; Walter was easily convinced to cooperate. Over the next weeks, Walter described how extortion and bribery worked in Nassau, drawing on his conspiracies with Francis O'Connor going back to the 1960s.

Genge developed a simple strategy to spring the trap on O'Connor. He phoned the general services commissioner and told him that his name had "come up" in the investigation of the "shakedown" of recycling plant contractors and that he might be indicted. The petrified O'Connor denied he had anything to do with the plant. Genge then told O'Connor to "get a lawyer. Have your lawyer call me, and we'll bring you down before the grand jury."

Soon after he finished his panicky conversation with Genge, O'Connor called Walter to arrange a meeting "first thing tomorrow morning." He wanted to make sure Walter would be "on board." FBI agent Michael Shay had carefully bugged Walter's phone so that no syllable of O'Connor's instructions would be lost.

The next morning, November 14, 1979, fifteen minutes before Walter was scheduled to meet O'Connor in a nearby Long Island City restaurant, Michael Shay fitted Walter out with a wire in his Clayburn office. Shay's encouraging words were unnecessary. Walter was now anxious to nail O'Connor, who had extorted thousands of dollars from him over the years in order to obtain work, which, without O'Connor's leeching, Walter felt he would have been capable of doing legally and at a smaller cost.

The transcript of the Walter-O'Connor restaurant sparring ran sixty-three pages. The tapes provided all of the corroboration needed to prosecute O'Connor, but getting the green light for that prosecution was not a simple matter. Once again, a sensational trial that would have destroyed D'Amato's career if it had been prosecuted before Election Day was delayed until several months after he had taken his senatorial oath.

On May 19, 1981, U.S. Attorney Ed Korman and strike force leader Tom Puccio held a press conference to announce that O'Connor had been indicted. Puccio stated that when O'Connor appeared before the grand jury on November 26, 1979, he had "falsely denied ever demanding any of these payoffs" and therefore had committed perjury. The indictment contained a terse statement that O'Connor had sought the money for himself and an unnamed Hempstead town official. The dozen reporters covering the story unanimously agreed that this was a reference to New York's new junior senator.

Before the day was out, their opinion had been confirmed. In a frenzy to minimize damage to his reputation, D'Amato released a letter written by Puccio stating that D'Amato *was* the unnamed official referred to in the indictment. The letter went on to state that federal authorities had uncovered no independent evidence that O'Connor was seeking money on D'Amato's behalf. Once again, D'Amato was in a familiar position: without a confession from O'Connor that he had been told by D'Amato to demand a kickback from contractors, the newest member of the Senate could deny that he had ever personally asked anyone for money.

The indictment stated that O'Connor sought the money for a Hempstead official, but D'Amato had forced Puccio to admit that although he had been confident enough of the truth of his charge to make reference to it in the indictment, he was unable to come up with enough evidence to risk trying D'Amato. To a man who had so frequently been accused, that was vindication enough.

From the start it was an extraordinary trial. Margiotta's friend George Pratt was the arraigning judge, recommended for his appointment by the boss after many years of faithful service to the Nassau party. That should have been grounds enough to have Judge Pratt remove himself from a case so fused to Republican politics. The judge did, in fact, disqualify himself. However, in chambers, when explaining why he was taking such a dramatic step, he made no reference to his association with the Republican organization. Instead, he told a story about an occasion on which he personally became acquainted with Francis O'Connor's larcenous nature.

In private practice years earlier, Judge Pratt explained, he had been the attorney for a man accused of a crime about which O'Connor, in his role as commissioner of the General Services Department, had information. Pratt's client had wanted O'Connor to testify, feeling that O'Connor's honest testimony would help his case. Judge Pratt explained that O'Connor had informed his client that he would ruin his case if put on the stand unless he was paid a substantial bribe. Although Pratt did not report O'Connor's extortion attempt to the authorities, many of whom were undoubtedly O'Connor's closest associates, he did not call him as a witness. As a result, he told the assemblage in his chambers, he knew that O'Connor was a thief from his private knowledge, and he was therefore removing himself from the case.

He was replaced by Judge Jacob Mishler, who had previously been involved in the early stages of the ABSCAM prosecutions. Mishler had a reputation among the Eastern District prosecutors of being an honest and able judge, grimly determined to throw the book at drug dealers and common criminals. Federal attorneys, however, were not anxious to try cases involving political figures in the court of the former president of the Astoria

Republican Club; the judge's moral indignation seemed to flag on those occasions.

Lothar Genge's case rested substantially on the testimony of Raymond Walter and the November 14, 1979, taped conversation in which O'Connor had attempted to get Walter to perjure himself before the grand jury. Genge introduced that crucial tape at the start of the trial. Apparently, O'Connor had consulted with an attorney before this rendezvous: His grasp of the legal subtleties of perjury, bribery, and extortion was complete. He spent over an hour trying to rehearse Walter for what he thought would be Genge's first interview with him.

Toward the end of his tendentious harangue, O'Connor's fear was suddenly exposed: "Did you ever mention my name to anybody?" he demanded.

Following Genge's scenario, double agent Walter replied that Treadwell's president Spitzer "had to know," since "he was gonna be putting his money out."

O'Connor concluded that Spitzer had given his name to the grand jury. That meant it was absolutely essential for him and Walter to tell the same story. If they did, there would be no way Genge could corroborate Spitzer's testimony.

Trying to make sure their "stories" would mesh, O'Connor told Walter: "Now, I think on the surface of it, of you as an old friend coming to me, making a recommendation to D'Amato is strictly good business. There's nothing wrong with that at all."

Walter then reminded O'Connor of the payoff proposal, and one can sense O'Connor's desperation.

O'CONNOR: Okay, but you and I never talked about that, did we . . .
WALTER: Well, come on, Frank . . .
O'CONNOR: Did we? No, wait a minute. Okay, sitting here, we did, but as far as anybody else is concerned, we never talked about it.

O'Connor was inviting Walter to commit perjury; unaware that his voice would someday be sounding in the ears of a jury. Walter told him the bad news immediately:

WALTER: Oh, they [the prosecutors] know about it.
O'CONNOR: Huh? [Shock drove the air out of his lungs.]
WALTER: They know about it.
O'CONNOR: They don't know I know about it.
WALTER: Oh, yes.
O'CONNOR: Huh, how do they know that?
WALTER: They were told.
O'CONNOR: By who?
WALTER: Either by Spitzer and then corroborated.
O'CONNOR: By who?
WALTER: And then corroborated by me. That we discussed that.
O'CONNOR: [His voice became surly.] What did you tell them that for?
WALTER: They told me.

Walter then said to the stunned O'Connor that Spitzer was apparently cooperating with Genge and he would have to tell the truth when called before the grand jury.

O'Connor scrambled to develop some strategy that would sound plausible. Since Spitzer had not been present at the meeting at which O'Connor and Walter had discussed the bribe, O'Connor suggested with a display of sham enthusiasm, Walter wouldn't have to admit it had influenced O'Connor or that he had agreed to accept the payoff.

O'CONNOR: This fifty cents an hour [the bribe] business with tickets and all that sort of shit . . . sure it was discussed, that was part of the conversation, but that certainly wasn't the . . . the reason why I called D'Amato.

He then breathlessly asked, "How does that sound, all right?" Walter's unenthusiastic response—"It's all right"—seemed to satisfy O'Connor.

As though to reassure his fellow conspirator, O'Connor then told Walter that he often got contractors to make "contributions" to the party because that was "how the system operates."

Now that he had shown the velvet glove, O'Connor thought it was time to reveal the steel beneath it.

O'CONNOR: Yeah, ya know, and uh, I don't want to see anybody get hurt, especially you or me . . . I don't want to see anybody get hurt. Because ya know, no matter how deep the prosecutors want to probe, a friend is still a friend . . . I'll go to the wall for you, you know, and I assume you'll go to the wall for me . . . A friend is a friend, and I live by that theory.

Judge Mishler was convinced that O'Connor had committed perjury. At one point, when O'Connor's attorney debated the meaning of the O'Connor–Walter discussion of a potential bribe, Mishler commented, "I don't care in what form. Why should anybody discuss [it] if they weren't talking about a kickback?"

On another occasion, Mishler directed a caustic remark at O'Connor's attorney after he had contended that his client had several times told Walter he should tell the truth. "Well, that's what he kept saying on the tape. . . . But the sense of it was; 'I want you to tell part of the truth.' "

Although O'Connor had condemned himself in his own words and in the process implicated D'Amato, Mishler insisted on excluding any reference to larger issues. O'Connor was the sole defendant, and Mishler had no intention of allowing Genge to introduce what he considered to be extraneous matters. The Republican party of Nassau County was not on trial; nor, with the exception of O'Connor, were any of its leaders.

Mishler's determination to narrow the trial's scope was shown in his treatment of two additional tapes Spitzer had made in his complexly bugged midtown apartment. The other person on these tapes was Peter Alevra, P & W's boss at Hempstead. Alevra, a delicate man accustomed to selling projects, not building them, was over his head in dealing with the rough-and-tumble of fieldwork. Born in Greece, a man of cultivated European temperament, he found it difficult to deal with teamsters and politicians.

As part of his instructions from Lothar Genge, Spitzer got Alevra to come to his apartment by refusing to complete work on one of the Hempstead boilers. Once Alevra had settled himself on the couch in Spitzer's living room, Spitzer explained that he had been forced to speak to Alevra directly because Francis O'Connor was demanding a large sum of money in order for Treadwell to continue working. This was going to force him to add that sum to future bills, Spitzer explained, and he felt it was necessary to clear this with Alevra in advance.

Alevra responded that he hadn't heard a word about this deal. He would, he said, have to take the matter up with D'Amato.

At a second meeting, which began in Spitzer's apartment but ended at a local restaurant, Alevra informed Spitzer that he had been told by D'Amato to tell Spitzer not to pay O'Connor. Since Spitzer had shown that he was willing to talk about the extortion money D'Amato's bagman was demanding, it would have been foolhardy for D'Amato to do anything but tell a supposedly irate Spitzer not to pay. But the news that O'Connor was an extortionist did not cause D'Amato to end their friendship. It soon became apparent that Spitzer's incriminating accusation had drawn them closer together.

Although this exchange clearly indicated D'Amato's iron-fisted control over the plant, Mishler refused to let the tapes be entered in evidence.

On August 20, 1981, a week after O'Connor's trial had begun, Sen. Al D'Amato, accompanied by his attorney, former Queens County district attorney Michael Armstrong, unexpectedly appeared in the Westbury courtroom. Armstrong gave his client one last confidence-boosting smile and headed for a front seat in the spectator's section. D'Amato walked briskly to the witness box.

Lothar Genge was startled to see D'Amato. Genge had been under the impression that the defense had concluded its case. He had worked late into the previous night preparing his summation, which he expected to deliver precisely at the moment that D'Amato's name was announced. "As I saw him smilingly enter the witness box," Genge said, "I thought: Now this should be interesting."

Genge described D'Amato's testimony as "a political speech. He rambled on about what a wonderful idea the Hempstead garbage plant was. [It had been closed down the previous year.] Judge Mishler allowed him to babble on."

Nevertheless, Genge was overjoyed. D'Amato wasn't appearing merely as a character witness, which would have limited Genge's ability to cross-examine him; he was testifying, albeit verbosely, about the facts in the case. That meant he had opened himself up to the broadest possible cross-examination.

When Genge's turn came, he approached the smiling, seemingly self-assured D'Amato with anticipation. The elusive target he had been trying to bring into focus for two years was finally in his sights. He fired off a barrage of accusatory questions. D'Amato calmly denied he had received money from any company in exchange for a plant contract. As far as Walter's testimony that O'Connor guaranteed him a contract for a kickback to D'Amato, the senator's only memory of the matter was that he had met with O'Connor "casually" in 1972, ten years earlier, at which time Walter's company had been discussed. "We either passed each other in the hall or something like that after a board of supervisors meeting," the senator remembered. "Commissioner O'Connor said he knew of a firm in Long Island City that was desirous of doing some work at the plant. Commissioner O'Connor wanted to know if I could have someone at Parsons & Whittemore contact them. We never discussed it again."

In effect, D'Amato told the jury that he, D'Amato, had been the man to speak to if you wanted a P & W contract. In addition, he conceded that although O'Connor was not a Hempstead official, O'Connor's "casual recommendation" had been enough to convince D'Amato to pass his endorsement on to the builders.

D'Amato admitted he had spoken to the P & W people about obtaining a contract for Walter, who would have been a subcontractor if the building of the plant had gone ahead in 1972. To have denied it would have risked the possibility that Genge was ready to produce a P. & W. witness to the conversation; down that tangled road lay a perjury indictment.

D'Amato was testifying about an event almost ten years in the past, yet his power of recall was so acute that he could effectively describe his conversation with O'Connor, a conversation that he had labeled casual and which, according to his account, couldn't have lasted more than a few seconds.

Under Genge's prodding, D'Amato confirmed Walter's testimony about the 1979 Treadwell deal. Yes, he admitted, O'Connor had recommended Spitzer's firm to him for the maintenance contract. Furthermore, he had personally recommended about six or eight contractors to P & W for work at the recycling plant.

132

Genge pressed on. D'Amato denied he had threatened P & W with cancellation of the project if they didn't hire certain companies he recommended. He also denied authorizing O'Connor to seek any kickbacks in exchange for sweetheart contracts at the plant.

Genge's voice rose as he attempted to force some damaging admissions. D'Amato's reaction during his ninety minutes on the stand was to alternately rock back and forth and look up at the ceiling.

"Did you ever assess any public employee a part of his salary?" Genge demanded. Paul Corcoran, O'Connor's defense attorney, looked back at Michael Armstrong and then reached out to protect D'Amato. "Objection," he cried out. "We're going outside the issues of this case."

"Sustained," Judge Mishler ruled. This was the closest the aging judge had come in five years to getting an issue in the 1 percent case before a jury, but he would not allow that slumbering case to be intruded into the O'Connor proceedings. Genge felt the two matters were closely associated, but his opinion did not control events in Judge Mishler's court.

"Did you ever travel to Europe while the project was being undertaken?" Genge continued cryptically.

"Objection!" Corcoran bellowed.

"Sustained," said the increasingly irritated judge.

With each question Genge's voice became louder. "Did you ever authorize Terrence Shine—"

Michael Armstrong leaped to his feet in the spectator's section and shouted his objection.

"Remove the jury!" Judge Mishler commanded the court clerk.

From this moment on, the judge informed the frustrated prosecutor, he would have to get prior approval for any questions he wanted to ask. Assured by the frown on Mishler's face that he had no choice, Genge said, "I have a series of questions relating to the senator: what, if any, role or dealings the senator had with a company known as Abdul Enterprises." There was an audible gasp from the spectators in the jammed courtroom at the reference to the ABSCAM bribery of officials that for months had dominated headlines in papers across the country.

Armstrong walked toward the judge's bench. "This is precisely the thing that, with all due respect, I suggest the senator needs

protection from," Armstrong remarked indignantly. "The senator
. . . is a man in public life; cheap shots can be taken by anybody.
. . . And now he is doing it in front of the press; he is going to list
off a whole lot of things having to do with Abscam and the Teapot
Dome scandal and whatever else."

"Your Honor," shouted Genge, raising his voice above the attorneys clamoring for the judge's attention. "The senator is like any
other witness. If he testified, he is subject to cross-examination.
Every one of these questions is asked upon good-faith information.
It bears upon his credibility."

Genge's questioning of D'Amato's credibility had made this a difficult decision for Judge Mishler. D'Amato was not Genge's witness;
the senator had volunteered to testify for the defense. Under these
circumstances, D'Amato had opened himself up to aggressive questioning by the prosecutor.

The argument between the attorneys raged on. Armstrong, who
had clashed with Genge repeatedly during recent months and
whose relationship with Genge was venomous, insisted he found it
incomprehensible that a senator's reputation could be dealt with in
such a disdainful manner. Genge retorted that in America's courts
there wasn't a separate set of rules for senators and another canon
for ordinary citizens.

Judge Mishler tired of the rhetoric: "All right, Mr. Genge. You've
had your speech. This is not a happy hunting ground. You
have the obligation, as a prosecutor, to be fair. . . . Now, I went
through the grand jury minutes, and I know your style." The judge
spoke angrily, pointing his finger at Genge. He had noticed in his
readings that Genge had "brought in the name of almost every
politician and asked Mr. O'Connor whether so-and-so was
involved."

Genge explained that in a grand jury setting it was the prosecutor's responsibility to follow up allegations of wrongdoings by all
who may have committed them. He hadn't brought up D'Amato's
name capriciously; it had been O'Connor who had spoken of
him in his taped conversation with Walter. O'Connor had also
brought in the names of other politicians. Genge saw it as his duty
to ferret out, in the "hunting ground" of the grand jury, fact from
fiction.

Mishler cut him off. He was not interested in hearing Genge's explanation. "You're not going to do that here or I'll hold you in contempt of court," he said in a harsh tone as D'Amato watched him.

Jacob Mishler was the incontestable authority in this Westbury courtroom; to challenge him was to risk going to jail before anyone whose case was then before a jury. Judge Mishler wanted it understood that he was not a man with whom one should trifle. His protection of D'Amato from a searching cross-examination was inexplicable, since as judge in the 1 percent case Burt Neuborne had shown him the smoking-gun letter that labeled D'Amato, in his own words, an extortionist.

Genge vainly attempted to convince Mishler to let him continue his cross-examination. Soon after the jury returned, D'Amato stepped down. With the air of an election-night candidate who has just read his opponent's concession telegram, he walked to where the defendant and his wife were seated. He ostentatiously kissed O'Connor's wife and smilingly wished O'Connor good luck.

Genge felt that with that dramatic gesture D'Amato was sealing his bargain with O'Connor. "He had paid his dues. He was showing his full support for O'Connor and his family. Now O'Connor should do the right thing."

While the attorneys had been arguing about whether D'Amato should answer Genge's questions, O'Connor, who had been sitting alone at the defense table, turned to his wife, Jean, and reporters heard him say with a shrug, "They've forgot about me."

O'Connor at that moment realized the truth about his dilemma: He was the forgotten man in his own case. Clearly, the chief actors in this demoralizing melodrama felt that there was a great deal more at stake in O'Connor's trial than his fate.

Even O'Connor seemed to have accepted their evaluation. He was convicted and went to jail without murmuring a word of protest against any one of a number of people whose actions had placed him there. The only witness on his behalf was Sen. Al D'Amato.

Years later, former county executive Ralph Caso still found it hard to believe that O'Connor had allowed himself to play the role of the fall guy. "The thing that has always amazed me is why Commissioner O'Connor took the dive for D'Amato," the diminutive former politician said in disbelief. "He was convicted of perjury. He went to jail for a year and a day. Why did Frank O'Connor pay the price?"

O'Connor's conviction did not satisfy Genge. He viewed it as an opportunity lost, a turning point in the fight against corruption in Nassau County. One of the party's top bagmen, O'Connor was on the inside of the political machine. A long sentence, such as George Boylan had gotten, might have induced O'Connor, as it had Boylan, to cooperate.

Genge explained with a rueful smile, "My hope always was to build the case up. If Mishler had given O'Connor more than a one-year sentence—a mere slap on the wrist—O'Connor might have been more willing to speak. The ultimate objective was to go higher. Unfortunately, that didn't work out."

Genge praised Mishler's ability but clearly disliked the way he handled the case. "I think Judge Mishler is an extremely competent judge. He, unfortunately, thought I was grandstanding. I wasn't. I had additional evidence that I couldn't approach Mishler with. As a result, he didn't have the background of our investigation. Normally, a judge, on cross-examination, will allow you latitude if you are acting in good faith, but the judge's suspicions led him to doubt our good faith. We wanted to get at the truth in the Hempstead case, but Mishler closed us down."

Genge explained what he had in mind when he asked D'Amato that cryptic question about his European trip while contracts were being handed out to build the Hempstead plant. "We understood that he took a trip to Europe with a supervisor at the plant, who our informants told us was the key man in the payoffs. We were looking at the possibility that he had some sort of consideration given to him while he was in Europe. It was a good-faith question."

Genge pointed out that his endeavor to question D'Amato on his possible connection to Abdul Enterprises was based on widely publicized statements made by D'Amato's friend Alfred Carpentier. "The FBI was actively pursuing D'Amato's connection as Carpentier stated it. The FBI gave some credence to Carpentier's statements. D'Amato got lucky when they shifted their focus to bigger fish— the congressmen and Senator Williams. That's why the presiding superintendent of Hempstead was not the target of the ABSCAM sting operation."

Genge spoke without heat, but it was clear that the passage of time had only confirmed his original skepticism about the case. "Mishler had a view of how a politician who had arrived should be treated; it was with respect. I saw it as an opportunity to get D'Amato, under oath, on the record. If you don't get someone near the beginning of the crime, they get insulated, the statute of limitations runs out, and they've escaped."

Senator D'Amato left the Westbury courthouse after Judge Mishler said he was no longer needed and flashed a winner's smile at the cameras. "I'm pleased that I finally had an opportunity to answer these charges," he said, ignoring the fact that Mishler had protected him from having to answer Genge's most embarrassing questions.

SIXTEEN

THE SQUIRE
OF OLD BROOKVILLE

O n November 24, 1980, when Joe Margiotta left his office in the Westbury building that the prosperous Nassau Republican party had recently bought for its leader, his heart was heavy. He returned to his newly purchased estate on the crest of a rolling hill in Old Brookville, and he must have gazed out over the neatly trimmed lawns, unconsoled by the splendor that met his eyes. That day, the unrelenting Ed Korman had asked the Brooklyn grand jury to indict him on five counts of extortion and one of mail fraud.

Margiotta could trace his troubles to an act committed by his dear friend Richard Nixon; although it was not intended to harm him or any other certified Republican leader, it had resulted in this pre-Thanksgiving calamity.

Nixon had first tried to become president in 1960 in a contest that pitted him against John F. Kennedy. During his thirteen years in politics Nixon had constantly been on the razor's edge of controversy; as a result, there was a multitude of reasons for Nixon's narrow 1960 defeat. But Ike's defeated vice president chose to think that victory had been fraudulently snatched from him by Democratic party leaders—chief among them, Chicago's mayor Richard Daley, who, Nixon maintained, held out the city's results until he saw how many votes were needed to overcome the GOP's downstate margins. In his biography *Six Crises*, the chagrined Nixon, with a strenuous attempt not to appear the sore loser, explained how "a swing of between 11,000 and 13,000 votes— properly distributed *in a few states* [italics mine]" would have made him president eight years before destiny placed that burden on his narrow shoulders. He concluded that it had been "fraud" that did him in. "What should I do with regard to the mounting charges of voter frauds and the demands that I ask for a recount in Illinois and other states?" he asked immediately after the election, before deciding against doing anything.

The humiliation caused by those eight years of repetitious explanations as to why he wasn't sitting in the Oval Office led Nixon, upon assuming the presidency in 1969, to seek some way to avenge himself. Since he was convinced that those urban Democrat politicos who had victimized him were all corrupt, he decided to invigorate the U.S. Attorneys' offices and turn them loose on his enemies.

Prior to Nixon's administration, U.S. Attorneys were mostly political hacks who considered that their primary function was to provide employment for down-on-their-luck lawyers who had worked hard for the party. It was unusual for a U.S. Attorney to seek an indictment against anyone, of either party, accused of political corruption.

Nixon's miscalculation, the one for which Margiotta paid dearly, was to overlook the fact that the new zealous U.S. Attorneys didn't understand the selective nature of the prosecutions he had in mind. Although the corrupt urban party leaders were largely Democrats, the corrupt suburban and rural party leaders were mainly Republicans.

An example of the mischief created by Nixon's desire for vengeance involves his appointee as U.S. Attorney in New York's Eastern District Republican David Trager, under whom Ed Korman served from 1974 to 1978 as chief assistant. Under Trager's stern command, his staff of thirty-two attorneys—quickly enlarged to ninety (including the new Organized Crime Strike Force)—proved indefatigable in pursuit of tainted politicians, specifically Nixon's loyal friends Joe Margiotta and Al D'Amato.

In September 1977, while Trager continued to serve as U.S. Attorney, the State Commission on Investigation (known as the SIC) began to investigate charges of irregularities in Nassau County government. As party witnesses were called before the SIC, Trager and Korman were kept informed about their testimony. Much of

139

that testimony involved the 1 percent kickbacks that Al D'Amato, now Hempstead's presiding supervisor, was overseeing. But some of it concerned the scheme created by Margiotta to squeeze bribes out of insurance brokers selling policies to Nassau County and Hempstead.

In 1978, at the conclusion of the SIC hearings, the commission referred the testimony of Margiotta, his assistant, Woolnough, and dozens of leaders of the Nassau party to Nassau district attorney Denis Dillon. Democrat Dillon reviewed the allegations against Margiotta in his usual fashion and declined to prosecute, claiming he found no evidence that state laws had been violated. This declination by Dillon led to the decision by the newly elevated U.S. attorney Ed Korman, in July 1979, to present the evidence collected by SIC and his own investigators to the Brooklyn grand jury.

It was Margiotta's continuing, covert involvement with the convicted former district attorney William Cahn that had convinced Korman to intensify his probe of the "Squire of Old Brookville." SIC investigators had discovered that the day after Cahn was turned out of office in 1975, because of his defeat by Denis Dillon, Margiotta had Cahn placed on the payroll of Richard B. Williams and Son, Inc., an insurance company handling most of the coverage for Hempstead and Nassau County.

Richard B. Williams and Son was willing to pay Bill Cahn $2,000 a month, although SIC agents discovered that Cahn was not a licensed insurance broker. Furthermore, testimony from father and son Williams, and the otherwise unemployable Cahn, revealed that the former district attorney performed no discernible services for his pay.

The SIC discovered that Cahn's $2,000-a-month honorarium had lasted until he went to jail for double-billing the county in April 1977. The state's investigators were even more startled to find that when the jail doors shut behind Cahn, his son Neil, then a recent law school graduate, became the recipient of his father's $2,000 stipend.

Ed Korman remarked, "Cahn told Mr. Margiotta that he wanted his son Neil to take over the retainer." It was as if the jailed Cahn felt he was finally able to tell the boss what he wanted without fear of being denied. A man with his knowledge of the deals and the payoffs, the suppressed prosecutions, and the inadequately pursued investigations was surely not overestimating the value of his continued silence.

140

Margiotta's order to the Williams agency to pay young Neil Cahn was risky; the Williams agency had almost no need for the services of an attorney. Indeed, during the two years Bill Cahn had been on the payroll, only one legal problem had arisen, and it had not been referred to Cahn. In the coming year the only legal advice Williams Jr. was going to need involved the settling of his father's estate, and Margiotta had already recommended that Margiotta's partner, Michael Ricigliano, handle that simple task.

While trying to find out why Williams and Son was so generous to the fallen district attorney, the curtain concealing a major portion of Margiotta's illegal activities was drawn back.

SIC investigators discovered that shortly after Margiotta became head of the county Republican party in 1968, he was approached by Richard B. Williams, executive leader of Garden City for thirty years, with a proposition he found impossible to resist. Williams wanted to be broker of record for Hempstead. Since all of Hempstead's insurance placement had to be done through the broker of record, Williams sought a major favor. In return, Williams proposed, he would split his commissions with Margiotta on a fifty-fifty basis. Margiotta was to take his 50 percent cut and distribute it to various committeemen, strengthening their dependency on him and consolidating his control of the party.

Ralph Caso, who in 1968 was still presiding supervisor of Hempstead, hadn't been at the meeting at which Margiotta decided who would be the new broker of record. However, a luncheon conversation with Margiotta at the Hempstead Golf Course secured Caso's never-denied consent to the boss's deal.

The SIC obtained documents from Williams Jr. that confirmed Korman's worst suspicions. In 1969, Williams and Son submitted an accounting to Margiotta showing that the firm had collected $31,200. Under a column marked "50% of commissions," Margiotta's share of the commissions had been duly entered. Also submitted was a list, sent to the Williams firm by Margiotta's office, designating the names of the recipients of the $15,600 and the amounts Margiotta decided they should receive. Similar lists, dividing up much larger sums of money, were produced for subsequent years.

As Caso was about to become county executive in 1971, Williams met with Margiotta to discuss the possibility of getting the insurance contracts for the Nassau Coliseum and the Nassau Medical

Center. Margiotta told him that nothing stood in his way, certainly not Caso. Margiotta then informed Caso, during lunch, that the new general services commissioner, Francis O'Connor, should instruct his director of insurance that all future county business was to go to the Williams agency. It was an item of such importance to Margiotta that Caso made it the first matter he dealt with when he assumed the county executive's office on January 1, 1971.

Margiotta seemed extremely pleased with the arrangement; not only had he been provided with a source of patronage for hard-working committeemen beyond the dreams of former party leader Joe Carlino, but Williams was amenable to any arrangement the boss wanted on how the boodle would be parceled out. This enhanced Margiotta's power and indirectly but substantially enriched him.

In 1971, for example, Margiotta admitted that he had asked Williams Sr. whether he could "see his way clear" to pay $5,000 to Richard Guardino, who had acted as Margiotta's counsel in private business matters. Although Guardino had never performed any services for Williams, the $5,000 was to be listed on the books of the Williams agency as a "legal fee."

It mattered not in the least to Williams how Margiotta wanted his 50 percent divided. Guardino's $5,000 came out of the share that would otherwise have gone to some committeeman; committee-men knew their first rule of conduct was that they must patiently stand and wait.

Margiotta had from the beginning thought the distribution of the Williams agency money was a matter completely at his discretion, but as time passed and he became comfortable with the bribes, his decisions about how the payoffs would be parceled out became less guarded, more gross. Looking back at his behavior, U.S. Attorney Korman remarked, "His [Margiotta] position was even more striking with respect to payments made by the Williams agency to another attorney, John Sutter."

This was the attorney that the party had hired in 1976 to defend Raymond Graber, the tearful deputy commissioner of conservation and waterways. "Hold on to a friend," he had urged his hysterical client as he embraced him. The suspicion remained, as he publicly tried to reassure the frail Graber, that Sutter had closer friends in the party hierarchy.

In 1977, when the SIC began its inquiry into the insurance practices in Nassau County, Margiotta told the Williams agency to hire
Sutter. Although Sutter would protect Margiotta's interests, Williams
would pay him.

During the SIC hearings and the subsequent grand jury sessions
that flowed from them, Sutter represented a number of Margiotta
lieutenants. Korman explained how Sutter was paid. "Mr. Sutter
never billed Margiotta or any of the other clients referred by
Margiotta except the Williams agency and Nassau County."
Williams paid all of the invoices submitted by Sutter, deducting the
exact amounts from the 50 percent commission "pot" available to
Margiotta.

Margiotta's apparatus to fleece Nassau taxpayers was finally
threatened with destruction because of a relatively smaller crime
committed by the now totally arrogant boss.

On November 8, 1976, Margiotta summoned Robert E. Dowler to
his office. Dowler was a loyal party worker who earned his living
as an insurance broker. Over the years he had received $5,000
annually as his share of the Williams-Margiotta scam. On this day,
Dowler noted in his diary, Margiotta began by telling him that the
cost of his daughter's education worried him. He then told Dowler
that he would be receiving a larger than usual check from the
Williams agency this year; $10,000, to be exact.

Since Dowler had done nothing more to earn this sum than he
had to earn the previously smaller payoffs, he sensed that he
shouldn't merely take the money and run. Instead, the prudent
Dowler suggested they split the payment in the same manner they
shared commissions on policies Dowler occasionally wrote for private clients Margiotta recommended to him. The boss coyly asked
Dowler what his opinion was about the propriety of such a proposal. Dowler assured him that it wouldn't have occurred to him to
make the proposal if he thought it lacked propriety.

Thus reassured, Margiotta sent Dowler off to Williams's office,
where, without any difficulty, the pliant messenger picked up a
$10,000 check that was already made out and dated November 8,
1976. Not even bothering to wait for the Williams check to clear,
Dowler wrote out a $5,000 check to Margiotta, dated November 9,
and delivered it to him along with a letter indicating that although

the $5,000 was "not part of our original brokerage agreement," the income was being "shared" on a "similar basis."

Margiotta then deposited the check into his account, which previously had insufficient funds. Despite his story to Dowler about the problem of paying for his daughter's education, Margiotta instead used it to pay his delinquent property taxes.

The SIC investigators had no inkling of this shoddy episode while they conducted their probe of the Williams agency. When they asked Margiotta why he had, in violation of prior practice, directed Williams to pay Dowler $10,000, he responded that "the spirit moved me to make a presentation to him at that time." By this stage in his ascendancy Margiotta had regularly come to express himself in such haughty terms.

Neither Margiotta nor Dowler told the SIC probers that the $10,000 had been split between them, nor did Dowler initially mention that Margiotta had raised his "fee" to $10,000.

Ed Hart, Margiotta's personal lawyer, who represented the party member recipients of the Williams agency "brokerage commissions" and whose legal fees were being paid by the Nassau Republican Committee, insisted that his clients had all "worked" for their commissions. As West Hempstead's executive leader Easa Easa, also head of Nassau's OTB, came close to admitting to the SIC questioner that he had been paid $20,000 in 1976–77 merely because of his party affiliations, Hart volunteered: "Plus the work he did." None of Hart's witnesses mentioned that Williams had been paying them because Margiotta submitted their names.

The whole matter might have been papered over with the aid of Attorney Hart's selective presentation had Dowler not been quite so honest with the Internal Revenue Service (IRS). In an attempt to pay only his fair share of the $10,000 "commission," Dowling had reported on his 1976 tax return that his Williams revenues consisted of $5,000. Korman's staff now focused on this inconsistency. The U.S. Attorney's office wanted to know why a $10,000 check, a copy of which they had, was reported as only $5,000 worth of income. Dowler could see the handwriting on the Leavenworth prison wall.

After what Korman described as "an excruciatingly long delay" by Dowler, the stressed insurance broker confessed to Korman that he had turned the $5,000 over to Nassau County's most prominent tax delinquent.

Ed Hart told me that Korman had no intention of prosecuting Margiotta until he found out about the $5,000 check. He described Korman as being some sort of fanatic on political corruption who became enraged when he found what he considered incontrovertible proof that Margiotta had been directly involved in extortion.

When I mentioned Hart's opinion to Korman, he smiled and commented, "I wanted a prosecutable case. That meant that I wasn't going to take a case involving such a prominent individual before a jury unless I thought the case was airtight. The $5,000 payoff made this case prosecutable. Margiotta showed, by his attempt to disguise the source of the money and his dissembling testimony before the SIC, that he understood what he had done was against the law."

Korman also saw that although the 1978 SIC report had denounced Margiotta's fee splitting with Williams, the practice, which Korman described as "a rape of taxpayers," was continuing: In 1979 the Cahns received $24,000; former assemblyman Joseph Reilly, who had succeeded Francis O'Connor as commissioner of the General Services Department, received $25,000 in 1979 and again in 1980; dozens of party hacks, posing as essential cogs in Williams's operation, found the delivery of their "commissions" as reliable as ever.

One of these hacks was Senator D'Amato's father, who in 1980 still worked for the county, now as "research director" in the Commerce Department. For this service Armand Sr. received $34,900. He also found time to run his insurance office and maintain the near stranglehold that he had on Island Park's insurance business. In an interview on WCBS-TV's *Newsmakers*, Al D'Amato responded to a question about his father's patronage job by saying, "I certainly recommended him for the position when it was there. He had the qualifications." He did not describe those qualifications, nor did he explain why his father continued each year to be listed on Margiotta's fee-splitting list.

SEVENTEEN

TWO POLS IN TUXEDOS

On December 3, 1980, Joe Margiotta was arraigned in federal court on extortion and mail-fraud charges. Ed Korman thought his case was airtight. The "ruthless" pro had been caught with his hand in the cookie jar. Margiotta was going to find it difficult to convince twelve jurors living in capitalist America that a hardheaded businessman like Richard Williams was giving away 50 percent of his profits without getting something in return. And since the 50 percent Margiotta got from Williams belonged to Nassau's citizens—the people who would sit on this jury—Korman believed that the boss's days in power were numbered.

It was Margiotta's bad luck to draw Korman as his adversary; it was going to be a battle between two Brooklyn boys, both tough, both brought up to fight hard for what they wanted.

Korman had been raised in East New York, on the other side of the borough from where Margiotta had years earlier learned to play stickball in Bushwick. His father, Korman told me reverently, was "a hand laborer in a laundry. He ironed shirts by hand, but not with an ordinary iron. He held his hand in a steaming glove."

Margiotta's Bushwick could not compare to young Korman's slum. East New York during the 1940s and 1950s began to absorb blacks from Harlem. Unemployment among the new population was higher than it had been during the Great Depression; marijuana and heroin were openly sold; violent crime rose, and teenagers

146

displayed little interest in the promise of education. When Korman graduated from Thomas Jefferson High School in 1960, the school, whose alumni listed over two thousand Ph.D.s and several Nobel Prize winners, was well on its way toward becoming a segregated facility, described by the Board of Education as the city's worst school.

From 1963 to 1966, Korman attended Margiotta's alma mater, Brooklyn Law, where he was the editor of the *Law Review*. His first job after graduation was as clerk to court of appeals judge Kenneth Keating, the former U.S. senator. In 1972, Korman became assistant solicitor general in the Nixon administration and spent two years representing the government in cases before the Supreme Court. He returned to Brooklyn in 1974 after his friend David Trager became U.S. Attorney and offered him the job of chief assistant.

When Democrat Daniel Patrick Moynihan became senator in 1977, he insisted on maintaining the smooth flow of prosecutions and allowed Trager to complete his term in office. He then nominated Korman to succeed Trager.

"He [Moynihan] made it clear to me," Korman recalled, "that while I was free to choose who I wanted for the major positions in the office, he expected me to run the office the way David did, and he didn't expect that there would be wholesale firings."

When he signed the indictment against Margiotta, Korman had married the previous February and had his life in order and his values firmly in place. He saw Margiotta as a thief and a threat to the commonwealth.

The Margiotta trial began on March 31, 1981, in the old federal courthouse, then still in Westbury. Margiotta was defended by a staff of lawyers headed by the ex-Brooklyn Democrat William G. Hundley, who, in a former life, was in charge of the Justice Department's Criminal Division in the Kennedy administration. He was now one of the country's most prominent criminal attorneys, capable of demanding a $300,000 fee from Margiotta. Al D'Amato helped organize dinners and cocktail parties around the county to pay off Hundley's fee. The fund-raisers were well attended by the party faithful, among whom were a large percentage of "insurance brokers." D'Amato expressed outrage that the government could not end street crime but instead was wasting its time prosecuting a politician whose ethics did not differ from his.

Hundley's assistant was Ed Hart, responsible for jury selection; Hart considered this process the main chance to win Margiotta's acquittal. Prospective jurors were asked if they knew who Margiotta was and how they thought a political leader should conduct himself. The "right" answers, from Hart's viewpoint, were: "The name rings a bell, but I don't know anything about him"; "I don't know too much about politics"; "I'm too busy to pay attention to politics"; or "I'm not interested in anything political."

Eight of the jurors were Republicans, two were not affiliated with any party, one was a conservative, and in one case Hart did not ask the female juror her political affiliation. "By the time I got through investigating those jurors," Hart bragged, "I knew just about how they were going to vote."

Korman's courtroom staff was led by Assistant U.S. Attorney Larry J. Silverman, soon to be struggling with the same temptations that had led Puccio, Hundley, and Armstrong to move on to the rewards of private criminal practice.

The chief prosecution witness was Richard A. Williams, who had tried to protect Margiotta at the SIC hearings, claiming, under Ed Hart's prompting, that the "brokers"—some of whom he only knew casually—all worked for their "commissions." This mendacity resulted in perjury charges against him, to which he pleaded guilty. As Margiotta's trial date approached, William's sentencing was delayed; Korman used the delay to pressure Williams to resist any temptation to repeat his SIC perjury before the Margiotta jury.

Margiotta countered Korman's psychological gambit by ordering Nassau's executive, Francis Purcell, and Hempstead's presiding supervisor, Thomas Gulotta, to retain the Williams agency as the broker of record despite the public confession of the younger Williams that he and his father had been systematically looting the county and town treasuries for over a decade.

Williams tried to protect the boss's interests, and his own, by delivering as many "safe" answers as he could. Frequently heard was "I don't recall." At one point, Judge Charles P. Sifton, a forty-six-year-old Jimmy Carter appointee, commented on "the very guarded and hostile testimony of the last few days."

During cross-examination Hundley dealt gently with Williams as he queried him about the large sums of money he gave to Margiotta each year. "When you were participating in this commission split-ting, did you think you were doing anything wrong?" he asked at the end of two hours. Williams softly said, "No, sir."

"Did you think Mr. Margiotta was doing anything wrong?" Hundley pressed on.

"No, sir."

Prosecutor Silverman then asked Williams if he would have split commissions with those politicians posing as brokers if Margiotta had not directed that they be paid. Reluctantly, Williams said no. He also admitted telling the State Commission on Investigation that he "would be excluded" from the town and county insurance busi-ness if he had not agreed to split the commissions.

Williams said he hadn't known the $10,000 Dowler check was to be shared with Margiotta. Silverman then asked whether he would have agreed to Margiotta's $5,000 payment had he known about it.

"No, sir," Williams responded hesitantly as he saw the trap but discerned no way to avoid it.

Why not? Silverman persisted.

There was a long pause, and then Williams slowly said, "Because I don't think that would be a proper thing for me to do."

On the seventh day of the trial, William Cahn described the arrangement by which he and his son received over $120,000 from Williams during a five-year period. Although testifying under a grant of immunity, the elder Cahn's fidelity to the boss was still apparent. He did admit that Margiotta was responsible for arrang-ing for the Cahns' "retainer" and that beyond "numerous" telephone calls to the agency, and a handful of correspondence, he and his son had no other proof of services performed for the "fees" they received.

A series of witnesses described a payoff from the commission-splitting fund that Margiotta made to an Albany political leader. The Albany politician knew about Margiotta's Nassau insurance scam and asked Joe whether he'd do an old buddy a favor and send him a $10,000 check from the pork barrel. Margiotta demon-strated his arbitrary, personal use of his 50 percent rake-off from the Williams agency by complying immediately.

Several Republican assemblymen and numerous town and county executives testified they had received tens of thousands of dollars over the years while doing "minimal" or "very little" work. Some said their contribution to easing the work load at the Williams agency had been to attend "conferences" on occasion.

Margiotta chatted freely with media people during each recess and at the end of each court day. During the three weeks of trial, he acted as though he were putting on a Uniondale street festival. His wife, daughter, mother-in-law, sister-in-law, brother-in-law, and dozens of relatives and friends were always present; they filled the first rows on either side of the courtroom, rows that were specifically reserved for them.

A large room adjoining the courtroom had been set aside for Margiotta; in it, surrounded by an adoring party claque, he held audience for the press. Tables were ladened with urns of coffee and pots of tea; there was an assortment of sodas. The solicitous were nourished with Danish and hot rolls in the morning; during the lunch hour, caterers brought in sandwiches and platters overflowing with delicacies. Reporters' notebooks were often out of sight as they struggled to balance beverage containers and dishes holding cannoli, spumoni, or tortoni. Anything the boss could do to win the approval of the multitude of journalists was done.

It is difficult to assess the value of these efforts, since so many other factors contributed to the generally neutral or affirmative treatment Margiotta received from the New York press. The *Times* was scrupulously fair in its coverage but used large amounts of space for pictures of the boss leaving the courthouse, his arm protectively around his wife's shoulders, a broad smile on his confident face. Occasionally, stories *Newsday* ran were sympathetic to the beleaguered local potentate.

Columnist Murray Kempton, soon to be awarded a Pulitzer Prize for thirty-five years of distinguished writing and whose most distinct theme during those years had been commiseration for the plight of the underdog, wrote repeatedly in *Newsday* attacking the prosecution and defending Margiotta. Kempton told me he thought Margiotta shouldn't have been brought into court on such a minor felony charge as "mail fraud"—the label Korman had used for one of the specific crimes among the many he knew Margiotta had committed.

Margiotta explained to the moiling press, when it became apparent Korman had the evidence to prove his charges, that what he had done was similar to what every political leader had always done. In effect, he asked, *Why condemn Joe Margiotta when you've let everyone in my position get away with it up to now?*

In addition, he and his lawyers tried to depict commission splitting as merely a normal type of party patronage. Wasn't it necessary to distribute patronage in order to keep people working for the party, they asked, and wasn't that a goal to strive for in our democracy? These specious questions were always answered by them affirmatively. Having advertised that false basic assumption as a truth, they went on to depict Margiotta as a man who differed from his predecessors only in the degree of his effectiveness.

Hundley led Margiotta through a routine on the witness stand emphasizing that fanciful view of extortion. When the prosecution cross-examined, that benign image of Margiotta's activities faded. Margiotta conceded that if Williams had balked at setting aside part of its fees for him to distribute, he would have called a meeting of the party's executive committee and recommended that the Williams agency be dismissed. "The risk could have been placed with different brokers, and everything would have been perfectly all right. . . ."

Korman observed, "Mr. Margiotta's answers, as self-serving as they are, plainly assumed that it was he who had the real power to decide who would be broker of record rather than the elected public officials."

Furthermore, after admitting he had recommended the appointment of the Williams agency only after the senior Williams had agreed to give him part of the commissions, Margiotta conceded that he understood such an agreement was illegal.

> SILVERMAN: Mr. Margiotta, would you agree that if you had made a deal to recommend Williams as broker of record based on him kicking back fifty percent of the business that he derived that that would be illegal?
> MARGIOTTA: If such a thing had taken place, it could be illegal.

Korman tried to introduce evidence about the more massive 1 percent kickback case "and Mr. Margiotta's involvement in this patently extortionate scheme." Korman felt that *Cullen v. Margiotta*, whose progress was stalled in Judge Mishler's court just down the hall, was part of what had brought Margiotta before Judge Sifton. In preparation for calling Al D'Amato to the witness stand, Korman asked Judge Sifton to allow the jury to see D'Amato's letter describing Robert Marcus's obligatory 1 percent salary kickback. Although the letter's authenticity was unchallenged, Sifton ruled that the "prejudicial value" of the letter and any reference to the 1 percent kickbacks would exceed its "probative value."

Once again Senator D'Amato's battered reputation had been shielded from further damage by a lucky bounce of the judicial ball. Had he testified, the prosecution would have required him to describe his role in Margiotta's commission-splitting racket. D'Amato had been executive leader of the Island Park Club for over a decade and often recommended to Margiotta committeemen-brokers who he wanted to share part of the loot. Imagine the spectacle if Armand Sr. had been called to the stand and, under oath, explained his son's part in getting him his insurance commissions.

The coconspirator in Margiotta's trial was Al D'Amato, but somehow the grand jury had failed to indict him.

After sixteen days of testimony by thirty-seven government witnesses and twenty-eight witnesses for the defense, the case went to the jury. Before the seven men and five women retired, Judge Sifton instructed them not "to judge the merits of a system of political patronage." They were, he cautioned, to think of this only as "a criminal case."

As the jury deliberated, Margiotta acted as if he were sure of exoneration, or perhaps failing that, he lightheartedly suggested, there really wasn't much at stake. He sat in the adjacent courtroom swapping stories with politicians; occasionally, people in the corridor would hear a roar of laughter. His wife and daughter, attended by relatives, sat in a nearby anteroom, distracting themselves with pickings from the festive board. After eight hours, it was announced that the jury had recessed for the night.

As the days passed and the jurors' indecision continued, Margiotta's appearance sobered; gone were the storytelling sessions. He stalked the courthouse lobby with his arms crossed over his chest, a weary, cynical look on his face. On the seventh day, after fifty-six hours of deliberation, the jury sent the judge a message: They were deadlocked. Judge Sifton sent the jurors home for the weekend after instructing them to return on Monday with renewed determination to reach a verdict. Margiotta's partisans informed the press that they were no longer confident and were now reduced to hoping for a hung jury. The boss looked glum.

Eight hours into the Monday, April 29, session, the jury again informed the judge, "Further deliberations are pointless." They were dismissed, and the judge set August 3 as the date for a new trial.

Outside the courtroom, a somber Margiotta told a crowd of reporters that he was "disappointed." Then, in an effort to offer an explanation of the jury's inability to exonerate him, he said, "You know, it's a very difficult climate for a political leader—we're not the most beloved people in the world."

William Hundley fell back on his extensive experience with the Justice Department to determine his next move. He announced that if U.S. Attorney Korman pressed for a second trial, he would urge the department, now controlled by Reagan appointees, to drop the case. In a tone of confidence that didn't seem misplaced, Margiotta's lawyer added, "I think I can convince the Justice Department not to go through this again."

Ed Korman was stung by the defeat. His knowledge of the full scope of Margiotta's illegal activity convinced him that the party boss belonged behind bars. But Judge Sifton had prevented the jury from learning the real nature of Margiotta's felonies. Shaking off his disappointment, he told reporters that he looked forward to the second trial. But, they demanded, wouldn't a Republican-controlled Justice Department refuse his request to retry the case? Korman said he didn't need Justice Department approval. He acknowledged that there was "always a possibility that I'd be overruled."

The way to overrule Korman was to have him fired. State Republican leaders called on President Reagan to do just that. Senator D'Amato, however, merely released a statement in which he said he felt Margiotta shouldn't have to face a second trial. "It would be a terrible ordeal to subject someone to that again, and it would be wrong."

D'Amato's press agent, Gary Lewi, when asked whether this meant that the senator would demand that Korman be fired, said, "We'd be guided by the administration's position." In short, despite D'Amato's press release asking the Justice Department to block Margiotta's retrial, he was unwilling to ask President Reagan to remove Korman from office and in this way make sure that his patron would never be retried.

His minimal press statement in support of Margiotta did not disguise the fact that he was distancing himself from the troubled boss. The Nassau regulars watched this charade in helpless rage. Mutterings about D'Amato's disloyalty and ingratitude were common in all the clubhouses, where behavior of this sort was so frequently observed that such a flagrant example of it was easily detected.

Two weeks after the trial, the county organization, still led by Margiotta, held its annual $150-a-plate filet mignon dinner; guest of honor: Joseph Margiotta. So anxious were the soldiers in the field to demonstrate a level of loyalty superior to D'Amato's that forty-three hundred people attended, most of them beneficiaries of commission splitting or some comparable "patronage." The previous year, Ronald Reagan had attracted forty-two hundred celebrants.

"As you know, these past six months have been difficult ones," Margiotta—in his dual role as guest of honor and host—said into the microphone. His beneficiaries sat in silent sympathy amid the five thousand balloons that festooned the ballroom. He thanked his family, staff, law partner, and defense attorneys and then, with no show of embarrassment on their part, named the public and party officials, union officers and religious leaders who "stood by me, shoulder to shoulder" as he had awaited the verdict. Recognizing the practical nature of their relationship, he concluded, "I certainly hope I will be privileged to repay you."

State chairman George Clark then stood to hail the Nassau party as "the greatest Republican organization in America" and the besieged Margiotta as "the best leader in this country."

D'Amato was told that the crowd might boo if he appeared. He was more concerned that his absence from this sacred party ritual would reinforce his image of infidelity to his mentor. And so he not only attended the tribute to the man he had abandoned; he arose on the dais, and to the most unresponsive forty-three hundred people he had ever faced, he delivered impromptu remarks assailing prosecutors for harassing politicians instead of fighting crime.

At the end of the affair, the boss posed for pictures with his supporters. D'Amato rushed up and threw his arms around the man he wouldn't otherwise help. They embraced, looking not at each other but out at the multitude of Nikons and Canons; two pols dressed in tuxedos, smiling faces cheek to cheek, the edges of their large bow ties crushed against each other, the front of D'Amato's frilled white shirt and his ruffled sleeve cuff boldly thrust out at the cameras' lenses.

Out in the lobby by himself, waiting for the valet to bring his car, the glacial-faced D'Amato was questioned by reporters as to whether he intended to do anything to stop his friend's second trial. He coolly responded, "It is not within my purview."

EIGHTEEN

HOW SENATOR POTHOLE OPERATES

Although it was six years off, D'Amato had already begun to worry about his campaign for reelection to the U.S. Senate. As D'Amato took his seat, the 1986 strategy for winning was already in place: at its heart, the TV ad. The canned commercial protected him from the risky convention of debating with his opponent; it allowed the clever people at the agency to develop the most appealing approach to the voters—whether it was an endorsement from his mother saying what a good boy he had always been or an actor playing the role of a streetwise taxi driver saying what a nice guy he still was.

He would have little to do in the campaign. He would seldom appear on the commercials, then only in carefully selected spots. During the weeks before election day he would speak to small club gatherings around the state or deliver speeches, written by his staff, at Bar Association and Chamber of Commerce dinners.

The only thing needed to bring this idyllic scenario to life was money. The millions he had spent to defeat Javits and Holtzman had reinforced Margiotta's lectures to him about the importance of fund-raising. The reelection campaign he envisioned might only require a small outlay of energy, but the six years spent raising those millions would be exhausting.

There was a pitfall. People objected when *campaign contributions* piled up in his bank accounts; there were rumors about corruption, about the need to pay back his contributors. To make matters worse, Elizabeth Holtzman had complained in October 1980, just a few days before the election, about four campaign loans he had gotten from the Bank of New York. The first of the unsecured loans, which eventually totaled $130,000, had been given to D'Amato at 10.5 percent interest when the prime rate for the bank's best business customers was 18.5 percent and less influential borrowers paid 25 percent. Furthermore, the loans had been posted in the bank's records as having been taken for personal purposes rather than for business purposes; business loans required a higher rate.

The *Village Voice*, which had uncovered the story, revealed that the bank's vice president, Robert H. von Elm, D'Amato's friend for seventeen years and a former Republican committeeman from Hempstead, had made the arrangements for the campaign loans, even though von Elm conceded he didn't normally handle such matters.

The propriety of von Elm's role was questioned by the *New York Times*, since von Elm admitted representing his bank in soliciting D'Amato for Hempstead deposits while D'Amato was the town's fiscal officer. The Bank of New York loved this kind of deposit. The *Times* pointed out that during one fifteen-day period in May 1979 the bank had more than $17 million in Hempstead tax funds on deposit while paying no interest to its favorite depositor.

Town records showed that during the 1970s, while D'Amato was a member of the town board, he repeatedly voted to designate the Bank of New York as a depository of these interest-free public funds. Although a number of other banks received *some* deposits, the Bank of New York was the largest beneficiary.

D'Amato's usefulness, from the Bank of New York's perspective, didn't end when he abandoned Hempstead for loftier venues. He had obtained a position on the Senate Banking Committee, such a good post from a banker's viewpoint for a man who had always rewarded his friends. (After Congress passed the 1984 Comprehensive Banking Bill, which legalized regional compacts formed by many states to keep out the gargantuan New York banks, the Bank of New York filed a lawsuit seeking to outlaw the compacts. Their friend, Senator D'Amato, filed a supporting friend-of-the-court brief.)

At the end of October 1980, federal prosecutors called in the FBI to determine whether Senator D'Amato had been the beneficiary of favorable loan terms from the Bank of New York. Its investigation was originally frustrated by a lack of cooperation from the Bank of New York. Ronald Mahaffey, the head of the Nassau FBI office, told *Newsday* that the bank had "been dragging its feet" in providing requested documents.

FBI agents visited D'Amato's Island Park home in February 1981 to question him and gain permission for access to his loan records. D'Amato complained that the bureau was taking too long to clear him. Reporters asking whether he had expressed his annoyance to the Department of Justice were told: "Damn right I have."

When the *Times* conducted an investigation into the apparent conflict of interest seven months after the election, the senator expressed surprise that anyone but Elizabeth Holtzman would object to his loans. In "hindsight," he told the *Times* on July 14, 1981, he probably should have sought financial help from a bank that hadn't done business with Hempstead. Anxious to explain that the matter was innocent despite appearances to the contrary, he said, "Who would think, you know, that that kind of situation would open up, where people could say, 'Well, here was your banker and he was dealing with the town on a municipal level and you dealt with his bank and you could be criticized.' " He added, "The fact, then, is, as a practical matter, I would probably have to not do business with any bank that did any business or substantial business with the town."

This decision required the breaking of an old habit, since he revealed that he had previously received two loans from the Bank of New York in 1972 while he was Hempstead supervisor: one for $9,000 and another for $145,000, which had been granted to a corporation in which he had a 50 percent interest.

The FBI was unable to document anything illegal about the bank's motives in granting loans to an official from whom they were seeking business. It was equally difficult to build a case, worth taking to court, that proved illegal D'Amato's motives for helping to grant the Bank of New York the lion's share of millions of interest-free deposits. At a minimum, D'Amato's ethics were questionable, but politicians never go to jail for that reason.

On February 1, 1982, the Justice Department announced it had been unable to discover any violation of law by Senator D'Amato in obtaining his campaign loans. The senator said he was pleased and described the department's decision to close its investigation as a complete vindication of "my actions and conduct."

Joe Margiotta was also creating problems for him. The boss was trying to convince President Reagan's Justice Department not to retry a Republican as faithful to the party as himself, and self-interest was forcing D'Amato to refuse to support Margiotta's petition. It was such a distraction from his main interest: suctioning up campaign contributions. His senate colleagues had already begun to call him "the Vacuum Cleaner."

While Margiotta awaited the start of his second trial, D'Amato busied himself erecting collection apparatuses, but some money began to flow in without apparent solicitation. For example: On January 20, 1981, Inauguration Day, John S. R. Shad, one of the top executives at the E. F. Hutton brokerage house and the chairman of the 1980 Reagan-Bush New York Finance Committee, sent a $1,000 check to the new senator, who would not face another campaign for almost six years. At that time, Mr. Shad actively sought the chairmanship of the Securities and Exchange Commission (SEC). Senator D'Amato was chairman of the Banking subcommittee charged with overseeing the work of the SEC and deciding who would lead the agency.

Mr. Shad was nominated to be chairman of the SEC one month after he made his D'Amato contribution, and although the senator conceded he had originally had someone else in mind for that position, Shad was, without any opposition, quickly approved.

On December 24, 1981, after the official relationship between the two men had been firmly established, Shad sent the senator an additional $1,000 check. Since federal law prohibits individuals from giving more than $2,000 to a senator in a six-year period, Chairman Shad had filled his quota.

When questioned about the contribution, D'Amato said, "We've become friends. Good friends. What should I do, give back the $1,000 and cause more of a fuss? A man of John Shad's stature would not expect me to act one way or another."

Shad recognized that this second check—which, in keeping with their new relationship, was made out to the Friends of Senator D'Amato Committee—might be improper. He consulted with the SEC lawyer responsible for advising commission members about ethics; he was told to go ahead with the gift. The advice, given privately to Chairman Shad, wasn't repeated when the matter became public. Fred S. Eiland, spokesman for the commission, thought it was legitimate to raise questions about Shad's contribution "from an ethical point of view," although he felt there was "nothing prohibiting it" in the election laws.

The senator did not need to consult any expert on ethics. When Shad's goodwill gesture was exposed, D'Amato observed that "his contributions are minuscule in comparison to the total." He insisted, "It's silly to try to think there was some sinister motive. It stretches credibility and imagination."

The *New York Times*, in an editorial, wrote:
Perhaps $2,000 doesn't mean much to Senator D'Amato. But when has price ever been the test of right and wrong? A Senator has jurisdiction over the work of an independent Federal agency. The agency head gives money to the Senator's campaign funds and the Senator gratefully accepts. . . . Even if the contribution does not actually sway the Senator's judgment about the agency, it gives the appearance of doing so. . . . The money should not have been offered, nor should it have been accepted.

It is difficult for a casual observer to decide exactly what does sway a senator's judgment, but six years later, on November 23, 1986, Chairman Shad had every reason to feel that his prompt contribution to Senator D'Amato's campaign chest six years earlier had served him well. On that late autumn Sunday a much harassed Shad had been summoned to appear before one of America's informal television grand juries, David Brinkley's ABC-TV program. Stories about the chairman had been front-page news for the previous week, competing for space with the burgeoning Iran-Contra arms scandal that was enveloping Reagan's administration.

Ivan F. Boesky, king of the arbitragers, had been caught using illegal inside information passed to him by Wall Street's junk bond specialist Drexel Burnham Lambert. That information gave him an edge in staging his corporate raids. Shad had agreed to allow Boesky to suffer as yet undescribed lesser penalties if he would "cooperate" with the SEC in an attempt to implicate other Wall Street manipulators.

Boesky's exposure had been years late in coming; he had been pillaging the stock market Shad was supposed to have been policing for the previous six years.

What appeared originally to have been a public relations coup for Shad suddenly was being perceived as a clumsy act of bad judgment. After Boesky privately confessed his crimes and agreed to pay a $100 million fine, he audaciously asked Shad for permission to liquidate $400 million in stocks controlled by him before Shad made public news of his crimes. Boesky was asking to be allowed to make one last trade based on inside information, in the knowledge that as soon as the news of his crimes surfaced, the value of his holdings would collapse.

Shad, for numerous reasons, none of which sounded convincing to brokers and small investors who had been caught with their options down, agreed to let Boesky make his profit at the expense of a multitude of the unwary. That multitude subsequently lost approximately one-third of its investment. The clamor that engulfed Shad when this act of undeserved generosity became known had placed him on notice that he was in for a hard time from Brinkley's panel of skeptical journalists.

In an endeavor to gain support for their attack on Shad, Brinkley invited an authority in the field of securities to supply an independent, unbiased judgment about the propriety of allowing Boesky to unload his stock holdings on the day before he was to be exposed. What better man, Brinkley decided, than the chairman of the committee charged with overseeing the SEC, Alfonse D'Amato?

Sam Donaldson and George Will wanted to know what Senator D'Amato thought of Chairman Shad's willingness to allow Boesky to trade on inside information? Oh, he responded, he didn't feel it was his place to express any view on that matter. "Shad is here, and he is going to answer to that." D'Amato added that the focus shouldn't be on Shad but on his own well-thought-out remedy for control of insider trading: Give the SEC additional resources; have his committee write legislation to provide more information to stockholders; and, finally, recognize that civil penalties were not enough for men like Boesky. Under repeated questioning, D'Amato could not be provoked into assailing Shad.

Chairman Shad soon resigned, accepting President Reagan's appointment as ambassador to a country some distance from Wall Street. By March 1989 the memory of Shad's financial rescue of Drexel Burnham's client Ivan Boesky faded, and the brokerage house, now about to be indicted for its role in the growing insider-trading scandal, announced the name of its new chairman, John S. R. Shad.

By the end of D'Amato's first year in office reports submitted to the Federal Election Commission showed that his four campaign committees had raised a total of $779,215, much of it from security firms and banking interests.

D'Amato organized a core group of bush beaters who sought $1,000 contributions through statewide senator clubs. They also sold tickets to frequently held $1000-a-plate dinners and cocktail parties, more intimate fund-raising breakfasts, and $1,000-per-ticket galas featuring party luminaries of the incandescence of President Reagan and Vice President Bush.

Small donations were solicited by a direct-mail operation. These drives were the least efficient way to raise usable money; they usually cost almost as much in postage, printing expenses, and fees as they brought in. D'Amato viewed them as good public relations and an easy way to tap the modest resources of the usually detached run-of-the-mill Republican voter.

He also received money from a number of conservative political action committees (PACs), among which was the Citicorp Political Action Committee. At D'Amato's request, that group of bankers wrote dunning letters to the names on its gold-plated list of the affluent.

Newsday sought an explanation for this tireless fund-raising and was rewarded with this practical slice of D'Amato's philosophy: "It isn't wrong to seek [contributions]. . . . I feel good [if] by my work there are people who say they want to help [because] we did something for you, to contribute."

The senator largely ignored other aspects of his job. His position on the Banking Committee required him to prevent the deregulated banks from engaging in risky practices. Savings and loans (S & Ls) were offering extraordinary interest rates to attract deposits that were insured by the government. Word that they were speculatively investing these deposits and might go broke had been circulating since the early 1980s. D'Amato had no interest in that part of his responsibilities. By the end of the decade the excesses of the banking industry, which he and others ignored, led to a cascade of bankruptcies.

He had similar oversight duties on the Housing Committee: Semiannual reports from Charles L. Dempsey, inspector general of the Department of Housing and Urban Development (HUD), pinpointed corrupt practices within the agency. They were filed with the committee, but D'Amato didn't bother to act on them. As far back as 1981, Dempsey had informed the committee of more than ten thousand instances in which HUD's Community Development Block Grant program had paid for work that was never done. The committee received fair notice from Dempsey that something was terribly wrong in HUD, but somehow D'Amato's interest could not be aroused. Years later, as federal prosecutors began to investigate charges of influence peddling, embezzlement, fraud, and mismanagement in HUD, retired inspector general Dempsey complained that he would like to see someone "force the damn congressmen and their lazy staffers to read the IG's reports."

Dempsey was being unjust to D'Amato's staff. They were a hardworking lot who handled matters as small as the late arrival of a social security check or a question about where a job seeker might go to obtain a civil service application. *D'Amato* had directed his staff's energies toward projects that detracted from the core duties of a senator. They spent their days performing minor constituent services that should have been handled by the agencies involved or, more often, in time-consuming services for wealthy favor seekers who helped D'Amato raise campaign funds.

His staff's attention to minutiae, to which a local councilman or alderman might normally devote himself, quickly earned D'Amato the nickname "Senator Pothole."

That name, with its less than flattering ring, didn't offend D'Amato. It suggested that he was a man of the people, someone who was concerned with the small events that filled the lives of those whose votes would return him to office. For a man with the conservative record D'Amato swiftly established, such a veneer of democratic concern was important. Call him "New York's Assemblyman in Washington" or "the Block Captain Senator." Each of these labels seemingly reflected his effort to be of service to a cross section of his state's voters.

Yet only a faction of grieving citizens ever bothered to contact his office. If his staff filled one of their potholes, the world was quickly informed of his effort by exuberant notices of self-congratulation to all media outlets.

Meanwhile, his antielitist pose diverted attention from senate votes that only inadvertently helped anyone except the superrich. In 1981 he voted to impose drastic cuts in social security, school aid, student loans, school lunches, low-income housing, and Medicaid. D'Amato's affirmative vote on Concurrent Resolution 115, President Reagan's first and deepest cut in domestic spending, slashed funding for those programs by $36 billion.

He was equally enthusiastic about any Reagan proposal to increase defense spending. Yes, he thought nerve-gas weapons systems should be modernized; the B-1 bomber developed; the neutron bomb artillery shell added to the arsenal; the MX missile given the green light; and just to show that his interest went beyond exotic weapons, he vigorously endorsed the buildup of the old-fashioned conventional navy to six hundred ships.

At the time he voted for military allocations that added hundreds of billions of dollars to the deficit, he supported President Reagan's proposal to cut taxes *across the board* by 25 percent. D'Amato's concept of economic justice considered it fair that a poor man whose annual tax was $100 would see his burden reduced by $25, not enough to pay for an increase in bus fare. It didn't disturb his sense of fairness that the middle-class householder who formerly paid a $1,000 tax bill now had only an insignificant additional $250 to play with at the end of the tax year. But he did consider it fair that his Park Avenue constituent, who had previously been obliged to pay a tax of $1 million, after his 25 percent tax cut suddenly had $250,000 in the pocket of his designer jeans.

Senator D'Amato's down-the-line support of Reagan's inequitable tax cuts and military buildup led to an average annual $200 billion shortfall in revenues and resulted, within five years, in doubling the national debt to $2 trillion; within ten years the debt had again doubled to $4 trillion.

As his first rocky year in the Senate drew to a close, D'Amato's association with shady underworld figures was being trumpeted to the world. Federal district judge Mark Costantino made public ABSCAM tapes on which Alfred Carpentier's voice was recorded. Earlier in the week, Judge Costantino had sentenced Carpentier to a four-year prison term. Reporters jammed into a conference room in the Brooklyn Eastern District courthouse to hear the tapes played by the Organized Crime Strike Force in which Carpentier said D'Amato had given him "the inside door" to distribute contracts on a $240-million hotel and industrial development at Mitchell Field and that D'Amato was "on the take."

Carpentier's assertion, heard for the first time by the media, that "D'Amato may look to shake you down for a little more [than most politicians]" did not help D'Amato's reputation.

D'Amato's spokesman Gary Lewi said, "It's unfortunate that in the climate we live in that if someone like Mr. Carpentier drops your name merely to puff himself up, you're tarred." The senator, Lewi said, had met Carpentier at Little League dinners, but "there was no business or personal relationship between the two men ever."

Murray Kempton, in his column the next day, remarked that "D'Amato's response was one more reminder that any public ventilation of allegations against his honesty at once disables the victim. He cannot afford to cry slander."

Abraham Hirschfeld, the New York City builder who contributed generously to politicians in order to grease the way for his commercial endeavors, explained the motivation of the men whose destiny D'Amato could now affect: "Nobody contributes hundreds of thousands of dollars not to get something for it."

Hirschfeld learned that lesson partly from dealing with Senator D'Amato, to whom he had contributed substantially for many years. On July 6, 1982, Hirschfeld applied the knowledge he had so expensively acquired. He took a group of his business associates to D'Amato's Washington office. He was seeking support for a luxury housing development on Manhattan's West Side. Wayne Barrett, in the *Village Voice*, described the meeting.

> They were armed with charts and documents to woo the senator's support, but D'Amato was "not interested in any presentation of the merits" of the 4,300-unit project. D'Amato said he would "back my friend Abe's project," and called Mayor Koch to endorse it while Hirschfeld [and his associates] sat in the senator's office listening to the phone conversation.

After the meeting, Hirschfeld's attorney, Leonard Bloom, returned to his Manhattan office, where he found a hand-delivered bill demanding $10,000. The bill was from Lawrence Elovich, who was a complete stranger to Bloom. A quick check revealed that Elovich ran a one-man Long Island law office. Bloom called and told Elovich that he had "no knowledge of what the bill was for."

Elovich's response: "That's for the D'Amato meeting."

Bloom was aghast. Bloom told the *Voice*, "I said, 'I beg your pardon; I wasn't aware there was a fee for meeting with a U.S. senator.' He [Elovich] explained that it had all been worked out through Abe Hirschfeld."

Bloom was so troubled by the influence-peddling implications of his conversation with Elovich that he took the matter up with his superiors. They refused to pay, warning Hirschfeld that if he continued to operate in this manner, his connection with the company would be severed. Hirschfeld was in an awkward position. His partners had received a bill they weren't going to pay, but D'Amato wanted Elovich to get $10,000. Hirschfeld knew Elovich and D'Amato had been political associates for thirty years. Elovich had coordinated D'Amato's Long Island campaigns as far back as the 1960s, when Hirschfeld had been state Democratic party treasurer.

In fact, the relationship was even closer. The senator had traveled with Elovich to Puerto Rico. One of D'Amato's favorite pastimes was to bicycle from Island Park down to Long Beach, where he would stroll on the boardwalk, display his celebrity presence, and flirt with promenading women. Elovich's nearby Lido Beach house was D'Amato's destination on those frequent excursions. He would park his bike there and have a bite to eat before venturing onto the boardwalk.

Hirschfeld knew that Elovich's $10,000 bill had to be paid if D'Amato's support was to be sustained. It was a cheap price to get their locally unpopular condominium built. In mid-September 1982, D'Amato's aide and campaign adviser, Richard Nasti, appeared before the New York City Board of Estimate; it had to approve the project. Nasti read D'Amato's statement of support. Two weeks later, Hirschfeld Realty, Abe's private account, sent a $10,000 check to Elovich. Abe Hirschfeld knew Al D'Amato needed money for his campaigns. He also knew that if you contributed there was a good chance you might "get something for it."

D'Amato was lucky that all of the following came in the first year of a six-year term: the probes by the FBI; a court appearance at Francis O'Connor's trial to deny he was soliciting bribes at the Hempstead Resources Recovery Plant; editorial attacks on his fund-raising ethics; an accusation connecting him with the ABSCAM scandal; and a voting record that appealed mainly to junk-bond salesmen. He could rely on the fleeting memory of the electorate to allow him to paper over these stains on his reputation. If he lowered his profile and let the creative people at the agency whip up a new image for him, there was an excellent chance that by the time voters reached for the polling lever, they would remember only what those thirty-second television commercials had to say about him.

NINETEEN
THE BOSS'S SECOND SHOT

There are few things so ordinary, or heartbreaking, as the ending of a friendship. For more than twenty years, Al D'Amato and Joe Margiotta had informed the world by speech and deed that each thought of the other as a trusted associate, a confidant, indeed, really a member of their family.

On that level of intimacy, expectations run high, perhaps more so since their relationship had been elevated to surrogate father and son. A good father gives and guides, hoping to see his offspring learn the ways of the world and prosper; in the traditional role—the role that Margiotta played—he expects to be honored and obeyed. D'Amato proved to be the type of son, seen too frequently in the real world, who accepts all the treasures offered in such a kinship but feels no obligation that survives the first strain on that kinship.

That strain had become most unbearable as the November 16, 1981, date for Margiotta's second trial approached. Loyalists in the party had tried to protect the boss from that added indignity by getting the Justice Department to end Ed Korman's prosecution. Cong. Norman F. Lent, of East Rockaway, spearheaded the endeavor. He described Korman as a "prosecutor run amuck" and exhorted supporters of patronage to rally to the boss's banner. "Good men," he said, "have to speak out lest the arrogance of these people go unchecked."

Lent would have preferred that Senator D'Amato, a man in a position to pressure the Justice Department, had gone directly to Atty. Gen. William French Smith and struck a deal that stopped Korman. But Lent gave up after months of pleading with D'Amato. In desperation, he drew up a letter to the attorney general asking him to investigate whether U.S. Attorney Korman was acting properly in his efforts to prosecute the Nassau leader.

Lent persuaded twenty-three area congressmen to sign the letter. Most of them were Long Island Republicans, but there were also House Democrats Mario Biaggi, of the Bronx (soon to be convicted of extortion), and Joseph Addabbo, of Queens, two buddies on whom the boss had always been able to count when the going got rough.

Lent was in an unenviable position: He was close to D'Amato *and* Margiotta. As a result, his most sincere effort was to support Margiotta while not criticizing D'Amato. He wanted everyone to know that D'Amato had been enthusiastic about signing the letter; he had even volunteered to talk to some members of the New York delegation to get them to sign up.

Finding it difficult to suppress his sorrow, Lent remarked that he hoped D'Amato would be "persuaded to submit alternative names" for Korman's job after the present trial ended.

The second trial opened in Judge Charles Sifton's court on November 16, 1981. In the interim between the two trials, a new Uniondale courthouse had been completed and was ready for business; Margiotta was to be one of its first clients. There was an irony in this. When Margiotta was at the height of his power and the most influential trustee of Hofstra University, he convinced the school's administrators to make a portion of the campus available to the federal government to build a courthouse on the corner of Hempstead Turnpike and Uniondale Avenue—the same building in which his fate was to be decided.

As Margiotta sat down at the defense table, the boss could comfort himself with the thought that the organization was still solidly under his control. Six weeks before the trial began he was unanimously reelected to a seventh term as head of the Nassau party.

Fortified by the opinion of those he most valued, Margiotta had walked into the Uniondale courthouse—through a large glass door held reverentially for him by a security guard—waved breezily to reporters, and proclaimed the commission-splitting arrangement for which he was about to be retried was nothing more than "traditional political patronage." In arranging to add 50 percent to the cost paid by Nassau taxpayers for their government's insurance, he was merely carrying out his "responsibilities as a party leader."

Assistant U.S. Attorney Larry J. Silverman, intent on learning from his first attempt to convict Margiotta, had polled the jurors to find out why they had deadlocked. The strategy that emerged, which had not been pursued at the first trial, was to emphasize two points: Margiotta had obtained $5,000 from Williams for his own use; and the Williams & Son agency was *forced* to "kick back a substantial portion of the commissions" whose illegal nature Margiotta implicitly conceded when he took steps to conceal "the true nature of what these payments really were."

In an attempt to prove this, Silverman presented his star witness, Richard A. Williams. Interestingly, Williams was still a Republican committeeman from Garden City and the official insurance broker for Nassau County. Clearly, Margiotta felt that Williams had behaved acceptably at the first trial.

In preparing for this trial, Silverman had informed witness Williams that his testimony at the first trial was unsatisfactory. In effect, Williams had concealed the true nature of the agreement between Margiotta and his father, which was continued by him after his father's death. Prosecutor Silverman reminded Williams that he faced convictions that could result in more, or less, jail time, depending on his testimony.

This tactic—used when dealing with witnesses who are as guilty as the person on trial but without whose testimony obtaining a conviction would be difficult—proved to be a bracing memory tonic for the younger Williams. On the stand he informed the jury that he believed that he "would lose the municipal business" Margiotta funneled to him if he had not distributed money to the party leaders on the boss's annual "commission" list.

Margiotta attempted to smile through such unequivocal testimony; appearances were important. When he entered the courtroom, he was accompanied by as large a crowd as had attended him at the first trial, and if his wife, Dorothy, was unavailable to act the role of an attractive, approving companion, then his law partner's wife, Michelle Ricigliano, would serve as a smiling stand-in.

Insurance agent Robert Dowler drove the second nail into Margiotta's political coffin when he told the jury he had given Margiotta $5,000 of the unexpected large $10,000 "commission" from the Williams agency. The $5,000 had "bribe" written all over it.

As the second week of the trial began, Donald Woolnough, Margiotta's administrative assistant, took the stand as "a hostile witness" for the prosecution. He reluctantly described how Margiotta drew up the list of those who would share the 50 percent kickback. In response to Silverman's relentless questioning, he confirmed that "everything went through his [Margiotta's] hands."

At this trial Judge Sifton allowed the prosecution to open up a small but damaging portion of the 1 percent case. Woolnough testified that before a non–civil service job could be filled in Nassau, he had to be told it was available and had to approve the appointee. He also cleared all requests for promotions and "salary increases involving more than $1,500" and had to be informed about "the extent of the promotion, the title, and the reason for the promotion." Woolnough's testimony proved extremely damaging, since it gave the politically unsophisticated jury a glimpse of the real, though unofficial, government of Nassau County.

He was followed to the stand by Ralph Caso, the former Nassau county executive, who again vehemently denied he knew the Williams agency was giving half of its commissions to party members selected by Margiotta. "I was not aware of it, no, sir!"

Somewhat less forcefully, Francis Purcell, Caso's successor as county executive, testified he had been aware of County Leader Margiotta's commission-sharing practices for years; though, he remarked, he hadn't known of the details of the arrangement. In an attempt to explain his role in county government, Purcell said, "Mr. Margiotta takes care of the politics, I take care of the government." Purcell, who wasn't known for the subtlety of his intellect, had been able to discern a division between politics and government that politicians generally pride themselves in ignoring.

At the end of two weeks, the prosecution rested. Hundley made a motion to dismiss the charges; Judge Sifton denied the motion. It was the testimony of Woolnough and Purcell that convinced him to let the trial proceed. Sifton remarked that the prosecution's evidence about Margiotta's power to influence the county's governmental affairs was "more ample" in the retrial than it had been in the first trial.

Margiotta was the first defense witness. Hundley carefully led him through a day of denials and then turned him over to Larry Silverman's cross-examination.

In a voice of injured innocence, Margiotta insisted that the prosecutor misconstrued his political activities. "This was a patronage system that had been carried on for years" he declaimed, adding that it had been "a widespread practice." This was the "widespread" theory of politics: If enough politicians practiced something that common sense, and the criminal law, would consider illegal, then it was legal, because it was "widespread."

Silverman's most persistent questioning was about the $5,000 kickback from Dowler with which Margiotta had paid his taxes. Margiotta maintained that the payment was simply part of political patronage, which was the way political parties operated. "No, sir," he asserted, "there was nothing illegal about it."

He admitted regretting taking the $5,000, not because it was illegal but because "it doesn't look good."

When Silverman was finished, Margiotta stepped down from the witness box with a spring in his step. He walked to the front row of the spectator's seats; smiling broadly, he kissed his wife and daughter before receiving the whispered congratulations, and thumbs-up signals, from his entourage.

Hundley's summation pivoted on the concept that Margiotta was innocent because he had carried on a "long-standing" patronage system. Margiotta's defenders had now been identified; they were Mr. Long-standing and Mr. Widespread.

The jury deliberated for eighteen hours over a period of three days and returned to the courtroom with a decision at 2:05 P.M., December 9; their verdict: guilty. Margiotta hunched his shoulders and dropped his head as if the enormity of his personal catastrophe had suddenly become too much to bear. Dorothy put her arm around his neck and whispered in his ear. Several relatives broke into tears.

Outside the courtroom Margiotta told reporters he was "shocked at the verdict. I feel that I've been convicted because I've been a successful political leader."

Later, in front of his Old Brookville home, Margiotta confided his elitist views of the jury to a crowd of reporters: "I was not convicted by a jury of my peers. They are not in the same station of life as me. They live in a different world, in which politicians are viewed with suspicion and antagonism."

A number of the jurors were interviewed. They revealed that, unlike the first jury, they had reached their decision immediately and with no dissent. Raymond Bonne, a forty-year-old dockworker living in Ronkonkoma and a member of the Conservative party, said, "All of us deliberated and took both sides of the case. We tried to put ourselves in the place of Mr. Margiotta and tried everything we could to find that man innocent, but the prosecution presented too much evidence that he was guilty."

The only Democrat on the jury, Rosalie Nolfo, forty-one, of Commack, said she was unfamiliar with Long Island politics and had not heard of Margiotta before the trial. "There was a lot of money that changed hands," she said, "and we felt the people of Nassau had been hurt."

Ed Korman issued a statement congratulating the jury. He called the conviction "a victory for the people of Nassau County, who have been victimized by years of institutionalized corruption at a cost to the taxpayers of millions of dollars."

On a personal note, federal district court judge Korman told me in his Brooklyn office on May 19, 1986, four and a half years after the trial, "There was a lot of pressure. There were attacks on my motive for bringing the case, but over the last few years my experience is that when you prosecute public officials, the first thing that is attacked are your motives." The forty-four-year-old, six foot-tall, 210-pound Korman had wavy black hair, and brown eyes peering out of horn-rimmed glasses. He complained about "political intimidation" that had been mounted against him in an attempt to head off the second trial by having him fired, describing it, in understated fashion, as "inappropriate."

Judge Korman felt that the news coverage of the trial had failed to focus on Margiotta's "real criminal activities." Instead, the media had gilded the image of Margiotta as a consummate political leader. "As a result, I fear that Mr. Margiotta was partially successful in portraying himself as doing something proper."

Korman then went on to underscore the importance of Margiotta's conviction. "I think, however, that the perception that is most important is that of other elected officials. I hope the message of this trial has gotten through to them."

Soon after Margiotta's conviction Senator D'Amato issued a press release from his Washington office. "I am deeply shocked, and I feel the courts will ultimately vindicate him."

The boss's confidants complained that as the trial approached D'Amato hadn't even called his mentor to wish him good luck. Furthermore, though everyone of consequence in the party had put in at least one appearance in court during the three-week trial, D'Amato had stayed away; in the twenty-four hours since the conviction, D'Amato hadn't called to console his *friend*.

When it became clear that the short written statement hadn't satisfied the boss's friends, Armand Paul D'Amato came to the defense of his silent brother. He acknowledged that there was a "strain" between his brother and Margiotta but thought it was of no consequence. It was unfair, he insisted, for party members to "try to make trouble" between the convicted felon and his brother by suggesting that the lack of contact was a major problem. Armand Paul wanted the world to know that his brother was always anxious to get the latest news about Margiotta's troubles. "My brother," he said proudly, "called three times a day to find out what was going on. He was genuinely concerned."

On the second day after the trial, Levittown North's executive leader Robert McDonald—Margiotta's public relations aide—said that after a number of people had remarked on this distant behavior by the senator, D'Amato had finally called Margiotta at Westbury party headquarters. The senator had explained to the still-numbed party leader that he had been out of touch because he was very busy in Washington.

When questioned about the contents of the call, Margiotta commented, "I'm busy thinking about the future." McDonald confirmed there had been a strain between the two. "It has been building for some time." However, he felt D'Amato "owed" his boss that call. "After all, Al is the first public official he made."

TWENTY

D'AMATO AND MARGIOTTA FIGHT FOR POWER

M argiotta's conviction raised questions about his continued leadership that created a psychological crisis in the party. The unscrupulously ambitious—who make up the ranks of party regulars—produced a number of luminaries who saw themselves being beckoned to assume the soon-to-become-vacant throne. Al D'Amato didn't want the throne, but he did want the power. Surely a felon couldn't lead a party that wanted the public to believe it was honest.

More powerful than individual ambition, however, was collective advantage. A coalition of political beneficiaries trembled at the thought of what might happen if the man from whose hand they had been feeding disappeared from the scene. This coalition included professional politicians whose livelihood depended on Margiotta's charity; businessmen whose prosperity depended on the boss's favorable decisions about the distribution of contracts, the granting of zoning changes, and tax abatements; and the marginal operators on society's underside who needed the assistance of the boss's appointees in providing them with lackluster inspections, averted eyes, and, most important, relatively reliable freedom from prosecution.

Now that Senator D'Amato had reestablished phone contact with the fallen boss, he presumed to speak for him. At a Buffalo news conference three days after the conviction, D'Amato said that the boss had "indicated that he will resign January 21, the day he is sentenced." Although he hadn't gotten the word directly from his old friend's mouth, he had been told that Margiotta had informed several Nassau committee members of his decision.

John McQuiston, intent on maintaining the high standards of the *New York Times*, contacted Margiotta to verify D'Amato's intelligence. Oh, no, Margiotta apprised the cautious reporter, he had "not yet made any decisions" about his plans. "I'm just waiting for the twenty-first," he said from his Brookville home, apparently unconcerned he was adding to the senator's reputation of being unreliable. "That's when I'll be sentenced. By then everything will be evaluated. Legally, a conviction doesn't take effect until sentencing. *At that time, I'll make a decision.*" Margiotta told McQuiston that D'Amato was "apparently referring to an option I have open to me." The boss wanted D'Amato to know that neither his conviction nor even his sentencing would force him to resign.

On January 20, Margiotta announced he had called a meeting of the Republican County Executive Committee for the next afternoon—soon after he was scheduled to be sentenced by Judge Sifton—whose purpose it would be to change party rules. He wanted to repeal the rule banning a party chairman who had been convicted of a felony. Spokesman McDonald explained that the chairman "would like to retain his post during the appeals process."

Thomas W. Wallace, the executive director of the New York State Board of Elections, pointed out that regardless of what Margiotta's friends on the Executive Committee did, state law required party leaders to be enrolled party members and that felons were no longer eligible to vote or to enroll in a party.

On January 21, 1982, Margiotta was escorted into Judge Sifton's court for sentencing by three congressmen, Hempstead's presiding supervisor Tom Gulotta, twenty top county officials, and most leading Nassau Republicans, with the exception of Senator D'Amato. Democrat Denis Dillon, Nassau's district attorney, who ran for reelection in 1981 with Margiotta's endorsement and who in his eight years in office had been unable to detect anything irregular in the manner that Margiotta ran the county, added his letter to those sent to Judge Sifton's desk asking that he show compassion when sentencing the fifty-four-year-old pol.

As the ashen-faced Margiotta stood before Judge Sifton, he heard himself excoriated for his "abuse of trust" and "sale of offices." The judge's words, however, were not a prologue to a draconian sentence. He ruled that the Nassau County boss must serve two years' imprisonment on each of six counts; but since he announced that the sentences were to be served concurrently, Margiotta's maximum sentence—which could have been 105 years—was two years. He would be eligible for parole after serving ten months.

Before this extraordinary day had ended, the sentenced Margiotta appeared before the Nassau County Executive Committee. He asked for the rules of the party to be changed so that he could continue to receive his $50,000 salary, retain his chauffeur-driven limousine, add to his pension, keep his generous expense account, and receive all of the perks that had been built into the chairman's job, while remaining the most powerful Republican in New York State.

Assemblyman Dean G. Skelos, of Rockville Centre, a member of the Executive Committee, thought this was the least they could do for their leader. "If it means changing the rules to get justice, we will." The committee agreed with Dean Skelos's view of justice; the vote was unanimous to have a criminal as chairman. Committee members explained that they were keeping faith with their boss because "he kept faith with us."

It was also announced that since Chairman Margiotta had hired the Washington attorney Edward Bennett Williams to handle his appeal, more fund-raising dinners and cocktail parties would be held to pay the boss's legal expenses, which had already cost $400,000 and were expected to soon exceed half a million. Al D'Amato took no part in arranging for these fund-raisers.

Margiotta's control over the livelihood of party leaders remained firm. As a result, their stake in keeping him in power was enormous. What difference did it make that some jury had mistakenly applied a code of political honesty to how things should work in county government. The boss still had the final say in how county workers made their livings.

The voters expressed their displeasure with Margiotta and the Republicans later in the year. In the November elections Nassau Republicans lost one congressman, a county court judge, and a state senate seat. This prompted Assemblyman Armand Paul D'Amato to hold a press conference at which he called for Margiotta's resignation. Margiotta's departure, he felt, would be in the best interests of the party.

To this point Margiotta had never publicly spoken out against his former friend. But Brother Armand's blast, transparently orchestrated by Alfonse, made him abandon discretion. Soon after Armand's press conference, Margiotta's office issued a statement.

> Even though their father, at the recommendation of Sen. D'Amato, participated in the patronage program which led to Mr. Margiotta's conviction, the D'Amatos have been plotting to unseat County Chairman Margiotta since his conviction in order to win control of the Nassau Republican Party, and, thus, to control the six Assembly votes from the county.

Driven by rage, Margiotta had become a witness against the D'Amatos. He was accusing Armand Sr. and his older son of taking part in the crime for which he was convicted.

> It's no secret in political circles that Assemb. D'Amato and his brother, U.S. Sen. Alfonse D'Amato, have used every means possible in an attempt to strong arm people around the state in their attempt to win the powerful minority leadership post.

Armand Paul issued the now repetitious defense of the accused D'Amatos: Margiotta's statements concerning the D'Amatos benefiting from county insurance commission splitting "were not worthy of a response."

Margiotta intervened in the assembly battle to determine who would be the Republican minority leader. Clarence Rappleyea, from upstate, received the unanimous support of the Nassau assembly delegation, and Armand Paul, his chief opponent, went down to defeat.

179

The appeals process, which could conceivably have gone on for years, was not quite that slow for Margiotta. By July 27, 1982, the U.S. Court of Appeals rejected his bid for a reversal. Judge Irving R. Kaufman, who years earlier had presided at the treason trial of Julius and Ethel Rosenberg, wrote a seventy-one-page decision in which he said the case raised "novel issues" concerning the legal obligations of a political leader who did not hold an official government office. Edward Bennett Williams had maintained that since Margiotta was not an elected official—just the head of a private political party—he "owed no fiduciary duty to the general citizenry of Nassau County." In short, in his private role he was allowed to pillage the public in a manner not open to him if he were an elected official.

Judge Kaufman rejected that argument, reasoning that although Margiotta wasn't an elected government official, he maintained a "stranglehold" on county government and had acted as a "de facto" official. Judge Kaufman concluded that Margiotta hadn't undertaken "the business of government" in a responsible or legal manner. He had, instead, used "his control over the appointment process and other aspects of municipal government" to generate a "slush fund" that he used to buy party loyalty and assist friends and some of his relatives.

Having received permission from Nassau Republicans to stay in office until his appeals were exhausted, Margiotta saw no reason to let Judge Kaufman's decision represent the last word. There was enough money left to enable Edward B. Williams to file an appeal with the U.S. Supreme Court.

Six months later, Margiotta was still sitting in the chairman's seat, as much in control of Nassau as he had ever been. On April 13, 1983, County Executive Purcell and the Republican-controlled board of supervisors, chaired by Margiotta's appointee Tom Gulotta, announced that the county would not exercise its right to sue Margiotta to recover the $700,000 he was convicted of robbing from taxpayers. Gulotta said that any attempt to reclaim the stolen money would be "too costly."

Margiotta's salary and perks had remained constant for the two years since his indictment, and now the county leaders had decided to forgo any attempt to sue him merely to recoup some of the

assau county district attorney William ahn, member of Al D'Amato's party hierar- ay, testifying before a Senate subcommittee n constitutional rights on February 27,)73, shortly before being indicted, onvicted, and sent to jail. (PHOTOGRAPH OURTESY OF THE ASSOCIATED PRESS)

County Republican leader Joseph Margiotta, Al D'Amato's mentor, leaves federal court in Brooklyn on December 3, 1980, after plead- ing innocent to charges that he had set up an insurance kickback scheme that allegedly involved, among others, Senator-elect D'Amato's father.
(AP PHOTOGRAPH BY DAVID BOOKSTAVER)

ep. Angelo Roncallo, Al D'Amato's ally in the Nassau County Republican party, on May 18,)74, after being acquitted in Westbury, L.I., federal court of conspiracy and extortion narges. He was soon defeated for reelection, given a county patronage job by the party, id then testified for William Cahn, the party's indicted county district attorney.
HOTOGRAPH COURTESY OF THE ASSOCIATED PRESS)

Sen. Jacob Javits (*center*) on October 19, 1980, debates Al D'Amato, the man who defeated him in the earlier Republican primary. Democrat Elizabeth Holtzman (*left*) waits her turn. Javits sought reelection on the Liberal party line and succeeded in splitting the liberal vote allowing D'Amato to win a narrow victory over Ms. Holtzman.
(PHOTOGRAPH COURTESY OF THE ASSOCIATED PRESS)

Senator-elect Al D'Amato and his wife, Penelope, meet with New York City Democratic mayor Ed Koch, November 6, 1980, at New York's city hall. This was the beginning of a close political relationship between the Republican and the Democrat, a key to D'Amato's electoral successes. (PHOTOGRAPH COURTESY OF THE ASSOCIATED PRESS)

Senator Al D'Amato stands behind his brother, Armand Paul D'Amato, at a political dinner in New York. It was September 1982 and the brothers were at a high point in their careers. The older brother was settled in the Senate, and his younger sibling was a state assemblyman and senior partner in a burgeoning Long Island law firm. (AP PHOTOGRAPH)

On July 1, 1983, Senator D'Amato joined Rep. Mario Biaggi (*left*) and Rep. Robert Garcia in announcing a $3 million grant to construct eighty-eight homes on Charlotte Street in the South Bronx. Both Democratic congressmen were subsequently convicted of felonies. D'Amato had a close relationship with Biaggi. Their dealings in the Wedtech scandal opened D'Amato to indictment for bribery. (AP PHOTOGRAPH BY DAVID PICKOFF)

Secretary of Housing and Urban Affairs Samuel Pierce stands to the left of Senator D'Amato as they kick off the New York Republican presidential campaign, May 29, 1984. D'Amato was state chairman for the Reagan-Bush ticket. By this time Pierce was D'Amato's puppet at HUD, using his "discretionary funds" to finance building projects of some of D'Amato's major campaign contributors. Many of D'Amato and Pierce's closest associates ended up in jail. (AP PHOTOGRAPH BY RAY HOWARD)

Special Assistant U.S. Attorney Lothar Genge in 1983. He was a member of the Organized Crime Strike Force based in Brooklyn that was prosecuting cases involving the erection of Al D'Amato's favorite project, the Hempstead Resources Recovery Plant. He seriously considered indicting the senator on extortion charges. (PHOTOGRAPH BY THE AUTHOR)

Former Republican committeeman Sol Goldfarb standing before the Oceanside Mountain garbage dump in 1985. Goldfarb had a patronage job at the landfill until he had a falling out with his clubhouse leader and cooperated with the prosecutors at the 1 percent trial. (PHOTOGRAPH BY THE AUTHOR)

Burt Neuborne, attorney for the members of the class who were suing the Nassau Republican party for triple damages for extorting 1 percent of their annual salaries in exchange for jobs, promotions, and salary increases, in August 1985. (WITH PERMISSION OF BURT NEUBORNE)

Federal district judge Jacob Mishler discussing the 1 percent case in his Uniondale, L.I., chambers on September 18, 1985. A product of machine politics himself, the judge presided at a trial involving the illegal acts of the Nassau Republican party. (PHOTOGRAPH BY THE AUTHOR)

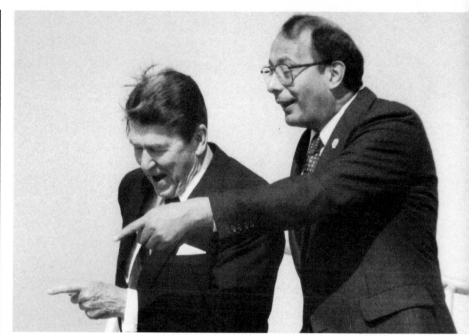

Pres. Ronald Reagan and Senator D'Amato step off a plane in New York on March 28, 1985, on their way to the New York Stock Exchange, where the president delivered a speech. This was two months after President Reagan began his second term. (AP PHOTOGRAPH BY CHARLES TASNADI)

Senator D'Amato publicly split with President Reagan over the latter's plan to attend a wreath-laying ceremony at the Bitburg cemetery in West Germany. The burial ground contains the remains of many World War II SS concentration-camp guards. The rally took place across the street from the United Nations in New York on May 29, 1985, and included a score of city, state, and federal officials, from Donna Shalala on the left, then head of Hunter College, to Mayor Ed Koch on the right. (AP PHOTOGRAPH BY FRANKIE ZITHS)

en. Al D'Amato and then U.S. Attorney Rudy Giuliani on July 9, 1986, as they pose
n Manhattan after going into a drug-infested neighborhood to purchase vials of crack
ocaine. D'Amato told Giuliani this would be a good publicity opportunity for him.
)'Amato was trying to convince Giuliani to run against Sen. Daniel Patrick Moynihan.
Giuliani was elected mayor of New York City in 1993. (AP PHOTOGRAPH BY RICHARD DREW)

Democratic nominee Mark Green shakes
hands with Al D'Amato, his Republican
senatorial opponent, before an October 22,
1986, debate in which Green accused
D'Amato of accepting contributions
from organized-crime figures.
(AP PHOTOGRAPH BY RICHARD DREW)

ames Nagourney, former member of the
Nassau Republican party leadership,
ecame Al D'Amato's rival before he went
nto private business.
PHOTOGRAPH BY THE AUTHOR)

Two political allies from opposite parties, Al D'Amato and New York City mayor Ed Koch, meet in Mother Antoinette D'Amato's Island Park house for a dinner on September 3, 1987. The Democratic mayor was soon to face his reelection test of fire. He would depend on the senator's covert support against his own party's candidate. (AP PHOTOGRAPH ED BAILEY)

Senator D'Amato prepares to vote on November 4, 1986, at the polling booth in the Island Park Volunteer Fire Department, a center of pro-D'Amato activists in the village. He wore his volunteer department jacket inscribed "Chief" on the left and "Senator Al" on the right. (AP PHOTOGRAPH BY DAVID BOOKSTAVER)

taxpayers' stolen money. The charm that the powerful exert over the lives of the weak was never more clearly demonstrated.

The *New York Times* was outraged. On April 18, 1983, it pointed out in an editorial:

> Other counties, notably neighboring Suffolk, are seeking recompense for similar betrayals through a Federal law, the 1970 Racketeer-Influenced and Corrupt Organizations Act (RICO). That law provides for civil lawsuits against racketeering politicians and triple damages for what their rackets have cost the people. It even requires the culprits ... to pay a county's legal bill.

That Margiotta would suffer some penalty was clear, but only within the jurisdiction of the federal courts. Within the boundaries of Nassau County, even out to the state borders, the powerful rose to delay his day of reckoning.

On May 2, 1983, seventeen months after his conviction, the Supreme Court declined to hear his appeal. Margiotta received the news in his Westbury office; Edward Bennett Williams had one of his colleagues call from Washington to inform him. Sitting on the couch when the anticipated call arrived was his close friend Hempstead town councilman forty-five-year-old Joseph N. Mondello.

Within six hours Margiotta had summoned the sixty-nine-member Executive Committee to his Westbury headquarters to announce his resignation. Following a scenario he had been preparing for months, he nominated the rotund Mondello to be his successor and had the pleasure of seeing his choice unanimously approved. The 2,006-member county committee would meet in ten days at Hofstra University to rubber-stamp the boss's nominee.

More than a year and a half after his conviction Margiotta was still in a position to choose his successor. He chose the most innocuous, weakest "yes-man" he could find. Mondello identified himself as a "Margiotta man," and it was understood he was keeping his chief's seat warm until that day when the unrepentant party boss could reclaim it.

Councilman Mondello, in his new role as county leader, wanted everyone to know that he wouldn't rule out a party post for Margiotta when he left prison. Mondello mused that Margiotta

181

might serve as executive director and de facto leader, although he couldn't, because of his felon status, hold party elective office.

Before he was scheduled to go to jail, party loyalists made one last effort to gain clemency from President Reagan. The president's White House adviser Lyn Nofziger publicly spoke of the possibility of a presidential pardon. (Within five years Nofziger had been convicted in the Wedtech scandal and was reduced to hoping for a similar act of mercy.)

In order to strengthen the call for clemency, Cong. Norman Lent mounted another letter-writing campaign, duly endorsed, this time, only by twelve congressmen, including the usual Democrat, Mario Biaggi, but prominently lacking Al D'Amato's name. Although he told reporters he thought the sentence was too severe, D'Amato insisted, "I'm not involved. I'm not making any recommendations."

At the end of the week in which Margiotta submitted his resignation, the Nassau Republicans held their annual dinner at the Colony Inn in Hauppauge; forty-six hundred persons paid $150 to hear Senator D'Amato tell guest of honor Margiotta, "Joe, we're proud to be here with you and to call you our friend in this difficult moment." Then he added, "He's in the heart, the minds, the prayers, of everyone here."

At midnight on June 15, in an endeavor to avoid reporters who had been told he would arrive after daylight, Margiotta slipped into Pennsylvania's Allenwood Prison Camp.

As though to underscore the casual manner in which *the law* views criminals who are politicians, Margiotta was sent to a prison that resembled a third-class hotel. The federal lockup at Allenwood made few demands on its select population. The prisoners' main restriction was an implied pledge not to walk away from the facility, which had no walls or guard towers. The favorite pastime for the less athletic involved growing tomatoes; for the rest, there was a variety of individual and intramural sports, of which tennis seemed the most popular. Television was available in the one-story brick dormitories, which were divided into cubicles, each with a cot and shelves; a modicum of privacy was guaranteed by five-foot-high partitions. Even the civilian rules of seniority had penetrated its cozy environs: old-timers who had no violations ticketed to them were provided with private units.

Some of President Nixon's Watergate associates had been housed there after their convictions. The alumni rolls included John Dean, Jeb Magruder, Charles Colson, and former attorney general John Mitchell. During Margiotta's stay Allenwood accommodated former congressman Fred Richmond, Brooklyn Democrat, who had been convicted of tax evasion, drug possession, and several varieties of payroll finagling. Also in residence were some ABSCAM politicians, most prominent, former Jersey senator Harrison Williams, who Margiotta told me he found to be "a fine gentleman."

It was still a prison, a place in which the fifty-six-year-old Margiotta didn't wish to celebrate his next birthday. His wife, he explained to me, "was frightened when I went away. She was really scared. She was convinced that I was never going to come back, 'cause I was prominent; that some of those hard-nosed—She was scared stiff."

Irving Long, *Newsday* reporter, told me that Margiotta had also been frightened about the prospect of going to prison. Margiotta had informed Long that he had enrolled in a gym program, prior to entering Allenwood, to toughen himself up.

When I told this to Margiotta, he seemed embarrassed by the suggestion that he might have taken that sort of reasonable precaution. "Eh . . . no, I never did that. Nah. . . . Let's face it, I wasn't concerned about that. I played a lot of football. I was a good athlete. You know, I could handle myself. My wife was afraid. You know, you read about these things. Somebody who knew I was part of the establishment . . . I was a Reagan supporter that they might do something. Some of them, I got a few flip remarks, but even then I was always defending the party and the president."

On August 13, 1984, Margiotta was enrolled in the work-release program at the Nassau County jail. After twelve months at Allenwood, Margiotta—looking trim and in better shape than he had been when he entered the compound—transferred to a facility he had helped staff, which was only a few miles from his Brookville home. He spent weekends at home and was only required to occupy the jail facilities on the other five nights of the week. His quarters consisted of a living room, three small bedrooms, and a bathroom, all with wood-paneled walls and furnished with lamps, couches, and television; he roomed with only one other inmate.

When he emerged from jail, Margiotta wanted to resume control of the party machinery he had turned over to Joseph Mondello, his obedient lieutenant. But Margiotta's absence had disoriented Mondello and given Al D'Amato an opportunity to become the state's most important party leader. D'Amato had wooed Mondello in an endeavor to block the reemergence of Margiotta. D'Amato convinced Margiotta's former servant that being the boss was better than working for the boss.

Mondello said that he had no intention of stepping aside and was planning to seek another two-year term as county chairman in September 1985. In his only affirmative reference to his former master, he said he was "delighted Margiotta has come home to be with his family and friends and to pick up the pieces."

With Mondello's decision to seek reelection as county chairman the party was effectively split between Al D'Amato's partisans and the still-dominant, although officially leaderless Margiotta camp. Margiotta's power resided in the loyalty of a majority of the sixty-nine clubhouse executive leaders, who had always viewed D'Amato as a ruthless, undependable rival.

Shockingly, except for Mondello's unexpected objection, there was little that stood in Margiotta's way—certainly not his conviction, his automatic disbarment, or his reputation for stealing money from the poor.

In many respects, Margiotta flourished. Important business and political associates continued to support him, if somewhat discreetly. He told me, "You know, some of our past presidents have been very good to me, a lot of people, prominent businessmen."

He became a "consultant" for a number of business accounts, including Hofstra University, guiding them in their dealings with county and state agencies. He also became an active lobbyist at the state legislature, quickly following a route laid out by former county leader Joseph Carlino.

He was still, however, confronted with the 1 percent case, in which he was the chief individual defendant. Even after fourteen months in jail, that sword of Damocles had been held back only by Jacob Mishler's willingness to accept any reason for a further delay of a trial for which his law clerks could find no precedent.

TWENTY-ONE
FORMING BATTLE RANKS

A l D'Amato and party leaders did everything possible to delay the opening of the 1 percent trial, hoping something would happen along the extended time track that would derail the juggernaut bearing down on them. Ed Hart's law office became a mill for manufacturing sheaves of motions that piled up on Judge Mishler's desk and were replaced by additional motions as rapidly as he could dispose of them.

Finally, in the middle of 1983, Mishler signaled he would brook no further delay. In denying the last of Ed Hart's motions, Mishler ruled that the case would continue, since "proof has been submitted of a practice on the part of the Republican party of conditioning appointment and promotion to an official position on a contribution to the Republican party."

It would have been simpler for the aging judge to grant Hart's motion to dismiss: He was a lifelong Republican, and he believed in the patronage system. The plaintiffs, led by Lorraine Cullen, were, giving them the benefit of his doubts, at best fuzzy-minded idealists who didn't understand why people were willing to engage in politics and how reasonable was their expectation of a reward for service performed. The case was unprecedented; his clerks had been unable to find another example of a trial against a political party on this issue in the entire history of the federal court system. Political parties trampled on the rights of citizens countrywide

185

every day; surely other judges had opportunities to deal with this issue, and just as surely they had avoided them.

Mishler was also disturbed by the aggrieved county and town workers' desire to invoke the triple-damage provisions of the Racketeering-Influenced and Corrupt Organizations Act (RICO). Congress passed RICO in 1970 to help the Justice Department fight the Mafia. The department had done a poor job of combating organized crime, partly because J. Edgar Hoover, head of the FBI, refused to recognize that the Mafia existed. Congress believed if it authorized individual victims to initiate *civil* actions against criminals who had harmed them, a more concerted attack could be made on crime. But since the victims of *criminal* acts are no less injured when their losses are caused by legitimate businesses that act criminally than when they are ripped off by mobsters, the triple-damage features of RICO were applied to enterprises such as General Motors, Shearson/American Express, E. F. Hutton, and Lloyd's of London, which had previously been able to avoid being hauled into court by "sore losers."

By the early 1980s, the American Bar Association estimated that less than 10 percent of RICO triple-damage suits alleging criminal activities involved offenses usually associated with the Mafia. For no reason other than its effectiveness, lobbyists for the National Association of Manufacturers and several insurance and banking groups began to ask Congress to limit the scope of the law.

The U.S. Court of Appeals for the Second Circuit—the court to which all appeals from Judge Mishler's district court had to be taken—was asked to rule on the question in 1984. The Second Circuit judges in their *Sedima v. Imrex Company* decision tried to limit the number of RICO suits by ruling they could be brought only when the damages sought involved traditional racketeering. Mishler, and all of the 1 percent attorneys, watched with fascination as the central issue in their decade-long case was considered by the Supreme Court. If the nine justices upheld the Second Circuit decision, Mishler could, with clear conscience, grant a new motion by Ed Hart to dismiss the 1 percent case, since no traditional Mafia involvement was alleged in the criminal acts committed by the Republican party against the citizens of Nassau County.

In July 1985, by a 5–4 vote, the Supreme Court rejected the Second Circuit's view on *Sedima*, holding that in pursuing criminal activity "Congress wanted to reach both 'legitimate' and 'illegitimate' enterprises." In effect, the Court affirmatively answered the question: Shouldn't lawbreakers be punished whether they are part of organized crime or a corporation?

This took the great obstacle out of the way of prosecuting the 1 percent case. It applied RICO penalties to groups of people who didn't wear alligator-skin shoes and smoke smuggled Havana cigars.

The Supreme Court's decision made Mishler's task more difficult. Lorraine Cullen and her 22,000 government cocomplainants had asked him to expand the scope of RICO to an enterprise that was neither an appendage of organized crime nor a corporation, a political party. Mishler saw this as an extraordinarily complicated and potentially too significant a case. Federal judges like to follow precedents, not make new law.

The impending trial also confronted Al D'Amato with the first great threat to his political career. To this point, the Nassau party organization had nourished and protected him. Local prosecutors Bill Cahn and Denis Dillon were not concerned with charges that he had tried to use his office to get the Nassau Medical Center janitorial contract for his father's firm, that he had put his father on Margiotta's brokerage commission-splitting list, that he was extorting money from contractors who wanted to get garbage-plant contracts, or that he was demanding a 1 percent annual salary kickback from anyone wanting government work or raises.

Now federal prosecutors were involved, and they didn't take orders from the Nassau Republican party. The government's specific target *was* the party, and the party's brightest luminary, Sen. Al D'Amato, was in the federal prosecutor's direct line of fire. He would have to testify. His name would be publicly tied to the party's extortion plot. Most threatening to D'Amato, it would happen just as he prepared to run for reelection to the Senate.

Burt Neuborne, attorney for *the members of the class*, now primed for the trial with a zeal previously absent from his efforts. He began to interview potential witnesses, deciding who they might be from Ed Korman's previous prosecutions of Margiotta's ring. If you had appeared before any of Korman's grand juries, you could expect a call from Neuborne's West Forty-third Street

American Civil Liberties Union (ACLU) office. Neuborne now headed the ACLU's legal department, and the ACLU had volunteered its assistance. No arm twisting; that was not Neuborne's style; just an intense, sincere endeavor—crooned in an alto voice—to explain his purposes and win your cooperation.

Ed Hart was equally convinced by Mishler that judgment day was approaching. There was a time when Mishler had been more convivial, willing to allow a relaxed atmosphere in his court, although one always knew he was the boss. "I tried many cases before Mishler," Hart mused aloud in a conversation with me. "He's grown more impatient with the passage of time." Hart once felt that Mishler responded to his charm, but recently he had begun to feel uncomfortable in his presence and was always prepared for a frown or a rebuke if he allowed himself to wander off the subject.

Edward Joseph Hart was another individual who had been swept out of Brooklyn by the postwar migratory torrent and deposited on Nassau's shores. He was born near picturesque Sheepshead Bay in 1926, and after attending Catholic elementary school, he enrolled at James Madison public high school, where he was considered a better than average student. He had a poor opinion of Franklin Roosevelt, since he felt FDR "really wasn't being candid" in his "impassioned speech" before the war in which "he indicated he would not get us involved in the war."

After serving in the infantry in World War II, he received a B.A. from Cornell and a law degree from St. John's. Somehow Harry Truman impressed him more than Roosevelt, and now ensconced in Nassau County, he joined the Young Democrats, eventually taking over as county chairman. The vivacious gabber was soon vice chairman of the state organization and in that capacity appeared at party functions featuring Carmine De Sapio and Hubert Humphrey. He said, "I thought Adlai Stevenson was a god."

During the Eisenhower years and through the 1960s, Hart was an active Democrat. "I got caught up in it," he told me with a flamboyance that was the mark of his most ordinary conversation. "In fact, I ran twice: once for district court judge . . . and I ran against Caso . . . town of Hempstead supervisor in 1960—the year that Gene Nickerson was elected county executive. I came very close."

He disengaged himself from the Democrats over a period of years. Ideologically he claimed to have soured on them. "I was disillusioned when the Democrats turned on the middle class." But there were also important business reasons. "My practice became very active. I wanted to be a trial lawyer. I wanted to try lawsuits and argue appeals."

As his reputation grew and he became politically more conservative, a friend introduced him to Margiotta, and the boss began to turn to him for legal advice. "One case led to another," he reminisced. "I first started to advise them around '75, '76."

He dealt with the early indictments of party leaders, but in 1976, Margiotta called him in to discuss the 1 percent case. Hart quoted Margiotta as saying. " 'I'm asking you to accept the defense of party officials and the party.' And that's how I got in it." Hart then remarked, "I've been counsel to the party since '78."

There had been attempts to reward him with a judgeship, Hart said. "When Senator D'Amato had his first opportunity, he asked me if I wanted to serve as a federal district judge. I went down to Washington to thank him, but one of the main reasons [he turned it down] was because of Mr. Margiotta's problems, and I was involved in helping his defense, and I didn't think it would be fair to abandon him. Secondly, maybe even more important to me, I like to be the participant rather than the observer. Why would Tom Seaver want to be an umpire?"

As Hart approached his sixtieth year, he still found it hard to remain seated or stand in one spot. After a lifetime of living by his wit and charm, he was the possessor of a confidence that seemed susceptible to challenge only by St. Peter's final judgment.

After Mishler had turned down Hart's 1983 motion to dismiss *Cullen v. Margiotta*, Al D'Amato often called Hart urging him to avoid a trial. The senator feared that accusations about other deals he had made might surface. He was worried that even if the party won, the exposure of how he had run Hempstead would be critically harmful to him.

As a result of D'Amato's pressure, Hart decided it would be wise to settle before the trial. He agreed that the case contained too many imponderables. Margiotta's conviction, D'Amato insisted, had set a bad example, and the party's 1 percent extortions were such common knowledge that picking a sympathetic jury would prove difficult. Besides, it was a no-win situation: Since a political party had never been tried, a conviction would thrust the party into terra incognita, an area in which attorneys hated to be. Who knew what kind of punishment might flow from this unique situation? Mishler might appoint a court officer to oversee the party, in the manner that some judges in desegregation cases were appointing caretakers to supervise school districts.

Hart thought reaching an out-of-court settlement would be difficult. He believed that an idealist of Neuborne's reputation would relish the opportunity to drag the Republican party before a jury. He visualized Neuborne stereotypically as an unyielding moralist who, having the opportunity to launch a crusade against corruption, would not pause until Jerusalem had been captured.

What Hart did not know was that the man who had tirelessly defended the civil rights of indigent litigants, whose professional life had been fixated on "causes," placed the 1 percent case in another category of litigation. As the attorney for the class, Neuborne thought of himself as a conventional lawyer representing a large group of people whose primary objective was to reclaim money owed to them. A secondary aim was to end the Republican party's forced tithing; but most important was the collection of the money due his anonymous clients. It was as though Neuborne the civil rights utopian had become—allowing for a dollop of habitual idealism—Neuborne the bill collector.

Neuborne had first exposed his shift in role to Hart when he called to set up a pretrial conference with Margiotta. During that call, Hart discovered, to his delight, that under certain circumstances, Neuborne was willing to grant Margiotta immunity.

The deal was struck during a meeting between Neuborne and Margiotta in Margiotta's Uniondale office. Neuborne described what he told Margiotta: " 'It's not my job to punish you. I'm not trying to punish you. My job is to win for my clients. You can help me do it. If you help me do it, I have no reason to continue to try to hold you personally liable for what you did—if you help end it and help get the money back.' "

"He said that he [Margiotta] understood. That he was willing to be completely candid about what happened. We went over a series of questions and talked about what his answers would be, and I allowed that if his answers were the way he said they would be, that after he testified, I would see to it that there was no personal liability."

Margiotta had always insisted on party loyalty; it was the standard to which—he urged the soldiers in his army—they must aspire. Some, like Francis O'Connor, had gone to jail proudly waving that banner. But when Neuborne put him to the test, regardless of the damage his testimony might do to the party, he took Neuborne's script and pledged to memorize it.

Neuborne then wrote what he characterized as 'a very strong memo to Hart . . . saying, 'I'm letting him [Margiotta] off but not because he deserves it. He's a . . . venal, lying bastard.' " There was always the distinct possibility that when Margiotta got on the stand he might not tell the truth; "venal liars" tend to be unreliable. If that happened, Neuborne warned, he would seek the strongest possible penalties against the backsliding rogue.

Endeavoring to explain why he was willing to grant Margiotta immunity, Neuborne spoke in the most practical, in fact, pecuniary, manner. "It didn't hurt my clients, because the money to pay them wasn't going to come out of Margiotta's pocket. I didn't need Margiotta to get the money to pay them. The money to pay them was going to come out of the town of Hempstead."

Neuborne had another, less practical reason why he was willing to grant Margiotta immunity. "I'm a softy," he confessed with a show of candor that was part of his personality. "No one ever accused me of being an effective prosecutor. An effective civil liberties lawyer, yes. But never an effective prosecutor. And I was essentially in a prosecutor's mode with Margiotta."

Hart's offer of a possible settlement was received warmly by Neuborne. Hart was overjoyed to discover that after more than a decade of living in a crisis atmosphere caused by Lorraine Cullen's suit, his clients' problems might be ending. It appeared that all Neuborne wanted was a little money. Was that a problem for the party? Certainly not! A few cocktail parties and an extra squeeze on the usual contributors would take care of that.

In mid-July 1985, as the trial date approached, horse-trading between Hart and Neuborne became frenetic. In an effort to encourage their efforts, Judge Mishler moved ahead with the selection of the jury. By July 20, the six jurors were chosen—two

Republicans, two Democrats, and two independents. Mishler had insisted on equality of party distribution, and as in the case of all matters in his court, he had his way.

On Tuesday, July 23, as Judge Mishler was about to begin the trial, Neuborne and Hart announced that a settlement had been reached. The judge listened soberly. No limit was to be placed on the money to be repaid. Hart said, "The people who say they want their contribution back would get it back. It's as simple as that." He didn't seem disturbed at the prospect of hordes descending on Republican headquarters, howling for their refunds. He revealed why getting money from the Republican party might be more difficult than giving it: "The claimants will obviously have to have some proof, like a canceled check or receipt of payment." This was clearly a settlement that favored good record keepers.

Neuborne called the settlement "a fair resolution of a long-standing issue." He admitted having no idea how much money was involved, since there was no way of determining how many intimidated government workers would accept his guarantee of anonymity and apply for a refund.

Al D'Amato told Hart that he was pleased with the settlement, since only harm to the party could come from publicly airing the 1 percent legal issues. It was worth the price to keep that from happening.

Mishler added only one requirement to the proposal: The accord was going to have to be reported back to Lorraine Cullen and John Jund, the only other named plaintiff. They must be given the chance to raise objections. If either objected, the attorneys must be prepared to go to trial the following Monday, July 29.

Outside the courtroom, tall, blond sanitation worker John Jund, standing by his young attorney, Julian Kaplan, expressed dissatisfaction with the Neuborne-Hart package. The pugnacious Kaplan informed the world that the proposed settlement "ignored" his client and he wasn't about to let that to happen. The soft-spoken Jund nodded his handsome head and said, "I still want my day in court."

Lorraine Cullen was worried. She had devoted ten years to fighting Margiotta's corrupt machine. Often her chief enemy had been the courts: The state court had dismissed her complaint; the federal court had allowed such long delays that she had wondered whether the case would ever be tried. But in the last month she had begun to hope that the party was finally going to be forced to account for the misery it had brought to the lives of thousands of people. Suddenly, Neuborne and Hart, neither one of whom represented her or Jund, were carving out a settlement between them, and it was obvious that the settlement they had reached didn't address her complaints. The Republican party was being allowed to escape without admitting any wrongdoing. That left Al D'Amato, Joe Mondello, and the behind-the-scenes Joe Margiotta with the power to continue punishing and extorting.

In addition, the Neuborne-Hart proposal didn't include relief for employees like herself and Jund who claimed they lost promotions and pay raises because they *refused* to contribute to the party. It only dealt with the grievances of the undeserving: a refund for those who had over the years *given* D'Amato and Margiotta money in the hope that they were buying an advantage. As a result, it offered restitution to those who didn't merit it, that is, those people who had benefited from their collusion with party leaders.

All the issues that brought her into this fight had been swept under the rug. D'Amato sat in the Senate posing as a concerned legislator, and the corrupt party apparatus still functioned largely undisturbed: Huge amounts of money continued to be squeezed out of government workers, though with greater finesse; D'Amato, Mondello, and Margiotta still dictated who received promotions and raises, and payoffs on government contracts still went to party loyalists.

It was time, she concluded, to draw on her last resources of strength and, by objecting to the settlement, force Judge Mishler to order the trial to begin.

TWENTY-TWO
FINALLY AFTER ELEVEN YEARS

On Monday, July 29, 1985, a half hour before the 9:30 A.M. scheduled start of the 1 percent case, the Uniondale courthouse was jammed with people. The story of how Al D'Amato and Joe Margiotta ran Nassau County for their own benefit was about to be made public. Under oath they would be forced to reveal the deals they had hidden from view. So many spectators tried to gain admittance to the lobby that a line had formed stretching back through the glass doorway toward the large concrete parking lot at the front of the building.

The courthouse was a circular structure, which created an interesting visual impact but made the internal architecture somewhat awkward. Since it was shaped like a pie, there were few absolutely square rooms in the two-story building. Each chamber, depending on its size, had to settle for some sort of slice from the center. Although it had the sparkle of something new, it had not been built on the gargantuan scale of a center-city courthouse; there were no marble pillars, no rotunda standing under an imposing dome.

Most of the Eastern District judges continued to occupy the larger courthouse in downtown Brooklyn. Judge Mishler was satisfied with these more modest accommodations: His Rockville Centre home was nearby, and he felt it was less of an imposition on his secretary, who—since the wearying, near disastrous surgery on his tumorous right ear—drove him to and from work each day.

During the half hour before the trial started, each of the attorneys stood in separate parts of the irregularly shaped lobby chatting with reporters and members of their retinues. There were four groups; three led by the independent counsels for the defendants: Ed Hart for the Republican party and Joe Margiotta; James Pascarella for Nassau County; and Daniel McCarthy for Hempstead. The fourth group was the plaintiffs' counsels, presided over by Burt Neuborne.

Neuborne stood in the center of the lobby and was explaining, to the largest audience, what he intended to say in his opening remarks.

His assistant, Carl ("Chip") Loewenson Jr. was a slender, brilliant young man, a Princeton graduate, and, in 1983, a graduate of Yale Law School; three years hence, as a member of Rudolph Giuliani's U.S. Attorney's office, he would be prosecuting one of the largest corporate-crime cases ever undertaken by the government. But at this moment, apprentice Chip Loewenson held his narrow, pale face motionless as he listened while Burt Neuborne, earnest and voluble, was answering the questions of even the humblest radio reporter from the weakest Long Island station.

"We're still talking about a settlement," Neuborne responded to a question. "I'm doubtful that it will ever happen, but D'Amato is putting pressure on the party to settle. He doesn't want to testify."

Ed Hart was holding sway over a contingent on the other side of the lobby. He seemed less relaxed than Neuborne, more prepared for a fight, somewhat reluctant to talk as his eyes darted around the lobby; but then, periodically, he would burst into a fit of authoritative declamation.

The town attorney, squared-jawed Daniel McCarthy, the tallest and heaviest barrister, remained half-concealed behind the bodies of his silent, inert staff near the corridor leading to the press room. He peered suspiciously at the other attorneys, occasionally voicing a "Humph!" in disapproval of something he was reluctant to communicate to the world.

James Pascarella, representing Nassau County, was an attorney with a successful criminal practice who had been hired by Francis

Purcell to defend the interests of the county, something Purcell didn't trust the county attorney to do. Pascarella was a dapper man of medium height whose shoulders were always sprinkled with dandruff, which seemed inexplicable because he appeared to be wearing a helmet-shaped toupee. He deftly avoided answering questions put by media inquisitors, radiating a reluctance to respond to any question not put to him by someone willing to pay a fee.

Lorraine Cullen and her husband, Frank, sat on a bench against the lobby wall with their attorney Evans Tilles. Although Lorraine and Frank talked to each other and to those who stopped by to encourage them, there was no exchange with Tilles. It was as though he were a complete stranger with whom they didn't feel completely comfortable.

While the lobby tumult was at its height, compact, peppy Julian Kaplan led his client, the towering, blond-bearded John Jund, into the courtroom. Facing his most important trial, Kaplan was intent on utilizing every second to prepare himself for his confrontation with the best that Margiotta's money could buy.

Jacob Mishler's courtroom had an air of the slapdash about it. There were no orderly rows of benches fastened to the floor. Instead, there were individual seats irregularly aligned in approximations of rows; each seat remained in line only until a shove from its occupant gave it an independent stance. The rear wall of the courtroom was a plastic accordion divider, which, when extended, cut down on the size of the room and allowed for only a few rows of seats for observers. Such an intimate space was unsuitable for a trial of this magnitude, and the divider had been rolled back on its tracks, almost doubling the room's size.

At the front, where one would expect to see the judge presiding, the witness box stood in splendid isolation. Because of the unusual shape of the building, the judge's elevated and majestic perch was thrust to the right and positioned in an oblique manner so that it squared off only with the wall against which it stood. The chamber had at least five walls and as many as seven, depending on whether the accordion divider was compacted or distended. Below the judge, the clerk and stenographer sat at a long counter that ran the full length of Mishler's desk.

To the left, the jury box clung to the wall; it had enough seats to hold six jurors and four alternates. A large attorney's lectern stood between the witness box and the visitors' section; it was on wheels, so that when a lawyer addressed the jury, he could turn the bulky lectern to his left; when examining a witness, he could swivel the lectern to face forward.

A line of shellacked oak tables had been positioned directly behind the lectern, forming a barricade that separated the front third of the court from the spectators' section. The thirteen attorneys in attendance sat at these tables, which were laden with cartons of documents, stacks of briefs, newspaper clippings, lists of questions, and compendiums of possibly useful cases.

The first irregular row of spectators' chairs was bivouacked approximately three feet behind the chairs on which the attorneys sat; that row was usually occupied by individuals who had some need to communicate with one or another of the attorneys. Lorraine and Frank Cullen sat in these seats, directly behind the ill-at-ease Evans Tilles.

Sol Goldfarb, the aggrieved garbage-truck weigher from the Oceanside dump, was also a disaffected Republican committee-man. He arrived early. This was the moment for which he had been waiting. He settled his enormous bulk on a seat at the left side of the courtroom, on the aisle that separated the press section from the spectators. Neuborne had told Sol, just before they entered the courtroom, that he wasn't sure whether he would call him as a witness. "Why?" Sol demanded in astonishment. "I'll tell everything. No one could be a better witness than me."

Neuborne had shrugged his shoulders and transparently struggled to avoid offending someone who had been so cooperative. "I don't know, Sol. I may have enough witnesses already. We'll see how things develop."

Sol had already discussed this unexpected turn of events with several reporters, some of whom he had known for years, as a result of contacting them to draw attention to his grievances. "Why shouldn't he want a witness like me, someone who he could depend on?" Sol called out to occupants of the press box. When he was finished with them, he rotated his massive body, wattled neck, and jowly cheeks in the direction of his neighbors in the main part of the spectators' section. A chorus of these ancient court regulars listened to Sol attentively, then offered their excited, authoritative responses.

There was a group of these older men who attended most trials of uncommon interest. They were retired lawyers, court clerks, accountants, and businessmen with an appetite for courtroom drama. There was a body of legal expertise among them exceeding that of any lawyer in the room. They were often on first-name terms with attorneys and judges, occasionally, in this suburban setting, visiting the judge's chambers and discussing some legal gossip over a cup of coffee. This was their Florida, their golf course, their crossword puzzle, and many a cheerful and intriguing day was spent in the confines of this, their Uniondale senior citizen's center.

Most other members of the audience were citizens who had a stake in the trial: They were potential witnesses, or they were former government workers who had an abiding anger about some indignity they had suffered at the hands of D'Amato or Margiotta. As in the case of Sol Goldfarb, this was a day for which they had been waiting; the desire for revenge smoldered in their eyes.

When Judge Mishler entered the courtroom at 9:30 A.M., the noisy chatter ceased. He slowly climbed the steps to his tilted perch, his white shoes showing briefly beneath the hem of his black robe. He sat in his tall leather chair and briefly stared across Neuborne's table to the far side of the room at the fully occupied press section.

The judge, staring at the cowed assemblage through his left eye, his right eye closed against his sagging cheek and sloping mouth, was a formidable sight.

Three women artists, their pastel chalks in hand, began to sketch the somber Mishler. The youngest, a chubby, attractive blonde in her late twenties, moved to the side of Neuborne's table, squatted down, and, balancing her three-by-two-foot pad on a bent knee, began her earnest efforts to capture the scene for television. The two older women, better established in their careers, since they were on the permanent payroll of NBC and CBS, rested comfortably in chairs they had placed in the aisle between Neuborne's table and the press box. The more experienced artists immediately began working on Jacob Mishler's eyes, while the younger one blocked out the judge's diagonal bench and the U.S. eagle seal in the circular plaque that was fastened on the wall above the judge's head.

Remarking that he had been informed that a settlement hadn't yet been reached, Mishler said he would stand for no further delay. Within moments Neuborne was at the lectern, hauling it around so that he faced the jury. As he spoke over the next two hours, Mishler intently studied his profile, occasionally reaching up to wipe away a tear that oozed from the corner of his closed eye.

Neuborne wanted the jury to understand that he represented government workers, none of whom were in the courtroom; he would refer to them solely as "the class." Although they were anonymous, they were, in reality, people much like themselves, with families, bills to pay, and fears about the future.

He said that the case was "about a machine that put extreme pressure on employees." Speaking in a gentle but eager voice that had a professorial reasonableness about it, he said that the party kept detailed records of those who gave and those who did not and that the records were made available to department heads who had the power to grant raises and promotions. The party, in fact, aggressively solicited campaign contributions in the workplace, often using supervisors, who were party officials, to enforce its demands.

Neuborne adjusted his metal-rimmed glasses and quietly stated that this corrupt system exerted its influence over the lives of innocent workers because the town of Hempstead and Nassau County had delegated its hiring discretion to the Republican party. The true government of Nassau County was the Republican party, a government whose leaders were not chosen by the people.

Ed Hart's appearance was in vivid contrast to Neuborne's: He wore a gray suit that didn't have the well-worn look of Neuborne's blue pencil stripe. The contrast was most noticeable in their speech. Neuborne spoke precisely in well-modulated, polished phraseology, careful not to overstate his position; Hart's voice boomed out to the farthest reaches of the court; he addressed the jury, but his real target was the universe.

He described the party's hiring and money-raising practices "as nothing more than political patronage," which, he claimed, was a "time-honored practice dating back to colonial times." This statement suggested that Hart's reliance on the "long-standing theory" was his major justification for the party's extortions.

The source of the party's problem, Hart said, was that when Eugene Nickerson had become county executive in the 1960s, he had fired all Republican employees. This was an overstated version of the facts, but it was, after all, Mr. Hart's turn at bat. In the league in which Hart played you were allowed any number of wild swings without risking the possibility that Jacob Mishler might call you out.

Standing near the jury box, his hands clasped in front of him, as though appealing for understanding, Hart explained how the jurors should view the party's activities. People gave what they did not because they were forced to but because they feared losing their jobs if the Republican party lost. He seemed to be suggesting that a person in fear of losing his job was justified in bribing those who were in a position to save it.

And then, in a burst of frankness typical of Hart, he added, "This might have been avoided if everyone was hired under civil service, but we don't have that system."

The other attorneys each had their opportunity to address the jury. James Pascarella, representing Nassau County and Francis Purcell, made a conventional appeal—"be open-minded." He wanted the jury to accept his contention that his client had nothing to do with the charges being made against the other defendants. He was instantly trying to distance himself from Hart and Town Attorney McCarthy. Pascarella signaled that it was every man for himself. Regardless of the bonds of friendship and self-interest that normally tied the defendants together, his voice would only be raised on behalf of the man who was paying his fee.

With tight gestures that appeared to be constrained by a fear that too much might be revealed, Pascarella told the jurors that he wasn't going to deny there had been "contributions." But, he added, there was no crime involved, since "we will prove that there was no coercion." Then, in a rash attempt to buttress his argument, he alluded to the U.S. Attorney's investigation of the 1 percent case. "No one was indicted," he remarked.

Pascarella's reference to a criminal investigation that was separate from this civil RICO action led to the first sidebar at Mishler's tribunal. All thirteen lawyers assembled beneath the judge's

Cyclopean gaze, accompanied by the stenographer and her recording machine. The judge activated a sounder that filled the room with a buzz. Henceforth, anything said at his bar could be heard only by the row of barristers, who stood like attentive students.

After five minutes of conversation, Mishler made a short motion with his hand, waved the attorneys back to their stations, and turned off the electronic static. In the polite, almost deferential voice he always used when addressing the jury, Mishler instructed them to wipe out Pascarella's references to an investigation. He advised them that that investigation had nothing to do with this trial. Indisputably, that contention was false. The trial stemmed from that investigation, and although Pascarella had been willing to concede the connection, Mishler, always anxious to narrow the scope of this unprecedented trial, was not.

Then, in a philosophical aside that seemed to come out of the blue, Mishler said that he wanted the jury to remember: "Our system today cannot exist without political contributions."

Burt Neuborne cringed; he turned and glanced at the press box, his head tilted, his eyes narrowed in barely suppressed exasperation. Frank Kenna's Astoria pupil had copied his long-dead Queens Republican boss's lessons in stone, and Neuborne suddenly realized that in this Uniondale court there was more than Al D'Amato, Joe Margiotta, and the Nassau Republican party to overcome.

TWENTY-THREE
HOW TO GET A JOB IN GOVERNMENT

S oon after the attorneys concluded their opening remarks, Judge Mishler announced two key decisions: He would limit the period of complaint to the three years between December 14, 1973, and December 14, 1976, and would allow Al D'Amato's June 9, 1971, smoking-gun letter to be introduced as Neuborne's first piece of evidence.

D'Amato's letter, which obtained a raise for sanitationman Robert Marcus by means of a bribe to the party, dramatically established that there was a 1 percent kickback conspiracy. Mishler might well have excluded this damaging evidence, since it was written over two years before the complaint period he had just established. But the party could take comfort in his other decision. By limiting the complaints to three years, now ten years in the past, the judge was shielding the party from a monetary catastrophe. Neuborne's "class" had suddenly been reduced to those who were working for Nassau or Hempstead during that short span, were still alive, and were in the grip of a record-keeping obsession. Mishler was also allowing party leaders to assume an air of hurt innocence: Perhaps this sort of conspiracy had existed during those three years in the dim past, but why tar the current Republican leaders, who were chaste, with the sins of men long gone from the scene?

Mishler's decision to narrow the time span was made although he knew that the party in settlement negotiations with Neuborne had conceded that the extortion was in place from 1976 to 1983. In pushing back the party's period of liability, Mishler was also ignoring the fact that Joe Mondello, Margiotta's successor, had repeatedly said he had ended the 1 percent practice when he took over from the boss in May 1983. Wasn't it clear, therefore, that the complaint period should have run at least through the middle of 1983?

It wasn't clear to Judge Mishler. The effect of his first decision was to limit the party's risk, although it still left a long line of individual Republican defendants swinging in the breeze and still allowed for the possibility of the first conviction of an American political party.

Neuborne began the plaintiff's case by calling Donald Woolnough to the stand. Woolnough had been a sheriff in Nassau County from 1961 to 1965, when Eugene Nickerson—exercising the right of a Democratic victor to imitate his Republican predecessors—fired him. Woolnough was swiftly provided with a snug berth as the assistant to the Nassau party chairman. He held that post during Joe Margiotta's reign and continued to serve in that capacity under Joe Mondello after Margiotta resigned in 1983.

Neuborne had interviewed Woolnough prior to the trial and had an agreement with him similar to the one he had made with Margiotta. Neuborne told me he had offered Woolnough "a terrific deal." Woolnough was "on the hook for potentially enormous liability," Neuborne said. But if he cooperated, Neuborne was going to allow him "to be immune to personal liability."

Neuborne said he viewed Woolnough as "the guy that always carries out the illegal orders and never has the guts to say no. He was the cog without which the machine couldn't work. He took orders from the boss. Whoever was in there was his boss. He just carried it out, and it was up to them to decide whether there was anything improper about it."

Neuborne didn't feel Woolnough was "a dummy." It was "self-interest" that explained the role Woolnough played for over twenty years. "There was some sort of vacuum in his mind where his sense of responsibility should be. I don't think he felt any guilt."

Since he had such a negative view of this key player in the conspiracy, why, I asked Neuborne, had he given Woolnough such a
"terrific" deal?

"I needed that testimony to ensure victory for the class," he
explained with his usual show of sincerity. "My principal responsibility was to establish on the public record in a way that was clear,
that this happened and it couldn't be denied."

Woolnough was a bespectacled, gray-haired man of average
height. He wore a dark business suit and a solid maroon tie, incon-
gruously highlighted by a pale pink shirt. He was sweating slightly
in the air-conditioned courtroom and answered all questions slowly
and only, in each instance, after a moment of deliberation. In 1971,
he said, Al D'Amato had recommended that Alfred Riehl, former
mayor of Island Park, be appointed as County Executive Ralph
Caso's personnel director.

When Riehl's name was mentioned, James Pascarella, who had
been perusing documents on his table, became attentive, almost
agitated. Riehl had been a county employee and therefore of special interest to the county's attorney. Riehl, working in an official
capacity, could tie the county directly to the conspiracy.

Woolnough told how he had called Riehl into his Westbury party
office to discuss his new government duties. County Executive
Caso, Riehl's new boss, wasn't present. Riehl clearly saw nothing
unusual about the fact that he was being briefed about his county
job by an official of the Republican party.

Neuborne stood in front of the witness box eying the nervous,
sweating Woolnough and asked, "Can you tell us exactly what was
said in that conversation?"

"It was to discuss how we were to fill any jobs that came our
way," Woolnough responded without smiling.

With that statement, at the very beginning of the trial, the party
had been irrevocably tied to the conspiracy.

Neuborne then had the ashen-faced, trembling Woolnough
describe how the party actually controlled county employment.
"Riehl called me and told me he had such-and-such job available.
For the most part they were in the labor class . . . electricians,
plumbers, carpenters. This was," Woolnough said in a voice so low
that it seemed aimed only at Neuborne, "up to a few years ago . . .
say, a year ago . . . ," at which point Riehl retired. Woolnough

would take Riehl's description of the job into Margiotta's office and discuss it with the boss.

"He'd tell me to call a particular leader. I'd do just that . . . and asked him [the leader] if he had someone . . . and they'd get back to me with a name. . . . I'd say, send them in to see me. . . .

"Margiotta would always see attorneys or if they wanted to be a deputy in one of the departments. [He] saw the people at the higher end of the salary scale."

As Woolnough's discomfort grew, Neuborne asked him, "What did you say during this interview?"

"I usually asked them whether they belong to the Republican club. . . . I asked them if they could be of assistance to the man [leader] who sent them to me."

Neuborne wanted to know how extensive these interviews had been. Was this merely an occasional practice?

"I'd say it [these interviews] was in the thousands."

As to the purpose of the interviews, why exactly were they being held?

"Of course, to indicate we were in the business of winning elections and that they should be of help."

If the applicant recited the correct answers, Woolnough would send the happy pilgrim to Riehl with a sealed letter authorizing employment. Since the questions had all been political and the applicants had been prescreened by one of the sixty-nine clubhouse leaders—such as Island Park's Al D'Amato—the possibility of a misspoken answer was remote. These sessions with Woolnough were to reinforce a lesson the applicant had already learned from teachers such as D'Amato and to overawe the supplicant with the majesty of Margiotta's chancellery.

Neuborne began a routine that lasted several minutes: He showed Woolnough forms that were filled out by applicants for government jobs, forms that existed solely for the use of the Republican party. Hart, Pascarella, McCarthy, Kaplan, and Tilles gathered around the witness box as Woolnough glanced at the documents. After he had authenticated them, Neuborne showed each member of the jury a sample copy.

Woolnough then informed the jury that the applicant's litmus test consisted of two questions on the form: Are you registered to vote, and are you a member of the Republican party?

Woolnough explained that the notation on the applicant's form assigning him to a specific job was always written by him, in his capacity as a Republican party official. In short, the individual's ability to perform the job for which he was being hired was, at best, a peripheral issue. Democrats with the most exquisite skills were ineligible for employment.

Although Hart and Pascarella, in their opening remarks, had insisted that a large number of jobs in Nassau were under the protection of the civil service—many of them requiring the successful completion of written and oral tests—Woolnough didn't agree with the party's advocates that those tests inhibited Margiotta from selecting a politically reliable work force. Since Democrats had been systematically excluded from entry-level civil service jobs, the subsequent promotional tests were not available to them.

Once ensconced in their sinecures, these certified Republicans—whose aspiration was now to obtain a raise or a promotion—only had to wait long enough to allow them to approach their political leaders without undue embarrassment. Although the request went through the employee's department head and thence to Mr. Riehl's office, the ambitious employee knew that eventually Woolnough would call his executive leader to see whether "he approved or disapproved."

At this point, Judge Mishler, who, despite age and infirmity, seemed less worn by the proceedings than any of the attorneys, brought the first day of the trial to an end, announcing that everyone should be at their station promptly at 10:00 A.M.

After the court session, Senator D'Amato's office released a statement in which a plaintive, anguished call for personal justice can be detected. "The so-called one percent contribution was there when I came into government." He was, in short, not an innovator, merely a man who recognized the value of a device that had been tested by time.

Trying to put things in perspective, D'Amato added, "It was generally considered that a voluntary contribution of one percent was a fair guide in support of the party." Then he concluded, "In retrospect, it may have been wrong."

The next morning, in an endeavor to make his case against the county as strong as possible, Neuborne's first question concerned

Woolnough's ability to approve or disapprove raises and promotions in the larger county as well as Hempstead: Woolnough responded that that power lay entirely within his office.

"Did local leaders have the power to disapprove raises for county workers?" Neuborne continued.

"Yes," Woolnough said. "The leader will call me, or write a letter, saying so-and-so wants to become, let's say, a maintenance manager. . . . I speak to Margiotta. If he approves, I call the department. They know, if I call, it's a Republican matter."

Neuborne began to explore the other face of the party coin, occasionally fingering his gold-rimmed glasses. He resembled a young Charles Laughton, fleshy lips, pudgy cheeks, quivering with sincerity. Woolnough had described how prospective employees got their jobs—and, eventually, promotions and raises—with party help; now, Neuborne wanted to know, what did they have to do to earn such favored treatment? After all, there were tens of thousands of registered Republicans who would have liked to work for the county, yet only a small number of them were honored with Margiotta's endorsement. What set that honored few apart from less fortunate party members?

The answer: money. Government jobs in Nassau County were bought, or to put it in the more lyrical phraseology of party collectors: "If you want to get, you have to give."

Neuborne established this point by asking, "While you worked for the Republican party, to your knowledge, were contributions to the Republican party solicited from workers while they were on duty."

Woolnough's answer escaped from him with a reluctant hiss: "Yes."

Plaintiff's Exhibit 6 was then introduced; it was a record of collections made at each employment site, including the name of the employee and the amount of his contribution.

Exhibit 7, dredged up from another carton by Chip Loewenson, consisted of thousands of receipts that had originally been made out in triplicate. One copy had been mailed back to the donor— these were the copies the good record keepers might someday have to produce. A second copy went to the Executive Leader—for example, Al D'Amato—so that a donation made on the job by his club member wouldn't escape his attention. The final copy was retained by Woolnough, a practice the party no doubt regretted, since it made possible this black moment in Judge Mishler's court.

Once a year, Woolnough testified, he would order computer printouts from government payroll offices (Exhibit 8). He then sent a copy of the printouts to the sixty-nine executive leaders, accompanied by a dollar figure, which was the quota required from each of the thousand election districts in the county. These payroll lists, Woolnough commented, were no longer sent to the leaders, "since the legal matters with Mr. Margiotta started."

Woolnough continued to punch holes in the defense case. The party, he testified, had two ways of bypassing civil service. Margiotta's office had the final say in the appointment of all provisional jobs, and according to the June 1985 state civil service audit, 53.3 percent of Hempstead's employees were provisional. The second technique was to use the loophole in the civil service law created by the "one-in-three rule." Woolnough would simply tell the department head which one of the top three candidates Margiotta wanted selected.

In an attempt to show the stranglehold that the party had on Nassau County government workers, Neuborne asked Woolnough to authenticate a letter addressed to him by Andrew J. Parise, the Lawrence-Cedarhurst executive leader. In a hushed courtroom, the June 21, 1973, letter was read aloud:

> Dear Don:
> Enclosed is my club check in the amount of $100 payable to the Town of Hempstead Finance Committee for Alfred Spitzer of 51 West Avenue, Meadowmere Park.
> I spoke to Al re his contribution. He was under the impression that the check he gave our club was going to be forwarded to Headquarters. He was never approached by any one else in his department.
> I would appreciate it if you would take him off the T.S. list. It really is my fault; I should have made sure he knew what his obligations were.

Neuborne asked Woolnough: What was the "T.S. list" to which Parise had referred? Margiotta's *keeper of the list* explained that the initials stood for "Tough Shit." The Parise letter made it clear that if you didn't pay off the party collectors, there was a penalty. Now that Parise's club member understood what his "obligations" were, he was once again eligible for the benefits unavailable to anyone whose name was on Woolnough's list.

Neuborne was pleased with Woolnough's testimony. After a conference with the judge during which he asked Mishler to strike Woolnough's name from the complaint as an individual defendant, he turned to an attentive Woolnough and said: "I offered to release you from personal responsibility in return for your testimony."

With that act of generosity, Neuborne was living up to his end of the deal, signaling to all future witnesses that he was as good as his word. Later, when I asked him whether he didn't think he was being too generous, he responded: "I think Woolnough, perhaps, should have been prosecuted."

The television artists, working with the same intensity as Michelangelo, spent the lunch hour finishing their Sistine Chapels while sitting cross-legged on the grass in front of the court. They were urged on by the mobile studio technicians, who rested nearby in their transmitting trucks, eating their brown-bag lunches. When the final pastel shading had been chalked in, the combat sketches of Mishler, Neuborne, Hart, and Pascarella were taped to the face of the building. Cameramen stood in front of them, adjusting their lenses to the bright sunlight, then photographing them for transmission to the Manhattan studios where they would be processed for the evening telecast. It was important to get these routine matters out of the way so that upcoming interviews, photographed after court had been adjourned, could be handled on a deadline basis.

At 1:50, Hart began a gentle and leading cross-examination of Woolnough. Wasn't it the custom for employees to make about 1 percent contributions to the Republican party? Isn't it true that since the mid-1970s contributions have not been carried on in the same manner? Hart seemed to be conceding the basic truth of the charges; his strategy was clearly aimed at damage control—to make it appear that the party's extortion tactics had been abandoned.

Daniel McCarthy, the town's square-jawed attorney, now rose, clearing his throat ostentatiously. Mishler was immediately restive.

He sat forward, as though prepared to rein in the tall, bespectacled McCarthy as soon as he made the first of what Mishler knew would be a long list of inevitable errors.

McCarthy tried to ignore the judge as he questioned Woolnough in a gruff voice, striving to appear confident. But his frequent, uneasy glances at Mishler suggested that his mind was occupied with the possibility that at any moment his longtime antagonist might interrupt with some sarcastic comment.

McCarthy followed Hart's strategy: He wanted it understood that the patronage practices Hempstead was being accused of may have occurred in the past, but they had been ended years earlier. Unlike the haughty McCarthy, Woolnough was under oath; at this moment he was the only Republican whose lies could result in a perjury charge. It was too much of a risk; therefore, within moments, Woolnough told McCarthy that contrary to the implications of the town attorney's question, during the last year he had made about a hundred job recommendations to the town's personnel director. As far as he knew, not a single one had been rejected.

A guilty look spread across McCarthy's reddening face as he sensed he had damaged his case. Glancing sideways at Mishler, McCarthy ended his cross-examination and stomped back to his seat, almost directly under Jacob Mishler's baleful glare.

Woolnough's two-day ordeal was soon completed; he stepped down at 2:53. During this recess Neuborne strolled over to the young blond artist and, with a charming, boyish look on his plump face, asked to see her drawings of him. He laughed gaily as she turned the pages of her sketch pad. Reporters joined them, and Neuborne discussed his reaction to Woolnough's testimony. Someone in the crowd told him that he thought that with Woolnough's testimony and the corroborating documents Neuborne had proved his case. Neuborne looked pleased but dubious.

Robert Livingston, who had taken over as Hempstead receiver of taxes when D'Amato had been promoted to supervisor in 1971, was the next witness. Livingston was an accountant by trade, and it was therefore his habit to save every document that had led to the preservation of the only extant copy of D'Amato's 'smoking-gun' letter. He was a slender man in his mid-fifties who looked like a well-turned-out waiter. During any pause, he would deftly smooth down his silver hair. He wore a blue pencil-striped suit and the Nassau version of the Eton tie.

Although he didn't testify as to the manner in which D'Amato had conducted their office, he described party practices that it seemed unlikely Livingston had invented. For example, from the moment he had taken over from D'Amato, employees in the tax receiver's office handed in their annual party contributions while on the job; he made no reference to this being his idea. "I'd forward them on to Republican headquarters," he remarked with pride in his efficiency. Furthermore, if someone wanted a raise, "then you might check with his leader to see if there was any problem," Livingston said, smoothing down his hair which was perfectly in place.

What kind of problem might require such a consultation? Neuborne asked. Responding as an accountant who knew his expert testimony would only be used against someone else, he said, "Maybe the individual did not help at campaign time. It could be contributions. . . ."

In his role as executive leader, he stated, when one of his committeemen recommended someone for a job, he would always contact Woolnough. Occasionally, Woolnough would phone and ask him to supply a candidate for a job available somewhere in the county.

As in the case of all sixty-nine executive leaders, he had received receipts from Woolnough indicating how much each member of his club had contributed at his place of employment. Livingston revealed that when he had taken over his club he had prepared index cards for all public employees living in his executive area; Woolnough's receipts were stapled to the back of these cards. "It was much easier to work on index cards," he said with the air of a man who knew how to handle paperwork.

Alfred Riehl testified on Wednesday, July 31, the third day of the trial. The balding, timid man sat in the witness seat with a Band-Aid pasted to the wrinkles above the bridge of his pendulous nose. His aged face was stamped with a pained look.

Neuborne had been uncertain of what D'Amato's Island Park crony would say. "He was never a defendant," Neuborne explained, "so I had no leverage on Riehl. I never had a chance to talk to him alone." But the threat of perjury was apparently enough to cause Riehl to describe his role in the conspiracy.

Riehl confirmed Woolnough's testimony tying the county to the conspiracy; he never authorized an appointment or a raise unless Woolnough approved it. Pascarella made a feeble attempt to resurrect the county's standing in cross-examination, but there was no way to refute the fact that for years Riehl had acted as the party's agent in the county's personnel office.

Hart's strategy of limiting the party's liability to the three-year period—1973–76—was also seriously damaged. Riehl, who had remained in his key county position until his retirement in 1984, said that the system of party committeemen recommending people for jobs remained in place "as long as I was there."

Woolnough, Livingston, and Riehl spoke about the corruption involved in job placement as though it were ordinary office routine. They had become so habituated to it that its illegality and unfairness seemed to have escaped their notice. When Neuborne brought it to their attention, they had difficulty understanding the nature of the problem. They had years earlier thrust aside the thought that their activities violated the law; after all, wasn't a U.S. senator and all Nassau County government officials taking part in it? And, most important, weren't they profiting from it? What did fairness have to do with making your way safely through the jungle out there?

The party had been reduced to the hope that the jurors' concern about legality and fairness would be as negligible as that shown by the trial's first witnesses.

TWENTY-FOUR
THE EMPEROR'S CLOTHES

J oe Margiotta was scheduled to come to the docket on the fourth day of the trial. Burt Neuborne decided to herald the boss's appearance with the testimony of a rank-and-file government worker, in this way showing the impact of Margiotta's brand of politics on an ordinary individual. Gaspar Cangemi, a tall, muscular garbageman with a receding hairline, too unimportant to be noticed by a politician like Margiotta, was the witness Neuborne chose as his prototypical victim.

Cangemi told a simple story. In 1968, in need of a job to support his young family, he had been told to speak to Uniondale committeeman John Pingle, soon to be president of Margiotta's club and soon after that director of the Coliseum. Pingle's most carefully executed responsibility at the Coliseum was to place applicants sent by Margiotta on the bloated payroll. But in this earlier case, Pingle placed Cangemi in the Sanitation Department.

In 1970, a year after Pingle got Cangemi a job on the back of a garbage truck, Cangemi approached his supervisor, Frank Castagnaro, and requested a promotion. Cangemi quotes Castagnaro as saying, " 'If you want to get, you have to give.' " Cangemi recalled, "He specifically said one percent of my salary."

Cangemi told Castagnaro that on a salary of $7,000, with four children to support, he couldn't scrape together the required $70. "I suggested installments, simply because I couldn't afford it at that

213

particular time." This satisfied Castagnaro, and he accepted a twenty-five-dollar check as a first installment.

When no promotion resulted and Castagnaro answered all his questions with a shrug, Cangemi sought relief in that desert called Hempstead sanitation commissioner William Landman. Returning from Landman's office as parched for sympathy as when he had entered, Cangemi sought out Pingle and asked him to arrange a meeting with Margiotta. Pingle told Cangemi that Margiotta was "unavailable."

While passing Margiotta's office one day, the desperate Cangemi noticed that the boss's car was parked on the street; he decided to go in. Cangemi told the jurors that Margiotta snapped at him: "I understand you're causing a lot of havoc."

Cangemi protested that he was trying to "do the right thing." The boss angrily retorted, "What, twenty-five dollars?" According to Cangemi, Margiotta knew exactly who he was and had spent a good deal of time working up his indignation over the garbageman's tardy installment payments.

Dejected, Cangemi returned to his home, a five-minute drive. He was shocked to find Committeeman Pingle and one of his job supervisors waiting at the curb in town cars. The two party potentates then read Cangemi the riot act; he would never get anywhere unless he contributed. Cangemi testified that Pingle said, "if I wanted my upgrading, I'd have to contribute my one percent." In order to get ahead in Nassau County, Pingle explained, you have to pay; one percent was " 'the name of the game.' " Cangemi told the jurors that it was the last time he ever contributed anything.

Within days of seeing Margiotta, Cangemi was transferred from his sanitation-truck job to the basement furnace pit of the Oceanside incinerator plant. Years later, Sol Goldfarb, who had worked at the Oceanside dump, took me there. I looked down through a grating in the floor of the plant where Cangemi had toiled. As I peered into the shrouded pit, the fire that roasted Cangemi was no longer burning. The bottom of the pit, twenty feet below me, was caked with ancient ash; the walls surrounding this Pompeian scene were blackened. Margiotta had found the proper setting for the inferno into which he had Cangemi placed.

Two months in the pit resulted in a back injury, and when, after a short recovery period, Cangemi came back to work, he was reassigned to his original duty as a helper on a garbage truck. The party allowed him to remain in that capacity for the next fifteen years, and it wasn't until the approach of the trial, in 1984, that he was moved up front and promoted to garbage-truck driver.

Margiotta suddenly made his entrance at the rear of the courtroom. The former boss had put on weight and lost the trim form he sported when he emerged from jail; but for a man of his bulk, he moved swiftly. He made his way to the far side of the room and seated himself in an empty part of the spectators' section. Everyone's attention was focused on him.

The confident resident of Old Brookville wore a three-piece dark blue suit and a blue shirt; he looked as if he had just come from having his beaming face shaved at the Uniondale barbershop. Heads of the defense lawyers bowed in his direction. Other well-conditioned souls began to follow suit, but a disapproving glance from Judge Mishler ended that display of homage. The lady artists immediately turned over their pages and, from long distance, began sketching the tanned defendant.

Squared-jawed Daniel McCarthy stepped forward to cross-examine Cangemi. Judge Mishler shifted in his seat and wiped a tear from his closed eye. McCarthy began to shower Cangemi with questions about his shortcomings as a garbage collector over his sixteen-year career. Isn't it true he had submitted unauthorized letters of absence during the early 1970s? Hempstead's defender pointed out to the jury that these vital notes had not been signed by Cangemi's doctor but by the doctor's nurse. Hadn't Cangemi complained against fellow workers for "being drunk at five o'clock in the morning," for "reckless driving," "for bullying workers," and "for being lazy"?

McCarthy implied that Cangemi was a chronic complainer; he agreed with Margiotta that Cangemi didn't know his place. Waving Cangemi's work record, which had through the years been peppered by Margiotta's handpicked supervisors with failings of similar moment, McCarthy demanded, wasn't it true he had used foul language against fellow workers and his supervisors? There was a burst of laughter from the spectators' section, where many sanitation workers had gathered for Cangemi's appearance. Sol Goldfarb slapped his knee zestfully over the thought that Hempstead's district attorney was shocked to learn sanitationmen used profanity.

Neuborne's rebuttal question for Cangemi: Was it his habit to curse his supervisors? Looking like a middle-aged choirboy, Cangemi said he never cursed them unless they cursed him first.

Applause rang loudly in the courtroom. Judge Mishler banged his gavel vigorously and with some heat demanded of the chastened spectators, "Where do you think you are?"

The jury was excused at 12:35 P.M. and told to return at 1:30. As soon as they had been led out, Judge Mishler addressed the packed courtroom. He was irate. "This is the first time in my twenty-five years as a judge that people have applauded or attempted to influence the jury." His one eye glaring at the miscreants, he warned, "If it happens again, I will not hesitate to hold you in contempt of court." Exploding from his chair, he stormed from the room, his white sporty shoes leading the way.

When court resumed, Margiotta was sworn in. Neuborne began by phrasing his questions politely, almost gently. Margiotta seldom responded without somehow referring to Neuborne as "sir." "Yes, sir," "No, sir," "That is correct, sir," rang respectfully from the bold sound chamber of Margiotta's mouth.

Each of Margiotta's responses was prefaced by a self-serving peroration. Neuborne had struck his bargain with the boss; as long as Margiotta didn't excessively deviate from the pact, the ACLU's director of legal services was willing to allow Margiotta his constitutional right to project himself in the best possible light.

Neuborne started by having Margiotta recite his résumé. With the exception of his eleven years in the state assembly and private law practice, he had been exclusively on the payroll of the Republican party. Tightening the noose, Neuborne asked:

But you never held any position either in the town or the county that had anything to do with personnel or hiring, did you?
MARGIOTTA: No, sir.

Neuborne then wanted to know whether Margiotta's assistant Donald Woolnough, and his staff, acted "on their own or did they act on orders?"

216

Margiotta seemed offended by the suggestion that anyone on his fourteen-member headquarters payroll would think of exercising an independent judgment. Ronald Reagan's defense in the Iran-Contra scandal—*Ollie North and Admiral Poindexter never told me what was going on*—was not for him. He raised his head and puffed out his chest. "They acted under my supervision and direction as the chairman of the party."

Neuborne then asked about Margiotta's relationship with Alfred Riehl, whom Margiotta described as "the personnel director in the county." Speaking of his power without shame or exaggeration, Margiotta remarked, "He [Riehl] was recommended for that position [by D'Amato], and I met with him, and I interviewed him, and he ultimately obtained the position."

Neuborne wanted to know what sort of criteria Margiotta used to decide whether Riehl would be a good man for Ralph Caso to hire.

NEUBORNE: Did you talk to him at all about winning elections for the Republican party?
MARGIOTTA: I always talked to everybody that I interviewed, that I would hope that he would help us win elections and work on behalf of the party to help us elect our candidates. (sic)

When Woolnough told Margiotta that Riehl had signaled that a vacancy had occurred, Margiotta described his invariable response:

MARGIOTTA: Well, first I would normally ask, do we have any pending applications from any of the leaders, and if so, he would tell me, and maybe we would allocate the positions to those communities, or if we didn't, I would designate the leaders.

Riehl never considered placing an ad in the local "Help Wanted" columns or alerting Democratic headquarters that the county needed workers. As far as Margiotta was concerned, although he had no official connection with the county government, it was his duty to fill all its vacant jobs.

NEUBORNE: Can you give us an estimate of how many of these interviews you conducted during your tenure as party chairman?

MARGIOTTA: Myself?

NEUBORNE: Yes.

MARGIOTTA: I would say probably several hundred.

NEUBORNE: When you sent someone over to the governmental person, as you put it, in the normal course, were they hired?

MARGIOTTA: . . . I would say normally they were.

Neuborne wanted to know whether Margiotta's power extended beyond the ability to dictate who was to be hired, and Margiotta pompously admitted he also controlled raises and promotions. Why would a clubhouse leader like Al D'Amato recommend giving a raise or a promotion? Neuborne asked.

MARGIOTTA: I know when I was a local leader why I [would] turn down a raise. [If] I was asked for political clearing of somebody who is not working for the party, that didn't . . . circulate petitions, didn't canvas and distribute literature, I would not be inclined to give them a political recommendation.

NEUBORNE: So the decisions of the local leaders were based on political considerations?

MARGIOTTA: Yes, sir.

NEUBORNE: And could contributions be one of those considerations?

MARGIOTTA: It could possibly, yes, sir.

To make sure the jury knew that this extortion was not only *possible* but that it was an unvarying practice, Neuborne got Margiotta to admit he sent club leaders printouts of the salaries and contributions of public employees living in their district. Neuborne felt that local leaders like Al D'Amato were the key operators in the party's extortion racket. Without their active participation, the squeeze couldn't work.

Margiotta had become squeamish. Neuborne asked, "What was the purpose of [local leaders] learning a salary, Mr. Margiotta?" As

218

though he were unaware of the 1 percent annual extortion, Margiotta lied, "I don't know what the purpose was."

Within moments he seemed to realize his answer wasn't credible, and in a fumbling, unconvincing manner, he added: " . . . the purpose was to enable the local leader who is in his area to try to encourage [government workers on the computer printout] to join the organization, to try to support the organization."

Neuborne turned the heat up a notch on his somewhat less self-assured witness:

NEUBORNE: Mr. Margiotta, have you ever heard of a custom or practice of contributing one percent of government employees' salary to the Republican party?
MARGIOTTA: Yes, sir.
NEUBORNE: . . . Have you ever called these one percent contributions "union dues," Mr. Margiotta?
MARGIOTTA: I could have made a statement that I thought that political contributions were like union dues.

Neuborne wanted the jurors to understood that if a government worker didn't pay his "union dues," he couldn't get promoted or receive a raise.

NEUBORNE: Wouldn't an employee feel pressured to give one percent when the person who was [asking for] the contribution also is a person who could veto his raise?

"I object," Hart interjected. Judge Mishler didn't wait for Hart to explain his objection. "I will allow it if you can answer it," he said, leaning expectantly toward the agitated witness.

Margiotta, apparently too flustered to take advantage of Mishler's invitation to invent some evasion, instead rose to the challenge implicit in Mishler's relentless one-eyed stare.

MARGIOTTA: I can see where a person's subjective frame of mind, he would feel a certain amount of pressure when the person who was soliciting the contribution also is a person who could make a recommendation in relation to his particular situation. (sic)

Having confessed he understood exactly what he was doing when he demanded 1 percent kickbacks from government workers, Margiotta now had to deal with a concrete example of that type of extortion. Neuborne read Margiotta the famous letter from Al D'Amato to Donald Woolnough. " 'I have spoken to Mr. Margiotta and he has indicated to me the raise for Mr. Robert Marcus of the Sanitation Department would be approved if he took care of the one percent. . . .' "

Neuborne was incapable of projecting menace or suggesting the nature of the terrible fate awaiting sinners who didn't tell the truth; he depended for his effectiveness on careful preparation, a knowledge of the law, and a bright mind. All of these excellent lawyerly qualities were undermined by his innate decency. "Do you remember having such a conversation with Mr. D'Amato?" he asked in an utterly reasonable voice.

Margiotta responded without a blink, "I do not have any recollection of any such conversation." It was, after all, a conversation fifteen years in the past.

"Are you saying," Neuborne asked mildly, "that the conversation did not take place or that you simply don't recall?"

"I don't remember," Margiotta answered calmly.

Anxious to take full advantage of his most dramatic documentary evidence, Neuborne asked:

> Did you have frequent meetings with him [D'Amato] in those days?
> MARGIOTTA: Oh, yes.
> NEUBORNE: You were on good terms with him?
> MARGIOTTA: Yes, sir.
> NEUBORNE: Do you know of any reason why Mr. D'Amato would be fabricating a story like that?

Although Margiotta was not his client, Pascarella jumped up and bellowed, "Objection."

Mishler responded, "Sustained," and that line of questioning was effectively aborted.

Thwarted in that direction, Neuborne continued to query his resuscitated witness.

NEUBORNE: If an employee failed to make a contribution to the party, Mr. Margiotta, would you feel less inclined to help him?
MARGIOTTA: That never entered into any recommendation I made, Mr. Neuborne.

One wonders what persuades a witness to lie so openly. Margiotta had already testified that whether an employee contributed to the party was a central issue when he decided to recommend or deny a salary increase.

Neuborne persisted: "Do you know the reason why these raises were turned down?"

"No, sir," Margiotta responded.

"But you do believe that political considerations . . . were the basis on which these decisions were made?"

"Yes, sir!" Margiotta snapped. "Because these people were political leaders and they were making a political recommendation and any leader worth his salt is not going to recommend someone who is not working to help the party win elections."

Confronted by a defiant Margiotta, Neuborne asked whether " . . . an employee could have a subjective frame of mind where he would fear that a local leader would turn the promotion down unless he contributes."

Acting as though he were almost bored by the suggestion, Margiotta responded, "An employee could have that subjective frame of mind."

In order to turn the greatest amount of pressure on employees to contribute, Margiotta had them dunned on their jobs. "By whom?" Neuborne asked.

"Basically by the department head or whoever he designated," Margiotta answered.

Neuborne soon had Margiotta admitting that by means of those terror tactics he had raised at least $1.2 million annually. With a polite bow of his head, Neuborne said, "Thank you, Mr. Margiotta. I have no further questions."

For the remainder of his time on the stand, Margiotta answered questions more expeditiously.

221

Judge Mishler turned reluctantly toward the town attorney. "Mr. McCarthy?" he said with a suggestion of foreboding. Under the whip, the town attorney jumped up and raced to the lectern, plopping down a handful of papers from which he apparently expected to gain more comfort than the judge was willing to supply.

"Good afternoon, Mr. Margiotta." He repeatedly pressed his metal-rimmed glasses on his nose as though they were threatening to spring off unless he compelled them to remain in place. "You know Al D'Amato, don't you?" he asked, his voice a touch too loud.

"Yes, sir," Margiotta answered. A wit in the press section wondered whether Margiotta would have recommended the appointment of McCarthy as town attorney if he had thought someday he would be forced, as a witness, to depend on his talents.

"Did you ever have any disagreements with him [D'Amato], sir, with respect to suggestions or recommendations that you made in connection with municipal employment?"

"Definitely," Margiotta responded.

"Who usually won those battles, sir?" McCarthy asked, sure that he was on the right track.

"If a recommendation is rejected, sir," Margiotta said firmly, "I would normally submit another name—keep submitting them until the elected official was happy with it."

McCarthy, although he didn't appear to realize it, had induced Margiotta to admit that government officials *never* had the final power to appoint whom they wanted; they just had the power to object when Margiotta told them whom to appoint—if they dared—and then, finally, acquiesce to some other Margiotta nominee.

When Neuborne returned to his examination, he focused on McCarthy's allusions to "disagreements you [Margiotta] might have had with some elected officials, Al D'Amato, Francis Purcell, about the recommendations that you would send over." Margiotta watched him warily as Neuborne framed his question:

NEUBORNE: Those recommendations generally involved high-ranking positions, didn't they?
MARGIOTTA: Yes, sir.
NEUBORNE: The positions on their staff, positions as deputy county executive, something like that. Did you ever have

222

an argument with Al D'Amato over someone who was sent over as a sanitation manager to be hired?
MARGIOTTA: No, sir.

The awful power that Alfonse D'Amato exercised over the lives of thousands of Nassau workers had been described by Margiotta. Although political activity in a democracy is theoretically a citizen's civic duty, in Nassau County, politics was a function of economics, primarily the concern of those interested in feathering their nest. Although D'Amato wasn't always able to get you a job as a deputy commissioner, if you were willing to settle for an entry-level job or the nearby rungs on the ladder—assistant foreman, foreman—he was the man to see.

Julian Kaplan's cross-examination of Margiotta on behalf of his client John Jund discredited one of the most persistent canards issued by Al D'Amato. When explaining why so many government workers kicked back to the party, D'Amato always blamed Eugene Nickerson. When Nickerson took over, D'Amato would proclaim indignantly, he fired all those innocent Republicans; therefore, present-day Republican job holders gave to the party to make sure that a change in administrations wouldn't bring about their firing.

Kaplan quickly established that a relatively small number of positions in Nassau government were "exempt" jobs, unprotected by civil service law and subject to discretionary firing. His fists clutched in front of his chest like a tense prizefighter ready to throw a punch, Kaplan challenged Margiotta:

KAPLAN: Do you recall testifying when Nickerson took over *exempt* employees were fired?
MARGIOTTA: Yes, sir.
KAPLAN: Now, do you know what percentage of the exempt employees were fired; were they all fired, virtually all; do you know?
MARGIOTTA: I know all of the department heads were terminated. The entire county attorney's office was eliminated. All our people were fired. Most of the deputy sheriffs were fired. And the deputy commissioners were fired.

In short, Nickerson's "carnage" had consisted of about sixty poli-cy-making *county* department heads and their deputies, a hundred or so party hacks in the county attorney's office, and a gaggle of deputy sheriffs. The county sheriffs were so well regarded by the party apparatus that a new "Department of Public Safety," with amorphous duties, was instantly established to hire them in Hempstead. The vast majority of the twenty-two thousand "protect-ed" civil service workers in the county didn't feel the slight tremble of the earth that rearranged the lives of a handful of Republican wire-pullers, most prominent among them, the youthful Al D'Amato.

Throwing one last punch, Kaplan demanded, "Do you have any knowledge as to whether, at the time of the Nickerson takeover, any *protected* employees were discharged?"

Margiotta hesitated. "Any protected employees?" he asked rhetor-ically.

"Yes," Kaplan persisted.

"Do you mean people with civil service status?" Margiotta stalled.

"Yes!" Kaplan retorted.

Hearing no objection from either Hart, Pascarella, or McCarthy, Margiotta was left with no alternative but to answer, "I have no actual knowledge as to that, sir."

"The boss," who was the most implacable foe of a genuine civil service system, had delivered, although reluctantly, some convinc-ing testimony about the value of that system.

After two hours of intensive questioning, Judge Mishler declared a fifteen-minute recess, and Margiotta stepped down from the wit-ness box. He went directly to a circle formed by Hart, Pascarella, McCarthy, and their legal assistants, who took turns pounding him on the back and shaking his hand. When he stepped away momentarily, I asked him how well he thought he had done on the stand. "I'm sorry," he said smiling expansively. "I've been advised by my attorneys not to speak to the press." We hadn't yet been introduced, and caution is always a good guide with strangers.

Margiotta had handled himself smoothly. His admissions were legally damaging, but they were said with such a show of pride and lack of remorse and he spoke of his actions as though they were so routine that it was hard to know what impact he had on the jury.

He smiled excessively and seemed indifferent to the suffering his decisions had caused thousands of people. The memory of Gaspar Cangemi roasting in the incinerator pit because he displeased the boss made it clear that if you were Cangemi or any of his humble peers, Margiotta was in control of your destiny. And the smile on Margiotta's face, if it meant anything, meant that he knew it.

TWENTY-FIVE

THE SPEAR CARRIERS

There were dozens of witnesses at the 1 percent trial, but none who created the emotional jolt of Al D'Amato's former deputy commissioner of conservation and waterways, a man with a name seemingly selected for its descriptive appropriateness—Raymond W. Graber.

Through the years Graber had become even thinner, more birdlike, with a bald crown and a protruding beak of a nose. His perjury and extortion conviction in 1976 and no-jail-time sentence by Judge Dooling had in no way diminished his loyalty to the party, which continued to provide him with a government job and pay increases, perhaps with his impending testimony in mind.

Graber strode to the witness box with an aggressive show of self-assurance. His first answers were delivered with precision. He had gone to work for Hempstead on September 29, 1966, as a provisional, in short, with Donald Woolnough's stamp of approval imprinted on his forehead. Within seven years he was the deputy commissioner of conservation and waterways.

"Have you ever held an office in the Republican party?" Neuborne asked, his tone no less gentle or kindly than it had been with every other witness.

"The answer is yes!" Graber exclaimed proudly.

He had been a committeeman briefly in the 1950s, chairman of the board of governors of his club during the 1960s, and never less than a committeeman since the 1970s.

"Were any employees you recommended for promotion ever turned down?"

"No," Graber responded after pausing fleetingly to review the strivers whose lives he had blessed.

Neuborne looked at Graber quizzically, as though he had a piece of information that was in conflict with the last answer.

"Were you aware that Michael Gribben had been turned down?" Neuborne asked. Graber cleared his throat. Neuborne continued: "Did you have a conversation with Muriel DeLac [Hemsptead's personnel director] about Mr. Gribben's promotion?"

Oh, yes, Graber recalled, as he undoubtedly simultaneously recalled the penalty for perjury. He had spoken to Mrs. DeLac because Gribben "was such a nice young man."

"What had Mrs. DeLac said?"

"Light."

What did that mean, Neuborne wondered.

" 'It should have been sixty-seven,' " Graber quoted DeLac as saying. Gribben had only contributed twenty-five dollars.

As he spoke, Graber's confidence disintegrated; his high-pitched voice became tremulous. He shortly interrupted Neuborne's questioning with a medical report that he said he felt compelled to give the court. He suffered from a peculiar condition: When he got nervous, "as all witnesses on a witness stand . . . ," his ear passage filled with mucus, and he found it hard to hear.

Neuborne nodded sympathetically, then asked Graber about his role as 1 percent collector in his department. Every year Commissioner Harold Udell had given him a "finance kit" from Margiotta's office—including a list of all employees' salaries in the department—and instructed him to collect the party's share of each worker's wages.

As Graber described the contents of the finance kit, he began to tremble visibly. Sol Goldfarb called out to the occupants of the press section, "That man is going to have a heart attack. He's sick." Then he turned to the assemblage of aged wise men and added, "He shouldn't be in charge of supervising people."

Judge Mishler raised a calming hand and told Graber, "Some witnesses find that after several questions their nervousness goes away. This does not seem to be happening with you." He then urged the quavering Graber to compose himself and offered to give him time to pull himself together.

Court clerk Martin Adler, prior to this moment distinguished only by an exaggerated show of disinterested and exactly doled out competence, without any instructions from Mishler, walked across the room, thermos in hand, and poured some water into a paper cup that he offered to the cringing witness.

Graber clutched at the cup and raised it unsteadily to his compressed lips. After a moment during which he seemed to be wondering whether he could trust its contents, he took a tentative swallow. He then stooped toward Neuborne, hiding behind the cup, which he held in front of his mouth and nose but slightly to one side, as though he were peeking around a shield to see what the nature of the attack would be.

Neuborne asked the terrorized Graber how he had established a departmentwide network to collect from hundreds of employees and what he did with the money turned in to him. Still holding his paper shield, Graber interjected that it was "never my idea to collect campaign contributions." He had done it only because he had been ordered to by Commissioner Udell.

Graber's anxiety level rose with each question. Finally, Neuborne asked a question that provoked an emotional crisis: Had Graber testified at previous hearings about "the collection process"? Graber's hands shook so violently that he was forced to lower the paper cup to the rim of the witness box. He rocked back and forth, then sideways, clutching and releasing the railing.

Defense attorneys rose en masse and objected. Mishler called them to a sidebar. After a short consultation, Mishler asked clerk Adler to lead the jury from the courtroom. When they were gone, he informed Graber that his 1976 perjury conviction could be introduced into evidence whether he acknowledged it or not. The judge apparently thought that knowledge of Graber's conviction wouldn't inflame the jury, although he had ruled against any reference to Margiotta's conviction on that ground.

Acting as though he were cornered, Graber sat gnawing at his knuckles as the jury was led back by the once again imperturbable clerk. Neuborne, now armed with the judge's permission, asked in an uncharacteristically, and unconvincingly, harsh voice, "Did you lie at that prior proceeding?"

"I can't answer yes or no," Graber squawked.

"Did you lie under oath?" Neuborne insisted.

"Are we talking about the grand jury?" Graber asked in a near scream.

"Did you lie to the grand jury?" Neuborne demanded.

"No, I did not!" Graber shouted, and began crying in loud, bleating gasps.

Except for the sounds of Graber's weeping, the courtroom was silent. Neuborne, clearly shaken and embarrassed, dashed to his desk, where Chip Loewenson handed him a document. "Your Honor, I offer Plaintiff's Exhibit twenty-seven," Neuborne called out, explaining that the paper in his hand was an official record of Graber's perjury conviction. He then bustled about, showing the conviction citation to the defense attorneys, who seemed much less disturbed than Neuborne, then to clerk Adler, who, as befitted his professional capacity, seemed least impressed of all.

Daniel McCarthy appeared puzzled about how to cross-examine the distraught witness. His dilemma led the town attorney to counterproductively establish that despite Graber's 1976 perjury conviction, the town had retained the party's bagman on its payroll. In doing this the town was merely following the example of Joe Margiotta, who—seeing no disgrace in a man lying about the illegal collection of money on his behalf—continued Graber in his party committeeman's post, apparently for life.

As Graber unsteadily made his way toward the exit, the completeness of the party's control over the lives of humanity's more fragile vessels became clear. Left to his own devices, it seemed hard to believe Raymond Graber would have ventured beyond the strictest interpretation of the law. Instead, Margiotta's flawed moral code, institutionalized by the party, had seduced him into acts that had destroyed his reputation and peace of mind, although it did seem to preserve his income.

Burt Neuborne reflected on Graber's torment some months later. Speaking with a mixture of indignation and regret, he said, "Here's a guy who took advantage of the system when he had a chance— puffed himself up into a position of more power than he could possibly have ever thought he was entitled to. He's a very little man, and when it exploded, he just couldn't face it.

"I'd been working on him for two years to come clean and tell me what he knew so that I wouldn't have to do that to him. And he wouldn't. So I did what I had to do. I was not happy about doing it to Graber. That's the softie in me. I was very distraught about what I had to do to him. But the jury had to see it. They had to see the conviction. And they also had to know how it [following D'Amato and Margiotta's orders to collect] could poison people's lives."

It seemed clear to me, as I saw the frenzied, bewildered Graber make his way haltingly out of Judge Mishler's courtroom, that this obedient party servant was being punished far more severely than his bosses were ever likely to be. In fact, Al D'Amato, who had been the instigator of every illegal act Graber committed, was sitting in the U.S. Senate.

Most of the plaintiffs shared a common characteristic: The majority were retired; only two or three were in their forties. As each witness took the stand, a disconcerting question arose: Where were the youthful activists who yearned to do battle with *the forces of evil*? Many of the gladiators who raised their fists against Nassau's Caesar came to court in sport shirts and slacks, as though they had just left the par 3 golf course. If they wore a business suit, it had a 1950s cut and fit poorly, as if it had been made for a different person who no longer existed; and even then, the few who donned their old business uniforms didn't meet dress standards—only two or three wore ties. But those observers of the traditional code were something to see: proud men with dazzling broad cravats, white shirts with starched collars, and suits pressed to perfection, showing no sign that they had been sat in.

Perhaps the absence of youthful protagonists was explained by an aging Elmer Davis, that extraordinary journalist of the post–World War II era. Asked why he was able to stand up to Sen. Joe McCarthy when President Eisenhower, Congress, and the rest of the media were avoiding a fight with that alcoholic demagogue, he responded: "It's easier to be an old lion."

At age seventy-seven, the white-haired Eugene Babiak was clearly an old, somewhat toothless lion, hard of hearing but with a smiling, good-natured face. His face had been creased by a lifetime of exposure to the winds of Great South Bay, on whose shores he had grown up and where, from the years 1963 through 1978, he had served as a waterborne constable for Hempstead's Department of Conservation and Waterways.

Babiak testified at the beginning of the second week of the trial. He was an absolute charmer, always on the verge of a smile, perfectly happy to answer any question about those years before retirement when he searched the bay for illegal clammers or helped day sailers in distress.

Dressed in a checked shirt open at the neck and a neat, worn gray suit, the relaxed Babiak described a competition for his money among politicians running his department. His immediate boss, the chief constable, had a simple technique. He would see him on the town dock and say, "If you don't make your yearly contribution, there will be no more overtime."

Babiak turned aside the chief's demands, since he had never made a contribution, although he had been a Republican for fifty years. Raymond Graber decided to try his collecting skills. "I was in the office reading the bulletin board," Babiak recalled. "Graber came over and said, 'It's time for the 1 percent.' " He also threatened to cut off overtime. This pressure from the deputy was more than Babiak could resist. "I said I'd give it to my committeeman. 'Oh, no,' he said, 'You've got to give it to me.' "

At that time, the somewhat intimidated lion was earning $9,000. With a smile on his face that suggested he saw his response to Graber's pressure only in terms of comedy, Babiak told the jury, "I decided I'd be a sport, and I sent in one hundred dollars . . . ten dollars more than I needed to."

Sol Goldfarb laughed along with the rest of the wise heads but remarked in a loud voice, "The last of the big-time spenders."

That was the sole contribution Babiak made to the party. Why was that? Neuborne asked. "I figure it was a form of kickback," Babiak explained, unsmiling. "I didn't like the idea of it."

This was the first time during the six days of the trial that the word "kickback" had been uttered. In a display of absolutely Orwellian discipline, the lawyers demonstrated their understanding that the word for kickback in Judge Mishler's courtroom was "contribution."

Neuborne concluded his examination by establishing that in all the years Babiak had worked in Graber's department he had never received a promotion.

Ed Hart recognized that Babiak had won the jury's heart. He approached the witness stand with a courteous smile on his face. He really just wanted to ask one simple question. Babiak cupped his hand to his ear, straining not to miss a word: "Did you make the hundred-dollar contribution voluntarily?"

Babiak did not hesitate. "Yes." He licked his lips. "Sure, you *had* to make it voluntarily."

Guffaws resounded in the courtroom; even Hart allowed a flicker of a smile to move across his craggy face.

Town attorney McCarthy attempted to picture Babiak as an employee with imperfections. Referring to a document from Babiak's work record that he held gingerly in his hand, McCarthy asked whether it wasn't true that the chief constable had once complained that Babiak had exceeded the five-mile speed limit at Zack's Bay.

An irritated Mishler called for a sidebar. While the attorneys conferred with the judge, Babiak smiled at the jury, then jammed one hand against an armrest of his chair, raised one shoulder defiantly, stared at the sidebar group, and burped.

Convinced it was better not to twist the tail of an old lion, the defense attorneys waived cross-examination, and Eugene Babiak left the stand. He made directly for the covey of retirees he spotted at the rear of the room; the occasion took on the aspect of a reunion. This was no paid claque of admirers; their affection for each other was obvious as they escorted Babiak from the chamber, leaving an impression that with their departure Judge Mishler's courtroom had suffered a loss of much-needed humanity.

During the lunch break, Neuborne chatted with reporters in the lobby. His cherubic cheeks quivered as he strenuously tried his case in that other court, the press conference. Babiak has been "a hit"—especially his remark ". . . you *had* to make it voluntarily." But Neuborne's greatest satisfaction so far in the trial had been Margiotta's admission that workers whose bosses asked them for contributions might have in their "subjective frame of mind felt pressured and in fear of losing their jobs."

A look of determination came into Neuborne's eyes. What he was really looking forward to, he said, "was Alfonse D'Amato under oath." He had waited until Congress was out of session to call D'Amato. "He is not a voluntary witness," Neuborne told the gathering of avowed cynics, most of whom knew D'Amato better than he did. "I had to subpoena him." The senator's testimony, Neuborne said, would make or break his case.

TWENTY-SIX

CULLEN AND JUND–
THEIR DAY IN COURT

As Lorraine Cullen entered the Uniondale courthouse on the afternoon of August 7 on the eighth day of the trial, the first rain in weeks was drenching Nassau. The entire Northeast had been in a prolonged drought, leaving farmers puzzled about why the wrath of God had descended on them and city dwellers with a feeling of well-being under a glowing sky. Lorraine mentioned she had heard on the radio in her husband Frank's car that 3.5 inches of rain had fallen on upstate New York. Always concerned about the welfare of the unfortunate, she remarked smilingly, "Isn't that good news."

Lorraine was not scheduled to testify. Neuborne wanted Thomas Gulotta, Margiotta's choice as Hempstead's presiding supervisor after Al D'Amato went off to the Senate, as his next witness; but Gulotta was nowhere to be found. The unctuous politician had actually slipped into the courthouse by the side entrance and was sequestered in an upstairs section of the pie, but he had neglected to inform Neuborne that he was in the building.

In desperation, Neuborne asked Evans Tilles if he would find some witness to put on the stand in the absence of Gulotta. Tilles, a man of transparent good nature, saw no reason to deny this request from a man on whom he had come to depend. Since he

234

was to contribute only three names to the list of 164 witnesses who appeared at the trial—one of whom was hostile and a second so inconsequential that he was off the stand within minutes—Tilles was therefore obliged to rush Lorraine Cullen into the breach.

It was apparent she was somewhat disconcerted to so suddenly be thrust into the limelight, yet there shone from her beneficent face a sense of pleasure at finally being given the opportunity to testify. She was wearing a simple blue linen suit, her blond hair was cut short in a cap style that framed her face, and she wore black leather, summery strap shoes.

Although Tilles was uncertain in his questioning, Lorraine was precise in her answers. In a well-modulated voice she told the jury that when she had passed the 1966 civil service test for a position in the County Probation Department she had been registered as an independent, a defect that couldn't be overcome simply because she placed high on the list. Although Democrat Nickerson was the county executive, the personnel division was still in the hands of the Republicans. It wasn't until months had passed and she had brought the matter directly to the attention of Nickerson that on July 22, 1966, she finally received her appointment.

The 1 percent requirement for promotion "was generally talked about in the office," she said. The power of that rule was made clear to her almost immediately. There were seven provisionals working as "Investigator 1" when she arrived. "They all failed the civil service test, but they remained in the position." Two people who had passed the test were also appointed, since there were nine vacancies. "The two off the list were dismissed after a six-month probationary period—all the provisionals were kept."

Her supervisor was a party committeeman, Allen S. Waters, with whom she had a good professional relationship. He often put her in charge of the office when he was on vacation. When Lorraine decided to take a promotional exam in 1970 for senior investigator, "Waters suggested it would be a good idea if I joined the Republican party. It was simply a matter of reality." She quoted Waters as telling her that "because he was active as a Republican committeeman and paid 1 percent, that was the reason he held on to his job." He had repeatedly failed the test for the position he held.

Lorraine refused to knuckle under to Margiotta's demand. She took her test, came out on top of the list, and watched while a provisional who had failed the test was appointed.

The test was given again later in the year; again she scored number one. At this point, Probation Commissioner Louis J. Milone, County Executive Ralph Caso's brother-in-law, called her into his office. Waving a paper at her, he said, "I guess you know why you're here."

Defense attorneys interrupted with objections, and Judge Mishler called them to a sidebar. After several minutes of argument, Mishler directed the jury to leave the room and instructed Cullen to continue her testimony so that he could determine whether he would allow the jury to hear it.

Taking up her narrative where Milone was waving a paper in her face, she quoted the irate commissioner as saying, "I have a key man on the list, and I'll have to break the list if I can't appoint him."

Looking directly at Mishler, she said, "Milone was encouraging me to decline, which was the way they could get rid of the list." The provisional they wanted to appoint, she stated, wasn't on the list.

Offering no explanation, Mishler ruled against admitting everything she had said about Milone's pressure tactics. With a stern glance, he quashed whatever impulse Tilles had to argue. Mishler then ordered that the jury be brought back.

The atmosphere in the courtroom was attentive. Lorraine Cullen was, after all, the Cullen of *Cullen v. Margiotta*. She was also clearly an intelligent woman, and her gentle mode of expressing herself was persuasive. In an obvious effort to destroy the almost hypnotic effect that her story was having, the defense attorneys began to object to almost all of Tilles's questions. The harassment increased; Tilles was befuddled. Almost every time he asked a question Pascarella was on his feet objecting or demanding a sidebar conference with the judge. Cullen had been a *county* employee and therefore was an especially important target at whom the county's attorney must aim an incessant fire.

Most of the last hour of the day was consumed warding off procedural objections by Pascarella, with an occasional assist from Hart; much of that time had been spent at the judge's bench. The pace of the trial lagged. Clearly, Pascarella and Hart were delighted with the havoc they were causing. The straight-line drive of the case

Neuborne had established had been broken. Cullen had not been allowed to explain her complaints; in fact, when Tilles indicated he had no more questions to ask, her story had been left incomplete.

The next morning, Pascarella started an intense cross-examination, since Cullen's complaint was against his client and he couldn't afford to ignore her, as he had most witnesses.

In an attempt to denigrate her civil service successes, Pascarella read off a long list of exams she had taken; it sounded as if he were reading from a police blotter about a series of crimes she had committed. One was left with the impression that it was Pascarella's view that in Nassau County it was a crime to take civil service exams for promotions but not illegal to advance oneself by bribing Republican politicians.

At the end of the morning session the jury was led from the courtroom, and the spectators who remained were treated to a public sidebar conference, this time audible, since there was no need to protect the jurors from possible verbal contamination.

An informal early scramble for endgame position developed. Mishler had told the attorneys that even as the trial proceeded he was writing a lengthy final charge to the jury. As a result, every sidebar became an opportunity for the opponents to obtain a ruling from Mishler that would, at that pivotal terminal moment, reflect favorably on their position.

At this sidebar, Hart was attempting to convince Mishler that the present leadership of the party could not be held responsible for acts of previous leaders.

"I know your argument that the committee changes every two years," Mishler said to the somewhat testy Hart. "But when they accept the office, they are accepting all the assets and all of the liabilities." Hart frowned as Mishler made this pro-plaintiff ruling. "This is a unique case in many respects," Mishler said, as though he were trying to help Hart think through the ramifications of a party's being charged with a crime for its political acts.

"A party is an *unincorporated association*," Hart shot back. Therefore, it was not subject to the legal actions that controlled incorporated associations. Mishler closed his one good eye. Hart walked away, waving his head, disgusted. "It's a waste of time," he muttered.

237

After a moment, Hart returned and tried again. "A party," he insisted, hands clasped tightly behind his back, "is the same kind of unincorporated association as, for example, a church."

Neuborne objected. "All we're trying to reach is the assets of the Republican party." And if the party was like a church, clearly its assets would be beyond his clients' covetous reach.

Mishler opened his eye and smiled jaggedly. "You're not only wrong because I say it," he told Hart, "but because Professor Neuborne says so."

Hart's vanity was clearly punctured. "Why don't you ever cite my qualifications?" he protested. Once again he turned away from Mishler and said loudly enough to be heard halfway across the room, "Nonsense!" It was the insurgency of an adolescent spirit; but since it took place out of hearing of the jury, Mishler handled this display of juvenile temper with a response no more severe than a Cyclopean blink.

John Jund was a six-foot-one, 215-pound, blue-eyed thirty-four-year-old, in the prime of life, who, if Margiotta and D'Amato had allowed him to pursue his career in the Sanitation Department, would be, at the time of the trial, at his most effective in keeping Nassau clean.

He was a hulk of a man, moving with muscular assurance; the type that enfeebled, in-bred monarchical families would occasionally seek out as a consort for some pale, fragile princess in the hope that an infusion from the wider genetic pool might reinvigorate the debilitated dynastic bloodline. But in Jacob Mishler's court he was merely one of the two remaining individual plaintiffs seeking restitution for injuries, which, as far as the judge was concerned, might just be imaginary.

Spiffed up in his blue suit and his blue-gray striped sateen tie, his blond beard and hair neatly trimmed, the youthful Jund was questioned by his attorney, Julian Kaplan. Feisty Kaplan knew every aspect of the case. Adding to his generally aggressive and effective performance was his personal affection for Jund and, more significant, his lack of fear of the glowering judge.

In a voice that occasionally rumbled with masculine discontent, Jund described the frustration of seeking employment in his late teens. Four years on the Allen Trees High School football team and six years of interscholastic wrestling didn't seem to qualify him for anything. He had finally followed the well-worn path to the Levittown North clubhouse and implored Committeeman Harry Norwalk to get him a laborer's job in the Sanitation Department. There was no other way to do it, since the Town's Civil Service Commission did not test entry-level garbagemen and the Nassau Republican organization, because of that omission, had been filling those jobs, with no sign of strain, for at least twenty years.

Several days later, Committeeman Norwalk came to his parents' home. Sitting in the family kitchen, Norwalk explained the facts of Nassau political life to the wide-eyed teenager. "He told me to register as Republican, be active in the club—sell tickets." With the inspirational admonishment that "one hand washes the other," Norwalk handed him a sealed letter and told him to take it to Donald Woolnough in the party's Garden City headquarters.

After receiving the usual pep talk from Woolnough, Jund reported for work on May 5, 1970, and at age nineteen found himself on the back of a Hempstead garbage truck. In exchange for the honest performance of a job the newly married Jund received $135 a week. The party expected that for relieving him of the need to take his minimal skills back into an unfriendly marketplace, Jund would buy an occasional pitcher of twenty-five-dollar beer at the monthly clubhouse meetings and purchase his fair share of raffles, plus tickets to cocktail parties, picnics, the annual dinner, and **A*NIGHT*AT* THE*RACES**. Norwalk not only expected him to buy every ticket he thrust into his hand; he began training him for the greater responsibilities of selling. Jund turned and faced the jury as he told of his first venture into political huckstering. "I sold ten football tickets a week during the football season." The one-dollar tickets "weren't easy to sell . . . usually my mother or father bought a ticket, and I bought the rest."

This catch-bag of dunning didn't exhaust the expectations of Margiotta's collection agency. Months after he went on the payroll his foreman ordered, "See Augie!" Jund found August Cosenza in the yard where the trucks were parked. "He asked me if I paid my one percent," Jund recounted. "I said no." Cosenza put on his Solomon hat and issued the following judgment: "He said, since I didn't pay last year, when I was earning $7,100, I should contribute $100."

After Jund made out a check and brought it to Cosenza, he received a provisional promotion, involving no additional pay, as a spare driver.

Jund said on April Fools' Day in 1973, after seven months of work as a spare driver, his supervisor told him he was being demoted, saying, "There's something wrong politically."

What was wrong politically was that Jund had not made any further 1 percent kickbacks after handing Cosenza his $100 check almost two years earlier.

Anxious to determine why other men with less time on the job were being promoted while he was being demoted, Jund went to see Cosenza. When Kaplan asked what had taken place at that confrontation, Hart objected, and Judge Mishler told the jury to leave the room while he listened to Jund's answer.

Kaplan repeated his question. "At that meeting, what did Mr. Cosenza tell you?"

Town attorney McCarthy was on his feet instantly. "I object!" he shouted. The courtroom resounded with laughter. Mishler smiled down at his favorite target. "The jury is out," he informed McCarthy. And then, as if he thought McCarthy would still have difficulty understanding, added, "It's out precisely so that you don't have to object."

Mishler turned to Jund and asked him to continue. "Mr. Cosenza said I didn't work for the Sanitation Department, I worked for the Republican party."

That was enough for Mishler; he called the jurors back and said he was going to allow them to hear Jund's testimony. Jund repeated Cosenza's information about who his real boss was and then added, "He told me not to make any waves."

There was a sidebar every few minutes. It was clear the defense attorneys had concluded that a strategy of delay and obfuscation which had disrupted Lorraine Cullen's testimony should be employed again to see if its spell would have a similar effect on Jund.

His morale destroyed by Cosenza's unwillingness to stand up for him, Jund continued to work on the back of a garbage truck until 1978. He had injured his back two years earlier and had been hospitalized, in traction for twelve days, but his request to D'Amato's sanitation commissioner, Landman, for "light service" while he was undergoing extensive physical rehabilitation was denied.

By this time Jund was involved in the court case initiated by Lorraine Cullen; he had also filed a complaint with Hempstead's moribund Equal Employment Opportunity Bureau and the Nassau district attorney's office. In an attempt to circumvent the party's obvious hostility toward him, Jund took two civil service promotional exams. He passed both in 1976 but watched himself being ignored while other men on the list were appointed. Desperation drove him to seek relief in the most unlikely place: Commissioner Landman's office.

Kaplan asked Jund what had happened when he sought the commissioner's aid.

"I asked Mr. Landman if the town had any work for me to do," Jund responded, taking a deep breath as he recalled the humiliating moment. "He said the town had no work for me and I should go on welfare. . . . I shouldn't have started this."

Shortly after, Jund resigned, convinced it was impossible to fight Margiotta's party and D'Amato's city hall on a battlefield chosen by them. He got a job as a real estate agent and was attempting to put back together a life that Sanitation Commissioner Landman had decided to throw on the trash heap.

A worried-looking Jund left the stand and headed for the exit. Mishler called a recess, and the courtroom emptied.

Out in the lobby Frank and Lorraine Cullen tried to reassure the upset Jund. Lorraine reached up and put her arm around his shoulders. At her touch, Jund looked up and began to speak. "The judge wants only *yes* or *no* answers, but that doesn't let me tell the jury how hard it is to be the helper on the back of a truck. We lift over a hundred thousand pounds of garbage a week. The smell from the cans would make the average person puke. There's broken glass, rusty, jagged metal. There isn't a load that doesn't contain something ugly—maggots, cockroaches, dead rats."

Lorraine murmured a reassuring "*Shush,*" as though she were trying to calm a disturbed youngster. Jund sighed, took a deep breath, and then, in a subdued voice, continued, "We stand on a bumper fastened to the back of the truck. It's three feet off the ground.

We're expected to jump off the moving truck even before it stops so we get a quick start for the can. Do you have any idea what that does to our legs? There isn't a guy working a route whose legs aren't a mass of varicose veins. And what for? So some thieving slime at party headquarters can leech off me."

TWENTY-SEVEN

FOR THE DEFENSE

W hen Neuborne called Hempstead's presiding supervisor Thomas Gulotta to the stand Friday afternoon, shortly after John Jund had completed his testimony, it had been his intention to make this thirty-fifth witness the scene setter for Al D'Amato's appearance. Against D'Amato's wishes, Gulotta had taken over D'Amato's Hempstead office when the new senator went to Washington. Neuborne hoped that under oath Gulotta would describe some of the corrupt practices he had found in place when D'Amato exited.

D'Amato had been scheduled to play the climactic role in the plaintiffs' case, but the anxious senator was resisting the day of his ordeal, hoping an out-of-court settlement might save him from that potential catastrophe. Though the trial was well under way, D'Amato's pressure on his ally, party chairman Mondello, to settle the case was unremitting. The previous night, party leaders had rejected a settlement to which Neuborne and D'Amato had agreed. The proposal included a $2 million cap on claims by the plaintiffs.

In the hope that it might yet happen, D'Amato invented improbable excuses—and fled to inaccessible reaches—trying to avoid Neuborne's judicial embrace.

Hempstead's incessantly smiling presiding supervisor now took D'Amato's place as the concluding attraction in the initial presentation of Neuborne's case.

Gulotta was born on April 27, 1944, into a political family headed by Frank Sr., former state supreme court justice and William Cahn's predecessor as Nassau County district attorney. As befits a second-generation politician, junior went to out-of-town college, Trinity, in Hartford, Connecticut; he graduated from Columbia Law School in 1969 and went to work for Cahn as assistant district attorney. He immediately joined the North Merrick Republican Club and by 1975 was the club's executive leader.

Gulotta was physically unimposing—of medium stature and trim build, forty-two years old, almost gray, with a sharply defined widow's peak. He had been elected to the state assembly in 1977, where he sat until 1981, when Margiotta picked him to take over Hempstead. As he sat in the stand, smiling constantly, staring good-naturedly in an unfocused manner at the space in front of him and tranquilly responding to Neuborne's questions, he appeared to be a pleasant, ineffectual nonentity.

With no hint that he felt he was putting his mortal soul in danger, Gulotta told Neuborne that during the years he served as one of the party's sixty-nine executive leaders he was never asked to approve or disapprove raises, promotions, or firings of government workers. It was a startling assertion in view of the contrary testimony of Margiotta and Woolnough.

In the next breath he told an incredulous Neuborne that as Merrick's executive leader he had received lists from party headquarters showing the precise amount of town workers' contributions. And then, stretching credulity beyond its limits, he said, "To be perfectly honest, I never knew exactly why I was receiving them, and I just disposed of them."

A call to party headquarters, with whom he was in daily contact, could have cleared up any confusion on that point, but to use one of Gulotta's most often employed phrases, "to be perfectly honest," the thought never seemed to have occurred to him.

Gulotta's answers grew in length as they shrank in substance. He wanted it known that since taking office as presiding supervisor in 1981, he had insisted that town employees be hired and promoted on the basis of merit, not political patronage. His smile did not soften the implication that his predecessor, Al D'Amato, had otherwise hired and promoted employees.

Neuborne had grown restive with Gulotta's extended, unresponsive answers and wanted to know why, if the presiding supervisor maintained he was so immune to the infection of patronage, he had dealt with Hempstead's public safety commissioner, Michael Limongelli, in such a benign manner. Limongelli had been pressuring workers in the Public Safety Department—a group scornfully described by Ed Hart as "parking lot watchmen"—to buy tickets worth up to $800 annually for Republican party affairs. Limongelli had done this in a Gulotta-controlled office, on town property, and he had linked the purchase of these tickets to the dispensing of overtime. In frustration, Hart's "watchmen" had blown the whistle on their commissioner, and his case was now in the hands of Denis Dillon, Hempstead's desultory Democratic district attorney.

When Gulotta could no longer ignore the "watchmen" protests, he attempted to quiet them by transferring Limongelli to the Parks Department, at the same salary, while the district attorney decided how to avoid handling the problem. Nine months had passed since Limongelli's case had been placed in Dillon's hands, but Gulotta told Neuborne that he hadn't even thought of asking his district attorney what he intended to do.

Neuborne asked Gulotta if he had ever disciplined Limongelli for forcing town employees to contribute to the party. In full oratorical splendor, Gulotta began, "Thank God, we are still in a country where—"

As he had several times previously, Neuborne cut in, "Yes or no, Mr. Gulotta."

The defense attorneys rose to protest. Mishler soberly told Gulotta that he did not have to give a yes or no response. "You had started to answer," Mishler said, "so you can go ahead and answer."

Gulotta said, "My answer was that we are still in a country where a person is still presumed innocent until proven guilty. At this moment, there are not even any charges against Mr. Limongelli."

Neuborne turned to the judge in exasperation. "Your Honor," he protested, raising his hand in a gesture of futility, "this is not an answer. It's a speech."

By the time Gulotta's ninety minutes on the stand had drawn to an end, Hempstead's leading Republican had uttered enough *I cannot recalls,* evaded enough direct answers, and lied frequently enough to place the party deeply in his debt. Party leaders seldom overlook debts of this nature, since they represent not only substantial obligations but, more important, proof that the creditor is someone on whom the party can depend, even under oath, where lying occasionally gets individuals in trouble.

A year and a half later, on January 16, 1987, the party paid its debt to Gulotta. After forty years on political payrolls, the party signaled that it was time for County Executive Francis Purcell to resign. His administrative acts had been shaped by the philosophy that today's pressing problems often solved themselves without interference from county government, a philosophy which he summarized with his frequently repeated remark "Snow melts." With this homespun philosopher out of the way, Gulotta was appointed by the county's party-controlled board of supervisors as the man most likely to perform the executive's role with the same vigor.

County Republican leader Joseph Mondello—Margiotta's treasonous former lieutenant—also had a personal motive when recommending Gulotta's promotion. Hours after Gulotta resigned to take up his new duties, Mondello had the Hempstead Town Board appoint himself as its presiding supervisor. This simultaneously made Mondello chairman of the county's board of supervisors. Since he saw no reason to abandon his post as party chairman, Mondello—by rewarding Gulotta—had more than doubled his own salary and strengthened his position as the most powerful man in Nassau.

When Judge Mishler adjourned court for the weekend shortly after five, Neuborne and I walked out to the parking lot together. It was a brilliant late-summer afternoon, and the television cameramen and reporters were clustered at the entranceway around the proud and accommodating Gulotta. Chip Loewenson was loading the plaintiffs' bloated briefcases into Neuborne's six-year-old sedan.

Neuborne was disturbed at his inability to pin down Gulotta. He glanced at the preening politician and commented that he felt he had been at his most ineffectual with Thomas Jr.

Why, I wondered, had Gulotta been allowed to make all those self-serving speeches when Mishler had previously been hostile toward anyone who failed to answer to the point? "Mishler is a fair, decent guy," Neuborne responded in his usual frank manner, "but there's no way he's going to treat a sanitation worker the way he treats a governmental official. His class bias showed."

Neuborne and Loewenson drove off, and I finished entering some of his remarks in my notebook. At this point Judge Mishler and his secretary approached, the judge in his white patent leather shoes and tennis slacks. It was our first conversation, at which time the judge made it clear that after the trial he would be willing to go on the record about the case.

On Monday, August 12, the start of the third week of the trial, Ed Hart began to present the party's case. He immediately offered a motion to dismiss the plaintiffs' complaint.

Mishler sent the jury from the room, and Hart spent several hours in this endeavor. The plaintiffs' witnesses, he insisted, were not credible: They had dirty hands; most of them had accepted the benefits of party patronage through the years. At the sound of the word "patronage," Mishler squinted his eye at Hart and asked, "What do you understand political patronage to mean?"

The conflict in Mishler's soul was summed up in that question. As he often told the attorneys, he sat at the head of this court only because of patronage. How could an upright man such as himself, who had benefited from the system, condemn it? He was challenging Hart to provide him with a definition of the practice that would make Margiotta's patronage sound like his recollection of the patronage distributed by his Astoria friend Frank Kenna.

Hart understood the judge's dilemma and attempted to define the word in the least obnoxious manner. "It means that political parties can make recommendations to members of their party who are elected to political office." It sounded like such an innocent exercise—a mere *recommendation*—something, perhaps, that even unaffiliated citizens might do.

There was nothing wrong with patronage, Hart told Mishler as he continued to apply the balm intended to soothe an unsettled conscience; it was just that the word had a bad connotation. "We have what I consider an unfortunate statement of President Jackson: 'To the victor belongs the spoils.' " It was that remark that had given the whole practice a black eye.

Neuborne countered that "patronage, as I understand it, does not mean a person should be forced to pay to get a promotion. It does not mean that Republicans can get promotions and others can't." Looking directly at Hart, he went on: "This case is not about isolated acts but systemic acts. The D'Amato letter sits in the record. A high-level executive of the party and the government knew of the 1 percent contribution." There was nothing innocent or innocuous about the D'Amato brand of patronage; it was pay or don't play.

Early in the afternoon Mishler denied the motion to dismiss. A somber-faced Hart then called the first of six low-level town supervisory witnesses who were to testify that day.

These witnesses were among a couple of dozen party members who had been standing around in the courthouse lobby through the morning, smoking, chatting, and laughing—until some stranger came too close—waiting their turn to testify. The lobby appeared to be the site of a clubhouse meeting.

Only the weakness of his cause could explain the strategy Hart pursued. Hart's six friendly witnesses testified that they had been started in their careers by recommendations from party leaders. Their testimony echoed the charges; the starting gate in the race for advancement was situated in their local clubhouse. Furthermore, most of them were committeemen, as were about 80 percent of the seventy-one witnesses Hart called to the stand in the next four weeks to swear that the party they revered depended for its sustenance solely on voluntary contributions.

We had a surprise visitor in midmorning, Murray Kempton, whom I hadn't seen in ten years. The world-renowned journalist and 1973 National Book Award author walked in as the trial was in session and stood for several moments in the aisle. He peered through his horn-rimmed glasses, benignly curious but detached, like a new schoolboy waiting for some kind soul to point out where to sit. At age sixty-seven he looked frail, not simply slender and esthetic, as I remembered him. His blond hair was now substantially gray; he was wearing a neat tan suit, with cuffed pants, black oxfords, and black socks. We waved at each other, and he came and sat next to me in the press section.

We had known each other for thirty-six years. In 1971 he wrote an introduction to my first book, *The Kingmakers,* which had germinated at the 1952 Republican convention in the Chicago stock-yard district where Dwight Eisenhower and Richard Nixon were nominated; Kempton and I had both attended that pivotal convention. When I began working at the *New York Post* as a copyboy in 1949, Kempton was already what he is today, a columnist who had a reputation as a stylist of elegant, droll essays, always tinged with sympathy for the underdog. Murray could write the most dazzling prose; the quality of his language has rarely been duplicated in the American press. In 1984 he was finally awarded the Pulitzer Prize for his accumulated lifetime work in journalism, but with equal justice a Pulitzer committee might have bestowed its award decades earlier.

I filled him in on what had been happening in Judge Mishler's court and then watched him open his loose-leaf notebook and begin to take careful, densely written notes. Murray's amused view of life was still apparent. He followed the action in Mishler's court as attentively as ever, chuckling when something occurred that seemed humorous to no one else. On those occasions, he always made some witty comment, invariably ironic or sardonic.

As the day wore on, Murray was increasingly concerned about what he would write: Hart's first clubhouse witnesses weren't the stuff from which columns are composed. His notes proliferated, but they were judged by him to be inconsequential. At one point, as Julian Kaplan cross-examined a witness without effect, Kempton muttered desperately, "Kaplan, give me *something!*"

During a recess, I introduced him to Lorraine and Frank Cullen; it seemed to me that they were the seeds from which Kempton columns most readily grew. But the pleasant chatter, dominated by Murray, signaled that although he might be willing to spend an evening drinking with his new acquaintances, they had not caught the imagination of his muse. He had, after all, come upon them more than two weeks after the beginning of the trial, after the main part of the plaintiffs' case had been completed. The subject of the day was the party's defense, not the distant charges of its accusers.

At the end of the day I drove Murray from the courthouse to the state supreme court building in Mineola. A *Newsday* typewriter and telephone were available there for his use. As the car slowly made its way through the heavy Nassau rush-hour traffic, Murray chewed on his pipe. I questioned him about Margiotta. He had covered both commission-splitting trials. He felt responsible, he told me with a trace of pride, for the hung jury in Margiotta's first trial. The jury was allowed to go home for the weekend, before returning to reach a decision. He thought they had read his column, which was favorable to Margiotta, and that it had swayed them. "The charges were thin," he said. "If Margiotta had sent his letters to Williams [the insurance agent in Oyster Bay] by messenger instead of the U.S. mails, he wouldn't have broken the law that sent him to jail."

It was the sort of clever, slightly skewed, antic remark with which he had amused me through the years. It seemed to me, I told him, that Margiotta had committed, in all likelihood, much more serious crimes than mail fraud. Crimes associated with, but not directly alluded to, in the five extortion charges on which he had also been tried and convicted.

"Margiotta has a good heart," he remarked, seeking a mitigating virtue with which to defend one laid low by the gods.

As we prepared to part in front of the supreme court building, I referred to his statement that Margiotta had a good heart and mentioned the ordinary, uneducated, defenseless people whom he had been extorting for years. I told him of Cangemi, who testified about going to see Margiotta at his office in an attempt to have the boss call off his party dogs. "No one gets in to see Margiotta," Kempton interjected. After explaining how Cangemi had accomplished that, I said, "When he told *good-hearted* Margiotta he couldn't afford the 1 percent, Margiotta threw him out."

Murray extracted his pipe from his mouth and said, "Margiotta is interested in power." And then he added, "D'Amato could have squelched the second trial. He didn't lift a finger for Margiotta."

Between the boss and his ungrateful recruit, Murray clearly preferred the fallen commander.

250

TWENTY-EIGHT
THE SENATOR REDEFINES PERJURY

A week passed before Alfonse D'Amato would allow himself to be led into the Uniondale court, without any visible handcuffs but under duress so compelling that without it he would have been elsewhere.

That Friday morning, August 16, 1985, prior to the opening of court, D'Amato, skittish and short-tempered, had rendezvoused with Burt Neuborne in the Coliseum Diner just south of the courthouse on Uniondale Avenue. Accompanied by Michael Armstrong, his lawyer, D'Amato explored the possibility of an agreement similar to the one Neuborne had reached with Margiotta; it might make the next few hours more endurable.

Armstrong's early reputation had been made prosecuting criminals in New York City. Now in private practice, he specialized in defending politicians accused of corruption. His most famous client was Donald Manes, tainted Queens Borough president, whose interests he represented until the tormented, about-to-be-indicted Democrat committed suicide by driving a kitchen knife into his heart.

During the previous weeks, Armstrong had several times phoned Neuborne to discuss the possibility of a Coliseum Diner meeting. The quality of Neuborne's reassurances was apparent in the fact that D'Amato's talented attorney allowed his client to attend this precourt breakfast. Each of them, Neuborne told me, envisioned this get-together as a potential dress rehearsal.

Neuborne stared across his coffee cup at the restless D'Amato and calmly explained he had no desire, when questioning the senator as a witness, to deal with issues that went beyond his need to recover money forced from his anonymous clients by the senator's party. If D'Amato would cooperate with him, Neuborne would make his interrogation as swift and painless as possible. Hearing no objection from a grim-faced D'Amato, Neuborne asked a series of questions. D'Amato responded as Neuborne had hoped he would and finally agreed to make the same statements under oath.

Having won the senator's cooperation, Neuborne was confronted with a difficult moral choice. D'Amato's answers had convinced Neuborne that D'Amato's 1975 grand jury testimony was perjurious; but since the statute of limitations had run out and D'Amato had finessed that perjury charge, the only opportunity to expose his true role in Nassau politics would come when the senator was on the witness stand. Didn't that obligate him, Neuborne wondered, to press ahead vigorously when D'Amato was under oath?

Neuborne later rationalized that the bargain he was offering D'Amato wasn't *legally* crucial to the worried senator. Since D'Amato's role in the 1 percent kickbacks was not known by him until 1977, after Judge Mishler had cut off the possibility of adding any new names to the list of the accused, the senator wasn't even a defendant; therefore, Neuborne held no club over his head. "The only leverage I had on him," Neuborne regretfully told me, "was his public image." If Neuborne grilled D'Amato and his appearance in court was prolonged, the possibility of many days of sensational headlines would increase. With the senator's reelection campaign about to start, that was, for him, a daunting prospect.

A few days earlier the *New York Times* had raised D'Amato's sensitivity to his political peril in an editorial entitled "The Senator and the Kickback Trial." The *Times* commented: "Beyond turning a beam on individuals, the trial offers the public a larger benefit: the chance to learn how much a powerful political machine operated local government as its private fiefdom."

The *Times*'s generalized statement about civic benefits that might flow from the trial of his closest political allies didn't concern D'Amato. What bothered him was the *Times*'s inference that he had lied. The thrust of the *Times*'s editorial was delivered in this judgmental declaration:

> Testifying during a Federal grand jury inquiry in 1975, Mr. D'Amato denied knowing of the kickback scheme. Now he says the practice was a fact of life when he came into government, and that a "voluntary contribution of 1 percent was a fair guide in support of the party. In retrospect, it may have been wrong." When Senator D'Amato takes the stand as expected, he'll have the chance to elaborate.

D'Amato was not anxious to confront the quixotic possibilities of that *chance* and saw an accommodation with Neuborne as his best opportunity to avoid it.

As Neuborne thought back to that crucial moment in the Coliseum Diner, it was clear that his conscience was still troubled. In describing his actions, he vacillated between being apologetic and aggressively defensive. "I could have gone after him real hard," he said. "I didn't know what to do. I was really in a quandary about which way to play it. The problem was, in order for me to attack him, I had to attack his credibility before the 1975 grand jury and show that it was different from his testimony in court."

Neuborne fully understood the nature of his predicament: "The only reason to do it was for the moral fact that this was a guy who shouldn't be allowed to masquerade as a public benefactor."

But in their diner summit, once D'Amato had assured the alternately troubled and exultant attorney that he was willing to testify against the Republican party, Neuborne discovered that what had been a simple moral choice had become an impossible practical one. Under those circumstances, Neuborne asked, "would I, as a lawyer, want to establish that his credibility was terrible? It couldn't help me collect any more money for my people."

Over a period of weeks, I had spoken to Burt Neuborne numerous times; his message was always the same: He wanted to collect money for his clients. There was never a moment, in those private sessions, when he spoke with passion about the need to strike a blow against political corruption.

At one point, while we were discussing the committeemen whom Hart had been monotonously parading to the stand for their fifteen-minute repetitious denials that their contributions, although never less than precisely 1 percent, were ever less than completely voluntary, Neuborne remarked, "They're all fundamentally decent people."

It seemed to me that he had missed the point. Their decency, real or only a figment of Neuborne's fancy created by his incomplete information about their character, was not a central issue in this trial. Nor was it an issue that shaped D'Amato's decisions about who would get jobs, be promoted, or get raises. Cartons of evidence had already been introduced revealing their participation in a corrupt enterprise that strongly suggested that the purported "decency" of these party hacks was notable mainly for its absence. Clearly, considerations about their possibly upstanding character had no part in D'Amato's calculus when he fitted them into his kickback operation.

The duties of all these committeemen were identically mercenary and almost completely asocial. They were, as former committeeman Sol Goldfarb said, "money raisers. If they didn't collect, they were out."

Neuborne was the quintessential ACLU lawyer. He was, by profession, tolerant of the guilty; he had spent years defending the marginal aspects of abstract principles. Mixed in with the worthy causes were the unworthy defendants, and he had early on learned to accommodate himself to the discomfort of being the white knight for Nazis, child abusers, and murderers. For him, their resemblance to the rest of humanity became a reason to extend to them the protection of the Golden Rule and a requirement that he give them his unlimited sympathy. He was their pacific defender, ready to heal what society would punish.

Neuborne's lack of fire was particularly notable that morning just after he had returned from his diner conference with D'Amato. Louis Milone, the retired director of the Nassau Probation Department, was to be the last witness before D'Amato. The seventy-two-year-old Milone was Ralph Caso's ungrateful brother-in-law; his lack of family loyalty still rankled the perpetually tormented former county executive.

Milone, shriveled and bent, his high, near skeletal forehead capped with a thin smattering of gray hairs, peered out at the courtroom with arrogant, bloodshot eyes. He was James Pascarella's witness for the county, here to deny Lorraine Cullen's charge that he had bypassed her for promotion because she had refused to contribute to the party.

In anticipation of D'Amato's appearance, Murray Kempton was in the courtroom. We spent the day together. He was in much better spirits because of the caliber of the docket. At the sight of Milone, he remarked with the wit of a southern rifleman at a turkey shoot, "Can you think of anyone who would be better to be head of the Probation Department than someone who looks like he should be serviced by it."

Neuborne sat at the lawyers' table inattentively watching Pascarella approach the prune-faced Milone. His back was troubling him, and his mind was occupied with his impending confrontation with D'Amato. Pascarella, in a praying mantis pose, his hands lifted in front of his chest, fingertips poised tensely against each other, head bent forward, asked the thoroughly imperturbable Milone how he had reached his decision to pass over Lorraine Cullen and select someone further down on the civil service list. Milone wanted the court to know that "the important thing here is that I exercised at this point my discretionary right, *one out of three.*" In short, he wanted it understood that he could pick whomever he wished without having to justify his decision. However, in an endeavor not to appear arbitrary, he added that he did consult occasionally with middle management to help him evaluate employees. "From time to time, you know, personal, mouth to mouth."

He went on to concede, "I didn't become too well acquainted with any of the professional staff, because I didn't have time for that."

When it was Neuborne's turn to step in and explore the secret avenues along which Louis Milone had meandered with the Nassau Republicans, he declined. Neuborne had raised his eyes to a different horizon and allowed the crotchety Milone to hobble past him without once attempting to detain him with a question that might have further inflamed his dour temperament.

During the luncheon recess, I asked Neuborne why he wasn't going after the party witnesses more vigorously. His answer came reflexively, with no sign of strain. "I'm pulling my punches with these witnesses. They are, after all, my clients—they are members of the class action. I don't want to humiliate them." And then, lighting up with that angelic smile displayed in times of adversity by religious martyrs in whatever cause, he added, "It's my job to win this case and not hurt these people."

Just before Judge Mishler prepared to open the afternoon session at 1:45, Gary Lewi, D'Amato's press agent, came over to where Kempton and I were sitting in the press section. The senator, he wanted us to know, would hold a press conference on the second floor in one of the vacant courtrooms immediately after he testified. Lewi left no doubt that of D'Amato's two appearances in the Uniondale courthouse, he considered the message to be delivered before the press corps the more important one: at most, there would only be a few hundred people watching his captain under oath in Mishler's court, but on television, millions would be addressed without any judicial penalty for lying.

Soon after the judge gaveled the packed courtroom crowd into silence, D'Amato—dressed soberly in a blue suit and gray-blue tie—became the hundredth person to occupy the witness stand. He sat there grinning at familiar faces in the audience; Margiotta's more unforgiving supporters stared back glumly.

Although Neuborne lacked the pugnacious tenacity of a seasoned prosecutor, there is no doubt he detested D'Amato and, as he prepared to ask his first question, had the power to destroy the freshman senator's career.

In a cozy voice he asked a series of inconsequential questions: How long had D'Amato served as presiding supervisor? How long had he been the town supervisor? It was almost as if Neuborne, habituated to shepherding his flock of beleaguered defendants, viewed D'Amato in his role as a "member of the class" and was attempting to put him at ease.

In a few minutes, D'Amato became more loquacious, his answers more expansive and irrelevant. By the time Neuborne had asked for an explanation of the supervisor's duties, D'Amato was clearly enjoying himself. In exquisite detail, he rambled on aimlessly about the county charter and why Hempstead was the only one of nine-hundred towns in the state to have two supervisors. Curious as to how far he could push this pointless trivia, D'Amato finally asked for permission to continue . . . "If I might?"

"Sure, go ahead," Neuborne responded with his usual conviviality.

Sometime later, after D'Amato had warned student Neuborne, "Now, this is very complex," the jury was treated to a beatified version of how logrolling and wire-pulling make the political world of Nassau County twirl more efficiently in its orbit.

At the height of D'Amato's digressive chatter, there was a pause as Neuborne looked at some cards his assistant had handed him. Taking advantage of the lull, D'Amato, obviously delighted with his performance, began to mouth something to Michael Armstrong, who was in the audience. He stuck his tongue out as far as it would go, then flapped it down over his receding chin and popped his eyes, simultaneously grinning, as though he wanted his lawyer to know he realized he was walking a tightrope but was confident he could successfully continue his balancing act.

Neuborne turned back to the clowning senator and resumed his interrogation. Suddenly, however, his questions were more pointed.

NEUBORNE: Now, Senator, in your capacity as an executive leader for Island Park, did you ever have conversations with Don Woolnough about filling employment vacancies at the town of Hempstead?

D'AMATO: Yes.

NEUBORNE: And with the county of Nassau as well?

D'AMATO: Yes.

NEUBORNE: And did those conversations take place over a period from 1970 to, say, 1976?

D'AMATO: Yes, about that time, I would say, '75, '76, yes. And there may have been instances thereafter, more isolated.

D'Amato had confessed that he sought town and county jobs from a private citizen. That admission might have made him look bad, but to have denied he knew government jobs were obtained only at party headquarters would have invited a perjury indictment. Looking bad is something politicians grow used to early in their careers, but it's more difficult to get used to serving hard time.

257

Neuborne tightened the screw another turn.

NEUBORNE: Could you describe the substance of those conversations [with Woolnough] . . . how did they take place?

D'AMATO: Well, more often than not it would be occasions when I would have someone seeking a job and might ask if there were any openings . . . in the county or town.

I might have heard of some and suggested that I knew of an opening that might be taking place and I would like to recommend someone.

Sometimes I would send in a recommendation on one of our committeeman's recommendation cards and wait for a call: *Yes, there is a spot.* It might take a month, sometimes longer.

NEUBORNE: Did he ever call you and say that we have got a vacancy, Hempstead Sanitation maybe, or County Parks?

D'AMATO: Yes.

NEUBORNE: Is there anybody you would like to recommend?

D'AMATO: Yes, that happened.

He then volunteered that on "other occasions Mr. Margiotta himself" would inform him of an opening. At that moment of betrayal, Kempton muttered, "D'Amato doesn't give a damn about anyone on God's green earth except himself."

As if D'Amato were anxious to emphasize that his reference to the boss was not accidental, in answer to Neuborne's question— "You would send them [recommended applicants] down to talk to whom, to Don Woolnough at party headquarters?"—the uncaged tiger offered, "Most often Don Woolnough. On some occasions, I believe Mr. Margiotta may have seen some."

The faint smile on Neuborne's cherubic face revealed his satisfaction with D'Amato's unexpected stiletto thrust into his former mentor.

NEUBORNE: Now, in addition to conversations with Mr. Woolnough about filling vacancies in either the town or the county, did you ever have conversations with Mr. Woolnough about *raises* or *promotions* for government employees in both the town and the county?

258

D'AMATO: I may have from time to time, yes. Yes, I did . . . I might get a phone call from Mr. Woolnough that so-and-so, a particular individual, had been recommended for a promotion, or a raise, what was my opinion.
NEUBORNE: Mr. Woolnough at the Republican party headquarters was soliciting your opinion as executive leader of Island Park?
D'AMATO: Of Island Park, yes.
NEUBORNE: As to whether those raises should go through?
D'AMATO: Whether or not I had any recommendations, any approval or disapproval.

D'Amato wanted Neuborne to know he couldn't remember ever turning down a party recommendation for a raise or a promotion.
"You yourself never turned anybody down?" Neuborne asked incredulously.
D'Amato grew uncomfortable as he eyed a card that Neuborne was perusing. "You know," D'Amato began tentatively, "well, you know when you say 'never,' that is a tough one, and I am trying to be very candid. To the best of my recollection, I did not. . . . There may be some person—I have to search my memory—who I saw as a troublemaker or something like that. . . ."
In order to underscore D'Amato's knowledge of the party's extortion, Neuborne asked, "When you were supervisor, Senator, you contributed one percent of your salary to the party, didn't you?"
D'Amato put his index fingers at either side of his glasses, lifted them off his nose, and carefully returned them to their accustomed spot before slowly answering. "I made contributions to the party, basically using the one percent as a guideline."
In 1975, before a grand jury in Brooklyn, D'Amato had been vague about contributions, even though he was involved in the mechanics of the kickback scheme at that time. When Assistant U.S. Attorney James Drucker asked D'Amato to tell the grand jury whether he knew who sent the contribution list over to the Republican Finance Committee, he responded, "I have no knowledge of that, nor did I know it was sent over to the Republican Finance Committee." And when Drucker asked him, "Have you put pressure onto anyone under you [to contribute]?" his answer was an unembroidered "No."

But ten years later, no longer concerned with what he had said to the grand jury, D'Amato's recollection was more precise.

> NEUBORNE: Do you know whether party headquarters kept records or lists of who contributed . . . who gave in the supervisor's office; who gave in the Parks Department?
> D'AMATO: You know, I have difficulty answering that whether or not I knew. I think there was a general knowledge that people—that the party kept receipts. I recall receiving, for example, receipts, little slips, Nassau County Republican Finance Committee, I believe they were. And they'd mail them right about in October or thereabouts in terms of what the contributions were. So obviously there was some record keeping, and I was aware of that, yes.

At the beginning of his answer he was not sure he knew that the party kept records of contributors, but within a few sentences the same mouth was informing the same ears that he was intimately aware of actual receipts, down to size and due date. He was even willing to elaborate. "My memory is they generally came in a packet, a small packet, and they were very thin slips." Regardless of their thinness, there was enough space on these informatory slivers to contain the name of the person who gave and "whether he or she was a county or town employee."

He had sworn to the 1975 grand jury that he had never put pressure on anyone to contribute, but now he was describing, if only inadvertently, one of the ways the pressure was applied.

> NEUBORNE: Senator, do you ever recall receiving, again in your capacity as an executive leader . . . receiving computer printouts showing the names and addresses and salaries of public employees living in your area?
> D'AMATO: Yes.
> NEUBORNE: Did you ever have any conversations with Mr. Margiotta or with anyone else in the Republican party about why the salaries of public employees were listed on those computer printout sheets?
> D'AMATO: No, I didn't.

There was an uncomfortable moment of silence, and D'Amato, sensing the implausibility of his answer, added, "I must say that I think that probably political party leaders would want to know what people were making. I don't think that—you know—an unusual kind of a thing." He clamped his jaws together, unwilling to explain why political leaders would want to know what people were making.

Neuborne pressed him: "Senator, as an executive leader . . . you were aware, weren't you, that employees for both the town of Hempstead and the county of Nassau were being interviewed at party headquarters before they got their jobs?"

D'Amato responded reluctantly, "Basically, yes."

Neuborne turned and faced the jury as he asked his next question: "And you were aware, weren't you, that employees . . . had their raises okayed by party headquarters before those raises went into effect?"

D'Amato stared off into space and spoke to the void: "Political approval was sought. I was aware of those that came to Island Park. So certainly."

NEUBORNE: You knew the other executive leaders were approving raises in their areas as well?

D'AMATO: I imagined and assumed that they were consulted, as well, for their political recommendations, yes.

NEUBORNE: And you were aware, weren't you, that copies of the receipts of campaign contributions of public employees were being sent out to the various executive leaders?

D'AMATO: I would have to say I assumed that if I got these receipts, I know certainly on several occasions—

In an attempt to keep D'Amato from describing those "several occasions," Hart objected. He didn't—he said without any sign he was offended—like the senator's use of the word "assumed." Mishler asked D'Amato, "Can you testify to the general practice and procedure, Senator? Do you know of the general practice and procedure?"

When the senator nodded, the judge overruled Hart, and D'Amato told Neuborne, "I have to say it was an assumption on my part that I was not the only person who received these."

Neuborne then reminded D'Amato he had testified that executive leaders received computer printouts showing the salaries of town and county employees living in their districts.

> Now, Senator, you've been in politics a long time and you've been engaged in both fund-raising and the administration of governmental employees for a long time. Does a system like that put pressure on employees to give?

Pascarella, sensing that Neuborne was now dealing with the heart of the case, objected. Mishler looked down at D'Amato. "Well," he asked, "do you have an opinion that you can express with a reasonable degree of certainty?" In an attempt to convince the judge he could not answer Neuborne's question with any degree of certainty, D'Amato responded, "Let me say that I believe, or—"
Mishler cut in abruptly. "I will allow him to testify to it . . . he may express an opinion."
D'Amato paused to see if Hart or Pascarella would mount another attempt to rescue him. With no sign of help coming from either of them, he finally said:

> I think there may have been some employees who could have felt they were under pressure to contribute. . . . It would appear that some people could feel that they were under pressure.

But in 1975, in answer to Drucker's question "Have you put pressure onto anyone under you?" he had said, "No."
D'Amato was growing increasingly restless. His answers became disconnected; there was seldom a straight flow of thought. Neuborne came close to the witness box and demanded:

> Senator, you said that raises were approved either at party headquarters or by executive leaders. Was payment or nonpayment of one percent contributions a factor in approving or denying raises?
> D'AMATO: . . . it was a consideration, there was no doubt. And some of the Republican leaders made [it] part of the consideration.

But in 1975, Drucker asked him a closely related question. "Do you yourself know of any policy within the town of Hempstead or with any of the departments whereby supervisors in the departments ever expected to collect from the men and the men are expected to give at the risk of possibly losing overtime or other benefits?" At that time, Supervisor D'Amato had responded, "I am not aware of any. . . . To my knowledge, officially and unofficially, no one has ever come to me and complained to me and made known that type of policy, and I think if it is the case, it certainly should not be collected. I would certainly use my influence to see to it that it would not be collected."

Other Republican leaders, he now conceded, took part in "certain situations that went by which were clearly abusive." Neuborne was unwilling to allow D'Amato to separate himself from the thundering Republican herd. "Were you aware, Senator, that the question of whether or not someone paid one percent was a factor in determining whether or not that raise would be approved."

D'Amato snapped: "I think that obviously the answer is that it was a factor, certainly."

Neuborne was leading up to the smoking-gun letter in which D'Amato had intervened to get Robert Marcus a raise denied by headquarters because Marcus hadn't made his "contribution." In that letter to Woolnough, D'Amato said he had "spoken to Mr. Margiotta . . ." and that Margiotta told him Marcus "would be approved if he took care of the one percent." With the letter in mind, Neuborne asked D'Amato, "Did you ever have a conversation with Joseph Margiotta about the connection between contributing one percent and the granting of raises or promotions to public employees?"

D'Amato fidgeted. "Well, I'm wondering if I can be a little more specific about that. Because there were many occasions during the course of several investigations where Mr. Margiotta would speak to the entire executive committee. *I never had a private conversation with him about the issue of the one percent*" (italics mine).

That seemed to contradict the simple language in the 1971 smoking-gun letter in which he wrote exactly the opposite. Furthermore, his current testimony contradicted his 1975 grand jury testimony. Drucker had asked him, "Have you ever had occasion to discuss the one percent matter with Mr. [Margiotta]?" At that time he had answered, "Yes." He had gone on to describe "our conversations" about "criminal action" arising from the 1 percent "matter," apparently additional conversations he had with Margiotta about the 1 percent kickbacks having nothing to do with Marcus.

Determined to pin down this obvious contradiction, Neuborne asked, "You spoke with Mr. Margiotta about a raise for a Mr. Robert Marcus, didn't you?" Referring to what he described as "the famous letter of 1971," D'Amato answered that "when I see the letter, which I've obviously seen, I recall writing that letter."

NEUBORNE: And do you have any question that the conversation took place—

D'AMATO: No. I would be—obviously if you look at the letter, certainly.

D'Amato explained that his action on behalf of Marcus had been sparked by a plea from two committeemen in his club. He had gone to Margiotta only when his attempt to get Marcus a raise by speaking to a willing but impotent sanitation commissioner—Landman—had failed. "And I might say, Mr. Neuborne," D'Amato added with a show of pride, "that Mr. Marcus never knew about that."

However, D'Amato's insistence on portraying himself as an anonymous benefactor was not true. After the Island Park committeemen's treasury had contributed seventy-five dollars in Marcus's name, a receipt acknowledging the contribution had been sent to Marcus by Republican headquarters. A notation of that receipt lay unheralded in the massive court records introduced by Neuborne. But D'Amato didn't need his attention drawn to that document for him to know that receipts were always sent to the person being credited with a contribution. It was a measure of D'Amato's contempt for the jurors' intelligence for him to say that he would ask for a favor for a member of his club without getting that club member to show his gratitude.

Within less than an hour it became apparent that Judge Mishler was anxious to complete the interrogation of the perturbed senator. D'Amato was beginning to babble; his incoherence had become noticeable as he strove to avoid answering questions.

NEUBORNE: You knew that if that contribution didn't go to headquarters, if they didn't get that one percent contribution, he [Marcus] wouldn't get that raise?

D'AMATO: Well, Mr. Neuborne, let me say that my thinking was a preoccupation in order to help this person. (sic)

NEUBORNE: In other words, would it be fair to say that you were trying to isolate him from the one percent—

D'AMATO: I wanted to help him. I didn't think I—how could I have conscientiously—or how could anyone approach him and say, "Look, I want to facilitate this." That was my purpose and that's why the—

NEUBORNE: He was so unsophisticated he didn't know he was supposed to give one percent?

D'AMATO: Let me say this: I know you've had him here. He is a nice person. Certainly not sophisticated. I think he was a good person. Had he had money, probably would have given. I don't know. We will never know that. I wasn't going to jeopardize it. I wanted to help him.

Kempton hadn't been impressed by D'Amato's show of beneficence. In an aside, he remarked sorrowfully, "No one should have that much control over someone else's life."

Neuborne's distaste for D'Amato's answers was manifested in the unaccustomed driving tone of his questions. "Can you recall a conversation with Mr. Margiotta in which you told him that it was wrong to require employees to pay money before they could get a raise?"

Since D'Amato had never counseled Margiotta that such a practice would be wrong, he licked his lips before nervously responding, "As I said, I believe I didn't have any conversations with him about the issue of one percent."

But that was not what he had told the 1975 grand jury. Mishler seemed disturbed. "Would you—" he said to the attorneys "—please come to the sidebar?"

The electronic buzzer went on, and the following conversation appears in the transcript:

Mishler: Now, I know that the lawyers would have liked to give the senator the chance to explain and give him probably a little more leeway than just the ordinary layman. But when you ask a question—Did you ever have a talk with Mr. Margiotta and tell him you thought it was wrong to solicit one percent for promotion?—what has that got to do with the case?

The judge had made a startling declaration: He did not consider everyone appearing in his court to be equal before the law. His playing field was tilted in favor of senators; an "ordinary laymen" could not expect to be given as much *leeway* as a Republican politician of D'Amato's stature. Equally startling was Mishler's reaction to Neuborne's attempt to find out whether D'Amato had ever told Margiotta he thought it was wrong to solicit 1 percent before a promotion would be granted. "What has that got to do with the case?" he had demanded obtusely. Neuborne attempted to explain:

> Because he was the supervisor of the town of Hempstead as well. And it's my position that he had this knowledge. He was obliged either to act on it, to try and stop the practice, or that if he didn't, his inaction can be charged as one of the factors in causing this to become a policy or custom of the town of Hempstead for the purpose of liability.

Before Mishler could further question Neuborne, he was distracted by noise in the courtroom. "This is an unruly crowd," he remarked. At which point, clerk Martin Adler interjected, "Judge, the senator was talking to one of the jurors. I don't know what the conversation was about."

The sudden commotion in the courtroom was caused by the extraordinary sight of D'Amato—after checking to see that the judge was preoccupied with the attorneys—turning and talking directly to a juror. The exchange went on for several seconds, interspersed with broad smiles and approving head bobs. Mishler, normally a stern enforcer of court decorum, decided not to even ask D'Amato about the subject of the conversation. Instead, he said, "All right. We better get to the questions. I see there is a lot of discussion here and the press is running wild. . . . It's fifty minutes already. . . . I want to get through with this."

The buzzer was turned off, and Mishler called out in a loud, chastising voice, "May we have order in the courtroom, please. Please be seated . . . your conversations are interfering with the jury's ability to hear the testimony. The public is invited. You are not here to participate."

Neuborne stood directly in front of D'Amato. Crossing his arms over his chest, he asked, "Senator, you recently were quoted as saying that the practice may have been wrong. In what way did you deem the practice may have been wrong?"

Town attorney McCarthy objected immediately; Mishler immediately overruled him. D'Amato was obviously disconcerted, embarrassed that his own publicized attempt to enunciate an ethical opinion was being thrown back at him—first by the *New York Times* and now by this ACLU tormentor. Grimacing, he spoke haltingly:

D'AMATO: Well, Mr. Neuborne, when we have the benefit of hindsight to look back and when there are those examples that have been proven in other matters—litigation, et cetera, supervisors collecting on the job, my feelings were always that people were making—I was making contributions. And I have said in previous testimony that the atmosphere was well known, that one percent was the standard of what was looked for as the guide for contributions, what would be appropriate, what you would give to be supported by your party. That was the guide. I knew that before I came into government in 1961. . . .

I have to suggest to you that in retrospect and that is what my statement—I tried to be truthful and candid and open with people, when you look back, although I think most people were giving voluntarily that certainly there could be some who felt that they were pressured, who weren't giving on a voluntary basis, and it comes down to when is something voluntary and when isn't it.

His tortured answer went on for several minutes. In the midst of it he explained why he contributed to the party, always in excess of 1 percent of his annual income. "I gave because I didn't want to lose my job, but not because the Republicans were going to jeopardize it, but because I felt I was helping that party and if we didn't win, I would be out." It was a rather direct expression of the role that greed plays in patronage: When the party wins, you get a job—if you paid for it.

D'Amato then described an incident in his life that he thought provided complete justification for the Nassau Republicans' patronage policies. He told of being fired as an eighty-three dollars-a-week law clerk when the Democrats had taken control of the county in the early 1960s. The primitive philosophy under which he was working appeared to be: They did it to me, so I can do it to them. Anxious to avoid dispelling the image of the long-suffering law clerk abused by Democratic bosses, D'Amato didn't volunteer that the law clerk's job had been given to him by Republican wire-puller Joe Carlino or that a better job had been handed to him by the same Carlino immediately after the Democrats had fired him.

Neuborne asked him—in view of his unwillingness to condemn the 1 percent kickbacks—why he had told the *Times* that he thought the practice was "wrong." His answer was as oblique as it was long, but as it wound down, still unanswered, he did say:

> Mr. Neuborne, in much of the information that has flowed, subsequent to '74, '75, '76, you begin to see that there may be some who do feel, and who feel, and did feel pressured, and I have to acknowledge that.

After once again assuring Neuborne, "I tried to be very candid with you," D'Amato insisted he had never considered whether a person contributed when deciding if he should approve a promotion or a raise. And then, as if to demonstrate what a reasonable man he was, he added, "I can't tell you that that was not something that Mr. Margiotta didn't do or that other leaders did factor in."

Appeased by D'Amato's last betrayal of his former friend, Neuborne ended his interrogation. With obvious relief, D'Amato heard the party attorneys state they had no interest in questioning him. Judge Mishler told him, "You may step down."

After several moments, he smoothed down the lapels of his jacket and departed. When he reached the jury stand, he stopped to chat with the jurors, an offense for which less august witnesses would have felt the sting of Judge Mishler's reprimand. D'Amato finally moved on, grinning broadly, his tongue again extruded from his mouth and flapping down over his lip, the press corps falling in behind him.

TWENTY-NINE

DAMAGE CONTROL

K empton and I had remained seated as Judge Mishler tidied up. After noting that the room had the shape of an octagon, Mishler warned the jurors not to speak of the trial over the weekend but to keep the case "within the eight walls of this court-room." He then dismissed them until Tuesday, August 20.

After they left, Tilles addressed the judge. "I was advised that while we were at the bench conference one of the reasons why the audience was a little noisy was that the senator, while on the witness stand, was engaging in banter of some sort with the jury." Frank Cullen, sitting at Lorraine's side in the first row, was nodding his head vigorously, urging Tilles on.

"What do you want me to say?" Mishler asked wearily.

Tilles seemed intimidated by Mishler's question. "I wanted to bring that to your attention," he replied neutrally.

"I will call that juror up," Mishler said, acknowledging the seri-ousness of D'Amato's infraction, but then, unexpectedly, he threw the responsibility for pursuing the matter on Tilles's frail shoulders. "*If you can identify him or her,* I will ask what was said and how it is going to affect their decision."

If the judge was too busy to personally probe for the identity of the juror, the court clerk, Adler, was in the jury conference room

270

with his wards and could have been delegated to ask which of his flock had spoken to D'Amato. Instead, Mishler had asked Tilles for the juror's name, which he couldn't produce, and the matter was pursued no further.

Kempton and I went out to the front of the sunlit building. We were looking forward to the more unrestrained give-and-take of D'Amato's press conference; it had been set for fifteen minutes after court was adjourned so that the senator would have an opportunity to freshen up. Kempton lit his ever-present pipe and began filtering out the fresh Nassau breezes. Through the plate-glass doors we caught sight of Ed Hart leaving the courtroom and racing down one of the corridors, followed by a pack of attorneys. Kempton remarked that Hart had come to him earlier and thanked him for printing his name in Tuesday's column. Kempton chuckled. "Unbelievable vanity," he said, and then explained that he felt his reference to Margiotta's attorney had been unflattering, but "vain-glorious" Hart didn't seem to recognize this.

In my conversations with Hart, he referred to Kempton as "Murray the Righteous." It was clear to me, though not to Kempton, that Hart had been toying with him, as the manipulative attorney did with most people with whom I had seen him deal. Hart's style called for disguising his true feelings, since to expose them risked the possibility someone might find them objectionable.

As we stood in front of the courthouse, warming ourselves in the midafternoon sunlight, Bob Teague, an experienced and well-respected reporter for NBC television, notebook in hand, came up to Kempton and requested a piece of information. Kempton dredged up the citation from some sharp neural curve in his brain and, as part of his normal routine with the dozens of people who ricocheted through his life every day, told Teague one of the lines that was to appear in his as yet uncomposed Sunday column. "No matter how high D'Amato climbs, he still calls Joe Margiotta 'Mr. Margiotta.' "

Teague laughed, which encouraged Kempton to tell him a story involving Hedrick Smith, a *Times* reporter, which I had already heard several times. "Smith and I were on assignment in the South twenty years ago during the desegregation fight. He had inter-viewed a black man in Albany, Georgia, who said that he knew when he came into a town for the first time that there wasn't any work if he saw a white man on the back of a garbage truck."

Kempton felt that this story communicated some truth about the status of Hempstead's corps of sanitation engineers. Teague rewarded him with another laugh, but suddenly his face became blank, and he began to recite in a subdued but intense voice something unrelated to anything he and Kempton had been discussing. After several moments of this startling behavior, Teague slowly turned and walked toward the courthouse doors. I looked at Kempton questioningly. "He's just memorizing his script," Kempton remarked tolerantly. Each media specialist, he knew, had craft problems, the nature of which only the specialist's peers could appreciate.

We went back into the courthouse and prepared to climb the lobby's circular staircase. At the foot of the staircase we found Neuborne talking to reporters. D'Amato's admissions that the 1 percent extortion system existed had made him decide not to question the senator about the obvious conflicts between his 1975 grand jury testimony, the Marcus letter, and his latest version of the truth. "I was quite satisfied," Neuborne said with a glowing face. "He conceded that workers had been pressured to contribute. And he conceded that whether somebody gave one percent could be a factor in whether they got a raise." There was in his explanation about why he had not pursued D'Amato an excess of ardor.

When we entered the large second-floor courtroom in which Gary Lewi told us the press conference was to be held, we found it had been emptied of furniture and was jammed with media people. They had formed a U-shaped space in front of a one-foot-high platform. A bank of microphones, hooked up to various radio and television recording units, stood at the front of the platform. The television cameras were about fifteen feet from the platform at the base of the U, behind them were technicians laden with battery power packs and sound booms.

Beneath the camera lenses knelt a dozen or so television reporters, at the ready to fire their questions. Members of the print media, including representatives from all the major wire services, lined the sides of the U. The *Washington Post* and *Newsweek* magazine had assigned special correspondents.

The artists who had worked for weeks in the cameraless court-room on the floor below were all there, pads opened, laboriously sketching a scene that a dozen still-cameramen were instanta-neously recording from every possible vantage point. Kempton and I stood at the right side of this elongated semicircle, outside the intense glow of the television lights.

Flanked by his press agent and his lawyer, the senator entered. Gary Lewi stationed himself against the wall at the back corner of the platform; Michael Armstrong took his position on our side, anchoring the end of the platform opposite Lewi. The press agent looked worried, but Armstrong glowed with attentiveness. They were prepared, if needed, to rescue their chief.

D'Amato, forty-eight years old, fresh-faced and beaming, slowly made his way through the crowd, exchanging greetings indiscrimi-nately. As he stepped onto the platform, he glanced around. When his eyes fell on Kempton, he waved his hand in apparent friend-ship to a man who had rarely had an unscathing word to say about him. Kempton nodded back, his face covered with the same toler-ant smile with which I had seen him beguile numerous scoundrels in the execution of his professional responsibilities.

The storm of questions broke immediately. How did he feel about being forced to explain his connection to the 1 percent scheme? Well, he would rather not be talking about that topic. "I would rather be announcing ... we had landed a new Toyota plant on Long Island"—he hesitated as if realizing that he now rep-resented more than the province of Nassau—"or in New York. I mean, that would have been, I think, a little more helpful than the name recognition that may come as a result of this."

The questions flew at the senator from every angle. To an experienced politician like D'Amato, this chaotic hustings was the perfect setting in which to discuss his involvement in the kick-back scheme: He had the luxury of answering whichever ques-tion he preferred. In that shouting, cacophonous bedlam, impu-dent questions were ignored, and if some clever reporter managed to come too close for comfort with his first question, it was always acceptable to the yapping dogs of the press if the senator disregarded the reporter's follow-up question and tried his luck with another straining wretch at the opposite end of the room.

Since his options were open, D'Amato chose to focus the thirty-minute conference on Robert Marcus. Adopting the pose of a folksy, small-town resident who came from a "little village," he pictured his clubhouse muscle flexing as merely a neighborly act. "He [Marcus] lived across the street from me in a little bungalow." D'Amato portrayed himself as a philanthropist trying to help someone who was unable to help himself. Moreover, in case it had gone unnoticed by those questers for truth who were calling out to him, he wanted it known that he had never even told Marcus who had performed this benevolent act.

As D'Amato brushed aside, or double-talked, the disconnected questions, Gary Lewi's concerned visage began to relax. He observed his boxer with the pleasure of a manager who saw that his meal ticket was ahead on points. Michael Armstrong seemed equally pleased, but without that air of desperation that marked the gratitude of the truly needy.

In an apparent effort to soften the impact of *the smoking-gun letter,* D'Amato said. "I never attempted to indicate I didn't send the letter." And then, with a casualness of delivery that comes easy only to those who conceive of themselves as invincible, he remarked, "The climate of that time was 'to the victor belongs the spoils.'" In an attempt to make that battlefield philosophy more palatable to an audience more concerned with honesty than he was, he added, "The traditional pattern of giving was based on that guideline, one percent. That word 'kickback' isn't the issue."

Kempton raised his hand and the press corps' riotous behavior subsided. "You viewed it as voluntary, but did the county leaders?"

D'Amato was grateful Kempton accepted his assertion that he viewed the obligatory 1 percent payments as voluntary, but that didn't produce any impulse to enlighten Kempton about the county leaders' frame of mind. "Obviously, I spoke to Mr. Margiotta," he began, but—the grin returned with deeper indentations around the corners of his mouth and eyes—how was it possible to know whether Margiotta viewed the 1 percent contributions with the same purity that he did?

In an endeavor to expose D'Amato's knowledge of the extortionary nature of the 1 percent extractions, I asked him, "Why did you think the seventy-five-dollar check would get Marcus the raise?"

I had called out during a lull toward the end of the conference, and D'Amato did not have a variety of questions to pick from. He looked uncomfortable for a moment and then responded, "I must have been given the assurance that it would get him the raise." Kempton patted me on the back; it was the closest D'Amato came all day to describing the reality of that dark practice.

The conference ended soon after; reporters headed for the telephones, and technicians began packing equipment. D'Amato and his exuberant acolytes shook hands with the cameramen, then made their way toward a dozen individuals who had clustered around Kempton. In full electioneering stride, he began glad-handing.

Reporter Irving Long remarked that Burt Neuborne just said that D'Amato's 1975 grand jury testimony conflicted with what he was now saying. D'Amato didn't seem to hear this account of Neuborne's allusion to his perjury. Instead, he turned to the artists, who were making last-second observations with their pastel chalks about his physiognomy. With a show of interest, he inspected a drawing of the press conference that had been scotch-taped to the wall and was being photographed by a television cameraman.

"My, do I really look that good?" he asked.

The traditional flatterers and improvers of the wart-skinned and cross-eyed effortlessly summoned up language to describe him as a handsome prince. One offered to give him any sketch in her portfolio that he liked. After a show of inspecting them for artistic merit, he selected one that memorialized a moment in his life when his honesty had been questioned and rather brusquely handed it back to Gary Lewi. He then thanked the artist for a gift it was impossible to believe he would ever again view, since it would always conjure up memories of an ordeal.

We accompanied him to the spiral staircase, then down its dizzying sweep to the floor of the lobby and out to the parking lot. During this processional, he informed us that although his test on the stand was behind him, he still planned to pressure party leaders to reach an accommodation with Neuborne. "A settlement, before the case goes to the jury, might still be the best thing." In a voice meant to convey his sense of fairness, he said, "I believe the interests of both sides might best be served by working out a settlement that encompasses those people who feel that they may have been coerced into paying."

The subliminal message was that a settlement would end the matter without further damaging preelection publicity. What did the leaders back on Post Avenue have to fear from a negative jury verdict? They weren't going to pay the bills. But he had to run for reelection, and if the fallout from this trial led to his defeat, that would be *his* personal catastrophe.

He informed *New York Times* reporter Maureen Dowd that his association with the trial and with the Nassau machine was "an impairment," but he wanted it understood that someone with his background could still succeed. "Maybe it is something I have to prove to people, that you don't have to be an Ivy Leaguer or come from a certain strata, that you can be an Alfonse Marcello D'Amato, and you can have been the product of a political machine—and certainly you made mistakes along the way—but that in the final analysis it's the kind of job you want to do."

Having expressed the opinion that the important thing when judging him was not what he did but what he—in the secret recesses of his mind—wanted to do, D'Amato hopped on a plane and within hours was campaigning at a farmers' fair upstate. The *Times* story carried a picture of the gleeful senator reaching for an ice cream cone at the fair grounds, but the editorial page contained a different message about D'Amato's role in the "sleazy system."

> In the teeth of compelling court evidence, Senator Alfonse D'Amato of New York continues to insist he didn't know something that in the 1970s every Nassau County politician had to know: public employees who wanted to be hired or promoted in the county had to kick back 1 percent of their pay to the Republican Party, which controlled the county.
> Indeed, it has become clear that the Senator not only knew about the kickback system while serving as a county and town official but also helped run it; and not only helped run it, but also misled a Federal grand jury that looked into the matter in 1975.

As Kempton and I drove away from Uniondale and made our way toward the press room in the Mineola court building, Kempton seemed somewhat disheartened. He chewed at his unlit pipe and squinted nervously at the congested island traffic.

"D'Amato tries to project the idea that the party has *reformed*," he said. "Of course, it hasn't. It's just applied some innovative thinking. They've changed the collection techniques, but they're still collecting. They can't send printout sheets to executive leaders and department heads. Too many grand juries have taken testimony. Now tickets constitute the major device, although undoubtedly some are still sending in 1 percent checks."

D'Amato bragged that his $1,000-a-plate Wall Street dinners, Meet-the-Senator fund-raising breakfasts, lunches, and cocktail parties, and hours spent every week on his Washington office phone dunning prospects had put over $8 million in his campaign accounts. So intimidating was this war chest that Brooklyn district attorney Elizabeth Holtzman—who had almost defeated him in 1980 and whom he contemptuously referred to as "Holtzperson"—withdrew from the race, citing her inability, because of the gross inequity of their financial positions, to wage a credible campaign.

The profits of sin were never more apparent than that day in mid-August 1985 when Al D'Amato confronted the federal judiciary and walked away convinced that the only time he would serve would be another six years in the U.S. Senate.

THIRTY

THE PIT IN WHICH SCORES
WERE TO BE SETTLED

A trial narrows the vision of observers; a murder, a rape, an audacious swindle, focuses attention on the perpetrator, while the motives, the lifestyle, the abilities of lawyers, judges, and jurors, are ignored. The pit in which trials are held is too small to allow for such a review; courtroom procedures, developed over hundreds of years, strive to exclude matters that are so difficult to appraise. Yet it is precisely those factors that determine the outcome of most cases. The 1 percent case was no exception.

On August 26, the beginning of the trial's fifth week, Judge Mishler seemed short-tempered. In his no-nonsense manner he announced, "I want to get this case over. I just told my wife we may not be able to go to the judicial conference." Mishler enjoyed the annual sociality of herding federal judges. Those few days were his only annual vacation, and he had no intention of letting verbose attorneys who didn't know when enough was enough deprive him of that pleasure. "I want to get the case on the road," he said in a tone that made clear he would brook no opposition.

Mishler's decree distressed Neuborne. He planned to call Francis Purcell as his final rebuttal witness. Purcell could tie the county to the 1 percent kickbacks. But Mishler was pressuring him to bypass a top Republican so that he wouldn't miss a minute of the judicial conference. Neuborne decided not to fight Mishler and shortly announced that Purcell would not be called.

The defense attorneys were under the same pressure to shorten their witness list. Pascarella wanted a political science professor to testify that patronage was a grand old American custom. Mishler frowned; it wouldn't be necessary to call an expert for that purpose. "I intend to charge the jury that our democratic system depends on the stability of political parties . . . and that political parties have a right to solicit from the general public—and that includes municipal employees. I don't think you need an expert on patronage."

The judge was lumping together two separate practices. One was not an issue at the trial—the right of political parties to solicit from the general public. The second practice was the central issue in the case—the use of patronage to reward individuals who kicked back to the party while withholding "patronage" from better qualified, more scrupulous people.

Although Neuborne felt the judge's open admiration for patronage undermined his case, he was not surprised by Mishler's statement to Pascarella. Neuborne told me later that "Judge Mishler lectured me at length on the fact that we were not trying the concept of patronage. And he made it very clear to me that if I started down that road I was going to have a very difficult time. In fact, he told us at the bench, 'Look, why do you think I'm here? I'm here through patronage. It's not such a bad thing.' He was smiling when he said it."

Mishler was suspicious of the jury's ability to deliberate dispassionately. "I know," he told Pascarella as the natty lawyer clasped his gold pinkie ring and rotated it back and forth, "that juries feel that everything political parties do is corrupt."

In an effort to soften the impact of that prejudice, Mishler told the attorneys that he had decided he would ask the jury to deliver a "special verdict." They wouldn't simply be asked to rule on the four defendants' innocence or guilt; they would be presented with fifty questions, which the judge had composed, and their answers to those questions would determine what verdict *he* would reach. If there were any inconsistency in their responses—fifty questions left ample room for that—he would choose which answer deserved consideration and which didn't.

The next day, August 27, as the deadline for the judicial conference loomed, Mishler watched Evans Tilles recall Lorraine Cullen to the stand with ill-disguised impatience.

Cullen's appearance two weeks earlier had been a disaster. Her lawyer had rarely asked a question without an objection from defense attorneys or a tongue-lashing from the irascible judge. She estimated that less than 10 percent of her case had been presented, and that small portion in a truncated, disconnected fashion.

Tilles inquired about Cullen's meeting with Commissioner Milone. Why did she feel he was warning her to contribute to the party if she wanted a promotion? "When he called me into his office," she replied, "he said I should start playing ball in their ballpark."

Hart and Pascarella were on their feet immediately. The objections flew from one or the other until Tilles managed to ask his witness what she thought Milone had meant by that phrase.

"I took this to mean that he wanted me to pay the one percent," she said, obviously relieved that she had finally been able to offer this explanation to the jury.

Having led Cullen through this rather sketchy recital, Tilles retired from the field, and Hart rushed forward to cross-examine. "When did you tell your lawyer about this meeting with Commissioner Milone?" he demanded.

Two years ago, she responded calmly. Hart was skeptical. Was there any proof Milone had made such a statement? Cullen said she had recorded the incident in her diary on the day the event had taken place. Hart seemed taken aback. He cleared his throat, but having come that far, he decided to press on. Could she produce the diary? It was in her car, she said. Did Mr. Hart want her husband to go and get it? It was a question to which a negative response would have been damaging. And so Frank Cullen was sent scurrying to the parking lot.

Ten minutes later, he breathlessly returned to the courtroom and gave his wife's diary to Hart, who pored over it at his table.

Pascarella, rotating his pinky ring aggressively, noted Hart's frantic exploration of the diary and took the opportunity to ask Lorraine Cullen to be specific about what Commissioner Milone had said to her.

"You're jeopardizing your position," she responded. "You're playing in our ballpark." She had taken that to be an attempt to get her to contribute. "It was always the context that I heard it in—play ball," she added.

Impatient at his inability to locate the entry, Hart rushed forward and challenged Cullen to find any reference substantiating her memory of that conversation. With the certainty of someone who had read this volume frequently enough to have memorized sections of it, she identified the page and in a clear voice read that Milone had stated, "I was jeopardizing my own position," but disaster could still be avoided "if I play in the same ballpark."

In an attempt to salvage something from this disastrous line of questioning, Pascarella returned to the front of the witness box, a calculating look on his narrow face. The use of baseball terminology—was that the way someone would ask for a political contribution? he continued perversely.

"Definitely," Cullen said in an even tone. "That is always how I heard that terminology used—baseball terminology."

When had she first heard it used in that manner? Pascarella asked, apparently unable to restrain himself.

"I first heard it in 1966," soon after she had started working for the county. "That was a common topic of conversation. It was discussed throughout the year, but more often in September."

Could she find any other reference in her diary to the use of baseball language, Pascarella persisted.

Thumbing through the small book with no show of doubt about its existence, Cullen quickly looked up and said, "January 30, 1974 . . ." A Republican stalwart in the office had told her during a discussion about the 1 percent kickbacks, "You know the score."

In rapid fashion she then read off the names of several coworkers with whom she had discussed the 1 percent payments. Finally convinced that a continuation of this exchange would gain him nothing, Pascarella went back to his seat. In effect, the trial was over; all that remained was for the jury to render its verdict.

While the jury was sequestered in its segment of the courthouse pie, Wednesday's session was spent arguing over Judge Mishler's ninety-page charge to the jury and the language of the fifty "special-verdict" questions he had composed. A twelve-page draft of the special-verdict questions was distributed to each attorney and to members of the press. As the attorneys raised objections, Mishler displayed a relatively intransigent attitude. He was willing to alter an adjective here, an adverb there—occasionally, if the reasoning was compelling, a phrase could be excised—but major surgery was not to be performed on the body of his laboriously assembled creature.

Neuborne was most concerned about one word that appeared in several questions, which was typified by question 1 (e):

> Did a *substantial* [italics mine] number of public employees fear that if they failed or refused to make the contributions to the Republican Party that they would lose opportunities for promotion, overtime and other requests for favorable consideration.

What constituted a *substantial* number? The word's imprecise nature gave the jurors no guideline to reach their decision; what was substantial to five of them might seem insubstantial to the necessary sixth vote. Furthermore, if only a few hundred—or even a handful—of the approximately twenty-two thousand members of the class had been deprived of promotion, overtime, and other favorable consideration, shouldn't that group be entitled to the protection of the law, even if they didn't constitute some amorphously *substantial* group.

Several hours of debate didn't sway the judge. When a lunch recess was called, Neuborne said to me with a weary shake of his head, "The judge has confused the issues. He's lost control of the case."

During the afternoon the debate continued about the special-verdict questions while the jury remained out of sight. In a moment of unexpected frankness, Judge Mishler remarked that the uncontradicted evidence showed that John Jund's career *was* affected by his lack of contributions. Hart snarled and said something that did not carry to the judge's lofty station.

Pascarella tried to summon up a mathematical argument, but Mishler fired back, "I know the figures as well as I know the Ten Commandments." Then, as if to show he was concerned with weightier matters than Pascarella's arithmetical conjurings, he continued: "The first one is 'Thou shall have no God but me.' God was jealous," he explained Talmudically. "He wanted to be the only God."

Mishler was being playful. He had made up his mind and was at peace with himself. Having heard as much as he wanted to about the special verdict, the judge adjourned court until the next day, suggesting that the attorneys attempt to keep their summations as succinct as possible.

The boundaries of the pit in which this trial was to be decided would be determined entirely by himself, and only the casual and uninformed observer would reach any other conclusion.

THIRTY-ONE

SUMMING UP

Mishler's cautionary note had little impact. Neuborne's summation lasted five hours and used most of Thursday, August 29.

Neuborne stood in front of the jurors, speaking emotionally. He rummaged through the boxes of exhibits on the floor as if they were a record of the torment each worker had endured. Holding aloft forms requesting promotions or raises that had been denied by Woolnough, he called out, "Each one of those denials was a human being. They represent human lives and aspirations."

Neuborne reminded the jury that when asked about the party's power Donald Woolnough had admitted, "Yes, we controlled hirings; yes, we controlled raises."

Furthermore, Margiotta had admitted everything when he had testified. "He is a charismatic man with a magnetic presence," Neuborne said as he gripped the jury-box railing. "But remember, he said he understood how a public employee could feel subjectively pressured." He paused. "That's a confession!" he roared.

The meaning of that confession had been reinforced when Margiotta had admitted that "no party official worth his salt would recommend someone who wasn't supporting the party."

And then Al D'Amato, the second most powerful man in the party, had testified that it was "reasonable" to think all public officials working for him knew about the 1 percent kickbacks. Gesturing expansively, Neuborne emphasized, "Al D'Amato admitted . . . that whether or not an employee contributed was a factor in whether you'd get a raise."

It was men like D'Amato who made possible the corruption in Hempstead and Nassau County. "The strongest political party could do nothing unless"—he turned dramatically from one juror to another—"unless the government is playing ball with the party. Officials had delegated to the party the function of the personnel departments for the town and county governments.

"D'Amato, with full knowledge of the one percent scheme, did nothing. The highest officials of the town of Hempstead knew about this scheme since at least 1971. D'Amato adopted this as the official scheme in the town of Hempstead." Neuborne insisted that D'Amato knew exactly how vicious the operation was but was unconcerned. "He knew Robert Marcus wasn't the only worker stuck in this trap. . . . He did nothing to try and stop it."

Shaking his head sorrowfully, he said, "The system essentially made employees into sheep ready to be sheared. These people are so vulnerable that they can't fight back. The system runs on fear: Fear is its engine, fear is its fuel."

Glancing at Judge Mishler, he said, "Patronage doesn't mean that you squeeze low-ranking workers or require workers to pay protection to keep the party from interfering. That's not old-fashioned patronage. There's a brutal word for it: extortion."

And that extortion was successful because of the fear D'Amato nurtured among government workers. "Acts induced by fear and threats," Neuborne said, "are not voluntary."

Neuborne scoffed at D'Amato's claims that the 1 percent kickbacks were "voluntary." He recalled that Soviet workers had once sworn to international observers that they worked on Saturdays without pay on a voluntary basis. The 1 percent system in Nassau, he said with conviction, "is the same kind of *voluntary.*"

Although D'Amato had rationalized that he paid his 1 percent to the Republican party because of his fear of the Democrats, the real fear on the part of most contributors was of the retaliatory power of the Republican machine. "It's not fear of the other party but fear of losing your job, or failing to get a raise, because the Republicans are going to stay in power."

After three and a half hours, Mishler recessed for lunch. The defense attorneys left for a nearby restaurant, but on the flagstone platform in front of the courthouse Pascarella allowed himself to be detached from Hart long enough to pose for the television cameras. He was asked about Neuborne's effectiveness during the morning. "Professor Neuborne teaches law at NYU," he said acidly. "It sounded to me like he was delivering a lecture."

At 2:07, Neuborne again faced the jury. Though the operation of the scheme had changed somewhat since the mid-1970s, he said, the same extortion was in effect. Local party leaders had stopped sending people down to Post Avenue headquarters for an interview. Now the interviewing was done directly by the sixty-nine executive leaders; but the hiring procedure was the same: The party cleared the applicant and then issued a "recommendation." Since all of the heads of town and county government are leaders of the party, each applicant knew that a favorable party "recommendation" was essential.

Now, instead of depending on a flood of election-eve 1 percent checks from workers, the party sells tickets. Tickets are a better way to extort money, Neuborne said. "They leave no paper trail." He pointed to the boxes of old receipts on the floor that, to the party's regret, had exposed the process. "The form has changed, but the substance remains . . . the reality hasn't changed."

The major exception after 1978, Neuborne interjected, was Commissioner of Public Safety Michael Limongelli; he had left a clear trail. He told his workers that if they didn't buy hundreds of dollars' worth of tickets each year, he would cut off their overtime or have them walking a wintery midnight patrol on the Great South Bay beaches. And when Presiding Supervisor Thomas Gulotta had been told about Limongelli's illegal acts, he ignored them. Confronted with the same type of complaints, "Al D'Amato hunched his shoulders and turned away," Neuborne said. Gulotta had merely followed his predecessor's example.

Neuborne's voice had grown husky, almost hoarse, when he concluded at 3:10.

Evans Tilles confessed to me that when he rose to sum up Lorraine Cullen's case, "I didn't know what I was going to say." Unlike Neuborne, Tilles used only twenty-five minutes to accomplish all he thought he could for his client.

"Our claim," he said to the attentive jurors, "is that the scheme existed and that Lorraine Cullen was affected by it."

In a straightforward manner, he described Mrs. Cullen's abilities; but her abilities, he said, didn't win her promotion. Her advancement had been blocked because she refused to kick back part of her salary to the Republican party. "It was a system that punished the people who didn't give," he said gravely.

Louis Milone had testified that in making up his mind whether to promote Cullen or an individual who had passed the same test with a lower mark, he hadn't gotten involved in evaluating the candidates; he couldn't remember whom he had talked to about the promotion. In fact, he said he didn't know much about the five hundred people in the Probation Department. It was more than coincidence, Tilles maintained, that the candidate Milone picked was the only one among the top three who had contributed to the party.

With his logical, low-keyed presentation, Tilles had done an effective job in this final moment of the trial.

Julian Kaplan, a bachelor in his thirtieth year, had brought his doting mother, Adele, to witness his oration to the jury. He introduced her to me and sat her next to me in the press box. Mrs. Kaplan was a thin lady wearing large, purple-tinted glasses. She listened to her darling son with her mouth gaping in wonderment, her hand clutching her fallen chin; she clearly believed more than ever that all her years of effort were worthwhile.

"John Jund had the courage to fight the system," Mrs. Kaplan's son proclaimed. Tremendous pressure had been put on Jund through the years, but he had not capitulated. The thrust of Kaplan's summation was epitomized in his statement "You can be coerced without being asked to do anything."

He listed "code words" used by supervisors who were pressuring Jund to contribute 1 percent without directly telling him he must. *"Don't make waves. . . . You're not going to work in this town. You shouldn't have started all this. . . . You can go on welfare as far as I'm concerned. . . . One hand washes the other. . . . There's something politically wrong on your end."*

If you were a young man trying to earn a living, "consider the threat in these words," he implored loudly.

After he had concluded a strident defense of his client's cause and Mishler had adjourned court until 10:00 A.M. Friday, the beaming attorney came directly to the press box, where he was embraced by his proud mother. For such kisses sons have always striven to conquer new worlds.

On August 30, the twenty-fourth day of the trial, minutes before the morning session was to begin, word spread through the courtroom lobby that Daniel McCarthy, who was scheduled to lead off the final day of summations, had informed Mishler he was too sick to go on. Substituting for him would be seventy-three-year-old Nicholas LaGinestra, who had attended only 20 percent of the court sessions.

LaGinestra stood near the court entrance, at the edge of a crowd of defense attorneys who were completely ignoring him. I asked him whether it was true he was going to deliver Hempstead's summation. "Yes," he said. "Town attorney Chave called me last night and said, 'McCarthy ain't feeling well. He's not up to handling the summation, so I guess you'll do it.' "

Did he feel up to the task? I asked. "I worked for an insurance company for forty years," he said, as if to explain the nature of his talents. "I was forced to retire when I was sixty-five. Then I came to the town in 1978. I handle the town's insurance cases—never anything like this."

Hart and Pascarella went past LaGinestra into the courtroom, not pausing to wish their cocounsel good luck. LaGinestra didn't seem to notice their slight. After they passed, he shook his gray head, clearly discontent. "A lousy boil," he said. "Can you imagine dumping out because of a lousy boil."

A few minutes later, Judge Mishler was introducing LaGinestra to the jury, remarking merely that "Mr. McCarthy fell ill" in a dry, vaguely disapproving tone.

Acting as if he understood that nothing more was expected of him than that he go through the formalities required by the occasion, LaGinestra spoke to the jury in a folksy, earthy manner, expressing the justification for kickbacks in theological terms.

Noting disapprovingly that committeemen were "being cursed instead of blessed," he wanted to suggest what he thought was an accurate comparison. "The committeeman has the screening process just as the FBI is the screening process for the United States Government [sic]."

LaGinestra wondered how such fine fellows could be rewarded for their "screening" efforts. "Now, a man obtains a job from the committeeman . . . and should he be thankful? Should he thank the party? How could he do it? By contributions when the committeeman comes around. 'I help you, will you help the party?' He does it by contribution."

Then, raising his explanation to the level of religious dogma, he added reverently, "That is thanksgiving. We do that, the only time you pray is for purpose: adoration, contrition, thanksgiving, and supplication.

"Supposing and assuming that individuals contribute, then he's on the job and he may want his son to get a part-time job during the summer. [sic] He may want a relative to be recommended for a part-time. . . . So if he needed somebody like that, he would have to ask supplication. Therefore, they had a reason; a reasonable person would fear that they should contribute for this particular purpose."

Having proved he was a grateful supplicant, the contributor has only one "fear" in mind. "The fact that the other party may get into power and deny him *that little right* that he may have."

Clutching his fists in front of his chest, he explained why contributors to the party held on to "that little right" so desperately. "They avoid the Long Island Railroad, where you wait in the station, change at Jamaica: train delayed, train derailed, strike, be stranded—they avoid that. Is that appreciated? They avoid the subways, and I need say no more about the condition of the subway except that many people are manhandled, murdered; that goes on down in that subway. They want to avoid that. Are they appreciative? Would a reasonable, prudent person be appreciative of the fact that the Republican party and the town of Hempstead has provided him an opportunity where he comes along and gets in his car in his home, goes to the place where he works, and he parks his car there, gets in his car at night, and goes home. Is that to be appreciated?"

He told the jury that Neuborne was cruel because Raymond Graber had broken down and cried when he was questioning him. But it was for Alfonse D'Amato, the man who was presiding supervisor in 1978 when LaGinestra was provided with a Hempstead job, that his gravelly voice filled with indignation. "Now, a big deal has been made about Senator D'Amato, Al D'Amato. It always amazes me that when one person does something a big deal is made out of it and he's condemned; another person who does the same thing, he's praised.

"Mr. Neuborne said that he [D'Amato] had two hats, leader of Island Park and the town supervisor in the town of Hempstead. And he wrote that letter; he wrote the letter as the leader of Island Park. He wrote the letter confirming the conversation with Margiotta, whatever it was.

"There was a rule among them, but the Republican party would not recommend anybody for a raise until there was a payment of a contribution. . . . So it was a supplication; asking a favor. Now, because it was done by D'Amato, oh, he's a scoundrel, this and that. If it had been by Joe Blow, the executive leader of X little village, he's a man, compassionate, and so on. Because it was done by Al D'Amato, oh, it's a crime and he's a criminal."

It is doubtful that if Daniel McCarthy's boil had not incapacitated him he would have been as impassioned as LaGinestra in his defense of Al D'Amato.

Judge Mishler recessed at 10:42 for a short break before James Pascarella would begin his summation for Nassau. Ed Hart was buoyant, a gladiator prepared for his test, fearful only that Pascarella would take too long and force him to address a weary jury.

Hart had not misjudged Pascarella. Twenty minutes into his summation he hadn't yet made any reference to the case. He was concerned with procedure. Preempting Judge Mishler's role, he explained to the jurors what they were expected to do, what special verdicts were, and what Judge Mishler was bound to tell them; his tone was entirely professorial.

Finally, at 11:05, he made reference to the central point in his plea: "Mr. Neuborne in his opening statement tried to lump the defendants together." Worse yet, he had tried to do that throughout the trial. Don't let him get away with it, Pascarella cautioned. "What I'm saying is, don't lump us together; the plain English of it, treat us all individually. . . . Nassau County is an individual defendant."

The evidence that had been presented, Pascarella claimed, was against Hempstead, not Nassau County. Witnesses like Gaspar Cangemi had been speaking about Hempstead. "He said nothing bad about Nassau County."

He named leaders of the Republican party who had testified about involvement in the 1 percent kickbacks—D'Amato, Margiotta, Woolnough, and Livingston. "None of them worked for Nassau County; none of them were a Nassau County government official." He read a list of government officials who were said to have "cooperated with and made it possible" for the scheme of the party leaders to work. Haff, Phears, Graber, "and finally Mr. Al Riehl. Well, who is the only one there that could possibly be considered a Nassau County government official? Alfred Riehl . . ." But Riehl was not the head of the county. He was only the "program staffing officer." There were government officials above him— Ralph Caso, Francis Purcell.

Pascarella's remarks annoyed Ed Hart. He had a sour look on his face. Pascarella's anxiety to separate his client from the other three defendants was strengthening Neuborne's case against Hart's client, the Republican party.

Most of the rest of the afternoon was filled with similar forays into theoretical distinctions that were based on assumptions that seemed plausible only if the listener had faith in Mr. Pascarella's impartiality. An example came at 2:45 when Pascarella launched a twenty-minute diatribe against Lorraine Cullen: Perhaps what Commissioner Milone meant when he referred to "playing in our ballpark" was that he wanted her to be more cooperative. Pascarella implied that Mrs. Cullen hadn't performed her job satisfactorily. But the defense had previously conceded she was a good worker, and Milone had testified that he didn't know what kind of work she did.

Citing Cullen's years-long effort to bring the 1 percent case to trial, Pascarella expressed his evaluation: "This is the pattern of a complainer."

At 4:10, after noting he had taken "a long time," Pascarella concluded his summation, remarking apologetically, "Obviously all the parties feel this is an important case."

"I feel like a pitcher who has warmed up three days in a row and got rained out," Ed Hart began at 4:20. So many of his points, he said, had been made by Mr. LaGinestra and Mr. Pascarella that he was reluctant to bring them up for fear of boring the jury.

Emphasizing his role as underdog, he jauntily remarked: "Yesterday, when Mr. Neuborne finished summing up, you probably looked over there and said, Ed Hart, why don't you give up? Run up the white flag, surrender, default, and we can all go home." He sneered, as if to emphasize the absurdity of such a suggestion.

Hart was the most flamboyant lawyer at the trial. He was not, however, the most coherent. For most of the next five hours he pranced around, gesticulating wildly at invisible opponents in the air above his head, sometimes shouting, sometimes whispering, but he seldom expressed himself lucidly for any extended period. He would start in one direction, interrupt himself, spurt off elsewhere, dodge around to a new topic, promise a return to it sometime, and then open up another soon forgotten issue.

At one point Hart seemed to be on the verge of explaining what he thought the case was about: "It's about—and I've said it many times—it's one of the things that I find kind of contradictory, is how the editorial pages, the media is always—and it's their job— criticizing the political party. I guess they figure to keep on their toes. But gee, come around Election Day and say can we have a page bought, we'd like the people who are running. You want the page? You have to pay. But I think it's a good one, the system, and you know why. (sic)

"And as I mentioned as it was mentioned in Soviet Russia yesterday, I hope Mr. Neuborne, I don't think he was accusing the Republican party of Nassau County of being, but I'll deal with it later, the same type of apparatus that is in place in a one percent system in Soviet Russia." (sic)

It is probable that the court stenographers didn't punctuate their account of Mr. Hart's words with the interpretive flair that those misty words required, but their task, the professional grammarian must concede, was formidable.

It is only out of a sense of concern for Mr. Hart's feelings that more extensive quotations from his summary remarks have been omitted; he was, like any lawyer, the captive of his case.

Because of the lateness of the hour, Neuborne informed Mishler that he was imposing a half-hour limit on his rebuttal summation; it was, however, the highlight of that contentious day. He spoke with the same emotional vigor that had characterized his original presentation, but the need to be concise, to isolate the important elements, added an edge to his remarks.

The court was almost empty as he drew himself up in front of the jurors and launched an attack on the Hempstead defense. "The town of Hempstead is implicated up to its neck in this case. The officials that ran it, the core of the activity, the solicitation on the premises, the conviction of the various officials, are all town of Hempstead people. And, of course, the single largest and single most important element in making the town of Hempstead liable is Al D'Amato's knowledge. He knew in '71, he knew the scheme was in effect. He knew that he had to pay in order to get a raise; indeed, he helped a neighbor by engaging in it, and he did nothing to stop it, and he was the supervisor of the town of Hempstead, one of the most powerful men in town, one of the strongest forces in both the town and the county."

He pointed at the defense lawyers. Hart and Pascarella stared back stoically; LaGinestra, still ebullient over his morning performance, smiled as if he expected a compliment. "What do they say?" Neuborne demanded, his accusatory finger still extended. " 'Yes, Al D'Amato knew, but he was acting in his Republican capacity when he wrote that letter, not in his town of Hempstead capacity. So please don't hang the town of Hempstead, because, after all, he wasn't acting as a town of Hempstead official.' "

He turned back to the jury and, bending toward them, spoke with intensity: "But when you get into the jury room, look at the letter, look at Exhibit 1. Take a look at the stationery, take a look at the heading, take a look at the official name—Alfonse D'Amato wrote that letter on the stationery of the supervisor of the town of Hempstead. He used his official stationery, used his official status.

"The truth of the matter is, you can't distinguish between the two. When the man wears two hats, he is a Republican leader and he is the supervisor in the town of Hempstead. He can't say that he had knowledge as a Republican leader but somehow blocked it out of his knowledge as the supervisor of the town of Hempstead.

"The man only had one brain, and when that consciousness was permeated with the knowledge of the one percent scheme, he owned that consciousness both as a leader and a supervisor of the town of Hempstead."

Furthermore, D'Amato had been the power broker who spread Hempstead's party monopoly over jobs and promotions to the county level. "Al D'Amato, when he was the supervisor of the town of Hempstead, also sat on the board of supervisors of the county of Nassau. He was one of the ranking officials of the county of Nassau. He knew as early as '71 what the Hempstead system was and he handpicked and put in place Al Riehl to take that Hempstead system into the county of Nassau."

To illustrate the effectiveness of Riehl's operation, Neuborne pointed to the large carton at his feet. "That carton is waiting there, waiting for one of us to trip on it." For the first time in hours, jury members laughed. "It is," Neuborne said, suddenly grim, "the paper trail for the county of Nassau. Mr. Pascarella tells us there are seventeen hundred pieces of paper in it. He says these are just applications. Well, they are not . . . these are cards kept by the central office of the Nassau County Republican Committee. Applications that have been accepted, applications where individuals have, in fact, been hired. Seventeen hundred of them; every single one of them is an individual who was hired between 1971 and 1974, not by the town of Hempstead but by the county of Nassau through the Al Riehl system. . . . And not one of them is a Democrat."

He reached into the box and dug out a handful of documents. "And if you look through these things you'll see time after time it says, 'Just enrolled, enrolled yesterday, enrolled last week—just enrolled.' These are people that need jobs, and they are tailoring their political lives to their employment needs."

At 10:28 P.M., Mishler cautioned the jury: "We have a long weekend . . . you are going to meet family, friends, strangers. Don't

294

make your task more difficult than it is by ... getting some outsider's notion of the way it should be decided." They would be
back in court on Tuesday, after Labor Day, at which time he would
prepare them for their deliberations.

The courtroom emptied rapidly. Sol Goldfarb and Nicholas
LaGinestra walked out together, exchanging caustic comments
about their mutually despised oppressor, the absentee town attorney. At the end, only Lorraine and Frank Cullen sat numbly in the
spectators' section, holding hands, staring at the empty jury box.

THIRTY-TWO

THE VERDICT

Judge Mishler's longtime secretary, Ruth Brennan, described her boss as "stern but fair." Those qualities were displayed in abundance at this trial, but when it came to his treatment of the jury, the word courteous must be substituted for stern.

Jacob Mishler dealt with the four women and two older males as though they were representatives of some aristocratic class, nowhere else observable in our democratic society, who must be addressed deferentially and whose every need must be anticipated. Their common sense and ability to arrive at a correct decision, although not previously demonstrated to anyone in the courtroom—and manifestly doubted by every attorney who had a role in picking them—was, for him, holy writ.

Mishler had promised Pascarella to tell the jurors that political parties were the cornerstone of American life, and he fulfilled his promise. "It is in the public interest to maintain the stability of political parties as the means of expressing the will of the citizenry. Political parties have a First Amendment right to solicit funds. That right includes the right to solicit funds from public employees."

Since jurors might read into this statement that Mishler thought *Margiotta's* political party had the right to do anything it pleased in order to maintain its "stability," the judge took pains to correct that impression. He wanted the jurors to understand that the plaintiff class was claiming "the solicitation went beyond the First Amendment rights of the Republican party and violated the First Amendment rights of public employees by compelling public employees to associate with the Republican party."

Soon the judge explained the meaning of each of the fifty questions in the special verdict. Question 1(a) required the jurors to decide whether forced "solicitation of contributions . . . existed during the period 1973 to 1976." Neuborne told the jury he thought this to be the pivotal issue, and if they answered *yes*, the class will have won.

Other questions cast doubt on Neuborne's declaration. Even if the jury decided a scheme to coerce public employees existed during those years, questions 1(c) and 1(d) wanted them to analyze the employees' "state of mind" at that time. "Did they generally understand that the Republican Party expected them to make a contribution of approximately 1%?" If the answer was "yes," then 1(e) also wanted to know whether "a substantial number" of them feared reprisals if they didn't contribute?

To describe the special verdict as being booby-trapped with caveats, encumbered with exquisitely shaded variations in language, honeycombed with categories divided into subsections, would do an injustice to the inventiveness of the legal mind.

Questions 7–10 involved violations of the Racketeer-Influenced and Corrupt Organizations Act (RICO). The judge's explanation—covering nineteen pages of his ninety-nine-page charge—was so convoluted that the eyes of the jurors quickly unfocused. The only attentive people in the court were the attorneys, who leaned forward over their barricade in a sincere endeavor to brush up on the law that was causing so much trouble for their clients.

The last twelve questions covered the claims of Lorraine Cullen and John Jund. Mishler treated the two plaintiffs differently. His first question concerning Lorraine Cullen's complaint was crucially at odds with the one the jury was being asked to decide in John Jund's case.

Was the practice and procedure of requesting or demanding 1% of a public employee's salary a *substantial* [italics mine] factor in denying Mrs. Cullen appointment as Field Investigator III in 1974?

Did the Republican Party oppose or participate *in any way* [italics mine] in the denial of the promotion of Mr. Jund to the position of Driver-Sanitationman II in 1972?

Mishler cautioned the jury that it wasn't enough for Mrs. Cullen to prove that her lack of contributions was *a* factor in her loss of promotion. If the jurors were convinced that was true, they could nevertheless vote against her, unless, by careful mental measurements, they determined that the party's prejudice had been a *substantial* factor in Milone's decision.

Mishler structured the jurors' thinking about Mrs. Cullen's complaint. They must accept that "under the discretionary authority of the Director of Probation, Louis Milone had the authority to appoint" the individual who scored lower on the civil service test than Mrs. Cullen. "Even if you find that the Republican Party recommended" her lower-ranking competitor, "it does not follow that the appointment was not within his [Milone's] sound discretion."

With these words, the judge had, for all practical purposes, instructed the jurors to vote against Mrs. Cullen.

After an hour and a half Mishler laid down his charge papers, smiled at the jurors, and said, "The first order of business is to give your lunch order to the marshal."

The jurors deliberated until 9:00 P.M., when Mishler sent them home with a solicitous wish that they have a good night's sleep.

At noon the following day, Wednesday, September 4, 1985, as the jury continued its deliberations, Ed Hart invited me to have lunch with James Pascarella and two other defense counsels, Hart's chief associate, John Ryan, and Pascarella's partner, Thomas Illmensee. We drove to Borrelli's Restaurant, a half mile from the courthouse, just east of Meadowbrook Parkway.

Borrelli's occupied a sprawling one-story building on the edge of Uniondale; it was built in 1955 on the site of an old hamburger stand by three brothers; one became the restaurant's waiter; the second, a cook; and the third ran the pizza oven.

The Borrellis had prospered. The exterior wall epitomized solidi-
ty and substance; it was a mass of blue tiles interspersed with
white bricks. Red window awnings advertised the menu: "Pizza . . .
Lasagna . . . Veal . . . Shrimp."

The original building had undergone many changes. There were
now four pizza ovens, a Roman Coliseum mosaic was plastered to
the largest wall in the otherwise brick-encrusted dining room, and
a terrazzo floor covered the public space. Hart led the five of us
past the bustling open kitchen to a Formica table directly in front
of the Coliseum mosaic.

Hart unmistakably liked Borrelli's, though he apologetically commented that he had selected it because it was close to the courthouse. His explanation was directed at Pascarella, but the disapproval couldn't be persuaded to leave the picky gourmet's face no
matter what the excuse. Pascarella was more accustomed to the
pretensions of the upscale North Shore eateries, and his delicate
appetite could never be satisfied by Borrelli's hearty fare.

Glasses of burgundy quickly appeared, orders for shrimp and
veal were carried back to the kitchen, and a discussion about the
trial began. Hart thought LaGinestra had done a good job summing
up, considering "he had missed most of the testimony." Pascarella
agreed: "He told a lot of cutesy stories."

Pascarella and Illmensee expressed disappointment that their
political scientist from a small Maine college had been barred from
testifying. "He had nine pages of credentials," Pascarella stated,
almost in awe. "He would have been sensational." The professor,
according to the man paying his fee, was prepared to state that the
Nassau Republican party was actually a weak political organization,
not at all up to the ironfist standards of parties he had studied.

I observed that party control over thousands of jobs seemed
rather complete, and although bodies were not being dumped in
the Great South Bay, the party apparatus seemed perfectly capable
of enforcing its decisions.

Hart, smug and self-assured as always in his public moments,
said, "I think the people of Nassau County are satisfied with the
kind of government the Republican party is giving them."

The hapless and unorganized citizens of politically despoiled
towns across America have frequently been depicted by their rav-

ishers as being content with corruption they are powerless to end. "I thought you were above that kind of argument," I told Hart. He was silent. I continued: "They can't be happy about paying exorbitant tax rates to support inflated payrolls."

They were a fascinating group, making their living by using their considerable skills in behalf of causes not requiring them to invest any belief. As they awaited the jury verdict, passing the time over tortoni, cannoli, and amaretto mousse cake, their major concern seemed to be how to convince their irritable clients, should disaster be the message delivered by the jury, that what appeared to be a defeat was, in reality, a victory.

The jurors sent a note to Mishler at 4:15 announcing they had concluded their deliberations; they were immediately ushered into the courtroom. Mishler asked Foreperson Fedele to stand and then queried her about the juror's decision on each of the fifty special verdict questions.

"Was there a practice and procedure in existence in Nassau County during the period January 1, 1973, to January 1, 1976, for the coercive solicitation of contributions of public employees, generally amounting to about one percent of their annual salaries?"

Ms. Fedele glanced down at her copy of the jury's decision. "Yes," she said crisply.

The spectators burst into applause. Burt Neuborne smiled and shook hands with Chip Loewenson; the defense counsels remained sober-faced.

The answer to question 1(b) began the subtle shading of the jury's guilty verdict. "The following defendants participated in the solicitation of coercive contributions," Mishler read. "The Nassau County Republican Committee?"

"Yes," Ms. Fedele responded.

"The Town of Hempstead Republican Committee?"

"Yes."

"The county of Nassau?"

"No."

Pascarella's narrow face stretched into a broad smile. Illmensee patted him on the back, but Hart's gloom was unrelieved.

"The town of Hempstead?" Mishler recited the name of the last defendant.

"Yes," Forewoman Fedele called out.

Three of the four defendants, including one of the two government entities, had been found guilty, but, unaccountably, not Nassau County.

The contradictions quickly set in. The jurors felt, according to their answer to question 1(c), that "a substantial number of public employees of the County of Nassau" generally did *not* understand they were expected to contribute 1 percent of their salary to the Republican party.

But in the broader question 1(e)—"Did a substantial number of public employees fear that if they failed or refused to make the contributions to the Republican party that they would lose opportunities for promotion, overtime, and other requests for favorable consideration?"—they answered, "Yes."

On the next question, the confusion multiplied. "Did more than ten percent of the public employees employed by the county of Nassau contribute to the Nassau County Republican Committee?" The jurors answered, "Yes."

One must conclude that the jurors did not feel that "more than 10%" of the work force contributing to the party was a "substantial number," or they felt it *was* a substantial number but that the substantial number had contributed voluntarily. Since in no other group in Nassau society had the contributors totaled even a remote fraction of that number, curiosity remained about how the jurors explained the volunteerism of Nassau County workers.

More contradictions. Although the jurors did not feel that the practice of soliciting contributions from government employees had continued "to the relatively recent past," they did find that Commissioner Limongelli had until 1984 induced Hempstead employees to purchase tickets to Republican fund-raising events with threats.

The jurors clearly believed that the crimes committed by the Republican party leaders and Hempstead government officials were serious and required extensive monetary recompense for its victims. In answer to a whole series of questions, they found that the three guilty defendants had also violated the RICO Act and were criminal enterprises that had "knowingly and willfully engaged in a pattern of illegal activity." Mishler was now free to apply triple damages in assessing the liability of the condemned defendants.

The town of Hempstead was specifically convicted of racketeering during the years that Presiding Supervisor Alfonse D'Amato had been its chief governmental official—now redesignated by the jury's verdict as its chief racketeer.

Toward the end of these decisions in favor of the plaintiff class, Mishler turned his attention to the individual plaintiffs. Lorraine and Frank Cullen were not present. Evans Tilles watched tensely as Mishler asked whether the practice of "demanding one percent of a public employee's salary [was] a substantial factor in denying Mrs. Cullen appointment . . . in 1974?"

Ms. Fedele hesitated and then said in a soft voice, "No."

Tilles's face paled. The jurors also decided that although the Nassau Republicans had tried to get contributions from all government workers, they had not attempted "to obtain a contribution to the Republican party from Mrs. Cullen . . ."

All eight questions dealing with John Jund's complaint were answered in his favor: The Republican party had participated in denial of his promotion; Commissioner William Landman's denial of Jund's promotion was not "within [his] sound discretion"; the failure of Jund to contribute 1 percent of his salary to the party was the "cause of his failure to be promoted"; the Nassau County Republican Committee, the town of Hempstead Republican Committee, and the town of Hempstead had all attempted "to obtain a contribution to the Republican party . . . by threatening" Jund; and that the threat was "one that would implant fear in the mind of a reasonable person."

What John Jund had proved to the jurors' satisfaction was found by them to require too great a leap of faith when evaluating Lorraine Cullen's struggle with the Republican hierarchy. Just as well at this moment that the accuser and her judges did not have to look into each other's eyes.

Judge Mishler seemed pleased with the jurors' responses. In dismissing them, he expressed his sincere thanks in a manner beyond the formal demands of chancellery ritual.

Turning to the barricade, he informed the commanders of the opposing forces that he must now consider whether damages should be awarded and if so, how much. The casual observer, when reading the newspapers that day, might have concluded that this long political trial had ended, but Judge Mishler had already signaled that was not true. He set October 4 for arguments by each attorney as to how he should interpret the jury's special verdict. *His* verdict would be issued some indeterminate time after that.

He was by no means sure his verdict would end the matter. "This was a difficult case," he told the attorneys after the jurors had left. "I don't know whether it's going to be decided here or in the appellate courts."

Months later, Judge Mishler explained to me that he had been surprised by the jury's verdict. "I never dreamed that they would find the county of Nassau was not part of the policy and did not indulge in it. I thought that they would find that they were all partners in this or none of them were. I didn't think they'd find three out of four guilty."

On the flagstone platform outside the courthouse a massive media inquest was being conducted. Several television camera crews and dozens of print-media reporters were separately interviewing Burt Neuborne, Ed Hart, James Pascarella, and an assortment of jurors who had finally emerged from behind their anonymous masks.

Genevieve Fedele, a docile smile on her face, said that the decision had been "very difficult" but that Senator D'Amato's testimony had eventually swayed her. She had reached her decision, she said softly, "because the evidence was there."

Eileen Carstairs had no such problem: She had made up her mind before she entered the jury room. It was D'Amato's smoking-gun letter, the first exhibit in the case, that had settled the matter for her. "It was pretty persuasive as far as knowing the scheme existed. Here was an official of the town at the time saying the one percent existed." She said other jurors had been impressed when D'Amato and Margiotta conceded that some employees might have felt pressured to contribute. As for the county participation in the scheme, Carstairs felt the plaintiffs "just didn't bring enough people in to prove the case."

Ed Hart, looking subdued, said he had a "mixed reaction." He was pleased the jury found that the 1 percent forced contributions had not continued past January 1976; however, nothing else was positive.

Burt Neuborne triumphantly said the verdict was "a reinforcement of the First Amendment right of employees to associate with the party of their choice." The case had meaning for the entire country. "This is one of the most important decisions involving political parties ever rendered," he said. "It is the first time that a political party—not an individual politician—has been found guilty of extortion."

The traditional excuses that political parties used to get money from government workers in exchange for favors no longer protected them from prosecution. Extortion now not only sent a corrupt boss to jail; it opened his party apparatus to civil damages and other penalties. Neuborne said, "Political crime can no longer masquerade as a traditional political right."

Hart's associate, John Ryan, voiced a similar opinion about the meaning of the trial. "This is the first case in which a political party has been found liable for unconstitutional activities in the soliciting of campaign funds. A political party has been found guilty of violating the First Amendment." He went on to explain the importance of the case, which he described as being "full of novel questions—virgin law." To begin with, "it is the first RICO political class action." In addition, "if Mishler applies RICO penalties to the jury's decision, for the first time a political party could be open to triple damages."

The plaintiff's attorneys, while overjoyed about their individual victories, expressed regret over the jury's inability to find in favor of Lorraine Cullen.

Neuborne fretted that "the victims in extortion cases never testify. They are fearful people—often weak individuals. But she had the courage to take on the whole party apparatus." Shaking his head regretfully, he said, "She was clearly the nicest person associated with the trial, and the most competent."

Julian Kaplan, glowing over his unadulterated victory in behalf of John Jund, tried to be affirmative about Cullen's years of effort. "I don't think she's heartbroken. She had an aim above money, and it was achieved."

Lorraine Cullen expressed much the same sentiments later that day after receiving a terse call from Evans Tilles informing her of the jury's decision. "It's ironic that I went through hell to get this case before a court, but with the jury's judgment, all those 'members of the class' who sat on the sidelines are now in a position to file claims for damages."

As her legal involvement in the 1 percent case came to an end, she made a remark that told a great deal about her character. "Even if I knew how it was going to come out, I would have done it again."

THIRTY-THREE

A HIGHER AUTHORITY

J acob Mishler had made it clear he wanted the 1 percent case, with its wild excursions into new legal territory, held as tightly under rein as possible. So many legal hornets' nests, which involved what were to him sacrosanct political parties, were being stirred up. He had come to dread the prospect of issuing a decision that would minimize the party's punishment, as he instinctively wanted to, and simultaneously invite an appeals court reversal. Getting past the court of appeals without suffering public humiliation by those smart-aleck second-guessers was a Mishler imperative.

On October 25, 1985, in his final brief to Mishler, Burt Neuborne explained what he thought the punishment should be. Since this was the first attempt to apply the RICO Act against crimes of a political party, Neuborne wanted Mishler to use the law to its fullest extent: triple damages and payment of all plaintiffs' costs, including lawyers' fees.

He also wanted Mishler to expand the liability period. "Given . . . the fact that the single most important item of evidence—the D'Amato letter—was dated June 11, 1971 . . . ," Neuborne felt the judge should push back the defendants' date of liability.

Ed Hart requested a new trial. He contended that the jury's decision would have a "chilling effect" on future party workers, who would shy away from fund-raising activities for fear of "not only civil liability but quasi-criminal sanctions, including the stigma of being a 'racketeer.'" Most important, he insisted, Mishler must reject the plaintiff's demand that RICO penalties be applied. He summoned up a vision of a weakened, perhaps destroyed American political system if the Democratic party and Republican party were subjected to the same law whose violation caused others who were convicted to empty out their Swiss bank accounts.

Months passed while the contending parties and the concerned multitude wondered whether Judge Mishler would accept the jury's decision in whole or in part. On its front page, the *New York Times* took note of the heightening anxiety:

> Jacob Mishler must now consider whether damages should be awarded, and if so, how much. . . . The jury also found that the town and the party had knowingly and willfully engaged in a pattern of illegal [RICO] activity, a finding that could enable the judge to award triple damages.

Finally, on December 20, 1985, four months after the jury had rendered its special verdict and as the senatorial campaign was about to get under way, Judge Mishler issued his twenty-eight-page decision.

In it he said: "The evidence in this case supports the jury's findings. . . ." He was therefore rejecting the request for a new trial. But what was Mishler to do with the jury's serpentine findings?

He exercised his arbitrary power with his usual decisiveness. "The RICO claim is dismissed in favor of all defendants and against all plaintiffs." He conceded that the jury had found that three of the defendants had "knowingly and willfully engaged in a pattern of illegal activity," which seemed to open them to RICO penalties. The jury had also found that there was "a pattern of racketeering activity" and that those three defendants had been found to be a racketeering "enterprise." However, as far as Judge Mishler was concerned, that wasn't sufficient to force him to establish a precedent that political parties were subject to the racketeering provisions of the RICO Act. The movie thug Rico may have slaughtered dozens in Chicago during the 1930s, but in Jake Mishler's court his namesake would never bump off a single politician.

In an effort to give some meaning to the jury's guilty verdict, Mishler wrote, "Burt Neuborne . . . is directed to submit a form of notice . . ." to be sent to all of his successful clients, the approximately twenty thousand class members eligible to file a claim.

In conclusion, he awarded Burt Neuborne a fee of $100,000 to be paid by the three guilty defendants. That sum was identified as only an "interim fee," since Mishler made it clear that Neuborne's work was far from done. "The additional proceedings which relate to the individual claims of the members of the class may take many months and possibly years to resolve."

In order to get on with that work, Mishler directed the attorneys still remaining on the case "to appear at a status conference to be held on January 2, 1986, to discuss the practical problems in identification of members of the class."

With no sign of diminishing vigor, the survivors of the 1 percent battalion prepared to march into another year.

The status conference was held at 3:30 P.M. on January 17, 1986, on the second floor of the Uniondale courthouse, in the small Courtroom B, in years to come the scene of another sensational D'Amato trial. No spectators or media people were present.

Wearing his blue pencil-striped uniform, Neuborne looked no more prosperous now that he was $100,000 richer. Joseph Jaspan, former county attorney, with close ties to Margiotta and D'Amato, represented the Republican party. Mishler, sitting in his usual perch above the contending attorneys, began by asking, "What does the class consist of?" Even that elemental question suddenly appeared unsettled.

Neuborne tried to redefine the class. Mishler interjected with zest, and the give-and-take of a legal joust took place.

Neuborne insisted on anonymity for claim filers. "The benefit of anonymity is that individuals will not fear coming forward. I've had people say to me, 'I have a nephew working for the town. I don't want to make trouble for him.' " More soberly, Mishler said, "I can't protect against the fears of what I conceive to be a very few." Suddenly, almost sternly, he added. "The individual must produce proof he contributed." The boxes of party receipts in his possession didn't seem sufficient proof for him.

There was a moment of silence; then Mishler seemed to relent somewhat. "The class was successful," he said to Neuborne. "The practice stopped after 1976. I'm sure if he doesn't succeed in anything else, Mr. Neuborne deserves his fee. Mr. Neuborne's success in this case far exceeds $100,000."

As the session wound down, Mishler became restive. With no effort to hide his irritation about the embarrassment to which these lawyers were about to expose him, he tartly remarked that since appeals from his decision were being planned, the attorneys should move promptly. "I don't think you should delay a moment in filing your appeals," he grumbled, mentioning that Chief Justice Warren Burger had assigned him to sit in place of Miami's indicted district court judge Alcee Hastings at the beginning of February; that would take him to Florida for three months.

The arguments before the U.S. Court of Appeals, Second Circuit, which took place on the seventeenth floor of the federal courthouse in Lower Manhattan on June 19, 1986, were on an exalted legal plain. They were heard as Al D'Amato's reelection drive shifted into high gear.

There would be no debate on facts; the jury had settled that in Mishler's court. The questions dealt with pivoted on the rightfulness of Mishler's decisions: Had he followed precedent correctly; had he applied the appropriate rules of evidence; and, most important, had he interpreted the jury's verdict properly?

Neuborne had frequently appeared before this three-judge panel. He believed he received a fair, although at times punishing, hearing. "They appeared to be annoyed with me," Neuborne remarked. He concluded, "They were annoyed that I allowed Mishler to draw up such a flawed special verdict."

Ed Hart presented the party's appeal smoothly. The panel was attentive and, in contrast to the rough manner in which they had dealt with Neuborne, asked few questions, which Hart had no difficulty answering.

The contending attorneys left the court together. Neuborne remembered: "Hart sneered at me. 'Are you satisfied now that you got your appeal?' "

On February 2, 1987, over a year after the appeals had been filed, the Second Circuit panel issued its ruling.

It upheld large sections of the jury verdict but, couched in the politest formal terms, was often harsh in appraising Judge Mishler's conclusions. "The *County* [italics mine] was not entitled to dismissal of plaintiffs' claims in their entirety because the court erred in ruling that the applicable statutes of limitations had [run out]." The statute of limitations could not run out while the plaintiffs were under duress from the defendants. "As duress is clearly an element of these claims, the court erred in ruling that all claims accruing earlier than December 14, 1973, were automatically barred."

That Lorraine Cullen had originally taken her case to the state court on December 2, 1974, pushed back the statute of limitations. Consequently, "plaintiffs are entitled to pursue claims against the County that accrued as early as three years prior to the date of the commencement of the state court action . . . on or after December 2, 1971."

Much more important: "We also conclude that the court erred in dismissing the RICO claims on the basis of the answers given by the jury to the special interrogatories, because those answers left a gap that should have been filled by the court.

"The jury was not asked whether any of the three [guilty] defendants had participated in the conduct of the affairs of an enterprise that did not include the County." That, in the eyes of the three-member panel, was a serious error. Mishler should have included a question *only* involving the possible RICO activities of the three guilty parties. "Had the court posed such a question, the trial record seems to suggest that the jury would have answered that question in the affirmative."

Having concluded that Judge Mishler's instructions to the jury were unduly "constrictive," the court decided that Mishler's "conclusion in the Post-trial Decision . . . was plainly overbroad." As a consequence, "we conclude that the court's decision to dismiss the RICO claims on the basis of the jury's interrogatory answers was factually, doctrinally, and procedurally flawed."

The judge, in their view, had committed an additional error. "Since the jury was not allowed to answer that question, the court itself should have answered it."

310

Pointedly, the lecture continued: "The ultimate question after trial is whether or not the plaintiff has proved its claim. If the interrogatories given to the jury do not include a factual question needed for a complete answer to the ultimate question, the consequence is not that the plaintiff's case is to be dismissed but simply that the right to have that fact issue determined by the jury is waived and any gap is to be filled by the court."

Because of Mishler's error, the court decreed, his dismissal of the plaintiffs' RICO claims for the years between 1973 and 1976 was "vacated." The plaintiffs' RICO claims were sent back to Mishler for his factual finding as to whether the plaintiffs' had, in the absence of that crucial question, proved their case.

Burt Neuborne was elated: The class's RICO triple penalties might still be paid, and the period of coverage was now six years instead of the scant three years that Mishler had allowed.

The Republican party, fearful of the anger of Hempstead voters if the town's taxpayers were forced to pay for the crimes of the party, agreed to pay Neuborne's fee in full.

But Ed Hart had found another door slammed in his face, and the only alternative for a man who did not like to accept defeat was an appeal to the U.S. Supreme Court. The forced march of the 1 percent battalion continued.

Although Hart was an able trial lawyer, his Supreme Court experience didn't match Neuborne's, whose ACLU assignments frequently brought him through those temple portals. In his thirty-page brief, Hart gave numerous reasons why the case should be heard. Neuborne filed a brief opposing a court review.

On June 25, 1987, the court rejected Hart's petition without comment, leaving the decision of the U.S. Court of Appeals for the Second Circuit to stand as a legal precedent on the liability of political parties when they act illegally.

The 1 percent case was now back in Judge Mishler's hands. He immediately decided to avoid a new trial on the RICO charge. Instead, he accepted the court of appeals' option: He reversed himself and declared that the Nassau Republican Committee and the Hempstead Republican Committee, having been found guilty by the jury, were now exposed to triple damages. Whatever damages individual claimants could prove would now cost the Republican party three times what it would have cost had Al D'Amato's advice been accepted and a settlement reached before the trial.

Mishler explained his reversal to me in his chambers after he had issued his new ruling. "Listen, whenever the court of appeals speak, I'm bound, no matter whether I agree with them or not. It's the law in the case."

District court judges view the court of appeals with the hurt sensibilities displayed by any player at that moment in a game where the umpire has the last word. Mishler's tone suggested unyielding repugnance about the need to capitulate to people who didn't sympathize with, or completely understand, his problems.

He refused, however, to place the convicted town of Hempstead under that RICO penalty umbrella, although he conceded that Neuborne would eventually try to get the court of appeals to overturn his decision. "I found that the municipality could not be assessed treble damages. There's very little law on this matter, but I felt that was the right decision. The poor taxpayer would have to pay it. He would be punished for something the officials did." It was an argument against a government body ever paying damages to any aggrieved citizen.

As to the party: "It could be a very, very serious liability," Mishler said solemnly.

On October 28, 1987, when Neuborne and Hart couldn't reach a consensus on what was to be included in the letter sent to the class members, Mishler took on the task. His guideline: "I didn't want to say, 'Make a claim, what do you have to lose.' "

The letter went out in February 1988; claimants had one month, until March 31, to file. At the end of that period, despite every caution Judge Mishler was able to insinuate in his letter to the awakening class, twelve hundred claims had been submitted. It was a substantial number, but the surprise was that almost all of the claimants were *retired.* Among the thousands of contributors still on the payroll, only a handful had the courage to come forward. Neuborne's prediction about what would happen if the anonymity of claimants was not safeguarded had proved to be accurate.

Significantly, Hart's and Pascarella's assertions to the jury that only four departments were involved in the extortions proved to be false. Claims showered in from former employees in all of the dozens of departments of Nassau County and Hempstead. Neuborne commented ruefully, "I suddenly have twelve hundred witnesses."

Over six hundred of those claimants had been county employees. Neuborne was moved to observe that, too late, the dispersed jurors must finally be convinced that they should have convicted Nassau County and declared in favor of Lorraine Cullen.

On St. Patrick's Day, March 17, 1988, I had a conversation with Judge Mishler in his chambers for two and a half hours. The dapper judge had made a minor concession to custom: His multicolored, diagonally stripped tie had a muted green line interspersed among four other pale colors. Judge Mishler was not one to be ostentatious about his sentiments.

He wore a white delicately embossed shirt, with a white dress handkerchief protruding from his shirt pocket. His full head of wavy gray hair, lined with black strands, was neatly combed. Behind his black-rimmed glasses his left eyelid still drooped, but the affected side of his face and lips had now assumed a relaxed, if immobile, cast.

Mishler insisted that claimants were not in a position to "simply come in here and say, 'Give me a check!' " The collection route was to be strewn with obstacles the judge was placing in their path. "First you have to prove that you paid your one percent . . . and you paid under pressure . . . or that you refused to pay your one percent, and because you refused to pay it, you're now entitled to damages, because of loss of appointment, there wasn't an increase in salary." A claimant must "prove that he was coerced into paying."

This reinforced the vision of a retrial of the 1 percent case not once but hundreds of times, exactly what a unified class-action suit was intended to avoid. "But how does he show a thing like that?" I asked. "I don't know," Mishler responded with his usual assertiveness. "But he'll have to show it."

Even John Jund, who had seemingly won, was far from collecting. He was going to have to face another trial. "He must prove that the violation of his rights caused him to lose his advancement," Mishler explained. "The defendants may very well show that he was a terrible worker. A fact question. And they may prove that this was the reason he wasn't promoted."

But I thought all of that was already proved, I said; the jury had heard those arguments and rejected them. He shook his head and continued: "Then the next step is that he's going to have to prove damages. How he does it is up to him."

"Is this case ever going to end?" I asked.

"Never," the octogenarian responded only half-jokingly. "I keep saying, I wasn't appointed forever, only for life. And this is going on forever, so I don't know if I'm going to make it."

As the interview was drawing to a close, the judge began to speak more passionately. "The RICO charge proved to be a terrible problem for the defense. And it proved to be a terrible problem for me." I remarked that political parties all over the country now had to be concerned with the possibility of triple damages if they committed criminal acts. His one good eye focused sharply on me. He was clearly worried that the law might be used unfairly to persecute politicians. His voice rising, he indignantly stated: "Too many of us say, 'Ah, he's just a politician.' I'll tell you something. In my experience, I have found that politicians are more ethical than some of our so-called businessmen. There are many things I'll find businessmen will do that politicians would never think of doing."

With an unswerving gaze he continued: "I was never a politician. I never got anything out of politics." The memory of his Astoria origins had apparently begun to fade. "But I respect the politician's role. There are some very fine politicians. There are some very awful politicians. There are some that would steal the eyes out of your head. I know that. But we're inclined to believe that every politician is a crook."

He suddenly mentioned the case of the Democratic leader of the New York State Senate, Manfred Ohrenstein, who had recently been indicted for using members of his office staff, during office hours, to regularly perform his personal political chores. Mishler felt this was merely a venial sin, no serious threat to a politician's mortal soul: "At election time he wants to win . . . so 'take off at two o'clock every day or don't come in on Thursday.' Now, I'm giving you the more sympathetic case. I know some of them don't even show up. Now all of a sudden a district attorney says, 'Ah, he's violating a statute. He's committing a fraud on the public.' "

Burt Neuborne had recognized this aspect of Mishler's character when, in his NYU office after the trial, he told me: "He was a very good judge. He was a fair judge. But I think I would have rather tried it with someone with a little greater sense of moral outrage than he had. His moral outrage was confined to the more venal aspects of it. Systemically, he didn't think there was anything wrong."

As I stood in the doorway of the judge's office and responded to the farewell of the tall, erect, warmly smiling Jacob Mishler, I couldn't help remembering Astoria's Republican boss Frank Kenna. Thirty years after the world had ceased to think of him, his hand had reached out from the grave and was still writing the record in the Uniondale court.

THIRTY-FOUR

HOW D'AMATO PLANNED TO WIN REELECTION

W hen my wife and I dropped into D'Amato's Washington office on February 24, 1986, we saw the private senator in operation. We had walked into his receptionist's office in the Hart office building at 10:00 A.M. and said we were constituents and would like to meet the senator. She summoned D'Amato's office manager, who asked where we were from and said if we would return later, she would schedule us to see him.

Later in the afternoon she ushered us through corridors and past numerous side offices and groups of desks in an open area into his large private office. The senator greeted us with firm handshakes and asked why we were in Washington. When I responded, "To visit you, Senator," his startling retort was a shouted, nasty rebuke. "Don't give me that baloney."

I explained that I had spent a year researching a book about him and that a visit to his office had seemed like the appropriate next step. He curtly motioned for us to seat ourselves in two chairs in front of his desk, but his bleak features showed no sign of hospitable intent. He would know better than anyone what my research might have uncovered.

During the next fifteen minutes we tried to lighten his mood. Knowing his keen interest in his upcoming reelection campaign, my wife asked him how he reacted to Harry Belafonte's announcement that he was thinking of running against D'Amato. The senator said with a smirk, "I'm planning to take singing lessons."

I told him I would like to interview him, especially about his formative years growing up in Island Park. The bold sneer, which he did not bother to suppress, and the grating tone in his voice belied his response. "Sure, sure, I'd be glad to do it."

At that moment he told his administrative assistant, Michael Kinsella, to take us into his adjoining office to make arrangements for a longer interview in New York. The parting handshake was just as firm, the uncompromising face just as calculating.

We spent the next half hour with Kinsella, discussing his boss, who he said was demanding and not easily pleased. During that time, D'Amato's angry voice often came through the open doorway of his inner office. Now and then one of his outbursts would send his secretary scurrying off on some quest.

At one point, I heard him bellow, "God damn it, that isn't the way I wanted that done." Instantly, he screamed for Kinsella, who leaped up from his desk and ran into the boss's office.

That day, I got a surprisingly clear view of the man I was to spend eight years investigating. Before he knew why I was in his office, he had fired off a snarling blast that exposed a quick-triggered temper. It was also obvious that he had his large office staff totally terrorized.

As his 1986 reelection campaign opened, Al D'Amato's only reference to the 1 percent case, as a result of which the jury labeled his Hempstead government acts a racket, was a sanctimoniously expressed sentiment that anyone who felt they had been coerced into contributing to him in the 1970s should get their money back. It was the generosity of a man who knew that although he had benefited from the service someone else was going to pay the bill.

Questions about the 1 percent racket would be brushed aside with comments such as "that's old hat" or "it was all settled last year." He preferred talking about what his ad agency called "his compassion." At the beginning of June 1986, months before his Democratic opponent was selected in the September 9 primary, he began a $1 million television blitz aimed at—an aide explained—showing he "is not just pothole centered, as some say."

The effort to sell "the New D'Amato" was pitched in four 30-second commercials. In the first he was shown in a friendly embrace with Clara M. Hale, the founder of Harlem's Hale House, for which he had gotten a small, well-publicized grant. In the second, he was pictured with the widow of a policeman killed by a parolee. The third showed him grinning at a Soviet Jewish émigré; and the last had him posing with an Elmira aircraft executive who had been able to add two hundred workers to his payroll because of the senator's widely broadcast pork-barrel efforts on his behalf.

Another commercial, released in July, was quickly withdrawn when protests arose because of its obvious attempt to mislead; it featured D'Amato's mother and father touring Ellis Island. The implication: His parents were revisiting a location that had special meaning for them. The reality: Neither Armand nor Antoinette was an immigrant.

By the time the Democrats had settled on Mark Green as their candidate, the D'Amato television blizzard had created a climate in which the most extraordinary opponent would have found it difficult to survive. According to statewide polls, Green began his abbreviated campaign with a 30 percent deficit in the polls.

The two candidates were worlds apart, although Green, like D'Amato, was born in Brooklyn, eight years after D'Amato, on March 15, 1945. Green's father was a real estate lawyer who settled in upper-middle-class Great Neck, twenty miles north of Island Park. Green said in high school that he was "in order of importance, interested in studies, athletics, and girls." He was captain of his tennis team both in high school and at Cornell, "where I studied my brains out even more."

In 1967 he gained his first Washington experience working as an intern for Jacob Javits. The next year, he went to Harvard Law School. After graduation in 1970, he joined Ralph Nader's staff as consumer advocate, ultimately becoming the director of Public Citizens' Congress Watch, Washington's largest consumer lobby. Green spoke of Nader in awed terms. "He is *my friend, my mentor, my hero.*"

Green returned to New York in 1980 and founded a liberal think tank called the Democracy Project. An unsuccessful run for

Congress in Manhattan's "Silk Stocking District" was his only campaign for office before taking on D'Amato.

Green was a brilliant debater, but D'Amato never allowed his opponent's advantage to be used effectively. After repeated prodding from his challenger, D'Amato finally agreed to two debates, but in exchange he demanded control over the dates and times at which the confrontations would take place.

D'Amato scheduled the first debate in Albany precisely as the first ball in the third game of the World Series was pitched. This was the exciting series between the Boston Red Sox and the hometown New York Mets; the Mets—who eventually won in seven games—had lost the first two games in their home stadium. There may have been some viewers in the state watching Green challenge D'Amato; I was not one of them: it was a mesmerizing ball game.

D'Amato's slick scheduling was the most effective thing he did on that night of October 21. The *Times* reported that Green came out swinging. In his first sentence he described D'Amato as a product of "Joe Margiotta's corrupt Nassau machine" who had "misled a grand jury" and habitually used the truth "sparingly."

Green hurled his bolts at a seemingly impassive senator; D'Amato sat on a stool five feet from him, head down, studying his notes. Green described the deadpan D'Amato as "a consumer fraud, because while he says that he brings home the bacon, in fact, New York has lost more federal aid than any other state per capita."

The Democratic candidate recited a list of D'Amato's votes for cuts in unemployment insurance, job retraining, mass transit, and urban redevelopment programs and charged that those D'Amato votes cost New York State billions. Although D'Amato "claimed to get things done," Green accused him of grandstand efforts to get a few million dollars for isolated projects that did not balance the damage he did by voting "less money for Social Security, less money for pollution-control enforcement, less money for student loans."

Green, speaking to the smallest prime-time television audience of the season, was particularly harsh when describing D'Amato's close relationship with Island Park's disco owner Philip Basile.

"He's a man whose nightclub had twenty drug arrests in one year. He's a man who was indicted and convicted of conspiring with an organized-crime member, a member of the Lucchese family, to get a drug dealer out of prison." Basile's connection to the Mafia was substantial. The man he conspired to get out of jail was murderer Henry Hill, whose grisly career movie patrons became acquainted with in Robert De Niro's 1990 gangster film *GoodFellas.*

Despite Philip Basile's ties to Lucchese godfather Paul Vario, when Basile was indicted in 1983 for fraudulently getting drug addict Hill out of jail, D'Amato came to his defense. "You know who his only character witness was?" Mark Green asked his minuscule TV audience rhetorically. "Al D'Amato. He exploited the position of U.S. senator, walked into court, and said this man, Philip Basile, was a man of integrity. What kind of signal does it send on the issue of drugs, on the issue of crime, when Al D'Amato testifies for such a man and then takes $1,000 from him."

The second debate took place fourteen hours later, during a weekday morning while honest citizens were at work. "The scheduling was so close," Green told me, "that if I had missed my flight, I would have missed the debate." When Green blasted D'Amato for scheduling the debates virtually back-to-back in order to minimize public attention, he didn't respond. His press secretary, Gary Lewi, stepped into the breach and commented to Frank Lynn of the *Times,* "It's an interesting theory, but it's ridiculous."

Green told me the debates were Kafkaesque and followed D'Amato's game plan for winning. "It was a bizarre experience. Al wasn't there. His body was there, and it was covered as if it was a debate between D'Amato and Green. The strategy was that he never engaged me, acknowledged me, or answered me or said anything controversial or in a loud tone of voice. He spoke in a monotone. He was so far ahead in the polls he wanted the debates to generate no interest."

In this respect Green thought D'Amato's strategy was successful. "I think it's fair to say that I won the debates if content counts, but politically he won the debates because the damage to him was negligible. The audience was negligible, and the print media did not write much because so few sparks flew."

Green pulled no punches during the fleeting days of October. He accused D'Amato of receiving a "pattern of gifts from members of organized crime." He quoted a *Newsday* article revealing "dozens of contractors and garbage haulers contributed to the 1980 campaign. More than thirty of these, from whom D'Amato accepted more than $30,000, have since been indicted or sued by state or county officials for allegedly profiting illegally from public projects."

That same week, the *Times* reported that New York's freshman senator had raised more money, nearly $8 million, than any other candidate in the history of the state. Green attributed D'Amato's fund-raising success to the fact that "his vote was for sale." He supported his allegation by documenting D'Amato's handling of a 1985 Senate proposal to restrict junk-bond sales.

The savings and loan (S & L) industry, which had been deregulated in the early 1980s, had attempted to recoup losses resulting from bad real estate investments by buying even riskier junk bonds. This had only accelerated the S & L decline. Partly in an attempt to limit losses caused by this harebrained flier into junk bonds, D'Amato chaired hearings before his Securities Subcommittee on a proposal to limit their sale. Although D'Amato had originally supported the proposal, he suddenly reversed himself and withdrew it. This happened one week after Drexel Burnham Lambert—the Wall Street company that pioneered in marketing such bonds—held a $1,000-a-person dinner for D'Amato.

Green was alerted to D'Amato's dealing with Drexel on September 25, 1986, by a devastating article on the front page of the *Wall Street Journal* in which that respected surveyor of the financial scene commented, "When it comes to shaking the money tree . . ." D'Amato ". . . has clearly become Wall Street's favorite senator."

The *Journal* stated that "according to a tabulation by this newspaper," since 1981 "more than $500,000 has poured into his reelection campaign from the partners, executives and political-action committees of Wall Street firms." The *Journal* concluded: "The big donations often coincide closely with his legislative actions—or inactions."

Assuming a virtuous pose, D'Amato admitted, "I have been a fighter for their interests," but he wanted it understood that the *Wall Street Journal's* charge that he was selling his vote was unfair. There was no "cause and effect" between those generous contributions and his decision to end any attempt to restrict the sale of junk bonds peddled almost exclusively by Drexel Burnham Lambert.

321

D'Amato's 1985 sabotaging of the attempt to curb the S & L banks from investing in junk bonds contributed to the eventual bankruptcy of a substantial part of that speculative industry. The potential loss to the taxpayers: something over an unimaginable $500 billion, to be paid off in installments over the next thirty years. Al D'Amato's rip-off of the taxpayers to benefit his bribers had finally assumed catastrophic proportions. He had gotten so out of hand that not only was he scavenging off the present generation, but he had invented a way to raise his "contributions" at the expense of people not yet alive.

D'Amato's administrative assistant, Michael Kinsella, a chubby bachelor then in his mid-forties, was a former lobbyist for the Securities Industry Association. During the 1986 campaign he spent much of his time as D'Amato's chief fund-raiser. He thought it was wonderful that his boss didn't have to be pushed into fund-raising endeavors. Other men he had worked for were shy about approaching potential contributors. How refreshing to work for a man who at the slightest suggestion reached for the phone to deliver an enthusiastic, if at times somewhat heavy-handed, sales pitch.

"I hadn't liked him at first," Kinsella told me in D'Amato's Washington offices as the senator, nearby, screamed invectives at a worker who hadn't carried out an assignment in precisely the manner he required. "But after a few months I got used to him."

The *Wall Street Journal* quoted a financial lobbyist as complaining that as far as D'Amato and Kinsella were concerned, "nothing is enough. It's continuous pressure. If you don't contribute, they don't return your calls."

Mark Green felt that his campaign began the national process of revealing D'Amato for what he was. "I always thought that Al D'Amato was one scandal away from losing his seat. I assumed that the media would investigate and expose a man who I regarded then, and now, as the sleaziest senator. I blistered him daily with documented stories. I thought everyone realized he was unethical and undeserving. But no one wanted to actually say it. Why? Few people—donors, civic leaders, elected leaders, or editorialists—wanted to take on a likely senator-for-life. You never know when you may need a senator. And he had, and *has*, a reputation for crude vindictiveness."

Documenting his charge that D'Amato frequently tried to intimidate reporters who wrote unflattering stories about him, he handed me an account of an interview between D'Amato and Murray Waas of the *New Republic*. Waas interviewed D'Amato in April 1986, as the campaign was getting under way. At the end of the interview as they were about to part, D'Amato made the following statement:

> "Let's turn off this thing," D'Amato says, pointing to my [Waas's] tape recorder. "Sheesus Christ, kid, I can't believe that story you did on Arlen [Specter]. If you ever wrote something like that about me, I'd come looking for you with a baseball bat. And if I'm not reelected, I'll just be another guy from Long Island. I won't think twice about coming looking for you. So if you write somethin' I don't like, you better hope I stay in the Senate for another thirty years."

Green said that this was "the way the senator routinely operates. It's his bullying style." When someone had the courage to confront the bully, Green said, he would lie and hurl accusations. "D'Amato is like a panicky passenger jumping off a sinking ship, grasping at anything to keep afloat. One of his shaky life preservers is his charge that people are against him because of his last name and his ethnicity. He never says explicitly, but he implies that the criticism of him is in large measure anti-Italian." Shaking his head at the memory of the effectiveness of those tactics in the 1986 campaign, Green added, "Of course, the issue has always been ethics, not ethnicity."

The quality of Al D'Amato's ethics was tested as the campaign proceeded. On October 18 he returned to the Brooklyn neighborhood where he was born. It was not a sentimental journey. The *New Republic* had printed a report that after he had refused to help get funds for low-income housing in Brooklyn, he said, "We didn't do too well with the animal vote, did we?"

The report upset Rev. Al Sharpton. He demanded a meeting with the senator.

Reverend Sharpton was a black minister whose view of ethics matched the senator's. He had no congregation, but he had supporters. At that moment, Sharpton had a hold on an issue that put him on the country's front pages—he was frenetically championing the cause of Tawana Brawley. Miss Brawley was a teenager who, according to the New York State attorney general and a grand jury investigating her charges, had concocted a story about being raped by white youths in the Hudson Valley town of Wappingers Falls in order to have an excuse for not coming home for several days. Sharpton was leading pro–Tawana Brawley demonstrations in Wappingers Falls, in Brooklyn, and in Manhattan. Television, hungry for action pictures, had converted him into a celebrity.

Sharpton's most effective weapon in his campaign against "racists," who were usually white but were sometimes Korean store owners, was his ability to transport several hundred people to some intimidated neighborhood where his fist-waving, bellicose supporters would jangle nerves and disrupt traffic. The likelihood that Reverend Sharpton's bus brigade would show up at his rallies caused D'Amato to accept Sharpton's invitation to confer.

The conference took place in the basement cafeteria of the Washington Temple in Bedford-Stuyvesant, where Sharpton had assembled a group of seventy-five, including some Brooklyn ministers. It was apparent Sharpton had been assured it wasn't going to take his usual bullhorned claque outside the temple to convince the senator to cooperate.

The audience warmly received D'Amato's assurance that he opposed drug abuse and supported sanctions against South Africa. He also wanted them to know he was against the Soviet Union, "that nation that would deprive us of the right to practice our religion." Then D'Amato denied that he referred to housing-project tenants as "animals" and concluded, "I assure you that I never made that statement."

Sharpton rose to denounce Governor Cuomo and the Democrats for taking blacks for granted. He announced that he would lead a group of ministers and the senator across the street to an abandoned dance hall where he wanted D'Amato to pledge his support for an effort to get federal funds to build a drug-treatment center. D'Amato promised to "take a look and see what can be done."

Reverend Sharpton then endorsed D'Amato for the Senate. Within a month D'Amato had obtained a $500,000 grant for the project from the Department of Housing and Urban Development (HUD). HUD's secretary Samuel Pierce had allocated that sum out of his "discretionary fund." The money was to be given to Sharpton's National Youth Movement. Sharpton was soon indicted for stealing at least $250,000 from that organization.

HUD made the grant, though the sponsors had no drug-treatment background and had no detailed plans for a drug center. In the letter communicating his success to Sharpton, D'Amato included a HUD application and wrote that "once the application is completed, [HUD] will release the funds." It was the dream of all supplicants that their applications be granted even before they apply.

When these Byzantine dealings were finally exposed, D'Amato's office issued a statement that "there was no connection" between Sharpton's endorsement and D'Amato's grant. But when queried on the same issue, Sharpton conceded, "If we hadn't endorsed D'Amato, I don't think [we] would have had access to D'Amato and any funding."

THIRTY-FIVE

WHY D'AMATO
WON REELECTION

F
ive days before the voters went to the polls in the November
1986 senatorial contest, Mark Green described part of a scandal involving his opponent whose dimensions it would take
years to measure. Al D'Amato, he charged, had received $11,000
since 1981 from Wedtech, a military contractor in the South Bronx,
for whom he had vigorously intervened with the Defense
Department.

Green revealed that the latest in a series of bribes had been made
in December 1985, when a Wedtech executive had given D'Amato
$3,000 in return for his efforts to obtain a $55 million naval pontoons order for the company. Green charged that D'Amato's activities on behalf of Wedtech reflected a "lack of ethics" and a "pattern
of pay-to-play deals with campaign contributors."

Green's knowledge of D'Amato's role in pushing Wedtech's
agenda with the Defense Department was sketchy. As a small
example of Green's ignorance, Green was unaware that D'Amato
had strenuously lobbied for the Wedtech contract with then navy
secretary John Lehman, insisting that he wanted the South Bronx
firm to become the *sole* supplier of the pontoons.

In fact, D'Amato was so proud of his exertions for Wedtech that
when a contract award was made in April 1984, he insisted on top

billing at the announcement ceremony, shoving aside his friend Cong. Mario Biaggi, who had lobbied at least as hard as the senator for Wedtech.

In August 1984, four months after the main contract was signed, Wedtech subcontracted $5 million of the pontoon work to Steamco, a Manhattan engineering firm that specialized in ship engines. Federal Election Commission records show that Steamco's president, James Johnson, made his first contribution to D'Amato in June 1984, two months before Wedtech sought out Steamco, a firm with which they had never done business. In an endeavor to keep D'Amato's goodwill, Johnson, Steamco officials, and their relatives gave $11,500 to his "campaign fund."

About that time, Steamco's president said he was approached by John Zagame, D'Amato's staff director, asking for a job as a consultant. Johnson had earlier met Zagame at a D'Amato fund-raiser, and he thought Zagame asked him for the job sometime between mid-1984, which would place the job request before Steamco got the Wedtech contract, and early 1985, by which time Zagame was working for the Republican National Committee.

In December 1985, Zagame opened a private consulting firm. One of his first clients was Steamco. Johnson explained, "We hired him because we were trying to get into government work and we were looking for help in approaching the right people."

Steamco was foundering and sought desperately to find someone with influence to keep the company afloat. Johnson paid Zagame $3,500 monthly for half a year to obtain government contracts, all to no avail. In October 1986, Steamco filed for bankruptcy.

Soon after going to work for Steamco, Zagame found another client, Wedtech. He received a $5,000 retainer fee from the South Bronx firm to act as one of its "government consultants."

Wedtech had grown in a few years from a small machine shop in a burned-out section of the Bronx to a major supplier of military equipment. To accomplish that miracle, Wedtech's owners handed out millions in bribes to bureaucrats and members of Congress who were in a position to influence the Reagan administration. Atty. Gen. Ed Meese had been used by his friend and personal attorney, Wedtech lawyer E. Robert Wallach, to coerce reluctant Defense Department brass into favoring the bids of the bribers. Some of Meese's closest associates had gone to work for Wedtech, and Wallach's successful investments for Meese had the appearance of payoffs to the attorney general. White House aide Lyn Nofziger, President Reagan's confidant for twenty years, was convicted in February 1988 of illegally lobbying for Wedtech in return for $909,000. Nofziger's influence had been vital in obtaining a $32 million army contract to build small engines, which the army had wanted to give to a better-qualified firm.

D'Amato's crony Democrat Mario Biaggi would soon be convicted of extorting millions from Wedtech. Like D'Amato, Biaggi had been repeatedly accused through the years of involvement in a series of corrupt activities but had managed to remain in Congress; that lucky string ran out on February 18, 1988, when the House Ethics Committee recommended that he be expelled. In March 1989, Biaggi began serving a four-year term in a Texas federal prison.

Biaggi's law partner in the firm of Biaggi & Ehrlich, Bernard G. Ehrlich, was a key player linking D'Amato to the Wedtech scandal. Ehrlich had represented Wedtech before government agencies, always making it a point to stress to officials of those agencies that Senator D'Amato had a special interest in Wedtech.

In return for his efforts, Ehrlich received $1.6 million in Wedtech shares and became one of the firm's directors. At the same time, Biaggi's son Richard, now an Ehrlich law partner, was rewarded with a similar number of Wedtech shares for services performed by his father.

One of Ehrlich's major Wedtech duties was to advise its moribund board which public officials should receive money euphemistically referred to as "campaign contributions." D'Amato, whose name rang through the halls of any agency under siege by Ehrlich, was the largest beneficiary of Wedtech "contributions."

Ehrlich's cozy relationship with D'Amato became apparent when he was appointed by D'Amato as his unpaid "military adviser." Decorated with that illustrious title, Ehrlich spent one day a week in D'Amato's Washington office. It was never clear what military advice the senator sought or needed. Ehrlich's credentials came from his brief role as commander of New York's forty-second National Guard division; hints of scandal at the armory forced him to resign. At that humiliating juncture Wedtech's director of political affairs had become available to serve in the unpaid military capacity required by the chairman of the Banking Securities Subcommittee.

The tie between the two became even stronger during the period between 1982 and 1984, when Ehrlich's daughter, Robin, became a full-time D'Amato staff member. Ehrlich's main job in D'Amato's office was to draft letters for the senator's signature used to file protests and initiate inquiries on Wedtech's behalf.

Mark Green's 1986 election-eve accusation that D'Amato had accepted $11,000 from Wedtech proved to be conservative. A fuller account of D'Amato's role in the scandal began to appear at Biaggi's Wedtech trial on March 23, 1988. At that time the congressman and six other defendants, including former Democratic Bronx borough president Stanley Simon, Biaggi's son Richard, and Bernard Ehrlich, were charged with turning Wedtech into a racketeering enterprise that paid millions of dollars to government officials.

At Biaggi's trial Wedtech's former vice chairman, Mario Moreno, testified in Manhattan federal court that he had for several years—after receiving advice from Commander Ehrlich—arranged for D'Amato to receive envelopes containing tens of thousands of dollars in checks and money orders. In exchange, D'Amato had repeatedly pressured the army, the navy, and the Small Business Administration. Moreno said that D'Amato's support proved crucial in winning the incompetent Wedtech company over $100 million in government contracts.

Moreno explained that Wedtech contributed to people like D'Amato "in exchange for favors we expected to get. . . . We expected to have the Republican party in our pocket." Moreno testified that he had conducted his business with D'Amato in the senator's office and that D'Amato often made three of his staff members available to him for Wedtech business. With Ehrlich and his daughter and Moreno constantly trekking through D'Amato's senate suite, it took on the air of a Wedtech branch office.

Moreno testified that his payments to D'Amato were always made under different names: It was illegal for individuals to contribute over $2,000 to his war chest during a six-year term, and corporations were prohibited from making any contributions. The prosecutor asked, "And you gave to Senator D'Amato contributions and money orders to his campaigns close to $30,000, is that not correct?"

"Yes," Moreno responded. "It might have been more than that." Because of the multiplicity of names he had used to funnel money to D'Amato, he couldn't recall how much more. In one of those moments of purification experienced by sinners on whom the prosecutors have the goods, Moreno added, "I felt we had violated the law."

It seemed reasonable to assume that D'Amato knew the limits on contributions better than Wedtech's vice chairman, and when accepting this shower of checks he also must have realized that he had violated the law.

Wedtech was not just another New York constituent D'Amato helped out—one of fifty-thousand constituents he claimed to service each year. If a New Yorker wrote the senator asking for a copy of a speech he made and a clerk mailed it, that person statistically become one of the "fifty-thousand" constituents he helped that year. Most of those constituent contacts were equally inconsequential.

Wedtech was "a constituent" with greater needs and clout: it absorbed a substantial amount of D'Amato's time and energy. Wedtech was a corrupt enterprise with which he shared an employee, to which he contributed staff, and for whom, in his large suite of offices in the new Hart Senate office building, he provided desk space. As he did not do for his other constituents, he lobbied vigorously for Wedtech's interests, and if he had not been restrained by his membership in the Senate, he would have been on Wedtech's payroll. Instead, his remuneration came in the form of large, illegal "contributions."

As soon as Green had hurled his bolt that D'Amato had received an "$11,000" bribe from Wedtech, D'Amato faded from the campaign trail. He referred all questions about Wedtech to Gary Lewi, who fended off those irritating reporters with the comment "We are hearing another silly accusation by a desperate candidate."

The rest of D'Amato's campaign was waged from the well of the Senate or in press releases handed out by Lewi.

In its October 28 editorial, the *New York Times,* one of America's most influential papers, came out with a less than ringing endorsement of D'Amato. The editorial recalled D'Amato's "incredible testimony that he didn't know, as a Long Island official, that the Republican organization required the faithful to kick back 1 percent of their salaries." It mentioned that "he was the sole character witness for a man convicted of conspiring with an organized crime figure," and it questioned "the aggressive fund-raising tactics that have brought him nearly $8 million in campaign contributions."

The *Times* conceded that "New York has been accustomed to senators who aspire to internationalism, eloquence, national stature." But this time New York voters must content themselves with a man who displayed a different brand of nobility. "Alfonse D'Amato has set himself a less glamorous goal. His slogan claims, He Delivers, and he does."

Newsday was offended by the thought that there was any validity to D'Amato's self-serving slogan He Delivers. The same day of the *Times's* tepid editorial on behalf of D'Amato, *Newsday* endorsed Green.

> D'Amato seems to regard the United States Senate as a larger version of the Nassau County Board of Supervisors, with the same parochial concerns and narrow interests. . . . During his six years in Washington, D'Amato has managed the nearly impossible: Despite repeatedly voting for cuts totaling billions of dollars in programs that benefit the people of New York, he has achieved a reputation for bringing home the pork. At the same time, he has voted for such dubious and horrendously expensive boondoggles as the Clinch River Breeder Reactor, the Tennessee-Tombigbee Waterway and the Garrison Diversion Project in North Dakota.

D'Amato had spent his first term as a backbencher in the Senate, trading his vote on bills important to his colleagues in exchange for their vote to protect the interests of his biggest contributors. The Tennessee-Tombigbee canal was the obsession of Republican majority leader Howard Baker. In exchange for assignment to the powerful Appropriations and Bank, Housing and Urban Affairs committees, each year D'Amato delivered his vote on Baker's pipedream, squandering $3 billions in an attempt to connect

Baker's state of Tennessee to the Gulf of Mexico. He also gave Baker his vote on the wasteful Tennessee Clinch River nuclear reactor on the same day in September 1982 that he voted to kill a federal jobs program for the unemployed. If those money-guzzling Tombigbee and Clinch River pork-barrel projects had not collapsed of their own weight, D'Amato's votes on issues of no interest or benefit to his constituents would have continued to be delivered.

Although concerned about his voting record, the *Newsday* editorial seemed more disturbed about the corruption issue. "D'Amato has looked out for the interests of defense contractors, Wall Street, real estate developers and the oil and chemical industries, and they in turn have contributed generously to his campaign." *Newsday* concluded:

> There is something less tangible but more troubling about D'Amato: the impression that his vote might be for sale, or at least for barter; that the government's role is to comfort the comfortable; that to be principled is to be dumb.

D'Amato worked hard to convince voters that "he delivers." Photographers were present when he gave Mayor Koch a check for a few million dollars he had obtained for a subway project. The media was informed when he dedicated a playground built with a stipend from Washington. With such simple political tactics, D'Amato had succeeded in establishing enough of an implication of utilitarian function to convince some voters that he was concerned about filling their potholes. Actually his vote in favor of the Gramm-Rudman Act all by itself resulted in a $700 million loss for New York in 1986 and 1987.

A study prepared by Fiscal Planning Services for the American Federation of State, County, and Municipal Employees in 1986 showed that New York State had received a cut of $11.8 billion in federal assistance between 1981 and 1986. That loss occurred because of Reagan administration budget cuts and the alteration of financing formulas. D'Amato's voting record was uniformly in favor of each of those cuts.

Cumulatively, Senator Pothole's votes slashed billions from New York's subways and buses and cost the state additional billions, leaving it short of money to repair roads, rebuild rusting bridges, and fight inner-city decay.

On November 4, 1986, D'Amato was reelected with 57.5 percent of the vote, .1 percent more than Javits's largest victory, in 1962. In a gesture of appreciation for the voters' verdict, D'Amato appeared before a rush-hour crowd in Grand Central Terminal and shouted that his triumph confirmed his decision to shun national and international issues and to fight for "bringing home the bacon to New York." He continued: "It was a vote by the people of New York that Al D'Amato is the kind of senator New York needs, the kind of senator who'll fight for the legitimate needs of New York, even if it means being called the 'pothole senator.' "

In a final attempt to explain why he had so decisively lost to such an "unethical" man, Mark Green handed me the official tabulation for 1986 campaign financing. D'Amato spent more than any candidate for the U.S. Senate; the final figure, $12,914,822.

Green said, "I don't mind losing to a guy who has thirteen million dollars when I spent only three. But I do mind when he has access to a trillion-dollar federal treasury in terms of the deals he can engineer for his donors or the grants he squeezes out of government agencies for his contributors. D'Amato has basically used our tax money to finance his political campaigns."

Green didn't mention that D'Amato was the eighth-largest recipient in the 100-member senate of contributions from PACs (political action committees) financed by defense contractors and that he was also the fifth-largest recipient of campaign contributions from the S & L industry.

Green had highlighted an important reason why D'Amato beat him, but there were others. D'Amato appealed unshakably to the largest bloc of voters in the state, Italian-Americans. His conservative stance on crime, welfare, and communism drew strong support from that community.

Jews voted for D'Amato in larger numbers than for any Republican candidate with the exception of Jacob Javits. His frequent trips to Israel and vociferous defense of the Jewish state against Yasir Arafat and the Palestine Liberation Organization (PLO) were classic politics in New York and paid off on election day.

Green's liberal position on social issues made him unacceptable to Reagan Democrats, who had deserted the party precisely because of candidates like him. For that group of lower-middle-class voters the contest was a mismatch: whereas Green was an elitist bleeding heart from an Ivy League college, entirely too glib, D'Amato was an ordinary guy, up from the streets, who knew how to handle himself in the real world. The cynics among them were not shocked by what they heard about D'Amato's sleaziness, because they thought anyone in his position would take advantage. These cynics believed they knew how things really worked, and they felt like realists when they cast their vote for a tough guy who had a reputation for paying back on his IOUs.

Added to Green's cup of hemlock was the incumbency factor. D'Amato's partisans knew that he had been a senator for six years, and despite the negative reports about him, they had survived. The incumbent, in spite of his opponent's low opinion of him, had not destroyed America. To that extent, New Yorkers *knew* D'Amato. They didn't know his opponent. If the new young man who had never served in any legislative office were elected, perhaps the county would continue to function. But why take the chance. An incumbent was like an old shoe; it might not look so good, but a new shoe could pinch your toes.

Finally, 1986 was a prosperous year. The Reagan recession of 1981–83 had became a distant memory. The economy was roaring along, fueled by tax cuts and out-of-control government spending. Good times and high employment always work to the benefit of the party in power. D'Amato fastened himself to Ronald Reagan, arranging for the popular president to campaign for him. Reagan's endorsement carried weight, but declining inflation and interest rates and a sense that the ship of state was in good hands were more significant.

After the results were announced, Green wondered what would have happened if he had as much money to spend as D'Amato. Since his cause had been lost from the beginning, a more suitable question would have been, how had he managed to come so close?

THIRTY-SIX

THE LETHAL THREAT

Armand Paul, Al D'Amato's younger brother separated by eight years, had not originally planned to be a lawyer. During his first three years at St. John's he studied to be an accountant. "I got bored with it," he told me. During those three years in the late 1960s he could see that Al's fortunes had changed. A penniless lawyer working as a court clerk had metamorphosed into a politician on the rise. Armand Paul suddenly found a law degree attractive.

After graduating from St. John's Law School in 1970 at age twenty-five, he taught accounting at a Rockville Centre Catholic high school while supposedly studying for the bar exam. "Actually I was a jock," he said. "I spent my time playing four-wall handball." He failed the bar. A hectic six months followed, teaching on the island and racing to evening prep courses in Manhattan.

Shortly after he passed the bar on his second try, Al obtained a seat for him in the assembly by asking his mentor, Joe Margiotta, to arrange Armand Paul's nomination as a personal favor. Al's influence was always at the service of his brother. In 1976, Armand Paul established his Mineola law practice. His major asset: Hempstead's supervisor, brother Al, whose clout with the board of

335

supervisors made lucrative rezoning fees a steady source of income.

Still, after four years, Armand Paul's firm could best be described as a modest partnership; in 1980 he had three partners and two associates. An ordinary graduate of law school without the political connections of Armand Paul could expect at this stage of his career to be on his own, handling divorces and drawing up wills, or an associate working for someone else. Prosperity flooded in on the firm after 1980, when Al was elected to the Senate. By the mid-1980s, there were six partners and thirteen lawyers on the staff of D'Amato, Forchelli, Libert, Schwartz, Mineo & Joseph F. Carlino, who, as party leader in 1961, had given Al his first government job.

In 1985, Joe Margiotta, seeking vengeance for Al's betrayal of him, thwarted Armand Paul's attempt to become Republican leader of the state assembly by throwing the Long Island votes he controlled to an upstate assemblyman. After that disappointment, Armand Paul established one of the worst attendance records in Albany. "I guess I had more pressing business in the district," he said in an attempt to explain his tardiness.

I asked why he became disenchanted with his assembly career. "I quit partly because I was bored," he confessed. "The assembly was controlled by the Democrats. We Republicans had nothing to do. We played and we ate, but after a while there was nothing to do. I just sat around all day."

He also said he was tired. His burgeoning law practice was absorbing more of his energy; in January 1985 he opened a Washington office with all its promise of easy access to Senator Al for his Long Island clients. And his brother's demands on him knew no limits; they were on the phone several times a day. Adding to the chaos, a frenzied Al, seeking reelection, had made his brother his campaign manager. In addition, he would be campaigning for his eighth term in the assembly. "I was being pulled in too many ways," Armand Paul complained. "On February 11, 1987, I wrote out my resignation, walked up to the assembly clerk, and handed it to him." Years later, when he described that ritual to me, he still sounded pleased with his decision.

By the late-1980s, lawyers in Nassau County ranked Armand's Mineola firm as one of the five largest on Long Island. Former county executive Ralph Caso explained the reasons for his success.

"Many people hire the firm because on Long Island the name Armand D'Amato is associated with Al D'Amato. People who want to have certain doors opened in government think it will be easier to do so with the D'Amato firm."

Caso's point was confirmed by Al and Armand Paul's relationship with Unisys, the megabusiness formed by the 1986 merger of Sperry and Burroughs, one of the country's largest defense contractors. Unisys is based in Great Neck, Long Island, and its former Sperry executives had been wooing D'Amato with contributions to his campaigns for years. In an endeavor to win Al's favor, Sperry quickly became a client of Armand Paul's new Washington office.

Since Alfonse was a member of the Armed Services Committee, which had power over defense contracts, Sperry felt it needed his support. Sperry's vice president, Charles Gardner, who handled such matters in Great Neck, knew what all well-connected businessmen on Long Island knew: that Senator D'Amato's support could be bought, most expeditiously by doing business with his brother.

As a result, when Armand Paul was unable to attract any other major clients for his Capitol Hill operation and his short-lived Washington office was closed down in March 1985, Sperry, still in need of Senator D'Amato's goodwill, shifted its "non-legal. . . . government relations work" to Armand Paul's Mineola *law* office.

In 1986 the Defense Department began a probe of fraud and bribery in contract procurement that included an investigation of Sperry/Unisys's contributions to Senator D'Amato's campaigns. In June 1986 the results of that probe were released. Unisys admitted that some of its executives had contributed money to D'Amato and then been told by corporate officers to "recoup the contributions by submitting false expense reports." A spokesman for the Federal Election Commission (FEC) stated that it was a crime for a corporation to make political contributions through a third party.

Unisys conducted its own investigation and revealed that at least five of its executives were told to falsify their expense accounts for submission to the Defense Department in order to get repaid for their D'Amato "contributions." This was a routine device used by D'Amato to circumvent the federal law prohibiting corporations from making contributions to political campaigns. He had used the same technique to harvest Wedtech's bribes.

SENATOR POTHOLE

In an attempt to disguise the illegal submissions, the "contributors" were told to spread out their expense-account items over a period of months.

Unisys stated that as a result of their investigation the firm had decided to enlarge its employees' ethics programs. "The current employee training program ... is being expanded to include a reemphasis on the prohibitions of entertaining government employees and obtaining reimbursement for any political contributions."

Senator D'Amato issued a statement: "If this happened, it's an outrage, and any contravention of the law regarding corporate contributions should be prosecuted. [It would be] absolutely unconscionable, wrong, and should not be tolerated. If people are putting pressure on other people to make contributions in violation of the law, they should be prosecuted."

The senator went on to deny he had ever received cash from anyone at Sperry or Unisys. The FEC records, however, revealed that his campaign had received $1,000 contributions from three Sperry executives in the 1983–84 period covered by the Defense Department probe. The FEC added that even its casual review of the senator's 1986 reports to them indicated that the D'Amato campaign had that year received $6,500 from Sperry or Unisys employees, consultants, and their relatives. That didn't include contributions of under $200, which did not have to be reported.

The FEC was controlled by President Reagan appointees, and since it had discretion about decisions involving prosecutions, it made no move against this bevy of prominent Republicans. The Defense Department, having discovered fraud in contributions accepted by D'Amato, was obligated to ask the Justice Department to present its evidence to a grand jury. But the Defense Department knew better than to go to war against a member of the Armed Services Committee, and the case against Senator D'Amato and Unisys was dropped.

Al D'Amato had publicly denied he ever received cash from anyone at Unisys, but at the moment of Al's denial that he had personally received money from the defense contractor, Armand Paul was on a concealed company payroll and had been since January 1985. Much larger amounts of Unisys money were being paid out to the D'Amatos than the few thousands openly donated to Al's campaign. Unisys's greatest generosity was showered on Armand Paul;

338

their beneficence was occasioned by his service as a hidden inter-mediary with his brother.

In 1986 the navy announced plans to build the Aegis, a ship defense system used to track and destroy missiles. Unisys wanted the $100 million contract to supply the missile's computers, and Unisys's vice president, Charles Gardner, a thief who was stealing from Unisys and was soon to end up in jail, was put in charge of landing that contract. Despite a carefully crafted proposal readied for the navy, Gardner watched for the opening of competitive bid-ding that did not come.

Gardner's problem was caused by a change in the perceived need for Unisys's product. By November 1987 the Defense Department was cutting its budget because of a diminished threat from the Soviet Union and the increased threat to the nation's eco-nomic stability from President Reagan's huge budget deficits. George Bush's presidential campaign was based on the pledge that although the country was falling into debt faster than a drunken playboy, if he were elected, there would be no new taxes. Therefore, belt tightening was the only remaining solution. As a result, a number of weapons systems were in the process of being terminated, and the Defense Department was looking for a way out of the Aegis deal.

In an attempt to get action, Charles Gardner turned to Armand, who was already on his secret payroll, ready to supply his broth-er's muscle in just such an emergency. Armand's activities suggest that at least in this instance Gardner was not wasting Unisys's money. On one trip to his brother's Washington office he carried in his briefcase a letter addressed to Navy Secretary James Webb com-posed by Gardner's coconspirators. Gardner wanted this letter, which urged Webb to award the Aegis contract without delay, retyped on brother Al's official stationery, signed by the senator, and then hand-delivered to Webb's office.

This December 1, 1987, letter from a prominent senator, whose "constituent" was Charles Gardner, was promptly sent. It concluded by demanding that the senator be "advised of your plans in this regard." Shortly, the bidding was held, and in April 1988 the navy reported that the Aegis contract had been given to Unisys.

On September 23, 1990, it was announced that a federal grand jury was investigating whether Armand Paul had used influence peddling to obtain defense contracts with the aid of his brother's office. Wiretap discussions about payments to Armand by Unisys were to be presented to the grand jury. Although a Unisys spokesman—no longer jail-bound Charles Gardner—said that Armand's firm had "never done any legal work for the company," he conceded that large payments had been made to Armand Paul going back to 1985.

Earlier company "contributions" to the senator suddenly appeared in a new light. Al D'Amato had pressured the navy to purchase a number of Sperry/Unisys weapons systems. In his war with the Pentagon aimed at getting its leaders to buy unneeded, even useless weapons, Senator D'Amato had been a dependable Sperry/Unisys ally. The 1983–86 contributions now appeared to be more than an illegal corporate donation to a senator Sperry/Unisys favored; it now appeared to be a payoff for service wanted and subsequently rendered.

The 1990 Brooklyn grand jury's investigation of Armand Paul's influence peddling with his brother on behalf of Unisys posed a lethal threat to Senator D'Amato. The statute of limitations had not run out on this crime. The senator issued a statement clearly aimed at distancing himself from his brother: "Since the investigation does not involve me, I have no knowledge of the facts. I have every confidence in the integrity of my brother, and I'm sure the investigation will confirm my faith in him."

Pulitzer Prize columnist Sydney H. Schanberg, a critic of D'Amato's, commented: "The only thing the senator left out was his promise to visit Armand regularly in the federal slammer and bring him his favorite foods."

THIRTY-SEVEN

THE PROSPERING
OF THE D'AMATOS

F ormer Nassau County deputy executive Jim Nagourney, whose negative opinion of Alfonse had been formed during years of close association, believes that "D'Amato is driven purely by a desire for power. He's the most power driven person I have ever known." He had a much more benign view of Armand. "Armand is not driven the way Al is." But Nagourney felt that Armand was dominated by Al. "He thinks Al is a terrific person. He's fiercely loyal to his brother."

Nagourney said he would be "shocked" to find money "going into Al D'Amato's pocket." Because "if you steal you get caught and you lose power." Money had one irresistible attraction to D'Amato, in Nagourney's opinion. "He raises funds for his campaigns, but that's part of his power play. He raises big money so that he can run for office so that he can get reelected so that he can keep his power and get even more power. That's the motivation for Al and the people like Al."

Mark Green, who lost to D'Amato in 1986, agreed with Nagourney about D'Amato's motivation. "There is an enormous amount of irrefutable evidence that he [D'Amato] has politically enriched his war chest, which most senators care more about than their bank account. Because it keeps them in office."

"As to whether Armand has gotten rich," Green continued, "there is no way to know; he doesn't have to file a net-worth statement. People have told me that he resigned from the assembly because the ethics rules were getting so strict that he couldn't make the income on the side that he wanted to. And the reporting requirements were getting so detailed he had to report more than he wanted to. In private practice he does not have to report."

Although Armand Paul has refused through the years to be interviewed about his law firm, a check of government records by Selwyn Raab of the *New York Times* showed that there is an unmistakable relationship between his brother's election to the senate and the increase in Armand's bank account. In practically every case, the firms signing on with Armand also become Al's contributors.

A short list of these symbiotic client-contributors includes:

- Cablevision: hired Armand in their quest to control cable television in Nassau County. It then formed a PAC that contributed $4,000 to Al D'Amato in 1986.
- The Bowery Savings Bank: uses Armand's firm to handle 15 percent of its Long Island mortgage closings. The Bowery Officers Non-Partisan Political Committee contributed $3,150 to the senator.
- The National Seatrade Company of Lake Success, L.I.: Armand's client obtained $30 million from Nassau for removal of sludge from county waste-treatment plants. Its owners, Leo V. Berger and James A. Johnson, and their relatives contributed $13,500 to Al D'Amato's campaigns.
- Stephen Sloan, New York marine developer: lost a bid in 1988 to provide ferry service to the Statue of Liberty. D'Amato then fired off a fruitless letter pressuring the National Park Department services director to change his mind. Sloan had contributed three times to the senator's campaign since 1985, including $1,000 donated two weeks after Sloan lost the bid competition: One never knew when the senator's help might be more effective. Sloan also retained Armand for legal work on a marina-condominium project.

- Johansen Organization of Hempstead: Officials and relatives of this major Long Island developer contributed $16,200 to Senator D'Amato's campaign kitty. Ronald K. Johansen, chairman of the Johansen Organization, said about his decision to hire Armand, "There is a presumed knowledge," that Armand's firm "knows how to get things through the political structure."

- The Redco Construction of Oceanside: thought Armand did such a good job handling their interests that its principal owner, Harold Lituchy, and his family gave Al D'Amato $11,000 to help him stay in the Senate. Before organizing Redco, Lituchy had built three federally subsidized HUD projects for the elderly in Nassau costing $16 million, including the first five HUD houses in Island Park.

Armand's firm was frequently retained by builders after they got work on HUD-financed projects with Al's pivotal aid.

The prospering of his family seemed to shape much of the senator's activity. His aim might seem to be the collection of campaign funds, usually by performing some "service" for a well-heeled constituent, but often there was an additional family advantage.

For example, the *Daily News* reported that "Sen. Alfonse D'Amato leases *the most expensive district office in Congress*—in a Manhattan building managed by a long-time friend and campaign contributor." The shabby building at 370 Seventh Avenue near the south end of the Garment District hardly seemed to be the appropriate place for the $250,000 annual rent that D'Amato was willing to let the taxpayers pay. Heavy contributor Jeffrey Feil owned the eighteen-story pre–World War I building.

Martin Bernstein comanaged the building with Feil. Bernstein had been a member of the Hempstead Town Council when D'Amato served as presiding supervisor. As leader of the Oceanside Republican Club, Bernstein was one of D'Amato's strongest supporters during his rise to power. His wife, Deborah, was a member of D'Amato's staff during his first term in the Senate, and to complete the circle, Bernstein was also a former law partner of Armand Paul's.

The *Daily News* pointed out that since he had become a tenant in September 1987, D'Amato had been grossly overpaying for his accommodations. He had committed the government to reimburse Feil and Bernstein at the rate of $29.07 per square foot, "but a half-dozen brokers and an equal number of tenants pegged the going rate in his building at between $18 and $23 a foot." D'Amato was giving his landlords a bonus of at least $75,000 per year, and in 1991, the last year of the lease, he had agreed to pay $40,000 more, raising the rent to $290,000, or in excess of $31 per square foot. This in the face of a weakening Manhattan real estate market.

Congress advises all its members to obtain their office space in government-owned buildings. And, in fact, D'Amato has four other offices around the state in federal buildings. However, he made no such attempt in Manhattan, where inexpensive government space was readily available. Cong. Ted Weiss had a suite in the Veterans Administration building at 252 Seventh Avenue, only a few blocks from D'Amato's office, for which he paid only $30,000.

Feil and Bernstein, their Garment District office adjacent to D'Amato's, were also Armand's clients. When Armand was asked about the fact that his brother rented from his clients, he responded that it was "purely coincidental."

Another "coincidence" was Armand's choice of abode.

In 1983, Feil and Bernstein, in partnership with Harold Lituchy, another heavy donor to Alfonse, decided they wanted to erect a luxury condominium on the shore in Island Park. This was the property on which twenty years earlier Jim Fazio wanted to build a village high school. As it worked out, D'Amato's opposition to that project had made the land available for Feil/Bernstein/Lituchy.

Since the plot was not zoned for that kind of development, the partners hired Armand Paul's law firm in 1985 to obtain state approval to build a marina essential for the marketing of the project. Armand's successful string pulling led to the construction of the Yacht Club Condominiums.

In December 1986, when Armand's relations with his first wife were souring, he purchased a two-bedroom apartment in Feil and Bernstein's condo. Sales price to Armand: $140,000. But in 1983, when the prospective condo first went on sale, the partners were selling that unit for $172,500, and by 1986, when Armand bought, the asking price for everyone else was $219,000. Nassau land records show that within five months of Armand Paul's discounted purchase, similar units sold for $172,500 and $203,000.

The lost profits suffered by the condo's partners because of their cut-rate sale to Armand were recouped by Feil and Bernstein a few months later when they rented Al D'Amato his Garment District office at an annual $75,000 over market value.

The advantage to Armand: The taxpayers were picking up a part of the cost of buying his apartment. The advantage to Al: He had performed several constituent services, even if one of those constituents was a member of his family.

The Yacht Club Condominiums deal that Armand Paul set up with the state had a socially constructive codicil in it that was used by him to make the condo deal float: Feil/Bernstein/Lituchy committed themselves to build senior citizen housing on an adjacent lot they owned. The senior citizens are still waiting for their housing.

Soon after the condo was built it became clear that the partners had no intention of honoring the agreement Armand had found it necessary to negotiate. In 1989 they contracted to sell the lot to Philip Basile, a friend of godfather Paul Vario and Senator D'Amato, who, as the sole character witness at Basile's 1983 trial, had characterized Basile as an "honest, truthful, hardworking man, a man of integrity." The man of integrity wanted to use it as a parking lot for his J. J. Sprats disco. Basile's singles bar was almost directly under the window of Armand's apartment, and with many lonely nights on his hands Armand often drank there and found it a reliable source of female companionship.

Instead of defending the senior citizens whose cause he, Armand, had used to get the Yacht Club Condominiums built, he signed up to represent convicted felon Basile. All of Armand's political contacts were now used to change the lot's zoning so that it could *not* be used for senior citizens housing. There was an outcry from village residents, and Armand Paul withdrew his proposal.

Regardless of whether Al D'Amato put money directly into his pocket, there is no doubt he profited by having his family prosper. Father Armand Sr. was a particularly good example.

Longtime neighbor Catherine Fazio had seen Armand Sr.'s insurance business grow through the years as her husband Jim had directed clients to his comember in the Public party. By the time

345

the mid-1960s rolled around, Armand no longer needed Jim's help. His oldest son was now head of the Island Park Republican Club and in a position to steer the village's business his way. On April 5, 1965, soon after Al became executive leader, he had his father appointed the village's insurance broker. Village clerk Harry Scully revealed that for the next five years Armand handled $20,000 in annual premiums. By the mid-1970s the figure had risen to $50,000. Armand's commission: 20 percent. The *Village Voice* checked that fee with other people in the field and concluded: "Insurance experts say that a 20 per cent commission is unusually high."

There was an insatiable quality to Armand Sr.'s appetite for new business and no limit to his older son's willingness to exert himself on his father's behalf. Catherine and Jim Fazio were active in school affairs during the 1960s, and Al's effort to corner the separate, lucrative school insurance account still rankled her.

"When we were involved in the school board," Catherine said, "even if we [the Fazios and Al] were supporting the same people, it was a known fact that he was interested only in getting the insurance business for his father and not whether it was a particularly good thing for the school. His whole purpose in trying to control the school board was for his father's benefit."

After Jim died in 1969, Catherine went to work as a law secretary. She also sought election to the school board, where she served from 1971 to 1989, always running unopposed because, she mused aloud, "people thought of me and motherhood at the same time."

The cost of insurance, she discovered, was lowering the quality of education the Island Park schools were able to offer village children. "Every year things had to be cut out because insurance costs were too high."

Jim Nagourney, who knew Armand Sr. during the 1960s and 1970s, said, "I had the feeling that the brains in the family comes from the mother. His father is a very nondescript person. He had a number of town and county jobs, certainly not on qualifications."

During Armand's career in government, which Jack Newfield in the *Village Voice* described as "his seldom-show job," he was known by his acquaintances as "Frenchie." His starting salary in 1972 came to $17,000, but by 1980 he was receiving $34,000, with no safe way to predict what his salary would be when he finally decided to legally retire. Even then there would be additional coin coming in from the insurance business he and his wife maintained in a building they owned in Rockville Centre. There are numerous grateful and hopeful people who think it's a good idea to be insured by a D'Amato.

George Ficke, an Island Park opponent of D'Amato's, estimates that the town's insurance bills during the 1980s had risen to $600,000 annually; the lowest estimate by others is not less than $300,000. "We've been fighting for the last four years to put our insurance out for bid," Ficke said. "Every other village on the island used to do it the same way [no-bid assignment to the village broker], but it got to a point where insurance just got so expensive that the villages had to put it out to bid. Not us." Armand D'Amato Sr. maintains his stranglehold on the Island Park no-bid bonanza.

Al D'Amato's profit by indirection took many forms. His proposal to build the Island Park pool illustrates that point.

In the fall of 1988 the senator wrote to village residents informing them that he had succeeded in getting HUD to allocate $1 million to build them a pool. No one had been campaigning for such a facility. After all, Island Park was surrounded by water. It had a fine beach. So unfocused were the village elders on the need for a swimming pool that no plans for such a project existed. D'Amato nevertheless perceived a need. The pool was to be within a short walk of his house, whose backyard was too small to build one.

While President Reagan had been cutting back on funds for housing and urban development for poor people, the president had placed millions of dollars of the remaining money in a "discretionary fund" controlled by HUD secretary Samuel Pierce. That allowed Pierce to allocate government money as he wished.

Building a swimming pool for a middle-class seashore community didn't remotely fit HUD's mission, which was to assist low-income individuals. This fact did not deter D'Amato from making his request to Secretary Pierce, nor did it deter the secretary from waving his approval. To show that he recognized good judgment, D'Amato wrote village residents that Secretary Pierce had made a "wise decision to approve this grant."

The wisdom of that decision was questioned only by most people Alfonse D'Amato did not know personally. The residents of

Island Park also came to doubt its wisdom. George Ficke, speaking for village opponents to the pool, said, "They should put that HUD money into housing. I have two married sons who can't afford a house on Long Island. One is moving to Florida. We need housing."

Amid the uproar, federal prosecutors announced they were undertaking an investigation of HUD projects on Long Island, including, most ominously for Senator D'Amato, Island Park. Within days, on June 30, 1989, village officials said they had decided to kill the swimming-pool project and return the $1 million to the secretary's "discretionary fund."

By that time there was a new secretary of HUD, former congressman Jack Kemp. His office issued the following statement: "We think the funds can be used for a purpose that will be more in line with assisting low-income individuals."

THIRTY-EIGHT
APPOINTING SAFE
PROSECUTORS

A s long as Bill Cahn was Nassau district attorney and the Eastern District's U.S. Attorney's office was in the hands of political appointees with more important things to do, Joe Margiotta could run his "pay-to-play" rackets with impunity. D'Amato knew that Margiotta's troubles had begun when David Trager became U.S. Attorney in the 1970s and that the boss had been brought down when Trager's successor, Ed Korman, decided to press on in hot pursuit.

D'Amato's fear of the prosecutor's dangerous role led him, soon after the 1980 election, to try to neutralize the U.S. Attorney's office. He was driven by the knowledge that Korman was investigating his role in Nassau corruption and was serious about indicting him. Although circumstances forced him to live with Korman for almost two years, until the 1982 expiration of his appointment, D'Amato began to express a preference for Korman's successor almost as soon as he took office. His man was Andrew J. Maloney of Mamaroneck, a modest, soft-spoken lawyer who had worked as Assistant U.S. Attorney in Manhattan from 1962 to 1972. Since then, he had been in private practice in Manhattan.

D'Amato faced a daunting obstacle: The experienced and effective Raymond J. Dearie, Korman's chief assistant, was widely spoken of as Korman's obvious successor.

In 1982, D'Amato was still haunted by the realization that he had barely won the 1980 election in a three-way race and was still too weak to defeat a single opponent. He knew that if he bypassed Dearie while Margiotta's extortion trial was before the courts, a firestorm would engulf him. Swallowing hard, he recommended Dearie's appointment. Although circumstances had thwarted him, he was determined to bring that dangerous office under his control.

Within two years his new strategy became clear. He recommended the promotion of a district court judge to a vacancy on the court of appeals, thereby creating a suitable position for Dearie on the district court bench. At the same time, he expressed the opinion that his old favorite Andrew J. Maloney would be an excellent replacement for Dearie as U.S. Attorney.

Events again conspired against D'Amato. Two more years passed before Senate approval was received; Dearie was sworn in on March 22, 1986. D'Amato instantly proposed Maloney as Dearie's successor. But President Reagan, perhaps to show D'Amato that it would be wise to be more compliant, took his time in sending Maloney's nomination to the Senate. The approval was delayed, and a young woman on Dearie's staff, Reena Raggi, assumed the role of acting U.S. Attorney. Months passed, and Ms. Raggi, vigorously performing her duties, began to make a reputation for herself. Her name and picture were frequently in the papers. Suggestions began to appear that she, and not Maloney, would make a suitably aggressive successor to Trager, Korman, and Dearie.

Confronted with this unwelcome prospect, D'Amato suddenly announced that he was nominating Reena Raggi as a federal district court judge. She was to be the first woman to sit on Jacob Mishler's fourteen-member Eastern District bench and at age thirty-five would be one of the youngest federal judges in the country. D'Amato simultaneously announced he was recommending Andrew J. Maloney as Dearie's *permanent* replacement. Within the week President Reagan nominated Maloney, and he was confirmed by the Senate.

Speaking to the press after he had been sworn in on June 26, 1986, Maloney made it clear that he was making no grand promises. "You're not going to wipe out crime, and you're not going to wipe out corruption. I'm a realist." Often referring to the Bible, he identified narcotics as his greatest concern and said he was going to focus on the top of a tall pyramid of dealers. Confirming D'Amato's judgment that it had been worth his years of persistence was Maloney's appraisal of himself. "You know, I really am a pussycat," he said, laughing. "I even cry at commercials."

D'Amato could breathe easier: The man with that awful RICO weapon in his hand was now beholden to him. Still a danger remained: The U.S. Attorney of the Southern District, with power to prosecute political corruption in Manhattan, the Bronx, and several counties north of the city, was Rudolph Giuliani. Giuliani was in the process of sending Bronx Democratic boss Stanley Friedman and a gang of assorted politicians to jail, and he did it with enthusiasm and vehemence. In addition, Giuliani had focused his attention on the Wedtech scandals in which D'Amato was deeply involved. People D'Amato knew intimately were being indicted, and stories appeared in New York papers that Giuliani was thinking of indicting him. He had to be replaced.

Giuliani's prominence—he had been on the cover of *Time* magazine—precluded solving the problem by offering him a mere judgeship. Urged on by D'Amato, the Reagan administration proposed making Giuliani FBI chief; he demurred. But Giuliani did have political ambitions: Men of influence within the Republican party were suggesting that he might make an ideal opponent of Patrick Moynihan in the 1988 senatorial election, and Giuliani didn't discourage the speculation. The idea pleased D'Amato. Moynihan, who had defeated his Republican opponent in 1982 by 1.5 million votes, was probably unbeatable, but if Giuliani wanted to resign as U.S. Attorney in order to challenge the popular senator, why, more power to him; he could expect D'Amato's outspoken support.

D'Amato was capable of extravagant displays of politically advantageous good fellowship. For example, when Burt Neuborne's daughter Lauren was lying in her hospital room recovering from surgery after the 1 percent trial in 1985, D'Amato filled her room with flowers. Yet in 1987, D'Amato did something that made Neuborne feel that he was, in reality, completely hostile to him.

Multimedia communications magnate Rupert Murdoch had hired Neuborne to initiate a case to overturn a federal law passed at the instigation of Sen. Ted Kennedy. It banned any individual from controlling more than one major media outlet in any urban area. Kennedy's law was aimed at Murdoch, who controlled a Boston paper and a television channel, both of which had been making negative editorial comments about the senator. Two days after being hired to overturn that law, Neuborne was fired.

Neuborne called Murdoch to find out why he had been fired. Murdoch said he heard that Neuborne and Murdoch's friend Al D'Amato did not get on well. That's why Murdoch fired him.

The smell of Lauren's flowers were still in Neuborne's memory. He was furious. He decided to call D'Amato and confront him. After informing D'Amato of what Murdoch had said, Neuborne told him that he didn't think D'Amato was the kind of man to carry a grudge about something Neuborne had done as part of his professional duties.

D'Amato was flustered and told Neuborne he would call Murdoch and set everything right. Demonstrating the power of a senator, Murdoch called Neuborne the next day and rehired him.

In 1988, a few months later, D'Amato felt free to ask Neuborne to file a *pro bono* suit on his behalf challenging New York State's primary law.

This sort of ritualistic support, motivated by nothing more substantial than self-interest, showered down on Giuliani in 1986. In order to encourage Giuliani's ambitions to run for the Senate against Moynihan, D'Amato proposed a publicity jaunt aimed at raising the U.S. Attorney's political profile. On July 9, 1986, the two set out on what the press kit advised was "an intelligence-gathering program." They donned disguises: Giuliani wore dark glasses and a Hell's Angel leather jacket, and D'Amato sported a United Parcel uniform, a billed cap, and sunglasses. Accompanied by thirty federal agents and police officers, they were driven to Manhattan's Washington Heights by a plainclothes female officer. The sports car blaring rock music came to a stop with its bogus hippy occupants in front of 555 West 160th Street, where three drug dealers were lounging on a stoop. The officer put a thumb to her nose and held up two fingers. The pusher recognized this signal as readily as an auctioneer at Sotheby's knew the meaning of a tug on an art lover's ear. He approached the car, took the twenty dollars offered to him first by the U.S. Attorney and then by the U.S. senator, and handed them each two vials of cocaine—or as they identified it to the cognoscenti in the press corps, "two vials of crack."

No arrests resulted from this illegal activity, since it was meant only to be "an intelligence-gathering mission," but a picture of the two intelligence gatherers appeared in newspapers across the country.

In the fall of 1987, Giuliani announced he was planning to resign either to run for the senate or to go into private practice. D'Amato was so confident Giuliani would run that he made the strategic error on October 25, 1987, of announcing that he intended to nominate his favorite U.S. Attorney, Andrew J. Maloney, as Giuliani's successor as soon as Giuliani resigned.

Maloney had been head of the Eastern District for little more than a year, but D'Amato's faith in him had been justified. A man of his cautious qualities could be of greater utility to D'Amato in the more activist Southern District, where some of D'Amato's most dependable Wall Street contributors and closest political allies were regularly being indicted by Giuliani.

Maloney declined the offer, but the fat was in the fire. Giuliani let it be known that he wanted Howard Wilson to succeed him. Wilson was chief of his criminal division during the previous two years and was in charge of the Wedtech prosecutions. D'Amato issued a list of seven contenders, including Wilson, but made it clear that only he would determine Giuliani's successor. When Giuliani held his ground, D'Amato floated a new list with thirteen names. The chief contender was revealed by D'Amato to be Charles Moerdler, whom he had encouraged to apply.

Moerdler, a former New York City buildings commissioner, had been Stanley Friedman's lawyer when Giuliani successfully prosecuted the Bronx Democratic leader in the city's Parking Violations Bureau scandal. During the trial, Moerdler ceaselessly attacked Giuliani. The mention of Moerdler's name upset Giuliani. According to D'Amato's friends, that was his intent.

Giuliani, obviously disillusioned by the rough game D'Amato was playing, fired a warning shot across the senator's bow on January 12, 1988: "It would be irresponsible to leave this office in a vacuum," he said crisply. "I have a very strong preference for filling it from within." He objected to some names on D'Amato's list because the candidates specialized in representing securities industries or white-collar criminals, principal targets of his investigations. "I've been trying to convey to the senator that I'm not being arrogant," Giuliani told the press. "I'm concerned about four or five very, very sensitive investigations."

There was in such talk an implicit threat, and D'Amato, not faced with an imminent reelection campaign, could afford to insist on a U.S. Attorney who would remove the menace. Howard Wilson was not that man; he was pressing ahead too vigorously on the Wedtech prosecutions. He would soon charge that the politicians being paid off by Wedtech treated Wedtech like "a gold mine. Some took a lot of gold, and some a little, but they all took." There was about Wilson that same unrelenting Giuliani quality. "This is a case about corruption and greed," Wilson insisted, "about the sale and purchase of public office." A man who expressed such sentiments threatened the soundness of D'Amato's sleep.

On February 8, 1988, Giuliani announced that he wouldn't oppose Moynihan but would stay on as U.S. Attorney. He had reluctantly reached this decision, he said, because Senator D'Amato had excluded him from the selection of his successor. He acknowledged to reporters that if his top aide, Howard Wilson, had been chosen, "I would probably have made a different decision."

Since D'Amato told him that wasn't to be the case, he said grimly, "it would be wrong of me to leave this office now, whatever the allure of another office or opportunity, because it would adversely affect some very sensitive matters still in progress." Then he added, "There are restrictions on the things I can say about those cases to anyone, including to the senator." In recent days, when speaking of D'Amato, that ominous note had often crept into Giuliani's remarks.

On Friday, May 6, 1988, D'Amato reluctantly gave the public a glimpse of the subterranean world in which he lived and the nature of the fear he had about Rudolph Giuliani. The Senate's most frequent witness in criminal prosecutions once again appeared in Manhattan's federal courthouse, where Cong. Mario Biaggi and his six codefendants were being prosecuted by Giuliani for turning Wedtech into a racketeering enterprise.

As in his former appearances, D'Amato was a witness for the prosecution, although evidence already presented made it appear he more appropriately fit the role of defendant. In four hours of testimony, which could only be described as a defense of Biaggi, against whom he had been called to testify, D'Amato answered mostly with long-winded civics lectures. He again used the guile he had practiced in his appearances before the 1975 grand jury, the trial of General Services Commissioner Francis O'Connor, and at the 1 percent trial. He behaved like a stump speaker, reciting his predictable speeches with broad gestures, thrusting his shoulders forward and holding out his arms to his audience. Prosecutor Ed Little quickly came to realize that D'Amato was not his ally against the accused, rather, he was Biaggi's accomplice. He repeatedly admonished D'Amato to "be concise" and "answer the question I asked."

But D'Amato, always the enemy of brevity in such trying moments, wanted the courtroom crowd to know how things were done in Washington, where annually he received thousands of requests for help from constituents. He equated all such requests as being equal: Someone who wanted a pass to the Senate gallery was listed as one of those "requesters" along with Congressman Biaggi and Commander Ehrlich who frequently called him and visited in his office to plead Wedtech's cause. He stated that his dealings with Biaggi on Wedtech matters were "always above board," and in a world known to be filled with rumormongers, there was "not a scintilla or suggestion of impropriety."

D'Amato conceded that he owed Bronx Democrat Biaggi a considerable debt of gratitude for his 1980 victory over Democrat Elizabeth Holtzman. Biaggi had refused to endorse his fellow Democrat and then revealed the intensity of his affection for her Republican opponent by organizing "Democrats for D'Amato." D'Amato felt Biaggi's aggressive support was "instrumental" in providing the votes needed for his narrow victory.

As to what he had done to earn the $30,000-plus illegal contributions from Wedtech, D'Amato was spared from answering that question. Judge Constance Baker Motley, illustrating the maxim that the restraints of the legal code effectively block from any trial much of its crucial information, ruled that the matter of Al D'Amato's illegal acceptance of Wedtech money was "irrelevant."

D'Amato lent credence to that other maxim of the legal system—that a man who commits one crime is likely to commit others—when he testified about his involvement with Coastal Drydock Co., a Brooklyn defense contractor. Biaggi had been previously sentenced to thirty months in prison for accepting bribes to help Coastal. From his perch in the witness box, D'Amato recalled that Biaggi had turned to him when he needed to show Coastal he could deliver value for his gratuity. With his usual concern for performing constituent services, D'Amato boasted that he had been glad to help Biaggi deliver on his Coastal commitment.

Assistant U.S. Attorney Little led the senator through a list of things he had done for Wedtech: arranging a conference in the White House through Ed Meese's office; helping to clear the way for a bank loan; obtaining a gasoline-engine contract; pressuring the Small Business Administration. Would he, Prosecutor Little asked, have devoted so much time to Wedtech's interests if he knew that Biaggi's son, Richard, and Biaggi's former law partner, Bernard Ehrlich, had been given 5 percent of Wedtech's stock? D'Amato wrinkled his forehead and with a show of thoughtfulness answered, "I don't know. I think it would have given me some pause to reflect. I just don't know."

On August 4, 1988, Biaggi and five of his codefendants were convicted of demanding million in bribes for helping Wedtech win military contracts. Biaggi resigned from Congress and was soon behind bars in a Texas prison, where he spent two years. His unindicted coconspirator, Al D'Amato, remained in the Senate.

The cry arose from state Republican party officials that D'Amato's intransigence on Giuliani's successor had guaranteed Moynihan's reelection. In November 1988, New York Republicans' worst fears were realized: Moynihan defeated the nonentity D'Amato preferred to Giuliani by the largest margin ever recorded in a Senate race.

When party leaders pointed their accusing fingers at D'Amato, he commented that those who blamed him were mistaken. "No one should say I stopped Mr. Giuliani's candidacy. I don't accept that. It's nonsense. Do you know a bigger booster of him than me?"

On January 10, 1989, Rudolph Giuliani announced that he planned to resign as U.S. Attorney and appoint Benito Romano as his interim successor. He pointed out that Congress would take months to make a permanent appointment and that Romano, who had served for seven years as chief of the corruption unit, would be a perfect replacement until then. D'Amato would have none of it. He again tried to get his favorite U.S. Attorney, Andrew J. Maloney, to transfer to the Manhattan office—with no success. On January 20 he announced that he was nominating Otto Obermaier to succeed Giuliani. Obermaier had been in private practice since 1970 and was one of the top defense counsels for white-collar criminals. In that capacity he spent a generation defending precisely the people Giuliani had been prosecuting. He was a specialist in winning acquittals for those accused of Wall Street insider trading, tax evasion, and government regulatory offenses.

Giuliani objected to Obermaier's nomination because so many of his clients had been his targets. He told D'Amato that Obermaier would be hamstrung if confirmed because of numerous conflicts of interest. D'Amato claimed not to see the problem.

Now that the Southern District's U.S. Attorney's office was in safe hands, D'Amato busily set about raising money for his reelection. By the beginning of 1988, his campaign treasurer, Arthur W. Jaspan, was able to announce that the senator's two finance committees—"D'Amato in '92" and "Friends of Senator D'Amato '92"—had accumulated $1,066,000. When put on his scale of practical politics, that good news clearly outweighed Rudy Giuliani's low opinion of him.

THIRTY-NINE

BLOWING UP
HIS MISTAKE

P oliticians accused of crimes always issue denials, which they repeat shamelessly despite damning evidence. They are occasionally reelected to offices they have despoiled after being convicted and sentenced. The votes for these future convicts come from their coconspirators, the gullible, and those who forgive, perhaps, in the hope of being forgiven. But it took Al D'Amato and the wire-pullers of the Nassau Republican party to invent a new way to wipe out the memory of their criminality: They blew it up.

By 1987 the Hempstead Resources Recovery Plant had stood deserted at the side of Meadowbrook Parkway for seven years after its last feeble attempt to burn garbage; its twin smokestacks served only to part the ocean breeze. "D'Amato's Folly" stoically displayed itself as a rusting reminder of a politician's pursuit of self-interest. Why not blow up the abomination and replace it with someone else's folly.

The time for such a good idea had come years earlier but had to wait until the conclusion of D'Amato's reelection campaign. It was easy to imagine what Mark Green would have done with enlarged pictures of an exploding D'Amato's Folly as a backdrop for his attacks.

While town supervisor, D'Amato had repeatedly pledged that Hempstead's residents would not pay "one penny" for the original plant, but a major provision of the contract for the new plant, whose construction was in the final planning stage, included a $35 million payment to the owners of the old plant—more than the old plant was initially supposed to cost. The cost of that indemnity to Parsons & Whittemore (P & W) was to be passed on to town residents, and when added to the higher price of the new plant, it would cause taxes for garbage removal in the next decade to exceed the current rate by 400 percent. D'Amato was intent on hiding these potentially demoralizing facts for as long as possible.

Therefore, it wasn't until 7:00 A.M. on Sunday, March 29, 1987, two months after the victorious senator had begun his second term, that seventy-two pounds of dynamite were strategically placed around the base of the smokestacks, in the bowels of the furnaces, under concrete foundations, and in all other man-made structures molded by political avarice. As dawn broke, a crowd of hundreds assembled at the side of Meadowbrook Parkway to watch a seven-second chain of explosions which removed that $140 million monstrosity from the Westbury plains. A cheer rose, cameras clicked, and videos whirred as the evidence of D'Amato's duplicity was buried beneath a heap of foul-smelling rubble.

The latest Republican Hempstead presiding supervisor, Joseph Mondello, then announced that within two years a new incinerator would rise from the same spot, this time, barring overruns, costing only $350 million.

The construction of the new incinerator would terminate the contract negotiated by Armand Paul D'Amato on behalf of Browning-Ferris Industries (BFI) to haul seven hundred tons of Hempstead garbage each day to a landfill 100 miles away in Goshen, New York. In 1984, Armand Paul and Thomas Gulotta, then presiding supervisor, had agreed on a five-year contract, which took $67 million out of taxpayers' pockets. BFI's bid had been the highest, but the D'Amato skill at negotiation convinced Tom Gulotta that town residents would accumulate incalculable advantages by paying more, rather than less, for another service provided by the D'Amato brothers.

According to *Newsday* reporter Mark McIntyre, Hempstead "did not check [Browning-Ferris's] legal history. As a result, the town was not made aware of the raft of civil and criminal actions against the firm around the country, actions involving allegations of bid-rigging, price-fixing, bribing of public officials and improper disposal of toxic waste."

There was no need to check too carefully, since no one in Nassau County was politically better connected than BFI's new attorney. After an interview with Armand, *Newsday* described the Mineola attorney as saying "he felt his brother's political status helped him get hired by Browning-Ferris."

The hauling of raw garbage would stop in 1989 when the new plant was completed. However, the senator's brother was also the attorney who had negotiated the contract to build the new $350 million plant, and his successful clients were BFI and American Ref-Fuel, their subsidiary.

Over a period of twenty years Armand Paul's clients stood to make almost $1 billion in profits from fees paid by Hempstead's citizens. In return, American Ref-Fuel would burn the town's garbage in the new plant and haul away its irreducible ash. In order to become eligible for that profit, American Ref-Fuel had to put up only $45.5 million, while nearly $300 million was raised by selling tax-exempt development bonds. The bonds, burdened with hidden interest costs, were to be paid off by Hempstead's residents, who, unlike the rich bondholders, weren't going to be allowed to arrange any tax-exempt status for themselves. To this deal American Ref-Fuel, unlike its competitive bidder, Signal Environmental Systems, brought no expertise.

The New York State Assembly Environmental Conservation Committee 1986 report, entitled "Organized Crime's Involvement in the Waste Hauling Industry," observed: "This is the first such effort American Ref-Fuel has undertaken."

The assembly report was no more impressed with Browning-BFI. "BFI has not had a good record, having used many of the same tactics associated with the organized-crime carters discussed in this report."

After exposing Armard's intimate connections to the unsavory characters in the garbage industry, the report added:

> Long Island's problem has been made even worse by the
> fact that its solid waste hauling industry has long been

dominated by what appears to be a tripartite working arrangement between organized crime, waste trade associations operating as fronts for organized crime and corrupt local officials.

This wasn't the first reference to Armand's dealings with someone connected to organized crime. In 1984 he had represented Philip Basile, friend of the Luccheses and the D'Amatos, in an attempt to regain the convicted Island Park nightclub owner's liquor license. Armand had raised the issue with Judge Robert Roberto, Bill Cahn's former dedicated massage-parlor sleuth, who had somehow made his way to a seat on the state supreme court. Justice Roberto saw nothing in Basile's history—certainly not the large number of drug arrests in his disco or his criminal attempt to get murderer Henry Hill out of prison—that would keep the judge from granting the request of his old friend's brother. Alfonse returned the favor in October 1987 when he nominated Roberto as a federal district court judge, a nomination uncharacteristically rejected by the Senate.

Armand Paul was offended by the criticism of the assembly's Environmental Committee. They had blasted two of his garbage-industry clients and tied him to unsavory characters in the garbage industry. Giving boredom and listlessness as his reasons, the Mineola legislator soon announced that he would not run for reelection to the assembly. Instead, he would devote his talents to negotiating contracts for his vast pool of clients who were interested in employing the brother of a U.S. senator.

Alfonse could only watch this scene with detachment. The state assembly had put a blot on his brother's reputation, but since it had no impact on his brother's ability to raise his fees, there was no real family loss. On the other hand, he had finally managed to blow up D'Amato's Folly, and that allowed him to remove an irritating mote from his eye. Given a little time, no one would remember his $140 million garbage boondoggle.

FORTY

THE FAST TRACK

A rmand Paul's clients' determination to profit by paying the
D'Amatos to exercise their political muscles became appar-
ent as the odor began to rise from the stables of Roosevelt
Raceway in the center of Nassau County.

The harness track had been the focal point of scandal since its
1940 opening. Politicians had been paid off to allow rezoning,
which was the only way the track could be built; there had also
been bribes to obtain reductions in county taxes and a multitude of
other favors.

As time passed, ownership of the huge track changed hands. In
1983, its relatively recent owner, Gulf & Western Corporation,
sought to sell its gambling subsidiary because it was no longer
meeting its required profit margins. A four-member consortium
interested in buying the track suddenly materialized. Charles Evans,
an investment adviser who specialized in raising tax-exempt
financing for housing and who had strong political connections,
was the chief architect of the developing scam.

William B. Hopkins, Gulf & Western's president of Roosevelt
Raceway, became a second pivotal member. Hopkins was in a
compromised position. He was, in effect, both the seller and the
buyer, which made him a potential conflict-of-interest time bomb.

In Hopkins's role as Gulf & Western executive, he had valued the track, in its annual report dated December 25, 1983, at $22.5 million. Yet the next month, in his role as a potential purchaser, he was offering to pay Gulf & Western over $51.5 million. There was a hint in these skewed figures of the consortium's real plan for the track that was nowhere mentioned in the original prospectus.

Gulf & Western's $22.5 million value estimate was for Roosevelt Raceway run as a track. But in an independent appraisal by accountant James G. Peel issued on January 20, 1984, a month before the consortium applied for financing on February 23, Peel had appraised the 172 acres *as an empty developable property with the track gone* at $56 million. Gulf & Western knew that the real value could only be realized in a land-speculation deal. If their employee Hopkins had tried to grab Roosevelt at a bargain-basement price based on the false assumption that the 172 acres would always be used as a harness track, he would have been shown the door.

However, the consortium had a more immediate problem: They did not have $51.5 million. The third member of the group was Barry Goldstein, strong in political connections but without deep pockets. The least important member of the consortium was David Stevenson, a former jockey whose sole function was to convince the State Racing and Wagering Board, the agency that licenses and regulates horse racing, that the consortium had a member with the practical knowledge of how to run a track. Soon after the sale was safely consummated, Stevenson was forced out, as much a pauper as he had been when the deal was hatched.

Each consortium member only supplied an average of $1,000 of his own money, not even a down payment on the deposit. But, more than money, the consortium had an innovative financing scheme. Charlie Evans's knowledge of how to get *tax-exempt* financing for private-profit projects was the scam's linchpin.

The town of Hempstead had created an Industrial Development Agency (IDA) that had the power to authorize the sale of bonds for "public benefit" purposes that would pay the bond purchasers tax-exempt interest: If the consortium could get IDA authorization, bonds could be issued at a lower rate of interest than ordinary private-sector bonds, thereby lowering the amount of money the track owners would have to repay bondholders. Without the tax exemption not only would the consortium's costs be much higher, it would have been difficult to sell such speculative bonds.

The consortium's clever innovation clearly benefited those well-heeled folks who could afford to buy the bonds; however, it victimized ordinary taxpayers. If the bonds were a private issue, they wouldn't be exempted from federal, state, and city taxes. The higher rate of interest the consortium would have had to pay bondholders in order to finance their scheme would then have been taxed by all three levels of government, and the public would not have been cheated out of that source of revenue. To compound the unfairness of the scheme, these were lost revenues that Hempstead had to make up by raising taxes on lower-income taxpayers.

The consortium's innovation depended on the willingness of Hempstead's political leaders to ignore the financial interests of almost all of its citizens. The Hempstead leaders also had to accept the lie that the sale of these bonds for a "public benefit" project would incomprehensibly benefit a wider public than the gambling fraternity.

The easiest part of the scheme was to win over the politicians. Although another bidder, Lawrence Kadish, was offering to put up private money and had proffered a serious first bid, his attempt to negotiate was quickly spurned by William Hopkins's Gulf & Western bosses. The Hempstead IDA then agreed to underwrite the bond issue that would give the track to Hopkins and his three partners virtually cost-free.

In turn, the Hempstead development agency's approval was important only if the federal government was willing to go along with the triple-tax exemption for the bonds that Hempstead would issue to finance the consortium's purchase of the track.

But that was going to be impossible. In 1984, just as the deal was about to go through, Congress was working on an amendment to the Industrial Development Agency Act prohibiting the use of local IDA bonds for projects proposed by land speculators. The amendment banned the issuance of tax-free bonds for any project for which the land cost more than 25 percent of the total price. Since without the track the land value of the 172 acres was really close to 100 percent, it was essential for the consortium to maintain the fiction that they were merely fanciers of the breed.

In addition, a more obvious threat to the scheme was another amendment that prohibited the issuing of IDA bonds for the construction of any "gambling facility," and no one had suggested that Roosevelt Raceway existed for any other purpose.

Enter Al D'Amato. With a display of energy, the senator started lobbying to add a "transitional rule" to the legislation. That tricky rule exempted from the proposed IDA ban any gambling facility not costing more than $57 million that had made substantial headway toward financing its plans before April 1, 1984. It was a time/money slot into which only the consortium scheme fit perfectly.

After strenuous logrolling and special-interest pleading, D'Amato succeeded in grandfathering the consortium's deal into the law that passed Congress. With D'Amato's blessing the IDA then issued $54 million in bonds for the consortium's purchase of the track. This was $2.5 million more than the purchase price, starting the consortium's enterprise off in the black before the ink was dried on the contract. It gave them the money to pay the Wall Street underwriters who actually sold the bonds.

The audacity of the operation was mind-boggling: On June 29, 1984, the consortium turned over $51.5 million of money not their own to Gulf & Western, which they were obligated to pay back to bondholders only with money they made from the track that they had been given as a political favor.

County politicians further indicated their concern for the prosperity of the track's consortium members by granting them a $1 million reduction in the following year's real estate taxes.

D'Amato's stated rationale for this sweetheart deal was that the new Roosevelt Raceway Associates had given a contractual guarantee to the Hempstead IDA that it would maintain the facility as a harness track "at all times" for at least twenty-five years. This would save the jobs of one thousand workers, D'Amato explained to critics. It would also ensure the collection of $2 million a year in taxes from the track. At the same time, D'Amato had ignored the fact that Hempstead's politicos had agreed to refund $1 million of those $2 million in taxes to the consortium, a practice likely to continue each year if the right wheels were greased. But even more absurd was D'Amato's implication that this valuable property would not have raised far more taxes and hired far more workers if its sprawling track had been allowed to disappear and the 172 acres devoted to other, more intensive commercial uses.

Within the year, Thomas Gulotta, D'Amato's successor as presiding supervisor of Hempstead, began receiving campaign contributions from the Roosevelt Raceway consortium amounting to $12,500. Consortium members, under their own names, also contributed a recorded $6,800 to Senator D'Amato's 1986 campaign.

The consortium's actions raised questions about other possible payoffs. In a November 1990 interview on Jack Anderson's weekly FNN show *The Insiders*, Charlie Evans was queried about the sudden increase in the amount of insurance that the consortium took out on their new property. Gulf & Western had only carried $60 million in insurance, but Charlie and his confederates, despite being short on cash, had immediately increased it to $130 million. This cost the consortium an additional several hundred thousand dollars a year despite the fact that when filing for property tax reductions they claimed the track's buildings were antiquated and badly deteriorating.

Memories of Joe Margiotta's insurance commission splitting immediately arose. Sydney Schanberg, *Newsday* columnist, commented on November 16, 1990:

> It has long been a practice in Long Island political circles to use insurance policies, especially inflated insurance policies, as vehicles for making payoffs to people who have helped grease the way to a lucrative deal.

Capping off its show of appreciation to the D'Amatos, in August 1987, shortly after Armand Paul handed the assembly's clerk his resignation, the consortium hired his law firm to represent its legal interests.

Columnist Schanberg, working to earn his second Pulitzer Prize, devoted most of his twice-weekly pieces after June 1990 to exposing the corruption of what he dubbed "the Gang of Four." He explained the consortium's hiring of Armand Paul thusly: "It regularly happens that when Alfonse sells his office to a favor-seeker and performs what is known in Latin as a *quo*, Armand turns up to collect what is known as the *quid*."

The consortium's hiring of Armand Paul had a more utilitarian purpose than merely to pay off two of its benefactors. Armand's clout in Nassau had become vital in the consortium's scheme to close down the track and sell it for development.

Although it wasn't apparent when Armand Paul went on the consortium's payroll, the purchase of the track had always been a venture in land speculation. It had never been the intention of the consortium to run the track for twenty-five years, as Al D'Amato had claimed, for the betting crowd. They had signaled their plans from the start when they got the Hempstead IDA to grant them the right to pay off the bondholders before the twenty-five-year life of the bond expired *without penalty payments*; an unheard-of concession that made the Hempstead politicians look as if they were holding a fire sale. The consortium had always schemed to sell the 172 acres at $1 million an acre for a profit of at least $100 million; a good return on no investment.

In an effort to justify, at some future time, the closing of the track, word began to surface soon after the consortium took over that the track was losing money. It was true that a sense of poverty had begun to settle over the once-sparkling facility. The consortium allowed medical waste to be trucked in and deposited on the infield. The rat population multiplied and could be seen scampering through the stands. The number of bathrooms for patrons was reduced. Maintenance employees were let go. Crucial repairs were ignored, while the reduced maintenance crew was assigned to do renovations on partner Barry Goldstein's Hewlett Harbor home.

Nevertheless, audits have revealed that track receipts enabled the new owners to meet their payments to bondholders, indeed, retire a substantial amount of the $51.5 million bond issue, thereby increasing their equity in a venture in which they originally had no equity.

Less than a year after its July 1984 purchase of Roosevelt Raceway, the consortium put out discreet feelers to potential commercial developers. In June 26, 1985, Charlie Evans and his attorney, Al Walsh, met with brokers at Manhattan's Eastdil Realty to work out a marketing plan, and Eastdil signed a contract with the consortium to sell the 172 acres. This was only eleven months after they had bought it and promised to keep it open as a track for at least twenty-five years, raising the question of whether the original purchase had involved a criminal fraud—in law, "a false-promise conspiracy."

By 1986, Canon USA has publicly stated that it had begun preliminary talks about the purchase of fifty or sixty acres of the track for the building of its North American headquarters. Despite the consortium's contract with Hempstead's development agency to keep the track open "at all times," its closing was the first condition of these negotiation. Canon, in fact, was planning to construct its headquarters building exactly where the grandstands stood.

The sale finally depended on Armand's ability to convince his political friends in Hempstead not to block it because the consortium was violating its contract to keep the track open. Equally important, he had to get town leaders to grant approval for the consortium's rezoning plans.

Armand began to firm up the deal with Canon, and by March 1988 the first draft was written. Canon was offering to buy fifty acres of the track at $1 million per acre. Though Armand was occupied with Canon's secret negotiations, he found time to file an application for the track's annual county tax reduction. Schanberg commented:

> They [Armand Paul's firm] left blank the section [of the tax reduction application] requiring them to state whether the property had recently been offered for sale and at what price. Does this not constitute a false document—in other words, a fraud?

Schanberg's question echoed in District Attorney Denis Dillon's office but received no reply.

Suddenly on July 15, 1988, without any notice to its one thousand employees or the Hempstead IDA, the track owners closed it down without any announcement of what plans they had for their property. Oblivious to the uproar that this violation of the 1984 IDA contract caused, Armand Paul continued to submit new drafts of the purchase agreement to Canon USA. On September 2, 1988, in the privacy of Armand Paul's office, both parties signed a "conditional agreement" for the sale. The Hempstead government's rezoning permission was the potential "conditional" fly in the ointment. Flyswatter Armand Paul was on alert against that possibility.

The Standardbred Owners Association, a group representing twenty-five hundred owners, trainers, and drivers of harness-race horses, charged that Armand's hiring represented a violation of the conflict-of-interest law. Since the alleged conflict arose because of Alfonse's role in jump-starting the conspiracy, the senator could not ignore the charge. On May 2, 1989, the indignant D'Amato characterized the association's charges as "absolutely ridiculous, unfair, and unjustified."

The Standardbred Owners Association claimed that the consortium had never intended to run Roosevelt Raceway as a harness track. Its president, Joseph Faraldo, stated that "from being one of the best racetracks in the country, in a matter of a couple of years it became a hellhole." It was the consortium's intention from the beginning, Faraldo alleged, to run the track into the ground, then shut it and sell it.

The next day, May 3, 1989, the *New York Times* printed an in-depth story on its front page about the closing of Roosevelt Raceway in which the major elements of the consortium's conspiracy were cogently outlined. The *Times* documented that the key to this successful manipulation was Al D'Amato.

The Standardbred Owners Association and track union officials demanded that prosecutors look into the latest D'Amato family scandal. But it seemed unlikely that the D'Amatos were overly concerned with this newest allegation against their probity. Nassau County's Denis Dillon, now a member of the Republican party, was in charge of the local investigation. The federal investigation was being handled by D'Amato's handpicked U.S. Attorney, Andrew Maloney, who informed the press that he had opened a "preliminary inquiry" but "refused to give further details."

In early 1994 the track remained closed but undemolished.

FORTY-ONE
TURNING A FRIEND
INTO AN ENEMY

It is possible to trace D'Amato's hard times to the incredibly clumsy manner in which he dealt with fellow Republican Rudolph Giuliani.

Soon after D'Amato entered the Senate he formed a working relationship with the unknown Giuliani, then an associate attorney general working in the Justice Department. This attempt to make contacts in government was typical of the way D'Amato operated. His clubhouse training in Island Park led him to place his staff members and personal friends in agencies all over the capital and in pivotal federal positions in New York. Giuliani was his friend in the sensitive Justice Department.

When the time came in 1983 to select a U.S. Attorney for the Southern District of New York, which included jurisdiction over Manhattan and seven adjacent northern counties, D'Amato picked his Justice Department friend. That decision was endorsed by D'Amato's judicial advisory group, which included Thomas Bolan, Roy Cohn's law partner, and Michael Armstrong, one of New York's leading attorneys for politicians accused of corruption. Giuliani had a strange group of patrons. It apparently never occurred to D'Amato that a clique so dedicated to selecting a U.S. Attorney who was willing to avert his eyes would endorse someone who would become the scourge of Wall Street high rollers and shady politicians. Giuliani appeared to be so unthreatening that Roy Cohn, the protector of the underworld, did not exercise his veto.

The senator and the new U.S. Attorney maintained a bond, motivated largely by self-interest, for several years. D'Amato was legally separated from Penny, although still using the basement bedroom in their Island Park home and infrequently appearing in public with her at ceremonial occasions, such as the fiftieth wedding anniversary of Mike and Sue Masone. But 90 percent of his time was spent in Washington, where he had a condo apartment, shared for a while with Staten Island congressman Guy Molinari. He used the condo as a base from which he wilded his way through the gamy preserves of de facto bachelorhood.

Giuliani was single. The two socialized occasionally. D'Amato, in keeping with his telephone mania, was constantly in touch with his protégé, and two of Giuliani's aides were occasionally assigned to work closely with the senator. In 1984, D'Amato became an honored guest at Giuliani's wedding to television newswoman Donna Hanover.

Giuliani's early stewardship of the Southern District was aimed at empire building. He wanted the Department of Justice to put the *independent* Organized Crime Strike Force in New York directly under his control. All of the thirteen U.S. Attorneys around the nation that had strike forces felt the same way, but Giuliani, with the help of his Washington friend, was the first of them to succeed. As morale declined among the longtime professional strike force prosecutors—now transferred to Giuliani's new Organized Crime Section—and they began to resign, D'Amato seemed delighted with the way his friend Giuliani performed.

Initially, D'Amato was much more concerned with gaining control over the Eastern District U.S. Attorney's office, which had for years threatened to indict him for a series of crimes in Nassau County. With Andrew Maloney safely in place in Brooklyn and the threat to D'Amato relieved on that front, the senator turned his attention to the rising specter in Manhattan. Giuliani had metamorphosed into a media star. Their relationship cooled as D'Amato began viewing the popular Giuliani as his only rival for leadership of the state's Republican party.

Yet, even as recently as 1985, D'Amato was making an attempt to act as though nothing had changed. They traveled together to Italy on a mission that was advertised as a sortie in the war on drugs. But as Yogi Berra might say, that was old history.

Fighting U.S. Attorney Rudy Giuliani had turned into a folk hero, the strongest potential Republican candidate in the state. Newspapers in New York City, where the Republican party was weakest, spoke of him as being "incorruptible," "indefatigable," "squeaky clean," and predicted that if he ran for public office he would be hard to beat.

D'Amato's attempt to capture control of the Southern District had first led him in 1988 to tempt Giuliani into a reckless bid to unseat Pat Moynihan. But when that slick invitation to disaster was turned aside, D'Amato's irritation with his protégé began to surface. His peevishness grew when Giuliani stayed in his office one year longer than he had intended, explaining that he did it only because D'Amato's choice of his successor endangered the conduct of several key cases.

Giuliani attempted to be discreet; he didn't mention the cases, but merely expressed concern that his successor carry on these prosecutions with the vigor that had characterized his efforts. At that point the thin-skinned senator turned on Giuliani with unrestrained, predictable fury.

By the end of 1988, Giuliani expressed an interest in becoming mayor of New York City. When reporters asked D'Amato what he thought of such a prospect, the senator replied that Giuliani would make "an excellent candidate."

Rudy's prospects seemed glowing. He was immensely popular. Polls showed that in excess of 70 percent of the city's voters thought he would be an outstanding mayor. Moreover, Ed Koch, who was finishing his twelfth year as mayor, had worn out his welcome. The media had been playing up scandals involving some of Koch's closest associates, a few of whom had been sentenced to jail, most often because of Giuliani's prosecutions. Though Koch's personal honesty was never challenged, editorial writers conveyed the impression that he was no longer an effective leader.

Koch encouraged the public image of himself as a loudmouth comedian, but for years most voters also thought he was a competent man, devoted to improving the city. He was widely viewed as

Senator D'Amato is questioned by reporters outside New York's federal courthouse on May 6, 1988, after appearing as a witness at the racketeering trial of his Democratic ally Rep. Mario Biaggi. D'Amato testified he would have interceded with the Pentagon on behalf of the scandal-plagued Wedtech Corporation even if he had never met Biaggi. (AP PHOTOGRAPH BY MARIO CABRERA)

Deborah Gore Dean, assistant to HUD secretary Samuel Pierce, testifies on June 13, 1989, before the House Government Operations Subcommittee. Dean, an ally of Sen. D'Amato's, was later convicted of felonies involving her HUD activities. (PHOTOGRAPH COURTESY OF THE ASSOCIATED PRESS)

Joseph Monticciolo, New York regional director of HUD, testified before the same House subcommittee on July 28, 1989, about his favors for his patron Senator D'Amato, with whom he maintained a direct telephone line.
(AP PHOTOGRAPH BY JOHN DURICKS)

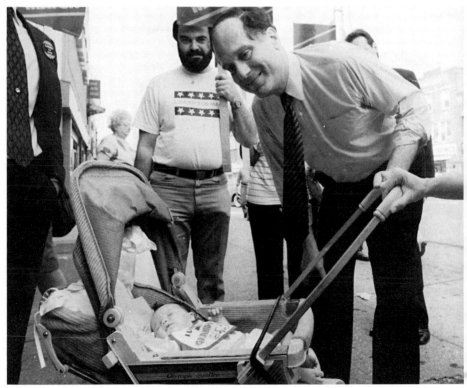

Ronald Lauder, Senator D'Amato's personal candidate to oppose Rudy Giuliani in the Republican primary for mayor of New York, looks at a sleeping baby in Bay Ridge, Brooklyn, on September 11, 1989. (AP PHOTOGRAPH BY MARIO CABRERA)

Senator D'Amato shows his passport to photographers after being turned back at the Lithuanian border by a Soviet guard on April 6, 1990. He was accompanied by the Lithuanian foreign minister, Algrinas Saudragis (*left*), who holds a visa for the senator. Jonas Bobelis (*right*) is from the Washington-based Committee for Liberation of Lithuania. (PHOTOGRAPH COURTESY OF THE ASSOCIATED PRESS)

Island Park housewife Annette Snow sparked the grand jury's investigation into Senator D'Amato's manipulation of the distribution of HUD houses to benefit his relatives and political supporters. (PHOTOGRAPH BY THE AUTHOR)

Roberta Scully, wife of Island Park village clerk Harry Scully, talked to the U.S. Attorney about Al D'Amato's illegal use of HUD funds. Mrs. Scully spoke in support of D'Amato's Integrity party opponents at the monthly meeting of the village board on August 16, 1990. (PHOTOGRAPH BY THE AUTHOR)

George Ficke, leader of Island Park's Integrity party in 1990, challenged Senator D'Amato's Unity party for control of village government. (PHOTOGRAPH BY THE AUTHOR)

Mike Masone, Al D'Amato's closest ally in Island Park. In 1990 he was playing poker with Senator D'Amato in the Volunteer Fire Department behind his house while trying to work out a strategy to defuse the government's civil rights suit growing out of the HUD scandals. (PHOTOGRAPH BY THE AUTHOR)

nate Ethics Committee chairman Terry Sanford (D-N.C.; *left*) joins with Sen. Warren
idman (R-N.H.) at a news conference on August 2, 1991. They reported that numerous
itnesses they wanted to hear in their investigation of ethics violations against Senator
Amato had invoked Fifth Amendment rights against self-incrimination and refused to tes-
y. That lack of cooperation thwarted the committee from getting at the truth on most
ounts. Nevertheless, the six Ethics Committee members unanimously found that D'Amato
ted "in an improper and inappropriate manner" by allowing his brother to use his office
r influence peddling on behalf of Unisys. (PHOTOGRAPH COURTESY OF THE ASSOCIATED PRESS)

enator D'Amato grasps the outstretched hand of President George Bush at a fund-raising
uncheon in New York on November 12, 1991. They were both about to begin their 1992
eelection campaigns. At this point, but not for much longer, Al D'Amato was still actively
upporting President Bush. (AP PHOTOGRAPH BY MARCY NIGHSWANDER)

Alfonse D'Amato and his Democratic opponent, Robert Abrams, engage in a radio debate on October 15, 1992. They spent most of the hour on the *Imus in the Morning* program, interrupting each other with accusations of improprieties and mudslinging. (AP PHOTOGRAPH BY MICHAEL ALBANS)

Norman Rosenbaum addresses a Brooklyn rally of four thousand Lubavitcher Jews protesting the murder of his brother Yankel and the acquittal of Lemrick Nelson. Nelson had confessed he was the killer after being caught at the murder site with a blood-smeared knife in his pocket. Standing to the left of the senator is former Democratic New York mayor Ed Koch and future Republican New York mayor Rudy Giuliani. The protest, two days before the polling on Senator D'Amato's bid for reelection, became an impromptu rally for D'Amato. (AP PHOTOGRAPH BY DAVID KARP)

nator D'Amato holds up the *Island Park Tribune* at a celebration of his come-from-
hind victory over Bob Abrams on November 4, 1992, the morning after the election.
nding next to him was Michael Long, chairman of New York's Conservative party.
? PHOTOGRAPH BY LUIS RIBEIRO)

nator D'Amato exhibits a photograph on March 28, 1993, at a news conference in front
New York's World Trade Center, where a month earlier terrorists had exploded a bomb
t killed six and injured over one thousand. D'Amato alleged that the photo shows
aham Elgabrowy months earlier at a street demonstration carrying an anti-D'Amato sign.
usin of Sayyid Nosair, accused slayer of Rabbi Meir Kahane, Elgabrowy was later tried
his role in the World Trade Center bombing. (AP PHOTOGRAPH BY FELICE QUINTO)

Antoinette D'Amato looks lovingly at her younger son, Armand Paul, after emerging from the Uniondale courthouse at the end of the fifth day of his trial on Monday, April 26, 199. His father, Armand Sr., follows to the rear. (PHOTOGRAPH BY THE AUTHOR)

A grim Armand Paul D'Amato heads for his car in front of the Uniondale court after being convicted on seven counts of mail fraud on May 7, 1993. The conviction resulted from influence peddling by Armand Paul through the use of his brother Alfonse's senatorial office to help Armand's client Unisys. (PHOTOGRAPH BY THE AUTHOR)

Senior U.S. District Court judge Jacob Mishler, at age eighty-one, in May 1993, presiding in the Uniondale courthouse at the mail-fraud trial of Senator D'Amato's brother, Armand Paul D'Amato. This was eight years after the judge had conducted the 1 percent trial involving Senator D'Amato in the same building. (PHOTOGRAPH BY THE AUTHOR)

a La Guardia-type politician, his outrageous style cloaking a matrix of civic virtue. By 1989 that consensus had vanished.

Giuliani's ambitions were also encouraged because no other Democrat, in this Democratic town, had stepped into the breach created by the beleaguered mayor. It appeared that all the Republicans had to do was nominate Rudy and then step aside and watch their knight joust some weak Democratic opponent onto the political junk heap. Giuliani delighted the state and city Republican hierarchy when he announced in March 1989 that he would run for that job-rich office. Clubhouse leaders from faintly breathing political organisms in Astoria and Riverdale began to dream about which commissioner's office they might fill.

Into this fantasy world of Republican opportunity stepped Al D'Amato, intent on leaving his fist's imprint on the Republican primary. The role played by D'Amato in that campaign reduces to inanity all of the claims made that he is a consummate politician; it vindicates those critics who see him mainly as a lucky bully who intimidated his way to power. Everything D'Amato did in that riveting campaign was predictably against his best interests and possibly catastrophic to his career.

To most observers, there seemed to be no reason to hold a Republican primary; Rudy Giuliani was the anointed candidate. He was conservative, although capable of maintaining the support of the liberals by calling for more state funds for education and AIDS treatment and favoring campaigns to rid the city of its malignant twins, drugs and crime. Not much there to outrage conservative Republicans. At the beginning of the campaign he even favored a modified pro-life position against abortion aimed at keeping the right-wing Conservative party at bay.

The leaders of the Liberal party, the infirm survivor of New York's 1930s radical wars, were expressing an interest in endorsing Giuliani and thereby recreating the fusion movement that elected Republicans Fiorello La Guardia in 1933 and John V. Lindsay in 1968. There would also be "Democrats for Giuliani," prepared to place an independent line on the November ballot. That would enable those Democrats disenchanted with Koch, who were convinced their hand would fall from their arm if they ever pulled a polling lever for a Republican, to find a nondisfiguring method of voting for Giuliani.

Into this euphoric Republican scene, even as the clubhouse bosses were counting the soon-to-be-delivered golden eggs, stepped a naysaying D'Amato. He thought that he could discern a much better candidate; it was someone named Ronald Lauder.

Nothing in Lauder's background suggested a reason why D'Amato was thrusting this nonentity into the Republican race. Lauder was the scion of the Estee Lauder cosmetic fortune, viewed widely as an only somewhat coherent ninny. In return for his generous contributions to Reagan's presidential campaigns, the Republican president had appointed him ambassador to Austria. As in the case of many such political appointees, Lauder had been protected against the consequences of his own bad judgment by the independent actions of his staff; in short, the civil service ran the Austrian shop as though the ambassador were on vacation. Why, then, was D'Amato so enthusiastic about Ronald Lauder?

Lauder had one irresistible attraction for the Senate's champion fundraiser: He had a passion for spending his mother's millions on any transitory pleasure. The pleasure of the moment was to see himself on the front pages and on television and to be everyone's topic of conversation. He had been idle since leaving his Austrian post, and suddenly here was the energetic junior senator from New York urging him to take center stage. Within the wink of an eye, D'Amato had obtained the Conservative party nomination for Lauder, and he was transformed into a "serious" candidate for the Republican nomination.

In January D'Amato offered an explanation of why he was sponsoring a neophyte against the party's strongest candidate. On John McLaughlin's TV show he charged that Giuliani was a "publicity hound" who had abused his role as a prosecutor. Showing his usual sensitivity for accused perpetrators, D'Amato said, "It becomes a question of a person who will go to any length to aggrandize himself, regardless of the guilt or innocence of a person. I'm for people's rights. And I don't think you take people and smear them the way Rudy Giuliani has without conscience." Recommending Giuliani as U.S. Attorney had been "the worst mistake I ever made."

For three months Lauder's incessant TV commercials hammered away at Giuliani, picturing him as unscrupulous and a threat to the republic. Giuliani's ratings in the polls declined with each day-and-night assault. He was no knight in shining armor, Lauder's public relations claque charged: he was really a Nazi.

On May 25, 1989, Giuliani tried to answer questions about D'Amato's reasons for spurring Lauder on. In the process, Giuliani shed new light on why he had refused D'Amato's invitation to take on Moynihan. He said it wasn't because he had wanted to pick his successor as U.S. Attorney, but rather that D'Amato had refused to tell him who his successor would be. "He said," Giuliani remarked cynically, " 'it's going to take a while. Trust me.' "

By then Giuliani had absolutely no trust in D'Amato and every reason to suspect his intentions. "It was a particularly sensitive period of time," Giuliani explained. His office was prosecuting three cases in which D'Amato had a strong connection with the defendants. Those defendants, Giuliani revealed, were the mob-ridden Teamsters Union, which through many conduits had become one of D'Amato's chief contributors; Drexel Burnham Lambert, another of D'Amato's heavy contributors whose junk-bond racket Giuliani was in the process of demolishing; and Cong. Mario Biaggi. Giuliani described the relationship between D'Amato and Wedtech's Biaggi as being "very close."

He also wanted it known that he had concluded his old benefactor was in reality "a scheming politician" who had taken on the role of self-appointed "political boss."

Furthermore, Giuliani didn't believe D'Amato really wanted to defeat Mayor Koch. Although of different parties, D'Amato and Koch were allies. As far back as November 14, 1988, D'Amato stated he would not be part of a Republican effort to form a fusion coalition against the Democratic mayor. "Thanks but no thanks," he told reporters. "It would be counterproductive for me to be involved in any such undertaking." He added: "Don't sell the mayor short."

"Their effort," Giuliani said bluntly about D'Amato and Lauder, "is an effort to help Koch. It is not an effort to elect a Republican mayor, because they don't believe that Lauder is going to beat Koch or [David] Dinkins." Although Giuliani was stating the obvious in only the most oblique terms, it was clear that D'Amato's real objective was to defeat him, regardless of who won the city contest.

Since he was inarticulate, Lauder's managers banned live interviews, allowed the press access solely for pictures, and let him appear on television only if he was paying for the time. The advertising bill for his harshly negative campaign against Giuliani eventually added up to over $14 million, $2 million more than John F. Kennedy had spent to become president in 1960.

Lauder's gaudy spending resembled nothing more than a gigantic potlatch. He had squandered a large chunk of his mother's money with no apparent benefit to himself. In the September 12 primary, he received barely 30 percent of the tally. Although he retained the Conservative party nomination and inertly carried it into the November election, in effect, after the primary, he left the cockpit of politics with a public reputation as much in tatters as his private one had been.

Giuliani made a grand effort to clean up the carnage of the D'Amato/Lauder blitzkrieg. His Democratic opponent was not to be Ed Koch: rather, the mild-mannered Manhattan borough president, David Dinkins, product of the Harlem machine, who had failed to pay his income tax for four years in the 1970s. As the final seven weeks of the campaign began, various polls had Giuliani losing to Dinkins by no less than 14 percent and as much as 30 percent. As the campaign wound down, it was still predicted by major New York papers that he would lose by at least 14 percent.

Already lost was an expedient friendship that Rudy and Alfonse appeared to be happy had ended.

FORTY-TWO

THE MAFIA CONNECTION

Two weeks before the 1989 mayoral election, the *Village Voice* exploded a bombshell. On October 25, Dan Collins wrote an article stating that a year earlier, while interviewing Giuliani for a proposed biography, the U.S. Attorney had told him that Alfonse D'Amato in late 1984 and early 1985 had appealed to him on behalf of mobster figures Giuliani was prosecuting.

If Collins's account was true, D'Amato's intervention was a serious violation of Senate ethics. Senators are prohibited from even making inquiries into any ongoing legal action. But what Collins was describing was much more serious: D'Amato was pleading for criminals at the highest level of organized crime.

The 1984 call concerned Mario .Gigante, who had, in June 1983, been convicted of extortion and sentenced to eight years in jail. Gigante was a Mafia captain, described by the FBI as a Genovese crime-family, "low-life loan shark," and brother of the family godfather, Vincent "the Chin" Gigante. The Chin had for years been warding off prosecution by posing as mentally incompetent. He would appear on Mulberry Street in Manhattan's Little Italy clad in a bathrobe, supported by his bodyguard, hesitantly taking a few steps while mumbling incoherently, his blank eyes suggesting he did not know where he was.

Vincent "Fish" Cafaro, a former Genovese soldier who turned FBI informer, told the government in March 1987 that following Mario Gigante's imprisonment, Vincent Gigante turned to Roy Cohn in an effort to get his brother's sentence reduced.

Cafaro said that Cohn told the Chin that it would cost "big bucks" to shave two years off his brother's sentence; the price quoted was $175,000. It was a contingency fee; if Cohn failed to get the reduction, there would be no payoff. Since such a reduction could mean the difference between eight years of hard time for his brother or, with time off for good behavior, less than three years, the Chin agreed to Cohn's *fee*.

In the fall of 1984, soon after the jail doors slammed shut on his client, Cohn filed a motion for a two-year reduction of Mario's sentence. Then D'Amato placed his call to Rudy Giuliani.

Within hours after the *Village Voice* was on the newsstands, Giuliani confirmed Collins's story. Yes, Giuliani said with no show of reluctance, D'Amato had called "about the Gigante case in which he asked me to look into the motion to reduce the sentence."

In Collins's article Giuliani stated he was very surprised by D'Amato's interest in the case. How did D'Amato explain his call, Collins wanted to know. "Well," Giuliani told his potential biographer, "he just wanted to bring to my attention what a lawyer [Cohn] had brought to his attention."

Giuliani's response: "I told him immediately that we would oppose, and oppose it in strong language."

Giuliani's office filed a document with the court fighting Cohn's motion. In a harsh comment that suggested that the prosecutors knew what criminality Cohn was capable of, they informed the court, "A reduction in this sentence would be greeted in these same criminal circles as evidence that crime pays and that justice can ultimately be bought and sold."

Closed off from Giuliani's aid, Cohn pursued his reduction petition in Federal Judge Charles E. Stewart's Southern District court. Judge Stewart was known for doling out lenient sentences. In January 1985 he approved, without comment, the two-year reduction Cohn was seeking. The *Village Voice* described the subsequent events:

Following the sentence reduction, Cafaro later told the FBI, he delivered $175,000 in cash to Cohn's office in three installments of $75,000, $50,000, and $50,000. Cafaro said he delivered the last payment to Tom Bolan, Cohn's law partner and a D'Amato confidant.

"I gave Bolan the remaining $50,000 in cash, and Bolan advised me, 'I know what this is for,' " Cafaro said in an affidavit to the FBI. "I advised Bolan at that time, 'This is it' [meaning that it was the last payment], at which time Bolan stated, 'OK,' and put the money in his desk drawer."

Cafaro said that both he and "The Chin" believed that the cash was to be used for a "reach" (a bribe).

Bolan took time from his busy law practice, and his responsibilities as a member of D'Amato's screening committee that recommended appointments of judges and U.S. Attorneys, to deny Cafaro's allegations.

D'Amato also had a denial to make. In July 1989, during the height of the Giuliani/Lauder primary contest, the *Daily News* received a tip that D'Amato had contacted Giuliani pressuring for Gigante's sentence reduction. It would be three more months before the *Village Voice* published the story, and it became a cause célèbre. In response to the *News's* inquiry D'Amato denied he had ever contacted anyone about Gigante. "I never called anyone about it," he swore to the *News.* "I never heard of it before."

It must have been clear to D'Amato that the most likely source for this *News* story was Giuliani, the man whose political career he was in the process of trashing. Did fear distract him even momentarily from his anti-Giuliani intrigue, or had arrogance so captured his intellect that he believed his lie to the *News* would end the matter?

D'Amato's second attempt to gain Giuliani's help for a Mafia leader occurred in early 1985. Giuliani told Dan Collins in 1988 that D'Amato had spoken to him for approximately five minutes, in person, about another Roy Cohn underworld client. The senator asked Giuliani to look into a murder charge pending against Paul Castellano. Castellano was the boss of the Gambino organized crime family and was considered by the FBI to be the most power-ful criminal in America.

Giuliani said D'Amato told him he was raising the question about the murder charges because he had been asked to by Roy Cohn. D'Amato warned Giuliani that the U.S. Attorney's office might be "embarrassed" by losing the case.

Although in 1985 the two were still friends and Giuliani was not anxious to affront his mentor, Giuliani nevertheless cautioned D'Amato in what he later described as "a lecture."

"I said to him that there was an open door in my office for lawyers to communicate on any problems in cases, that that's the way it should be done, that it would be better for him and better for the office if he didn't talk to me about these things."

D'Amato and Cohn had again run into Giuliani's stone wall and had to accommodate themselves to the sight of the nation's leading criminal moving steadily in the direction of a trial. In December 1985, during Castellano's trial, he and his bodyguard were mur-dered on the street outside a Manhattan steak house.

Once the October 1989 *Village Voice* article appeared, D'Amato was besieged with demands for his side of the story. At first, his only response was a short written statement insisting he had done nothing wrong. But as the cries of outrage rose on all sides, he finally told the *New York Times*, "I acted properly. Rudy did noth-ing wrong, and I did nothing wrong. I'm not happy with this. I'm not saying there's not a negative impact. Who needs it? Hindsight is a wonderful teacher."

I asked Assistant U.S. Attorney Lawrence Noyer, a member of Andrew Maloney's staff, what he thought about this special plead-ing by D'Amato on behalf of the Mafia. I first asked whether his office hadn't been concerned when Mafia turncoat Henry Hill had said on television that D'Amato's reputation was that he "could be reached." The mafiosi used the word "reached" to mean *bribed.* "Wasn't that a red flag?" I asked Noyer.

"Sure it was a red flag," the earnest Noyer answered frankly. He attempted to explain his office's lack of action. "Let's assume for the moment that that's true. What does he [Hill] mean by 'reached'? Was he [D'Amato] reached in a criminal way?"

Noyer was searching for language that would satisfy the conflict between his moral code and the inaction of the Eastern District

Attorney's office. "There were allegations that Senator D'Amato called up Rudy Giuliani and that he—"

I interrupted: "They're not allegations. They've both said it happened."

"Okay," Noyer agreed, now that his memory had been refreshed. "Is that outrageous?" he asked rhetorically. "Of course it is. . . . If the call from Senator D'Amato came from 'wiseguys,' then obviously you could say—"

"It came from Roy Cohn," I said.

His training at Fordham Law School and editorship of the law journal came to his aid. "That's outrageous, and that's disgraceful," he said, "but it's no crime."

In an effort to get his keen legal mind to revisit the issue of whether D'Amato might have committed a crime, I said, "No senator has ever called up a U.S. Attorney and asked him to call off a murder case against a Mafia godfather."

Noyer went along with my premise. "I regard myself," he began firmly, "as familiar with federal criminal code as any U.S. Attorney you'll ever talk to, and I know of no statute that would make that a crime." After considering the implications of his legal opinion, he added, "Maybe that should be a crime."

Mark Green was seething when he discussed with me D'Amato's phone calls to Giuliani. He accused his former opponent of pandering to the Mafia. "Why would any senator testify in open court as a character witness for a mob-related criminal like Philip Basile?" he asked, referring back to D'Amato's 1983 court appearance on behalf of a man who had arranged to get Lucchese crime-family murderer Henry Hill out of jail. "Would any other senator have lifted a finger, much less made two phone calls to help two leaders of organized crime, like Paul Castellano and Mario Gigante?"

"He says he was innocent and uninformed," Green continued with heavy sarcasm. "You don't make a phone call to help a convicted felon unless you know who he is and why you're calling. He claimed he didn't know who Paul Castellano was. It's like a public leader saying he doesn't know who John Gotti is. Assume that's true. Then why did he make the phone call? D'Amato's answer is that a lawyer asked him to do it. Well, isn't that nice that a senator will do anything that any lawyer asks him to do. Who was the lawyer? D'Amato's answer: Roy Cohn. Roy Cohn is not any old Cohn. He is the sleaziest lawyer of the modern era, which is documented by his disbarment by the New York Bar in 1987."

Mark Green's indignation was reaching the boiling point. D'Amato's direct effort on the part of these mob figures was fueling his anger, but it was D'Amato's involvement with the HUD scandals, news of which was simultaneously making front-page headlines across the country, that made him seriously consider an attack on D'Amato that would place the senator's whole career in jeopardy.

FORTY-THREE

AL'S HUD HOUSE OF CARDS

D'Amato's blunders in New York made him vulnerable to a changing public perception. On November 7 the Republican outcry against D'Amato intensified when it was announced that in an overwhelmingly Democratic city Giuliani had almost defeated David Dinkins, losing by forty-seven thousand votes, a margin of less than 2 percent. State Republican strategist Richard Bond, soon to be George Bush's presidential campaign manager, commented, "I believe—and Rudy does—that if it were not for Al's manipulation of Lauder, Giuliani would be mayor today. A lot of people are still upset with that."

D'Amato's New York City disaster encouraged a host of Democrats, otherwise timidly sitting on the sidelines, to consider running against him in 1992. The revelations about his pleadings for Mafia capos exposed him to a full-scale attack on his honesty. These were political problems—serious, possibly career-ending problems—but his more serious legal peril came from the mushrooming HUD scandals.

D'Amato's earliest efforts to misuse federal housing funds date back to the 1970s, when he instituted what became known as Island Park's "Black Removal Program." Jim Nagourney, who was then city manager of nearby Long Beach, described the scheme: "Al D'Amato was the sole architect and implementer of the Black Removal Program in Island Park. I'll tell you what they did. If there was a building with a high black population, the village condemned it. 'Well, they're in a slum building and let's condemn this substandard building.' And say it with a straight face and just go and do it because the blacks are not powerful enough to make a stink about it."

Nagourney said the whole scam was operated with federal funds. The village did not have the financial resources to reshape its demographics. Washington had to be convinced that D'Amato's plan had a socially constructive motive that merited support. "Every opportunity they had," Nagourney said, "they ripped down buildings in Island Park where blacks were living and built parking lots—God knows for what. They never had enough businesses for parking lots. They must have had ten parking spaces for every resident in Island Park. Then the blacks had no choice but to move to Long Beach."

Nagourney said D'Amato laughed when he complained to him about the burden that his Black Removal Program was placing on Long Beach. "He thought that was very funny, that he was, *quote*, 'pushing an Island Park problem into Long Beach.' "

Parking lots were only a temporary expedience. As soon as D'Amato could obtain federal money, new housing went up. One of the buildings where twenty-two black families had been living was razed in 1976; by 1980, D'Amato had obtained a HUD subsidy to erect a forty-apartment senior-citizen building on the site. None of the evicted blacks were eligible under D'Amato's rules.

Al's longtime friend, contributor, former campaign aide, and agent for his overpriced Manhattan office, Martin Bernstein, was chosen to build and run the senior-citizen apartments. Al appointed his friend Geraldine McGann head of the Island Park Housing Authority, which handed out the generously subsidized apartments. And like everything else in Island Park, the distribution of these low-rent apartments was based on political connections.

Al's cousin Francine Ciccimarro Sniffin got her in-laws an apartment; Geraldine McGann and her husband, "Doc," found a place for one of their relatives. Joe Ruocco, village justice, had a grandfather in the senior citizen center. According to Nicholas Goldberg of *Newsday*, "A local Republican 'executive leader' had a sister in a HUD apartment. . . . The former deputy village clerk's mother lives in one of the apartments, as does the mother-in-law of the former village justice."

Goldberg went on to quote Mike Rizzo, whose uncle was a village trustee: "I got my mother an apartment in the senior-citizen home through politics. I had done a lot of running around for Doc McGann, getting petitions signed and handing out literature, and I thought it was time I got a favor for myself. That's the way the system works in Island Park."

The Federal Housing and Urban Development Act offered D'Amato a temptation impossible to resist. It was a program meant to provide housing for the poor, but it was so laxly administered that its original objective was easily perverted by politicians, consultants, and builders.

D'Amato's exploitation of HUD began in 1977, when he was elected presiding supervisor of Hempstead. Jimmy Carter's HUD officials were battling Hempstead's politicians who did not want to put low-income housing for poor blacks and Hispanics into middle-class white communities like Island Park. D'Amato wanted HUD money to build forty-four single-family houses; he just didn't want black and Hispanic families to accompany the money.

Cong. Bill Green, Manhattan Republican and HUD's New York regional director under Presidents Nixon and Ford, remembered D'Amato's intervention. "My understanding was that D'Amato offered to break the deadlock by meeting the HUD requirements. That's why I was rather upset at what happened in Island Park. Because those units were supposed to be part of the solution to provide housing opportunities for minorities outside areas of minority concentration. Instead, they all went to the friends of the powers that be in Island Park."

By the end of Jimmy Carter's administration D'Amato had succeeded in getting a grant to build the forty-four HUD houses. The duplicity involved in D'Amato's promise was not yet exposed, nor was his plan to distribute most of the forty-four houses to his friends, supporters, and relatives.

An indication of what D'Amato had in mind came on March 25, 1980, the day applications were supposed to be delivered to the village hall for the first five of the forty-four houses. A slew of applications were under village clerk Harry Scully's office door before it opened at 9:00 A.M. Most of the successful applicants came from these early risers.

Among them were two children of Antoinette D'Amato's sister, Violet Ciccimaro, née Cioffari. Violet and her children were living across the street from Antoinette and Armand in grandfather Alfonse Cioffari's old house. Scully stamped their applications as numbers three and four.

William Sniffin, ex-husband of Al's cousin Francine Ciccimarro, told FBI agents that he listened to his then wife call cousin Al D'Amato and ask him for one of the HUD houses. When she hung up she said, "We got it." A few days later, Sniffin and his wife were taken by a village employee to select one of five vacant sites for their new home. The site they selected was a parking lot that had previously been occupied by a boardinghouse in which seven blacks had lived.

Although he operated behind the scenes and communicated his orders directly to Harry Scully, D'Amato's approval about who was to get a house was more important than any paperwork done in the HUD regional office. This was *his* project in *his* town, and only *his* people were eligible.

In January 1981, as D'Amato took his back-bench Senate seat, Jimmy Carter's HUD regulators were packing their bags and leaving town. The new crew coming on board at HUD consisted of inexperienced Reaganites philosophically antagonistic to federal programs in general and determined to implement Reagan's policy of "getting federal regulators off the backs of the people." By 1988, Reagan had cut HUD's budget from $30 billion to $7.5 billion, but D'Amato's formative 1981 vision was of a bloated agency run by political hacks on the lookout for senators with blueprints bulging out of their pockets.

In those early days D'Amato was pleased to discover that President Reagan wanted New York's new senator to recommend appointees to replace Carter's agency heads. The ripest plum on that appointment plate was New York's regional director of HUD.

The person who occupied that office had control over hundreds of millions of dollars, 950 jobs, and the power to decide which housing projects would be approved in New York, New Jersey, Puerto Rico, and the Virgin Islands—for administrative purposes the latter two had been placed under the control of the New York office.

D'Amato chose Joseph Monticciolo, his longtime Nassau fundraiser, and lobbied strongly for his appointment. Samuel Pierce, the new secretary of HUD, made no attempt to pick his New York lieutenant. It was more important for him to maintain the goodwill of a senator whose reputation as an enemy was nasty and who had managed to get himself assigned to the Housing and Urban Affairs Committee, which had power over HUD.

Pierce was a bad manager, disorganized and not in the slightest interested in keeping his eye on the shop. He appointed as his department second-in-command Deborah Gore Dean, a twenty-eight-year-old former Washington bar hostess who had a taste for approving grants to friends who were private housing consultants. Pierce couldn't care less. One of his favorite activities in the afternoons was watching TV soap operas, and he was often too enervated by these exertions to remain at work past four o'clock.

D'Amato's control over the New York office is epitomized by Monticciolo's decision to install a special button on his telephone that connected him directly to a phone in D'Amato's Washington office. D'Amato was literally wired into HUD.

Annette Snow found out about D'Amato's plan to get HUD houses built in Island Park in 1980 only when she saw construction start on the first five houses. Annette was twenty-five and pregnant with her daughter. She and her husband, Peter, lived in a one-bedroom house owned by her grandmother Antoinette. When Annette's son was born a year and a half later, she and her husband gave the bedroom to the children and slept on the living-room floor. From the moment Annette glimpsed the cement trucks pouring foundations, a HUD house seemed like the answer to her prayers.

Grandma was "very proud," said Annette, her eyes shining with love. "She was a woman who would give you the shirt off her back." She migrated from Palermo, Sicily, in 1917. "She was seventeen when she came to this country. Her parents died in the 1918 influenza epidemic. They left eight kids; the youngest was two—

she brought them all up." Antoinette married a Swedish tailor. In 1925, three years before the village became incorporated, they moved to Island Park. From her grandfather Annette got her blond hair and Nordic features; from her grandmother, a feisty spirit.

"Grandma used to fight with the village board," Annette recalled. "She was head of the PTA and was against what they were doing in the school. She always said that the group that was in, the Unity party, were nothing but a bunch of bums. They were out for themselves, destroying the village."

She remembered Al D'Amato during the 1960s in his role as a Republican committeeman. "My oldest memory of the senator is when I was ten years old. He was basting my mother's turkey and baby-sitting for us while she went and voted. He made sure that everyone got out to vote. When she came home, he went on to the next house."

During her adolescence Annette helped out at her father's dry cleaning store. Occasionally, she saw D'Amato in the store. "He'd walk right behind the counter and take care of the customers. That was just Al. This was *his* town. He ran it. If the deli was busy, he'd jump behind the counter just to try and make himself look good. 'I wouldn't want to see you wait in the cleaners. I'll take care of it for you. I know this place like the back of my hand.' My father didn't care. He knew him for years. He was always friendly with him. That was him."

It took D'Amato's manipulation of the HUD houses to get Annette angry with him. "When I first started fighting the village, they nicknamed me 'Antoinette' after my grandmother and said I was just like her, but only worse."

As befits the secretive character of Island Park's rulers, information about the HUD project was known only to a small group of village insiders, and Annette was not among that elite. But as soon as she saw the first five houses going up, she decided to inquire. "Peter and I stopped in to see the mayor, Mike Parente. We asked him if they were building any others. And he told us they weren't building any more, maybe a few on the railroad, and they were already gone."

The Snows walked away from Parente's office feeling that they had missed an opportunity; they were resigned to solving their housing problems elsewhere. A village board variance to build a second bedroom on Grandma Antoinette's house seemed like the best bet. When village officials turned down Grandma, Annette wanted to find out why; she saw variances being given out for similar additions all over the village. Walter Foster, then on the village zoning board but soon to be a major player in the HUD scandal, told Annette, "You're going to be living in a one-bedroom house for the rest of your life." Foster was a family friend, and he confided in her. "There's someone on the village board that had something against her [Grandma Antoinette], and they blackballed her."

In August 1981, Annette recalled, "they began to break ground down the block from me on the beach. It was a second section. We had specifically asked the mayor, and he said no other ones were being built, and I see that they're breaking ground. So I started making phone calls. Every time they banged a nail, I made a phone call to HUD. I got furious. I couldn't find out about applications. What were the regulations about getting one? I called HUD in Washington, in Albany, I called New York HUD. I went through the U.S. blue pages in the phone book, and I called everything labeled HUD."

Annette began tracking the program. "I started to keep a notebook—a black-and-white hard-covered school notebook—about everyone who was getting a house, who they were related to."

She also contacted newspapers and television stations. No one was interested. "Finally, I began calling Ray Malone in Hempstead." Malone was the Nassau County director of housing, a Margiotta party appointee completely under D'Amato's control. Annette complained that she couldn't get an application for the proposed housing. She quoted Malone, " 'Oh, the applications are all done. The houses are all taken.' I said, 'They're not even planned and not even built, how can they all be taken?' "

Annette persisted. Wasn't everyone allowed to file an application? Who determined who got the applications that had been secretly distributed? "After a number of calls he told me, 'If you lived in Island Park so long, you must know the senator. If you want a house so badly, Mrs. Snow, get off my back. Leave me alone. Call the senator. He'll get you a house.' "

Annette's response: "Oh, you mean I got to go through favors. So I'm right in my assumption that it's who knows who and who's getting what under the table."

Annette said this ended the conversation. " 'I don't wanna discuss any of this,' " she quoted Malone as saying. I guess he figured I had a tape recorder. I told him, 'I already know all I want to know.'

"Everyone was telling me, 'Call the senator. Have your father talk to him.' I said, 'Why? I gotta owe someone to own a home in a village my family has been in for so many years?' I should be able to get an application and get on a list and maybe get my name picked in a lottery. That's all I wanted. I gotta owe favors to somebody? I wouldn't ask that man for a favor for anything."

Peter worried that Annette was getting too involved, too upset. He said, "Let's go down to Florida and stay with your aunt for a couple of days."

They bought their tickets, but the day before they left, Annette again became indignant. She read an article in *Newsday* about HUD that listed the qualifications needed to get a house. "I looked at it and I said, 'This is crazy.' It said you had to have two children, so much money, you had to be married. I started looking through my book. And I said, Geraldine McGann's son is running for justice of the peace because he's *not* married. How the hell is he getting a house? One guy down the block is married but has no children. Joe Ruocco is a lawyer. Why does a lawyer need government help to buy a house? It was unbelievable. Nothing matched up to what Newsday's story said."

Annette decided to make one last effort to expose what was going on. "Before we got on the plane I called Channel two, Channel seven, and Channel five. 'I dare you to go down to the village of Island Park and find one application for those houses.' "

She thinks that calls from those television stations to D'Amato's office broke the logjam. "We were at my aunt's house in Fort Lauderdale, and we got a phone call from Walter Foster. He and my father were like brothers. He knew where to find me."

Peter got on the phone with village zoning board member Foster. "He told Peter to put a muzzle on me and get the first flight back, because the house is ours if we're there at nine o'clock in the morning. We were living in one bedroom. We weren't going to kick ourselves. We forfeited our tickets, got on the plane, and came right home."

The next morning, Peter went to see Harry Scully, the village clerk. Annette's voice became sarcastic. "Suddenly the application appeared, and there was a house available. Miraculous. They had me fill out the application after they gave me the house. It was the last house, cost $63,000. The original ones went for $40,000."

Scully had a message from Senator D'Amato. "Harry Scully told me in the village office to use Armand D'Amato as my closing lawyer."

Annette said, "I refused. I used my own lawyer. There were twenty other couples at the closing, and Armand was running around from one to another in the village hall, but they were all around me and my lawyer. 'Is everything all right?' et cetera. I told Scully, even as we were signing the papers, 'It doesn't mean I'm stopping. It doesn't mean I'm not going to pursue what I've been pursuing. This is wrong and it's illegal.'"

Scully had heard people complain before. What difference did it make? D'Amato told him what to do, and he did it. Island Park's powerhouse was controlled by D'Amato, and Scully knew complaints shouted against the walls of that house by Annette Snow would not blow it down.

FORTY-FOUR
THE COVER-UP

Annette Snow kept phoning newspaper and television reporters and HUD officials. The Integrity party was formed to oppose D'Amato's entrenched Unity party. Protesting voices began to be heard at the monthly village meetings. There was so much noise coming out of Island Park that HUD could no longer look the other way. In 1983, Washington ordered an audit of the forty-four Island Park houses.

When auditor Jeffrey Pless showed up in Harry Scully's office and asked for access to all records involving the HUD program, the village clerk did not feel threatened. D'Amato had always assured him that HUD did what he wanted it to do. Hadn't he seen proof enough of that? This was merely a farce staged by HUD bureaucrats to make sure they were covered.

Auditor Jeffrey Pless did a thorough job. His 1984 report cited numerous violations by the village against its agreement with HUD. Pless pointed out that the houses had to be advertised in local newspapers so that low-income people from nearby towns could apply. Instead, he reported, favored applicants were told when the ads were to appear, and on that day, before dawn and before any outsider had a chance to buy a newspaper, they slipped their applications under Harry Scully's door.

Furthermore, although the village had agreed to reserve seventeen houses for minorities, only three homeowners had a Hispanic spouse, and no blacks had been selected.

Pless discovered that most applicants had received "preferential treatment" based on "relationships with village officials." Among them, Pless disclosed, were two of D'Amato's cousins, Anthony Ciccimarro and his sister, Francine Ciccimarro Sniffen. Daniel McGann, son of village trustee and HUD official Geraldine McGann, was the other celebrity on the list, which also included, in its short version, the following Island Park gentry:

- Tricia Holtje, niece of Harry Scully.
- Mary Ellen Guerin, niece of village trustee James Brady.
- Michael DeLessio and Joseph DiDomenico, village workers.
- Joseph Ruocco, a lawyer who became village justice.
- Donna Moore, daughter of village employee Mary Digiacomo.

Subsequent investigation revealed that another house had gone to the son of Miriam Madden, D'Amato's personal secretary.

Pless concluded: "The program was a mockery. It took everyone's tax money and gave it to the people who didn't need it."

D'Amato had bestowed on his favorites a glittering prize. Joe Ruocco, for example, put down $2,000 to buy his $40,000 house in August 1980. In 1986, he sold it for $150,000, reinvesting the profits in a $275,000 waterfront house. Twelve of the owners made similar profits, some on even quicker resales.

The 1984 audit singled out HUD official Geraldine McGann for condemnation. Mrs. McGann had been a close friend and political ally of neighbor Al D'Amato since she was a young woman. She lived in a house on the waterfront, and from the late 1970s on she acted as a party giver for D'Amato. She has said of him, "He's a very dear friend."

The senator's small house and his wife Penny's abhorrence of playing hostess to a political crowd from whom she felt alienated made Mrs. McGann an important fund-raising asset. It was a common sight for neighbors to see luxury cruisers glide up the channel and park at the McGann dock.

Mrs. McGann's early reward came when she was made the liaison between the county, for whom her politically active husband

Edward "Doc" McGann worked, and the Island Park senior citizens luncheon program. When D'Amato became presiding supervisor of Hempstead, he appointed her deputy commissioner for the aging. The entire family income now depended on D'Amato's inclination to give or to withhold.

On October 19, 1981, soon after D'Amato secured the New York regional director's job for Joe Monticciolo, he had Monticciolo appoint Mrs. McGann as his "special assistant," a high-level job and her first paid position in housing.

D'Amato also picked her to be a village trustee; she served in that capacity from August 19, 1982, until 1989. The trustee's position was the source of much of auditor Pless's criticism of Mrs. McGann. The problem arose because as a paid trustee Mrs. McGann voted on HUD-related issues while she was on the other side of the fence as a HUD "special assistant," and, for her, the fence did not exist.

Mrs. McGann's inability to keep her two adversarial roles separate was dramatically demonstrated by the manner in which her son Daniel obtained a house in the third and last section.

At first glance, Daniel seemed ineligible for HUD housing. He was not married, and single persons could not normally take part in the program. In fact, he lived with his mother, making it difficult for her to be unaware of his single status.

Daniel McGann made no effort to apply for any of the twenty-four houses in the first two sections. He had no need for one, at least not until, as Mrs. McGann subsequently explained, "my son was engaged to a young lady." Daniel suddenly wanted one of the seventeen houses in the last section, and since his mother was now a trustee and her best friend was handing out the houses, Daniel felt encouraged. However, in addition to being single he had another major problem. Since no minority members had been given any of the first twenty-four houses, HUD's Washington office had set strict guidelines for the distribution of these last houses.

There were 120 applicants who had applied for the initial twenty-four houses; they had not been legitimately considered, since insiders had been advised to file in advance. Auditor Pless said the public ads had also been misleading in that they "stated only that persons interested should write the village." By the time Harry Scully received their letters, he had stamped in the applications of the early risers. Therefore, Washington decreed, in deciding who would get the last seventeen houses these 120 misled applicants had to be given first consideration. Again, young McGann was shut out.

Daniel McGann had no intention of letting technicalities stand in his way. As the auditor put it, his "handwritten/hand-delivered letter of interest was delivered to the village office." The letter "was not numbered or time stamped." Daniel's hope to overcome petty regulations was summed up in the auditor's observation that in his letter McGann "stated that he would be getting married on Dec. 4, 1982."

The clearest sign that Mrs. McGann was allowing her motherly concern to blind her judgment came on March 17, 1983. In her capacity as Island Park trustee she voted for the sale of village land, at the token sum of $500 per lot, to the builders of the last seventeen houses, among which was her son's house. It's admirable for a mother to be generous with her child, but in this case Mother McGann's generosity was being funded with other people's money.

In addition, before the third phase was started, Mrs. McGann and the other trustees sat down with village clerk Scully and "went over the whole list of everyone interested in a house." In summary, Mrs. McGann decided on the elimination of people who were competing with her son for a HUD house, and she showed no sign of detecting a conflict of interest.

Although HUD had prohibited Mrs. McGann from voting on issues involving the forty-four houses, Pless reported that village board minutes showed that she "had participated." Pless's 1984 audit concluded: "There appears to be a Standards of Conduct violation by Mrs. McGann" and he recommended "appropriate disciplinary action."

Al D'Amato was Mrs. McGann's assurance that "disciplinary action" would never cloud her future. The only question was how he and Monticciolo would handle this negative audit report.

The first opportunity to bury the audit occurred within days when it was reviewed by several auditors in the regional inspector general's office. The regional inspector generals approved Pless's findings. A frustrated Monticciolo then tried a new tack. He assigned HUD regional counsel Steven Love to get some responses from Mrs. McGann that might be used to rebuff Pless's charges against her.

Mrs. McGann denied everything. She told Love that she hadn't intervened for her son. She denied ever speaking to Scully on her son's behalf or that she had any inside information about the houses. The village minutes showing her votes were "in total error." She told Love, "As a village trustee I did not at any time vote on any HUD-related decisions." But, Pless said, the board minutes showed she had.

Trying to resolve the conflict between McGann's claims and the written record, Love interviewed Scully. Not only was Scully D'Amato's ally; the village clerk had been singled out, along with Mrs. McGann for the auditor's sharpest criticisms. Scully was enmeshed in the board's attempt to subvert HUD regulations. Nevertheless, HUD counsel Love, at a loss to find anyone who could corroborate Mrs. McGann's version of the truth, decided to depend on Harry Scully. Love solicited a letter from Scully, dated March 16, 1984, stating that his minutes were wrong. Scully lied that Mrs. McGann's votes were "inadvertently recorded by me as 'aye' rather than 'abstain.'" He claimed he was a "cavalier" note taker.

Armed with these *facts*, Love sent Monticciolo, New York's regional HUD administrator, a report saying there was nothing improper about an eligible child of an employee receiving a HUD house and recommended the closing of the case. When Philip Schulman of the Washington inspector general's office read Love's opinion, he wrote that the real question ignored by Love "is whether Ms. McGann improperly used her influence to help her son." Schulman recommended further investigation, but Monticciolo decided to rely on Love's contrary advice.

Although Love's opinion was the only one absolving Mrs. McGann, Monticciolo concluded that not even a reprimand was called for. Instead, in September 1984 he ordered the investigation closed. Mrs. McGann continued as his special assistant.

In October 1986, Steven Love resigned as counsel to HUD's New York regional office and went on the payroll of Armand D'Amato's Mineola law firm.

After one year as an associate in Armand Paul's office, Love became restless. At that point, Emanuel Popolizio, chairman of the

New York City Housing Authority, received a call from Armand Paul D'Amato. The Nassau lawyer-brother of Senator D'Amato asked Popolizio to put Steven Love on his New York City payroll. Although there was no job for Love, Popolizio created a new post, director of intergovernmental relations, and Love started collecting $60,869 per year, even as New York City found it increasingly difficult to pay its bills.

When the *New York Times* asked Armand Paul's firm to explain why he had urged Popolizio to hire Love, the official response was: Because Mr. Love "desired to be there." Popolizio knew that a $60,869 job was a small price to pay to keep a member of the Senate Housing and Urban Affairs Committee happy.

The internal HUD audit was squashed in September 1984. Within a few months, Jeffrey Pless quit his job as New York regional auditor, saying he was disgusted because no action was taken. In fact, the damning audit was not made public. The loose threads of this affair had been tidied up.

FORTY-FIVE

THE SENATOR
FROM PUERTO RICO

D
uring the spring of 1989 newspaper accounts began to
raise doubts about the manner in which HUD was being
administered. The testimony of President Reagan's former
secretary of the interior James Watts before the House Subcommittee on Employment and Housing led to negative editorial reaction
about the politicizing of HUD.

Watts was asked to explain a $400,000 payment to him from
HUD for his services as "a housing consultant." Since Watts's expertise was in the mating habits of spotted owls and his most strenuous efforts had been made to convince the public that the national
forests could best be managed by the lumber industry, what, committee members wanted to know, had he done to receive $400,000
in the nonrelated field of housing.

Well, Watts responded with a broad smile in front of television
cameras, he had "made two or three telephone calls" to HUD
officials he knew recommending people who wanted to build a
project.

Suddenly, the spotlight was on the way Samuel Pierce ran HUD.
Was Pierce so lax that a well-placed politician with a sliding-scale
moral code had only to pick up the phone to make millions flow
from the secretary's discretionary fund?

That question filled the air as attention abruptly shifted from "consultant" Watts to Senator D'Amato when, on May 25, 1989, the *Wall Street Journal* printed a story headlined:

> *Favored Friends*
> PROGRAM AIDED PUERTO RICANS
> WHO FINANCIALLY BACKED
> NEW YORK SEN. D'AMATO

The *Journal* said that within HUD, D'Amato was known as "the senator from Puerto Rico." So effective was he in procuring grants for Puerto Rico that from 1984 to 1988 the offshore common-wealth, with 1 percent of the eligible population, had "snared" 7 percent of the subsidies. During this period, D'Amato was satisfied with 4.9 percent for New York, the state he officially represented, although it was entitled to 13.6 percent.

HUD's program to provide housing for the poor, The *Journal* declared, "may be better remembered as a pot of gold for fat-cat Republican contributors, well-connected developers and powerful Washington consultants." The *Journal* identified D'Amato's real "constituents" for whom he did "constituent service," always for a fee usually described as "a campaign contribution" but sometimes listed as a retainer for brother Armand Paul.

D'Amato immediately issued a denial. "I never as much as made an inquiry on behalf of any developer in Puerto Rico."

This denial came precisely as D'Amato was attempting to destroy Rudy Giuliani's effort to become mayor of New York. D'Amato had wasted so much of his credibility on his vendetta against Giuliani that his denial only encouraged reporters to dig deeper. A number of newspapers around the country quickly discovered that New York's junior senator had found the Caribbean island fertile ground for his type of retail politics.

D'Amato's first venture into the tropical underbrush of Puerto Rican housing came in 1984. Cleofe Rubi, a local developer, want-ed a share of HUD projects that were going to friends of Interior Secretary James Watts. In order to obtain housing subsidies, Rubi formed Alameda Associates with Eduardo Lopez Ballori, a public relations executive familiar with the Washington labyrinth.

Years later, at Lopez Ballori's trial for conspiracy involving contributions to D'Amato, a cooperative Rubi testified that in order to get HUD subsidies, Lopez Ballori told him they had to "get in contact with Senator D'Amato." And the only way D'Amato would help was if they collected large "contributions" for him.

Assistant U.S. Attorney Lawrence Noyer, who prosecuted Lopez Ballori, told me, "When we asked him [Rubi] whether all these contributions to the senator would influence the senator to help them with their HUD applications, he said, 'Of course! Why do you think I did it?' That was his plot. That was their motive."

At his June 1992 trial Ballori claimed he knew nothing about American campaign laws. Since individuals could only give $2,000 and Rubi's bag held $75,000, a plan was needed for passing the money to D'Amato in smaller sums.

When confronted with this problem in the past, D'Amato had often used dummy "contributors" to hide the real giver. For example: Unisys executives donated to D'Amato after being told by a company representative they would be reimbursed by writing off their "contributions" on their expense accounts; and the Wedtech checks for D'Amato from strangers, never in excess of $2,000, were all reimbursed by the head of Wedtech. These are just two cases in court records that illustrate how D'Amato violated the election law. The person who made out the check had established a paper trail, but the trail led only to the illegal contributor, not the senator. D'Amato knew he could always claim he never would have accepted the money if he knew it wasn't legitimate.

Lopez Ballori, self-professed campaign finance innocent, came up with the identical scheme. He had twenty-seven of his friends, relatives, and business associates mail checks never exceeding $2,000 to the Friends of D'Amato Committee. He then reimbursed each and every one of them.

Prosecutor Noyer described how widespread was this practice employed by D'Amato and his "contributors".

"Having worked with a lot of election commissions, I'm willing to bet that a significant portion of every elected official's contributions are illegal. The law is a joke. The law says it's illegal to reimburse anyone for making a contribution and corporations can't make contributions. What happened in the Lopez Ballori case to circumvent the campaign laws is obvious to everyone. You are a small corporation that has ten employees, and as president of the corporation you're a big supporter of Senator D'Amato, and those ten employees depend on you for a job. Ask them to write checks for 1,000 bucks to Senator D'Amato: Do you think they're going to care? Of course not!"

Lopez Ballori's former brother-in-law Raphael Llera testified that over time he had made out $4,000 worth of such checks. "Did you know who Senator D'Amato was?" the prosecutor asked. Mr. Llera reviewed long-forgotten checks and then responded, "At that time, no."

Contributors often donate to politicians they don't know personally, but making out a check to someone you never even heard of seemed incomprehensible. It became comprehensible when Lopez Ballori's defense counsel made the following statement: "Lopez Ballori does not contest the government's allegation that he reimbursed people for making contributions to the D'Amato campaign committee." The defendant's own lawyer could afford to be so candid because the statute of limitations had run out on that violation of the federal election law. His client was ironically being tried only for misleading Senator D'Amato about the source of his contribution because D'Amato had filed a report with the Federal Election Commission falsely identifying the contributor.

Lawrence Noyer described D'Amato's tactics to me in the following manner: "An old friend of mine had a saying which I think is pretty apt: 'Never write it if you can say it; never say it if you can wink it.' "

By setting up these phony contributors, Lopez Ballori was conceding that he knew what he was doing was illegal. Otherwise, he would have sent D'Amato one check for $75,000, with his signature boldly inscribed.

Rubi testified that the money had been well spent; D'Amato had delivered. HUD subsidies meant for low-income housing came pouring in, allowing Rubi to rehabilitate luxury Alameda Towers on the outskirts of San Juan. Rubi said that he made a $4 million profit, while he gave his noninvesting partner Lopez Ballori $700,000 for using his "political contacts" with D'Amato's office.

Prosecutor Noyer's charge that Lopez Ballori had "willfully and knowingly" misled D'Amato into filing a false report seemed petty to the jury. Undermining Noyer's case further was that D'Amato, the linchpin of the scheme, was not indicted and wasn't even called as a witness.

Noyer attempted to explain why he had steered such a wide path around the senator. "The fact that D'Amato had acted to help Ballori was irrelevant. All that was relevant was what Lopez Ballori had done. He wanted the senator's help, so he gave the illegal campaign contributions.... The charge was *giving the contributions* [italics mine].... So that whether D'Amato did anything to help Ballori becomes irrelevant." Legally irrelevant no doubt, but the decision to go after the man who was "giving" and not the man who was *receiving* gave a mixed message to the jury.

Lopez Ballori's attorneys were so confident he would be acquitted that they didn't put a single witness on the stand. They depended on the jury's inability to sort out the legal fine points, all of which they pictured as being written for the benefit of mainland lawyers who were trying to convict a hometown boy.

The jury was deadlocked. Judge Gilberto Gierbolini discharged them and scheduled a second trial. At that trial, in November 1992, Noyer depended on testimony from Carmen Maria Ferre, one of Lopez Ballori's employees. At the first trial, in exchange for immunity, Ferre had testified that she knew Ballori was cochairman of the Dole for President Committee and was therefore completely familiar with the technicalities of the Federal Election Law. At the second trial, Noyer said with remorse, Carmen-Ferre "stabbed us in the back. She said to us at the end of the first trial—outside on the sidewalk—she couldn't wait till the whole thing was over so she could tell us to go (expletive) ourselves.... The day that she testified at the second trial—lunchtime—she told us that she had helped us too much at the first trial and at this trial she was going to help Eduardo.

"When we got to the question 'Did Eduardo have a position with the Dole for President Committee?' and she had testified previously under oath that she knew he did ... this time she begins her answer with a long-drawn-out 'Well, I think—' and then almost as if on cue, the defense attorneys get up and object. 'Well, Your Honor, she has no personal knowledge. She's guessing.' "

Attempts to rephrase the question were cut off by Judge Gierbolini. "Within short order it became a circus, and we realized exactly what was happening. We tried every traditional method to impeach her or refresh her recollection, and the judge wouldn't let us do it."

Judge Gierbolini dismissed the charges against Lopez Ballori without allowing the case to go to the jury. No one was going to pay for the crimes that Al D'Amato had programmed and which Lopez Ballori's attorneys said he committed.

FORTY-SIX

THE WAR AT HUD

D'Amato's control over HUD's Washington's headquarters was exercised through Deborah Gore Dean, Secretary Pierce's executive assistant. On July 8, 1992, a federal grand jury indicted Ms. Dean on thirteen criminal counts of fraud, perjury, and conspiracy to hand out HUD grants to favored developers and consultants. Before her lawyer silenced her, she bluntly described the way she ran HUD. "It was set up and designed to be a political program. . . . I would have to say we ran it in a political manner." She added that Monticciolo and D'Amato "did what they could for people who raised money and supported [the senator]. I'm not worried about that. It's the system of spoils and favoritism." On October 26, 1993, a Washington jury convicted her of defrauding the government, taking bribes, and lying to Congress.

Other hands were in Deborah Gore Dean's till besides Al D'Amato's. Former Kentucky governor Louie B. Nunn had testified at her six-week trial that he had been paid $644,000 as a "consultant" to get developers grants from HUD. He said he did little work for the money and that he had paid $184,000 of his fees to John N. Mitchell, Richard Nixon's jailed attorney general, who was romantically involved with Deborah Gore Dean's mother. Many fought for their share of the pot she was ladling out, but none with the effectiveness of Al D'Amato and the allies he had parked in various offices in New York and Washington.

D'Amato's battle plan for HUD spoils was alluded to in a scribbled note to Deborah Gore Dean from Thomas Broussard, a California lawyer who specialized in using political influence to help HUD developers. On January 7, 1985, Broussard reported to Ms. Dean that Joseph Monticciolo, D'Amato's New York HUD appointee, "is putting me in contact with a group in old San Juan that is working on units through Joe and D'Amato."

For weeks after The *Wall Street Journal* printed its story about D'Amato's tropical housing obsession, the senator's denials suggested that if handed a map of the Caribbean he would be unable to find Puerto Rico. Then, on July 28, 1989, Monticciolo was called before the housing subcommittee investigating political favoritism at HUD, and grand juries in several states again began looking in Senator D'Amato's direction.

The toughest questions asked of Monticciolo concerned his relations with D'Amato, and they came from Republican members of the committee. Connecticut's representative Christopher Shays wanted to know whether D'Amato had ever called him to push specific projects. Monticciolo seemed unable to answer. For half a minute he said nothing. Then he haltingly spoke: "It's possible. . . . I can't remember. . . . It is likely."

During six hours of grilling, Monticciolo admitted that as HUD's New York director he had gone outside regular channels to advance ineligible projects favored by D'Amato. HUD's rules mandated that Section 8 Moderate Rehabilitation projects were not to be "developer driven." They must be applied for by local housing authorities. These authorities had to assess community needs, request funding from HUD, and if their plans were approved, advertise the projects for competitive bidding. All of D'Amato's projects, including his plan to build a swimming pool in Island Park, had been approved by HUD without any application from a housing authority. They were all "senator driven," and in each case the senator knew who he wanted as developer.

Monticciolo attempted to evade a direct answer about his cozy relationship with D'Amato until he was warned he was coming close to committing perjury. Finally, Congressman Shays said, "Obviously, you were working hand and glove with Senator D'Amato."

It was impossible for Monticciolo to deny D'Amato's overwhelming influence with HUD. The House panel had released a HUD memo before the hearing in which Deborah Gore Dean informed Secretary Pierce that her Washington office was prepared to offer millions to subsidize five projects approved by Monticciolo, labeled in her memo as "Senator D'Amato's."

There was also written evidence from Assistant Secretary of Housing Thomas Demery showing D'Amato's and Monticciolo's determination to obtain those five housing grants. On March 4, 1987, Demery sent a memo to Deborah Gore Dean detailing funding decisions for the rest of the year. All of the grants had been requested by public housing agencies except, as the memo stated, that "Senator D'Amato's requests had no record of a public housing agency application on file." Attached was a list of the five rogue projects; the three largest were in Puerto Rico.

Demery, not one of D'Amato's allies, decided that since the applications were defective, he couldn't approve them. The result of his rejecting D'Amato's requests to subsidize housing projects appears in his office telephone log.

March 13, 1987. Monticciolo calls for Demery. Wants return call.

March 14, 1987. D'Amato calls for Demery. Wants return call.

March 15, 1987. D'Amato calls for Demery. Wants return call.

March 16, 1987. Monticciolo calls for Demery. Please call back.

March 17, 1987. Monticciolo calls for Demery. Wants return call.

Demery felt the pressure. Since he had earned his political credentials as a fund-raiser for the 1984 Reagan-Bush reelection team and was fighting Deborah Gore Dean for power within HUD, he was hardly a novice in this game. Furthermore, he was running his own scam. On June 19, 1993, forty-three-year-old Demery pleaded guilty in Washington District Court on two felony counts that he had steered $148 million in HUD funds to Michigan and Colorado developers in return for monetary considerations.

In March 1987, however, Demery was riding high. He told his deputy assistant secretary, Hunter Cushing, to check his sources and see if he could discover what these two persistent message leavers wanted. On March 19, Cushing called Demery and left a note: "[The] only thing he could find out about why D'Amato wants to meet with you is Sec. 8 Mod Rehab." No reference to Monticciolo. Clearly, Demery understood that the pressure, as in numerous other matters involving HUD, came from D'Amato.

The same day, another Demery aide called and left a message: "Did some 'snooping' about the purpose of the Sen. D'Amato meeting: re: Sec 8 Mod Rehab for 3 villages in Puerto Rico . . . and 2 in NY."

For some inexplicable reason, Demery discovered, D'Amato wanted 525 low-income housing units in Puerto Rico; he thought New York could get by with only 130.

Demery had enough information and no desire to further inflame D'Amato's notorious temper. His log shows that later that day, March 19 at 5:00 P.M., he went to D'Amato's office, room 520, Hart Building, where he agreed to the senator's requests but not before, D'Amato told an interviewer, he "gave him heck." An April 8, 1987, memo from Demery to Hunter Cushing spelled out the terms of surrender; it contained an amended list of HUD 1987 grants. D'Amato's five requested projects were to be funded. On May 7, Demery sent Monticciolo a letter authorizing an increase in his regional budget to include the following spoils items for D'Amato:

Puerto Rico Housing Finance Corp.: 150 units.

City of San Juan: 50 units.

Bayamon Housing Project, Puerto Rico: 50 units.

Sackets Harbor, N.Y. Housing Authority: 50 units.

Spring Valley, N.Y. Housing Authority: 50 units.

When first questioned in June 1989 about the March 19, 1987, meeting in D'Amato's office, Demery claimed he only had a faint memory of what was discussed. As a result, for the next three months D'Amato felt his denials were still plausible.

Even when informed on September 17, 1989, that *Newsday* had copies of Demery's memos and logs, D'Amato issued another outraged denial that he had battled for any Puerto Rican project. The phone calls to Demery and the meeting in his office were not made or held to seek any specific Section 8 grants, only to obtain more housing for the city of San Juan. "You may find this hard to believe," D'Amato said, "but neither I nor any member of my staff ever wrote or requested these things on the Demery memo."

D'Amato told a television interviewer that he had reluctantly concluded that his old friend Joe Monticciolo had used his name without his permission to gain approval for the Puerto Rican projects. "You can say that the senator is angry and annoyed at the misuse of his name," D'Amato exclaimed. "It was wrong of him to do this, because it created something where there was nothing and casts a cloud over all the good things I've tried to accomplish."

A week later, however, Thomas Demery found that his hazy recollection of his March 19, 1987, meeting with D'Amato had sharpened. He had become concerned that he, along with Deborah Gore Dean and former Secretary Samuel Pierce, had been targeted for prosecution by the Justice Department. Demery now recalled that D'Amato had discussed all five requests at the meeting in his Senate office. He even remembered that there was a witness, D'Amato's top aide, Michael Kinsella. The purpose of the meeting, Demery said, was to discuss D'Amato's concern that the HUD housing grants go to the Puerto Rico Housing Finance Agency. D'Amato had found a housing agency to sponsor his "senator-driven" projects. Although he had never before claimed to be a housing expert, D'Amato assured Demery that it was the best of several competing Puerto Rican housing agencies.

The bulk of the HUD grants was given to Cleofe Rubi, who by this time had staged fund-raisers in Puerto Rico that harvested $160,000 for Senator D'Amato. Rubi and his associates contributed $18,000 to D'Amato on the same day in February 1987, a month before D'Amato started lobbying Demery on their behalf.

Questions about the grants ran into a stone wall in Puerto Rico. San Juan housing director Maria Judith Orquendo was unable to supply any information about the units. In 1987, Joe Monticciolo moved HUD's San Juan office into a building owned by Cleofi Rubi, with a ten-year, $7 million lease. Ms. Orquendo explained why she couldn't supply any information: "The files have disappeared," she said. "It seems they didn't guard them well."

Former New York regional HUD director Monticciolo's July 28, 1989, testimony before the Housing Subcommittee was a public relations disaster for him and D'Amato. At one point he admitted, "I made recommendations to Washington that ultimately benefited people who are partners of mine now." Monticciolo was referring to work he took up after he left HUD in January 1988. In the month before he resigned, he told the committee that he had contacted a group of men who had profited by his governmental decisions and proposed that they form a business. "I was retiring from HUD, and I was interested in potential opportunity," Monticciolo explained.

The opportunity seeker got the type of response he expected. A few days after Monticciolo left HUD, he formed Eagle Capital Group Ltd. with these grateful investors. One of them was Puerto Rico's favorite HUD developer, Cleofe Rubi, who while Monticciolo was in office received $60 million in HUD grants, the largest total issued by Monticciolo. Eagle Capital planned to develop two senior-citizen projects in New York, a hotel complex in Puerto Rico, and a rental housing project in New Jersey, all scenes of previous Monticciolo transgressions. For his knowledge of how to bring off this next series of HUD rip-offs, Monticciolo nearly doubled his government salary and was given a 15 percent share in the business, although he invested no money and the others kicked in nearly a million dollars.

Monticciolo also told the congressional subcommittee that when he left HUD, with a legal obligation not to lobby the agency for two years, he had his wife form a company to lobby the agency. His wife had previously worked as a bookkeeper in an unrelated field. Armand Paul D'Amato became the lawyer for Mrs. Monticciolo's soon prosperous company.

At the end of the day, Cong. Christopher Shays scathingly told Monticciolo, "A lot of smelly things happened on your watch. I'm hopeful and will expect that the attorney general's office will look at what you've done, because you've cashed in, it seems to me." He then added, "I'm a little surprised that you didn't take the Fifth."

There was a suggestion in Shays's caustic comment that Monticciolo should be afraid of what the Eastern District U.S. Attorney might do. But having been a reliable fund-raiser for Al D'Amato through the years and having always acquiesced to anything demanded of him, Monticciolo clearly felt that Andrew Maloney, who had been handpicked by the senator, wasn't a man he had to fear.

FORTY-SEVEN

SCANDAL ROCKETS
BURSTING IN AIR

J oe Monticciolo's efforts to help D'Amato's friends knew no limits. One of the senator's closest buddies was Michael Puntillo, owner of a Great Neck, Long Island, construction company called JOBCO. As early as 1983, D'Amato tried to obtain for JOBCO a $12 million HUD contract to rehabilitate the low-income Winbrook housing project in White Plains, New York. Work on the 450 run-down units in the nine-story buildings could not begin until Monticciolo gave his approval.

Puntillo had a problem. Polera, a local firm which had done major projects in the area, was low bidder and was chosen by the White Plains Housing Authority. Puntillo's JOBCO was listed in last place. Authority chairman Myron Simon recalled that after the vote JOBCO's agent said, "You haven't heard the last of this."

White Plains mayor Alfred DelVecchio stated that as soon as the vote was in Monticciolo began pressuring him. "I said to Monticciolo, 'If you people want to pick the construction manager, just tell us. Why have us waste six months getting bids?' "

Chairman Simon added, "We found JOBCO incompetent. There's no question that it was being forced down our throat."

Three months later, HUD's regional office informed Chairman Simon that among the bidders only JOBCO was considered qualified. The decision was issued under the signature of Alexander Naclerio, Monticciolo's chief assistant. Naclerio was not part of Monticciolo's inner circle, having been appointed by the previous director. As such, Naclerio represented a threat to D'Amato's control over the New York office. Feeling the heat, Naclerio retired from HUD in 1986 and became a private housing consultant in White Plains. He has since told a congressional committee that Monticciolo ordered him to select JOBCO for the White Plains job.

Worried about Puntillo's political clout and resigned to JOBCO's eventual victory, White Plain officials tried to get Monticciolo to put caps on profits and deadline–pay incentives in the contract; to no avail. Mr. Simon said, "JOBCO didn't negotiate in good faith, and HUD didn't seem to care."

Puntillo began work in 1984; he was supposed to be finished in thirty months but fell further and further behind schedule. The HUD inspector showed no concern. Mr. Simon said that "all through things we felt that there was a higher force behind JOBCO." He told the *New York Times*, "Circumstantial evidence points to D'Amato." He deduced this, he explained, because of common knowledge of strong ties between the senator, HUD's New York office, and JOBCO.

D'Amato made the evidence less circumstantial when he admitted that his office had a role in the White Plains controversy. According to the *Times* D'Amato "said his office's only role was reconciling JOBCO and White Plains when contract negotiations between the two broke down in 1983."

By January 1989, JOBCO had been paid $2.2 million for managing a job on which they had originally bid $600,000. The project was $4 million over budget, three years late, and still, unfinished. The federal government canceled JOBCO's contract, and the project was discontinued. D'Amato's friend Michael Puntillo had been enriched beyond his original expectation, but many of the senator's noncontributing constituents at Winbrook continued to live in wretched conditions.

Another Puntillo-D'Amato arrangement, Sackets Harbor, contains many elements of any deal involving the senator: family benefit, "contributions" in return for favors, the Mafia, HUD milking, indifference to ethical concerns, protestations of innocence in the face of damning evidence to the contrary, and an inability to distinguish the legal from the illegal.

Sackets Harbor is a waterfront hamlet on the shores of Lake Ontario in upstate New York. Its twelve hundred inhabitants live on the eastern end of the lake, two hundred miles from the spectacle of Niagara Falls. The falls attract the attention of the world; Sackets Harbor barely increases its population during what is usually a short but lovely summer. Sackets Harbor, however, caught Al D'Amato's eye.

For one thing, Michael Puntillo had a consuming interest in Sackets Harbor. Puntillo wasn't just the senator's friend. He and his family members had through the years given thousands of dollars to D'Amato's campaigns; he had also organized a fund-raiser for D'Amato that brought in thousands more.

The year of that fund-raiser, 1986, Puntillo decided to build a project in Sackets Harbor. The site was an abandoned army base containing stone barracks built during the War of 1812. Puntillo wanted to put up a resort that included a 100-room country inn, luxury housing reconstructed from the old barracks, a 132-boat marina, and a shopping mall containing boutiques and restaurants. Puntillo needed financing, but the stressed-out S & L banks that in more high-flying days would have backed his speculation were overextended. Puntillo turned to HUD as a likely source of cash. The White Plains deal had shown Puntillo that Monticciolo was amenable to any of his proposals endorsed by D'Amato.

Sackets Harbor treasurer James Yuhas confirmed that Puntillo handled all applications and negotiations for the HUD award. From the beginning, Puntillo's project was "developer driven."

The first sign that D'Amato had zeroed in on Sackets Harbor came in a July 15, 1986, letter that he wrote to Secretary Pierce in which he requested a grant for this most inconspicuous part of his domain. He stated his "strongest support for . . . the application . . . of Sackets Harbor," ending with: "I ask your urgent consideration of this request." Pierce rejected it on a technicality but assured him it would be given consideration in the November funding period.

Puntillo hired Armand Paul D'Amato to deal with HUD. In a November 3, 1986, letter to Puntillo, Armand Paul wrote that the fee for his law firm's services to obtain the HUD grant would come to $150,000.

Alfonse's next public effort on behalf of Puntillo's resort appeared in a March 4, 1987, Thomas Demery memo to Deborah Gore Dean. In it Demery remarked that "Senator D'Amato's requests" included "Sacketts [sic] Harbor, N.Y., 50 [housing units]." After Demery had been chastised by D'Amato in his Senate office on March 19, 1987, Sackets Harbor, along with the more munificent Puerto Rican grants, was approved. However, D'Amato's Sackets Harbor plans were again blocked when Monticciolo passed Demery's approval along to HUD's Buffalo office. Buffalo manager Joseph B. Lynch rejected it. "It came through, and it was a big surprise to us," Lynch explained. "There is no Sackets Harbor Housing Authority." It was the same *lack-of-housing-authority-sponsorship* hang-up that got Demery into difficulty with D'Amato.

In an endeavor to break the deadlock, Puntillo applied for an Urban Development Action Grant and a low-interest Section 312 rehabilitation loan, which Congress had set aside to be used in assisting individual homeowners. These programs did not require the input of a local housing agency and since 1984 were made solely on the basis of Secretary Pierce's discretionary powers.

New York City had applied for the same Section 312 funds to revive ailing homeowner neighborhoods. The city had received $3 million under the program in 1987–88 and depended on it to meet commitments made in several deteriorating neighborhoods. Months before Puntillo applied for the Sackets Harbor grant Monticciolo had told Abraham Biderman, New York City's housing commissioner, that he would receive an increase in Section 312 support.

In October 1987, Monticciolo informed Biderman that New York City wasn't going to get the 312 funds. Biderman was disappointed but attributed the change in plans to a shrinking Reagan housing budget. Two months later, Monticciolo announced that Puntillo's Sackets Harbor resort would receive $6.5 millions. It was the second-largest package of loans given in 1988 under the Section 312 program. Unlike New York City's proposal, Puntillo's project was not aimed at lower-income families. "They are basically restoring buildings to restore buildings," Sackets Harbor mayor Vincent Capozzella said, describing Puntillo's plans. "The fact that people are going to live there is an afterthought."

Biderman was outraged; the grants were "incredible." He said: "We had a large, successful program. Many people went through a complicated process to document our needs and costs. Then we were just left hanging out there. We could've met all our commitments and then some with what they gave to a village of twelve hundred people."

Puntillo quickly formed a partnership with Inner City Drywall, a New Rochelle carpentry firm once owned by reputed mobster Vincent DiNapoli, then under indictment in Manhattan on conspiracy and bribery charges. Antonio Rodriguez had taken DiNapoli's place as president of Inner City Drywall. In August 1989, Rodriguez was indicted on racketeering charges. The Manhattan district attorney alleged that Rodriguez had paid $9,000 in bribes to union officials. Inner City Drywall was also charged in the indictment. It was described by a state law enforcement agency as controlled by the Genovese crime family.

Armand Paul's law firm handled all of the partnership's dealings with HUD. The firm applied for and received several waivers, including one that exempted the village from requiring bids. Armand Paul obtained another unusual HUD concession: HUD agreed to divide the package into forty-five separate agreements. In a December 5, 1988, letter to HUD, Armand Paul's firm said that the breakup of the loan was needed to take advantage of federal tax laws.

Al D'Amato, through spokeswoman Zenia Mucha, claimed to be unaware that his brother had done any legal work for the Sackets Harbor project. Proclaiming the innocence of her boss, Mucha said that D'Amato "was not personally aware" of the HUD awards to Sackets Harbor. It was possible, she conceded, that at some point HUD had been targeted with a "pro forma letter of support."

In the face of the overwhelming need for low-income housing and the decline in money available, Al D'Amato had siphoned off a large percentage of HUD funds to create a luxury development in the wilderness.

On the surface, efforts to perfect the Stirling experimental engine seemed to be a worthwhile way to respond to the 1970s Middle East oil crisis. The engine was named after a Scottish minister, Rev. Robert Stirling, who patented the prototype in 1816. Its great attraction was that it ran on any fuel: Texas sweet crude, olive oil, or bathtub gin. But for 175 years many engineers had unsuccessfully tried to perfect it. It was too large to put in passenger cars. It cost too much to build and operate; its hydrogen cooling system leaked so that it had to be refilled, and parts had to be replaced every week.

But none of this was certifiable in 1976 when the Department of Energy awarded a contract to Ford Motors to see if a useful Stirling engine could be developed. Two years later, Mechanical Technology Inc. (MTI) of Albany, New York, a firm that worked with gears and bearings, also received a contract to perfect the Stirling engine. Ford was required to supply its own money; MTI sought and got Department of Energy funding.

By 1980 the worst fears about the Stirling were realized. Ford discontinued its four years of experimentation. The General Motors (GM) director of research, after reviewing MTI's engine several times in 1980, stated, "It has not shown competitive fuel economy. And it is too big." GM announced it had given up on Stirlings.

Because of the lack of progress, federal funding for MTI was about to be shut off. At this point, MTI's chairman, Harry Apkarian, decided if science wasn't a compelling enough reason to fund his company's efforts, politics might be. Since New York's new senator had a reputation for defending the interests of his contributors, in March 1981, Apkarian gave a $1,000 check to D'Amato's campaign fund. The company's representative later explained that they wanted to be "first in the door."

D'Amato quickly showed his appreciation. Reagan was proposing to cut $3.1 million from MTI's Stirling research as part of his attempt to reduce the deficit. In a no-holds-barred fight, D'Amato beat back the cuts and actually won funding for an MTI generator unrelated to the Stirling engine. This happened while Reagan was cutting appropriations to New York that meant the loss of billions, cuts D'Amato enthusiastically supported.

Apkarian was so grateful that the following year he arranged an Albany fund-raiser for D'Amato. The senator expressed his pleasure with Apkarian's effort and asked him to conduct a series of similar events. Apkarian happily complied and soon gained a reputation for being D'Amato's Albany money man. "I don't think it's stretching it that I could bring out $100,000 in one night," Apkarian bragged.

It was important for Apkarian to keep D'Amato content. By 1982 the government had spent $60 million on Stirling, yet no working model had been successfully tested. At that point, the Office of Management and Budget recommended an end to the program. The assistant secretary of the Department of Energy told Congress that his agency could find "no reason for the federal government to continue to spend money on the Stirling engine."

Although the Department of Energy annually opposed any further funding of the program, claiming there was no prospect of getting the engine into wide-scale use, D'Amato always managed to overcome White House opposition. From his position on the Appropriations Committee he successfully lobbied to gain funding approval for $13 million in 1983 and $14 million in 1984. In 1985, the year after the program was originally supposed to end, D'Amato obtained $23 million for additional "research work."

Apkarian always knew that he was skating on thin ice with D'Amato. When asked about the quality of D'Amato's friendship, he responded realistically, "If you ask me if he'd do as much [without fund-raising], maybe not."

It wasn't as if the Senate were unaware of MTI's inability to produce a workable engine. Experts had visited the monster in its Albany work shed, surrounded by puzzled engineers, and then reported to Washington that the breath of life didn't course through its external cylinders. Sen. Bennett Johnston (D-La) described D'Amato's project as pouring money "right down the rat hole." D'Amato was certainly willing to trade his vote on some other senator's pork-barrel project for an additional year of MTI funding.

Apkarian continued working just as hard for the senator. In June 1988 he held a fund-raiser that brought in *at least* $17,725. The caveat is raised about the total because the report only listed offerings of $200 to $1,000, but there was one executive who was quoted as saying that he attended several of Apkarian's functions for D'Amato and at times he gave $100 at the door. Such donations were not reported.

The next month, July 1988, D'Amato made an impassioned plea to the Appropriations Committee to approve one final year of funding. One million dollars was granted, bringing the total since D'Amato entered the Senate to $78.3 million and the overall total to $140 million. Rolf Meyer, an engineer considered a pioneer in Stirling technology, who had struggled for over a decade to get his firm a total of $1 million in funding, complained, "They've [MTI] gotten nearly all the [research] money. We don't know how that was possible, but it was." On April 9, 1989, William Beale, a former MTI consultant, in a statement to the New York *Daily News* summed up what D'Amato's special pleading had accomplished. It was "an utter waste. An absolutely obscene use of taxpayer money."

FORTY-EIGHT
AL'S DOOMED LEMMINGS

On June 8, 1989, two weeks after the *Wall Street Journal* labeled him "the senator from Puerto Rico," Al D'Amato's world was on the verge of collapse. The *New York Times* printed a front-page story by Michael Winerip that went beyond the HUD Puerto Rican scandal and coolly reported the wider nature of his corruption. Winerip's exposé appeared in the midst of the Giuliani-Lauder war. It reported on Jeffrey Pless's squashed 1984 HUD audit of D'Amato's illegal distribution of forty-four Island Park homes.

Assistant U.S. Attorney Lawrence Noyer described the impact of Winerip's story. "Bob Begleiter came into my office with a copy of the paper and said, 'We've got to do something about this.' When you see something like that, and you hadn't known about it and the *Times* article is quoting verbatim from an internal HUD investigating report that had been done in 1984, this is not just one or two people running to a newspaper and making allegations. This was facts created by the agency itself. Yet it had lain there for five years. That was the beginning of it."

Noyer was referring to a civil suit that his office began preparing that day against twenty-two officials and residents of Island Park. "By the time these matters came to our attention, the five-year federal statute of limitations had passed. So there was nothing we could do criminally." But, he added, " . . . the claim of housing discrimination under the civil rights act has no statute of limitations at all."

Why, after five years, had this story suddenly appeared? Winerip explained that "a copy of the HUD audit was anonymously mailed to the *Times*." Annette Snow, who was still trying to interest media people in D'Amato's Island Park HUD swindle, got a call from Winerip as he prepared the June 8 story. He wanted information about the material in the audit. "He said he had gotten a tip about the audit," she recalled. "My first suspicion was that Giuliani was trying to get D'Amato off his back, and what better way than to start a big investigation."

After speaking to Annette, Winerip contacted Harry Scully, the retired village clerk, a different Scully than the dutiful clerk who had scratched his quill pen across the village ledgers for thirty-one years. Harry had had a falling out with D'Amato; it was entirely personal.

When Harry was thinking about retiring, his wife, Roberta, decided to make up for his diminished pensioner's income by going into the real estate business. Since Island Park had only one major real estate office, owned by one of D'Amato's closest supporters, the senator was displeased. He called the village clerk and berated him for allowing Roberta to contemplate such an act of treachery. Their children were grown; their mortgage was paid off; they didn't need the money. Why were they being so greedy?

Harry's Irish temper exploded. This was his personal life. It had nothing to do with being village clerk, and he'd appreciate it if the senator minded his own business.

Soon stories were being told that Harry, who was also village recorder of death certificates at $5,000 per annum, was calling his wife in her Century 21 office when someone died and telling her to scramble over to the deceased's house to see if she could get a listing. It was the kind of calumny bound to permanently infuriate Harry. After he retired in 1985, he spoke with candor and repugnance about the way D'Amato ran the village and began to encourage insurgents in the Integrity party to fight the senator.

When reporter Michael Winerip caught up with him in early June 1989, Scully was anxious to tell him what he knew about D'Amato's corrupt distribution of the HUD houses. Scully admitted he did not tell the truth in the 1984 letter he wrote for HUD's counsel Steven Love absolving Geraldine McGann of using Island Park subsidized housing to help D'Amato's friends. He said he had written it, offering the Eichmann defense, "because I was told to. I was an employee of the village, and I just followed orders."

In his more candid retirement role, Scully said that trustee McGann *had* exerted pressure on him to get her unmarried son Daniel his house. "I received a phone call from her stating that her son was thinking of applying for a HUD house. She said she checked it out with someone in HUD and there was no conflict. My response was: 'Then go for it.' "

Scully said Mrs. McGann knew he had never approved the application of an unmarried person. She also knew he had been instructed by HUD to select people from the preexisting list of the 120, which didn't contain her son's name. He therefore concluded she was politely ordering him to give her son a house regardless of whether it violated directives issued by her agency.

Contradicting what he had previously said, Harry Scully told Winerip that Mrs. McGann *had* endorsed giving houses to people on D'Amato's list. She had also voted on a number of HUD issues in direct conflict with her status as a HUD official. "We bailed her out," Scully said, revealing that he had changed the record on her HUD votes. "She voted when she shouldn't have."

Mrs. McGann stuck to her story. When the *Times* discovered that she had voted on a new set of Island Park HUD issues at least three times in 1988, she maintained her composure and continued to take the same position, "I did not vote on any HUD-related matters, never."

Scully told Winerip that despite D'Amato's denials he had repeatedly checked the list of applicants, approving some and blackballing others.

Even after he became a senator, D'Amato continued his tightfisted control of the village. He frequently called Scully with instructions for local officials.

I asked Noyer whether he believed Scully's accusations. He said, "It was my belief as a U.S. Attorney that he was at all times truthful and forthcoming with us."

Noyer referred to Scully's deposition under oath in which he stated "that the selection of houses had been influenced by outsiders. In that respect," Noyer observed, "Al D'Amato was no different than any outsider for purposes of our legal theory. . . . The village board allowed themselves to be influenced in the selection of owners by those who should have had no influence in that selection."

I told Noyer that I had seen a copy of the civil complaint and that it was obvious to me that D'Amato's name, after having been listed, had been whited out. "That's correct," he admitted. "We played around with the question whether there was a civil legal theory that . . . was properly pursued against Senator D'Amato in court. And in an effort to analyze that, I drafted a complaint naming him as a defendant and put in legal claims that we would assert against him."

Noyer had shown a good deal of courage in even considering the possibility of indicting his boss's patron but finally concluded "It was not a proper claim to assert against a United States senator."

By June 1989 it was realistic to describe Al D'Amato as the de facto head of HUD. Before he left to become a private "consultant," Alexander Naclerio, a top executive in the New York office, told the House Government Operations Subcommittee on September 27, 1989, that D'Amato's control over the regional office was complete. "Monticciolo always told me he cleared things with him [D'Amato]."

Naclerio said that Monticciolo kept a list of priority projects that D'Amato wanted funded; New York City's official requests were on a separate list. Before Monticciolo made a major decision, Naclerio testified, he used a phone on his desk with a direct connection to the senator's office so he could gain clearance expeditiously. They were "extremely close," according to Naclerio, often meeting on weekends and after office hours.

When Monticciolo left office in January 1988, D'Amato lobbied to sidetrack Secretary Pierce's proposed replacement and had an even closer ally, the more pliant Geraldine McGann, selected as regional director. He now had the Washington and New York offices filled with friends and ex-members of his staff.

- Donna Kaufman, his secretary from 1981 to 1983, about whom rumors of personal involvement with D'Amato had surfaced in the press, was placed by him in HUD's pivotal Washington office of congressional liaison. That contact allowed him to stay in touch with day-to-day developments in the department.

- Jerome Blue, after three years of working as D'Amato's administrative assistant, moved to HUD in 1987 as Monticciolo's executive assistant and D'Amato's personal watchdog. Within a month of the transfer memos released by the Housing Subcommittee reveal that Blue and Monticciolo pressured the Washington office to fund D'Amato's Puerto Rican projects.

- Susan Zagame became a deputy assistant secretary of HUD in 1985. She was the wife of John Zagame, D'Amato's first chief of staff from 1980 to 1984 and D'Amato's campaign aide in 1986.

John Zagame played an increasing role in D'Amato's money harvesting. In 1989 he helped organize the Committee for New York while a Washington lobbyist and political consultant to D'Amato. In one year he raised $160,000, most of it spent to pay D'Amato's speechwriters, aides, and pollsters. One of those speechwriters was former navy secretary James Webb, to whom Armand Paul's 1987 Unisys letter had been addressed while Webb was in the process of deciding who would get the Aegis contract. Zagame's committee paid Webb $5,000 for writing one speech for D'Amato. The Committee for New York also paid Ron Finkelstein, head of D'Amato's personal polling firm, $60,000 in 1989. *Newsday*'s investigating team, which uncovered the story, commented: "All but $8,500 of the money raised [by Zagame] would have been barred by the Federal Election Commission from being contributed to D'Amato. . . ." Most of the contributors had already made the maximum amount of contributions to the senator's campaign committees. Zagame was handling a back-door operation that funneled "soft money" to D'Amato.

The teamwork of D'Amato's HUD allies was best described by New York's HUD economist David S. Burns in an interview he gave to the *Times* on October 26, 1989. He was a career civil servant who had worked for the agency for twenty years; it was his duty to evaluate potential housing sites and determine project feasibility. In 1987 and 1988 he reviewed two Manhattan projects with ties to D'Amato, both of which he decided to reject.

The 1987 proposal was to build a senior citizens development on the Lower East Side. "It was a low-income area with an overriding concentration of assisted housing," he said, adding that he only rejected a site if it was "a complete disaster."

Mr. Burns wasn't overstating the area's problems. It was one of the worst slums in the country, infested by drug addicts and victimized by violent crimes, especially against the elderly.

After Burns filed his rejection, he was summoned by Geraldine McGann, who showed him a memo supporting the East Ninth Street and Avenue C site. There was also a letter at the agency from D'Amato strongly endorsing the project. Burns resisted Mrs. McGann's demand that he reverse his decision, saying only that he would seek another opinion. An agency analyst reviewed the site and filed a report agreeing with Burns.

"Then Monticciolo told me we were going to take a ride and look at the site," Burns told the *New York Times*. "And took along McGann and Jerry Blue." Burns knew of their direct connection to D'Amato. "They really wanted this project for whatever reason. We hadn't left the garage when Gerry McGann said to me, 'David, try to be objective.' I said, 'You try to be objective.' Monticciolo told me to shut up."

The view of the devastation on the Lower East Side quieted D'Amato's friends. Burns described them as being glum. They returned to the office in silence. But two weeks later Monticciolo's spine had been stiffened. He told Burns, "Look, David, you're going to have to change your recommendation."

Burns confessed that he had "caved in." On August 26, 1987, Monticciolo announced that the project was approved and was on Secretary Pierce's "discretionary list" for funding. The best surprise was kept for last. A few months later it was announced that JOBCO of Great Neck, represented by its counsel, Armand Paul D'Amato, had been chosen as general contractor. In a city filled with capable builders looking for work, Michael Puntillo's out-of-town firm had not been required to submit a competitive bid.

The second time Burns was coerced by Geraldine McGann the tie to Al D'Amato was more personal. It involved a project on

105th Street and First Avenue in Manhattan sponsored by the New York Foundation for Senior Citizens. The project had originally been approved by Monticciolo in 1985, but Washington HUD—alerted by the 1984 audit of Island Park's swindle—was so displeased with Monticciolo's selections that it revised the 1985 list, eliminating the foundation's project as well as several others. This was an unprecedented Washington rebuke to Monticciolo, since it had never intervened in HUD's nine other regional offices.

Later that year, D'Amato's mother, Antoinette, and his former aide, Deborah Smith Bernstein, joined the board of directors of the New York Foundation for Senior Citizens. Mrs. McGann and the two ladies knew each other very well. During Al's 1980 election campaign they had traveled together around the state, the two women acting as companions for the senator's mother.

The foundation's project was resubmitted. Monticciolo again wanted it approved but had to contend with the possibility of another humiliating Washington turndown. Burns, who described himself as a man of malleable disposition, was assigned by Monticciolo to evaluate the project. After a careful review, he rejected it, calling the area dangerous. Most of the neighborhood consisted of abandoned houses. The rest "was ninety percent subsidized housing. It wasn't a place for the elderly," he said.

Burns said he began to get pressure from Mrs. McGann to change his evaluation. It was obvious to him that Monticciolo wanted the cover of his expert opinion to help the foundation's badly located project escape Washington's scrutiny. Without his endorsement, Burns said, "Monticciolo would have had to provide something in the record, and Washington would be able to look at it. He'd rather have his technicians lie for him."

Burns again caved in, explaining, "When you're in any organization, you want to belong and not just be considered an outcast. And I hate to admit it, the bonus system was a factor."

When Geraldine McGann became head of HUD's New York office in 1988, she used the "bonus" carrot to change Burns's opinion about three new projects. This time his initial rejection was overturned with even greater ease. At year's end, Burns received an "outstanding" evaluation from Mrs. McGann, his first in twenty years. He also received his largest bonus, nearly $2,000. Mrs. McGann said she was very happy with Burns. "She told me I was loyal," Burns recalled. "It made me almost sad. I felt that I had to some extent prostituted myself, and I was getting a bonus."

D'Amato issued statements denying he had ever tried to influence anyone about any project. Usually in a few days some newspaper using the Freedom of Information Act uncovered a letter that he had written bluntly exerting influence for projects in which his mother or brother had an interest or for which his major contributors later became the contractors.

During a December 7, 1989, interview on WABC radio, D'Amato attempted another bogus defense. "By the way, no one comes forward and says, 'D'Amato supported a bad project, something was wrong with it.' No!" Two months earlier, on the front page of the October 26 *New York Times*, the HUD economist had accused D'Amato's allies of forcing him to approve two flawed projects that would have made senior citizens prisoners in violent communities. Burns charged that in the fifteen years he had been evaluating proposals these D'Amato projects were "the worst sites I'm aware of that were approved."

Cong. Jack Kemp, a politician with a reputation for honesty, was brought into the cabinet by President Bush to succeed the disgraced Samuel Pierce. Soon after, he said, "Some of these people [at HUD] should go to jail." He pledged a cleanup of what he described as HUD's "swamp." Al D'Amato owned the deed to the deepest part of that swamp. An audit of the New York regional office revealed that between 1986 and 1988 two-thirds of the approved senior citizens projects had at least one major developer who was a D'Amato contributor.

Kemp knew D'Amato's flagrant tampering with HUD had to stop, but trying to end it presented him with a sticky political problem. President Bush needed every vote Republicans could muster in a Democratic-controlled Senate. Bush occasionally depended on D'Amato, who stayed close to the party line, to provide the margin required. Action to curb such a man would require finesse. In an effort to diminish D'Amato's influence, Kemp transferred control of Puerto Rico and the Virgin Islands to the Atlanta office.

Kemp's cautious hand was forced by Winerip's June 8, 1989, HUD exposé. The next day, Kemp announced, "I have asked the

inspector general to reopen his investigation of the situation surrounding Geraldine McGann and the allocation of subsidized housing in the Village of Island Park." He also placed Mrs. McGann on
paid leave of absence. A week later, Mrs. McGann resigned as village trustee, citing Kemp's directive that "prohibits employees of
the department to hold local or state office."

A four-month departmental investigation of Mrs. McGann
seemed aimed at not upsetting her neighbor, Senator D'Amato,
who still had so much power over HUD. The department report
found "suspicious and disturbing facts" about how the houses had
been distributed but no "direct evidence that she called or requested" that her son obtain a house. Scully's word was apparently not
"direct" evidence, although his original lies on behalf of Mrs.
McGann had been enough to clear her.

Inspector general offices exist to ferret out wrongdoers.
However, they are fundamentally in business to protect the reputation of their agencies. If exposure of the culprits will make the
agency look good, the inspector general can be expected to beat
his drum loudly, but since the mud from most scandals splatters all
in the vicinity, the inspector general's drums are usually muffled; it
was so in Geraldine McGann's case.

After reading the deftly balanced inspector general's report, the
agency's counsel decided that Mrs. McGann had voted on several
HUD-related matters in Island Park despite instructions by HUD's
lawyer not to do so. He also said that he "did not accept Mrs.
McGann's explanation that her votes were improperly recorded."
HUD's counsel then tossed the hot potato to Andrew Maloney and
Denis Dillon, noting that the U.S. Attorney and Nassau County dis-
trict attorney were both conducting "investigations."

Secretary Kemp, a conservative who often avowed concern for
society's orphans, told reporters, "She will not be beheaded."
Pending action by Maloney and Dillon, she was being removed as
regional director, transferred to Washington, but would continue
receiving her full salary, $68,572. Kemp was clearly seeking a polit-
ical solution to a criminal problem.

A year later, on November 16, 1990, in the absence of any action
by Maloney or Dillon, Kemp's office announced that Mrs. McGann
had been demoted from management rank and transferred to a
field office in Newark, New Jersey. Her salary had been cut by

$18,000 to $55,381 after an audit found that she had violated HUD's "standards of conduct," the exact charge made by Jeffrey Pless in his 1984 audit, a charge that for six years had not caught the attention of any inspector general.

Kemp's mild treatment of Geraldine McGann came a little more than three weeks before Harry Scully gave his sworn deposition to prosecutors about Mrs. McGann's role in the Island Park scandal. But it was Scully's revelations in his 395-page deposition about D'Amato's control of all elements of that scandal that made sensational reading.

Scully gave his deposition in Brooklyn before the defendant's counsel and Lawrence Noyer in two full-day sessions on December 13 and 17, 1990. After months of editorial criticism from the New York press, U.S. Attorney Andrew Maloney had finally recused himself from the Island Park investigation and given Noyer some scope to indict everyone in the village—except his mentor, Al D'Amato.

Scully testified that the premature beginning of the race for the first five HUD houses in 1980, before the starting pistol had been fired, was not accidental. A week before the houses were advertised, he was told by D'Amato's minions on the village board to "tip off" those who were to be selected. Scully had called the well-placed candidates, including four of his relatives, and told them that the early birds would find their worm under his door.

The prosecutor asked Scully, "Did you understand that act would subvert the process that HUD had required with regard to advertisements?"

Scully responded, "Yes."

The former village clerk told Noyer that two of D'Amato's cousins had been selected by him at the senator's insistence. "Al D'Amato came in the office and said he wanted his cousins to get a house," Scully deposed. "He looked at the list and said, 'I want Mr. and Mrs. Sniffen and Mr. and Mrs. Ciccimarro to get homes.' "

Furthermore, Scully told the prosecutor, in "late '79 or early '80" D'Amato picked the builder for the first five houses, Harold Lituchy, one of his most reliable contributors. Even *after* D'Amato was elected to the Senate in "1982–83" he reviewed with Scully the specific sites on which the homes were to be built.

No one got a house without D'Amato's careful scrutiny. Politics and family connections were the central considerations, but whim also played a role. Scully gave as an example a tow-truck operator whom he had tentatively approved for a house. D'Amato said no when he saw his name on the list. The guy was hardworking and a lifelong resident of the village, but the master of Island Park had the feeling that he *might* leave his tow truck in his driveway, and this was enough reason for D'Amato to exercise his veto.

Scully charged that despite D'Amato's and McGann's pledges to provide seventeen houses for minority members, they had no intention of allowing a black family into Island Park. "They wanted to provide homes for their residents and to keep blacks out."

D'Amato's standards for acceptability were actually much more restrictive. You not only had to be a resident; you had to be the senator's political supporter or a well-connected relative. Large numbers of white Island Park residents did not fall into either category.

Scully testified that his former deputy clerk, Ann Leonard, was present when D'Amato came to his office and decreed how the HUD units were to be distributed, including when he reserved two houses for his cousins. Ms. Leonard, now the village clerk, invoked her Fifth Amendment rights against self-incrimination and refused to answer the prosecutor's questions.

Throughout D'Amato's public career there were people who had lined up to take their turn to lose their reputation and their livelihood, who had even gone to jail so that Al D'Amato could escape unscathed. Ann Leonard and a phalanx of Island Park lemmings now joined the doomed line.

FORTY-NINE

A NIGHT IN ISLAND PARK

The night of August 16, 1990, a tense crowd gathered on the sidewalk outside the village hall for the monthly meeting of the village board. Their leader, George Ficke, head of the Integrity party, said they were there because they "refused to take it anymore." At eight o'clock Ficke's community warriors marched into the citadel of their adversaries and seated themselves in rows of folding chairs.

At this congregation of the ruled and their rulers, members of the Integrity party temporarily outnumbered Al D'Amato's surrogates in the Unity party. The senator's stalwarts had not emerged in numbers, since many of them were under investigation by Larry Noyer's federal prosecutors and therefore cautiously apportioned the time they devoted to public appearances.

George Ficke is six feet two and nobody's fool. He speaks boldly, with wit and eloquence. He waged the first campaign against D'Amato's candidate for mayor in 1986 and knows that village meetings often resemble a gladiator arena in which combatants strike each other with bloody intent and discourse is interspersed with howls. Will Ficke's friends be heard? Absolutely. Will they change village policy? A doubtful proposition.

Ficke had lived in the village since 1967 and managed one of the marinas that nestle in the coves. He owned a modest house in a hamlet in which only an occasional grandee has a mansion. Nearby live Al D'Amato and his long-suffering wife, Penny, who by legal certification occupy separate bedrooms under a common roof. He has told reporters that he sleeps on a bed in the basement. Appearances have always been important to the politically ambitious, and to a man of D'Amato's professed religious orthodoxy, it is easier to maintain the appearance of a conventional marriage than it is to defy the church and its multitude of voters by obtaining a divorce from the mother of his four children.

The village board members sit on a raised dais facing the discontented: the mayor—matronly blond Jackie Papatsos—and four trustees. They are newly empowered. The previous board members were all entangled with the 1989 HUD scandal, and since those local potentates have been summoned before the bar of justice in Assistant U.S. Attorney Noyer's civil rights suit, D'Amato has seen fit to replace them with allies equally reliable but visibly unstained.

"The Star-Spangled Banner" was sung with gusto by the congregation. The drunk at the rear slurred everything but *"the bombs bursting in air."* Ficke's Integrity party stalwarts leaned forward in their chairs as Mayor Papatsos called on trustees to report on items for which they were responsible. The discontented waited, for the rule in this congress is that the agenda is completed before the citizenry is allowed to express an opinion.

For twenty minutes the prim lady village clerk sat on the dais reading various proposed local laws and noted the unanimous vote by which they all passed. Their thrust seemed uniformly to protect Mrs. McGann and previous board members against any loss they might suffer if an increasingly aggressive Noyer obtained their convictions, to pay lawyer's fees arising from the village's complicity in an assortment of HUD felonies, and to authorize bond issues that would raise the money to settle these obligations. The Island Park way of paying for all but the most ordinary expenses is to issue a bond, the theory being that today's voters are likely to protest any increased taxes, while a bond issue shifts that onerous duty to persons beyond the political horizon whose protests will be inaudible to those politicians who have saddled them with debt.

As soon as Mayor Papatsos signaled that the important part of the meeting was concluded, Roberta Scully rose to her feet. Roberta was there to represent her husband, Harry. Harry stays at home during these monthly confrontations: He is the chief witness against D'Amato and saves his energy for judicial appearances. In the conspiratorial world of Island Park, Harry Scully reasons that a thrust from an enemy's stiletto is always possible, and he mostly remains hidden behind his drawn venetian blinds.

Roberta is a steady gray-haired woman, slender, with a quick smile, who seems to be without fear. Her decision to open a real estate business in direct competition with D'Amato's ally proved her valor. She needs an intrepid spirit, because people D'Amato dislikes have occasionally had their houses defaced or, as during the Black Removal era, demolished, and the senator doesn't merely dislike the Scullys; he despises them.

Roberta firmly but politely asked Mayor Papatsos why Island Park citizens who had no role in the corruption surrounding the HUD crimes were being taxed for the wages of other people's sins.

Mayor Papatsos glanced at her watch as Mrs. Scully spoke. The squires of Island Park have legislated a limit on each speaker's time: three minutes, and it was clear that the mayor was attentive to nothing more in Roberta Scully's oration than the pending expiration of her time.

The mayor's answer was a model of memorized legalisms, and the pallid, balding, palsied village lawyer of many decades sitting in the front row nodded in approval. All questions addressed to barrister Jules St. Germaine during the evening were answered by the mayor.

George Ficke rose to ask the mayor about the liability policy obtained by the village's insurance broker Armand D'Amato Sr. Why had it been canceled just at the time that Island Park was being sued and most needed its protection? The answer: Armand Sr. hadn't told the underwriting insurance issuer about the potential liability the village had because of its HUD manipulations, and therefore the company canceled the policy when the *New York Times* supplied the information Armand had withheld. Hundreds of thousands in annual premium payments had been wasted while village residents lived under the illusion that Armand's expensive policy protected them.

However, the mayor wasn't interested in explaining any of this. She continued to be absorbed with concern about the three-minute rule and provided an evasive answer that lasted only until Ficke's time had expired.

Roberta Scully again claimed the floor, and it became apparent that the strategy of the members of the Integrity party was to conduct themselves as though they were playing a Ping-Pong game; the ball, which took three minutes to get from one side of the net to the other, was in constant motion; first Roberta Scully swung her verbal racket, then George Ficke; then some other person of integrity kept the ball flying.

Each time Mrs. Scully spoke, the drunk in the back of the room taunted her. "Canary!" he growled. "You're a canary!" This referred to Harry's singing to the prosecutor. For some in Island Park the code of honor does not allow citizens to speak to this instrument of the carabinieri. Several times the heckler lurched out of his seat and made a menacing thrust in Roberta's direction.

At the end of the forty-five minute meeting George Ficke's forces had made no impact on village affairs. Members of the Integrity party followed their leader out to the sidewalk. Ficke remarked, "This is what we go through every month. You never get a straight answer." He characterized the meeting as "a mild one."

Roberta Scully told me she was proud that so many residents were willing to confront D'Amato's cohorts. Harry's fight, she explained, was being waged in a different venue, where D'Amato would eventually testify under oath, possibly under indictment.

Hugh Roehrig, who was the Integrity party candidate for mayor in 1989, wanted it understood that D'Amato's forces had been on their best behavior because they had seen a stranger in their midst. "Politics in this town can get pretty rough," he said. "During the campaign last year they paint-bombed my house, and a couple of my windshields were knocked out."

In Ficke's group there were strong statements made about how the town had been oppressed by D'Amato and his clubhouse allies. Fears were voiced that he might manage to escape, leaving his minions to take the fall, but there was almost no sympathy expressed for Mrs. McGann now that retribution seemed to be catching up with her.

Yet even among D'Amato's enemies there was an occasional expression of pity for his HUD aparatchik. Catherine Fazio had watched Geraldine McGann grow up, get married, have children. She knew Geraldine's father as one of the few Democrats in the village, a close friend of her husband, Jim. During the last few years, when commuting to her apartment in Manhattan, Catherine had often traveled with Geraldine on the Long Island Railroad. "We talked mostly about family. Never about D'Amato. She should have known better. The conflict was right out there. But I can't help feeling that she was manipulated."

FIFTY

HIS FRIENDS
CALL HIM RICHIE

Richard Rodriguez would have liked to share Catherine Fazio's sympathy for Geraldine McGann—his mother schooled him in the need to forgive your enemy—but his normal good nature wasn't capable of meeting such a demand on it.

Richie, thirty-seven had lived in Island Park since he was ten. He was always hardworking, first as a shoeshine boy with his younger sister when he was nine in the Long Island Railroad station in Long Beach, then, between the ages of thirteen and eighteen, as a counterman at the Village Luncheonette, and in 1991 as a longtime Federal Express employee at Kennedy Airport.

Rodriguez was an anomaly in Island Park: a Hispanic married to an Italian, imbued with love of the village, who thought, "naively," he now says, that he was accepted. He coached the Little League, was head of the auxiliary police, and radiated optimism about life. "I've always been lucky with people. They always trusted me. That was the way I was raised. My mother says, 'Never hurt anybody and always have respect.' "

"Richie," as he is known to most people, was a longtime admirer of the D'Amatos. Armand used to breakfast every day at the Village Luncheonette, which was only a couple of blocks from his house. Richie remembered him as "a sharp-looking gentleman with a wax mustache with points on the end" who liked to wear black cashmere winter coats and black fedoras.

Richie also remembered Armand's order. "He had a bagel or a corn muffin. Every time he came in he didn't even make it to the counter before I had his coffee there for him. And he said, 'Good morning, Rickie.' He always called me Rickie. And I like the name. I had a lot of respect for him."

Rodriguez said the patriarch of the D'Amatos was an isolated man. "Every time I saw him walking, it was by himself. Every time he came to the luncheonette, it was by himself."

Richie's relationship with Alfonse was more distant; when passing him, D'Amato would wave mechanically. But he never stopped to talk, as he did with almost anyone else. Richie was not offended. He went about his business, trying to earn respect.

One of the great thrills in his life came in the late 1970s, when D'Amato was Hempstead supervisor. There was a bad snowstorm, and Richie, in his capacity as the nonpaid head of the auxiliary police, had been picking up stranded police officers and nurses to take them to work. "I just dropped my partner off after working twelve hours straight," Rodriguez said proudly. "He [Alfonse] beeped the horn and rolled down his car window and said, 'By the way Mr. Rodriguez, you're doing a fantastic job. Keep up the good work.'

"It shocked me," Rodriguez admitted. "I couldn't wait to come home to my wife and tell her. 'You're not going to believe this. Mr. D. Amato [sic—common pronunciation of D'Amato's last name in his hometown] said I was doing a fantastic job.'"

Although the senator's house can be reached by jumping over Rodriguez's fence—"he's just on the other side of the street"—and D'Amato's daughter, Lisa, whom Al visits Sundays, lives next door to Rodriguez, over a decade passed before D'Amato spoke another word to his admirer.

It was shortly after the snowstorm that Richie got word about the HUD houses. "I believe I heard about it from the very beginning, because my office was right next door to the mayor's in the village hall."

It wasn't that he was being taken into anyone's confidence. "If you live in Island Park, you know one thing," Rodriguez said. "Everyone keeps their mouth shut. The CIA should have such good security. I believed then, and now, it's like a code of silence."

But it was hard to maintain perfect silence in a building as small as the town hall. "All I heard was rumors. 'There's going to be a new program.' Men talking back and forth. And I was happy. This was going to be my chance to get a home."

"I began to ask Mayor Parente about it. He said, 'It isn't a matter of public record, but Rickie [sic], don't worry about it. Guaranteed you're going to get one. Just keep doing a good job.' "

He spoke to trustee Francis R. McGinty, who told him, "Richie, you know the senator. Why don't you go see him." Richie held off. "I wasn't really that close to Mr. D. Amato. I didn't know the ropes."

Rodriguez was shut out of the first section, but when rumors circulated that more houses were going up, he anxiously began his efforts again. This time he didn't depend on informal contacts with village officials. He wrote to Scully asking for information and an application. Scully wrote back advising him to read an ad that was to appear in *Newsday.* On the day the ad appeared, "I got up at six. The ink wasn't dry on the paper. I went to Scully as soon as the place opened up. I was the only person there. I told him, 'I went to get the first paper, and I'm here to apply for a house.' He said, 'They're gone already.' I said, 'Wait a minute. How could they be gone? It just came out.' I didn't know they'd all slipped their applications under the door."

Even while Rodriguez was being deceived, D'Amato continued to wave when they passed on the street. Now that all the houses were taken, Richie settled down with his family in the bottom-floor apartment of his uncle's house. There was only one bedroom, which he and his wife, Lavinia, shared with their three children.

That room also contains a homemade altar. Although he is deeply religious—he wears a crucifix ring on his right pinkie and a St. Christopher's medal on a gold chain around his neck—Richie no longer goes to Sacred Heart. "I'm not going to take communion from a regular man whose daughter owns one of those homes and he's going to give me the bread and forgive my sins."

When Michael Winerip's story appeared on June 8, 1989, Richie Rodriguez finally understood he was the victim of a conspiracy. Annette Snow's conversation with Winerip had led the *New York Times* to Rodriguez, and after they printed his story on June 20, the television cameras turned Richie into a celebrity.

A few days later, as he was sitting on his front steps having a cup of coffee, he saw D'Amato's black limousine draw up to the curb next door and his two bodyguards emerge. Rodriguez assumed this was the senator's usual Sunday night visit with his daughter Lisa, her lawyer-husband, and his two grandchildren. Rodriguez was surprised to see Penny get out of the car with him, since he knew they were separated and he hadn't seen them together for years. He was even more surprised to see D'Amato, dressed in shorts, stroll to the front of Rodriguez's house and lounge against his car. D'Amato called up, "Richie, can I talk to you for a minute."

Rodriguez was stunned. He walked down the steps and came to a halt in front of the senator.

"Richie," D'Amato said, "you know I had nothing to do with none of this." Richie remained silent as D'Amato continued. "Whatever they did they did by themselves."

"Then," Rodriguez said, "he puts his hands on my shoulders, and he looked me straight in the eye. He says, 'Richard, the next time you get interviewed by camera, just say that maybe you should've came to me and I would've found out what was going on.' "

Richie was skeptical. "So I said to myself, wait a minute, maybe he's saying, 'I didn't know anything about it, and if you would've come to me, I would've found out what was going on.' "

Richie found his tongue as he tried to sort out who was responsible. "You know me," he told D'Amato. "I never done anything to you. I never mentioned your name. But every village official was responsible."

"Not everybody," D'Amato cajoled. "Scully was the one who did everything."

Rodriguez stood face-to-face with his nemesis in the darkness. "No," he said, "it was everyone."

D'Amato insisted, "You're wrong. It was Scully."

Richie's voice firmed. "He was used as a scapegoat."

"Well," D'Amato said, "that's your opinion."

"Yes. That's my opinion. My true belief."

D'Amato turned and started to leave. "Well, Richie, have a good evening."

Richie Rodriguez had made his passage from innocence. What had stripped the veil from Richie's eyes was D'Amato's claim that he didn't know anything about what was going on in the village he controlled absolutely. To the retreating figure, Rodriguez called out, "Have a good evening, Mr. D. Amato."

The next week, Ted Koppel interviewed them both on his nationwide TV show *Nightline*. Just before Richie's appearance, D'Amato patronizingly said, "Richard Rodriguez, who I happen to know, is an outstanding young man. If he was discriminated against, that was wrong."

That was a wrong Rodriguez wanted corrected. He filed a $4 million lawsuit against Island Park, its mayor, and trustees, citing violations of federal civil rights, fair housing, and racketeering laws. As usual, those in the line of Richie's fire all stood in front of their commander. This time it wasn't necessary to raise a new bond issue to pay off Richie; the judge ruled the case couldn't come to trial, since the statute of limitations had run out.

FIFTY-ONE

PROSECUTORS ON D'AMATO'S CASES

Meanwhile, D'Amato's troubles multiplied. Atty. Gen. Dick Thornburgh was being urged to appoint a "special prosecutor" to investigate HUD corruption. Although D'Amato was not part of the executive branch, an investigation of HUD aimed at Secretary Samuel Pierce, Pierce's executive assistant Deborah Gore Dean, Assistant Secretary Thomas Demery, and New York's regional directors Joseph Monticciolo and Geraldine McGann would inevitably expose D'Amato's role in the scandals.

The 1978 Ethics in Government Act, however, required the process to be initiated by Attorney General Thornburgh, and Republican Thornburgh showed no interest in starting an independent probe into President Reagan's housing department appointees. Thornburgh had shown a similar reluctance to pursue the S & Ls and thieves who were stealing from the Bank of Credit and Commerce.

The attorney general is the federal officer charged with defending the country against crime. The FBI is under the attorney general's control. The ninety-four U.S. Attorneys around the country cannot undertake major prosecutions without his approval; yet the office is often run by political hacks most responsive to the needs of the party. They consider themselves the president's lawyer and favor their client's interests, occasionally at the expense of the public. The one cabinet officer the nation expects to be spotless in his conduct is frequently asked by the president to tidy up the messes left by well-connected party figures. Thornburgh performed up to the standards of his predecessors.

Despite the steady eruption of HUD outrages during the spring and summer of 1989, Dick Thornburgh resisted congressional demands for the appointment of a special prosecutor. The *New York Times* wrote on July 30, 1989:

> The Justice Department has never seemed eager to take on the H.U.D. situation. . . . Nothing would be more in Mr. Thornburgh's or the Administration's interest than to pursue the political abuses at H.U.D. like a junkyard dog.

In the fall of 1989, an exasperated House Judiciary Committee petitioned the Justice Department to appoint a special prosecutor. Despite the rising demand for action, Thornburgh held out until February 1990. He finally went to a three-judge panel appointed under the provisions of the 1978 Ethics Act and requested that they select one.

Thornburgh was able to define what he wanted investigated, thereby narrowing the special prosecutor's scope. He was to limit himself to discovering whether HUD secretary Pierce and his aides had "conspired to defraud the United States" by diverting hundreds of millions of dollars in rent subsidies to projects backed by Republican consultants. Thornburgh was pointing the finger away from D'Amato toward the people who had done D'Amato's bidding.

When the three-judge panel announced on March 2, 1990, that it was appointing Arlin M. Adams as special prosecutor, it restricted Adams to investigate only one HUD program, Moderate Rehabilitation of low-income housing. That meant White Plains and Sackets Harbor might be investigated, but it was only D'Amato's lemmings who would undergo that scrutiny, limiting his risk.

Arlin Adams, sixty-eight, had never worked as a prosecutor. He had been appointed to the U.S. Court of Appeals in Philadelphia by Richard Nixon, where he had served for seventeen years. Since retiring in 1986, he had been in private practice. He was described by his friends as "thorough."

The attempt at damage control by Attorney General Thornburgh was upset in May 1990 by startling testimony from a witness before the House Subcommittee on Housing. Under the chairmanship of Cong. Tom Landos (D-Cal.) the committee had been doing much of the basic spadework in exposing corruption at HUD. The witness was DuBois L. Gilliam, former deputy assistant secretary of housing under Pierce, who was serving an eighteen-month prison sentence after pleading guilty to accepting payoffs from contractors. Claiming to be repentant, Gilliam was now willing to cooperate with prosecutors.

Gilliam testified that political favoritism at HUD went far beyond the Moderate Rehabilitation program. Pierce, he said, had directed millions of dollars in grants to projects promoted largely by Al D'Amato. "The Department of Housing and Urban Development was the best domestic political machine I'd ever seen. We dealt strictly in politics."

Gilliam described the importance to Pierce of having D'Amato as chairman of the Banking Committee, citing among other favors that D'Amato had pushed through Congress over $100 million in "discretionary funds." D'Amato then told Pierce how the funds were to be distributed, always to his contributors or Armand Paul's clients. Gilliam stated that D'Amato's assistant Jerry Blue would bring over a shopping list of fat-cat applicants whose projects were usually ineligible. This didn't deter HUD administrators who had been told by Pierce to "keep him happy, take care of Al." Inside the agency, staffers cynically referred to the senator as "Secretary D'Amato."*

Thornburgh suddenly became concerned. He wrote a letter to Arlin Adams stating that in view of Gilliam's revelation that political corruption had pervaded other HUD programs, he thought the special prosecutor should expand his investigation. Adams agreeably responded that "it may be appropriate to redefine" his mandate. The mandate was now to include HUD's operation of the multi-billion-dollar Urban Development Action Grant for the construction in

---

*In April 1991, Gilliam told Mike Wallace of *60 Minutes* that D'Amato's ineligible favorites were given copies of previously successful applications and told to erase the name and substitute their own. "You would think, well, my God, maybe they might change it a little bit, but they never did." Gilliam concluded: "Basically we became an extended arm of Senator D'Amato's staff."

distressed cities of residential and retail buildings *and* Pierce's use of his discretionary fund.

D'Amato's career, if not his freedom, was in serious jeopardy. Adams was now going to look into every aspect of his raid on HUD.

The one quarter from which D'Amato saw no threat was the investigations by U.S. Attorney Andrew Maloney's New York office. After nine months of probing into the fraud involved in the distribution of HUD's forty-four Island Park homes, Maloney's subordinates had only filed a civil lawsuit against the village government and some of the homeowners. But D'Amato, who masterminded the fraud and who was named in Lawrence Noyer's draft of the indictment, was nowhere mentioned in its final version.

Although Arlin Adams was now in charge of most aspects of the HUD investigations, the Island Park civil suit remained in Maloney's office. Larry Noyer was in charge. For almost a year it was his only case. Noyer, though bright, competent, and ethical, was in a difficult situation. He was a young man, barely twenty-nine, in the early stages of building his career. He wanted to marry Pamela Davis, who was also an Assistant U.S. Attorney on Maloney's staff. Maloney, because of his known ties to D'Amato, had officially removed himself from the case, but he was still Larry's and Pamela's boss.

Noyer told me of his reaction to D'Amato's wider HUD involvement: "People who work in HUD have enormous power to award hundreds of millions of dollars in contracts. They have power over billions of dollars. If Senator D'Amato, or any other senator, effects that process by bullying, getting his allies into positions to effect those decisions, using every single political strategy he can think of to get his way, and effecting it to the point where, say, Puerto Rico gets thirteen times more Section 8 grants than it should get and deserving communities in New York and Cleveland and depressed cities throughout the country don't get, well, then, shame on them, and maybe they shouldn't be holding federal office, but that's a long way from saying that someone has committed a crime."

"Al D'Amato can engage in things that as a private citizen I find absolutely disgusting, but as a prosecutor I have to say: Are these crimes?"

Also reassuring D'Amato that Maloney was still under his thumb was the lack of action on the proposed indictment of his brother. Armand Paul had been investigated for over a year about his use of the senator's office to get the Aegis contract for Unisys. After the original prosecutor had been transferred to Washington, Noyer was put in charge of this even more sensitive case. Maloney apparently thought Noyer had the right cautionary attitude toward matters involving D'Amato indictments. His judgment about Noyer must have been shaken when *Newsday* obtained a memo from anonymous prosecutors on Maloney's staff saying there was enough evidence to indict Armand Paul in April 1991. *Newsday* was told that this leak was a deliberate effort by Maloney's staff to pressure their boss and the Justice Department into authorizing the prosecution of the case.

Noyer told me he wasn't the source of that leak, but D'Amato thought he was, and although nine months later, at the end of 1991, the U.S. Attorney had still not made a move, the sound of worry beads could be heard through the walls of all D'Amato domiciles.

Maloney's effort to protect D'Amato was most blatant in his attempt to intimidate one of the senator's most damaging accusers. Former New York HUD executive assistant Alexander Naclerio had testified under oath before Tom Landos's House committee that D'Amato controlled New York's HUD office and used it to pay off his contributors. But a year had elapsed since that sworn testimony about D'Amato's alleged criminal activity, and Maloney showed no interest in hauling Naclerio before a grand jury to testify; in fact, his FBI agents hadn't even spoken to Naclerio.

In October 1990, Maloney had a change of attitude motivated entirely by a desire to shield his patron-senator. Word reached him that Naclerio was speaking to Arlin Adams about D'Amato's influence-peddling abuses. Maloney's response: an October 15 letter to Naclerio's attorney, Raymond Grunewald, declaring that since Neclario was talking to the special prosecutor, "we see no reason why he should not submit to an interview by the Department of Justice on the same terms."

The exchange of letters that followed, which mysteriously came into the possession of columnist Sydney Schanberg, revealed an extraordinary effort by Maloney to shield D'Amato. The "terms" he offered didn't come close to the deal that Neclario had made with Adams. Maloney's office rejected the broad immunity the special prosecutor was willing to grant and instead proposed that Neclario be quizzed by FBI agents "for the purpose of obtaining leads to other evidence, which evidence may be used in any prosecution and sentencing of client [Naclerio]."

Grunewald charged in his letter to the Brooklyn prosecutors that the Justice Department had clearly decided to pursue his client like a junkyard dog in an effort to protect D'Amato and his "cronies." He saw the Justice Department's approach "as serving no useful purpose except to shield a powerful U.S. senator and his underlings at HUD from exposure and indictment by stalling the investigation with roadblocks to essential witnesses."

Grunewald's plea-bargain negotiations, first with Special Prosecutor Adams and then with Maloney's office, assumed Naclerio was guilty of something. Although Grunewald was conceding that his client had taken part in the crimes he was describing, he insisted that Naclerio wasn't a central figure in the conspiracies. Therefore, he felt the Justice Department should follow its usual practice when trying to indict ringleaders: Grant Naclerio immunity so that his testimony could be used to catch "the obvious targets," whom he identified as D'Amato, Monticciolo, and McGann.

Instead, the Justice Department was telling Neclario that it planned to prosecute him, potentially the government's prime witness. Grunewald, a former federal prosecutor, knew the game being played: "[Y]our actions indicate the Justice Department does not want him [Naclerio] to testify and, to ensure it, have made it impossible for him to do so, for if he does, without unrestricted-use immunity . . . Alexander Naclerio will be subjected to the tender and obvious mercies of an investigation that seeks to somehow discredit a key witness and forfeit the possibility of a successful investigation and prosecution of a politically powerful U.S. senator and his underlings."

President Bush and Dick Thornburgh owed Senator D'Amato a favor. In the last week in October, D'Amato voted against overriding Bush's veto of the 1990 civil rights bill. Bush's veto survived by only one vote, D'Amato's.

Dick Thornburgh resigned as attorney general in the summer of 1991 and returned to Pennsylvania, where he had formerly been governor, to run for the U.S. Senate. Although expected to win easily in November, he lost. Pundits attributed that loss to the deepening recession for which Republican president George Bush was being blamed and the skillful use of the national health insurance issue by Thornburgh's Democratic opponent. Add to the list of causes that helped defeat him *the D'Amato/S & L/Bank of Credit and Commerce factor.*

FIFTY-TWO

THE SENATE'S ETHICS

In the summer of 1989, Mark Green watched with mixed emotions as scandal after scandal involving D'Amato hit the nation's front pages. There was so much more being unearthed about Al D'Amato than he had known during his 1986 senatorial campaign.

The *Wall Street Journal* and the *Times* had taken on D'Amato. Even television anchormen, limited by time constraints to news blinks, sent "investigative reporters" to look into the senator's affairs. In his Manhattan Democracy Project think-tank office Green was surrounded by cabinets crammed with examples of political villainy that had never been punished. He had spent twenty years working on issues of public ethics and campaign financing, the worst aspects of which were embodied in Al D'Amato's career. He set about drawing up a complaint to the Senate Ethics Committee.

Anyone can file charges with the Ethics Committee. If there is "substantial evidence" that a senator has "violated a law," "engaged in improper conduct which may reflect upon the Senate," or "violated the Senate Code of Official Conduct," the committee chairmen can appoint a counsel to investigate. If his investigation suggests a basis for action, the committee then votes for a full probe in preparation for a formal hearing.

That hearing is not a trial, but it has all the trappings of a trial: A special counsel (always a member of the private bar) functions as a pseudoprosecutor; the six members act as a jury, and the chairman serves as presiding judge. The jury can acquit or recommend to the Senate a change of committee assignments, a motion of censure, or expulsion. None of these actions approaches capital punishment; in fact, the Senate doesn't have the power to put a miscreant in jail. In the committee's proceedings the rules of criminal law do not apply, only the more relaxed Senate rules.

The committee, unlike any other in the Senate, is composed of three Democrats and three Republicans; it is supposed to be nonpartisan. In 1977, its hand was strengthened by a new Senate code of ethics. It has frequently acted as a layer of protection for its often accused, but seldom punished, members.

Green's thirty-two-page complaint requesting a "preliminary investigation" was filed on July 17, 1989. It included nine major charges against D'Amato involving HUD, Wedtech, Drexel Burnham Lambert, Unisys, Mechanical Technology Inc., Steamco, Roosevelt Raceway, Sackets Harbor, JOBCO, Armand Paul D'Amato, and D'Amato's Manhattan office rent. Green included an appendix consisting largely of newspaper clippings but pointed out that the full extent of D'Amato's derelictions couldn't be uncovered by newspaper investigations. "Journalists lacking subpoena power have taken these stories as far as they can. And federal prosecutors in New York selected by him may be predictably wary of investigating their patron. Consequently, only a Senate inquiry can now determine the truth by subpoenaing documents and witnesses and by asking Senator D'Amato questions under oath."

Forestalling the senator's criticism that the charges in his complaint were old hat and had been decided in D'Amato's favor by the voters in 1986, Green made a point of insisting that "this complaint is based almost entirely on public evidence disclosed *since* his 1986 reelection. The issue is not politics but ethics."

Although the brief was professional, as befits a Harvard Law School graduate, Green wasn't confident it would fire up the committee; its history of avoiding its responsibilities reinforced his doubts.

The first senator to be disciplined by the "revitalized" committee was Georgia's Herman E. Talmadge. After a protracted hearing before the committee in 1979, he was "denounced" by the entire Senate, but not expelled, for misusing campaign and office funds.

In 1981 the committee took its strongest action. It voted to expel New Jersey Democrat Harrison A. Williams, a twenty-three-year-member of Congress. Williams fell into the ABSCAM net when he agreed to accept a hidden interest in a titanium mine as his price for helping one of those phony FBI sheiks get a large loan. But it had taken Williams's court conviction and an impending jail sentence to overcome his colleagues' reluctance to act.

Williams's tardy expulsion seemed to have sobered committee members: What an awful power they had. A lifetime of campaigning in rain and snow, years of negotiating with enemies, countless sleepless nights caused by eating indigestible fund-raising meals—all of it made meaningless by the vote of six men. Such power palsied all politicians who had ever strayed.

The next charge against a member suggested that the committee's reluctance to act was based less on an absence of evidence than an unwillingness to believe poorly of a colleague. Mark Hatfield, Republican of Oregon, a Senate member since 1967, was accused of selling his vote to Greek financier Basil A. Tsakos. Mr. Tsakos wanted Hatfield's support to build a $12 billion trans-African oil pipeline. Hatfield showed no interest in moving oil across Africa until his wife, Antoinette, a real estate agent, received $55,000 from Tsakos for finding him an apartment.

Despite closed-session testimony supporting the charges, the committee unanimously voted on September 25, 1984, to end a preliminary inquiry into the payment. The members, four of whom were still serving on the committee in 1991, claimed they couldn't bring themselves to believe that a man with Hatfield's reputation for morality could have done anything seriously wrong.

The senator had prepared the way for his exoneration by conceding he had made "an error in judgment" when he failed to consider how the public would view his support for the pipeline after it discovered the payment to his wife. He then donated the $55,000 to the Portland Shriners Hospital for Crippled Children.

With this gesture Hatfield established the survival drill for accused senators: Contrition and restitution obtain absolution. Absolution, however, did not mean, in his case, abstaining from future sin. On June 6, 1991, the Ethics Committee initiated preliminary hearings on charges that between 1983 and 1987 Hatfield had accepted $15,000 in airline tickets and gifts from the University of South Carolina; they included Steuben glass, an Audubon print, and a porcelain statue. The university also granted his younger son a $15,000 scholarship. This generosity, none of it disclosed to the Senate, showered down on Hatfield while the university was seeking a $16.3 million grant from the Appropriations Committee he headed.

David Durenberger, Republican of Minnesota, a member of the Ethics Committee that had absolved Hatfield, was the next subject of its public investigation. In 1989 he was accused of arranging a phony book deal to skirt legal limits on accepting honoraria. Durenberger knew better than to attempt to refute the irrefutable. After a full hearing, when the committee's vote for some sort of conviction was assured, he pleaded guilty, stood before the full Senate, and delivered an abject apology, accepting his condemnation, which did not include expulsion. Durenberger decided it was possible to endure a series of humiliations as long as the final deadly one was not delivered. He subsequently decided not to run for reelection in 1994.

The committee rarely met and left most of its decisions in the hands of Democratic chairman Howell Heflin and Republican vice chairman Warren Rudman. They reviewed a large number of complaints against Senate members before dismissing them. In 1985 Warren Rudman, committee chairman at the time, had set the standard when he said, "We're not supposed to be the national nanny down here. We're supposed to look for true breaches of ethics by people who have stretched the law for their personal advantage."

When complaints arose about misuse of campaign funds or franking privileges or the selling of a vote for a contribution, Heflin or Rudman would privately discuss the limits of such behavior with the offending senator. In effect, they cautioned him and gave him a second chance.

As time passed, the committee that senators had originally viewed as someone's bad joke took on the aspects of a reliquary of spiritual purity, the defender of all who were *essentially* honest, and the source of forgiveness for the repenter who professed to be willing to make amends.

Mark Green suppressed his skepticism. On September 26, 1989, in an attempt to keep the fire stoked, he filed supplemental material with the committee aimed at updating and reinforcing his July 17 charges. He believed that if he could confront the members with a substantial case, they would be forced to act.

On November 17, 1989, the committee announced it had retained Robert S. Bennett as counsel to determine if investigations of influence peddling by D'Amato and "the Keating Five" senators were warranted. The rotund, sartorially indifferent Bennett had been the special counsel in the 1981 probe of Harrison Williams and in the hearings earlier in the year involving Senator Durenberger. In making the announcement, Chairman Heflin said a decision hadn't been made as to whether a "preliminary inquiry," the first step in an ethics investigation, would be authorized.

Two weeks later, on November 27, Bennett withdrew from the D'Amato case after learning that clients of his law firm had contributed to D'Amato's campaigns. This was the most important development for D'Amato in the investigation. It took an experienced, no-nonsense counsel out of the process.

Bennett was left to deal solely with the Keating Five: Alan Cranston (D-Calif.), Dennis DeConcini (D-Ariz.), Donald Riegle (D-Mich.), John McCain (R-Ariz.), and John Glenn (D-Ohio). Each of them was accused of pressuring bank regulators to help financier Charles Keating keep his bankrupt S & L in business in exchange for contributions to their campaigns. By this time the government had seized Keating's California Lincoln Savings and Loan at a $2.5 billion loss to the taxpayers.

D'Amato's role in the S & L debacle was larger and more significant than any of the Keating Five's. As chairman of the Banking Security Subcommittee, D'Amato, at the behest of his contributor Drexel Burnham Lambert, blocked the Senate's move to ban the S & Ls from trafficking in risky junk bonds. The loss of value of these junk bonds was a major reason for the bankruptcy of the "thrifts." A more rigorous Ethics Committee might have concluded that its Keating Five investigation should more properly have included D'Amato and been called "the S & L Six." But timidity made the Keating Five more palatable; D'Amato got another reprieve.

In place of Bennett the committee on November 29, 1989, appointed Henry F. Schuelke III as special counsel for D'Amato's investigation. Schuelke sharpened his legal skills during the 1970s when he was an assistant U.S. Attorney in the District of Columbia.

He changed sides in 1979, representing Jimmy Carter's budget director Bert Lance in a messy scandal involving charges of bank fraud. By the time of his Ethics Committee appointment, Schuelke was a partner in the Washington firm Janis, Schuelke and Wechsler and a member of an elite group of Capitol lawyers who specialized in defending those accused of white-collar crimes.

To no one's surprise, D'Amato announced that although he was innocent of "sore loser" Green's charges, he was hiring his long-time confidant Michael Armstrong to defend him. He had chosen a lawyer who wasn't going to have to spend a lot of expensive legal hours in his office at Lord Day & Lord, etc., getting up to speed.

For D'Amato that expense had never been large. On May 22, 1991, the Associated Press (AP) reported that although other senators forced to seek legal aid had paid their attorney's hundreds of thousands of dollars, Michael Armstrong, during a year and a half of working on the inquiry, had never billed D'Amato. This raised the question of whether Armstrong's normally substantial fee should be reported on D'Amato's financial disclosure form as a liability or, if no payment was to be made, as a gift.

The AP phoned D'Amato to get an answer. " 'I will be billed appropriately,' " D'Amato responded without answering. When asked if the arrangement constituted a liability that must be reported, D'Amato became angry. " 'I will go to the Ethics Committee and ask for their opinion,' he shouted, and hung up."

The AP then turned to Michael Armstrong in quest of a more informative response. Despite his many services to D'Amato over the previous ten years, Armstrong said he couldn't remember ever billing the senator. "My relationship with Alfonse all along is that I help him on my own time."

On December 13, 1989, Green filed an eighteen-page supplemental brief "in response to the generous request of Henry Schuelke Esq. that I provide any further information and insights which might assist him and the Committee." Green added two new charges:

1. "Phone calls on behalf of organized crime figures ... Paul Castellano, the reputed head of the Gambino crime family ... and Mario Gigante, the (jailed) brother of Vincent (the Chin) Gigante, reputed boss of the Genovese crime family."

2. "Senator D'Amato helped obtain approval for a half-million-dollar federal [HUD] grant for ... a group of black ministers led by Al Sharpton, who a month earlier had endorsed the Senator's 1986 campaign."

After months of preliminary investigation, Schuelke informed the committee that there were sufficient grounds for a formal investigation, and in the spring of 1990 the six members voted to authorize one. This meant that at the conclusion of Schuelke's probe the committee would put D'Amato "on trial."

In a January 15, 1991, interview, on the eve of the outbreak of the Persian Gulf War, Mark Green told me that although he had been fully occupied for over a year with his duties as New York City's consumer affairs commissioner, he still kept his eye on what the Ethics Committee and HUD Special Prosecutor Arlin Adams were doing.

From November 17, 1990, to January 15, 1991, Ethics Committee counsel Bennett conducted a fair and exhaustive public "trial" of the Keating Five senators. The charges against the senators were aired in thirty televised sessions. Millions of Americans watched the eyelids of the accused blink and their brows submerge in sweat as Bennett accused them of pressuring regulators to do what Charles Keating wanted in exchange for $1.3 million in campaign contributions. The humiliating exhibition of the Keating Five signaled that D'Amato was about to become the isolated target of an even more intense national public scrutiny.

Green said, "Although Schuelke has been researching his brains out on D'Amato, it's hard to predict where the committee is going to draw the line. They've all done *some* of what D'Amato has done to raise campaign contributions, although to a much smaller extent. How far is too far? You can obviously find out what happened to grandma's social security check, which is the kind of constituent service most of them like to have their staffs do. Also, obviously, you can't beat up a regulator."

In an attempt to define that gray area between inquiries about grandma's check and beating up regulators, Green said: "If an eight-hundred-pound gorilla comes along to a park bench and asks people sitting on a bench if there's a seat, it's not just an ordinary *sta-*

SENATOR POTHOLE

tus inquiry. That's the kind of distinction that the Ethics Committee is going to have to make, and although most people with common sense won't find any difficulty in making that distinction, it's hard to predict whether they'll do it."

D'Amato pressured his colleagues not to make that distinction. He lobbied them mercilessly. Implicit was the threat that if they forced him into a television defense of himself, such as the Keating Five had undergone, his well-known, easily triggered temper would force him to fire accusations against them. Defendant D'Amato had access to his "jury" and did everything possible to intimidate them.

With a touch of whimsy Mark Green remarked, "It's like a jury of pickpockets deciding whether pickpocketing is a crime or a profession."

In mid-March 1991 the Ethics Committee decided pickpocketing was a profession. It unanimously ruled that four of the Keating Five deserved only letters of reprimand. Democrat Cranston, who had already announced he was retiring, was to be referred to the Democratic-controlled Senate for unspecified action. Nine months later, the Senate decided to listen to the Ethics Committee's conclusion that Cranston's behavior was "improper and repugnant" but not to vote "punishment" in view of Cranston's imminent retirement. In a two-hour session Senator Cranston, speaking "with deep remorse in my heart," put the Senate on trial. He asked rhetorically, "How many of you, after really thinking about it, could rise and declare you've never, ever helped—or agreed to help—a contributor close in time to the solicitation or receipt of a contribution? I don't believe any of you could say, 'Never.' "

Mark Green believed that in Arlin Adams's probe of D'Amato different forces were at work. Green said, "People who know D'Amato have told me he's privately frantic . . . sweating bullets. A prosecutor he doesn't have control over is in charge of his case.

"Periodically he tells journalists, 'My only problem is a vindictive sore loser, Mark Green.' I'm not his problem. His history of scandals is finally catching up with him. He obviously shook down cabinet secretaries and undersecretaries to help his family and cronies. It's laughable to say he would do it for anyone. He energetically goes to bat for his buddies. He built the bomb. I just lit the fuse."

On August 2, 1991, more than two years after Green filed his charges, the fuse sputtered out. Warren Rudman, flanked by the vaguely present new chairman of the committee, seventy-two-year-old Terry Sanford, assembled a press conference to announce that the investigation was at an end. Committee counsel Scheulke had studied 250 boxes of papers provided by D'Amato and fourteen boxes from the Senate Banking Committee. Lawyers on Schuelke's staff had "reviewed" about 1 million documents. Even counting that number, much less *reviewing* 1 million documents, seemed to require a battalion-sized staff. In addition, they had subpoenaed documents from seventy-one other people and had listened to wiretaps on forty-one suspects in New York, Washington, and Virginia. All to no avail.

Sanford, clearly not the man he had once been, appeared to be struggling with a task beyond his abilities. Rudman was feisty, combative, and arrogant. The ethics problem of the Senate was summed up in their contrasting styles. Sanford didn't seem to understand the nature of the problem; Rudman didn't seem to care whether there was a problem.

During the previous month, as the time came to make a decision about open hearings on D'Amato, the committee had disintegrated. Members had for months defended themselves against the nation-wide disgust with the manner in which they had settled the Keating Five affair. Howell Heflin, chairman for years, resigned, complaining of stress, as did David Pryor, who two weeks after resigning suffered a heart attack. Jesse Helms left the committee because of its lack of action and issued a 247-page blast concluding: "I seriously question, as one who sat on the committee for more than a decade, the reasonableness of any senator being asked to sit in judgment of five fellow senators and to serve in effect as both judge and jury."

The remaining members of the committee were so on edge that they made their decision the night before the press conference during a four-hour secret session in an electronically swept room on the fourth floor of the Capitol. Their main worry: A mean-spirited, bullying D'Amato had made it clear he would turn a trial of him into a trial of the Senate.

In a testy mood, Rudman curtly read from the unanimous committee report. His effort was to show that its decision had been reached only after the most extensive investigation. Instead, however, he revealed that despite spending over $800,000, little progress had been made toward uncovering the facts. The staff had tried to interview sixty-eight witnesses: Twenty-five had declined to testify, claiming Fifth Amendment rights against self-incrimination. Ten additional witnesses didn't even cooperate to that extent; they said that *if called* they would invoke their Fifth Amendment privilege. Over half the witnesses the committee believed had information refused to speak, and the committee had declined to grant immunity to even *one* of them to compel testimony that might force D'Amato out of the Senate.

The committee, Rudman declaimed, had investigated sixteen charges. He conceded that there was some basis to four of them, all of which accused D'Amato of exploiting his office to "financially enrich contributors, cronies, and relatives."

One of the four charges was that Senator D'Amato had rigged the distribution of forty-four Island Park HUD homes to benefit "friends and family." The committee's amorphous nine-page report stated that "there is insufficient credible evidence to provide substantial cause to conclude that a violation within the Committee's jurisdiction had occurred." D'Amato might well have committed some violation of the law prior to becoming a senator, but that was before "the Committee's jurisdiction had occurred." As to whether any of those violations had continued after he became senator in 1981: "There is insufficient evidence." Harry Scully was ready to supply that evidence.

In response to questions from reporters, Rudman admitted that most of the key witnesses in Island Park had refused to testify and that the committee had not made an effort to obtain their testimony for fear that it might upset U.S. Attorney Maloney's effort to prosecute his case. D'Amato was being doubly protected. In New York's Eastern District, Maloney was breathing heavily on Lawrence Noyer; in the Senate the Ethics Committee refused to press a diligent investigation because it might interfere with Maloney's cover-up.

The same standoffish treatment was applied to a second "charge of some weight" that D'Amato had "engaged in improper conduct" regarding HUD projects in Puerto Rico. Sanford read off the report's "Finding." It complained that "the committee has been disadvantaged by the unavailability of several essential witnesses, who have asserted their constitutional privilege against self-incrimination." In the face of this intransigence on the part of D'Amato's Puerto Rican friends, Sanford conceded, the committee still could have acted. He continued: "Of course, the committee is empowered by law to seek judicial orders of immunity and to compel the testimony. . . . With respect to these particular witnesses, however, the committee . . . determined that judicial orders of immunity might jeopardize ongoing criminal investigations or put contemplated prosecutions at grave risk."

As a result, the committee decided its hands were tied. "Absent the testimony of these crucial witnesses and based on the evidence available to it, the Committee finds that there is insufficient credible evidence to provide substantial cause for the Committee to conclude that a violation within its jurisdiction has occurred."

The committee had similarly been blocked on the third somewhat meritorious charge: that D'Amato had failed to introduce promised restrictive legislation on junk bonds after Drexel Burnham Lambert had made large contributions to his campaign. Every member of the Senate Banking Committee was aware that D'Amato had promised them he would introduce that legislation and then gone back on his promise after a Drexel fund-raiser. They could all have been witnesses against him. But the Ethics Committee report averred that "based on the available evidence . . ." it had no choice but to absolve D'Amato of even engaging "in any improper conduct."

It was only on the last of the four charges—that Unisys had illegally used D'Amato's office to secure a contract—that the committee found the courage to criticize him. But it was precisely this finding that most vividly exposed the senators' reluctance to deal with unethical—even illegal—acts by their colleagues when the issue of "contributions" is involved.

The thrust of the charge was that "actions by the Senator may have been improperly influenced by allegedly illegal campaign contributions [from Unisys]." There was nothing "alleged" about the illegal contributions. Unisys had conceded that some of its senior officers had given D'Amato contributions that had then been repaid to them on inflated expense-account vouchers.

Senator Rudman read the committee's response to the charge. "While the senator's office did provide some support for Unisys, that support consisted of actions, such as letters of inquiry to Executive Branch officials, that were ordinary and routine." Rudman implied that a letter on D'Amato's official stationery urging support for a defense contractor, who was also a major contributor, was akin to a telephone call from his office to inquire about grandma's missing social security check. All senators did this sort of thing all the time. It was "ordinary and routine."

As to allegations of misconduct by the senator in "the use of the senator's office by his brother on behalf of Unisys, the committee does not find that on the basis of the evidence available to it Senator D'Amato violated any law of the United States or rule of the Senate."

Senators had been careful not to write such a law, concerned that consequently some of them would end up in jail. The same caution kept them from writing any "rule of the senate" preventing D'Amato from servicing his wealthy constituents in exchange for "contributions." It was as if the fox had been told to write the rules under which the chickens were protected, and when cries were raised that he had eaten the chickens, he responded that he hadn't written any rules against eating chickens.

Only in Armand Paul's use of his brother's office did the Ethics Committee issue a clear-cut denunciation:

> The committee notes that it is the duty of every United States Senator to conduct his or her office in a manner that precludes its systematic misuse by members of his or her family for personal gain. The activities of Senator D'Amato's brother on behalf of Unisys constituted such a misuse.
>
> Senator D'Amato conducted the business of his office in an improper and inappropriate manner. Based on the evidence available to it, the Committee finds that Senator D'Amato was negligent in failing to establish appropriate standards for the operation of his office.

Beyond this, nothing. There was to be no recommendation to the full Senate for even the mildest formal rebuke. In fact, the only recommendation Senator Rudman would make to the Senate was that it should adopt a rule that would "require more in the way of affidavits and sworn statements before we accept this kind of complaint again."

As to the rest of the twelve charges, Rudman described them as "frivolous." Among them was D'Amato's public admission that he had asked U.S. Attorney Rudolf Giuliani to end the murder prosecution of a Mafia godfather. The senator had also admitted that at a different time he had asked Giuliani to help gain the release from prison of another mobster.

Rudman said that the remaining list of charges had been based on "insufficient information." A reporter wanted to know, "What was the 'insufficient information.' "

Rudman glared at him. "Do you have three months?" he answered sarcastically.

The reporter said, "Yes."

"Well, I don't," Rudman shot back as he stood up and abruptly ended the press conference.

This abbreviated statement to the press was the committee's only explanation for its action. All requests for documents were rejected. Counsel Schuelke was unavailable for interviews, and the committee refused to release his report. Transcripts of witnesses' sworn statements were sealed.

Despite the committee's efforts to cover up for D'Amato and itself, months later *Newsday* correspondent Josh Friedman revealed that D'Amato and his assistant Mike Kinsella had testified under oath in July 1991 before a secret session of the committee.

Eleven months after the Rudman-Sanford press conference burial of the D'Amato ethics investigation, a partial description of D'Amato and Kinsella's secret testimony emerged. Assistant U.S. Attorney Lawrence Noyer submitted documents at Eduardo Lopez Ballori's June 1992 trial that showed that D'Amato and Kinsella had lied. In a letter to the court, Noyer stated that in D'Amato's sworn testimony before the committee he "denied knowledge of defendant's [Ballori] interest in any H.U.D. project and denied attempting to influence any H.U.D. employee to act favorably toward any project in which the defendant had an interest."

But a handwritten note from Lopez Ballori to Michael Kinsella, submitted into evidence by Noyer, showed D'Amato's denial was preposterous. In his April 2, 1985, letter Lopez Ballori wrote,

"During the Senator's visit to Puerto Rico, we discussed the situation described on the attached 'white paper,' which he asked me to prepare." Ballori went on to describe what he had discussed with D'Amato: money for 610 units of housing that Ballori and his partner, Cleofi Rubi, wanted steered to their Alameda Towers project.

In a 1989 interview with *Newsday*, D'Amato denied he had ever discussed housing grants with Lopez Ballori.

> We never discussed housing. The major thread was G.O.P. politics. I was supporting [Bob] Dole [for president] at the time, and Eduardo was very active in connection with that.

There was something in the characters of D'Amato and Dole that made them natural allies. D'Amato's wooing of the Republican Senate leader had gone so far that D'Amato had arranged to have Lopez Ballori stage one of his reimburse-the-contributors fund-raisers for the Kansas senator.

Prosecutor Noyer also introduced Kinsella's phone logs for July 8, 1986, which said: "Eduardo called. His rehab project is called Alameda."

Cleofi Rubi cooperated with the government. He testified at Ballori's first trial that Ballori "kept me posted about conversations he had with the senator's office about our efforts to bring units to Puerto Rico. . . . 'I have talked to Mike [Kinsella].' That kind of thing."

In another letter introduced into evidence by Noyer, Lopez Ballori wrote to "Mike" Kinsella about a Section 8 application Rubi was trying to get approved. He ended by saying, "I very deeply appreciate your efforts on this regard, and look forward to seeing you soon. Best regards, Eduardo."

Kinsella's testimony before the Ethics Committee was clearly contradicted by these documents.

In that same letter to "Mike," Lopez Ballori brought up the name of D'Amato's HUD ally Joseph Monticciolo. "I have talked to Joe Monticciolo, who assures me that this was the appropriate way to present it [the Alameda Towers project]."

Newsday provided another witness to Monticciolo's avid interest in Cleofi Rubi's project.

San Juan Mayor Baltasar Corrada said that Monticciolo told him repeatedly in 1985 that if he did not award the city's allocation of HUD Section 8 units to Cleofi Rubi's Alameda Towers project, San Juan would be cut off from further HUD money for housing.

Monticciolo didn't make a move in his HUD office without picking up the phone and clearing it with D'Amato. When asked by the press why he appeared to be lobbying personally for Rubi and Ballori's project, D'Amato said that he had been "unfairly used" by his former fund-raiser Joe Monticciolo. Without his permission, D'Amato protested, Monticciolo had misinformed Washington HUD that he wanted Rubi-Ballori projects approved.

Monticciolo had long since learned to play by the Hempstead rules: He made as few damaging admissions about D'Amato as he could before congressional investigators and, in retirement, was rewarded with a Cleofi Rubi partnership.

On May 6, 1993, Mark Green summed up his reaction to the Ethics Committee's behind-the-scenes cover-up. "I frankly never expected much out of the Senate Ethics Committee . . . but it was the only forum a citizen could go to to blow the whistle on a senator who had repeatedly exploited his public office for private gain.

"I'm surprised and pleased that they launched a formal investigation, put him under oath, and then reprimanded D'Amato for the Unisys scandal . . . but they obviously flinched at the other charges, since their final report was such a lightweight whitewash. For example, they called very few of the witnesses who knew about his HUD scandals. D'Amato escaped many charges because his implicit argument of 'there but for the grace of God go I' worked on the panel."

Within the year the two leading figures in the committee investigation were out of the Senate. Warren Rudman said he was tired and decided not to seek reelection. Terry Sanford was defeated. The remaining committee members who had decided against taking on New York's junior senator made a point of erasing from their résumés any reference to their association with the committee. The new Ethics Committee members acted as though they were unaware that the Rudman-Sanford report had pledged to reopen the matter of the HUD charges "without prejudice" when Lopez Ballori's trial was concluded and the committee could compel previously reluctant trial witnesses, now granted immunity, to testify.

The underlying message: The Senate was not prepared to act on most charges against a senator and most likely never against a senator accused of illegally soliciting campaign contributions. If there were to be any penalty suffered by Al D'Amato, it would have to be inflicted by his constituents.

FIFTY-THREE
THE SURVIVAL FRENZY

A ssistant U.S. Attorney Lawrence Noyer had a rationale for not indicting Al D'Amato: "This is an elected official. The citizens of the state of New York put him in office." If elected officials misbehaved, then you had a remedy. "If you don't like the way they are exercising their authority, then kick them out."

Democratic societies are based on that theory. When a majority disagrees with a politician, they can vote him into a different line of work. But Al D'Amato had specialized in covert *criminal* behavior, and what criminal wouldn't prefer to avoid facing a jury in a court, where lying is counted as an additional crime, and instead seek absolution through campaigning, where lying often wins re-election. D'Amato's third-term campaign in 1992 tested Larry Noyer's theory about elections providing an effective method for getting rid of politicians who have violated the law.

At the start of the 1992 campaign it was impossible to find a savvy political leader who thought D'Amato could win. The state Republican party was split. Larry Rockefeller, a fourth-generation heir to the Standard Oil fortune, announced he would challenge D'Amato in the Republican primary.

"I knew," he said, "that significant majorities of Republicans were, unlike him, pro-choice and pro-environment and dismayed at the never-ending parade of scandals associated with his name."

Unwilling to face even that inexperienced contender, D'Amato went into court accompanied by a battalion of election-law specialists. They managed to cite enough signatures on Rockefeller's petitions without their "i's" dotted and "t's" crossed to have him taken off the ballot.

"I want to tell New Yorkers," Rockefeller complained, "you are being set up. Right now, the system is rigged to protect incumbents and prevent choice."

Nevertheless, a general-election defeat still seemed certain. In a poll taken two months before the election by Arthur Finkelstein, D'Amato's campaign strategist, he was losing by 20 percent. D'Amato was depressed and in a panic. All stories referring to his prospects contained some variety of these words: "If the election were held today, Senator D'Amato would lose."

D'Amato's only hope came from the likelihood he would run against a weak Democratic opponent. Eighteen months before the election fifty-four-year-old Robert Abrams, the New York attorney general, announced he wanted the Democratic nomination. Abrams was a product of the gamy Bronx machine; between 1970 and 1978 he had served as borough president, the party's patronage dispenser. Although Abrams had been in political office for over half his life, his recent safe campaigns on Gov. Mario Cuomo's ticket had been so routine that the short, balding pol had lost any sign of a competitive spirit. If D'Amato had selected his opponent, he would have chosen the plodding, play-it-safe Bob Abrams.

D'Amato's outlook became particularly bleak when Geraldine Ferraro announced she would run against Abrams in the Democratic primary. Ferraro was a substantial political presence. A former member of Congress, she had been the first serious woman nominee for vice president, running with Fritz Mondale in 1984. If she won the primary, her Italian ancestry ensured that she would cut into D'Amato's core support in the general election. Equally daunting, she was a feisty debater, a charming stump speaker, and with her all-out support of freedom of choice on abortion, she was bound to attract large numbers of Republican women for whom that issue was decisive.

With Nelson Rockefeller's relative out of the way, D'Amato went into his frenetic campaign mode. If there was a funeral for a prominent Jew, he attended, wearing his yarmulke. Puerto Ricans seeking someone to carry the island's flag in the Fifth Avenue parade found him ready to snatch it from any contender. Were the Greeks worried about the Turks? He would fly into Athens Airport to rally the sons of Apollo.

Jim Nagourney, Joe Margiotta's Republican party protégé, described what he thought D'Amato was capable of in this survival-frenzy mode: "If genocide became popular tomorrow, he'd be for it."

The Democratic primary reached its climax seven weeks before the 1992 November election. It was an early Christmas gift for D'Amato. Eventually, Bob Abrams had three opponents: Mrs. Ferraro, Elizabeth Holtzman, who lost to D'Amato in 1980 and was now the comptroller of New York City, and Rev. Al Sharpton, whose support D'Amato had bought in his campaign against Mark Green. As primary day approached, Ferraro held the lead. But in a series of rancorous televised debates Abrams and Holtzman ganged up on her. Holtzman sought the same bloc of women who found Ferraro appealing and in sharp, malicious attacks repeatedly questioned Ferraro's personal integrity and family finances. Instead of allowing a desperate Holtzman to do his dirty work and remaining above the battle, Abrams slyly joined the attack.

The smear campaign against Geraldine Ferraro worked. She lost to Abrams by less than 1 percent. Abrams had spent $4.2 million on TV commercials to defeat the Democrat D'Amato feared most, and his money had won him a diminished image and a resentful Geraldine Ferraro. He spent much of the campaign trying to win her endorsement and dunning contributors for the $3 million that he was able to muster against D'Amato's $12 million.

D'Amato had a series of vicious commercials ready to air regardless of whether Abrams or Ferraro won. The day after the primary, D'Amato's off-the-shelf barrage against Abrams pictured the attorney general as "hopelessly liberal." D'Amato's campaign against

Abrams was brutal. The *New York Times* remarked about the "far rougher form of warfare" Abrams encountered in his campaign against D'Amato:

> But Mr. D'Amato had already conveyed that message privately, accosting the Attorney General at three events before the primary election and warning him, in his customary blunt manner, not to attempt to raise the issue of ethics. Mr. Abrams, aides said, was taken aback by Mr. D'Amato's fury. [The senator later boasted about the confrontation to friends, dismissing Mr. Abrams contemptuously as a "wimp."]

In Binghamton, at one of his rare, poorly attended rallies, an exasperated Abrams attempted to fight D'Amato on his level of invective. He blurted out that his opponent was a "Fascist." The next day was Columbus Day. D'Amato seized that ethnically correct occasion to denounce what he characterized as Abrams's slur on all Italians. In no time, television commercials ran statewide showing Mussolini's jutting jaw and gesticulating fist, while the copy made the point that when Abrams described D'Amato as a Fascist, he was exposing an anti-Italian prejudice.

D'Amato's first tracking polls after the ethnic-pride ads ran showed that he had moved up three points. *New York Times* reporter Alessandra Stanley noted that "while Mr. D'Amato was snatching up the moral high ground, publicly lamenting the insult, his aides were privately skipping with glee." She quoted Anthony W. Marsh, whose firm had produced the ads. " 'We turned it into an anti-Italian attack, and we kept it alive for a week and a half,' adding, 'It was sheer gall.' "

D'Amato was always in the game for himself, as Joe Margiotta learned to his sorrow. When the presidential polls showed that New York State would go for Bill Clinton by 15 percent, D'Amato abandoned George Bush to his fate. Confirming Jim Nagourney's jaundiced view of his political morality, he attached himself to Democrat Clinton's coattails, pointing out that they both supported the death penalty, welfare reform, and reductions in military spending. He claimed he was closer to centrist Clinton's positions.

Three days before the election, Democratic party leaders overcame Geraldine Ferraro's bitterness toward Abrams and coerced her into a public endorsement. But her grim television commercial on his behalf only served to remind voters that she had been the victim of the man who now wooed her.

The decisive event in D'Amato's campaign to win a third term happened on Sunday, November 1, 1992, two days before the election. But the catastrophe that made that event possible began a year and a half earlier on a summer day in Crown Heights, Brooklyn.

A few thousand Hasidic Jews have for over forty-five years lived in a small area of Crown Heights bordering Eastern Parkway, one of the few grand boulevards in a borough otherwise interlaced by a cobweb of narrow streets. These Hasidim are descendents of a relatively recent offshoot of orthodox Judaism. They appeared for the first time in eighteenth-century Poland, where their founder wanted to energize Judaism by infusing the staid rituals of that era with activities that would appeal to the hardworking members of their community. Hasidim dance (although separated by sex), they sing, they laugh, and they worship their God with an intensity present in all isolated groups of mystics.

In Crown Heights the Hasidim found a uniquely isolated environment in which to practice their beliefs. After 1955, their Jewish neighbors moved to the suburbs, and the Hasidim were surrounded by an African-American and Caribbean-black community that moved south from nearby Bedford-Stuyvesant. The manorial Lubavitch World Headquarters at 777 Eastern Parkway, in which their ninety-year-old rabbi made occasional, silent, iconic appearances before worshipers, was their unornamented spiritual home.

During the years they have lived in Crown Heights, Hasidim have sometimes been assaulted by bands of blacks usually inspired by an insult, real or imagined. Many blacks perceive them to be arrogant and seekers of special favors, like police protection, which they insist is not afforded to the Bedford-Stuyvesant community, where black-on-black crime is endemic. The Hasidim have responded to what they see as an ongoing threat from Bed-Sty hoodlums by organizing an unarmed neighborhood patrol.

Crown Heights is an integrated community in which blacks and whites frequently occupy adjoining apartments. Jews make up only 10 percent of the Crown Heights population, and within the area where a majority of them live, they are outnumbered two to one by blacks.

On that summer day, Monday, August 19, 1991, at 8:22 P.M., as twilight was approaching, the ancient grand rebbe Menachem Schneerson was returning from his weekly visit to his wife's grave in a nearby Cypress Hills cemetery. As his three-car motorcade crossed Utica Avenue, four blocks from Rabbi Schneerson's home, the third car bounced off a parked car, swerved out of control, and ran up on the sidewalk. Two seven-year-old black cousins, Gavin and Angela Cato, were struck. Gavin was crushed under the wheels of the car, and Angela was severely injured.

It was a tragic accident, similar to one six months earlier on the same streets, that time with a black driver and a Jewish child dead under the wheels of his car. But whereas that accident had been mourned and then placed in a private family niche for perpetual sorrows, Gavin Cato's death caused a riot.

Bands of young blacks rampaged through Crown Heights hurling stones and bottles, breaking into businesses, and assaulting pedestrians. The police had been ordered by Commissioner Lee Brown to be passive and "not to take independent actions." State director of criminal justice Richard Girgenti, in his July 21, 1993, report on the riots, stated: "The fact that the police were not fully deployed until well after midnight had significant consequences . . . a rapid mobilization of sufficient forces would have provided a better opportunity to end or limit the disorders."

Three hours after the accident, at approximately 11:20 P.M., a roving gang of blacks began to chase Yankel Rosenbaum, a twenty-nine-year-old Hasidic scholar from Australia. They screamed, "Kill the Jew!" He managed to stay ahead of them for three blocks, but finally he was cut off and surrounded. After taunting and beating the frail Rosenbaum while chanting "The Jews killed the kids" and "Death to the Jew," someone pounced on him and four times thrust a knife into his body.

The police, who had been watching passively, immediately began chasing Lemrick Nelson Jr., a teenage member of the gang that had been assaulting Rosenbaum. They quickly caught him and found a knife covered with Rosenbaum's blood in his bloody pants pocket.

They took Lemrick Nelson back to Yankel Rosenbaum, who had been placed on a hood of a car, where he was slowly bleeding to death. Was this the person who stabbed you? the police asked. "That's him," Rosenbaum said. "Twenty to one. Why did you do it?" he demanded, and spat at his assailant.

Subsequently, Lemrick Nelson confessed to the police that he had stabbed Rosenbaum.

The Girgenti report charged that during the first twenty-four hours after Yankel Rosenbaum's murder, "roving bands terrorized parts of the neighborhood for prolonged periods. The aggression was systematic, intense, and injurious." Yet Police Commissioner Brown refused to act; instead, three days later, he issued a statement praising his police for showing "great restraint."

The restraint had gone on while police logged 411 crime complaints from Crown Heights Jews. Television news programs carried extensive coverage of the violence; newspaper front pages were covered with pictures of the rampaging mobs. Mayor David Dinkins had independent sources of information that detailed the fury of the assaults. Joseph Gonzalez, director of the emergency unit of the mayor's Community Assistance Unit, and Robert Brennan, a member of his staff, acted as the "eyes and ears" of City Hall on the streets of Crown Heights. They reported directly to Deputy Mayor Bill Lynch.

Girgenti stated: "On Monday night and Tuesday, he [Gonzalez] tried to impress upon Lynch . . . the severity of the situation and that the police were not reacting in a strong and effective way. On Tuesday and Wednesday he repeatedly told Lynch . . . that the situation was 'out of control' and that the police were not reacting . . . and that the riots would continue or get worse until the police took action to 'shut it down.' "

Brennan had a separate tale of horror to tell his superiors. "On Tuesday evening," Girgenti reported, "Brennan called Lynch and related the following events to him:

"He was standing with Chief Gallagher, outside the Cato residence, when they were bombarded with rocks and bricks. He went to a telephone booth to call Lynch. The barrage became more intense. The captain in charge of the task force ordered the police to 'hold the line.' Things were totally out of control.

"Brennan described how 'cops went down all over the streets,' and he began to run. Then something happened which Brennan said he had never seen before: The police ran, too. He said the police were 'in full retreat; they gave up their positions and ran.' "

A few minutes later, Brennan, a police captain, and another officer responded to an emergency call they heard on a police radio. Girgenti continued: "Bricks and rocks were raining down from the rooftops. Brennan was hit in the face with a brick and lost consciousness. The police dragged him into a hallway, where he subsequently regained consciousness. Brennan got to his own car, which had its windows shattered and its tires blown . . ." and drove to the seventy-first Precinct, where he called Lynch at City Hall and " 'laid out' the entire situation to him. . . . He told Lynch that 'all hell is breaking loose' and the situation is 'totally out of control.' "

Mayor Dinkins visited Yankel Rosenbaum on his deathbed in Kings County Hospital, held his hand, and assured him that he would recover, but for three days after Rosenbaum's death he did nothing to end the rioting. Although he must have been concerned, publicly he appeared indifferent to the fate of the beleaguered Jews.

At 5:00 P.M. on Wednesday the mayor spoke to a largely black audience in the auditorium of P.S. 167, three blocks from the Lubavitch headquarters. He called for a restoration of peace. Violence had spread, intensified by a relatively small number of people who felt it was an acceptable response to personal or group unhappiness. Police cars had been overturned and burned on Eastern Parkway. There had been shootings, robberies, arson, assaults, and looting. A paramedic described the scene as "a war zone."

On his way out of P.S. 167 the mayor was pelted with bottles thrown by black bystanders, who booed as he called for peace. This personal assault infuriated Dinkins. Later that night, after visiting eight wounded police officers at Kings County Hospital, he ordered Chief Brown "to take all steps necessary to end the violence." The police were directed to "take back the streets." Determined action ended the rampage within hours without serious injury to any rioter. But in the intervening four days of mob violence Yankel Rosenbaum had been killed and eighty Jews were injured, as were numerous police officers who had been ordered to "restrain" themselves even as they were being assaulted.

In due course Lemrick Nelson was indicted for Rosenbaum's murder. He went on trial in October 1992. The twelve-member jury, eleven of whose members were blacks and Hispanics, found him innocent despite his bloody knife, Rosenbaum's "deathbed" identification of him as his assailant, the police testimony that he was a member of the mob that killed Rosenbaum, and his confession that he was the killer.

This incendiary verdict came on Thursday, October 29, five days before the 1992 senatorial election. In a defiant display of the passion that they had brought to their verdict, the following day eleven of the jurors hosted a party for Lemrick Nelson and his attorneys, embraced him joyously, and raised wineglasses to toast their vindication of him.

New York Jews, among others, were stunned. The case had been so clear-cut. How could such a miscarriage of justice happen?

The Hasidim made no public comment, because they were muted by Sabbath observance on Friday and Saturday. D'Amato's Democratic opponent, State Comptroller Bob Abrams, an orthodox Jew, remained similarly silent. On Saturday night, October 31, as the Sabbath curfew ended, Abrams met in the Crown Heights Community Council headquarters with Hasidic representatives who dealt with secular matters and for an hour and a half privately expressed his distress at the verdict. He then left unobtrusively, stating ambiguously, "There is a deep need to ensure that those responsible for this terrible killing are going to be pursued." He apparently felt that he had done the right thing by discreetly stating his empathy for the Hasidim, and since he speaks fluent Hebrew, he must have felt that the nuances of his sentiments were clearly conveyed.

At the same time that Saturday night a loudspeaker, mounted on a car, circulated through Crown Heights announcing that "an emergency demonstration" would be held the next day on Eastern Parkway in front of the Lubavitch World Headquarters.

Sunday, November 1, the pivotal event in the 1992 election took place at high noon. A noisy crowd of forty-five hundred Jews assembled on the boulevard while police stood vigil on surrounding roofs. What made it pivotal was the presence of Alfonse D'Amato on the speaker's platform, flanked on one side by former mayor Ed Koch, his close and enduring ally, and Rudy Giuliani, his former friend and enemy and from this moment on again a member of the team.

D'Amato's presence at the front of the podium was not the result of last-minute opportunism. He had been bellowing for the mayor and his police commissioner to act for days. He was a well-known defender of Jewish causes. That fact had infuriated the terrorists who, the following March, exploded a truck filled with explosives under the World Trade Center, killing six and injuring a thousand. They were also accused of planning to kill him. D'Amato flaunts a picture of Mahmud Abouhalima, described by authorities as the mastermind of the plot, picketing him during the campaign with a sign reading D'AMATO KISS YOUR SEAT GOOD-BYE, while next to Abouhalima stands a picketer with a sign proclaiming D'AMATO SOLD OUT TO THE JEWS.

Norman Rosenbaum, who had come from Australia to seek justice for his dead brother, delivered an angry speech in which he said that the verdict had a larger meaning, since it was so blatant in its anti-Semitic bias that all Jews must tremble. "It was not just Yankel who was a victim," he said. "What we had in this neighborhood was a pogrom. Yankel's murder is a symbol of the outrageous anti-Semitic violence that was permitted to be perpetrated not only in Crown Heights but against Jews of this city, this state, and this country."

Rosenbaum then introduced D'Amato, embracing and being embraced by his most vociferous ecumenical supporter. After D'Amato finished his exhortation, there was no doubt where he stood on "the pogrom" in Crown Heights or his defense of the Jewish community. Al D'Amato and Ed Koch joined hands and raised them in salute to the cheering crowd at what had become an impromptu D'Amato rally. When the pictures of the senator and the former mayor appeared on television, the Jewish vote, and the vote of those distraught by what had occurred in Crown Heights, moved in D'Amato's direction.

Two days later, D'Amato gained a narrow victory, he and Abrams dividing 6 million votes almost evenly, 49 percent to 48 percent. Three percentage points were shared by four other candidates. Aside from the fundamental demographics of the New York electorate that favored Al D'Amato, the result was caused by a combination of singular factors: Abrams joining with Elizabeth Holtzman in a vicious attack on Geraldine Ferraro during the Democratic primary; D'Amato's skillful exploitation of Abrams's reference to him as a Fascist; a tremendous disparity in campaign treasuries that allowed D'Amato exclusive access to television for five of the last six weeks of the campaign; and, decisively, Abrams's timidity in Crown Heights as the campaign's climax was reached.

The day after the election, on the 11:00 P.M. Channel 4 television news program, reporter David Diaz asked the victorious senator whether he was concerned about charges that he conducted a vicious, lying campaign. D'Amato said, "I'd be concerned if I came out on the wrong end of the count. Come on, get real."

A month before the election D'Amato had pledged that this would be his final campaign. It was his attempt to neutralize anti-incumbent sentiment so effectively being mobilized by Ross Perot's term-limits crusade. "This will be the last time I run for public office," D'Amato said on October 17 as he emerged from a debate with Bob Abrams. Hours after his victory D'Amato abandoned his pledge, announcing that he might seek a fourth term, in fact, he said the chances were "fifty-fifty or better" that he would run for governor of New York against Mario Cuomo.

He was exhilarated by his upset victory. How could he allow himself to be required by a promise to limit his options?

FIFTY-FOUR

THE D'AMATOS' TRIAL

On March 18, 1992, Armand Paul D'Amato, senior partner in the firm of D'Amato, Forchelli, Libert, Schwartz, Mineo & Joseph F. Carlino, was arraigned in Nassau federal court on twenty-four counts of mail fraud. The indictment, which had been handed down by an Eastern District grand jury the previous week, had been delayed in U.S. Attorney Andrew Maloney's office for over two and a half years as the D'Amato family sought ways to escape its stain. Even after the arraignment, stalling continued. Senator D'Amato's campaign would be devastated if his brother's trial was in progress as he sought reelection.

The trial didn't start until April 20, 1993, three months after D'Amato began his third senatorial term. Handsome, preppy Larry Noyer and soft-spoken Joshua Hochberg were the two Assistant U.S. Attorneys in charge of the prosecution in the Uniondale court-house. Federal district court senior judge Jacob Mishler, now eighty-one, presided.

It was an extraordinary occasion: the first time that the D'Amatos, who can only be thought of as a family enterprise, were the lead actors in such a melodrama.

It was also an opportunity to talk to family members. Attempts to interview them in surroundings of their choice, where they could decide which questions to answer or they could break off the interview, had been repeatedly rejected. Suddenly, they were available under perfect circumstances. The D'Amato way of exploiting the public's trust *was* the subject. Questions they might have refused to answer in another venue had to be answered under threat of a judicial penalty. Not only were they available; they were functioning under stress, and the defenses that normally shielded them were bound to be less rigorously policed.

Courtroom B is on the second floor of the courthouse, directly above the chamber in which the 1 percent case had been heard eight years earlier. It was smaller, and its more modest slice of the pie-structured building only required five walls. I sat in a chair to the right of the three rows of spectator benches, close to the witness box and four feet from Armand D'Amato. He was attended by his lawyer, Stephen Scaring, a man never offended by any charge made against his clients. Directly behind the defense table, separated from me by an aisle, sat Armand Paul's mother, Antoinette, and her aged husband, Armand. As Judge Mishler opened the trial, Armand Paul's second wife, Audrey, and a number of relatives sat beside the family's matriarch and patriarch. Missing at the starting line was the family's luminary.

In his opening remarks to the seven-woman, five-man jury Larry Noyer showed a fiery aspect of his personality previously concealed by institutional etiquette. D'Amato, he charged, had defrauded Sperry-Unisys from 1986 to 1988 by claiming to do work he didn't do and had no intention of doing. He had been hired purportedly as a Washington consultant, a subject about which he knew little. The real reason he was hired was to influence his brother, a member of the Senate Military Appropriations Committee, which had jurisdiction over contracts vital to the company.

Noyer insisted that higher-ups in the company weren't aware that Sperry's executive vice president, Charles Gardner, had hired Armand Paul. He charged that Armand Paul was being paid to buy his brother's vote.

Defense counsel Scaring countered Noyer by picturing Armand Paul as "a political novice" who was innocently doing exactly what he was asked to do by Charles Gardner.

On the second day of the trial, Noyer produced a witness who established the fraudulent nature of Armand Paul's association with

Unisys. Robert Littlefield was the former president of Coastal Energy Enterprises, a subsidiary of Sperry that Gardner had set up to handle his payoffs. The Coastal slush fund was used to pay bribes to government officials, to buy $1 million worth of tickets given to influential politicians and contractors, or, in Armand Paul's case, to issue purchase orders in 1986 and 1987 that paid him $88,000.

Littlefield testified, in response to questions from Joshua Hochberg, that he never met with Armand Paul and that he never saw any reports prepared by him or his firm. "Did you have any need for these types of services at Coastal?" asked Hochberg.

"Not that I was aware of," Littlefield said.

On the third day of the trial the prosecution produced a witness who told why the Coastal payoff mechanism had been necessary. Dennis Mitchell, former Unisys marketing manager, who had served a ninety-day sentence for illegal campaign contributions and was part of the inner circle of Gardner's Washington lobbying operation, testified that by billing D'Amato on a "purchase order" for "a technical service," only Gardner's signature was needed to obtain D'Amato's $6,500 monthly payoff.

When Unisys had acquired Sperry in 1986, it had been unaware of Charles Gardner's illegal activity. But careful scrutiny of company records aroused Unisys's suspicions and led to the appointment of Lawrence Cresce, an expert investigative accountant. Gardner was his target.

Gardner worried that the larger fraud in which he was participating might be exposed. He was less concerned about Armand Paul's being discovered, since his name never appeared on a Unisys payroll. But when Unisys decided to close down Coastal Energy near the end of 1987, as a result of Cresce's initial probe, Gardner had to find a new way of paying Armand Paul. Unisys's more rigorous ethical regulations made it clear that payment to political lobbyists had to be approved at an executive level above Gardner. Further closing off Gardner's ability to operate as a freebooter, Unisys now demanded that all consultants who provided a "technical service" had to submit a monthly report about what they had done. Dennis Mitchell testified that under the new regime "we couldn't have paid the invoice without a report."

Since Gardner knew the company would never pay a bill with Armand Paul's name on it, he had Armand submit his bill and "the report" signed by, and paid to, Jeffrey D. Forchelli, Armand's partner and closest friend. Although the last of the five "purchase orders" signed by Forchelli were accompanied by "a report" supposedly written by Forchelli, a government wiretapped conversation between Charles Gardner and Dennis Mitchell, taped on April 11, 1988, revealed the identity of the actual writer. Gardner is heard praising the report's brevity. "Who wrote those? D'Amato?" he asked Mitchell.

"Uh, no, uh, [James G.] Lynch and I wrote them." On the stand he corrected this self-aggrandizing fib: Lynch, another member of Gardner's Washington lobbying operation, had written all of Armand's "reports." His vacuous, ghostwritten efforts never exceeded two paragraphs and contained information broadcast hourly on CNN, but they enabled D'Amato to squeeze another $32,000 out of Unisys, for a total of $120,500.

The following day, April 22, 1993, Charles Gardner, the prosecution's star witness, made his first public statement about his Unisys boiler-room operation. In the four years since his resignation from Unisys, Gardner had been in prison for two years and four months after pleading guilty in 1989 to charges of bribery, conspiracy, and filing false income tax returns. In connection with that guilty plea Unisys had paid a $190 million fine. Among his crimes, Gardner had bribed Assistant Secretary of the Navy Melvyn R. Paisley and Cong. Joseph Addabbo, a Queens Democrat and confederate of Al D'Amato's. Addabbo was then chairman of the House Military Appropriations Subcommittee, for Gardner's purpose Congress's most influential committee. Gardner, whose forthright gaze signaled that he hadn't been chastened by prison, said he had "tremendous clout" with Addabbo, and when the congressman suggested in 1984 that he try to win over Al D'Amato, Gardner set his Washington lobbyists to work on the task.

D'Amato's aid became imperative in 1985 because Gardner was fearful that the navy had decided it didn't want two of Sperry's antimissile radar systems, the Aegis and the MK-92, the latter because it was obsolete. Since these were the mainstays of Sperry's

Great Neck plant, which he headed, Gardner needed D'Amato to cram the missile systems down the navy's throat.

Even though D'Amato bragged he was the "Pothole Senator" who always helped his constituents and Sperry was one of the largest employers of his constituents, he refused to deal with Gardner's lobbyists. That Washington crew included a former congressman, former congressional staff members, and a host of full-time employees. Gardner told the transfixed jurors that D'Amato was miffed because Sperry hadn't contributed to his 1980 campaign. If they wanted to deal with him, they were advised, it would have to be through his brother.

Gardner said he was perfectly willing to accommodate the senator, but since he was running an independent scam that was skimming $2.5–$3 million annually from Unisys, he feared the larger swindle might accidentally be discovered should the red flag of D'Amato's name cause Unisys's auditors to look closer.

His disgrace didn't dim Gardner's exuberant nature. After leaving prison, he found work suited to his talents: He was a car salesman in a local dealership. Dressed in a gray suit that matched his close-cropped hair and a red paisley tie he might have worn to a Unisys board meeting, he peered out through his gold-rimmed glasses, occasionally glancing defiantly at Armand Paul, who glared back at him. In a firm voice, and in elaborate detail, he described his operation. It had only been with the help of Congressman Addabbo and Senator D'Amato, among others, that he had been able to get millions in allocations out of a navy bureaucracy dead set against buying his flawed products.

The key to his success with Senator D'Amato was the connection to his brother. Before that, a locked and bolted door; afterward, access. Noyer asked how Armand Paul reacted to an offer from a company with whose business he was unfamiliar. "He didn't blink an eyelash," Gardner said, looking at the defendant and smiling broadly.

"What did you communicate was your principal reason for hiring him?" Noyer queried.

"For support on the Appropriations Committee."

"How was he supposed to do that," Noyer continued.

Gardner said: "By working through the senator's office."

The payoff arrangement had been made with Coastal in order to avoid "having the D'Amato name in the company." He patiently explained, "We were hiding the name essentially. It represented political activity I did not want known."

In his second day of testimony, Gardner was asked by Noyer, "Did you hire Armand D'Amato because of his experience on Capitol Hill."

"No," Gardner answered. He pointed out that Armand didn't have any experience on Capitol Hill, only influence with his brother.

During the two years he paid Armand Paul, Gardner said, he had done almost nothing to earn his $120,500. He had only arranged to have two letters, which were drafted by Gardner's staff, sent to navy officials on the senator's stationery. Gardner also had Armand transmit legislative language to his brother that Gardner wanted inserted in bills, a constituent service not available to ordinary citizens.

Noyer then played recordings that the government had made from wiretaps on Gardner's phone in the spring of 1988. The taps had been installed after Unisys had informed the Defense Department of their investigator's conclusion that Gardner had procured contracts illegally. The roof, groaning under the weight of auditor Cresce's tentative accusations, hadn't fallen, but Gardner was nervously eying its ominous cracks.

"The hell with that goddamned D'Amato," he told one of his lobbyists. "You know, for his two letters a year, we can use somebody else."

The senator was not performing up to his expectations. The lobbyist responded to Gardner's complaint: "Well . . . yeah. Because he can't really help us too much on . . . where it counts, 'cause he doesn't have enough . . . respect from his colleagues."

"Let's drop him," Gardner concluded.

It was a bruising day for Armand Paul. At the end of the session his mother came to reclaim her raincoat, which hung from a rack next to my chair. She seemed to be tiring. As I helped her on with her coat, she became more animated and volunteered, "They're trying to get at Al this way because they can't get him any other way." In one sentence she had found the trial's focus: It was really all about her elder son.

We chatted for five minutes about their short stay in Brooklyn after Al was born, the seven years in North Jersey, and then the move to Island Park because her father wanted them to live there. She was approximately five feet tall and had a matronly figure crowned by wispy brown hair. During our conversation she often smiled and displayed a warm personality, which led me to comment that her neighbor Catherine Fazio had described her to me in the most complimentary manner. This pleased her.

In response to my question about the young woman sitting next to her, she said it was Armand Paul's second wife, Audrey. Four years of marriage had produced two children. "Very supportive" she said, looking at Audrey a few feet away, talking to her balding husband.

As she was about to leave, she wrapped a red scarf around her neck, and I noticed a black onyx gold ring on her finger. I expressed my admiration for it, and she remarked, "A gift to myself . . . a long time ago."

The next witness was Gardner's Washington lobbyist James G. Lynch, who earned $90,000 annually and had a company car and an expense account. "I wrote off political contributions on my expense account," he said, unconcerned about the penalty for such frankness because he was testifying under a grant of immunity. Lynch had led the good life until he was fired in 1991 because he had illegally obtained navy documents for the company.

Lynch confirmed much of what Gardner had said. He had been introduced to Armand Paul at the end of 1985 and had been told by Gardner to educate him about the Aegis program. But for Lynch the important part of that meeting was summed up in a brief exchange. "I said we'd like to get Al D'Amato's support for the program. He said, 'Yes.' "

He conversed with Armand Paul a number of times but had never been given any reports about what he was doing. This didn't bother Gardner's coconspirator. "He was the interface between us and the senator."

Lynch described how it worked: He told Armand he wanted a letter from his brother to the secretary of the navy telling the secretary to start the Aegis program. The letter was not to mention

Unisys directly; that would open the brash letter writer to influ-ence-peddling charges.

Larry Noyer later told me, "My understanding after reading all kinds of these letters from all kinds of corrupt officials . . . you did-n't mention any particular contract. You mentioned the program." But since Unisys was the sole supplier, if the navy decided to go ahead with the program, there was only one company that would benefit. The letter would say: Congress wanted you to do some-thing. You haven't done it, do it. Lynch told the jury that the letter he drafted and gave to Armand Paul was the "identical" letter sent out on the senator's stationery. Larry Noyer finished his comment about the letter to me by remarking, "The real deal making and arm twisting isn't in a letter. It's in a phone call. It's in a hallway."

When Armand Paul's attorney, Stephen Scaring, cross-examined, he asked, "Would you describe Mr. D'Amato as a charismatic per-son or low-keyed?"

"Low-keyed" was lobbyist Lynch's character analysis.

The answer cut two ways. It depicted Armand as someone who wouldn't initiate the scheme of which the government accused him. It also reinforced the image of a pliant Armand Paul habituat-ed to doing anything demanded by his older brother.

When it was his turn to cross-examine, Assistant U.S. Attorney Joshua Hochberg had two questions. "Did you supply other letters to senators?"

"Yes," Lynch answered.

"Did you ever go through other senators' brothers?"

The emphatic "No!" sounded through a silent courtroom.

That day, Armand Sr. returned to court from a solitary lunch at 2:15 P.M. He was small, about five feet four inches, wore a hearing aid in his right ear, and forcefully strode toward the front bench. His thin gray hair was combed across his bald pate. He was still a dandy after all these years, though the pointy waxed mustache was gone.

Larry Noyer, who had been cross-examining a witness, watched the senior Armand walk in. "The place was packed," Noyer told me. "You know where Mama and Papa sat—in the middle of the front row. People were sitting in that seat, and he walked in and just about sat down in a guy's lap and said, 'Front row is for family only.' You'd have thought it was an Italian funeral."

After the old man cleared out a space for himself, he sat down at Antoinette's left. As he turned to face Judge Mishler, a toothpick in his mouth came into view. For the next two hours he sat slumped on the bench, his feet thrust against the fence separating the spectators from the participants. Antoinette ignored him completely, although she frequently held animated conversations with Audrey. Armand spent his time sucking on his toothpick, occasionally resetting its position in his mouth.

At 4:15 P.M., during a sidebar, he stood up to leave. As he moved past a disinterested Antoinette, he reached over the waist-high fence and tapped junior on the shoulder. Armand Paul had been sitting docilely by himself, staring at the attorneys conversing with Judge Mishler. With elaborate staginess, father D'Amato extended his right arm, grasped his son's hand, and shook it vigorously, but the expression on his face remained strangely remote, almost as though he could think of nothing to say. Armand Paul was also at a conversational loss. After an awkward moment, Armand walked away.

Herbert Chodosh had worked for Sperry-Unisys from 1958 until his forced retirement as a marketing director in 1989. He was Gardner's closest contact with Armand Paul. A convivial fellow, he was the only prosecution witness who turned to Armand Paul with a smile, which was returned in kind. He and Jim Lynch had presented the idea of working for Sperry to Armand Paul at a lunch meeting in the Salisbury Restaurant in Nassau's Eisenhower Park, where the health enthusiast had been jogging.

Chodosh gave the jury an example of how networking between congressmen increased lobbyists' power. He had given Armand Paul a letter Gardner wanted his brother to send to Acting Secretary of Commerce Clarence Brown. Armand Paul said that the senator's legislative assistant thought this would be imprudent for the senator but offered to get Cong. Norman Lent (R-N.Y.), D'Amato's close ally, to send it out over his name. On July 28, 1987, Lent dispatched the letter. Until this moment, D'Amato's role in that influence-peddling episode had not been exposed.

During the two years of their business relationship Chodosh and Armand Paul met "six or eight times," usually with Jim Lynch, and had a few telephone contacts. The meetings and calls were inconsequential, sometimes concerning Armand Paul's attempt to get Chodosh to buy tickets to the senator's golf outings or cocktail parties. More often, Armand Paul was calling because his monthly check hadn't arrived punctually and he wanted Chodosh to light a fire under Coastal's payroll department.

Armand Sr. came back into the courtroom at three o'clock. A sidebar was taking place, and he took the opportunity to converse with an old family friend sitting on the bench behind him who was present throughout the trial. He was Armand's size, dressed in a black sport shirt, black slacks, and green Nike sneakers. They spoke loudly in Italian, Armand gesturing broadly as he made his points, never once removing the toothpick from his mouth.

Antoinette had moved away, and after several minutes the lonely Armand Paul came to where his father was seated and spoke to him haltingly. Senior was haughty; Junior, fawning. At one point Junior drifted away, then returned and loudly offered, "Pop, you and Mom ought'ta go on a cruise after this."

Senior retorted, "We're booked on a Mediterranean cruise in July." Junior, who lived in a Lloyd Harbor mansion on the North Shore, forty miles from Island Park, knew nothing about this family voyage, and Senior did not appear to expect that he would.

Senior then gave the cruise's agenda in a swaggering, overbearing tone. "Genoa, then France ... Nice, Spain, North Africa, back to Naples and Genoa."

At this point, Antoinette approached me to retrieve her coat. She said, "I'm leaving," as if she had enough for one day.

Armand Sr. now sprawled out on the half-empty bench. His arms were slung over the backrest, his feet spread and propped up against the divider separating him from the lawyers. Throughout the session the toothpick jauntily protruded from his mouth. It didn't seem to interfere with the conversations he held with his diminutive friend or with his intimidated son. Late in the afternoon, Alfonse D'Amato's daughter Lisa came into the court. She went directly to her grandfather, bent down, and kissed his regally offered cheek; but he did not remove his toothpick.

Court was adjourned for the weekend. I took the opportunity to cross the hall to Judge Mishler's chambers and say hello. I mentioned that he looked better than he did when I last saw him five years earlier. He responded, "That proves to me that your eyesight isn't as good as it used to be."

I asked to be brought up-to-date on the 1 percent case. He reeled off details as if he had just emerged from listening to Burt Neuborne and Ed Hart summarize the case. He had set Neuborne's fee at $1 million, which Neuborne refused as being too large. Neuborne later told me he had finally accepted $620,000.

Ed Hart, Mishler said sarcastically, had received his reward from the party. "He was chosen by the clubhouse boys last year to run for state supreme court judge." Nassau's Tom Seaver was now refereeing all those boring decisions involving contract disputes and marital bickering.

Mishler had forced John Jund to go through two more trials to prove his claims, the first in 1989, which ended indecisively; the second in 1990, which resulted in a jury verdict for Jund. He had awarded Jund "about $125,000," which was upheld after a 1991 Republican party trip to the court of appeals.

Mishler had finally granted triple RICO damages to the members of the class. He had given the responsibility of establishing who the members were to Neuborne, who spent three years checking boxes of party receipts and, in the absence of receipts, deciding whether notarized affidavits would be sufficient. Despite what Neuborne described as his "generous" guidelines, he eventually verified only 750 claims. That cost the Republican party $1,200,000, which was paid out in three annual installments of $400,000. The settlement covered claims of extortions only up to the mid-1970s, leaving the possibility of new RICO suits by more current complainants that would more seriously affect the solvency of the party.

Jessel Rothman, Mishler's perpetual antagonist, had asked the judge for $754,000 as his fee for representing "the class," a job entirely done at the trial by Burt Neuborne. Mishler countered with an offer of $188,177, which he thought was sufficient for the earlier work that Rothman had performed for the class, and for Julian Kaplan's fine effort on behalf of John Jund. Rothman was outraged and took the matter to the court of appeals, where it remains unresolved. "So," Mishler said sardonically, "after twenty years the one percent case still has some life, if not much."

On Monday, April 26, 1993, Judge Mishler opened court in the absence of the jury and listened to attorney arguments about the jury charge. He said that he had not yet decided whether he would charge the jury or even allow the case to go on after the prosecution had concluded. He also wanted it understood that "he's [Armand Paul] not being charged with lobbying." He was being charged with mail fraud. Then, displaying his tolerance for marginal political activities, Mishler added an opinion no one had asked him to render: "Lobbying is not unlawful." Unmentioned were a number of lobbying activities that are unlawful; bribery, for example, which was the reason, when legalisms are stripped away, that Armand Paul sat beneath Mishler's steady gaze.

At 11:15 A.M. there was a recess, and Antoinette, who was sitting by herself on the front bench, approached me, holding her coat in front of her. I took it and hung it on the coat rack. We spoke about her father's life in Rome and Armand's family in Naples. "They had hard times," she said in summary. Armand Sr. walked into the court and came to where we were chatting. "Is this the lunch break?" he asked his suddenly glum wife.

"No," she answered impatiently, ". . . just a short break."

The old man wisecracked, "Oh, it's just to go to the boys' and girls' room."

He went to his place on the front bench and occupied himself chewing gum while the ubiquitous toothpick simultaneously jutted from his mouth.

The prosecution's next witness was Andrew Henry, who had been general counsel for Unisys when the forensic accountant, Lawrence Cresce, had been hired to investigate Charles Gardner. Henry had blond wavy hair, wore gold wire-rimmed glasses, and spoke only after carefully weighing his choice of words. He was unsmiling and took every opportunity with grimaces and words extruded through pursed lips to demonstrate his disapproval of Armand Paul's activities.

The supposed reports by D'Amato and Forchelli were "plagia-rized." Cresce had discovered that "paperwork didn't show actual work accomplished." Neither D'Amato nor Forchelli are listed as consultants, and no record of payments to them was found in Great Neck files.

His sense of managerial decorum seemed to be offended. Hidden lobbying activity, he said in the way of a legal opinion, potentially harmed Unisys. The company had been deprived of the ability to check on the honesty of its lobbyists.

This reference to a marginal political activity aroused the judge. "Only the employees of Unisys had to live up to the code of ethics," he expounded. "Armand D'Amato was not an employee of Unisys." In Judge Mishler's crucial opinion, being an employee of a Unisys subsidiary, Coastal, didn't obligate Armand to measure up ethically. Furthermore, he concluded, "lobbying is a democratic right. It is not illegal."

Larry Noyer's last witness can only be described as hostile; he was Jeffrey Forchelli, managing partner of Armand Paul's law firm. Forchelli was tall and husky, with a full head of graying kinky hair. He had grown up in Queens and graduated from Flushing High School in 1963. After obtaining a degree from Brooklyn Law School, his first substantial job was with the New York State Assembly, where he served as a legislative counsel from 1972 to 1975, the same position Armand Paul held in Joe Margiotta's Albany office. The two lawyers became acquainted and in June 1976 organized a firm in Nassau County. They soon began to spe-cialize in land use and zoning, two disciplines requiring the heavi-est kind of political connections. Alfonse D'Amato was then town supervisor of rapidly growing Hempstead, and Armand Paul's Albany boss, Margiotta, controlled all of Nassau County.

Forchelli seemed extremely nervous. He glanced at Armand Paul and attempted a smile, but he couldn't sustain it and quickly turned back to Noyer. The thrust of his testimony was that he real-ly didn't know what his partner was doing. He had never met Charles Gardner or any of Gardner's employees.

Noyer asked, "What kind of work did you think he was doing?"

"Government work," Forchelli responded softly.

After Unisys shut down Coastal in December 1987, Armand had casually mentioned he would like him to sign the "purchase orders" and "reports" Unisys now required. Forchelli said that in signing the forms he was stating "we" had performed the work based on Armand's statement to him that the work had been done.

Noyer was curious about the apparent subterfuge. "Did you ask him why not his name?"

Forchelli said, "I kind of figured it out for myself." An idiot, he implied, could figure it out. "There was a sensitivity in Unisys about the D'Amato name," he added delicately.

This was a crucial moment in the trial, because it confirmed that Armand Paul was trying to hide his name from Unisys. The bills were also submitted circuitously. Instead of being sent directly to the company's accounting department, they were addressed to Dennis Mitchell, one of the conspirators.

Noyer wanted to know whether D'Amato ever asked him to send out any other bill without his name on it? "No," Forchelli conceded. And then, in response to Noyer's suggestion that this was extraordinary, he admitted, "It was extraordinary."

At 3:10 P.M., Larry Noyer rested the government's case. The jury was sent out of the room, and Scaring immediately asked Judge Mishler to dismiss the case. It was apparent that this wasn't a simple pro forma motion. Mishler had previously expressed doubts about letting the trial go on after the prosecution concluded. Scaring knew this was his best opportunity to win. In an oration that lasted eight minutes and took on the air of a summation, Scaring's major argument was that *Gardner* had chosen the manner in which Armand Paul was paid. And it was simply a way to get him paid; it had never been a "scheme" to defraud Unisys.

Noyer answered Scaring by quoting Gardner's testimony: "*We devised a scheme. . . .*" He was impassioned. He characterized Armand as "a no-show employee." For twelve minutes he blasted forth his rebuttal. "Mr. D'Amato cannot set up as an excuse that he didn't read the paperwork." Without doubt, "Mr. D'Amato had the criminal intent to take part in Gardner's scheme."

Scaring seemed deflated. But since he practiced in a profession that allowed no concession to the obvious, he steeled himself to address the judge in banal legalisms. "We don't have to prove that Mr. D'Amato visited Washington or did any work." He had to be presumed innocent until the jury ruled otherwise.

The judge seemed offended by this gratuitous lecture. As Noyer began to counter, Mishler interjected. He would take Scaring's advice and let the jury decide. "The motion is denied without any further discussion," he pronounced with Mishlerian finality. "There is no doubt the government has made a case."

The family filed out of the courtroom in varying degrees of shock and dejection, without even the comfort that might have been produced by the presence of their senatorial luminary.

When Scaring returned to the almost empty chamber at 3:30 P.M. to prepare for the opening of the defense, he was disconcerted. Bent over his records, he spoke loudly enough to be heard by Larry Noyer, Joshua Hochberg, several reporters, and myself, for whom he had a self-deprecating message. "I surely love to introduce witnesses," he remarked cynically. His voice was pessimistic, suggesting he had little faith that those who were about to testify would be of any help.

When he called his first witness at 3:46 P.M., it became apparent why he had made that woebegone remark. It was Lawrence Cresce, the scourge of flimflam accounting. Why did Scaring think that the man who had connected Armand Paul to Charles Gardner could help D'Amato's cause?

Scaring's defense rested on the premise that Armand could not be accused of mail fraud when the top men at Unisys knew after Cresce began his investigation why he was mailing them bills, even if his name wasn't on the bills. He hoped Cresce would lend credence to that supposition. At best, this dubious premise suggested that D'Amato should not have been in the docket by himself.

Unisys was determined not to allow Scaring to smear its upper echelons. In order to prevent this, a glittering array of America's most accomplished attorneys sat in the spectator's section ready to object should attempts be made to include Unisys executives in the accusations against Armand Paul.

Charles ("Chuck") Ruff, chief counsel to Unisys, was the most dramatic legal presence in the courtroom. Mr. Ruff was stocky, middle-aged, and spent his productive days in a wheelchair. He sat in the aisle next to me, warmly and graciously instructing a staff of three about what he wanted done. Mr. Ruff had been mentioned as a possible nominee to the U.S. Supreme Court prior to President Clinton's selection of Ruth Bader Ginsburg.

Earlier in the trial Judge Mishler announced: "The law protects privileged communications between a lawyer and his client. . . . It's proper for Unisys to assert its privilege." So the matter was settled by the time Lawrence Cresce was sworn in, and it was hard to imagine what Scaring thought he was going to accomplish with a hostile witness who sought comfort from Charles Ruff whenever privileged territory was approached.

Cresce told Scaring that in a discussion with Gardner in November 1987 he had learned about Gardner's payment plan for his Washington lobbyists. Although Gardner informed him that he used worthless reports as "window dressing" to pay his staff, he never mentioned that Armand Paul was working for him.

The next month, Cresce interviewed David Osterhout, Unisys's vice president for business development, who told him that Gardner had "covert consultants to lobby on the hill." Osterhout had set up the Washington lobbying office for Sperry but no longer had anything to do with it and didn't know how Gardner operated.

Scaring had come up against a stone wall. Was Cresce's information passed up to a higher level of the company? Cresce was not obligated to say. Scaring began to fumble with a tape recorder, trying to get a tape between Cresce and Gardner to play. He spent the next thirty minutes at this fruitless task, at which point Judge Mishler put him out of his misery by calling an adjournment for the day. It had been an inauspicious beginning for the defense.

A night's rest and time to regroup produced no better results. Scaring tried to establish that Unisys's top executives knew what was going on, but within twenty minutes Mishler upheld Cresce's assertion of client privilege, and Scaring gave up.

Joshua Hochberg's cross-examination brought out that in the December 1987 interview with Osterhout, Cresce was told of the senator's "edict." D'Amato had decreed he must "go through my brother on your program requests." But Osterhout didn't know anything about what had resulted from that demand.

Why, Hochberg asked Cresce, hadn't he gone directly to Senator D'Amato to confront him with Osterhout's allegation. "I wouldn't think of it," Cresce answered, apparently horrified. The senator, he explained, had control over Unisys contracts.

Cresce found out from Gardner in November 1987 about the existence of Coastal's covert payment apparatus, but Gardner blocked him from gaining access to Coastal's records. He immediately informed Henry Ruth, Unisys's ethics counsel, but the company wouldn't fire Gardner on the basis of the initial fragmentary information he had gathered. He was urged, however, to intensify and speed up his investigation.

It wasn't until Cresce had a second formal interview with Gardner, on March 9, 1988, that he was told Unisys money was going to Armand Paul. Even then, when Gardner handed him a list of his lobbyists, the list didn't include the senator's brother.

Charles Ruff was happy with Cresce's testimony. From his wheelchair during a sidebar that began at 9:52 A.M. he beamed a smile of satisfaction at Cresce.

When testimony resumed, Cresce said that in his May 1988 report he concluded that the billing arrangement with Armand Paul, especially with the Forchelli purchase orders and reports, was "a cover" to gain Gardner access to Senator D'Amato. Unisys informed the Justice Department of Cresce's conclusions, and on June 14, 1988, the government raided Unisys's offices and seized records.

After Hochberg concluded, Scaring asked for a sidebar with Judge Mishler. Armand Paul sat deserted at the defense table, eying Charles Ruff as he wheeled his chair past him to join the conference at Mishler's podium. When Judge Mishler ruled against Scaring and a host of lawyers darted for their posts around the courtroom, Armand Paul's blinking eyes glanced in all directions.

Shawn Smeallie, the senator's former legislative assistant in charge of defense, was Scaring's next witness. He was a tall, thin man, not yet out of his twenties. He wore the gold-rimmed glasses sported by most of the successful men who had testified.

Smeallie was there to talk about Gardner's Aegis letter that Armand Paul had brought "to my desk and asked that it be sent out to Secretary James Webb." He felt it was a "pro forma letter," similar to others he regularly handled.

On cross, Hochberg brought out that although Smeallie claimed the letter was routine, he didn't handle it routinely. He first called the Unisys Washington lobbying office to find out if they wanted the letter sent. Then, still not satisfied, he had taken the letter to D'Amato's chief of staff Michael Kinsella to find out whether he should process it.

Why had he done that? Hochberg asked.

Because, Smeallie answered, this was "not a normal channel."

Henry Ruth, prestigious counsel to Unisys's ethics committee, had been Watergate special prosecutor in the mid-1970s. He was dapper, understated, self-confident, and without a sign of pomposity. Ruth told Scaring that he had supervised Cresce, whom he described as "a terrific investigator." In fact, he added, "Larry and I had constant communication." But what he had told his Unisys superiors about Cresce's findings was locked in a secret part of his brain, protected from disclosure, since it was "a privileged communication." Again a dead end.

Prosecutor Hochberg brought out that Ruth had been responsible for Unisys's disclosure to the government of Gardner's activity. By the lunch recess Ruth was excused, with no sign that he had helped D'Amato. A few minutes later, I saw Ruth on the parking lot, jogging to his car, a broad smile on his face.

Headed in the other direction were Antoinette D'Amato and her daughter-in-law Audrey, deep in conversation as they crossed Uniondale Avenue on their way to lunch at Roy Rogers.

At 1:25 P.M., Judge Mishler climbed the steps to his pulpit and immediately asked Scaring if Armand Paul planned to testify. Scaring said he hadn't made up his mind and wouldn't until later that night. Such a torturous decision, he implied, required the outcome of future testimony and the alchemic weighing of all the trial's elements.

He had only asked, Mishler said, because he wanted to make a judgment about his schedule for next week. In an attempt to be helpful, Scaring added, in any case he expected to conclude his case "tomorrow." Mishler expressed surprise, saying he thought the defense would be on through the beginning of next week "at least." Scaring shook his head as though to say that such a lengthy time would not be needed to prove his client's innocence.

Professor Geoffrey Hazard Jr. was one of the trial's most fascinating witnesses. He had taught legal ethics since 1977 at Yale Law School. Scaring had hired him months earlier and was paying him a substantial sum to offer an opinion that each of Armand Paul's covert acts was legally ethical.

Professor Hazard began by reciting his accomplishments. He needed no prompting, but rattled on about his Columbia Law School degree in 1954, through his teaching stint at Berkeley and the University of Chicago. The man's credentials were intimidating. No doubt that was why he had through the years made a good living as an expert witness.

Responding to Scaring's questions, he said he didn't think it was unusual for a person to do business with a subsidiary. As to Forchelli's signing bills in the name of one of the partners: "It was unusual . . ." but if the client wants to do it that way "that's their business." One sensed that Professor Hazard had a nonjudgmental attitude toward the ethics of his clients. It seemed to come down to, if it wasn't illegal, it was ethical.

Since he was clearly an honorable man, he added, "unless you have a signal that something is amiss," you take the client's word. "Your job is not to run the company." Well, what was Armand Paul's correct role? When dealing with bureaucracies, the professor said, "you make the paper fit the requirements."

Larry Noyer was polite but persistent in his cross-examination. He showed the professor a purchase order that Forchelli had signed on February 2, 1988, to obtain payment for Armand Paul. Was this a retainer agreement? Noyer asked.

"I don't know what it is," Hazard answered.

Noyer wanted Hazard to comment on bogus "reports" Armand Paul had filed. "Would it be 'a signal' to you" if the purchase order says that you should provide "reports" and a corporate officer (Gardner) says he'll write the reports for you? Should Forchelli have taken this as "a signal that something was wrong."

Scaring objected. Mishler called a sidebar and four minutes later announced he would allow Noyer's question to be answered. "In cross," he said, "a lawyer may hypothesize."

"That could be 'a signal,' yes," Hazard told Noyer.

The prosecutor put forth a hypothetical: Assume a lawyer over a year and a half has performed no services but receives raises. "Would that be 'a signal'?"

"Yes," Hazard responded.

At 2:46 P.M., the professor left the stand, having skillfully been turned by Noyer from an expert retainer for the defense into an effective witness for the prosecution.

Antoinette D'Amato didn't seem concerned about Professor Hazard's double-edged testimony when she wandered over to the coat rack. She volunteered that someone had told her that coats might disappear. "They better not take mine," she said in a jovially threatening tone. "I'll have to go back to London to get another." She quickly explained that she had been to London four years earlier on vacation with her daughter Joanne. They had shopped at Harrods.

Scaring's last three witnesses testified for a total of eighteen minutes. That included walking in and out of the courtroom, being sworn in, fidgeting in the witness box, and a sidebar called by Judge Mishler.

Donald Murphy had worked for Charles Gardner for twenty-five years. He had been told to go to Armand Paul's office and brief him about Aegis. The thing that he remembered most clearly about the meeting, he said on cross-examination by Noyer, was that Armand had told him and his companions that they were expected to buy tickets to the senator's next golf outing.

Two character witnesses were called: Dr. Barbara Feingold, executive director of Little Village House for disturbed children, and Vivian Mannis, executive director of Hi Hello Child Care Center in Freeport. Both stated that Armand Paul performed free legal services for their facilities, that he was "highly respected" and "regarded highly in the community for honesty."

At 3:24 P.M., Judge Mishler called an early end to the day. Unless Stephen Scaring had second thoughts about putting Armand Paul in the witness box, the testimonial part of the trial was at an end.

FIFTY-FIVE

OUT, OUT, DAMNED SPOT

A t 9:00 A.M. on the eighth day of the trial, Armand Paul D'Amato, dressed in a navy blue suit, white shirt, and blue tie, raised his hand to be sworn in by the court clerk. Scaring had concluded that the accused would offer a better explanation of his acts than had his defenders.

Scaring's first questions evoked an image of a prudent, respectable man who devoted time to charitable efforts on behalf of disabled children. Armand Paul answered calmly, in a smoothly modulated tenor voice; he frequently gestured in an attempt to emphasize and persuade. He kept his answers brief, seeking to avoid the damage often self-inflicted by those who do not realize they had already answered the question.

He described meeting Sperry vice president Charlie Gardner's lobbyists Herb Chodosh and Jim Lynch during lunch in Nassau's Salisbury Restaurant. The get-together was arranged by the senator's chief of staff, John Zagame. Zagame wanted to become a consultant for Sperry, and Armand Paul was there to impress these influence seekers with his important, well-connected friends.

According to Armand Paul, Zagame had miscalculated the impact of his presence. Armand Paul shortly received a call from Chodosh, who told him Gardner didn't want Zagame but wished to

494

retain him at a monthly fee of $3,000. "I had no idea what they wanted me to do," Armand Paul remarked, but he nevertheless, without hesitation, abandoned Zagame.

Did you ask for an increase from three thousand to five thousand dollars? Scaring queried. "No," Armand responded innocently. "We had a cordial relationship. . . . and I thought that was the reason."

As to the origin of the infamous Aegis letter: "I recall meeting with Jim Lynch at the Garden City Hotel for breakfast. . . . He showed me a letter. . . . addressed to the secretary of the navy. . . . I told him I would try to get the letter sent out on Senator D'Amato's letterhead." And then, perhaps to put the folks in the jury in his gastronomic debt, he added, "The Garden City Hotel is a beautiful place to have breakfast."

He then explained how he had advanced the process. "I flew down to Washington to speak to Shawn Smeallie [Senator D'Amato's legislative assistant]. I spoke to him and Michael Kinsella [D'Amato's chief of staff]."

The conversation with Kinsella placed Armand Paul almost at the door of his brother's office, yet Armand maintained he didn't dash in to greet the senator, an act of sibling courtesy that the jury might think would have required an explanation of his presence in Washington. That was a dangerous conclusion for them to reach, since Al D'Amato insisted that he knew nothing about his brother's visits to his office.

As to the reason Gardner wanted Forchelli to sign the invoices instead of Armand Paul, he felt it was because he was the senator's brother and "*Newsday* was giving him a hard time."

At eleven o'clock, after a twenty-five-minute recess, Scaring focused on Armand Paul's "appointment books." These small spiral-bound volumes, which resembled schoolboy pads, became the center of his effort to prove that his client *had* worked for the $120,500 Unisys otherwise seemed to have charitably mailed to him.

The accounting included thirty-two citations, which first listed "Lunch Herb Chodosh—Salisbury." The second item began the padding of the account: It showed "Zagame/Chodosh lunch" as a separate item. But according to Armand Paul's testimony, this was the same lunch mentioned in the previous listing.

Item 7 introduced a cryptic category of labor. It simply inscribed the date July 17 with the single word "Washington." What exactly did that word mean? It seemed to mean, and Armand Paul said nothing to disabuse the jury of this interpretation, that he had gone to Washington on business for Unisys.

Scaring had said that this was a catalog of work Armand Paul had done for Unisys, so that when item 13 was recited, "March 8 [1987] leaving for Washington D.C.," the jury could only conclude he had gone to Washington on behalf of his client. There were eight more solitary "Washington" listings. It appeared that Armand Paul, touting Unisys's cause, had become one of the shuttle's frequent fliers.

At 11:25 A.M., Scaring concluded by eliciting denials from Armand Paul that he did anything wrong.

The key role of cross-examining the star witness was given to the tall, older member of the prosecution. Joshua Hochberg was the kind of attorney that Judge Mishler liked. He never raised his voice, appeared to be reasonable, and negotiated with the judge in a posture that suggested he was schooled in court etiquette. In addition, he appeared as a man of substance. This prosecutor would not likely batter the witness to a point where the jury's sympathies would be aroused.

Hochberg immediately focused on the appointment book. He had noticed that item 30, dated February 29, 1988, was unusually specific. It read: "Unisys 'important' send invoices to Dennis Mitchell." Mitchell was Gardner's fellow conspirator, and Hochberg wanted the jury to note how "important" D'Amato thought it was to make sure the bills were routed through him.

Armand Paul's gestures had become restrained, and his face had grown pale. Hochberg now sought to discredit the appointment book. Wasn't it true that many of the entries were unrelated to Unisys business? For example, "How many trips to Washington did you take on Unisys's behalf?"

Armand Paul was now blinking constantly. "No more than two or three," he coughed out.

Had he, in his role as a consultant seeking information, ever met with naval officials?

"No" came the quiet answer.

Did you ever meet with any congressmen besides your brother?

Another muffled negative.

And although he considered the Aegis letter "routine," Hochberg asked with raised eyebrows, he had waited in his brother's offices for two hours until Smeallie told him it would be sent to Secretary Webb?

"Yes."

He had also never told his brother he represented Sperry, Hochberg asked skeptically, and, furthermore, dealt with his brother's office but never told his brother?

"That's right." Armand Paul nodded as he blinked.

Then a major surprise for the laypersons of the jury. When the government had subpoenaed Armand's appointment books, he had been allowed to white out anything he thought applied to other clients. In making those decisions his sole guide was *the honor system.* Concerning this process of redacting, known to non-lawyers as erasing, Hochberg asked, "Are you the one who made the redactions in the diary pages in front of you?"

Armand Paul acted as though he must check to make sure. He thumbed through the pages. Yes, he finally responded. "I was scared," he added, as if to supply an excuse for what he anticipated was coming.

Hochberg used an overhead projector to display the pages of the appointment book on a screen facing the jury. He first exhibited a copy of the document Scaring had offered into evidence and then showed the jury what he described as "the original." On his copy there was a March 24, 1986, entry not visible on Scaring's. The courtroom was in turmoil. Had Armand Paul altered the evidence?

Scaring seemed bewildered. He asked for a sidebar: "Maybe we should approach, because I'm getting confused," he said.

After the conference, Scaring appeared even more worried. Hochberg pointed out to the nervous witness that on his redacted copy there was nothing below "Herb Chodosh," leaving the impression he had met with Chodosh on some business matter he had been handling for Unisys. But in the original version there was a reference to ten tickets being sold to a party affair. "Do you recall selling ten tickets to Mr. Chodosh," he asked.

"Yes."

"You made the legal judgment to white out the other part?"

"Yes," Armand Paul said, stifling himself.

Hochberg pressed ahead. "Did it [the whited-out material] have any relevance to explaining the above entry 'Herb Chodosh'?"

"It certainly explains it," Armand Paul conceded.

With that concession, Armand Paul undermined whatever credibility his notes might have had. Hochberg had proved he tampered with relevant evidence. Hanging in the air was the question What else had he whited out? In addition, were other telephone calls merely dunning requests for his brother? And finally, was he going to suffer any penalty for a perjury committed with white-out fluid?

Hochberg drove the point home by noting that an item indexed in D'Amato's redacted copy only as "D.C." was followed in the original version by the words "seminar Rick."

"Do you think the 'seminar' notation casts some light on why you were in Washington?" Hochberg asked, implying that a charge of tampering with evidence was on his mind.

"Yes," he affirmed in a low voice.

Hochberg cited another redacted "Washington" listing that in the original included Armand Paul's words describing it as a planning session for a trip to New Orleans having nothing to do with Unisys.

Of all these trips to Washington, Hochberg reflected, how many had actually been on business for Unisys? "Two or three," D'Amato repeated in a failed attempt to appear casual.

Hochberg returned to his desk, where Larry Noyer handed him a note. He read it and then went back to the witness box. There was, he said, a glaring problem with the diaries Armand Paul had produced. Each volume represented one month, but there were a number of volumes missing. These diaries had been in the possession of Armand Paul's first attorney, who had returned them to Armand when he had been indicted in March 1992.

Judge Mishler interrupted. He wanted to know whether the diaries had been intact when Armand Paul had *given* them to his previous attorney? D'Amato answered that when he turned them over to his first attorney, "none were missing." He didn't know why some volumes were now missing.

Scaring seemed more perturbed than ever. As the judge called a lunch recess, Scaring asked for permission to speak to his client during the break. Judge Mishler said he would allow it but warned

Scaring that Hochberg could inquire about what they discussed, since Mr. D'Amato was still testifying.

When the afternoon session began at 1:29 P.M., Judge Mishler politely addressed the jury. "The government asked me to advise the jury that there is no implication of mishandling of these diaries by Mr. Scaring."

The good implication for Scaring was a bad one for Armand Paul. Someone had caused a number of volumes to disappear, and since he was the only one who benefited from their disappearance, suspicion settled easily on his shoulders.

Scaring was on his feet immediately to underscore the implication. *He* had asked Judge Mishler to announce the government's absolving of him in open court. There was, he seemed to be suggesting, no purpose in putting anyone else but his client at jeopardy.

Hochberg made one last reference to the diaries. On March 25, 1987, the diary contained a note "Herb Chodosh" and a telephone number. Underneath, however, whited out in the copy Armand Paul had submitted but visible in the original, was the intriguing handwritten "Lunch with Al," followed by "D.C."; "D.C." was the only visible remains of Al's lunch. Why had the reference to his brother been erased? Armand couldn't remember.

Although Hochberg usually phrased his doubts in the form of questions, he couldn't restrain himself from letting his skepticism show through his narrowing eyelids before he moved on.

He was curious about the lack of a retainer form signed by Gardner or a "retainer fee" paid by him when he hired D'Amato. Most attorneys paper their files with those badges of honor. What possible reason but a sense of guilt could have kept him from such a traditional display?

And why was it that Armand's office files showed almost no work done for Unisys? "Are you a careful and meticulous person?" the prosecutor asked.

"No. . . . not all the time," D'Amato answered.

But he had been meticulous about one thing: His brother's Aegis letter pressuring the navy wasn't in Armand's Unisys file. He had been careful to obliterate the connection between his work for Unisys and his brother, although that file did contain Congressman Lent's letter to the secretary of commerce.

Hochberg wanted to establish why Armand was so frequently in Washington if it had nothing to do with Unisys. "Is it true," he asked, "in 1986 many of your trips to Washington were in your capacity as your brother's campaign manager?"

"Yes," Armand responded docilely.

Referring to his law firm's records, Hochberg remarked that the initial $3,000 monthly fee had been raised to $5,000 after only one month. Within a few months it was again raised to $6,500. He must have been an expert consultant for Coastal Enterprises to get such a large raise so quickly.

"Did you know what Coastal did?" Hochberg asked.

"No," Armand answered.

"Did you ever make any presentations to Coastal?"

Again: "No."

"Well, then, why the raise?" Hochberg wondered.

"I never asked for the raise," D'Amato volunteered.

"Did you find it unusual?"

"I did find it unusual," D'Amato said, as if he were still puzzled by it. "Usually with a client it's like pulling teeth."

After a twenty-minute recess, at 3:05 P.M. Assistant U.S. Attorney Hochberg concluded with this exchange:

"Was it usual for the Forchelli invoice not to have your name on it?"

"It was unusual," Armand Paul admitted.

"Did you ever ask anyone at Unisys why the Forchelli invoice wasn't in your name?"

"No."

Scaring closed his case without asking further questions.

Judge Mishler announced that he would hear summations on Monday at nine o'clock. He cautioned: "I expect to charge on Monday if summations don't run too long." It was the kind of warning, at this crucial stage of the trial, that attorneys took seriously.

On Monday morning I took a seat on the spectator bench directly behind Antoinette D'Amato, where I had a better view of the jury. The jurors filed into the court rapidly, most of them glowing in the attention focused on them.

Joshua Hochberg was first to summarize. He delivered a reasoned presentation to the attentive jury. His basic contention:

Armand Paul had been hired "solely and uniquely" to get his brother to provide favors for Unisys.

Furthermore, D'Amato knew that his "technical services" were "a sham." He taught business law and had an accounting degree. Armand's eyes blinked nervously as Hochberg went over the evidence, no longer asking questions but now analyzing his conflicting answers and condemning his pay-to-play extortion.

Coastal, Hochberg said, was Gardner's "shell" corporation, used to pay bills Sperry did not want to know about. "It was a bogus, sham company." Everything D'Amato had done during the years he had taken money from Sperry-Unisys was controlled by his desire to conceal his identity from the company, for which he performed no services except to give Gardner access to his brother.

Hochberg went to the prosecutor's table where D'Amato's 235-page Sperry-Unisys file, subpoenaed by the government, lay in isolated splendor. In deliberate fashion he took out all the pages Armand Paul had not prepared, which he described as "file stuffers." He was finally left with two sheets of yellow paper covered with Armand's scrawl. "One hundred and twenty thousand dollars to a prominent attorney—two pages of notes," Hochberg's normally composed face contorted with mock surprise.

And when Cresce comes on the scene and begins to discover the connection to Alfonse D'Amato, "Was Cresce supposed to call up Senator D'Amato and say, 'I hear you're engaged in unethical, illegal activity'?"

Hochberg charged that the empty file proved that Armand Paul had merely been a conduit for his brother. During his entire employment by Gardner his sole effort had been to act as his brother's agent.

"He thought it was important to put down Herb Chodosh's name," Hochberg said, "but erased that it was to get Chodosh to buy ten tickets to his brother's affair."

"The two letters from Alfonse are not in Armand's file, nor is there any reference to his brother."

Armand's bare file proves that "it was not only Charles Gardner who wanted to conceal the relationship," Hochberg insisted. "It was a seamy relationship that was truly corrupt and ugly from its very inception."

501

Hochberg made his only attempt at the dramatic as he finished. "To call what the defendant did consulting work is to dignify it. To even call it lobbying is to dignify it. He traded not on his skill or knowledge. . . . The only thing he traded on was the familial relationship he had with his brother, the fact they shared the name *D'Amato*."

By 10:32 A.M., Hochberg had finished. From beginning to end Mother Antoinette stared straight ahead, unimpressed.

Joey Buttafuoco—Scaring began with that hot-button name—is a topic discussed around the kitchen table. What did he do with teenager Amy Fisher? It's all just speculation. He seemed to be drawing a parallel: "Where's the proof that he [Armand Paul] knew?" The government's case, in his eyes, was the same kind of kitchen-table speculation.

"We are not talking about a scheme to defraud," Scaring suggested delicately. "We are talking about modifications of procedures, not going precisely by the book. Everybody doesn't go precisely by the book, and it doesn't make you a schemer or a crook or a criminal."

At this point, at 10:57 A.M., Armand Sr. shuffled into the courtroom and discovered that the front bench was occupied. Space was squeezed out for him next to his wife. As he prepared to sit down, he snapped at Antoinette in what appeared to be an ongoing argument: "You couldn't save a seat for me."

Antoinette coldly stared at him. "Why weren't you here on time?" she demanded, and when he started to respond, she commanded, her eyes filled with fury, "Shut up!"

He did.

Scaring was oblivious to the family drama. He stood next to the lectern, leaned his left elbow on it, and tried to prove Armand Paul innocent by analogy. "Someone goes out and hires a pitcher for two million dollars, and he never pitches an inning. So what! It's their money. They can do what they want with their money." This was the "it's their money" theory of business: If businessmen practiced something that common sense, and the criminal law, would consider illegal, it was nevertheless legal because "it's their money."

Continuing with the baseball terminology, he added, "If Unisys wanted Armand D'Amato in reserve, that's their choice." Scaring seemed to feel that Charlie Gardner wanted D'Amato for some future ninth-inning crisis; Charlie's team could always use another strong arm in the bullpen.

As to the Forchelli purchase order appearing to hide Armand Paul's name. "By itself this is suspicious," he conceded. But remember what Professor Hazard said about the method of payment. "It's up to the client." A weighty opinion, since it was backed by the authority of the Yale Law School.

At 12:07 P.M., Scaring requested an adjournment for lunch. When he returned to the lectern at 1:30 P.M., he started a labored reconstruction of the records. By 2:00 P.M., he seemed weary. "It's getting hot in here," he said, turning to the judge. "Is there anything we can do about it?"

"We're doing our best, Mr. Scaring," Judge Mishler said, cool as a cucumber. Armand Sr. seemed equally unconcerned about the heat as he chewed gum and stared at his son's lawyer. By 2:24 P.M., Scaring had slowed noticeably; occasionally, he was silent for a minute at a time as he studied material on the lectern.

Over the next hour and twenty minutes Scaring gave the impression he was stalling. He repeatedly discussed points he had made earlier, trying his best to absolve D'Amato by labeling company representatives of Unisys as liars for not admitting they knew he was on their payroll.

He frequently returned to Professor Hazard's version of what was legally ethical, as opposed to what the world might consider morally ethical. He ignored the fact that often the problem in maintaining a fair, orderly society was not in defending against what was illegal but resisting what was legal: Tobacco producers and gun manufacturers personify that problem.

After harping endlessly on themes enunciated by Professor Hazard, Scaring finally ran out of steam. "I'm about out of things to talk to you about," he said, looking up from his papers. And then, in little more than a whisper, he remarked, "You have to live with yourself. . . ."

Mishler, whose sternness and fairness were proved each day in his court, seemed offended by Scaring's violation of a pledge to him. After excusing the jury, he chastised the defense attorney. "You took far more time to sum up than you said you would. I'm not going to force the government to go ahead while they're off balance."

After ascertaining that Noyer would only take one hour for countersummation, he adjourned the court at 3:50 P.M. until the next day, Tuesday, May 4, at 9:00 A.M.

Larry Noyer's style was in complete contrast to Hochberg's and Scaring's. He was dynamic. He wasn't merely weaving a logical tale of corruption. He was accusatory. He wanted the jury to remember D'Amato's answer to the question "Did you ask any other senator besides Senator D'Amato to help Unisys?" The answer had been: "No."

At that point, six minutes into Noyer's attack, Antoinette rose indignantly from her seat and, followed by Audrey, stalked from the scene where her youngest child was being abused. Armand Sr. serenely continued to chew his gum.

Noyer wanted the jury to note that although Scaring had read extensively from the court transcript, he had not once quoted from his own client's or Jeffrey Forchelli's testimony. Instead, he had thrown up "a smoke screen." He had been intent on making "a phony, corrupt, sham relationship look normal."

Denigrating Cresce's investigation was part of Scaring's smoke screen. Cresce started digging into Gardner's shady dealings in the latter half of 1987, but "there was no record in the corporation's files from 1985 through 1987 bearing Armand D'Amato's name." It wasn't until "March 1988 that the defendant's name comes up for the first time."

Noyer conducted his rebuttal ferociously. Almost every time he referred to an aspect of Armand Paul's relationship with Unisys that was suspect, he pointed his finger, and a spark seemed to leap across the room at the defendant.

"This defendant [the arm shot out, and the finger pointed] wasn't consulted [by Unisys]. He produced no work."

For emphasis, Noyer quoted a question to Gardner: "Was the defendant one of the people who worked the Hill for you?" Gardner's answer: "No." The finger remained raised throughout that interlude.

At 9:39 A.M., Antoinette had steeled herself enough to return to her seat, intent on giving her son the moral support of her presence. However, her resolve lasted only thirty seconds. She jumped up and said grimly to Armand, "I can't stand him [Noyer]," then

504

stormed from the room. Later, Noyer gave me an enhanced version of this episode. "I'm told—I didn't see her getting up—I hear that Mama D'Amato got up and left. . . . One of the reporters told me that she said, 'I don't have to listen to this shit.' "

Noyer quoted Jeffrey Forchelli's testimony: "Nothing our office does is connected with Senator D'Amato." But Noyer insisted that the facts contradicted that assertion, since Forchelli's partner had been hired only to work on his brother.

Noyer walked over to where D'Amato was sitting and pointed at him. "When you analyze motives, analyze that man's motives."

By this time, Armand Paul's blinking eyes were painful to watch. When I interviewed Noyer, he recalled that moment. "They [the jury] were all looking at me. I was making eye contact with every one of them." He spoke with the enthusiasm of a vigorous thirty-three-year-old and the spirit of a conqueror. "I knew I was on a roll. I was barely looking at my notes."

A buoyant Noyer felt the jury was in his hands. He decided to explain why there was little tangible evidence that Armand understood exactly what was expected of him. "Someone who knows what is going on from the start can be passive." This was a standard Al D'Amato technique: *Don't put anything in writing; don't say it if you can wink it.*

Gardner didn't need a signed declaration from Armand committing himself to influencing his brother. Noyer quoted a bit of Gardner dialogue with Armand Paul: "But above all, it's a product [Aegis] that comes through the Senate Appropriations Committee." And Armand's one-word answer: "Right."

Noyer charged: "The answer 'Right' . . . tell[s] you Armand knew what was expected of him."

"Strip away all the veneer from this relationship, strip away the paperwork, strip away the diaries, strip away the legal files, and what do you have? You have cash paid by a corrupt corporate official to a lawyer, the brother of a United States senator, for the purpose of creating the appearance of access."

"Everything else was created to give an appearance of regularity, normality, meaningfulness, and substance to an operation that was corrupt and a fraud and a sham from the start."

Noyer pointed. The defendant knows he can't get paid for what he *is* doing, so he makes out false documents that conceal what he *is not* doing. His only absolute imperative was "making sure there are no Senator D'Amato letters in his files."

"The defendant never did a bloody thing," Noyer said as his voice rose. "He just collected money." He then concluded:

> "The only people that ever benefited by this relationship were Armand D'Amato and Charlie Gardner. Charlie Gardner got to walk around knowing he had a senator's brother in his pocket that he had bought and paid for with corporate money. And Armand D'Amato got $120,500 by billing through the mail for work he never did."

At 10:05, Judge Mishler called a ten-minute recess. I went out into the upstairs lobby where Armand Paul was standing by himself. "What did you think about Noyer's summation?" I asked.

"It was tough listening to it," he answered. He became volatile, apparently wanting to persuade me of his innocence. "The whole thing's ridiculous. Would I risk my whole career for $120,000?" And then the accountant's mind kicked in. "After expenses—traveling back and forth, office expenses—I didn't even clear $5,000."

Overlooked in his accounting was the share of $120,000 that went to his partners and the return share of profits given to him from business they brought into the firm. There must have been some reason, despite his brief audit to me, why he had publicly boasted that Unisys was his "best account."

Ruth Brennan, still the judge's loyal and efficient secretary, had made up copies of Mishler's charge, which were distributed to the jury. Mishler stood at the lectern on his dais and read it as they followed along.

He gave "the raincoat analogy" to illustrate direct and circumstantial evidence. If you looked out the window and saw it was raining, that would be direct evidence. But if you were unable to see outside, you could still conclude it was raining if someone just coming in from outside was wearing a wet raincoat.

"Did the defendant close his eyes to what was happening?" Mishler asked calmly. Then he balanced it off by admonishing the jury: If the defendant "knowingly" filed false reports, the government must prove he did it "knowingly."

Judge Mishler evenhandedly led the jurors through the technicalities of the mail-fraud laws, telling them they must be convinced "beyond a reasonable doubt," the most demanding standard, before they could bring in a guilty verdict.

As he spoke, it became apparent that there was still a trace of damage from the ear operation, now almost a decade in the past. As he tired, the judge's mouth still sagged in a downward slope from right to left. He nevertheless conducted himself with great competence.

When Mishler sent the jury out to lunch, Armand Sr. swiveled around and peered at me. "How did you feel about Noyer's blast?" I asked.

"It was nasty," he answered. "My wife couldn't take it." Perhaps, I suggested, he should also have left to avoid the unpleasantness.

He grimaced and shook his head; tough guys face the music.

My wife and I ate at Cody's Restaurant, two blocks east of the court. During the 1 percent trial it was called Maxx's and was a hangout for the press. We sat in a narrow mezzanine, looking down at the first-floor tables and bar. About halfway through the meal Antoinette and Armand came in.

They sat near the door, Antoinette's back to the street. She had a farmer's omelet, and Armand ordered a hamburger. There wasn't a smile exchanged; Antoinette did most of the talking.

On our way out, I stopped at their table. "*Buon appetito,*" I said.

Armand stuck out his hand to shake mine, then didn't let it go as he asked: "What's your name?" I told him. "I didn't get it," he said. I leaned over the table, close to his right earpiece, and repeated my name. "Who are you working for?" he persisted, still holding my hand.

"I write books," I told him. "I'm writing one on Nassau politics." This seemed to satisfy his curiosity.

Remembering that he had a heart condition, I asked, "How's your health?"

"Never been in better shape," he claimed. "You're a young man, but I'm going to be eighty."

I turned to a dour Antoinette and said, "It must be hard to handle health problems."

She glared at Armand. "It's hard to put up with him!" she said grimly.

I felt like a mediator at a fight that had been going on for decades. In order to moderate the level of misery, I said, "Well, good luck."

Armand responded as though he were accepting my boilerplate remark at face value: "Thank you. From your mouth to God's ears. I believe in the power of prayer. I believe the vibrations sent to heaven make a difference."

Jury deliberations dragged on for four days. Occasionally, the jurors would return to the courtroom for a reading of some testimony or to see a document. Publicly the jurors were unusually convivial, but as each day passed, Armand Paul looked more dejected. The company of family, good friends like Jeff Forchelli and his wife, Sadie, and Armand Paul's eighteen-year-old son Andrew offered only a reprieve from melancholy.

Joe Mondello, Hempstead's presiding supervisor, did provide some diversion. On April 26, at the start of the second week of the trial, Mondello had resigned as presiding supervisor to become president of Nassau's OTB organization. Mondello's reasons for vacating that powerful office were debated in the corridors of Judge Mishler's domain. The OTB job was a tempting plum: It paid a $139,000 salary and had no regular office hours. The OTB jackpot provided the fifty-five-year-old Mondello with a 40 percent pension increase. If Mondello could get a good second-in-command, as Jim Nagourney had been, there would be plenty of time for golf and open-ended lunches. Mondello also announced that he was holding on to his $75,000 job as county Republican chairman.

According to corridor talk among reporters and political friends of the D'Amatos who had mounted a death watch, the real reason for Mondello's resignation as Hempstead's chief officer was that Joe Margiotta had reemerged as the behind-the-scenes power in the party. Tom Gulotta, whom Margiotta had picked as county executive, unlike Margiotta's former minion Mondello, had remained loyal. For the six years Mondello had been presiding supervisor, the Margiotta-Gulotta forces had made him pay for abandoning his former boss. When informed that Mondello was taking the money and running, Margiotta told the press, "It's a logical move."

The next logical move in Margiotta's war against the D'Amato-Mondello camp was to dump Mondello as county chairman and drop him through the same trap door used to dispose of former country executive Ralph Caso. How Margiotta would gain the satisfaction of revenge against his "tiger" would depend on his opportunities, but what he intended to do was preordained by the merciless rules of party politics.

The bubbling and boiling in this political caldron was the witches' brew of Nassau politics. In the late afternoon on the third day of deliberations, the significance of these maneuverings was being discussed with *Newsday* reporters Craig Gordon and Andrew Smith in a small room directly behind the court. Suddenly, Armand Paul appeared in the open doorway. He looked edgy and bored.

He opened the conversation by asking: "Does anyone know what the Yankees did last night?"

After we delivered the box scores, I asked, "How do you think it's going?"

Armand eased himself into the room, walked around the table where we sat, and leaned against the wall next to my chair. "I came here today fully expecting to be convicted," he said with startling frankness. "Today was going to be the day."

This was an extraordinary statement to make in the presence of two reporters, without any precondition that his remarks were to be off the record. A politically experienced man like Armand Paul D'Amato surely understood that his extraordinary quote might easily be staring at him the next day from *Newsday*'s front page.

During the next twenty minutes it became apparent that Armand Paul was functioning in his role as chief lobbyist in his own cause. He wanted to persuade us that he was a victim. How could the jury convict him? he asked.

I responded, "Logically it's easy to convict you. You collected $120,500 over a two-year period from Sperry-Unisys, and for all that money you only produced two letters from your brother."

The suggestion of criminal behavior between him and his brother and the felons in Charlie Gardner's office was stated gently and obliquely, but he seemed to have understood its implications. Little hope appeared in his wide, staring eyes when he said, "I would be happy with a hung jury."

The subject turned to his brother, since so much of the trial had been devoted to him. "Money's not his thing," Armand Paul explained loyally. "He's a political animal. He's blunt. He makes enemies."

According to him, that also explained the source of his troubles. "I was indicted because Al had enemies in the Republican-controlled Justice Department. They were trying to get back at him."

If he got his wish and the jury deadlocked, he didn't think the Democratic-controlled Justice Department would retry him. Why? I wondered. If a Republican Justice Department indicted him, why should he expect Bill Clinton's Justice Department not to pursue him?

With absolute certainty he responded, "Janet Reno is a professional."

The next day, May 7, the jury returned with its verdict. Guilty on seven counts of mail fraud. The family showed no reaction; they left the court in a silent group.

The sentencing maneuvering now began. Since D'Amato's fraud conviction had involved more than $50,000, Mishler had to sentence him to a maximum of eighteen months, but no less than twelve months. Scaring began to submit motions aimed at reducing the penalty. He argued that since Armand Paul had *successfully* lobbied his brother, the work he had done for Unisys had real value. Therefore, the money he had *earned* should be subtracted from the total fraudulently received, lowering his potential sentence. The prosecutors argued that this was "Alice in Wonderland" reasoning, since it reversed D'Amato's position at the trial, where he insisted that Unisys officials had never told him they had hired him to gain access to his brother.

Judge Mishler toyed with Scaring's sophistic arguments. The original sentencing date of August 6 was postponed to October 12, then rescheduled for October 28, and finally set for November 5, three days after Tom Gulotta and the Republican machine had to face the voters.

Judge Mishler came down on Scaring's side: The two letters Armand Paul had gotten his brother to send allowed Mishler to subtract enough money from the fraud to lower the time served to five months. That hard time would be spent in the Allentown country-club prison, where he would have ample space to do his daily jogging. It would be followed by five months' confinement to his Lloyd Harbor mansion, where the former partner of Long Island's most prestigious law firm might have to wear an electronic-surveillance ankle bracelet. He would always have access to a phone so that he could stay in touch with Al, who had been absent throughout the trial and whose only comment on hearing his brother's penalty had been a one-sentence press release: "I love my brother very much, and I believe he will be found innocent upon appeal."

FIFTY-SIX

TO THE MEMBERS
OF THE CLASS

On April 28, 1991, Mike Wallace did an exposé of Al D'Amato on CBS-TV's *60 Minutes.* Thirty-five million people watched former Mafia soldier Henry Hill tell Wallace that in the Mafia Senator D'Amato's reputation was that "he could be reached." As for D'Amato's convicted Island Park nightclub friend Philip Basile, at whose trial Alfonse·had testified he was "honest, truthful, hardworking," Hill told Wallace, Basile "was hardworking. He was industrious. He was also a wise guy."

Assistant U.S. Attorney Larry Noyer remembered the Basile trial vividly. He was twenty-five years old and clerking for the presiding judge, Joseph M. McLaughlin. "Basile was charged with conspiring with Paul Vario [Mafia godfather] to provide a no-show job for Henry Hill so that Hill could get out of prison," Noyer recalled. "At the trial, Senator D'Amato came in as a character witness for Basile. He used the courtroom as though it was a political rally, waving to everybody. He tried to kiss one of the prosecutors—Laura Ward— on the cheek. He gave a big 'Hello' to the judge. He walked in, glad-handed everybody, waved to the jury, got on the stand. 'Phil Basile is a wonderful guy. Phil Basile is a great guy. I've known him for years. I've been out with him and his wife many times.'

And then he gets up off the stand and glad-hands everybody on the way out . . . smiling at everybody."

Basile's trial took place in 1983, and by the time Mike Wallace interviewed Henry Hill in 1991, Hill was in the Witness Protection Program, testifying against his former Mafia pals and giving his opinion about Al D'Amato's honesty.

The next day, D'Amato defended himself on television across the country. As for Hill's charge that he could be bought by the Mafia, D'Amato's only answer was: "I never even met him."

Wallace's accusations about D'Amato's HUD corruption were dismissed with a counterattack on Wallace's honesty. "He'd have you believe I slammed the phone on him."

Charges that Senator D'Amato had ties to the Mafia had circulated for years. Mike Wallace's investigation of these charges came as the Senate Ethics Committee was weighing more comprehensive allegations about his Mafia involvement. The Ethics Committee avoided an open hearing on the senator's admission that he had intervened on behalf of Mafia figures, but it did condemn the senator for sending a letter to the secretary of the navy lobbying for his brother's Unisys client.

Al D'Amato soon revealed how little he was concerned about the committee's chastising words. On November 26, 1991, three months after the Senate Ethics Committee had berated him, the *New York Times* reported that Senator D'Amato sent a letter to the Resolution Trust Corporation (RTC) "to lobby on behalf of a businessman with reported strong ties to the Gambino organized-crime family."

The businessman was Peter Castellana, cousin of Paul Castellano, the assassinated head of the Gambino crime family, the same Castellano that Senator D'Amato had tried to get U.S. Attorney Rudy Giuliani to stop prosecuting for murder.

Although Peter Castellana did not have the extensive criminal record of his dead cousin, he was convicted in the 1950s of selling adulterated meat and served five years in prison for bankruptcy fraud and tax evasion in the 1960s. A 1986 presidential commission on organized crime said that Mr. Castellana and the meat company he ran had strong ties to the Gambino family.

Peter Castellana wished to buy a Long Island meat-processing plant that had been taken over on December 7, 1990, by the RTC when it closed down the bankrupt Central Federal S & L. Central Federal had loaned money to the now-closed-down meat processor, and prosecutors in New York were investigating to determine whether there was fraud involved in the Long Island bank's collapse. Castellana's bid to buy the defunct plant had been rejected by the RTC. He wanted Senator D'Amato to use his influence to reverse that decision.

The November 1991 letter on the senator's stationery, bearing his signature, was a particularly powerful form of lobbying on Mr. Castellana's behalf. Senator D'Amato was the ranking Republican on the Senate Banking Committee. He had a role to play in confirmation hearings for the RTC's senior officials and in determining how much money the agency would receive to bail out the insolvent S & Ls. His membership on the Appropriations Committee reinforced his power over the agency.

The RTC's officers had reason to be fearful of Senator D'Amato. In the previous year he had taken part in a key maneuver to determine who would control the S & Ls. When former S & L regulator M. Danny Wall, who had been lax in policing his S & L wards, was to undergo a public confirmation hearing as director of the Office of Thrift Supervision, Mr. D'Amato voted, on April 19, 1989, to block the confirmation hearing. Those hearings would have sounded an alarm alerting the public to the gargantuan dimensions of the S & L scandal and Mr. Wall's unwillingness to deal with the problem.

The RTC officers were wary of any communication from New York's junior senator. They knew that he was one of a handful of the biggest recipients of contributions from the S & L industry. When they received his November 1991 letter, which in capital letters demanded that the federal agency respond to Peter Castellana's complaints "within four weeks of your receipt of this request," they felt the senator's pressure. Jim Bolster, the government's managing agent for Central Federal after the bank was seized, said, "When members of Congress write such letters, they're trying to put the heat on."

Senator D'Amato explained to the *New York Times* that his letter in support of Mr. Castellana's cause was merely another constituent service. His office "has lobbied on behalf of other constituents nearly one million times over the years."

The senator had previously claimed that his office performed fifty thousand constituent services annually. When the math was done, that meant that in his twelve years in the Senate he and his staff members had performed approximately 600,000 such services, about 400,000 short of his latest claim. In addition, the senator was now raising these "1 million" responses to the level of *active lobbying.*

Al D'Amato's repeated efforts to portray himself as the senate's champion performer of constituent services—fifty thousand annually—appeared to be self-puffery. He had never provided a breakdown of those services, leaving the figure floating in ambiguity. Now he had provided the *Times* with a new figure about his constituent lobbying that was so grossly exaggerated it inadvertently raised the question about what he was actually doing in Washington.

His lobbying on behalf of Peter Castellana was all to no avail; the RTC continued to reject Castellana's bid. Senator D'Amato might be willing to help a person with strong ties to the Gambino crime family, but the RTC was not ready to perform that constituent service.

The D'Amato saga began in Island Park. But the meaning of his saga can only be understood when it is placed in the context of a $4.5 trillion national debt, a half-trillion-dollar potential loss from S & L bankruptcies, still-untotaled billions stolen in junk bond rip-offs, billions in Defense Department procurement swindles, and a $3 billion HUD raid on the Treasury. In each of these calamities Al D'Amato had a role, sometimes as a supporting actor, often as a lead player.

D'Amato is temperamentally unstable, blunt, and belligerent in language and brutal in execution. Those characteristics were all publicly displayed on June 12, 1993, during a rally at the Plattsburgh Air Force Base in upstate New York. A crowd of seventy-five hundred people had gathered to protest defense cuts that were going to cost area jobs.

Both of New York's senators had agreed to attend the outdoor rally, but Daniel Patrick Moynihan was detained on other business. He asked Senator D'Amato to convey his regrets to those assembled. However, on the rally platform a Moynihan aide gave the same message to Democratic lieutenant governor Stan

Lundine, who promptly passed on Senator Moynihan's regrets to the audience.

Senator D'Amato was livid. He felt that he had been upstaged. Plattsburgh's mayor, Clyde Rabideau, thought "Big Al" was going to assault the lieutenant governor. He described the senator's reaction. "D'Amato charged straight at Stan, put his finger in his chest, and just started saying, 'F—you! F—you!'"

The *New York Post* printed an AP photo showing Mayor Rabideau separating Senator D'Amato from the lieutenant governor under the headline "Foul-Mouth Al Is on the 'F'-ensive."

Mayor Rabideau, a former college wrestler, told the *Post*, "D'Amato said 'f—' quite a bit, and he said it really loud. Stan responded, 'Don't push me.' He was flushed. At that point, I thought it would be best to intercede."

The senator's spokeswoman Zenia Mucha said that the senator's hot-tempered reaction had been fueled by resentment left over from the 1992 senatorial campaign when Lundine had described him as sleazy.

Al D'Amato resides in a town that resembles a medieval fortress whose political leaders peer out at the countryside in search of opportunities for plunder. Yet it is also a community that nurtures hardworking, honest folk. The hypocrisy of Island Park's ruling class is in contrast to the deeply held humanity and genuine morality of most of its townspeople. Al D'Amato could have been as upright as any of them. Instead, he chose a vocation that made it possible for him to become *powerful*. If a lieutenant governor offended him, his power allowed him to poke him in the chest while shouting curses.

Benjamin Franklin, on June 2, 1787, at the sixth session of the Constitutional Convention, expressed the opinion about politicians held by most of his peers: "And of what kind are the men that will strive for this profitable pre-eminence, through all the bustle of cabal, the heat of contention, the infinite mutual abuse of parties, tearing to pieces the best of characters? It will not be the wise and moderate; the lovers of peace and good order, the men fittest for the trust. It will be the bold and the violent, the men of strong passions and indefatigable activity in their selfish pursuits. These will thrust themselves into your Government and be your rulers."

Franklin seemed to have a vision of Al D'Amato as he spoke of the dangers the new country would face when it selected its leaders. He warned: Fear the hack politician: "Place before the eyes of such men, a post of *honour* that shall be at the same time a place of *profit*, and they will move heaven and earth to obtain it. . . . The struggles for them are the true source of all those factions which are perpetually dividing the Nation. . . ."

D'Amato never viewed his post of honor as anything but a place of profit. There were so many honeypots from which to draw sustenance: lecture fees from groups seeking his favors; substantial lifestyle benefits charged to the swollen campaign treasury; lunches and soirees as guest of expense-account lobbyists; ski trips to Utah resorts and vacations at Palm Beach watering holes; dinners and gifts from financial types on the make—all of this annually added tens of thousands of untaxed dollars to his real income and brightened his prospects after leaving the Senate when a mountain of IOUs could be cashed in.

While in the Senate he lives the power fantasies of a Roman senator. Marbled and wood-paneled gymnasiums are provided to condition his body. The Philip A. Hart office building in which his suite of offices is located is the newest of the massive Senate office buildings. It is farther from the Senate than the two more august buildings occupied by his mostly junior colleagues but is connected to the chamber by a private underground subway. Hart's enormous ground-floor atrium is filled to its nine-story ceiling with an Alexander Calder mobile and stabile entitled *Mountains and Clouds*. It was Calder's last work and consists of four black-painted metal sheets of clouds—one is forty-two feet long—hanging over five-story-high flat steel mountains. His offices at Hart, and in five locations around New York State, are filled with dozens of workers conditioned to react to his barked orders.

Substantial monetary rewards will be reaped when the retired politician, whether convicted like Joe Margiotta and Armand Paul D'Amato or defeated for reelection, joins a prestigious law firm or sets up a free-lance "consulting" operation. As a lobbyist, he will be able to exploit political relationships made through the years. The resulting huge fees will quickly make him a millionaire.

Senator D'Amato also has an insurance policy, should some unforeseen disaster occur. He will receive a large pension from

Nassau County for his years as court clerk, deputy town attorney, receiver of taxes, Hempstead supervisor, and presiding supervisor and a second federal senatorial pension in excess of $100,000.

The family advantage was immediate. His father spent years on a Nassau payroll collecting a salary for work not done while collecting insurance fees he was entitled to only because his son said he was. Armand Paul became a rich man because of his older brother. If you wanted something done, requiring political influence, you came to Armand's door with your checkbook in hand. He could do it for you in New York, or his brother could do it for you in Washington. And organized-crime ties were no obstacle; for a price, the A-Team would do it.

So much of D'Amato's behavior can be explained by his narrow view of family advantage. The family could ask for his favors, but the rest of society had to shift for itself. More accurately, it had to be prepared to defend itself against his predatory instincts. He never rid himself of that primitive clan trait that saw the family as a blood brotherhood and the rest of mankind as the enemy.

If you weren't a member of his family, the question really came down to whether you were of use to Al D'Amato. It didn't matter that Joe Margiotta had made him a senator. That was yesterday's favor. As soon as the boss was in trouble, "his son" abandoned him. Close as he thought he was to his "tiger," Margiotta was not a member of the family.

In return for the honor of being selected for his office, D'Amato offered the key to the door of the U.S. Treasury to anyone willing to pay for it. And he had a rationale for why it was a good idea for him to take money from the generous rich. He explained it on C-Span TV on January 3, 1991, in answer to a caller who asked why congresspeople were getting raises when the country was in a recession. He began defensively, with that skintight control he exhibited when under attack that barely allowed his lips to move: "The House took a large twenty-five percent raise, but not the Senate. We took a three percent raise." But when senators limited themselves to a 3 percent raise, he added, lowering his voice as though to reduce the risk of further antagonizing his questioner, "we kept our right to earn an outside income. In this way the taxpayers don't have to pay."

Americans pay senators with checks issued by the Treasury; the constitution mandates that procedure because senators work for all taxpayers. D'Amato, however, clearly saw himself as having two patrons: the ordinary body of voters who put him in office and private individuals with the money to keep him there. Neither group had a compelling grip on his allegiance, since they weren't members of his family, but on the field where their interests did battle, they were in his eyes equal.

Since private and public interests are frequently at odds, money a senator obtains from private sources is usually intended to weaken his dedication to the public. It always reduces the politician's obligation to his constituents while increasing his subservience to his contributors. Alexander Hamilton expressed the theory with perfect clarity when he said, "He who pays is the master of he who is paid."

But here was a senator who bluntly proclaimed that "taxpayers don't have to pay" him because he had made other arrangements. There was a suspicion of a family prospering in this alternate way of paying a senator. However, the cost to the community for his family's prosperity was always substantially more than Al D'Amato wanted anyone to know.

A case in point was Al D'Amato's attempt to use his influence for Easa Easa, a Hempstead political ally who had helped advance his career through the years. That the senator's influence peddling complicated U.S. relations with one of the new republics of the former Soviet Union did not restrain him.

On December 7, 1993, the *New York Times* revealed that three years earlier a fledgling Hempstead, Long Island, company, Videotel Think Tank Corporation, had mysteriously obtained a $45 million contract to set up an international telephone system in the former Soviet Republic of Georgia. The mysterious aspect of the deal was how a new company with only seven employees, which had no experience in the telephone business, had managed to capture a monopoly that might logically have belonged to AT&T, MCI, or Sprint.

Equally mysterious, how did Easa Easa qualify to be head of an international telephone company? He was the former executive leader of the West Hempstead Republican Club and along with Al D'Amato had been for years one of the sixty-nine members of the party's County Executive Leaders Committee. His major work experience had been eighteen years as head of Nassau's OTB organization.

His partner in the Videotel venture was Joseph L. Schwartz. The *New York Times* identified Mr. Schwartz as a computer consultant who met Mr. Easa in the late 1970s, when he received the contract to develop a data transmission system for Nassau's OTB. The *Times* also stated that Mr. Schwartz was indicted three times in 1974 on charges that he passed $300,000 in forged and bad checks. He pleaded guilty and served two months of a one-year prison sentence.

It is not clear how these two Nassau county figures managed to obtain the Georgia contract that guaranteed Videotel 80 percent of any profits.

In order to make the project viable, in October 1992 the Georgian government applied to the World Bank for a $40 million loan to upgrade its phone system. The World Bank investigated and described Videotel in a memo as a "bottleneck" to Georgia's future. The World Bank concluded that Videotel appeared to lack the experience and financial backing to meet its contractual obligations.

In March 1993, after Eduard A. Shevardnadze, former foreign minister of the Soviet Union, became the leader of Georgia, he terminated the contract. He sued Videotel for fraud, charging that it delivered faulty equipment, siphoned off thousands of the venture's dollars to its own bank account, and submitted phony invoices. The Georgian government then opened talks with AT&T and other companies to provide phone service at substantially lower consumer rates and larger returns to the government.

Mr. Shevardnadze, contacted on the battlefield where he was attempting to win a civil war, said he believed that bribery might have been involved in the letting of the contract. "It is either ignorance, huge ignorance, or there is some dirt."

Nodar Kharatishvili, the first deputy of Georgia's Ministry of Communication, told the *New York Times* that Videotel's contract created a board of directors but that five of the seven board seats went to Mr. Easa, Mr. Schwartz, their wives, and Jack Easa, Mr. Easa's brother.

Kharatishvili complained: "This means we had lost control of a strategic industry." He also thought bribery might have originally been involved.

At this point, Senator D'Amato publicly became a player in the controversy. He explained through a spokesman that Easa Easa had contacted him and told him that the company's lawyers thought it would be helpful if he made the State and Treasury Department heads aware of Videotel's problems with the beleaguered Georgian government.

The senator was happy to oblige. It is not clear exactly how he did this, since phone and hallway conversations leave no permanent record of their substance. But in mid-August 1993 the senator wrote to Secretary of State Warren Christopher and Treasury Secretary Lloyd Bentsen thanking them for taking an interest in Videotel. The senator's gratitude was being expressed for the secretaries' reactions to his prior contacts. "The continuing efforts of this administration in relation to this matter are very much appreciated," Senator D'Amato told them.

Suddenly, massive pressure focused on Mr. Shevardnadze. American ambassador Kent Brown visited Mr. Shevardnadze on the battlefield to discuss Videotel's complaints. The World Bank was told by Videotel's lawyer, former secretary of defense Caspar Weinberger, that if Mr. Shevardnadze nullified its contract, the American member on the bank's board would be required under federal law to oppose any future loans to Georgia.

The *New York Times* stated that should the Georgian government be forced to buy out Videotel's contract, Mr. Easa and Mr. Schwartz "could profit handsomely."

There seemed to be a good possibility that might happen, since a besieged Mr. Shevardnadze said that in deference to American officials, he had decided not to investigate the company.

He explained, "I did not want to create a scandal, because this company is associated with America, and they are our great friend."

Senator D'Amato has had an undistinguished tenure in Washington. In its biographical sketch of the senator, the *Almanac of American Politics* described his style. "He is loud, persistent, he pinches cheeks and puts his arms around shoulders and stands just a little too close when he speaks, he uses lushly vulgar expressions and is utterly shameless in his bids for popularity."

His quest for popularity never prompted him to sponsor important legislation. Instead, he ignored nationally important issues, and when he did become involved in initiating legislation, focused on the trivial or on narrowly tailored legislation aimed at pleasing a small group of voters. Two measures that he cosponsored with Republican minority leader Bob Dole typified the public relations attitude he brought to the Senate.

On September 29, 1987, a vote was taken on their bill to ban all imports from Iran. Since the Iranian government considered America an imperialist devil and did not allow commerce with their enemy and since America considered Iran a terrorist nation from the moment Ayatollah Khomeini's disciples had invaded our Tehran embassy in the late 1970s, it hardly came as a surprise that the Dole-D'Amato resolution passed with a 98–0 vote. Only a few sacks of smuggled pistachio nuts ever made their way from Iran to America in the 1980s, which made Senator D'Amato's efforts to ban Iranian imports seem, at the least, frivolous.

On September 29, 1993, Senators Dole and D'Amato joined together again to introduce a sense of the Senate resolution urging Atty. Gen. Janet Reno to press a civil rights investigation into the August 1991 killing of Yankel Rosenbaum in Crown Heights.

While the vote was in progress, C-Span cameras in the Senate showed Al D'Amato standing to the right side of the well, several yards from the clerk's desk, isolated from other senators. He occasionally exchanged a word with Bob Dole when the voluble leader was not engaged in other conversations.

Every member of the Senate voted their approval on an issue many of them viewed as being morally significant, but since it did not have the force of law, they understood that Al D'Amato saw it mainly as an issue of importance to his future campaign successes. After raising their hand in the well so that the clerk could record their vote, they turned and chatted with their colleagues, but almost never with the solitary, unsmiling sponsoring senator from New York.

Senator D'Amato was treated with the same disdain by each of the presidents who served during his tenure. His vote was sought by Republican leader Dole, but he was one of the least frequent senate visitors to the White House during the Reagan and Bush administrations. He was rewarded with campaign visits by both presidents during the Mark Green and Bob Abrams contests because his vote was important and this kind of recompense was what he most valued.

In return, on April 30, 1985, he provided the decisive vote on the Dole-Domenici amendment affirming President Reagan's decision to cut domestic social programs while approving a 3 percent real growth in military spending. This amendment represented the ideological heart of Reaganomics and was a major reason for the tripling of the national debt; it passed, 50–49. He also cast the deciding vote for Star Wars, the MX missile, and nerve gas as well as President Bush's veto of the 1991 Civil Rights Act.

His voting record during his first ten years in the Senate was conservative. He voted in favor of all amendments aimed at diluting or delaying an increase of the minimum wage to $4.45. He voted in favor of Jesse Helms's amendment to reduce social security payments by 6.5 percent on June 29, 1982. On July 9, 1985, he voted for the McClure-Volkmer proposal to weaken the 1968 Gun Control Act. He also voted to lift the ban on the interstate sale of handguns. By 1990 the gun lobby contributed over $100,000 to his campaigns.

His votes on abortion have consistently been against a woman's right to make a choice on that issue. In 1982, during a memorable Senate debate on abortion, he voted in favor of Jesse Helms's bill that stated that the Supreme Court had "erred" in *Roe v. Wade.*

But his record does not reveal a consistent ideological dedication. When he first entered the Senate in 1981, he sponsored a bill to withhold federal housing funds from cities with rent control. After receiving a great deal of criticism on his position, in 1983 he voted against an identical bill introduced by another senator. In 1985 he voted against tougher economic sanctions against the South African apartheid government, but as public opinion came to support those sanctions, he reversed himself.

As he approached what he expected to be an extremely difficult race for reelection in 1992, he began to move somewhat toward the center. The *Almanac of American Politics 1994* printed statistics showing his shifting approval rate among key lobbying groups.

In 1991 the liberal Americans for Democratic Action said he voted correctly from their viewpoint 15 percent of the time. But in 1992 their approval rate changed dramatically, doubling to 30 percent. The Consumers Federation of America, a pro-consumers group that opposed business-oriented lobbies, showed a similar startling reversal of the senator's previous ratings: in 1991, 39 percent; in 1992, 67 percent.

The American Conservative Union, which gauges the conservatism of members of Congress, detected a similar shift in the senator's votes on foreign policy and social and budget issues: in 1991 they approved of his votes 86 percent of the time, but in 1992 only 52 percent of his votes met their standard of excellence.

His move toward the center also seemed predicated on the possibility that he might run for governor of New York against incumbent Mario Cuomo. During the later half of 1993 he frequently attacked Mr. Cuomo as being the head of "the taxasaurus and spendasaurus capital of the nation." This from a politician whose patronage-driven budgets, when he was in charge of Nassau County, resulted in one of the highest tax rates in the country.

As part of his preparation for a gubernatorial race that would not require him to resign his seat in the Senate, on September 27, 1993, he staged a fund-raising dinner at Manhattan's Sheraton New York Hotel attended by a thousand people. They each paid $1,000 for the privilege. The main speaker was his senate friend Bob Dole. Novice senator Kay Bailey Hutchison had also been scheduled to speak but had to cancel when she was suddenly called back to Texas after being indicted on corruption charges.

The invitation to the fund-raising dinner was unusual. It provided a detailed explanation of state and federal campaign-contribution laws, and it supplied a sheet of paper with boxes to be checked if the donor wanted his or her money used to test the practicality of a 1994 race for governor, a 1998 Senate reelection campaign, or, for the truly worldly, a box to check if the donor wished to leave the decision up to Al D'Amato.

On January 4, 1994, after three months of conflicting remarks on the subject, Mr. D'Amato announced that he was seriously thinking of running against that Democratic taxasaurus in Albany. This despite Mother Antoinette's public statement that she was against such a race because the family had been through enough.

TO THE MEMBERS OF THE CLASS

One question is often asked about Al D'Amato: How does he continue to get elected despite the fact that scandals involving him have appeared time after time in newspapers and on television and have been used by his political enemies in their campaigns?

The 1 percent case goes a long way toward providing an answer to that question. That case exposed a seamy part of American politics rarely alluded to in the press and seldom seen on television. It is a world in which dwells former county executive Ralph Caso, sequestered in his melancholy office, shuffling his prayer cards, with little chance of being disturbed by friend or foe, thinking that if it had not been for the opposition of Joe Margiotta and Al D'Amato, he might have held Richard Nixon's and Ronald Reagan's scepter.

It was in that seamy 1 percent world that Al D'Amato learned the flawed morality of clubhouse politics, a morality that has since been his guide in every public act. It was a morality based on the party hack's practical view of what was necessary to win office.

He quickly realized that the Nassau Republican party existed almost exclusively to collect money. The 1 percent case demonstrated that fact conclusively. The party subsisted on kickbacks from workers and bribes extorted from contractors; it was organized to collect money through small indignities like raffles or larger ones like tickets to testimonial dinners, golf outings, and cocktail parties.

The key to Al D'Amato's early success lay entirely in Joe Margiotta's well-disciplined, scandal-ridden party organization. The Nassau Republican party controlled access to elective office. Democrats and Independents didn't stand a chance. Once Margiotta decided who was going to receive *his* endorsement for a place on the Republican ticket, that person was elected.

Therefore, D'Amato stayed close to Joe Margiotta, the source of power. He crooned praise into his ear over the phone. When in his presence, he hugged him, pinched his cheek, did whatever he asked, in fact, did it before being asked. His praise and show of adoration for the boss was not a demonstration of loyalty in the sense most people understand the meaning of the word. Although for many years Margiotta did not realize it, D'Amato viewed him as a competitor. The rising Island Park politician was engaged in a cold-blooded form of competition, waiting only for the most advantageous moment to betray him.

525

The scandals that surfaced throughout Al D'Amato's senatorial career were soon submerged in the heavy flow of stories printed each year. Political scandals, unless they are of the dimensions of Watergate, Iran-Contra, or Whitewater never have a lengthy front-page life. As a result, the damage to D'Amato caused by his scandals was effectively defused by the senator's routine comment as his political opponents dredged them up: "Oh, that's old news."

Al D'Amato's strategy in dealing with his "problems" was similar to the stage magician who practices to make the audience watch his wildly gesticulating hand in which nothing is happening while his concealed, motionless hand is accomplishing the artful deception. There was always a hot-button issue waiting to be exploited as soon as some atrocity came to light. An example of such distracting shrewdness was his trip to the Lithuanian border to challenge a solitary, bewildered guard while cameramen were recording the confrontation. There was also always time for a filibuster in the Senate just prior to adjournment for the year to show the folks back home that their senator was fighting for them, even if the issue was of minor import and his political opportunism annoyed his colleagues.

His campaigns were successful despite the scandals partly because of the demographics of New York. The racial, ethnic, and religious deck was stacked in his favor. He never sought the votes of blacks or Hispanics. By 1992 blacks represented 14.3 percent of the state's population; Hispanics, only 12.3 percent. That small percentage of the total vote reliably went to his opponents. He courted whites, who comprised 69.3 percent of the electorate and were more likely to vote.

Furthermore, according to studies by the Voter Research and Survey, a consortium of four television networks, in 1992, 70 percent of Italian-Americans voted for Senator D'Amato. They provided over one-quarter of all the votes cast, the state's largest single voter bloc. He also held a strong lead among Irish-Americans, the second strongest bloc, providing approximately one-quarter of the total vote. The third component of his success was the Jewish vote. Although he did not win a majority of that vote, his astute defense of the Crown Heights Hasidim and aggressive support of Israel resulted in a large deflection of normally Democratic votes to his Republican column.

TO THE MEMBERS OF THE CLASS

There was finally one resource he had that made it difficult to oust him. He was the incumbent and therefore had a near stranglehold on renomination. That meant he was always going to be one of the two major party candidates with the *only* possibility of being elected. Consider the impact of that advantage. In the last forty years I have never failed to vote on election day. Although I am usually an easily pleased person, during those years I can count on one hand the number of candidates with whom I have been completely satisfied. I believe that many voters are similarly unhappy with the choice party leaders present to them. Yet, along with me, they vote. And the incompetents and rascals who are elected with our vote claim that we love them and have given them a mandate. They do not seem to understand that we had little choice. On election day we either had to vote for them or their opponent, who somehow managed to be even more unacceptable than they were.

Mix this witches' brew together—demographics, party monopoly of access to nomination, and an unscrupulous huckster's intuitive understanding of how to manipulate crowds—and you have Alfonse D'Amato's formula for success. His scandals, which invariably resulted in other people going to jail, were never sufficient to cancel out those enormous advantages.

His margins of victory were almost always narrow. New York's senior senator Daniel Patrick Moynihan repeatedly won with substantially larger totals. In an off-year election in 1982, Moynihan polled 3,232,146, a 2,5354,381 margin of victory. In 1988, despite Republican George Bush's presidential victory, Democrat Moynihan won reelection with 4,048,649 votes, a 2,172,865 margin over his opponent. In contrast, Al D'Amato largest margin of victory was 654,981 in 1986 over Mark Green. His total vote that year was 2,378,197, substantially below Moynihan's worst showing.

The precedent-setting 1 percent case revealed the difference between the democratic aspirations of most Americans and the government provided for them by party bosses like Al D'Amato; a difference about which many disenchanted voters express themselves when they speak of politicians as being "crooks."

In his professorial office at NYU, attorney for the *class members* Burt Neuborne told me that he saw the lesson to be drawn from the 1 percent case in the same light: "I think the Nassau County

527

experience is not unique. I think it's probably the norm, although we dare not admit it. There is an essentially corrupt civil service, an essentially corrupt governmental structure throughout the country. The only people who get promoted are the people who play ball. And the only people who get contracts play ball."

Neuborne's negative view of professional politicians is older than the republic. The men who wrote our Constitution were repelled by the thought that the country they were shaping would be dominated by clubhouse patronage dispensers.

Abraham Lincoln in an 1837 speech to Illinois legislators showed the durability of that revulsion when he said politicians are "a set of men who have interests aside from the interests of the people, and who, to say the most [for] them, are, taken as a mass, at least one long step removed from honest men."

The U.S. Supreme Court finally came to grips with the issues raised in the 1 percent case on June 21, 1990. In a 5–4 decision in *Rutan v. Republican Party of Illinois,* the majority decided that the Constitution prevents the hiring, promoting, or transferring of most public employees on the basis of party affiliation. Those illegal practices were precisely the ones used by Al D'Amato in his climb to power. The principles of honest government service that Lorraine Cullen fought for in the Uniondale courthouse, which Al D'Amato always subverted, suddenly seemed enforceable.

As a result of the 1 percent case, the penalties of the RICO Act were finally extended to political parties. Convicted politicians could now be labeled criminals, not merely violators of some subtle civil statute but "racketeers." The party itself could be a "racketeering enterprise." It was extraordinary, after two hundred years of Boss This and Boss That extracting bribes out of Boston trolley-car workers and Kansas City slaughterhouse owners, to finally have the courts recognize what Americans have always known: On the local level politicians like Al D'Amato are a threat to the well-being of the state, and on the national level corrupt habits of a lifetime undermine the possibility that they might contribute to the country's honest administration or prosperity.

Judge Jacob Mishler is a man with great respect for the law. He is commanding in his direction of lawyers and witnesses and possesses a sly, often punishing sense of humor. Yet he illustrates the weaknesses of a system in which access to appointment is controlled by men such as Al D'Amato. Mishler spent his adult life, before donning his robe, moiling around in Queens County clubhouse politics, learning to accept its standards and habituating himself to its methods of operation. When he gazed down from his pulpit on witness Joe Margiotta, he saw aspects of his revered political mentor Frank Kenna. Senator D'Amato deserved his respect and indulgence because he had won it at the ballot box. Lorraine Cullen appeared to him to be a Queens Democrat who didn't know that she was now living in a Republican borough. And all the committeemen were like the good old guys from the Astoria Republican Club from whom—through twenty years of an otherwise shy lifestyle—he had received some measure of pleasure, occasionally playing poker and drinking beer.

It is from the clubhouses of America, inhabited by pale versions of Jacob Mishler and darker ones of Al D'Amato, that political power radiates: first to the county leader and then, from his den to each nervous merchant and bureaucrat who has come to appreciate the leader's ability to deliver and to withhold.

In every community in the country, local D'Amatos affect the lives of Americans. They firmly believe that it is their right to dictate how people will earn their livelihood and mandate how much money the tax collector will leave in their pay envelop.

At the 1 percent trial Murray Kempton had listened to Al D'Amato describe how his party had forced Robert Marcus to ante up seventy-five dollars before he could get a raise that he needed to feed and clothe his family. Kempton's sorrowful comment, "No one should have that much control over someone else's life," was a recognition of the power exercised by party leaders. Within three years after his appearance at the 1 percent trial Marcus was forced off the Hempstead Sanitation Department payroll, a victim of D'Amato's taste for revenge, even against an "unsophisticated man" who had only unintentionally been a source of discomfort to him.

Richie Rodriguez, who knew Marcus for twenty-five years and had worked for him as a driver when Marcus was a dispatcher for the Island Park Taxi Company, remembered "a happy-go-lucky man" in those days. "We were like father and son." But everything had changed. "They made his life miserable. They forced him to resign. He's completely beaten down. Now he's doing absolutely nothing. He drifts through town, and no one talks to him. I stopped him on the sidewalk a couple of weeks ago, and my heart went out to him."

But Marcus's tormenter remained in the Senate, where his power grew. On weekends in Island Park he occasionally occupied a middle-class, unpretentious home, but most of his life was spent on Washington's and Manhattan's more opulent, power-driven stages. His clubhouse was more jammed than ever with flunkies, who understood that if they learned to play the game the way Senator Pothole had—raised money for campaigns by extorting anyone who wanted a job, a raise, a promotion, a contract, or a service— someday they might get the vital support of their local boss to run for office; someday they might be called Senator Pothole.

In those nationwide facsimiles of the Island Park and Astoria Republican Clubs, in all those haunts of shady dreams, our judges, our mayors, our congressmen, and our presidents are picked. It is there that the first decisions about who will run our governments are made. It is there that unqualified job seekers find their niche, where failed lawyers search for a last chance to make good, where inflated contracts for public works are handed out, where self-aggrandizement raises the cost of government and encourages the production of counterfeit services.

The scope and comprehensiveness of corruption in Nassau County is unusual only because of the massive amounts of money involved. There are hundreds of less affluent Nassau Counties spread over the nation's landscape and many towns and states that have their D'Amatos.

On January 7, 1994, at 9:00 A.M., Al D'Amato called WFAN in New York to chat with talk-radio host Don Imus. Four hours of *Imus in the Morning,* carried on twenty radio stations, was simultaneously telecast nationwide on C-Span. Senator D'Amato's style was relaxed, since Imus was a supporter and had been announcing for almost three hours that his friend Al would soon speak.

The senator opened with a caustic remark about seven-year-old Andrew Giuliani, who had been unrestrained in his joy when his father, Rudy Giuliani, had been inaugurated as mayor on the steps of New York City Hall earlier in the week. Republican D'Amato's absence was notable because along with Democratic senator

Moynihan most prominent state and city leaders of both major parties *were* present. Instead of explaining his absence, Senator D'Amato chose to ridicule a child.

Imus is unrestrained in his pursuit of a laugh and soon provoked his friend with remarks about how he had dodged a few indictments by ducking under the statute-of-limitations curtain. The senator agreed that this was one of his better skills and had kept him out of a good deal of trouble.

The HUD scandal, a subject Imus did not raise, was voluntarily broached by the senator. "I helped my cousin get a HUD house. Well, if you didn't help your cousin, who would you help?" There was in this gleeful revelation a suggestion that another statute of limitations had run out.

As to whether he was going to oppose Mario Cuomo in the November governor's race, well, he may or may not run; his decision would come later. "I'm going to wait around for a while, because I want to torment him."

There have undoubtedly been greater scoundrels in American political history, and the competition of ambitious men does encourage bad temper, but few of his colleagues exhibit his frank displays of mean-spiritedness, and when it comes to ethics, none is quite like Alfonse D'Amato.

EPILOGUE

During the winter of 1994 Alfonse D'Amato discovered someone else's scandal, Whitewater. With a notable lack of information at his disposal, D'Amato began to attack the president and his wife concerning an investment they had made in an Arkansas real estate development in the late 1970s with James B. McDougal, and a business relationship Mrs. Clinton had with the same McDougal when he was later owner of the Madison Guaranty Savings and Loan.

For years the Clintons maintained they had lost $60,000 in their Whitewater Development partnership with McDougal. When they finally released their 1977 and 1978 income tax returns on March 25, 1994, their half of the partnership's loss was $43,635; McDougal lost $92,200. Although they were supposed to share Whitewater's profits equally, the losses were disproportionally borne by the partner not living in the governor's mansion.

The importance to the owner of a struggling S&L of having the governor of his state as his business partner was demonstrated in a February 5, 1985, memo, printed in the *New York Times* March 25, 1994. From McDougal to Bill Clinton:

Kathy called yesterday to ask for my recommendation for two people to fill the vacancies on the State Savings and Loan Board.

For the industry position from the 2nd Congressional District, I recommend John Latham, who is chairman of the board of Madison Guaranty Savings and Loan Association. . . . He is a major contributor to your campaign. . . . For the consumer position from the 4th Congressional District, I recommend Dr. Jerry Kendall of Camden.

Bill, we are down to only about 15 state chartered savings and loan institutions and I am about the only one around who has any interest in this board.

Mr. McDougal seemed to have lost sight of the interest of the taxpayers who were guaranteeing his overextended loans. In 1989 Madison Guaranty S&L failed, costing taxpayers $60 million.

Questions about the propriety of the Clintons' involvement in Whitewater rose during the 1992 presidential campaign, but candidate Clinton's news conference presentation of his version of the facts, and a media perception that the public was more concerned with how Clinton's program might effect the nation's faltering economy, ended further discussion of the matter at that time.

Interest was revived in July 1993 when Vincent Foster, President Clinton's friend and deputy counsel to the president, committed suicide in Washington. Speculation appeared in the media that Foster had been driven to his destructive act by a guilty knowledge of professional improprieties he had committed on behalf of the president. More rabid partisans suggested he had been murdered in a administration safe house and his body then transported to a bank of the Potomac River.

When it was announced in October 1993 that the Treasury Department was looking into the failure of Madison Guaranty, interest in the story redeveloped. Alfonse D'Amato began to attack the administration's "cover-up," a charge echoed by his Senate mentor Bob Dole in a less blunt, somewhat more elegantly caustic manner.

It wasn't until late December 1993 that Whitewater took on the aura of a scandal. It was revealed that White House counsel Bernard Nussbaum, a New York corporate litigator, had supervised the removal of all Whitewater files from Vincent Foster's office after his suicide. The phrase "appearance of impropriety," which subsequently became a mantra in Whitewater stories, made its presence felt for the first time.

The president added to the perception of a cover-up when he avoided answering questions about Whitewater and initially opposed D'Amato's and Dole's demands for the appointment of a special prosecutor.

The public remained largely uninterested, partly because the events had taken place sixteen years earlier, but more significantly because the issues were submerged in a fog of legalisms. There was also an absence of any unimpeachable evidence of wrongdoing. D'Amato's charges were always prefaced with references to rumors—*some say, reportedly, it has been suggested*—and that old standby of the unauthenticated, *allegedly.* It was difficult for most Americans to credit Al D'Amato and Bob Dole with a nonpolitical purpose in the bruhaha they were orchestrating. D'Amato even publicly conceded that he thought there might be "little if anything" at Whitewater's core. There seemed to be an incongruity in the spectacle of the Senate's most unethical member posing as defender of the nation's ethics.

Nevertheless, each time a Republican spokesman was needed, Al D'Amato was thrust forward. He was constantly quoted. Articles about him appeared in magazines and in papers. Daily, over a period of months, he was on television.

Why had the Senate Republican leadership chosen Al D'Amato as its spokesman? The answer seemed to be that no one else wanted the job. Picking on Bill Clinton when his approval rate in the polls was almost 60 percent was not an assignment sought by cautious pols. The president was delivering on his campaign promises. The deficit was declining, employment was rising, NAFTA had passed, and a push for universal health insurance was progressing for the first time since Harry Truman proposed it. Taking on a popular president seemed like a thankless task better assumed by a senator not up for reelection who had an attack-dog personality.

When New Jersey Democratic senator Bill Bradley and other members of his own party began calling for the appointment of a special prosecutor, President Clinton yielded, selecting Robert B. Fiske Jr., an eminent attorney and lifelong Republican. The president turned over all documents related to Whitewater, and pledged his full cooperation, including testifying under oath if Fiske felt that was necessary.

Until the day Fiske was appointed, D'Amato and Dole had repeatedly said an independent investigation would satisfy them. But within days after the special prosecutor hired his staff and moved to Little Rock, D'Amato and Dole broadcast a new demand: they wanted Congress to hold public hearings. The trumpet call for a political circus had sounded. It became obvious that their real intent was to destroy the president's credibility as the nation's leader.

D'Amato was particularly vituperative. He claimed to be "outraged," accusing Clinton of uttering "lies," "distortions," and "deception" in dealing with disclosures about his role in Whitewater. The president had created "secret cabals" in the White House that were generating "fairy-tale versions" of what had happened. This was really "as great if not greater than Watergate!" He demanded publication of all reports about the affair, and televised hearings. Conveniently forgotten were his strenuous efforts to reject calls for a public Senate Ethics Committee investigation of the much more numerous and serious charges against him.

The hypocrisy of D'Amato's demands became apparent on March 13, 1994. NBC-TV reporter Lisa Myers asked D'Amato whether he would agree to the release of the August 1991 report of the Ethics Committee on its investigation of his more current scandals. D'Amato, suddenly defensive, said that he would not withdraw his objection to its publication because it was not "standard procedure." It was not standard procedure only if the senator being investigated insisted on senatorial privilege to suppress the committee's findings. With D'Amato's permission the Ethics Committee's report could instantly be made available. As political commentator Mark Shields observed, the moral high ground is a place where D'Amato is "subject to nosebleeds."

Bill Clinton's willingness to "play the game" when raising money in Arkansas for his election campaigns suggests an insensitivity to conflict-of-interest rules. But to have D'Amato, the most investigated senator in American history, sanctimoniously draw these lapses to the attention of the public he has so frequently imposed on in a much more egregious, often criminal manner detracts from the seriousness the subject deserves.

Representative Jim Leach of Iowa, who was leading the House Republicans in investigating Whitewater, had been as moderate in his public statements as D'Amato had been immoderate. On *Meet the Press*, on March 27, 1994, months after he had begun calling attention to the Clintons' unattractive financial deals, Leach was still attempting to be temperate in assessing what the president had done. "This is a breach of public ethics before the president took office. There is a difference between ethical lapse and a breach of the law."

The president ignored Leach. Al D'Amato instead became Bill Clinton's easy target. "The Republicans have decided that Senator D'Amato will be the ethical spokesman for the Republican party in Congress," the president said ironically. "That is their right to do that." His comment subtly drew attention to the risk of such a strategy and barely concealed his gratitude for what the Republicans had done.

Al D'Amato's cries that he was "shocked, shocked" that a politician had done favors for his major contributors do not cause heads to nod in agreement but rather evoke smiles. When dealing with people who gave him money, he never showed the slightest interest in drawing any kind of line between what was criminal and what was merely revolting.

D'Amato's warning to his opponents in March 1994 was "Don't try to shout me down. Don't try to beat me down. I don't stop." It foreshadows what can be expected from him in the remaining four years of his third term in the Senate, where he has become a senior member and assumed the status of Bob Dole's tiger. Americans will have many opportunities to be blinded by the glare from his brass.

INDEX

Abdul Enterprises, 90–91, 133, 136
Abortion, 464, 523
Abouhalima, Mahmud, 472
Abrams, Robert, 464–67, 471, 472, 473, 523
ABSCAM, 90–93, 133–34, 136, 165, 167, 183, 449
ACLU (American Civil Liberties Union), 188, 254, 311
Adams, Arlin, 441–45, 453, 454
Addabbo, Joseph, 169, 477
Adler, Martin, 228, 229, 266, 270
Aegis defense system, 339, 423, 444, 477, 480, 490, 493, 495, 497, 499, 505
AHA Consultants, 53
Ailes, Roger, 101
Alameda Associates, 399
Alameda Towers, 401, 460–61
Albano, Vincent, 98
Alevra, Peter, 116, 117, 120, 130–31
Allenwood Prison Camp, 182–83, 511
Almanac of American Politics, 521–22, 523
American Civil Liberties Union. *See* ACLU
American Conservative Union, 524
American Ref-Fuel, 360
Americans for Democratic Action, 524
Apkarian, Harry, 416, 417
Armstrong, Michael, 106, 131, 133–34, 148, 251, 257, 273, 274, 370, 452
Associated Press (AP), 452
Astoria Republican Club, 80–83, 529
Attorney general, 440–41

Babiak, Eugene, 230–32
Baker, Howard, 109–10, 331–32
Ballori, Eduardo. *See* Lopez Ballori, Eduardo
Bank of New York, 157–59
Barrett, Wayne, 166
Basile, Philip, 104, 319–20, 345, 361, 381, 512–13
Beale, William, 418
Begleiter, Bob, 419
Belafonte, Harry, 317
Bennett, James, 108
Bennett, Robert, 451, 453
Bentsen, Lloyd, 521
Berger, Leo, 342
Bernstein, Deborah Smith, 425
Bernstein, Martin, 343–45, 384
BFI. *See* Browning-Ferris Industries
Biaggi, Mario, 169, 182, 327, 328, 355–56, 375
Biaggi, Richard, 328, 329, 356
Biderman, Abraham, 414
Black, Clawson, Inc., 74, 75, 115–18
Black Removal Program (Island Park), 383–84, 432
Blacks, 324, 383–84, 385, 393, 429, 467–73, 526
Blankman, Norman E., 47
Bloom, Leonard, 166
Blue, Jerome, 423, 424, 442
Boesky, Ivan, 161–62

Boklan, Kenneth, 92
Bolan, Thomas, 106, 370, 379
Bolster, Jim, 514
Bond, Richard, 383
Bonne, Raymond, 173
Borrelli's Restaurant, 298–99
Bowery Savings Bank, 342
Boylan, George, 112–15, 121, 123, 124
Boyle, Terry, 19–20, 36, 100
Bradley, Bill, 534
Brawley, Tawana, 324
Brennan, Robert, 469–70
Brennan, Ruth, 296, 506
Brinkley, David, 160, 161
Broussard, Thomas, 405
Brown, Clarence, 482
Brown, Lee, 468, 469
Brown, Kent, 521
Browning-Ferris Industries (BFI), 359–60
Burger, Warren, 309
Burns, David, 423–26
Bush, George, 339, 426, 445, 446, 466, 523, 527

Cablevision, 342
Cafaro, Vincent, 378, 379
Cahn, Neil, 140–41, 145
Cahn, William, 44–50, 62, 140–41, 145, 149, 187, 244, 349
Calder, Alexander, 517
Cangemi, Gaspar, 213–16, 225, 250, 291
Canon USA, 368
Capozzella, Vincent, 414
Carlino, Joe, 15, 16, 23, 30, 63, 142, 184, 268
Carpentier, Alfred, 91–93, 136, 165
Carstairs, Ellen, 303
Carter, Jimmy, 385, 386
Casey, William, 25
Caso, Ralph, 55, 58, 204, 217, 254, 291, 525
  on Armand D'Amato's law firm, 336–37
  as county executive, 27, 28, 29, 34–41, 47
  on D'Amato, 105
  ending of career, 77, 78
  on Javits, 99, 104
  Nagourney on reelection, 22–23
  naming of Roncallo to Nassau Board of
    Assessors, 49
  on Nickerson as county executive, 16
  on O'Connor, 135–36
  rift with Margiotta, 72–73, 98, 509
  and Williams and Son case, 141–42, 171
Caso, Virginia, 39
Castagnaro, Frank, 213–14
Castellana, Peter, 513–15
Castellano, Paul, 379–80, 381, 452, 513

Cato, Gavin and Angela, 468
CCS Services, 52–53
Central Federal S & L, 514
Chodosh, Herbert, 482–83, 494, 495, 497–99, 501
Christopher, Warren, 521
Ciccimarro, Anthony, 393
Ciccimarro, Violet Cioffari, 4, 5, 386, 428
Cioffari, Alfonse, 4, 13
Cioffari, Mrs., 5
Civil service, 528
  See also Nassau County politics, civil
    service
Clancy, Pat, 82
Clark, George, 154
Clark, Paul, 60
Clayburn Construction Company, 115, 117–18
Clinch River Breeder Reactor, 331, 332
Clinton, Bill, 466, 510, 532–36
Coastal Drydock Co., 356
Coastal Energy Enterprises, 476, 479, 483, 486, 487, 490, 500, 501
Cohn, Roy, 371, 378–82
Collins, Dan, 377, 378, 379
Collins, James, 53
Commercials, 317–18, 465, 467
Committee for New York, 423
Constantino, Mark, 165
Consumers Federation of America, 524
Corcoran, Paul, 133
Corrada, Baltasar, 461
Cosenza, August, 64, 65–66, 239–40
Cranston, Alan, 451, 454
Crean, Agnes, 60
Cresce, Lawrence, 476, 479, 485, 488–91, 501, 504
Crime, 45
Crown Heights (N.Y.), 467–73, 522, 526
Cullen, Frank, 196, 197, 241, 249, 270, 280, 295, 302
Cullen, Lorraine, 79, 83, 185, 187, 191–93, 196, 197, 234–37, 241, 249, 255, 280–81, 287, 291–92, 295, 297–98, 302, 304–5, 310, 313, 528, 529
Cullen v. Margiotta, 79, 151, 189, 236
Cuomo, Mario, 473, 524, 531
Cushing, Hunter, 407

Daily News, 343, 344, 379, 418
Daley, Richard, 138
D'Amato, Alfonse
  ability to escape prosecution, 64–71
  and ABSCAM, 91–93, 165, 167
  Almanac of American Politics on, 521–22, 523

INDEX

anticrime stance, 45
appointing safe prosecutors, 349–57
ascension, 72–78
on Banking Committee, 110, 157, 163,
    442, 457, 514
CCS case, 53–54
college years, 14–15
and Crown Heights affair, 472
and District Attorney Cahn, 44–50
early career, 15–21
ethics, 323
family background, 3–8
family ties, 518
fund-raising, 109–10, 156–60, 162–63,
    165–67, 322, 341, 524
and Giuliani, 351, 352–54, 356–57,
    370–81, 399, 530–31
and Hempstead garbage dump, 73–76,
    95–96, 111, 115–37, 167, 358–59
and Hempstead taxpayer rip-off, 58–59
on Housing Committee, 163
and HUD scandals, 382–415, 419–34,
    436–46, 460–62, 513, 531
influence peddling, 30–32, 123, 451, 519
on insider trading, 161–62
lobbying for Castellana, 513–15
luck, 105–10, 121, 152, 167
and Mafia, 377–83, 512–13
and Margiotta, 107–8, 122, 153–55, 159,
    168–69, 174–76, 179, 184, 258, 268,
    271, 274, 518
Mitchell Field deal, 93–95
monetary rewards, 341–48, 517–18
and MTI contract, 416–18
and Nassau County politics, 15–43
    passim, 87–88, 101–3, 222–23, 244, 248,
    293–94
and Nassau kickback trial, 185, 187, 189,
    192–94, 202, 206, 230, 233, 243,
    251–77, 285, 290, 291, 293–94, 302, 303
and O'Connor as bagman, 123–37
and OTB/Nagourney incidents, 55–58,
    69–71
perjury, 60–63, 87, 102, 126, 252, 275
publicity-seeking, 51–52
reelection, 316–34, 463–67, 472–73,
    525–27
relationship with brother, 8, 30, 341
Roosevelt Raceway deal, 365–66, 369
scandals, 525–27
and Senate Ethics Committee, 447–48,
    451–62, 513, 535
and Senate legislation, 522–24
Senate runs, 98–104, 109, 156–57, 316–34,
    463–67, 472–73
on Senate salaries, 518

Senate voting record, 164–65
Senator Pothole nickname, 163–64
temper, 317, 515–16
TV commercials, 317–18
Unisys case, 337–40, 400, 457–58, 461,
    477–80, 499, 501–2, 505, 509–10, 513
Wedtech scandal, 326–30, 351, 355–56,
    400
and Whitewater, 532–36
youth, 8–11
D'Amato, Antoinette, 3–5, 9, 11, 13, 18, 109,
    425, 475, 479–80, 482, 483, 485, 491,
    493, 500, 502, 504–5, 507–8, 524
D'Amato, Armand M., Sr., 3–8, 11, 13, 15,
    16, 18, 29, 52, 53–54, 105, 122, 145,
    152, 179, 187, 345–47, 432, 475,
    481–83, 485, 502–4, 507–8, 518
D'Amato, Armand Paul, 4, 8, 10, 11, 18,
    104
    CCS case, 52–54
    and Hempstead waste haulage, 359–60
    and HUD scandals, 396–97, 413, 415, 424,
        442
    law practice, 335–36, 366
    mail fraud trial, 474–511
    on Margiotta, 174, 179
    prospering of, 341–45
    relationship with brother, 8, 30, 335–36,
        518
    Roosevelt Raceway deal, 366–69
    in state assembly, 29–30, 40–41, 74, 335,
        336, 361, 366
    Unisys case, 337–40, 423, 444, 458,
        475–511
D'Amato, Audrey, 475, 480, 482, 491, 504
D'Amato, Joanne, 5, 11
D'Amato, Penelope Collenburg, 15, 20,
    27–28, 371, 393, 438
Davis, Elmer, 230
Davis, Pamela, 443
Dean, Deborah Gore, 387, 404–6, 408, 414,
    440
Dearie, Raymond, 350
DeBremont, Leon, 119–20
DeConcini, Dennis, 451
Defense contracts, 326–30, 337–40, 479
Defense Department, 326, 327, 337, 338,
    339, 479
Defense spending, 164–65, 515, 523
DeLac, Muriel, 227
DelVecchio, Alfred, 411
Demery, Thomas, 406–8, 414, 440
Dempsey, Charles, 163
DeVito, Tony, 92
DeVivo, Thomas, 59
Diaz, David, 473

Dillon, Denis, 47–48, 77, 109, 140, 177, 187, 245, 368, 369
DiNapoli, Vincent, 415
Dinkins, David, 375, 376, 383, 469, 470
Dole, Bob, 522, 524, 533–36
Dole-Domenici amendment, 523
Donaldson, Sam, 161
Donovan, Brian, 39, 40
Dooling, John F., 50, 64–69, 226
Double-billing, 47–50, 140
Dowd, Maureen, 276
Dowler, Robert, 143–44, 149, 171, 172
Drexel Burnham Lambert, 161, 162, 321, 375, 451, 457
Drucker, James, 18, 49–50, 60–64, 67–68, 259, 262–64
Drugs, 324–25
Dump trucks, 58–59
Dunne, John R., 77, 78
Durenberger, David, 450, 451

Eagle Capital Group, 409
Easa, Easa, 144, 519–21
Eastdil Realty, 367
Economy, 334
Ehrlich, Bernard, 328–29, 355, 356
Ehrlich, Robin, 329
Eiland, Fred, 160
Elovich, Lawrence, 166–67
Energy Department, 416, 417
Environmental Conservation Committee (N.Y.S.), 360, 361
Environmental impact statement, 109
Errichetti, Angelo, 92
Ethics in Government Act, 440, 441
European-American Bank, 29
Evans, Charles, 362, 363, 366, 367
Executive Relaxation (massage parlor), 46
Extortion. See Nassau County politics, job kickbacks

Faraldo, Joseph, 369
Fazio, Catherine, 5, 7–9, 14, 15, 18–19, 20–21, 30, 345–46, 434, 435, 480
Fazio, Frank, 8
Fazio, Jim, 6–7, 10, 14–15, 16, 18–19, 20–21, 344, 345–46
FEC. See Federal Election Commission
Fedele, Genevieve, 300–301, 302, 303
Federal Election Commission (FEC), 337, 338, 401, 423
Federal Housing and Urban Development Act, 385
Feil, Jerry, 343–45
Feingold, Barbara, 493

Ferraro, Geraldine, 464–65, 467, 473
Ferre, Carmen Maria, 402

Ficke, George, 347–48, 430–33
Finkelstein, Arthur, 464
Finkelstein, Ron, 423
First Amendment, 296–97, 304
Fiske, Robert B., Jr., 535
Forchelli, Jeffrey, 477, 486–87, 490, 495, 500, 503, 504, 505, 508
Ford Motors, 416
Foster, Vincent, 533, 534
Foster, Walter, 389, 390
Franklin, Benjamin, 516–17
Friedman, Josh, 459
Friedman, Stanley, 351, 353

Gambino family, 513, 515
Garbage disposal plant (Hempstead), 73–76, 89–90, 95–96, 111–37, 358–59
Gardner, Charles, 337, 339, 340, 475–80, 485–506 passim, 509
General Motors, 416
Genge, Lothar R., 90, 111–13, 120, 124–37 passim
Georgia (former Soviet republic), 519–21
Gierbolini, Gilberto, 402–3
Gigante, Mario, 377–78, 381, 452
Gigante, Vincent (the Chin), 377–78, 379, 452
Gilliam, DuBois, 442
Girgenti, Richard, 468, 469
Giuliani, Andrew, 530–31
Giuliani, Donna, 371
Giuliani, Rudolph, 383, 472
    and D'Amato, 370–81, 399, 420
    first mayoral race, 372–76, 383, 419
    Senate ambitions, 352–54, 356
    as U.S. Attorney, 351, 357, 371–72, 459, 513
Glenn, John, 451
Goldberg, Nicholas, 385
Goldfarb, Sol, 89, 197–98, 214, 215, 227, 231, 254, 295
Goldstein, Barry, 363, 367
Gonzalez, Joseph, 469
Gordon, Craig, 509
Graber, Raymond, 64, 66–69, 142, 226–32, 290, 291
Gramm-Rudman Act, 332
Green, Bill, 385
Green, Mark, 318–23, 326, 329–31, 333–34, 341–42, 358, 381–82, 447, 448, 450–54, 461, 465, 523, 527
Gribben, Michael, 227

Grunewald, Raymond, 444–45
Guardino, Richard, 142
Gulf & Western Corporation, 362–66
Gulotta, Frank, 244
Gulotta, Thomas, 108–9, 177, 180, 234,
   243–46, 286, 359, 366, 508
Gun control, 523

Habib, Yassir, 91
Haff, Harold, 72, 291
Hale, Clara M., 318
Hamilton, Alexander, 519
Hart, Ed, 144, 145, 148
   and Nassau kickback trial, 185–312
     passim, 484
Hart office building (Washington), 517
Hasidim, 467–73, 526
Hastings, Alcee, 309
Hatfield, Mark, 449–50
Hazard, Geoffrey, Jr., 492–93, 503
Heflin, Howell, 450, 451, 455
Helms, Jesse, 455, 523
Hempstead (N.Y.), 16, 18, 23, 27, 117, 118,
   141
   control of, 108–9
   employees, 38–39, 41
   garbage disposal, 359–60
   See also Hempstead Resources
     Recovery Plant
   kickback trial, 208, 257–58, 261, 285, 291,
     293–94, 300–302
   Roosevelt Raceway deal, 363–69
   tax funds, 58–59, 157
   See also Nassau County politics; specific
     villages
Hempstead Republican Executive
   Committee, 108–9
Hempstead Resources Recovery Plant,
   73–76, 89–90, 92, 95–96, 111–37, 167,
   358–59
Henry, Andrew, 485
Hertzberg, Dan, 59
Hilgendorff, Elizabeth, 59
Hill, Henry, 320, 361, 380, 381, 512–13
Hirschfeld, Abraham, 165–67
Hispanics, 385, 393, 526
Hochberg, Joshua, 474, 476, 481, 488–91,
   496–502, 504
Hofstra University, 169, 184
Holtzman, Elizabeth, 98, 104, 121, 157, 277,
   355, 465, 473
Hoover, J. Edgar, 186
Hopkins, William, 362–63, 364
House Military Appropriations
   Subcommittee, 477

House Subcommittee on Housing, 442
Housing, 345, 348, 384–415, 419–34,
   436–46, 523
HUD (Housing and Urban Developmment,
   Department of), 163, 324–25, 347–48,
   382–415, 419–34, 436–46, 456, 460–62,
   513, 531
Hundley, William, 147–49, 151, 153, 171–72
Hutchison, Kay Bailey, 524

IDA. See Industrial Development Agency
Illmen. See, Thomas, 298, 299, 300
Imus, Don, 530, 531
Industrial Development Agency (IDA;
   Hempstead), 363–65, 367, 368
Inner City Drywall, 415
Insurance, 105–6, 122, 140–53, 170, 179,
   345–47, 366, 432
Integrity party, 392, 430, 431, 433
International Boilermakers Union, 112, 114
Irish-Americans, 526
Islanders hockey team, 94
Island Park (N.Y.), 4, 5–6, 13–14, 15, 21, 36,
   48, 56, 74, 259, 261
   Black Removal Program, 383–84
   insurance, 346–47
   subsidized housing scandal, 384–97,
     419–21, 427–29, 436–39, 443, 456
   swimming pool, 347–48, 405
   village board meeting (1990), 430–34
Island Park Republican Club, 17–18, 30, 61,
   152
Italian-Americans, 333, 466, 526

Jaspan, Arthur, 357
Jaspan, Joseph, 308
Javits, Jacob, 97–104, 318, 333
Jews, 333, 471, 472, 526
   See also Hasidim
J.J. Sprats disco, 345
JOBCO (co.), 411–12, 424
Johansen Organization, 343
Johnson, James (National Seatrade official),
   342
Johnson, James (Steamco official), 327
Johnston, Bennett, 417
Jund, John, 192–93, 196, 223, 238–42,
   287–88, 297, 302, 313, 484
Junk bonds, 321–22, 451, 457
Justice Department, 153, 159, 168, 169, 186,
   370, 371, 441, 445, 490, 510

Kadish, Lawrence, 364
Kaplan, Julian, 192, 196, 205, 223–24, 238,
   240, 241, 249, 287–88, 304, 484

Kaufman, Donna, 422
Kaufman, Irving, 180
Keating, Charles, 451, 453
Keating Five, 451, 453, 454, 455
Kemp, Jack, 99, 348, 426–28
Kempton, Murray, 150, 165, 248–50, 255, 256, 258, 265, 270–77, 529
Kendall, Jerry, 533
Kenna, Frank, 81–83, 247, 315, 529
Kennedy, Robert F., 23
Kennedy, Ted, 352
Kharatishvili, Nodar, 520–21
Kickbacks. See Nassau County politics, job kickbacks
Kikkert, Daniel V., 31
Kinsella, Michael, 317, 322, 408, 459, 460, 491, 495
Koch, Ed, 332, 372–73, 375, 472
Kohlepp, Dean, 117
Koppel, Ted, 439
Korman, Ed, 105–8, 121–24, 126, 138–54 passim, 168–69, 173–74, 187, 349, 350
Kravco, Inc., 109

LaGinestra, Nicholas, 288–90, 292, 293, 295, 299
La Guardia, Fiorello, 81, 373
Lance, Bert, 452
Landman, William, 31, 72, 116, 120, 125, 214, 241, 264, 302
Latham, John, 533
Lauder, Ronald, 374–76, 383, 419
Leach, Jim, 536
Lehman, John, 326
Lent, Norman, 168–69, 182, 482, 499
Leonard, Adele, 38–43
Leonard, Ann, 429
Levy, Morton, 74
Lewi, Gary, 108, 120–21, 153, 165, 256, 272, 273, 274, 275, 320, 330
Liberal party, 104, 373
Lido Beach (N.Y.), 25–26
LILCO. See Long Island Lighting Company
Limongelli, Michael, 245, 286, 301
Lincoln, Abraham, 528
Lindsay, John, 373
Little, Ed, 355, 356
Littlefield, Robert, 476
Lituchy, Harold, 343, 344, 345, 428
Livingston, Robert, 87, 210–11, 212, 291
Llera, Raphael, 401
Lobbying, 485, 515, 523
Loewenson, Chip, 195, 206, 207, 229, 246, 247, 300
Long, Irving, 183, 275
Long Beach (N.Y.), 32, 55

Long Island Lighting Company (LILCO), 113, 122
Long Island Power Company, 74
Lopez Ballori, Eduardo, 399–403, 459–62
Love, Steve, 395–97, 421
Lundine, Stan, 515–16
Lynch, Bill, 469, 470
Lynch, James A., 9
Lynch, James G., 477, 480–83, 494, 495
Lynch, Joseph B., 414
Lynn, Frank, 320

McCain, John, 451
McCarthy, Daniel, 195, 200, 205, 209–10, 215, 222, 224, 229, 232, 240, 267, 288
McClure-Volkmer proposal, 523
McDonald, Robert, 108, 174–75, 177
McDougal, James, 532–33
McGann, Daniel, 390, 393–96
McGann, Doc, 384, 385, 394
McGann, Geraldine, 384, 390, 393–96, 421, 422, 424–25, 427–29, 431, 433–35, 440, 445
McGinty, Francis, 437
McIntyre, Mark, 359
McQuiston, John, 177
Madden, Miriam, 393
Madison Guaranty Savings and Loan, 532–33
Mafia, 45, 104, 186, 320, 377–83, 459, 512–13
Mahaffey, Ronald, 158
Mail fraud, 146, 150
See also D'Amato, Armand Paul, mail fraud trial
Malone, Ray, 389–90
Maloney, Andrew, 349, 350, 351, 353, 357, 369, 371, 410, 427, 428, 443–45, 456, 474
Manes, Donald, 251
Mannis, Vivian, 493
Marcus, Robert, 30–32, 61, 88, 102, 103, 152, 202, 220, 263–65, 274, 285, 529–30
Margiotta, Joseph, 58, 60, 62, 64, 66, 71–73, 77, 79, 87, 93, 105–8, 114, 115, 122, 127, 159, 349, 529
  appeal, 180, 181
  and Armand Paul D'Amato, 335, 336
  and D'Amato's Senate run, 98–99, 101–2
  first trial, 138–55 passim, 250
  Hart's defense, 189, 195
  Kempton on, 249–50
  and Nassau kickback trial, 206, 208, 215, 216–25, 232, 284, 303
  immunity, 190–91, 194, 291

as Nassau Republican boss, 23–50 passim, 176, 178, 180, 181, 193, 194, 205, 214, 229, 247, 263–66, 508–9
in prison, 182–83
rift with D'Amato, 107–8, 122, 153–55, 159, 168–69, 174–75, 179, 184, 258, 268, 518
second trial, 168–75, 250
sentencing, 177–78
Marsh, Anthony, 466
Masone, Mike, 9–10, 11, 371
Meadowbrook Parkway, 73–74, 358
Mechanical Technology Inc. (MTI), 416–18
Media, 352
Meese, Ed, 327–28, 356
Meyer, Rolf, 417
Meyerson, Bess, 98
Milone, Louis, 73, 236, 254–55, 280, 281, 287, 291, 298
Milone, Sal, 73
Miranda, Richard L., 27
Mishler, Jacob, 528–29
  and ABSCAM case, 93
  and Armand D'Amato Unisys case, 474, 475, 482, 486–93, 496, 498–500, 503, 506–7, 510
  and Astoria Republican Club, 80–81, 82–83, 529
  background, 80, 82–83
  and class-action suit, 83–84, 86–88
  and Cullen v. Margiotta, 79, 151
  and O'Connor trial, 127–28, 130–31, 133–37
  and one percent kickback trial, 185–315 passim, 484–85
  and "smoking gun" letter, 101
Mitchell, Dennis, 476, 477, 487, 496
Mitchell, John N., 404
Mitchell Field, 73, 91–92, 93–95, 116
Moerdler, Charles, 353
Molinari, Guy, 371
Mondello, Joseph, 180–81, 184, 193, 203, 243, 246, 359, 508–9
Monticciolo, Joseph, 387, 394, 395–96, 404–14, 422–25, 440, 445, 460–61
Moreno, Mario, 329–30
Motley, Constance Baker, 355
Moynihan, Daniel Patrick, 107, 147, 351, 352, 354, 356, 372, 375, 515–16, 527, 531
MTI. See Mechanical Technology Inc.
Mucha, Zenia, 415, 516
Murdoch, Rupert, 352
Murphy, Donald, 493

Muskrats, 51–52
Myers, Lisa, 535

Naclerio, Alexander, 412, 422, 444–45
Nader, Ralph, 318
Nagourney, Jim, 341, 466
  background, 25–26
  on Black Removal Program, 383–84
  on D'Amato, 22, 26, 32–33, 70–71, 100, 465
  on D'Amato, Sr., 346
  and Mitchell Field deal, 93–95
  as OTB director, 55–58, 69–70, 508
Nassau Board of Assessors, 49
Nassau Coliseum, 39–40, 76, 94, 141, 213
Nassau County (N.Y.), 13
Nassau County Medical Center, 52–53, 141–42, 187
Nassau County politics, 15–18, 22–33, 57, 108, 223, 509, 525, 530
  civil service, 25, 34–43, 83–84, 200, 206, 208, 223–24, 235–37, 255, 298
  committeemen, 17, 30, 42, 48, 59, 142, 289
  county executive, 16
  and D'Amato, 15–43, 87–88, 101–3, 222–23, 244, 248, 293–94
  district attorney, 44–50
  double-billing, 47–50, 140
  job kickbacks, 47–48, 60–68, 76–77, 80, 83–84, 87–88, 101–3, 114–15, 124–27, 133, 139–45, 151–52, 525, 527, 528
  trial, 185–315, 484–85, 529
  under Margiotta, 23–50, 176, 178, 180, 181, 193, 194, 205, 214, 229, 247, 263–66, 508–9
  See also specific towns and officials
Nassau Republican County Executive Committee, 177, 178
Nasti, Richard, 167
National District Attorneys Association, 47
National Seatrade Company, 342
Nelson, Lemrick, 468–69, 471
Neuborne, Burt, 84–88, 101, 135, 351–52
  and Nassau kickback case, 187–314 passim, 484, 527–28
Newfield, Jack, 346
New Republic, 323
Newsday, 39–42, 47, 48, 52–54, 58–59, 119, 150, 158, 162, 321, 331, 332, 360, 390, 408, 423, 437, 444, 459, 460, 495, 509
New York City
  housing funds, 414, 424
  mayoral race, 372–76, 383
  police, 468–70

New York Foundation for Senior Citizens, 425
New York Post, 516
New York State finances, 332–33
New York Times, 150, 157, 158, 160, 177, 181, 252–53, 267, 268, 276, 307, 321, 330–31, 369, 380, 397, 412, 419–21, 426, 432, 437, 441, 447, 466, 513–15, 519–21
Nickerson, Eugene, 16, 23, 24, 26, 29, 38, 39, 200, 203, 223–24
Nightline, 439
Nixon, Richard, 138–39
Nofziger, Lyn, 106, 182, 328
Nolfo, Rosalie, 173
Norwalk, Harry, 239
Noyer, Lawrence
  and Armand D'Amato Unisys case, 474, 475, 478–79, 481, 486–88, 492–93, 498, 504–7
  on D'Amato and Mafia, 380–81, 512
  and Island Park housing case, 419, 421–22, 428, 430, 431, 443, 456
  and Lopez Ballori case, 400, 401–2, 459, 460
  on not indicting D'Amato, 463
Nunn, Louie B., 404
Nussbaum, Bernard, 534

Oceanside (N.Y.), 51
  dump, 74, 89, 214
O'Connor, Francis, 116–18, 123–36, 142, 167, 191, 355
Office of Management and Budget, 417
Office of Thrift Supervision, 514
Off-Track Betting (OTB), 55–57, 69–70, 76, 93, 508, 520
Ohrenstein, Manfred, 314
Oil crisis, 415
One percent case. *See* Nassau County politics, job kickbacks
Organized crime. *See* Mafia
"Organized Crime's Involvement in the Waste Hauling Industry" (report), 360–61
Organized Crime Strike Force, 76, 111, 113, 114, 123, 124, 165, 371
Orquendo, Maria Judith, 409
O'Shaughnessy, John, 53
Osterhout, David, 489–90
OTB. *See* Off-Track Betting

PACs (political action committees), 333
Paisley, Melvyn, 477
Papatsos, Jackie, 431–33
Parente, Mike, 388, 437

Parise, Andrew, 208
Parsons & Whittemore, 89–90, 118–21, 122, 124, 125, 132–33, 359
Pascarella, James, 195, 200, 201, 204–6, 212, 220, 224, 236, 237, 255, 262, 279–303 passim, 312
Patronage, 25, 30–32, 37, 40, 73, 86, 151, 172, 185, 245, 247–48, 268, 279, 285, 528
Payoffs. *See* Nassau County politics, job kickbacks
Peel, James, 363
Phears, William, 64–65, 72, 291
Pierce, Samuel, 325, 347, 387, 398, 406, 408, 413, 414, 422, 424, 426, 440, 441
Pingle, John, 39–40, 213, 214
Pless, Jeffrey, 392–97, 419, 428
Polera (co.), 411
Police, 468–70
Political parties, 84, 296, 304
Politics, 15
Popolizio, Emanuel, 396–97
Pratt, George, 121, 127
Prostitution, 46
Pryor, David, 455
Public party, 6–8, 18, 19, 20, 21
Puccio, Thomas P., 90, 91, 93, 126, 127, 148
Puerto Rico, 399, 401, 405–9, 426, 443, 456–57, 460–61
Puntillo, Michael, 411–15, 424
Purcell, Francis, 27, 28, 41, 58, 72, 73, 77, 78, 93, 95, 171–72, 180, 195–96, 200, 222, 246, 278, 291
Pyne, William E., 52–53

Queens (N.Y.), 81

Raab , Selwyn, 342
Rabideau, Clyde, 516
Racketeering-Influenced and Corrupt Organizations Act. *See* RICO
Raggi, Reena, 350
Rahman, Kambir Abdul, 91
Rappleyea, Clarence, 179
Reagan, Ronald, 98, 99, 106, 107, 153, 159, 162, 164, 182, 332, 334, 338, 339, 347, 350, 351, 374, 386, 416, 440, 523
Redco Construction, 343
Reilly, Joseph, 145
Reno, Janet, 510, 522
Republican party, 15–18, 34, 35, 37, 60, 127
  See also Nassau County politics; *specific party officials*
Resolution Trust Corporation (RTC), 513–15
Richard B. Williams and Son, 140–45, 149–51, 170–71

INDEX

Richmond, Fred, 183
Ricigliano, Michael, 141
RICO (Racketeering-Influenced and Corrupt Organizations Act), 186–87, 200, 297, 301, 304, 306–8, 310–11, 312, 314, 351, 484, 528
Riegle, Donald, 451
Riehl, Al, 36–37, 44, 204–5, 211–12, 217, 294
Rizzo, Mike, 385
Roberto, Robert, 46–47, 361
Rockefeller, Larry, 463–64
Rockefeller, Nelson, 24, 44, 97, 98, 99, 100
Rodriguez, Antonio, 415
Rodriguez, Richard, 435–39, 529
Roehrig, Hugh, 433
Romano, Benito, 357
Roncallo, Angelo D., 49, 50
Roosevelt Raceway, 74, 362–69
Rosenbaum, Norman, 472
Rosenbaum, Yankel, 468, 470, 471, 522
Rosenthal, Sidney, 59
Rothman, Jessel, 484
Rubi, Cleofe, 399–400, 401, 408–9, 460–61
Rudman, Warren, 450, 455–56, 457–59, 461
Ruff, Charles, 488–89, 490
Ruocco, Joe, 385, 390, 393
Rutan v. Republican Party of Illinois, 528
Ruth, Henry, 491
Ryan, John, 298, 304

Sackets Harbor (Lake Ontario, N.Y.), 412–15, 441
St. Germaine, Jules, 432
Salary
 kickbacks. *See* Nassau County politics, job kickbacks
 Senate, 518–19
Sanford, Terry, 455, 456–57, 459, 461
Savings and loans, 163, 321–22, 440, 451, 514
Scaduto, John, 29
Scaring, Stephen, 475, 481, 487–500, 502–4, 510
Schanberg, Sydney, 340, 366, 368, 444
Schneerson, Menachem, 468
Schuelke, Henry, 451–53, 455
Schulman, Philip, 396
Schwartz, Joseph, 520, 521
Scully, Harry, 386, 390–96, 420–21, 427–29, 432, 433, 437, 438, 456
Scully, Roberta, 420, 432, 433
Seaver, Tom, 484
Securities and Exchange Commission (SEC), 159–62
Sedima v. Imrex Company, 186–87
Senate Armed Services Committee, 337, 338

Senate Banking Committee, 110, 157, 163, 442, 455, 457, 514
Senate Ethics Committee, 447–62, 513, 535
Senate Housing and Urban Affairs Committee, 163, 387
Senate legislation, 522–24
Senate Military Appropriations Committee, 475, 505
Senate salaries, 518–19
Shad, John, 159–62
Sharpton, Al, 323–25, 453, 465
Shay, Michael, 125, 126
Shays, Christopher, 405–6, 410
Shevardnadze, Eduard, 520, 521
Shields, Mark, 535
Shine, Terrence, 119–23, 133
SIC. *See* State Commission on Investigation
Sifton, Charles, 148, 152–53, 169, 171–72, 177–78
Signal Environmental Systems, 360
Silverman, Joy, 45
Silverman, Larry, 148–49, 151, 170–72
Simon, Myron, 411, 412
Simon, Stanley, 329
Six Crises (Nixon), 139
60 Minutes, 442, 512
Skelos, Dean G., 178
Sloan, Stephen, 342
Smeallie, Shawn, 490–91, 495, 497
Smith, Andrew, 509
Smith, Hedrick, 271
Smith, William French, 169
"Smoking gun" letter. *See* Marcus, Robert
Sniffin, Francine Ciccimarro, 384, 393, 428
Sniffin, William, 386, 428
Snow, Annette, 387–92, 420, 437
Social programs, 523
Sorley, Ralph G., 47, 48, 49
South Africa, 523
Sperry (co.), 337, 338, 340, 475, 477–78, 482, 489, 494, 497, 509
 See also Unisys
Spitzer, Robert, 113–15, 124–25, 128–31, 132
Standardbred Owners Association, 369
Stanley, Alessandra, 466
State Commission on Investigation (SIC), 139–41, 143–45, 148, 149
Steamco (co.), 327
Stevenson, David, 363
Stewart, Charles, 378
Stirling, Robert, 415
Stirling engine, 415–17
Supreme Court, 186–87, 311, 528
Surrogate system, 23
Sutter, John J., 64–65, 67, 68, 142–43
Talmadge, Herman, 448–49

545

INDEX

Teague, Bob, 271–72
Teamsters Union, 375
Tennesee-Tombigbee Waterway, 331–32
Thornburgh, Dick, 440–42, 445–46
Tilles, Evans, 196, 197, 205, 234–35, 236, 270–71, 280, 287, 302, 304
Trager, David, 60, 88, 139, 147, 349, 350
Treadwell Corporation, 113, 124, 125, 130, 132
Tsakos, Basil, 449

Udell, Harold, 66–68, 227, 228
Unisys (co.), 337–40, 400, 423, 444, 457–58, 461, 475–511, 513
United Parcel Service, 94
Unity party, 18, 19, 20, 392, 430
Urban Development Action Grant, 442
U.S. Attorneys, 106–7, 108, 139, 147

Vario, Paul, 104, 320
Videotel Think Tank Corporation, 519–21
Village party, 6–8, 19–20
Village Voice, 157, 166, 346, 377–80
Von Elm, Robert, 157
Voter Research and Survey, 526

Waas, Murray, 323
Wachtler, Sol, 24, 44, 45, 50
Wall, M. Danny, 514
Wallace, Mike, 442, 512, 513
Wallace, Thomas, 177
Wallach, E. Robert, 327–28
Wall Street Journal, 321, 322, 399, 405, 447
Walsh, Al, 367

Walter, Raymond, 115, 116–18, 124–26, 128–30, 132, 134
Waste haulage, 359–61
Waters, Allen, 235
Watts, James, 398–99
Webb, James, 339, 423, 490, 497
Wedtech, 326–30, 337, 351, 353–56, 400
Weinberg, Mel, 90–91, 92
Weinberger, Caspar, 521
Weiss, Ted, 344
White Plains (N.Y.), 411–12, 441
Whitewater scandal, 532–36
Will, George, 161
Williams, Edward Bennett, 178, 180, 181
Williams, Harrison, 183, 449, 451
Williams, Richard, 141, 146, 148–49, 170
See also Richard B. Williams and Son
Wilson, Harold, 353, 354
Winbrook housing project (White Plains), 411–12
Winerip, Michael, 419–21, 426, 437
Woolnough, Donald, 36, 140
indictment, 64
and job kickback trial, 203–11, 216, 217, 220, 226, 239, 244, 257–59, 263, 284, 291
and "smoking gun" letter, 32
and Williams and Son case, 171–72
World Bank, 520, 521

Yacht Club Condominiums, 344–45
Yuhas, James, 413

Zagame, John, 327, 423, 494–95
Zagame, Susan, 423